THE PAPERS OF

WOODROW WILSON

VOLUME 57

APRIL 5-22, 1919

SPONSORED BY THE WOODROW WILSON
FOUNDATION
AND PRINCETON UNIVERSITY

THE PAPERS OF

WOODROW WILSON

ARTHUR S. LINK, *EDITOR*

DAVID W. HIRST, *SENIOR ASSOCIATE EDITOR*

JOHN E. LITTLE, *ASSOCIATE EDITOR*

FREDRICK AANDAHL, *ASSOCIATE EDITOR*

MANFRED F. BOEMEKE, *ASSOCIATE EDITOR*

DENISE THOMPSON, *ASSISTANT EDITOR*

PHYLLIS MARCHAND AND MARGARET D. LINK,
EDITORIAL ASSISTANTS

Volume 57
April 5-22, 1919

PRINCETON, NEW JERSEY
PRINCETON UNIVERSITY PRESS
1987

INTRODUCTION

THIS volume opens amidst the first great crisis of the Paris Peace Conference. It is occasioned, on the one hand, by the seemingly intransigent French demands for annexation of the Saar Basin and for either sovereignty over German territory west of the Rhine or the establishment of a Rhenish republic under French control, and, on the other hand, Wilson's adamant refusal to tolerate what he considers palpable violations of the Fourteen Points. Wilson, recovering from a viral infection, resolves to break the impasse on his terms, even at the risk of a rupture of the conference.

On April 7, he orders Admiral Benson to take the *George Washington* out of dry dock at Hoboken and to dispatch her to Brest under full steam. Wilson is careful to see that his order is published in the newspapers. When Wilson returns to the Council of Four on April 8, his acrimonious and lonely struggle with the French intensifies. Finally, he sends House to Tardieu on April 12 to warn Clemenceau that he, Wilson, will leave the conference if Clemenceau does not yield. At the same time, Wilson enables the Tiger of France to stand down Marshal Foch and other French military leaders, who have been unyielding in their demands for annexation of the Rhineland. This Wilson does by defining the terms of a treaty between the United States and France, by which the United States will come to the immediate aid of France in the event of unprovoked German aggression against her. Moreover, Wilson agrees to the details of a plan for a three-staged Allied occupation of the Rhineland.

The bargain is struck, in fact, on April 14. France will receive ownership of the Saar mines in compensation for wanton German destruction of French mines in the Nord (all along, Wilson has agreed that such reparation was due to France). German sovereignty over and administration of the Saar Valley will be suspended and transferred to a League of Nations high commission, on which Germany will be represented. Moreover, local government of the area will be in the hands of an assembly elected by the Saarlanders. After fifteen years, they will vote whether to join France or go back to Germany. In the latter event, Germany will have the right to purchase the Saar mines from the French government.

This, the most important compromise of the Paris Peace Conference, effectually settles all important differences between Wilson and Clemenceau and saves the conference from disruption. There are, of course, continuing disputes between Wilson and his advisers and the Anglo-French bloc over the issue of reparation, which drag on almost until the signing of the Versailles Treaty. Wilson keeps up a drumfire of arguments in favor of a fixed sum and a time limit to Germany's payments.

Meanwhile, about April 9, Orlando and Sonnino begin a campaign to force the Council of Four to award to Italy, not only those territories conceded to her by the Treaty of London of 1915, including the Dalmatian islands and littoral, but also the strategic port of Fiume. That treaty had awarded Fiume to Croatia, now part of the Kingdom of the Serbs, Croats, and Slovenes. Wilson, from the outset, makes it clear that he is not bound by and will not respect the terms of the Treaty of London, although he had earlier consented to the transfer of the Austrian South Tyrol to Italy in order to give her a secure northern frontier. In the early stages of the discussion of the Adriatic question, Wilson uses his most persuasive arts and appeals movingly to the idealism and highmindedness of his Italian colleagues. When it turns out that these qualities are in short supply, Wilson says that he will leave the conference before seeing Fiume and Yugoslavian territory turned over to Italy. As this volume ends, Wilson has drafted an appeal to the Italian people, over the heads of their leaders, in a ringing reaffirmation of the principle of self-determination.

Not long after the Italian leaders launch their initiative, the heretofore taciturn Japanese demand that the Council of Four ratify secret treaties and other arrangements which awarded Japan all German concessions in China—most particularly the German leasehold in Kiaochow Bay and control of the Tsingtao-Chinan Railroad in the province of Shantung, sacred to the Chinese because it was the birthplace of Confucius. Wilson and all of his advisers strongly support Chinese claims for the full restitution to China of former German rights in Shantung Province. However, as this volume ends, it is becoming increasingly clear that Wilson faces the hard choice of either agreeing to a compromise acceptable to the Japanese or of forcing the Japanese delegates to go home and negotiate a separate treaty with Germany.

Still seeking to find a solution to the Russian problem after the cold reception accorded the proposals by Lenin that William C. Bullitt brought back from Moscow, Wilson falls in with the so-called Nansen plan. It provides that northern neutrals would organize and administer the sending of food and civilian supplies to Russia through the Bolshevik government in return for a ceasefire in the Russian civil war and the withdrawal of all foreign troops from Russia. Wilson secures the approval of the other members of the Council of Four to this plan and takes decisive steps to quell Herbert Hoover's efforts to sabotage it.

During all these turbulent days, Wilson, with the indispensable support of Lord Robert Cecil, pushes changes in the Covenant through the League of Nations Commission—changes which former President Taft and others have assured him will guarantee the speedy consent of the Senate to the ratification of the peace treaty. These changes include recognition of the Monroe Doctrine, the right of a member to withdraw from the League after due notice, and exclusion of the League's jurisdiction over such domestic policies as tariffs and immigration. At the same time, in order to win Lloyd George's support for the League, Wilson, through Colonel House, gives vague and ambiguous assurances that he will not permit the United States to challenge British world-wide naval supremacy by building a navy larger than Britain's.

The only significant controversy at home during this period is the bitter struggle between the Industrial Board of the Commerce Department and the Railroad Administration over the issue of whether the former should exercise the right to determine the price which the Railroad Administration should pay for steel rails. In the end, Wilson agrees that the Railroad Administration should buy steel rails at competitive prices, and this effectively ends all efforts by the Industrial Board to stabilize prices in general.

"VERBATIM ET LITERATIM"

In earlier volumes of this series, we have said the following: "All documents are reproduced *verbatim et literatim*, with typographical and spelling errors corrected in square brackets only when necessary for clarity and ease of reading." The following essay explains our textual methods and review procedures.

We have never printed and do not intend to print critical, or corrected, versions of documents. We print them exactly as they are, with a few exceptions which we always note. We never use the word *sic* except to denote the repetition of words in a document; in fact, we think that a succession of *sics* defaces a page.

We usually repair words in square brackets when letters are missing. As we have said, we also repair words in square brackets for clarity and ease of reading. Our general rule is to do this when we, ourselves, cannot read the word without having to stop to puzzle out its meaning. Jumbled words and names misspelled beyond recognition of course have to be repaired. We correct the misspelling of names in documents in the footnotes identifying those persons.

However, when an old man writes to Wilson saying that he is glad to hear that Wilson is "comming" to Newark, or a semiliterate farmer from Texas writes phonetically, we see no reason to correct spellings in square brackets when the words are perfectly understandable. We do not correct Wilson's misspellings unless they are unreadable, except to supply in square brackets letters missing in words. For example, he consistently spelled "belligerent" as "belligerant." Nothing would be gained by correcting "belligerant" in square brackets.

We think that it is very important for several reasons to follow the rule of *verbatim et literatim*. Most important, a document has its own integrity and power, particularly when it is not written in perfect literary form. There is something very moving in seeing a Texas dirt farmer struggling to express his feelings in words, or a semiliterate former slave doing the same thing. Second, in Wilson's case it is essential to reproduce his errors in letters which he typed himself, since he usually typed badly when he was in an agitated state. Third, since style is the essence of the person, we would never correct grammar or make tenses consistent, as one correspondent has urged us to do. Fourth, we think that it is very important that we print exact transcripts of Charles L. Swem's copies of Wilson's letters. Swem made many mistakes (we correct them in footnotes from a reading of his shorthand books), and Wilson let them pass. We thus have to assume that Wilson often did not read his letters before signing them, and this, we think, is a significant fact.

We think that our series would be worthless if we produced unreliable texts, and we go to considerable effort to make certain that the texts are authentic.

Our typists are highly skilled and proofread their transcripts carefully as soon as they have typed them. The Editor sight proofreads documents once he has assembled a volume and is setting its annotation. The Editors who write the notes read through documents several times and are careful to check any anomalies. Then, once the manuscript volume has been completed and all notes checked, the Editor and Senior Associate Editor orally proofread the documents against the copy. They read every comma, dash, and character. They note every absence of punctuation. They study every nearly illegible word in written documents.

Once this process of "establishing the text" is completed, the manuscript volume goes to our editor at Princeton University Press, who checks the volume carefully and sends it to the printing plant. The galley proofs are read against copy in the proofroom at the Press. And we must say that the proofreaders there are extraordinarily skilled. Some years ago, before we found a way to ease their burden, they queried every misspelled word, inconsistencies in punctuation and capitalization, asbence of punctuation, or other such anomalies. Now we write "O.K." above such words or spaces on the copy.

We read the galley proofs at least four times. Our copyeditor gives them a sight reading against the manuscript copy to look for remaining typographical errors and to make sure that no line has been dropped. The Editor, Senior Associate Editor and Associate Editor Boemeke sight read them against documents and copy. We then get the page proofs, which have been corrected at the Press. We check all the changes three times. In addition, we get *revised* pages and check them twice.

This is not the end. The Editor, Senior Associate Editor, and Dr. Boemeke give a final reading to headings, description-location lines, and notes. Finally, our indexer of course reads the pages word by word. Before we return the pages to the Press, she brings in a list of queries, all of which are answered by reference to the documents.

Our rule in the Wilson Papers is that our tolerance of error is zero. No system and no person can be perfect. There may be errors in our volumes. However, we believe that we have done everything humanly possible to avoid error; the chance is remote that what looks at first glance like a typographical error is indeed an error.

We call the reader's attention to Sterling J. Kernek's "Woodrow Wilson and National Self-Determination along Italy's Frontier . . . ," *Proceedings of the American Philosophical Society*, CXXVI (Aug. 1982), 243-300. We have greatly profited from the insights in this monograph and mention it here lest it be overlooked in a footnote.

We are indebted to many persons for invaluable aid in the preparation of this volume. John Milton Cooper, Jr., William H. Harbaugh, Richard W. Leopold, and Betty Miller Unterberger all read the manuscript carefully and were, as always, helpful critics. Barbara Brooks translated the telegram from Keishiro Matsui to Viscount Uchida of April 22, 1919. Catharine Vera Bligh, Assistant Archivist of the Record Office of the House of Lords, who has been of great service to us in the past, found for us the document printed as an addendum on page 631. We are grateful to Arthur Walworth for calling our attention to the two memoranda by Wellington Koo printed as addenda on pages 631-37. We continue to be indebted to Philippe-Roger Mantoux for reviewing our translations of his father's notes of the conversations of the Big Four. Alice Calaprice served as editor of this volume for Princeton University Press. Finally, we want to reiterate our deep thanks to the proofreaders of Princeton University Press for their assiduous attention to our text.

THE EDITORS

Princeton, New Jersey
February 20, 1987

CONTENTS

Introduction, vii
Illustrations, xxi
Abbreviations and Symbols, xxiii

The Papers, April 5-22, 1919
The Paris Peace Conference

General Diplomatic and Military Affairs

Domestic Affairs

Personal Affairs

ILLUSTRATIONS

Following page 358

From the collections of Princeton University Library except where otherwise noted

The Inquiry Division Chiefs
National Archives

André Tardieu

Baron Sidney Sonnino

Baron Nobuaki Makino

Ignace Jan Paderewski
National Archives

Ion I. C. Brătianu

Eduard Beneš

Nikola Pašić

Ante Trumbić

Vi Kyuin Wellington Koo

Viscount Sutemi Chinda

ABBREVIATIONS

ACNP	American Commission to Negotiate Peace
ALI	autograph letter initialed
ALS	autograph letter signed
ASB	Albert Sidney Burleson
BMB	Bernard Mannes Baruch
CC	carbon copy
CCL	carbon copy of letter
CCLS	carbon copy of letter signed
EMH	Edward Mandell House
FLP	Frank Lyon Polk
FR	*Papers Relating to the Foreign Relations of the United States*
GFC	Gilbert Fairchild Close
HCH	Herbert Clark Hoover
Hw, hw	handwriting, handwritten
JPT	Joseph Patrick Tumulty
MS, MSS	manuscript, manuscripts
NDB	Newton Diehl Baker
PPC	*Papers Relating to the Foreign Relations of the United States, The Paris Peace Conference, 1919*
RChw	Lord Robert Cecil handwriting, handwritten
RG	record group
RL	Robert Lansing
T	typed
TC	typed copy
TCL	typed copy of letter
THB	Tasker Howard Bliss
TI	typed initialed
TL	typed letter
TLS	typed letter signed
TNP	Thomas Nelson Page
TS	typed signed
WBW	William Bauchop Wilson
WCR	William Cox Redfield
WJB	William Jennings Bryan
WW	Woodrow Wilson
WWhw	Woodrow Wilson handwriting, handwritten
WWsh	Woodrow Wilson shorthand
WWT	Woodrow Wilson typed
WWTLI	Woodrow Wilson typed letter initialed
WWTLS	Woodrow Wilson typed letter signed

ABBREVIATIONS FOR COLLECTIONS
AND REPOSITORIES

Following the National Union Catalog of the
Library of Congress

CaOOA	Public Archives Library, Ottawa
CSt-H	Hoover Institution on War, Revolution and Peace

CtY	Yale University
CU-B	University of California, Berkeley, Bancroft Library
DGU	Georgetown University
DLC	Library of Congress
DNA	National Archives
HPL	Hoover Presidential Library
MH-BA	Harvard University Graduate School of Business Administration
NjP	Princeton University
NNC	Columbia University
PRO	Public Record Office
SDR	State Department Records
WC, NjP	Woodrow Wilson Collection, Princeton University
WP, DLC	Woodrow Wilson Papers, Library of Congress

SYMBOLS

[April 5, 1919]	publication date of published writing; also date of document when date is not part of text
[*April 16, 1919*]	composition date when publication date differs
[[April 9, 1919]]	delivery date of speech if publication date differs
**** ***	text deleted by author of document

THE PAPERS OF

WOODROW WILSON

VOLUME 57

APRIL 5-22, 1919

THE PAPERS OF
WOODROW WILSON

From the Diary of Dr. Grayson[1]

Saturday, April 5, 1919.

This morning the President's temperature was 101, but he was showing signs of improvement. His bronchial tubes were filled up with mucus, and he could notice a wheezing sound while breathing. It worried him considerably and he sent for me, asking me if I would tell him what that meant. I again made a thorough examination of his lungs and assured him that they were not involved. I now began administering an expectorant mixture in order to clear up the mucus. The complete physical examination which I made revealed the fact that outside the acute nature of the disturbance, the President's other functions were practically normal.

The President called my attention to the great benefit that he had received from the deep-breathing exercises in which I had commenced to instruct him six years ago, and which he has continued without cessation to the present time. He said: "I notice the difference, not only in the fact that my chest has increased in size, but when I speak I never get out of breath." He also said: "Don't you think that these deep-breathing exercises have helped me perhaps from suffering from bronchial troubles or influenza or possibly an attack of pneumonia?" And I told him that I did think so. He said: "I think it is remarkable though that since I have followed out the line of treatment which you have given me, this is the first real cold I have had in three years.[2] Before I came to Washington, and the first winter I was in Washington, I would have sometimes as many as two colds a month."

With the President's consent I gave to the newspaper correspondents the following official statement:

"The President has come very near having a serious attack of influenza, but by going to bed at once, by my direction, he has apparently escaped it. He is still necessarily confined to his bed."

During the afternoon the President indicated that he was getting along nicely by taking a distinct and decided interest in everything that was going on. Among other matters he called for some of the people about the house and found that they were all out except one. This made him distinctly irascible, which was one of the most favorable symptoms possible, showing that he actually was getting well, because a very sick person does not pay much attention to matters of daily routine.

While the President was in bed the Council of Four continued their meetings, with Colonel House sitting in, but they made substantially no progress, it being admitted that the absence of the President, while necessary, was a very decided handicap. The general peace situation at the present time was very disquieting inasmuch as the criticism was increasing in volume, both in Great Britain and France, and there was a very evident effort being made through the inspired press of the two countries to throw the blame on the President, so that Clemenceau and his followers, and Lloyd-George and his would seem to get out from under.

Immediately after dinner Bernard M. Baruch called in to see me. The President heard me say that Mr. Baruch was here, and he said to me: "I would like to have a word with Baruch. Ask him to come down here. I want to speak to him." When Baruch appeared in the room, the President raised his head up on the pillow, and he said: "Baruch, I want you to give me the plain facts as to how things are going." Baruch spoke very freely to him and said: "When you get ready to act I would suggest that you do as you always do—not threaten, but perform." The President said: "That's exactly what I have in mind of doing, and I want you to think it over and give me any confidential advice that you have on the subject in the next twenty-four hours."

I was with the President until after midnight, talking with him at the side of his bed. He was feeling comfortable and in good spirits, notwithstanding his burdens and trials.

T MS (received from James Gordon Grayson and Cary T. Grayson, Jr.)
    [1] About this document, see n. 1 to the extract from it printed at Dec. 3, 1918, Vol. 53.
    [2] An astonishing statement!

From the Diary of Ray Stannard Baker

Saturday the 5th [April 1919]

There is some slight evidence to-day that peace will be made because peace must be made—a peace written on paper & signed by a few old men none of whom will believe in what he is doing—but it will solve nothing, decide nothing—

Wilson is still in bed. Col. House is still chirping hopefully—& has set another date for the conclusion of negotiations (while Bavaria is setting up a Soviet Republic).[1] The only hopeful man I saw to-day was Dr. Nansen the Norwegian who has a plan for feeding the starving Russians.[2]

The only hope left of this Conference is that Wilson will come out with a last terrific blast for his principles, and their *specific application* & go down in the ruin. *I fear he won't.* And that is complete failure. For what good will be a League of Nations unless the settlements upon which it rests are just? A League the only purpose of which is to guarantee "grabs" of land by France, Italy, Poland &c &c is doomed to speedy failure. I have been here mostly because I saw a chance to help along the reconstructive movement, with the organization of a L of N. to keep the peace of the world. It now looks as though the League would be so weak, its foundations so insecure, that I could not myself support it.

It will make very little difference *now* what peace is signed, for nothing essential will be settled.

Hw MS (R. S. Baker Papers, DLC).
    [1] Ever since the assassination of the Bavarian Prime Minister, Kurt Eisner, on February 21, 1919 (about which see EMH to WW, March 4, 1919, n. 1, Vol. 55), the political situation in Bavaria had been characterized by utter chaos and confusion, by the absence of any single source of power and authority, and by the lack of any consensus among the various moderate and radical left-wing parties and revolutionary councils which determined the fate of the Bavarian Republic in the spring of 1919. For weeks, Munich witnessed a fierce struggle between proponents of a parliamentary form of government and advocates of a socialist soviet republic ruled by workers', soldiers', and peasants' councils. Finally, a medley of radical leaders seized the initiative and, in a meeting on April 5, 1919, decided to establish a Bavarian soviet republic. Proclaimed on April 7, the first Bavarian Soviet Republic was headed by Independent Social Democrats, leaders of the Bavarian Peasants' League, and a number of socialist intellectuals without party affiliation. Ironically, the Communists refused to endorse what they called a "pseudo soviet republic," created by a revolution "proclaimed from a green table." As it turned out, the first soviet regime in Bavaria, which was marked above all by "raucous and at times ridiculous confusion" and disarray, lasted but six days. As a result of an abortive Putsch by the moderate left, the Communists seized power and, on April 13, proclaimed the second Bavarian Soviet Republic and the dictatorship of the proletariat. For a detailed discussion, see Allan Mitchell, *Revolution in Bavaria, 1918-1919: The Eisner Regime and the Soviet Republic* (Princeton, N. J., 1965), pp. 273-331.
    [2] See F. Nansen to WW, April 3, 1919, Vol. 56.

Hankey's and Mantoux's Notes of a Meeting of the Council of Four[1]

I.C.-170H.   President Wilson's House, Paris,
                                        April 5, 1919, 11 a.m.

The Conference had before them a Memorandum attached in the Appendix, which had been substantially agreed to by the American and British representatives, but which was not accepted by the French representatives.[2]

    [1] The complete text of Hankey's minutes is printed in *PPC*, V, 21-30.
    [2] For the comments and "reserves" of the various delegations about this tentative Anglo-American agreement on reparations, see the Enclosure printed with N. H. Davis and V. C. McCormick to WW, April 4, 1919, Vol. 56.

§ Mantoux's notes:

Clemenceau. I ask M. Klotz to report to us about the state of the question [reparations].

Klotz. Following the conversation which took place here the other day,[3] a memorandum was drafted through the good offices of Mr. Lloyd George.[4] The French delegation presented certain observations on the subject of this memorandum;[5] the American delegation then examined the text, with the French annotations, and it proposed a new draft, which was then the object of a common discussion of the English, American, French, and Italian delegations. The observations formulated by our delegation brought out some rather important differences.[6] I will explain the Anglo-American plan, with the French observations.

Article 1 of the Anglo-American text is a declaration of principle, which has political significance. According to this article, the Allied and Associated Powers recognize that the enemy's resources are not unlimited, and that consequently it will be impossible for him to provide a complete reparation for all damages caused. Is it appropriate to place a clause of this kind in a financial agreement, which should be composed of precise stipulations? I do not believe that it would be politically advisable to place such a declaration here, although it could be advantageous to insert it—in a form to be studied—in a general preamble. I fear that if it is put among the financial clauses, it could only create an unfortunate impression.

Lloyd George. I have some sympathy for the point of view M. Klotz expresses. This Article 1 is insufficient to permit us to face the political difficulties which we can expect from both British and French opinion.

I transmitted to M. Clemenceau an account of the debate which took place in the House of Commons on this question of reparations,[7] and he could see the violence of feeling which arose. Mr.

---

[3] See the minutes of the Council of Four printed at March 28, 1919, 11 a.m., *ibid.*

[4] See Appendix III to the minutes of the Council of Four printed at March 29, 1919, 3 p.m., *ibid.*

[5] See L. L. Klotz to WW, March 30, 1919, n. 2, and the minutes of the Council of Four, March 31, 1919, 11 a.m., both printed in *ibid.*

[6] See the first draft of an Anglo-American accord on reparations, April 1, 1919; the second draft of an accord on reparations, April 2, 1919; and, again, the Enclosure printed with N. H. Davis and V. C. McCormick to WW, April 4, 1919, all printed in *ibid.*

[7] The debate of April 2, 1919, had been the most recent onslaught in the continuing offensive by a group of Conservative M.P.s against Lloyd George's alleged lack of resolve on the question of obtaining a full indemnity from Germany. See, e.g., n. 1 to the extract from the Grayson Diary printed at March 26, 1919, *ibid.* This latest attack had been precipitated by an article in the London *Westminster Gazette* of March 31, 1919. Written by Sisley Huddleston, the paper's Paris correspondent, it included an interview with a "High British Authority," who, it soon turned out, was none other than Lloyd George himself. In the days following the submission of his Fontainebleau Memorandum (printed at March 25, 1919, Vol. 56), Lloyd George, in the hope of building popular support for

Bonar Law wrote to me, after this session, that Parliament showed itself to be rather dissatisfied with his declarations.

The English public, like the French public, thinks that the Germans must above all recognize their obligation to compensate us for all the consequences of their aggression. When this is done, we will come to the question of Germany's capacity to pay; we all think that she will be unable to pay more than what is required of her by this document.

Clemenceau. I do not entirely agree with you about that. But undoubtedly Germany will not be able to pay all that she will owe.

Lloyd George. It is important to state clearly that, if the definition of reparations claimed by us is limited, that is only because we recognize the sheer impossibility of a complete payment.

House. I believe we can agree about that.

---

his new course of moderation, had made repeated efforts to have the main thesis of the memorandum disseminated. On one such occasion, he had given one of his frequent off-the-record interviews, during which he had virtually repeated the major arguments of the Fontainebleau thesis. However, among the correspondents present, Huddleston, himself an advocate of a peace of reconciliation, had been the only one who had actually seen a copy of the memorandum and who had realized the significance of Lloyd George's remarks and had considered them worth repeating.

As in the Fontainebleau Memorandum, the dominant theme of the interview was a call for "moderation" in the peace negotiations, for a "practical treaty" and a "sane peace," regardless of the inevitable disappointments which would result among the Allied peoples from such a settlement. Among other things, the "High British Authority" pointed out that the Allies could not go on "stripping Germany bare," and that the question of indemnities beyond the mere reparation of material damages could not even be considered.

The publication of what has become known as the "moderation interview" created a furor in Britain's conservative press, and the jingoistic London *Morning Post* immediately revealed the identity of Huddleston's source. As a result, a group of so-called punitive Members of Parliament, led by Lt. Col. Claude Lowther and Kennedy Jones, Conservative M.P.s from Lancashire and Middlesex, respectively, initiated a debate in the House of Commons for the purpose of "forcibly reminding" the British delegates in Paris that 400 members of the House were solemnly pledged to their constituents to exact the "uttermost farthing" from Germany. They demanded that Lloyd George keep his election promises, and they called on Bonar Law to assure the country that the government had not abandoned its original intention to make Germany pay for the full cost of the war. In response, Bonar Law stated that, contrary to the assertions by Lowther and others, neither Lloyd George nor any other member of the present government had ever promised to claim a full indemnity from Germany; they had only pledged to "exact from Germany whatever Germany was able to pay." He continued: "There is no change whatever up to this hour in the attitude of His Majesty's Government on this question. The intention still is to obtain, as part of the debt which Germany owes, whatever can be got from Germany."

However, Bonar Law was under no delusion that his assurances had succeeded in quelling the mushrooming rebellion in the House of Commons. In a telegram to Lloyd George, he admitted that he had just had "a bad time about indemnities," and he concluded: "I do not think I convinced anyone and probably nine out of ten, of the Unionist Members at least, were very disgusted." *Parliamentary Debates*, Fifth Series, Vol. 114, House of Commons, Cols. 1304-49. For a detailed discussion, see also A. Lentin, *Lloyd George, Woodrow Wilson and the Guilt of Germany: An Essay in the Pre-History of Appeasement* (Baton Rouge, La., 1985), pp. 50-52; Arno J. Mayer, *Politics and Diplomacy of Peacemaking: Containment and Counterrevolution at Versailles, 1918-1919* (New York, 1967), pp. 623, 627-30; Robert Blake, *The Unknown Prime Minister: The Life and Times of Andrew Bonar Law, 1858-1923* (London, 1955), pp. 406-407; and Sisley Huddleston, *Peace-Making at Paris* (London, 1919), pp. 137-56.

Davis. It is not the American delegation which wanted to introduce that sentence into the text. In drafting it, we were trying to respond to the desire expressed by Great Britain and France.

Clemenceau. Then we must indicate in this sentence that Germany *acknowledges* the totality of her debt. It is not sufficient to say that we affirm it.

Lloyd George. We must say that the Allies affirm their claim and that the Germans acknowledge their debt for the entire cost of the war.

House. That would be contrary to our agreement prior to the Armistice, and to the note which you addressed to the American government.[8] We must not draft this text in such a way that it appears to violate our own commitments.

Davis. We can write that Germany is morally responsible for the war and for all its consequences and that, legally, she is responsible for damages to property and persons, according to the formula adopted.

Clemenceau. It is a question of wording; I believe we can find a way out.§

It was agreed to add in the first line after the word "affirm" the following words "and the enemy Governments accept." The Clause as amended reads as follows:

"The Allied and Associated Governments affirm *and the enemy Governments accept* the responsibility of the enemy States for causing all the loss and damage to which the Allied and Associated Governments and their Nationals have been subjected as a consequence of the war imposed upon them by the aggression of the enemy States."

M. KLOTZ read the following extract from the remarks by the French delegation on the Scheme of the American and British Delegations:

"The note brought forward by Mr. Lloyd George on the 29th of March, 1919, and the memorandum of the British and American Delegations of the 1st of April asserted both the right for the Allied and Associated Governments of getting full reparation for all the loss and damage caused to the persons and to the property whatever may be the cost for the enemy States. But the terms of Article III were inconsistent with that principle, since they compelled the Inter-allied Commission to limit the amount of the payments to be made by the enemy by taking into account its financial capacity during 30 years."[9]

[8] See EMH to WW, No. 12, Oct. 30, 1918, and No. 42, Nov. 4, 1918, both printed in Vol. 51.

[9] A CC MS of Klotz's full statement, entitled "Remarks of the French Delegation about the Scheme of the British and American Delegations" and dated April 5, 1919, is in WP, DLC.

MR. LLOYD GEORGE said that this was merely intended as an expression of opinion that Germany can pay in 30 years. If she can pay in that time it is better than in 40 years. The Clause, however, was not intended to limit the sum to be paid to the amount that Germany could pay in 30 years.

M. CLEMENCEAU said that the British Financial Experts had taken a different opinion.

M. KLOTZ explained that the view of the British Experts had been that the whole transaction was limited to 30 years. Hence, he said, if the Commission estimated that 50 milliard of dollars represented the amount that Germany could pay, and in fact, it was only found possible to make her pay 30 milliards, in 30 years there would be a dead loss to the Allied and Associated Powers of 20 milliards.

MR. LLOYD GEORGE said that it was no use his arguing about a point which we were not endeavouring to sustain. Supposing Germany could pay 60 milliards in 40 years, but only 50 milliards in 30 years, we should not propose to limit the total that she must pay to 30 milliards, and this document did not say that we should.

MR. DAVIS said, in this case, he did not understand this position, for the British delegates had made it quite clear that the document did so limit it.

LORD SUMNER did not admit this.

MR. LLOYD GEORGE said that according to Lord Sumner, our view was that Germany ought to pay within 30 years, but that if she could not do so, the Commission should have the right to extend the time of payment.

§ Mantoux's notes:

Klotz. I have some important observations to make about Articles 2 and 3. Mr. Lloyd George's note dated March 29 and the American note of April 1 affirmed Germany's responsibility for damages caused to property and persons "whatever the financial consequences might be for the enemy." Now what is proposed is to limit the actual payments to Germany's capacity to pay during thirty years.

Lloyd George. That limitation does not seem to me to proceed from the text I have before me.

Klotz. I beg your pardon. Let us suppose that the inter-Allied commission concludes that the sum due from Germany is 50 billion dollars but that, on the other hand, it estimates that in thirty years Germany can only pay 40 billions or 30 billions. According to this text, the difference, that is 10 billions or 20 billions, would be irretrievably lost to the Allies.

Lloyd George. It is pointless to debate with me about something which I do not support. Let us suppose that Germany can pay 60 billion dollars in forty years, or only 50 billions in thirty years. I am not proposing that we reduce her debt to 50 billions. Note that

Article 4 says that the period of payment can be prolonged if that is necessary. If then Germany can pay all in forty years, I will not reduce the total in order that the payment might be made in thirty years.

I just said a word about this to Lord Sumner; he thinks that Germany should pay in thirty years, but if she cannot manage to fulfill her obligations in that period of time, the commission can prolong the period of payment. §

M. LOUCHEUR said he entirely agreed with Mr. Lloyd George, but the British Delegation had not taken the same attitude in the discussions of the experts. The matter was explained clearly by the following example. Supposing the amount that Germany ought to pay was estimated by the Commission at 50 billions of dollars, and the Commission found that Germany was only capable of paying 40 billions in 30 years, it had been clearly explained that 10 billions had been lost.

LORD SUMNER said that the difficulty arose out of a misunderstanding of terms. Mr. Montagu had agreed to the insertion of a limit of 30 years because he had been given to understand Mr. Lloyd George had agreed to this limitation. (MR. LLOYD GEORGE interjected, that of course he preferred a period of 30 years if it were practicable to obtain the sum within that time. Everyone had agreed to this.)

Lord Sumner continuing said that the French Delegates had then put the question—if the total was not paid in 30 years would the balance be remitted? The British Delegates had replied in the negative. He had then understood Mr. Davis to say that the balance would be immediately payable. Then a further amendment had been introduced, namely, Clause 4, which was put in to enable the total amount to be paid by some means. It was by no means the desire, however, of the British Delegation, that Germany should escape.

MR. LLOYD GEORGE said that Lord Sumner had presented his view perfectly correctly.

M. LOUCHEUR said if this were the case this meeting would hardly seem to have been necessary. The French Delegation were quite ready to accept Mr. Lloyd George's view, but when Article 4 had been drafted it had not really applied to this but to something else. The hypothesis had been that the Commission would estimate the total amount that Germany could pay at 50 milliard dollars, but that the amount which she could pay in 30 years was only 40 milliard dollars. Supposing, however, it was found in practice that even the 40 milliard dollars could not be paid, then it was proposed that the time might be extended for the payment of even the 40.

MR. DAVIS said he was willing to accept this draft which had been prepared by the British Delegation, but he wished to have no doubt as to what it meant. The Commission would have to decide: (1) the total estimate of the amount to be paid; (2) if they considered this amount in excess of what Germany could pay in 30 years they must say the amount we estimate she could pay in 30 years is what Germany is required to pay, but if in practice she cannot pay in 30 years she must be allowed more time but, nevertheless, must pay it. When President Wilson agreed to include Pensions he thought it would not run up the total amount which was limited by Germany's ability to pay.[10]

MR. LLOYD GEORGE said that the difference of opinion was not very substantial. By May 1921 the claims for reparation would have been examined and adjusted. Suppose these amounted to 70 milliards of dollars and suppose the Commissioners thought that Germany could only pay 50 milliards of dollars. Germany might be able to pay 60 milliards in 60 years, but only 30 milliards in 30 years: in this case she would have to pay the balance after the end of the 30 years.

MR. DAVIS said she would only have to pay the amount of the default.

MR. LLOYD GEORGE asked whether, when you arrived at the capacity of Germany to pay, you took the amount of 30 years into account.

MR. DAVIS replied in the affirmative.

MR. LLOYD GEORGE said that in this case he took the French view. If you said that Germany could only pay 30 milliards in 30 years but could pay the total of 50 milliards if the time were extended, say to 50 years, then he would unquestionably say that 50 milliards was the right sum that Germany should pay.

MR. DAVIS said that if you took so large a capital sum Germany would not even be able to pay the interest on it. It was essential to hold out a ray of light to Germany somewhere.

MR. LLOYD GEORGE and M. KLOTZ pointed out that this was a difficult point.

M. LOUCHEUR said that Mr. Lloyd George's point was that Germany should pay according to the Commissioners' view of her total capacity to pay, not on the limitation of what she could pay in 30 years.

M. CLEMENCEAU said that the conclusion of the Commission ought to be confirmed by the Governments which alone could take the responsibility.

[10] See the memorandum by J. F. Dulles, particularly n. 3, and the extracts from the diaries of V. C. McCormick and T. W. Lamont, all printed at April 1, 1919, Vol. 56.

MR. DAVIS said that the only difference now was between the view that the Commission should base its estimate on what Germany could pay in 30 years rather than what she could pay in 40 or 50 years. The American view was that for a period longer than 30 years the interest would eat up the amount she could pay. They felt that if the Germans were not given something to lead them into this scheme they would absolutely reject it.

M. KLOTZ agreed that you must hold out something to the Germans, but pointed out that you must also give the French and British people something that they could accept. They would not expect to pay what it was Germany's acknowledged duty to pay. The Armistice laid down that Germany should pay reparation for damage, and it was very undesirable that she should get off what she could not pay in 30 years. It would require a genius to discover in 1921 the capacity of what Germany could pay 30 years later. It was only in 1930 or 1940, when we should be confronted with Germany's incapacity to pay, supported on evidence, that a definite opinion could be expressed. Hence, he demanded that we should adhere to the excellent text of April 1st. If the Commission should definitely find that a prolongation of the period of payment was necessary, they could apply to the Governments concerned for instructions.

§ Mantoux's notes:

Loucheur. We are completely in agreement with Mr. Lloyd George. But in our discussions among the experts, the British delegation did not support this point of view. I will explain.

The estimate of damages is made. A total of 50 billion dollars is reached. Our commission says: "In thirty years, Germany will only be able to pay 40 billions." What has been said is that, in this case, the difference, 10 billions would be lost to us.

Sumner. I believe that there is a misunderstanding arising from the terminology used. Mr. Montagu accepted the limit of thirty years because he had understood that Mr. Lloyd George would desire this figure. The French delegates say: "If, in thirty years, everything is not paid, will the remainder be abandoned?" I answer: no, because of the power given to the commission to prolong the duration of payment and to accept payment if necessary in German treasury bonds. It is not our wish that Germany be able to evade us by not paying what she owes in thirty years.

Loucheur. If you had expressed yourselves as clearly as that, our discussion of today would not have been necessary. I should do justice to the American delegation, which did not leave any doubt about the meaning of its declarations.[11] Article 4 does not apply to

---

[11] In the American notes of this meeting, this sentence reads as follows: "However,

that loss of 10 billions which I envisage hypothetically. Let us suppose that the commission declares that in thirty years Germany can only pay 40 billion dollars, instead of the 50 billions that she owes us. It was observed that perhaps Germany would not manage to pay these 40 billions which the commission will have said was her capacity to pay over thirty years. Our colleagues then said: "The commission will have the power to prolong the period until complete payment of the 40 billions. But the 10 billions difference between the commission's estimate of her capacity to pay and the sum actually due from Germany will be lost to us."

Davis. In fact, this text was drafted by the British delegation, and here is how I understand it. Two years from now, the commission must declare the total sum due us. If it finds that this sum exceeds Germany's capacity to pay within thirty years, it will decide what Germany should pay according to that capacity. But that last sum will have to be paid in full, even if it is later found necessary to prolong the period of payment.

Lloyd George. I do not think there is a real divergence between our views. In 1921, we will not only have examined but fixed all our claims. I suppose that the total will reach 70 billion dollars, but that the commission will arrive at the conclusion that it is impossible for Germany to pay more than 50 billions; we will have to be satisfied with these 50 billions. Once this conclusion has been reached, we can study the period over which this sum should be divided.

Davis. That's it.

Lloyd George. I agree with the French delegation. Obviously, if you say to the commission: "You must restrict yourselves to seeking what Germany can pay in thirty years," you are imposing a limit upon it.

Loucheur. Mr. Lloyd George seems to be admitting that the commission will be able to limit the total figure according to Germany's ability to pay.

Clemenceau. I would not leave that right to the commission without the governments being consulted.

Davis. There is no real difference between a period of thirty years and a period of forty years, because of the role of compound interest, and we should try to present the Germans with something acceptable.

Klotz. Yes, but it must also be acceptable to the French, who will never admit that part of the financial responsibilities which Germany will have acknowledged be thrown back on them. I recognize as you do that it is highly desirable that Germany be able to acquit

the American delegation clearly expressed the contrary view." "REPARATIONS; MEMO-
RANDUM OF CONFERENCE HELD APRIL 5, 11 A.M. . . . ," T MS (J. F. Dulles Papers, NjP).

herself in thirty years; but if that is impossible, we should not be the victims.

The commission must be able to grant extensions. I do not think that we can arrive at a satisfactory total estimate as early as 1921. It would require a superhuman genius to know at that date what Germany will be able to pay during the following thirty years. In my opinion, it is in 1930 or 1940, faced with a recognized and justified inability, that the commission will be authorized to grant delays. I recall the formula of the note of April 1: "We must determine the enemy's debt, whatever the financial obligations it imposes upon him." This principle having been stated, if the commission judges an extension necessary, it will have to turn to the governments. §

COLONEL HOUSE said that all the experts seemed to think that a 30 years basis was a right one for the Commission to take in fixing the amount. Everyone was agreed that if the Germans could not pay in 30 years, then they must pay the amount in 40 years. He did not understand, therefore, what the discussion was all about.

M. LOUCHEUR said that there was one obscure point. When the Commission met, what figure was it to arrive at? According to the American Delegates, this figure was the amount that Germany could pay in 30 years, but the French Delegates maintained that it was to ascertain the total amount that Germany could pay.

COLONEL HOUSE said they would have to pay it in 50 years if not in 30 years.

M. CLEMENCEAU said the question was whether the Commission was to fix in 1921 only what Germany could pay in 30 years, or what the total amount was that she had to pay.

MR. LLOYD GEORGE said they were to work out their estimate of the total that Germany could pay, although it was, of course, desirable that she should pay in 30 years.

MR. DAVIS said the Commission would be very liberal to the Allies in its estimate of what Germany could pay in 30 years. The Commission, however, must have some basis for its work.

M. CLEMENCEAU said he did not accept that point of view.

MR. LAMONT agreed with Mr. Davis that the subjects being discussed were largely academic. We were arranging for a Commission to do two years hence what we had been trying to do lately, and had failed.

In all the Conversations of the Commission it had been agreed that it was not worth while considering a period exceeding 30 or 35 years. It was now only proposed to instruct the Commission to take the same time limit as had been taken in all recent discussions. It did not pay to figure the matter out beyond that. Of course, if it turned out that Germany could not pay in that period, then time must be given to them.

MR. LLOYD GEORGE then proposed the following re-draft of the last part of Clause 2 [3], proposed by Lord Sumner:

"The Commission shall estimate Germany's capacity to pay in the future, and shall also concurrently draw up a schedule of payments up to or within a period of 30 years, and this schedule of payments shall then be communicated to Germany."

He pointed out that the sequence was as follows: First, you determine Germany's capacity to pay. Second, you try to get the amount within 30 years. And third, if you cannot get it in 30 years you extend the limit. But the basis of calculation was Germany's total capacity to pay.

M. KLOTZ said that Mr. Lloyd George opposed the proposal to limit Germany's capacity to pay to her capacity for 30 years. The first point was to determine Germany's capacity to pay, and the second point was to spread the amount over a period of 30 years.

MR. DAVIS said that you had either to fix for the Commission a limitation of years or a maximum of money to be paid.

COLONEL HOUSE agreed.

MR. LLOYD GEORGE rehearsed the argument against fixing a period of 30 years. There would be a general dislocation of business everywhere, and particularly in Germany. Germany's ships would have been taken away; if Germany undertook to repair the damage done in Belgium and in Northern France, her workmen would have been taken away. It was not as though conditions were as in 1913. It would take Germany ten years to find her feet. If you said 30 years from the year 1929, it would be a different thing. But you could not tell Germany's capacity to pay until she found her feet. He hoped, therefore, that we would not limit it to the next 30 years, but to a period of 30 years under normal conditions. He agreed that Germany must know what she was in for. But she could obtain this from the schedule giving the items on which she had to pay. After all, Germany had been in Northern France for four years and probably had a pretty good idea of the damage she had done. She knew what ships she had sunk. She could obtain the amounts of the pensions she would have to pay. Hence, she could form a rough estimate. If she were to say "I will take no estimates from the Allies, but will make good the damage myself," she was in a position to get the requisite information.

COLONEL HOUSE asked, then, why it was necessary to have a Commission.

MR. LLOYD GEORGE said that there were a certain number of things in regard to which Germany would have no information, e.g., the amount to be paid for sailors and for the restitution of things she had stolen. The Commission would really work within the limits of this class of reparations, supposing that we accepted, as he understood M. Clemenceau had, Germany's offer to make good the damage.

COLONEL HOUSE said he understood that all estimates of Germany's capacity to pay had been on the basis of Germany as she was in 1914; that she still possessed Alsace-Lorraine, Silesia, etc. At any rate, such had been the assumption in the American estimates.

MR. LLOYD GEORGE said that was not the case. He had asked our Delegates, and he found they had made allowance. Lord Sumner's paper,[12] for instance, which was before the Conference, had made allowance for Silesia, the Saar Valley, etc.

COLONEL HOUSE said that a few minutes ago agreement had appeared imminent. President Wilson had always understood that the estimate was to be based on what Germany could pay in a period of 30 years.

MR. LLOYD GEORGE said he never understood this.

MR. DAVIS said President Wilson had understood that by including pensions, the total amount was not increased, owing to the 30 years limit, but that their inclusion only formed a more equitable basis for distribution.

MR. LLOYD GEORGE said this was not the case. He could not face his people and say that human life was of less value than a chimney. You could rebuild a house in a year or two, but you could not supply an efficient man in less than 21 years.

MR. HOUSE said President Wilson accepted this view.

MR. DAVIS said that nevertheless, you do not thereby increase Germany's capacity to pay.

MR. LLOYD GEORGE said he had always discredited the assumption of those who said it was possible for Germany to pay the whole of the war debt, but there was all the difference between this and making all adequate reparation.

He again read Lord Sumner's re-draft of Clause 3. He pointed out that Germany expects to have to pay a very big bill. If we were to put in a bill for reparation and human life, she will know her position.

COLONEL HOUSE suggested that the clause should be drafted in that form, and that nothing should be said about the 30 years limit.

(The Conference then adjourned for a consideration of Lord Sumner's draft of Clause 3, and for Colonel House to prepare a fresh draft, based on the above remark.)

[12] That is, Baron Sumner's memorandum on reparations printed at March 18, 1919, Vol. 56.

§ Mantoux's notes:

House. All our experts seem to agree in thinking that a period of thirty years should be the basis of all our calculations. The commission fixes the sum that this period represents; if that sum is not paid within thirty years, the commission can divide the payments over forty or fifty years. If that really is it, what are we debating?

Loucheur. There remains an obscurity. The commission meets. What will it do? According to the American delegates, it will determine the sum that Germany can pay in thirty years.

Lloyd George. Is that what Colonel House thinks?

House. Yes.

Clemenceau. Will the commission be charged with declaring the amount which, according to its estimates, Germany is capable of paying in thirty years?

Davis. That's it.

Loucheur. Then the difference between that sum and the actual amount of damages is lost to us?

Davis. What we are now proposing to have the commission do in two years is simply what we have tried to do among ourselves, namely to determine what Germany can pay and, consequently, what one can demand of her.

Clemenceau. I do not accept the way you state the question.

Orlando. I have a precise objection to make to Mr. Davis. I am examining this text as a jurist and I read in it: "The Allied and Associated Governments demand that the enemy make compensation to the very limit of his capacity." This sentence signifies clearly that the limit of our claims is none other than the limit of Germany's capacity to pay.

Now, when we come to expressing this capacity in figures, we cannot take account solely of the present wealth of Germany, but of her future capacity, which depends upon her power of production. It follows that the capacity for payment, when we envisage a long period, is related to the will of the debtor. It would be dangerous to adopt a formula which would, as it were, reward bad faith and a refusal to work.

Lamont. It seems to me that our discussion revolves above all around a point of pure theory. We are proposing to confide to the commission the very task which we had undertaken here. In our discussions, we always recognized that it was not worthwhile to consider a period longer than thirty or thirty-five years. What I hear now contradicts what we said among ourselves.

Lloyd George. Since there are doubts about the meaning of the text submitted to us, and about which much could be said, I think, in favor of Mr. Davis' interpretation of it, I propose to modify the draft in the following way: the commission will fix Germany's total capacity to pay and will draw up a plan for periodic payment over thirty years, with the right to modify the annual payments and to extend the period if that is necessary. First of all it must be stated what Germany must pay, to try to obtain what she can pay in thirty years and, if she cannot manage to do that, to reserve the right to prolong the period.

Loucheur. I understand that Mr. Lloyd George contrasts the total capacity with the capacity to pay in thirty years.

Klotz. Here is how I understand the thing: (1) the commission establishes the amount of the debt; (2) the commission estimates the total capacity to pay, and divides the sum over a period of thirty years; (3) if the payment is not completed in thirty years, the commission can prolong that period.

Davis. I think it is preferable that thirty years remain the limit.

Lloyd George. I must present a rather strong argument against this conception. We will all be in a rather bad state for a number of years, and Germany will need ten years to get back on her feet. We cannot really say what Germany's capacity to pay will be! We do not know what Germany will be able to pay in the next thirty years.

Mr. Davis tells us: "Germany must know where she stands and what she will pay." But the Germans know very well what they have destroyed; they know better than we do the state of the devastated regions, for they have stayed there longer. They know the ships they have sunk; they know the pensions we have to pay. So they have an approximate idea of what they owe. If they say today that they themselves will rebuild destroyed houses, that eliminates one of the most uncertain elements from the calculations.

House. In this case, why name a commission? Why not simply draw up such a list?

Lloyd George. The commission will have to be concerned with compensation for the lives of sailors lost at sea, for the restitution of stolen or damaged property. But obviously its work only concerns part of the reparations due.

House. As Mr. Davis said a short time ago, if the period envisaged is too long, the accumulation of interest will make payment nearly impossible.

Lloyd George. I recognize the importance of this observation. Perhaps there is no advantage in prolonging the payment for a hundred years instead of fifty years. But because of the circumstances in which we find ourselves, there will be a great difference between the next thirty years and a period of fifty years, for example.

House. Have not all the estimates of capacity to pay been made according to the estimates of Germany's wealth in 1914, when she had Alsace and Lorraine, Silesia, and her entire merchant fleet?

Lloyd George. No; Lord Sumner's report took account of the difference resulting from the loss of Alsace-Lorraine, the mines of Silesia, the merchant fleet, etc.

House. It seems to me that a few minutes ago we were close to a conclusion.

Lloyd George. We had thought so; but now I no longer think so.

House. President Wilson has always thought that our estimates were all based on a period of thirty years.

Davis. That is what I had thought, and we think on the other hand that, by admitting the right to reimbursement for pensions, we will not obtain any noticeable difference, except perhaps in regard to the distribution, and that because Germany's capacity to pay is limited.

Clemenceau. No one can say today what that capacity is.

Lloyd George. I have fought against those who go on repeating that Germany can pay all that the war cost; but I do not want her to pay less than the extreme limit of the possible.

House. Perhaps it would be better to make no mention of the period.

Lloyd George. I shall have a text drafted which will have as its major points: The Reparation Commission will estimate Germany's capacity to pay in the future, and at the same time will prepare a plan for annual payments within the limits of the total sum due us, fixing according to its opinion what Germany should pay over thirty years. Believe me: Germany will not create the anticipated difficulties about payments; she knows that she must pay, and she is prepared to face the situation.

House. Why, in this case, not say simply that Germany acknowledges her obligation to pay reparations for damages caused to property and persons, without enumerating all the categories that have been suggested and without indicating the limit of thirty years? A text of this kind can be drafted in three lines.

Klotz. We could also return to the first Anglo-American text.

Clemenceau. I propose to adjourn the rest of the debate, in order to discuss a text written according to Mr. Lloyd George's suggestions. §

APPENDIX.

1. The Allied and Associated Governments affirm the responsibility of the enemy States for causing all the loss and damage to which the Allied and Associated Governments and their nationals have been subjected as a consequence of the war imposed upon them by the aggression of the enemy States.

2. The Allied and Associated Governments recognize that the financial resources of the enemy States are not unlimited and, after taking into account permanent diminutions of such resources which will result from other treaty clauses, they judge that it will be impracticable for enemy States to make complete reparation for all such loss and damage. The Allied and Associated Governments, however, require that the enemy States, to the extent of their utmost capacity, make compensation for all damage done to the civilian population of the Allied or Associated Powers and to their property by the aggression of the enemy States by land, by sea, and from the air, (and also from damage resulting from their acts in violation of formal engagements and of the law of nations).

3. The amount of such damage for which compensation is to be made shall be determined by an Inter-Allied Commission, to be constituted in such form as the Allied and Associated Governments shall forthwith determine. This Commission shall examine into the claims and give to the enemy States a just opportunity to be heard. The findings of the Commission as to the amount of damage defined in Article 2 shall be concluded and communicated to the enemy States on or before May 1st 1921. The Commission shall also concurrently draw up a schedule of payments up to or within the total sum thus due, which in their judgment Germany should be able to liquidate within a period of thirty years, and this schedule of payments shall then be communicated to Germany as representing the extent of her obligations.

4. The inter-allied commission shall further have discretion to modify from time to time the date and mode of the schedule of payments in clause 3 and, if necessary, to extend them in part beyond thirty years, by acceptance of long period bonds or otherwise, if subsequently such modification or extension appear necessary, after giving Germany a just opportunity to be heard.

5. In order to enable the Allied and Associated Powers to proceed at once to the restoration of their industrial and economic life, pending the full determination of their claim, Germany shall pay in such instalments and in such manner (whether in gold, commodities, ships, securities or otherwise) as the inter-allied commission may fix, in 1919 and 1920 the equivalent of $5,000,000,000 gold towards the liquidation of the above claims, out of which the expenses of the army of occupation subsequent to the Armistice, shall first be met, provided that such supplies of food and raw materials as may be judged by the Allied and Associated Governments to be essential to enable Germany to meet her obligations for reparation may, with the approval of the Allied and Associated Governments, be paid for out of the above sum.

6. The successive instalments paid over by the enemy States in satisfaction of the above claims shall be divided by the Allied and Associated Governments in proportions which have been determined upon by them in advance, on a basis of general equity, and of the rights of each.

7. The payments mentioned above do not include restitution in kind of cash taken away, seized or sequestrated, or the restitution in kind of animals, objects of every nature and securities taken away, seized, or sequestrated, in the cases in which it proves possible to identify them in enemy territory. If at least half the number of the animals taken by the enemy from the invaded territories cannot be identified and returned, the balance, up to a total of half the number taken, shall be delivered by Germany by way of restitution.

8. The attention of the four Chiefs of the respective Governments is to be called to the following:
   (a) That necessary guarantees to insure the due collection of the sums fixed for reparation should be planned; and
   (b) That there are other financial clauses which this conference has not been charged to deal with.[13]

CC T MS (E. M. House Papers, CtY); Paul Mantoux, *Les Délibérations du Conseil des Quatre* (2 vols., Paris, 1955), I, 151-58; used with the approval of the late Mme. Paul Mantoux and Philippe-Roger Mantoux and Jacques Mantoux.

[13] Here follow the American and British drafts for categories of damages, "Annexure to Clause 2" and "Interpretation of Clause 2." They were discussed by the Council of Four in the afternoon session of April 5, 1919. The former is printed at April 3, 1919, and as an Annex to the Enclosure printed with N. H. Davis and V. C. McCormick to WW, April 4, 1919, both in Vol. 56; the latter is printed at April 2, 1919, *ibid.*

Hankey's and Mantoux's Notes of a Meeting of the Council of Four[1]

I.C.-170I.   President Wilson's House, Paris,
                                                April 5, 1919, 4 p.m.

MR. LLOYD GEORGE drew attention to paragraph 6 of the annexure to Clause (2) proposed by the American delegation (Appendix 1).[2] The wording of this Clause is as follows:

"(6) Damage resulting from acts in violation of international law (as found by the Commission on Responsibilities) and in violation of formal engagements."

He asked what the meaning of this Clause was? He pointed out that under this could be included the whole of the trade lost owing to submarine warfare, as well as the whole costs of the war, since

[1] The complete text of Hankey's minutes is printed in *PPC*, V, 31-38.
[2] Not reprinted; see n. 13 to the preceding document.

the violation of Belgium was a violation of international law. Under these circumstances, he himself, would be the last person to object to it, but he thought it right to point out what it entailed.

§Mantoux's notes:

Lloyd George. I see in the American text presented to me that reparation is due for the consequences of acts committed in violation of express agreements and of principles recognized by international law. This was aimed especially at the invasion of Belgium. But this text would allow claims to compensation for all losses suffered by trade as a result of submarine warfare and a host of things to which we have renounced claim. It was not I who proposed this text: I note that it permits claiming all that the war has cost.§

MR. MCCORMICK said that the intention was that under this Clause Belgium would be the only country to benefit, and she was entitled to the whole of her war costs.

MR. LLOYD GEORGE said that if this Clause was adopted he would be bound to put in his claim as stated above. South Africa, for instance, maintained that the whole of her trade had been stopped by the submarine warfare. Under these circumstances she could claim reparation for the whole. He felt bound to give warning of this.

MR. DULLES said that what the draftsmen of this Clause had had in mind was that the Commission on Responsibilities had made certain recommendations relating to all kinds of breaches of the laws of war, as well as the murder of Captain Fryatt, Nurse Cavell,[3] and other cases, and it was thought that Belgium alone would benefit.

(At this point M. Clemenceau, M. Klotz and M. Loucheur entered)

MR. LLOYD GEORGE pointed out that the Report of the Commission on the breaches of the laws of war[4] also included the violation of Belgium as a breach, besides the submarine warfare.

MR. DULLES said that the United States Delegation put in the reference to the report of the Commission on the Breaches of the Laws of War on the understanding that the Clause would only apply to direct and immediate damage. If it was interpreted as extending to stoppage of trade the Clause must be ruled out.

MR. LLOYD GEORGE said that the cost of the war and the stoppage

[3] About whom, see, respectively, n. 9 to the Enclosure printed with RL to WW, Aug. 22, 1916, Vol. 38, and R. U. Johnson to WW, Oct. 22, 1915, n. 1, Vol. 35.

[4] Actually, the Commission on the Responsibility of the Authors of the War and on Enforcement of Penalties in its *Report Presented to the Preliminary Peace Conference,* about which, see n. 4 to the minutes of the Council of Four printed at April 2, 1919, 4 p.m., Vol. 56. This commission had appointed three subcommissions, one of which was the Subcommission on the Responsibility for the Violation of the Laws and Customs of War.

of trade were direct results from breaches of the laws of war, namely, the violation of Belgium and the submarine warfare respectively.

COLONEL HOUSE suggested the Clause should be entirely eliminated with the understanding that Belgium should be properly provided for.

MR. LLOYD GEORGE drew attention to the interpretation of Clause (2) provided by the British Delegation (Appendix II) which he said provided for reparation for everything in the King of the Belgians' list.[5] He himself had objected to nothing in the King of the Belgians' list, neither had Colonel House, nor M. Clemenceau. Nevertheless, if the vague words were put in Clause 6 of the draft of the American Delegation, he and M. Clemenceau would both have to put in the claims they were entitled to under it. To say that Belgium was entitled to one class of damage, and France and the British Empire to another class, was impossible.

MR. MC CORMICK said that the United States Delegation had made this proposal as applying to Belgium which was entitled to all the war costs.

MR. LLOYD GEORGE pointed out that France and Great Britain had paid every penny of Belgium's war costs, even down to the salaries of the Ministers.

LORD SUMNER pointed out that Belgium was not a party to the Treaty of 1839 which had only been signed by the Guaranteeing Powers, and hence was not specially entitled to all war costs.

PROFESSOR MANTOUX at Mr. Lloyd George's request then read the British draft of the interpretation of Clause 2 in French.

COLONEL HOUSE said that if Belgium was properly provided for the United States Delegation would accept the British draft provided the French were willing to.

M. KLOTZ said that very long conversations had taken place on this subject. It was true that two texts had been evolved, namely, the American and the British. The American text, however, had been discussed line by line and in great detail, and had finally been agreed to by the French subject to additions and by the Italians subject to one addition.[6] The British text had not been studied in the same detail, consequently if this were adopted the ground would have to be gone over again in detail. Hence he thought it would be better to work on the American text. The British representatives, however, would have the right to suggest additions.

COLONEL HOUSE suggested that as the British text had been submitted at the same time as the American text and both had been

[5] See the minutes of the Council of Four printed at April 4, 1919, 11 a.m., *ibid*.
[6] See the Annex to the Enclosure printed with N. H. Davis and V. C. McCormick to WW, April 4, 1919, *ibid*.

discussed, there was no particular reason for adopting the latter.

MR. LLOYD GEORGE asked if M. Klotz accepted Mr. McCormick's interpretation of Clause 6 of the American text.[7]

M. KLOTZ replied that he did not.

MR. LLOYD GEORGE said that this was proof that it had not been properly examined. He then read Clause 2 of the British text. He said that Clause (2) of the British text appeared to him to be a better draft from the public point of view.

Mr. Lloyd George suggested that if the British text was to be taken as the basis it should be studied carefully and he suggested that a meeting should take place to consider the matter.

(It was agreed that the British text should be adopted subject to a detailed scrutiny and examination by the experts.)

M. CLEMENCEAU then made the following statement:

"I do not accept that the Commission should have power to declare the capacity of payment of Germany. I would say this: Germany owes me X for damages to persons and property. The Governments will have the right to reduce that sum in the course of years if they deem it just. But we are not prepared to accept any reduction now. We shall see what is possible and what is not, we shall take into account the question of accumulated interest (we may have to abandon our claim to interest altogether). We are willing to let the door open to every liberal solution.

But I ask, in the name of the French Government, after consultation with my colleagues, that what the enemy owes to us should be declared (if not by means of ____ sum, at least by determining categories of damage to be compensated for). We shall retain our faculty of allowing time to pay. Let us fix a limit of 30 years, as thought desirable by most of us. If everything has not been paid for during 30 years, then the Commission will have the right to extend the period."[8]

§Mantoux's notes:

Clemenceau. I ask that we return to the discussion of the proposal drafted by Mr. Lloyd George at the end of this morning's session. I do not recognize a commission's right to fix Germany's capacity to pay. I would say this: Germany owes me X for damages caused to property and to persons. This sum X can be reduced by the governments in the course of time if they find it right; but I am not prepared to accept that it be reduced at the present time. We shall see what is possible and what is not; we shall take account

---

[7] Mantoux's notes here read as follows: "Lloyd George. Does M. Klotz accept the interpretation given by Mr. McCormick of Article 6, namely that this article would permit Belgium, and not France, to receive complete compensation?"

[8] An undated CC MS of this statement is in WP, DLC.

of the element of interest, which I am inclined to renounce if we deem it necessary. The door will be wide open to liberal solutions.

But I ask in the name of the French government, and after having consulted my colleagues, that the peace treaty fix what Germany owes us, indicating at least the nature of the damages for which reparation is due us. We shall reserve to ourselves the freedom to make adjustments. We shall fix a period of thirty years, according to the desire expressed by most of us, and we shall give the commission a mandate to require payment during these thirty years of all that Germany owes us. If that is recognized to be impossible, the commission will have the right to prolong payments beyond thirty years.

Mr. Lloyd George's text seems to leave to the commission the right to fix a figure below that which is due us; that I could not accept.§

COLONEL HOUSE suggested that this was a very important statement which might form the basis of an agreement.

At Colonel House's request M. Clemenceau's statement was read a second time.

MR. DAVIS said that it seemed to him to be very similar to the proposal of the United States Delegation.⁹

M. LOUCHEUR said that this was not the case. There was an enormous difference. M. Clemenceau said "What Germany owes she owes. The Commission shall have no right to reduce the amount but the Governments will. The Commission will be only entitled to alter the time of payment. We instruct them to arrange for full payment in 30 years if possible."

M. CLEMENCEAU said he quite approved of this interpretation of his remarks.

MR. DAVIS reminded the meeting of the history of this question. The Commission had begun by considering two things, namely, what Germany owed, and what Germany could pay. They had always acted on the principle that she could not pay all that she owed. The basis of their calculations, was, therefore, always the amount that Germany could pay, and the limiting period had generally been taken as from thirty to thirty-five years. After that period the amount

⁹ In his annotations to the peace treaty in David Hunter Miller, *My Diary at the Conference of Paris, with Documents* (21 vols., New York, 1924), XIX, 301, Preston William Slosson, then the assistant librarian of the A.C.N.P, also attributes this remark to Davis. However, both the American notes "REPARATIONS; Memorandum of Conference Held April 5, 4 P.M. . . ." T MS (J. F. Dulles Papers, NjP) and Mantoux's minutes (printed below) attribute it to House. Paul Birdsall, who interviewed Davis in 1940, supports the latter view. Moreover, according to Birdsall, Davis stated during the interview that his own subsequent remarks at the afternoon meeting of April 5, 1919, were "prompted by indignation at Colonel House's inability or unwillingness to see the difference" between the French and the American proposals. Paul Birdsall, *Versailles Twenty Years After* (New York, 1941), pp. 257, 327.

became so large that the annual instalments were swallowed up in interest. The estimates of the amount that Germany could pay varied enormously, as much as from 25 billion to 50 billion dollars.

As no agreement could be reached as to the figure and as developments seemed to render the fixing of a figure inadvisable, it was decided to try and deal with the matter in another way. In doing so the principle previously adhered to of ascertaining what Germany could pay had been departed from. If some basis of calculation was not fixed, the principle would be dropped.

§Mantoux's notes:

Lloyd George: Could M. Klotz read his proposal?

Klotz. I will respond to the question asked this morning by Colonel House: "Why not limit ourselves to declaring that Germany will have to compensate for damages to persons and to property, without fixing a period of payment?" If Germany's capacity to pay requires that payments be divided over a period of fifty years, we are ready to give her fifty years. Let us suppose that the commission arrives at a figure of 60 billion pounds sterling [dollars] for the total of Germany's debt to the Allies; it will determine if that can be paid in thirty years or if it will take forty.

Clemenceau. That is not very clearly expressed.

Klotz. I mean that the capacity to pay should be taken into account, in order to fix the number of annual payments.

House. It seems to me that M. Clemenceau's conclusion is close to the American proposal.

Loucheur. Here is what M. Clemenceau said: what is due is due; the commission does not have the right to declare that Germany will pay less. The governments, on the other hand, reserve to themselves the right to reduce the sum that they claim. The commission will have only the right to change the duration of the period of payment. We will suggest to it a period of thirty years, to which it will be held, on the condition however that the total can actually be paid in thirty years.

McCormick. In other words, all will be paid, whatever period is necessary.

Davis. This carries us away from the principles which have served as the basis of our work for three months. We had always spoken of taking into account, on the one hand, what is due, and on the other hand, capacity for payment, which we always considered to be less than the debt. We have constantly worked with the idea that Germany would have to pay what she could pay in thirty years or, at most, thirty-five. For after that, the accumulation of interest would become so enormous that the problem is impossible to resolve.

Regarding the capacity to pay, we have made estimates which varied, at least in the American delegation, between a minimum of 25 billion dollars and a maximum of 35 billions. These figures were determined without taking any account of the debt; we only tried to imagine a Germany in good condition and able to pay. We then arrived at the conclusion that it was better not to fix a figure at all. But by working on this new basis, we are ending by abandoning our constant principle, which was this: Germany must pay what she can pay. At the same time we are renouncing the attempt to fix a minimum and a maximum between which the commission can operate. If none of this remains in our proposals, we are abandoning our principles. §

MR. LLOYD GEORGE then gave an historical résumé differing somewhat from Mr. Davis's.

§Mantoux's notes:

Lloyd George. I will observe that we were then in fact trying to find out what Germany could pay, without trying to establish categories of damages which should be compensated. By doing that we were doing our best to satisfy the principles laid down by President Wilson, in their strictest interpretation. We had to reach a solution: hence the choice of the other method.

Mr. Davis wants today to superimpose the limits that both methods would impose upon us. May I tell him that the difficulties which he fears do not exist? If we allow Germany to pay in goods, herself reconstruct buildings, restore machinery, we solve a great part of the problem. For Germany, the difficulty is not finding money, but money which can serve for payments abroad; through payment in kind, payments abroad are considerably reduced and this almost eliminates the question of capacity to pay. §

(After a short interval spent in an informal exchange of views and final drafting amendments, the following clauses, based on a draft prepared by M. Klotz to carry out ideas expressed by Colonel House at the morning meeting, were adopted:[10]

Note: Words inserted in the original draft are underlined. Words omitted from the original draft are in brackets.

(1) The Allied and Associated Powers require and the Enemy Powers accept that the Enemy States at whatever cost to themselves make compensation for all damages done to the civilian population of the Allied and Associated Powers, and to their property by the aggression of the Enemy States by land, by sea, and from the air, and also for all damages resulting from permanent injury to the health of any of their nationals [and for all damages resulting from

---

[10] That is, adopted as a basis for further discussion.

the acts of the enemy in violation of formal engagements and of the law of nations].

(2) The amount of damages as set forth in the specific categories annexed hereto, for which compensation is to be made, shall be determined by an Inter-Allied Commission to be constituted in such form as the Allied and Associated Powers shall forthwith determine.

This Commission shall examine into the claims and give to the Enemy States a just opportunity to be heard.

The findings of this Commission as to the amount of damages shall be concluded and communicated to the Enemy States on or before May 1st, 1921.

The schedule of payments to be made by the Enemy States shall be set forth by this Commission, taking into account in the fixation of the time for payment their capacity for payment.

On Lord Sumner's suggestion, it was agreed that the following preamble should be added to the schedule:

"Compensation is to be made in accordance with this schedule as hereinbefore provided."

M. KLOTZ said that as the result of the previous discussion there would be consequential alterations in Articles 2, 3 and 4, but in regard to Article 5 he had some comments to make. He considered the wording of this article politically dangerous. He then read Clause 5 as follows:

"In order to enable the Allied and Associated Powers to proceed at once to the restoration of their industrial and economic life, pending the full determination of their claim, Germany shall pay in such instalments and in such manner (whether in gold, commodities, ships, securities, or otherwise) as the Inter-Allied Commission may fix in 1919 and 1920, the equivalent of $5,000,000,000 gold towards the liquidation of the above claims, out of which the expense of the Army of Occupation subsequent to the Armistice shall first be met, provided that such supplies of food and raw materials as may be judged by the Allied and Associated Governments to be essential to enable Germany to meet her obligations for reparation, may, with the approval of the Allied and Associated Governments, be paid for out of the above sum."

What he objected to was the inclusion of money for the expenses of the Army of Occupation and the supplies of food and raw material for revictualling Germany. If, after saying to our peoples that we were obtaining from the enemy a certain sum of money we were to deduct a considerable sum to pay for the Army of Occupation, the effect on public opinion would be bad. In two years the cost of an Army of Occupation would amount to 14 milliards [francs]. If you added to this the cost of revictualling Germany, nothing would remain. If it was impolitic for the French people it was, in his view, equally impolitic for the German people. If we asked them to make an immediate effort to supply a certain sum of money, it was not desirable to tell them that a quarter of it would go back to them. Hence he would like in some way to separate from the total figure, the amount for revictualling and for the cost of the Army of Occupation.

MR. LLOYD GEORGE points out that the figure 14 milliards was calculated for an Army of Occupation of the size now occupying the Rhinish provinces. It would be absurd to maintain so large an army when Germany only had an army of 40,000 men. He asked if M. Klotz's objection was to supplying food and raw material. Without those Germany could not make reparation.

M. LOUCHEUR was quite in accord with Mr. Lloyd George in regard to the necessity of giving Germany food and raw material, otherwise they would not be able to pay. Nevertheless, it was necessary to fix a limit. His idea was to fix a sum which Germany should pay for food and raw material.

MR. LAMONT said that the text of Article 5 had been suggested after a very long discussion by the British Delegation. M. Loucheur had made his present suggestion in the course of this discussion. He had been met with the reply that the Allied and Associated Powers were fully safeguarded by the following words:

"Provided that such supplies of food and raw materials as may be judged by the Allied and Associated Governments to be essential to enable Germany to meet her obligations for reparation may, with the approval of the Allied and Associated Governments, be paid for out of the above sum."

MR. LLOYD GEORGE pointed out that under this clause the enemy could not obtain an ounce without our permission. The Allied and Associated Powers retained absolute control. To fix a definite amount was to encourage the enemy in making their reparation to say "We are ready to finish the job, but we cannot do so unless you give us another fifty million." They would be continually doing this.

M. LOUCHEUR questioned whether it was desirable to have the clause so worded in the Peace Treaty as to enable Germany to come to us at once and demand food and raw materials.

M. KLOTZ said the political objection was that if we asked for $5,000,000,000, it would have the appearance to Germany of paying a far greater sum because part of it was to be paid for the Army of Occupation and for their own revictualling. He would prefer to fix a sum without saying how much Germany was to have. As the clause now ran the German people would not see that part of the money was for their own benefit, whereas the Allied population would expect to receive more than they would get. Hence he would rather reduce the figure and make a special allowance for the Army of Occupation and for revictualling.

MR. LLOYD GEORGE preferred the present article. It would give us complete control over Germany for two years. It was better that the German assets should be controlled by us than by some German Government of very doubtful authority and stability.

M. CLEMENCEAU said that undoubtedly there were great inconveniences in the present proposal, and these had been pointed out by M. Klotz, but he thought that Mr. Lloyd George had shown that there was still greater danger in dividing the figures.

M. KLOTZ said that there was one serious omission from the draft. Nothing was said about guarantees. In the case of debts between individuals, securities or some other form of guarantee were always given for the payment of the debt. The question of political and military guarantee was outside the present enquiry. There were, however, some technical guarantees that could be taken, such as the revenue from ports, customs, railways, and the control of other sources of revenue. The British and United States experts when addressed on this subject said that no mandate had been considered. Nevertheless, he believed that these technical guarantees should be in the Treaty as well as military and financial guarantees.

MR. LLOYD GEORGE said that, supposing you occupied the Customs Houses, what would you get? Goods? Or Marks? He could not see what would be gained by this proposal. It was really part of the whole question of the enforcement of the Treaty of Peace. It seemed to him, therefore, irrelevant to the Financial Terms. It was worth consideration, perhaps, whether some form of paper bonds should be issued, but that was entirely a different proposal and one for the Financial Experts.

M. LOUCHEUR said that this was part of the question of the means of payments.

MR. BARUCH said that on the question of control they were waiting for the Report of the Commission. If, however, a promise were received from Germany to pay, very little would be gained by occupying territory.

MR. DAVIS said that the utmost that could be done would be to occupy a certain amount of territory.

MR. LLOYD GEORGE suggested that something ought to be put in about the right to restitution.

M. CLEMENCEAU said that this was a very important point.

M. LOUCHEUR said it was vital for the French, Belgian and Italian Governments to have the faculty of choice between the various means by which payment could be made.

One method of payment was the rebuilding of houses; another

was to take certain classes of goods. In this latter connection the question of coal was of the utmost importance, both to France and Italy. France would have a deficiency of 18,000,000 tons of coal, even supposing she obtained the produce of the Saar Valley, and after making allowance for the normal importation from Great Britain. The same applied to Italy, which had been asked to put down the amount of coal she required from Germany. Another form was replacement of machinery taken away.

§Mantoux's notes:

Klotz. Articles 2, 3 and 4 should be corrected, as a consequence of the change made in Article 1.

I have a word to say about Article 5, referring to the down payment. I do not argue now about the amount of this down payment; but the formula used seems to me impolitic and dangerous. The same figure will include compensation for us and sums destined for the maintenance of the army of occupation and the victualing of Germany. It is not very politic to say to the peoples who have suffered the most: here are 25 billion that we are getting immediately—then to withdraw from this sum that which is necessary to maintain the armies and to pay for food destined for Germany.

If the army of occupation were maintained in its present state, in two years, its maintenance would cost 14 billions. Add to this what is necessary for the victualing of Germany; practically nothing would remain for our invaded populations. That formula would be impolitic not only as far as the French people are concerned, but for the German people as well; it will appear to them that a huge sum is being required, when in reality one third or one quarter would be destined for their own use. It seems to me preferable to divide the total under two distinct rubrics.

Lloyd George. Your figure for the expenses of the army of occupation is exaggerated, because that army will not remain long at its present strength.

Loucheur. We agree to leave Germany enough to buy food and raw materials. We only think that the figure must be fixed for these purchases; otherwise, Germany could spend most of the 25 billions on that and excuse herself from working. We must allot her, say, five billions, and from the rest, which will be reserved for us, deduct expenses for the army of occupation.

Lamont. You recall that this wording was previously suggested by the British delegation. You had already made the same objection; but it was answered, further on in the same text, that a reservation is made which gives us a complete guarantee, for it is said that the sums spent for Germany will have to be recognized as necessary by the Allied and Associated Powers.

Loucheur. Yes, but I remember the recent discussion on the

victualing of Germany. In order not to repeat this discussion end-
lessly, I would prefer a lump sum.

Lamont. Germany has no more interest than we do in dissipating
all she has.

Lloyd George. If you give Germany a fixed sum, I believe that it
will go against what you are seeking. The Germans will spend that
sum and will come and tell us afterward: "You did not give us
enough; we can no longer buy raw materials to reconstruct your
houses." So they must be given a supplement. Five billion francs
is a large sum. I would prefer that they come to ask us in detail
and that each time they have to justify their request.

Loucheur. I see a danger in encouraging the Germans to make
repeated demands on us.

Klotz. I return to the danger of seeming to inflate the sum which
we are asking the Germans to pay immediately. I would prefer to
say that we are demanding from them 20 billions, instead of 25
billions, without fixing the figure for the victualing of Germany.
The Economic Commission would examine their requests as their
work proceeds, according to the established rules. If we should
keep this text, we would seem to be demanding more from the
Germans than we are in fact demanding, and our people would be
disappointed when they compare the published figure with what
is reserved for them.

Lloyd George. I prefer a system which permits us to keep control
of German purchases in our hands; our draft gives us this control.
I prefer that to giving a lump sum to a government which we do
not even know.

Klotz. Another question: it seems to me indispensable to specify
guarantees. Among individuals of whom one is indebted to the
other, mortgages or securities are required. This is not a matter of
military guarantees; but are there no guarantees which could be
found in the revenues of railways, ports, and customs? The American delegation says that it does not have a mandate to discuss
these questions. I believe that a stipulation along these lines should
be inserted into the treaty.

Lloyd George. I do not see what we would gain by that. If we
seize the customs, what will we get?

The truth is that we must foresee the problem of the means of
forcing Germany to fulfill her obligations. But it seems to me useless
to concern ourselves with customs and ports. It is up to the governments to see what they want to do if Germany refuses to execute
the treaty or if, without refusing, she does not execute it. But I
would place nothing about this subject in the specifically financial
articles of the preliminaries. We can study the question of whether

we must accept German bonds as a means of payment. It is another question, which should be handed over to the financial experts.

I am surprised to see nothing about the subject of direct restoration or reconstruction.

Baruch. If Germany commits herself to paying a sum X and gives her signature, I do not see what we can gain by requiring guarantees of the type suggested by M. Klotz.

Davis. The real sanction is the occupation of a part of German territory until the first payment.

Clemenceau. Like Mr. Lloyd George, I wish to have the restoration of buildings expressly mentioned.

Loucheur. That question is especially important for France, Belgium, and also for Italy. It is in reality that of the right to choose among the means of payment. We must be able not only to demand reconstruction of buildings, but also certain supplies which are necessary for us. One vital supply for France and for Italy is that of coal. Even if France can exploit the entire Saar Basin, her coal deficit will be 18 million tons, taking account of all that Great Britain normally furnishes her. If we turn to Germany, she can refuse to furnish us with coal, or propose to sell it at an exorbitant price. What will we do then? It is the same for certain materials necessary to our industries in the east of France.

We have asked Italy to inform us about her coal needs. This question is no less important for her than for us. We must be able to claim from Germany supplies and works such as the reconstruction of railways, bridges, roads. What we ask is that it be clearly stated in this text that we have the right to choose the means of payment, in such a way as to assure us direct reconstruction of destroyed cities and the supplies necessary to our industry.§

M. CLEMENCEAU proposed that M. Loucheur should prepare a text on this subject for consideration on Monday.

MR. LLOYD GEORGE suggested that the experts should meet to consider this text first.

(It was agreed that M. Loucheur should prepare a text which should be considered by the experts before the next meeting on Monday, which was arranged to take place at President Wilson's house in the Place des Etats-Unis at 11.0 a.m.)

(The Meeting then adjourned.)

T MS (SDR, RG 256, PPC, 180.03401/103, DNA); Mantoux, I, 159-65.

From the Diary of Colonel House

April 5, 1919.

I sat both morning and afternoon in the Council of Four. The only subject discussed was Reparations which instead of being called by that name might well be terms [termed] the question of "loot."

In the morning session I made a proposal and we thought we had arrived at a solution, but when our experts got together in the interim, it was found not to work. Then Clemenceau made a statement which I seized upon and said if he would stick to it I thought we might come to an agreement. I had his remarks carefully written, then typed, and it is on that basis that our experts will go into the conference tomorrow and report to us on Monday.

I went in and out of the President's room at various intervals so as to keep him informed as to the progress we were making. He is very much better and will perhaps be able to sit in himself Monday. Lloyd George, weather-cock that he is, expressed the hope that the President would not sit in with us again until we had finished settling the financial question, saying, "you have gotten the thread of the situation and it would be much better for you to carry it through than to have him come in at this stage."

George is insistent that Belgium shall not have priority over either France or Great Britain. I have instructed our experts not to argue the question of Belgium but to put our position to their associates and if they decline to come to it, to make a minority report which we will give to the Belgians and which we will take occasion to have published. George, and even Clemenceau who has followed him somewhat in this, seem indifferent to Belgium and her economic condition.

I suggested to the President today that in the event there was no agreement by the end of next week that he draw up a statement of what the United States is willing to sign in the way of a peace treaty, and give the Allies notice that unless they can come near our way of thinking, we would go home immediately and let them make whatever peace seems to them best. My suggestion was to do this gently and in the mildest possible tone, but firmly. At first blush, the President approved this course, but said he would like to think it over. As a matter of fact, I doubt whether it will ever come to this and I would not advise it except as a last resort.

The sitting of the Council of Four yesterday discussing the amount which Germany was to be forced to pay,[1] reminded me of a lot of children telling one another what they intended to do when they "grew up." Nothing is being done toward settling the Russian question, which is a burning issue. Without recognizing the Soviet Government or doing anything to which the conservatives could reasonably object, an arrangement might be made now by which fighting on the Russian fronts could be immediately stopped and the advance of Bolshevism westward checked. But no one has the courage to go forward in the matter.

Sir William Tyrrell had an interview with Clemenceau yesterday. He told Clemenceau that in his opinion he had made a great mistake in trying to have an understanding with Lloyd George rather than with President Wilson. He also told him that he had "prostituted his friendship for Colonel House in making such an attempt." I mention this in order to show how completely the British are in revolt against Lloyd George. It starts with Balfour and runs down through Cecil, Tyrrell, Wiseman, Montagu, and many others. The only people who uphold Lloyd George, as far as I know, are his immediate secretariat. Montagu threatens to resign as Secretary of State for India and has sent Lloyd George a sharp letter telling him he is going home and giving some of the reasons why. I advised against his resignation for the reason that he has a chance to do a great work for India. He is one of the few Englishmen I know who wants to give India a responsible government as fast as she is ready for it.

In yesterday's meeting,[2] I did just the things our experts told me would bring about a sharp division between the English and French. They were much chagrined, however, to find they had misinformed me. Their only excuse was that the British and French had come to an understanding between themselves about which they knew nothing.

I am pressed these days in so many directions that it is impossible to chronicle the happenings as I would like. I can only touch what seems to be the "high lights." I have stopped trying to keep in touch with my fellow Commissioners of the American Delegation. I have not seen Lansing for days and I see Bliss only when he has some matter to report. White usually comes up in the morning to get the news of the preceeding day. This Conference so far has been run by the President, Lloyd George, Clemenceau, Balfour, Tardieu and myself. Orlando has never been assertive. It is a pity perhaps that he has remained in the backgroun[d], for he has both good feeling and good sense. Balfour comes to the front every now and then and does good work, but is then submerged until needed again. Cecil has been of great service in the making of the Covenant. The other Delegates one seldom hears of and they might just as well be in Patagonia. I do not approve of the method which has brought this about. Everyone could and ought to have a niche in which they could help. But there is no organization to permit of such cooperation.

T MS (E. M. House Papers, CtY).
   [1] House obviously meant to refer to the meetings of the Council of Four on April 5, not April 4. The meetings of April 4 (see the minutes printed at that date in Vol. 56) did not deal with the question of reparations. House probably dictated this latter part of his diary entry for April 5, 1919, on the next day, April 6.
   [2] Again, House meant the meetings of April 5, 1919.

From William Harbutt Dawson[1]

Sir,   [Paris] 5 April, 1919.

   I am in Paris at the wish of Mr. C. P. Scott, the editor of the Manchester Guardian, who is very desirous that my views on the Polish-Danzig and other German questions should be brought to your knowledge. Mr. Scott intended to give me a letter for you, but as I came at very short notice that was impossible.

   May I say that I am entirely at your disposal and would be most glad to wait upon you at any time you might decide? I will add, in view of the unfortunate turn which political controversy has taken in England—or rather in London—that I would like to bring home to my countrymen the immense importance of a continuance of most cordial cooperation between your country and my own which is so essential to the gaining of a just peace.

   In order to identify myself may I mention the fact that you were good enough to accept a copy of my book "Problems of the Peace"[2] a year ago and again in December last (through Lord Bryce) a memorandum from me on "America's Duty to Europe."[3]

   I remain   Yours faithfully   W. H. Dawson

ALS (WP, DLC).
   [1] Author of numerous books on German thought, life, and institutions, with particular emphasis on the German response to social, economic, and industrial questions.
   [2] W. H. Dawson, *Problems of the Peace* (London and New York, 1917).
   [3] It was, in fact, W. H. Dawson, "America's Debt to the World," Dec. 23, 1918, TS MS, enclosed in Lord Bryce to WW, Dec. 28, 1919, ALS (WP, DLC).

From John Joseph Pershing

Dear Mr. President: [Chaumont] April 5, 1919.

   The American Army, with the encouragement of the French government, has sent 2,000 students, officers and soldiers, to take advantage of the opportunities in Science, Literature and Art at the University of Paris.

   To enable these students to profit more fully by their residence in Paris, it is desired to invite a certain number of eminent men of France, England and the United States, to address them upon some of the grave questions of the present hour. The lectures will take place in the grand amphitheatre of the Sorbonne during the two weeks of the Easter vacation.

It will be for the students and for the American Army, as well as for the lecturer of the day, a great honor if you will be present at the first meeting, April 14th, to speak a word of greeting to the American students and to present Lord Robert Cecil, who has been asked to deliver the first lecture.

I appreciate the heavy responsibilities which engage your attention at the present moment, but I hope that you will find it possible to give to the students this great opportunity, which will meet full appreciation.

With high esteem, I remain

Your most obedient servant,   John J. Pershing.

TLS (WP, DLC).

Joseph Patrick Tumulty to Cary Travers Grayson

The White House, April 5, 1919.

In my opinion the President must in some dramatic way clear the air of doubts, misunderstanding and despair which now pervade the whole world situation. He must take hold of the situation with both hands and shake it out of its indecision or political sabotage and scheming will triumph. Only a bold stroke by the President will save Europe and perhaps the world. That stroke must be made regardless of the cries and admonitions of his friendly advisers. He has tried to settle the issue in secret, only publicity of a dramatic kind can now save the situation. This occasion calls for that audacity which has helped him win in every fight.   Tumulty.

T telegram (WP, DLC).

Charles Henry Grasty to Cary Travers Grayson, with Enclosures

Dear Grayson: [Paris] April 5, 1919.

Following your advice, I went home and "beat out" my talk to you. You will know what use to make of it or whether to make any. Much of it has been said to me, in substance, by other people, and generally speaking it represents the prevailing American view in Paris.   Sincerely yours,   Charles H Grasty

ALS (WP, DLC).

E N C L O S U R E   I

Memorandum No 1.

French were persuaded on February 14th. They accepted the League of Nations. They lapsed back because they have Government without mandate. They are playing military game because they are a government in which politicians vie with each other, threaten each other in artificial competition for false ends. Clemenceau if convinced would be unable to stand because he would be afraid that his rivals would take position abandoned by him and beat him.

French Government is French politics and French politics is rotten. Its incapable of sound thought. I know of no man with possible exception of Joffre who could lead. Mental perversity creates false atmosphere and on top of that there is a plague of talk. They're orators and when they've said a thing they've done it. They brought German financiers here[1] for the chance of "orating" to them in the full belief that they could put matters so beautifully Germans would fall at their feet.

French political mentality is hopeless. To argue with them is to attempt sweep air out of the house. And they're beggars of the moon. If you gave them the Rhine and beyond, they would immediately prove by irrefrangible logic that you were compelled to guard it for them as it is, to use the language of some of their papers, "really an American frontier." And if you conceded that point they'd have you for proportionate share as per population of all war expenses from August 1914 till Doomsday in the afternoon.

Personally I don't believe results can be achieved by contending to end in this mumbo-jumbo of continentals. They're experts in logic but strangers to reason.

In all my comings and goings among Americans in Paris, I get one impression and that is that they think President has dealt admirably. He has gone over ground that had to be gone over. He has conciliated. He has kept open mind. He has made allowances for everybody's viewpoint, for the sufferings and sacrifices of all, for their pride and ambition. He has loyally considered them first and tried to conform his views and plans to theirs. But American opinion in Paris, as far as I can make out, is that if President's diplomacy is to be made useful, he shouldn't go on with private negotiations which may involve him as one government head among many, each contending for his particular viewpoint.

President must stand apart from these European politicians. He asks nothing and he represents a nation which asks nothing.

American opinion is that he should state the case publicly (for private statements don't carry conviction with European diplomats to whom all negotiation is bluff). He should say to them with a power that only he is capable of that America came to Europe to prevent German conquest, to disarm Germany and thereby crush German militarism, and to bring to bear American influence as an associate (but not as an Ally) in effort for reparation, security and restoration of world on Peace basis. First two ends have been accomplished and President has gone to limit of his own and American conscience and judgment for the other ends. Time has come when apparently European governments are not satisfied to accept utmost that America can give. President has told European governments that he will pledge himself with consent of legislative branch to League of Nations. Something more and different is wanted. Something that would face world toward new lease of militarism and that would compromise future free will and independence of America. Such a commit[t]al American people would never enter into. There is nothing left for America to do in Europe, her Army and Navy having completed what they came to do. They have aided in preventing German conquest and in disarming Germany. We have exhausted all means at out [our] disposal for reconciling Allies to some common plan for making peace and maintaining it.

Our staying here except to wait for ships to take us home simply gives Entente Militarism false ideas of its own power, encourages military enterprise, and throws Europe out of balance. With America definitely out of it the map of Europe, as looked at in Paris, would not be foreshortened and distorted as it is now.

As we turn our faces homeward, a farewell address by President Wilson, enunciating the great principles of world Democracy would form the platform against militarism and Bolchevism. Europe needs a broad platform, broad enough for all the war-weary and forward-looking in all countries to stand on. It should assume the fundamental goodness of the majority. It is time for a gospel of faith to take the place of the gospel of hate. After such a war we need both the Fztherhood [Fatherhood] of God and the Brotherhood of Man.

Not the Rhine, but the Right is the dividing line.

No matter where the buffer states are erected, provided they are moral and mental states in which those of us in the world who love law, order and decency—with America at the head—can know and aid all those of like minds. If a line were clearly drawn in Germany between the sheep and the goats, who doubts on which side the majority would stand? Instead of a "buffer state" with one-tenth of Germany in it, we would have a buffer state with all of Germany in it that was worth while. And such "buffer states" in Germany, Russia and elsewhere, instead of being coverts for war would be guarantees of peace.

The fight for the League of Nations has been won. The people are for it and will find a way to adopt it either through the back number governments or over their heads.

¹ See n. 1 to the extract from the Grayson Diary printed at April 2, 1919, Vol. 56.

ENCLOSURE II

[April 5, 1919] 11:30 Saturday morning.

MEMORANDUM NO 2.

C.T.G.—

When your messenger arrived I was trying to put the matter written last night in better form, but I think the other is better. I send this along in case you should find something in it.

C H G

President Wilson's course, from the viewpoint of an outside observer, has the advantage of not leading into an impasse. He has gone along with the european heads patiently and tactfully and, while open-minded to what they contended for, has tried to get them to accept the essentials of his peace policy. There has always been an alternative, up to this time, and for the adoption of that alternative Mr. Wilson's work was as necessary as it was for the effort for concert with the four Allied governments.

The alternative is to play a lone hand.

If the bright blue banner of Democracy, American style, were lifted in the hands of President Wilson, the masses of Europe would flock to it.

"The United States of Europe" is not such a wild dream as it may have appeared when it was first mentioned.

As the Peace Conference has proceeded the great masses with the insight characteristic of the juedment [judgment] of great masses have perceived that governments without popular mandates and out of touch with their peoples, were attempting to play the same old game of militarism. They conceived that the defeat of militarism in Germany meant simply a transfer of the same power, and that it was now their inning. In order to conceal the play, they and their Press and the "conservative" class have sought to make the public believe that the war was still going on and that a Germany, broken and beaten to her knees, was still the greatest menace. This propaganda has been successful for the purpose for which it was intended.

But a great and trusted leadership can bring the truth home to the people and they will follow it.

I don't think that this movement should be "personally conducted." In fact, in my opinion, it will go better to the music of

"Our boys are marching home." We have done our part in this war, on the military side. We have prevented the conquest of Europe by Germany, enabled the Allies to disarm her and collect from her the full amount of indemnity that she can pay and still pay at all.

Our staying here except to wait for ships to take us home simply gives Entente Militarism false ideas of its own power, encourages military enterprise, and throws Europe out of balance. With America definitely out of it the map of Europe as looked at in Paris would not be foreshortened and distorted as it is now.

As we turn our faces homeward, a farewell address by President Wilson, enunciating the great principles of world Democracy would form the platform against militarism and Bolchevism. Europe needs a broad platform, broad enough for all the war-weary in all countries to stand on. It should assume the fundamental goodness of the majority. It is time for a gospel of faith to take the place of the gospel of hate. After such a war we need both the Fatherhood of God and the Brotherhood of Man.

Not the Rhine, but the Right is the dividing line.

No matter where the buffer States are erected provided they are moral and mental States in which those of us in the world who love law order and decency—with America at the head—can know and aid those of like minds. If a line were clearly drawn in Germany between the sheep and the goats who doubts on which side the majority would stand? Instead of a "buffer state" with one-tenth of Germany in it, we would have a buffer state with all of Germany in it that was worth while. And such "buffer states" instead of being coverts for war would be guarantees of peace.

I believe that the withdrawal of America from field of war in Europe accompanied by a mighty blast on the trumpet would result in putting the real people of Europe in charge. The militarists are producing the Bolchevists while the great sound masses await leadership. Peace and Democracy expounded in plain terms, that is Americanism set before their eyes, would give them a platform and a definite program. And they should know the truth about the war situation. Germany is beaten and broken, disarmed on sea and land and must take on the burden of indemnity. To suppose that this enemy will rise again against all Europe is to attribute to him superhuman powers. He does not possess them.

T MSS (WP, DLC).

To Carter Glass

Paris April 5, 1919.

For Glass: If there are any pending applications for loans or any kind of financial accommodation from France or England please do not take favorable action before consulting me.

Woodrow Wilson.

From Carter Glass

The White House, 5 April 1919.

Following from the Secretary of the Treasury QUOTE
I have received your cable of this date.

First: In order to obtain sterling required by our Army at current rates have already made commitments to British for establishment of credits within limits you have approved and for temporary advances to be repaid through sterling furnished us and dollars paid them by War Department for transportation of troops, and for wool. This arrangement will in my judgment provide for all British requirements here up to July first when I should in ordinary course expect British to finance their requirements through private channels.

Second: In connection with arranging to procure from French Treasury at current exchange rates large amount of francs which our Army will need, I am committed to make certain further loans to France. Our requirements for francs alone would provide dollars for all French war requirements here and with one hundred and ninety million dollar credit in favor of Bank of France would also provide for French reconstruction expenditures in United States to consideration [considerable] amount. In view of limitations imposed by Congress, France cannot expect considerable advances from Treasury beyond those I shall be obliged to make in pursuance of commitment mentioned. I am constrained to advise you that at most nothing more than mere temporary inconvenience could result to France if comparatively insignificant requirements for loans were refused that might possibly be needed by France beyond existing commitments of Treasury UNQUOTE   Tumulty.

From Carrie Clinton Lane Chapman Catt

Washington [April 5, 1919]

Number fortyone Following just received from Mrs. Chapman Catt Quote When message from President Wilson[1] was received by

National American Women Suffrage Association in St Louis entire
convention arose and cheered for several minutes and immediately
instructed that cablegram of thanks be returned to him to express
gratitude and appreciation of convention for his continued efforts
in behalf of women suffrage stop Resolution was also passed unanimously indorsing principle of the League of Nations stop Convention represented the women of every state in the union with membership of about two million five hundred thousand unquote.

Tumulty.

T telegrams (J. P. Tumulty Papers, DLC).
  [1] See WW to JPT, March 22, 1919, Vol. 56.

From Walker Downer Hines

Dear Mr. President: Washington April 5, 1919.

It is not improbable that the question of purchases of coal by the
Railroad Administration will be presented to you so that I take this
occasion to put before you the facts as I understand them.

Broadly, the question is whether there shall be a reasonable degree of competition in the coal business, (to the extent that it is
not prevented by the tacit concurrences of view among the coal
operators) or whether competition shall continue to be completely
eliminated through the fixing of governmental prices at which the
Railroad Administration must buy. During the war Doctor Garfield
emphasized that the coal prices were maximum prices and that it
was permissible even then for any operator to sell at a less price
upon the strength of any legitimate commercial consideration. The
present movement, however, seems designed to remove even this
element of competition and to force the fixing of an absolute price
without permission to seek by competition the obtaining of lower
prices.

The practical difficulty about the plan of the coal operators is that
it will require necessarily a uniform price in each district with the
result that the price will have to be high enough to sustain the coal
operators having the higher costs, and therefore will produce prices
which will yield excessive profits to the coal operations [operators]
with lower costs. This would serve to perpetuate to a substantial
degree the very high profits existing during the war. Any such
governmental standard would, of course, become the standard for
coal prices in general and would greatly facilitate the maintenance
for the general public of an unduly high level of coal prices for an
indefinite period. In my opinion the plan would be directly opposed
to the public interest, which I believe needs a progressive read-

justment to lower price levels so that the factors contributing to the present high cost of living will the more rapidly become less oppressive.

I am keenly alive to the necessity of avoiding action which will force a reduction in wages and I think the problem is to find a way which will reasonably protect the wage situation while not perpetuating a price situation directly opposed to the general public interest.

I believe this desirable middle course can be substantially accomplished, as far as the Railroad Administration's purchases of coal are concerned, by the continuance of the policy now established. The various elements of that policy are as follows:

1. The Railroad Administration is not using the guaranty of a car supply as a leverage to secure low prices, this plan having been abandoned last summer as a result of your decision. It is only fair to add, however, that under existing conditions of car surplus, everybody can count on 100 per cent. car supply for all purposes, and therefore the guaranty of 100 per cent. car supply would not be a consideration of much present value anyhow.

2. The Railroad Administration is not concentrating the coal purchasing power of all the railroads so as to create an oppressive condition, but on the contrary has redistributed that purchasing power so that each railroad buys its own coal. The only influence which the Central Administration is exerting is to make the respective railroad managements more solicitous to avoid oppression than they were in the period of private management.

3. The Railroad Administration has no purpose to obtain lower prices than other large industries can and will obtain on account of the volume and regularity of their demands. The notion has been persistently encouraged by the coal operators that the Railroad Administration's action is on the theory that the Government must obtain coal at relatively lower prices than other consumers who use coal in large and regular quantities, but there is no basis for this view.

4. The Railroad Administration permits the purchasing agent of each railroad to ask for bids, stipulating that no bids shall be made or shall be accepted that will operate to cut the existing level of wages. Each purchasing agent is expected to buy his coal on his own line as far as practicable and to make among the mines on his line as wide a distribution of the tonnage as the conditions will permit, considering quality, transportation and price.

5. The Railroad Administration requires that no price shall be accepted which would involve the cutting of the existing scale of mining wages. Further than this, in order to satisfy the suspicions

of the miners that some operators might give unduly low prices for the purpose of disturbing reasonable distribution or for the purpose of creating a condition which would force wages lower, the Railroad Administration has instructed that any price actually contracted for shall be open to the inspection of the representatives of the employees and also to the inspection of any interested coal producer.

Of course, in the operation of nearly 250,000 miles of railroad through perhaps 150 different railroad organizations there will be instances of a failure to carry out the spirit of these policies. At all times we have invited the coal operators and the coal miners to present to the Central Administration any cases of such departures. Comparatively few cases have been presented and they have been promptly dealt with.

Notwithstanding the policies thus put into effect by the Railroad Administration, and without bringing to my personal attention any specific instance of a disregard of those policies, and despite the fact that the few complaints presented to Mr. H. B. Spencer,[1] Director of the Divison of Purchases, were promptly dealt with, the National Coal Operators Association on March 27th issued a formal statement charging that the United States Railroad Administration had adopted unfair practices which would drive the price of railroad fuel below the cost of production and necessitated advancing the price of coal for the general consuming public. This unjust charge against the Government appears to have been made for the purpose of coercing the Railroad Administation into abandoning entirely the invitation of bids and adopting instead the plan of some uniform price for each district. I feel that the plan thus sought by the coal operators is highly opposed to the interests of the Government and to the general public interest; to the interest of the Government because of the excessive costs for railroad fuel which will result, and to the general public interest because of the creation and maintenance in this way of a high artificial price level which will exert an injurious influence for a long time to come against a reasonable reduction in the price of coal to consumers generally.

Although the coal operators have such an obvious selfish interest in maintaining an unreasonably high price level for coal, they appear to base their demand in this respect exclusively upon the theory that they are solicitous for the interests of labor. The argument is that the present is an exceedingly critical period when many miners are unable to earn enough to support themselves and that therefore there should be the widest possible distribution of coal orders so as to make the relatively small amount of mining now in demand go as far as possible in protecting the general situation. My own judgment is that the careful carrying out of the plans above outlined will reasonably meet this situation and that any theoretical additional benefit which might come to the labor situation from a wider distribution of coal purchases at uniform Government prices would be obtained at a serious sacrifice of the important permanent interest of the general consuming public.

In weighing this matter I think it is important to bear in mind that the factor of railroad purchases is at the moment much less influential than general statistics suggest. The great problem in this regard that confronts the country is for the next four or five months. During that period coal purchases will be relatively small because many manufacturing enterprises have large stocks of coal obtained during the war. Generally speaking these stocks are likely to be exhausted in the next few months and probably by July or August there will be such a resumption of demand for coal as will alleviate to a very great extent the existing condition of small production. During these months a very large percentage of the Railroad Administration's consumption of coal will not be controlled in any event by any present policy but by contracts which were made many months ago and which have many months to run. Besides, the railroad purchases are limited to mines producing the appropriate quality of coal. Moreover, the conditions vary greatly in different parts of the country. Perhaps in some parts of the country the purchases which the Railroad Administration will have to make upon the basis of new contracts in the next two or three months will be relatively large and the mining conditions will be relatively unfavorable. In these cases intensive application of the liberal policies already adopted by the Railroad Administration will be able to meet any local embarrassments in the matter of distribution.

But I earnestly advise that there is nothing in existence or in prospect which justifies the Government adopting a policy that will give the coal operators throughout the United States the continued benefit of a high Government price, and any Government price must be high because it must be high enough to sustain all mines remaining in operation. If the Government price is not high enough to do this the result will be that the Government will be charged with responsibility for reducing the wages of the miners in the high cost operations. If the Government price is sufficiently high to avoid this charge, then it will be so high as to give abnormal and unjustifiable profits to the low cost operators and a general price level for coal will be built up which will have an injurious influence for a long time to come upon the public interest.

The policies of the coal operators, and indeed to some extent of other producing interests, bring out sharply an important difficulty with Government control of such an extensive enterprise as the railroads. The operators are quick to use the Government as a target for the purpose of holding the Government responsible, on account of any price policy which it adopts, for the maintenance of wage levels. The more the Government enters into price fixing, especially in an enterprise such as the coal industry where there are perhaps fifteen thousand different producers, the more it will be charged with responsibility for the labor situation. I have felt that decidedly the best course to avoid this embarrassment and also to protect the general public interest has been for the Railroad Administration to decline any responsibility for the price of coal and to say that it would leave the prices to be named by the operators who chose to bid, but would accept no price insufficient to maintain the existing wage scale.   Sincerely yours,   Walker D Hines

TLS (WP, DLC).
  [1] Henry Benning Spencer.

From Edward Field Goltra

Dear Mr. President: [St. Louis] April 5, 1919.

In furtherance of the accomplishment of the thing proposed to be done in Missouri which I mentioned in bidding you goodbye in your room at the Capitol—the following steps have been and will be taken: Seeing that he[1] was departing from his speeches handed in advance to the press and these departures being vitriolic and sarcastic attacks on you, ingeniously worded so as no one could mistake who was meant, but veiled so as not to be charged with open attack on the President, as for instance in his address in St. Louis[2]—he having arranged to be invited by Zak Lionberger[3] and some other lawyers of St. Louis to address the citizens of St. Louis on the subject of a League of Nations, the Odeon being filled to overflowing with republicans, some democrats being present out of curiosity—it was arranged to give him a chance to perform in the new State House at Jefferson City by being invited to address the Senate and House in joint session in order to materialize opportunity for effective protest. The republican applause he received at the Odeon meeting stimulated him to greater invective so that he was in fine form to play his part at Jefferson City.[4] The new hall of the Lower House made a wonderful theatre. He soon began the attack and had proceeded but a short time when Frank Farris, the most able democrat in either body, a country lawyer from Phelps Co., arose and, in ringing tones, protested that "this is abuse of the President of the United States and I for one shall not remain and listen." Immediately another democrat, and then two or three others, and then a half dozen and so on were all on their feet protesting and, forming themselves in a body, walked out. The principal actor had worked himself up to a point where not only did he express his malice and hate by word of mouth, but by facial performance. The majority of the republicans applauded him, some of them I am glad to say sat in silence, the performance being clearly not to their liking. Fifty-one democratic members caucassed and adopted resolutions at once stating that the democracy of Missouri was being misrepresented and calling upon the senator to forward his resignation to the Governor[5] which they would likewise do and asked the state committee to call a convention to determine whether his or their resignation should be accepted. We gave widespread publicity to this challenge and the reply to it was that a handful of democrats at Jefferson City did not represent the democracy of Missouri.

I then caused a letter to be addressed to State Chairman Neale,[6] signed by Farris and forty-seven other democrats requesting that a convention be called by the state committee. It was arranged that this letter be sent to me for transmittal by me to Chairman Neale, to afford me the natural and plausible opportunity for drawing an indictment, and copies of these two letters you will find inclosed herewith. The Senators supporters getting ahold of Neale persuaded him to procrastinate in his reply as it would "tear the party all to pieces if a convention were called." I wait[ed] a few days and not hearing from Neale addressed a letter to each county chairman inclosing copies of the Farris letter and my letter to Chairman Neale, all of which is herewith inclosed.[7] The county chairmen are sounding the sentiment in each county and reporting as fast as they hear from the townships. Twenty-nine counties had reported up to last night, all are for a League except one, five are doubtful as to whether it is better to hold a convention now or after the final draft is submitted, the balance are insistent for an immediate convention, all are for President Wilson.

At this writing it would seem that a most remarkable democratic convention will be held at St. Louis within the next ten days or two weeks. The Senator thought he would come to Missouri and stampede the democracy in the state. What took place, however, started a stampede in an opposite direction and had its effect throughout the country. When the replies are in, demand will be made by me that the state committee call a convention. If the chairman refuses, the writer acting under and by virtue of his prerogatives as National Committeeman will call the convention. I hope it may be convened and action taken before the final draft is sent out from Paris, as I want the democrats of Missouri to endorse in advance. A wringing [ringing] and complete repudiation of the Senator by his own party, in his own state, cabled to Paris, may be of some little real assistance to you by reason of its effect on those with whom you are negotiating.

I know you are going to win out over there; I also know that the entire country here, in overwhelming percentage, is for a League of Nations and such a Constitution as you endorse.

Secretary Baker has kindly offered to personally see that you get this.   Faithfully yours,   Edward F. Goltra

P.S. We have 114 counties in Missouri.

TLS (WP, DLC).
[1] That is, Senator James Alexander Reed. About this matter, see also JPT to WW, March 22, 1919, n. 1, Vol. 56.
[2] On January 7 or 8, 1919.
[3] That is, Isaac Henry Lionberger, Princeton 1875, lawyer of St. Louis and long active in Missouri Democratic party politics.
[4] When he spoke to the Missouri legislature on March 18, 1919.
[5] That is, Frederick Dozier Gardner.
[6] Ben M. Neale.
[7] F. H. Farris *et al.* to B. M. Neale, March 25, 1919; E. F. Goltra to B. M. Neale, March 27, 1919; and E. F. Goltra to the chairmen of the Missouri Democratic County Committees, March 31, 1919, all TCL (WP, DLC).

Joseph Patrick Tumulty to Newton Diehl Baker, with Enclosure

My dear Mr. Secretary: The White House April 5, 1919.

When you reach Paris will you please hand to the President the enclosed copy of a telegram which I have received from Senator Phelan?   Sincerely yours,   J. P. Tumulty

TLS (WP, DLC).

E N C L O S U R E

San Francisco, Calif. April 4, 1919.

A bill denying Orientals the right to own or lease land in California and another bill prohibiting the immigration of socalled Japanese picture brides who are coming into California in great numbers under the guise of wives have been submitted for introduction in the State Senate. I have been waging a hot campaign against the Japanese demand at the Peace Conference for racial equality and addressed a joint session of the legislature last Monday night. Governor Stephens had declared the time inopportune for such legislation and is using the power of his office to defeat these measures. His floor leaders have denied the authors of these bills the right to even introduce these bills. The Committee today decided to cable Secretary Lansing asking if the introduction and possible enactment into law of these bills would embarrass the American Peace Delegates. It is a political trick of a Republican Legislature to embarrass the President. I strongly urge that you immediately communicate with the President suggesting to him that the Legislature act on its own responsibility. I cabled him to this effect today[1] and would appreciate it if you would reinforce my request. Under the immigration laws the wives of alien residents may enter the United States and the Japanese have devised a marriage between a resident Japanese and a woman in Japan who has never met the prospective groom until her arrival. I believe the object is to breed a race on our soil because born on the soil the children are citizens and the alien father can then buy land in the child's name and circumvent the State law. In nineteen thirteen there was objection when Bryan came to California on the Japanese question and now they are inviting interference which shows the insincerity of their action. Please wire me what action you take.   James D. Phelan.

TC telegram (WP, DLC).
  [1] J. D. Phelan to WW, April 4, 1919, T telegram (WP, DLC).

From the Diary of Dr. Grayson

Sunday, April 6, 1919.

The President had a good night's rest. His temperature was one degree above normal, and he continued to show signs of improvement. He expectorated very freely, which gave him considerable relief in his throat. With a merry twinkle in his eyes he said: "I suppose you are going to cause me to set a bad example to the world today and not consent to my going to church." I told him that I would shoulder the heavy responsibility.

The President said: "While you have me on my back I have been doing a lot of thinking, thinking what would be the outcome on the world if these French politicians were given a free-hand and allowed to have their way and secure all that they claim France is entitled to. My opinion is that if they had their way the world would go to pieces in a very short while. I hope that I can get things in hand and that we can work them out when I get up. But if we don't within a specified time, I am going to tell all of the Peace Commissioners plainly what I am going to do. And when I make this statement I do not intend it as a bluff. I am trying to formulate in my mind the exact procedure I am going to take." He added: "I wish you would communicate with Admiral Benson and find out what the movements are of the u.s.s. GEORGE WASHINGTON. If she is in an American port, order her to proceed to Brest, France, at once." "When I decide, doctor," he said, "to carry this thing through I do not want to say that I am going as soon as I can get a boat; I want the boat to be here."

The President said: "If you don't think it would hurt me, I would like to have the members of the American Peace Commission here for a conference. I can lie in bed and talk to them." I impressed upon him the necessity of not fatiguing or over-exerting himself. He said: "I have got some steam inside of me that if I could let off I think you would find it would help me physically." He turned to Mrs. Wilson and said: "My dear, will you be good enough to call the various members over the telephone and tell them I wish them to come here at five o'clock?" She replied: "Can't I tell Colonel House to do it?" He said: "No," (emphatically), "because that would mean that he would detail it to Auchincloss, and he (Auchincloss) has such an exalted opinion of himself these days that I don't care to have him do any business in my name." The conference lasted for an hour, at the conclusion of which Mrs. Wilson served tea to them. When the members of the Commission got back to the Hotel Crillon they were distinctly serious in their demeanor and declined to make any statements to the newspaper men regarding what transpired at the conference.

After the conference had adjourned I went in to see the President and asked him how he felt. He made this brief reply, rolling his eyes at me: "Better—the steam's off." Thereupon I proceeded with my professional business with him.

The President asked me to have dinner with him and Mrs. Wilson, and I had dinner on a table by his bed. He was in good spirits and acted as if he had not a care in the world. After dinner, I said: "I hope you will have a good night's sleep"; to which the President replied: "It is difficult to put things off your mind when you cannot personally handle them. To lie in bed and think of problems that you cannot pitch into and dispose of naturally make the mind more active and prevents sleeping. When you can handle them in person it is easy enough to dismiss them after you go to bed. To know that I am responsible for them and cannot take part in the proceedings makes me restless."

The President said to me: "I wonder if you can locate Baruch." I reached him over the telephone by the President's bed. Baruch came in and stood at the foot of his bed and talked with the President over the international situation and the latest crisis which has enveloped it. The President asked Mr. Baruch whether he thought he (the President) was right in the stand which he has taken on the Saar Valley problem and on the French demand for the creation of a buffer state to be known as a Rhinish Republic, located between Alsace and Lorraine and the Rhine River. The President was opposed to both projects. Mr. Baruch endorsed the President's position and said: "If you stand by your principles as laid down in the 14 points and the right and justice which you stand for for all, and which you have explained to me in the various matters which you have put up to me for investigation, I am absolutely convinced that the whole world will endorse your stand regardless of what the other countries' peace commissioners may do or say."

The President said to Mr. Baruch: "I wish you would study the controversy between the Railroad Department and the Commerce Department.[1] They have laid the matter before me and I wish you would take it and give me your advice as to what I should do.["]

I gave the President his treatment before leaving him for the night. I found that the excitement had had no very serious after-effect, which demonstrated to my mind that he was coming back fast.

[1] About this controversy between the Industrial Board of the Department of Commerce and the Director General of the Railroads over the price of steel rails, see the numerous documents in Vols. 55 and 56.

From the Diary of Ray Stannard Baker

Sunday the 6th [April 1919]

Colonel House was as busy as busy could be seeing people today. Lord R. Cecil & Orlando in the morning & in the afternoon a conference of our commissioners with the President, who is still in bed, but much better. It is the first time in days, if not weeks that old Mr. White has even seen the President: & the first time [in] days, certainly, that Mr. Lansing has seen him. Lloyd-George is excitedly proclaiming that a settlement has been reached, but so far as I can see, there has been no agreement whatever on any essential point, though the Four may be close to an understanding upon several. The pressure of public opinion is becoming overwhelming for some issue.

From the Diary of Colonel House

April 6, 1919.

As it was Sunday I had counted upon a restful day, but it has been anything but that. Orlando, by some misunderstanding, wanted a meeting of the Committee to select a site for the League of Nations and called it in my apartment at ten o'clock. The mistake was the fault of Cecil. Smuts being away, Cecil did not know that he and I had already settled the matter and had obtained all the guarantees we thought necessary.

While I had Orlando and Cecil together I took occasion to present the Russian matter to them and succeeded in getting their approval of what Hoover and I have done regarding the Neutrals headed by Dr. Nansen. Cecil and I had a long talk on the economic condition of the world. He is considering going back to England and making a speech in Parliament which will open the eyes of that body.

I went to Versailles to lunch, but I had hardly gotten there before the President telephoned he would like to see me at four o'clock. He had our fellow Commissioners there and we discussed at great length the best possible means of speeding up the Peace Conference. It was determined that if nothing happened within the next few days, the President would say to the Prime Ministers that unless peace was made according to their promises, which were to conform to the principles of the Fourteen Points, he would either have to go home or he would insist upon having the conferences in the open. In other words, to have Plenary Sessions with the delegates of all the smaller powers sitting in.

I took up with him the question of Reparations which the experts have been working on today, and got him in agreement with the plan, with slight modifications, which they had worked out.[1] If we can get George and Clemenceau to accept it the thing will be done. I doubt, however, whether we shall ever be able to do so.

I advised our experts to "throw a scare" into the French and English by telling them that tomorrow would be the last day that I would sit with the Council of Four; that on Tuesday the President would be there himself; that in their opinion they would get better terms from me than from him; that he was in a belligerent mood and that they would be well advised to settle on the agreement that had been drawn up.

[1] A CC MS of this draft, dated April 5, 1919, is in the J. F. Dulles Papers, NjP. Wilson's most important revision pertained to Article I, in which he deleted the italicized words in the following opening sentence: "The Allied and Associate Governments affirm, *and the enemy States accept*, the responsibility of the enemy States for causing all the loss and damage. . . ." In addition, Wilson changed the word order in Article IV, and he deleted the following sentence from Article VII: "If at least half of the number of the animals taken by the enemy from the invaded territories cannot be identified and returned, the balance, up to a total of half the number taken, shall be delivered by Germany by way of restitution." As revised by Wilson, this draft was discussed by the Council of Four on April 7, 1919, 4 p.m. (see the minutes of this meeting printed below) and is printed in *PPC*, V, 55-56.

A Memorandum by Charles Homer Haskins and Others

[April 6, 1919]

THE SAAR BASIN

In accordance with the instructions given by the President and the Prime Ministers 31 March, Messrs. Tardieu, Headlam-Morley, and Haskins have had four meetings to consider possible arrangements with respect to the mines of the Saar basin.

The following were the terms of reference:

It is agreed in principle

1. That full ownership of the coal-mines of the Saar Basin should pass to France to be credited on her claims against Germany for reparation.

2. That for the exploitation of these mines the fullest economic facilities shall be accorded to France, including particularly:

(a) Exemption from taxation on the part of Germany, including import and export dues.

(b) Full mobility of labour, foreign and native.

(c) Freedom for the development of adequate means of communication by rail and water.

3. That the political and administrative arrangements necessary to secure the foregoing results be enquired into.

In accordance with these terms M. Tardieu submitted a draft of articles for the acquisition and exploitation of these mines by France.[1] These articles were discussed in detail, and several modifications were suggested by Messrs. Headlam-Morley and Haskins and accepted by M. Tardieu. In this amended form they are annexed hereto.

The articles fall into two sections: articles 1-8 are confined to technical and economic provisions; articles 9-17 involve more general political and administrative arrangements.

While the draft is subject to changes in technical detail, it appears to contain in substance the just and necessary basis for working these mines, regard being had not only to the greatest efficiency of operation but also to the interests of the workmen and the general prosperity of the basin.

If these articles, the substance of which appears economically and socially necessary, were to be applied without the establishment of some special political and administrative régime, serious friction and conflict would inevitably arise.

[1] It is printed in David Hunter Miller, *My Diary at the Conference of Paris*, VIII, 34-40.

Article I.

Right of Ownership.

From the date of the signing of the present Treaty all the deposits of mineral substances which under existing French legislation are classified under the heading of mines, and which are situated within the Saar Basin as it is defined below, belong to the French State, which will have the perpetual right of working them or of not working them, or of transferring to a third party the right of working them without receiving any previous authorization or fulfilling any formalities.

Questions arising respecting the rights of the French State under the preceding provision will be decided according to the German law in force 11 November 1918.

Article II.

Definition of Ownership.
Indemnification by Germany for public and private property.

The right of ownership of the French State created by article I. applies not only to the deposits which are free and for which concessions have not yet been granted, but also to the deposits for which concessions have already been made, whether they belong to the Prussian State, to the Bavarian State, to other corporations or to individuals, whether they have been worked or not, that is to say, to all deposits for the working of which there has already been created a right distinct from the right of the owners of the surface of the soil.

The German State will have to indemnify the Prussian State and the Bavarian State as well as private proprietors of the said mines, the ownership of which is hereby transferred to the French State.

Article III.

Ownership of Mines covers subsidiaries and accessories.

As far as concerns the mines which are being worked, the transference to the French State of the ownership of the mines resulting from the preceding clauses applies not only to the ownership of the mines but also to that of their subsidiaries and accessories, that is to say, all their plant and equipment as well as on as below the surface, in particular their extracting machinery, their plants for transforming coal into electric power, coke, and bye-products, their workshops, means of communication, electric lines, water conduits, land, buildings such as offices, workmen's dwellings, schools, and hospitals, their stocks and supplies, their archives and plans, and in general everything which those who own or exploit the mines possess or enjoy for the purpose of exploiting the mines and their subsidiaries and accessories.

The transference applies moreover to the debts owing for products which shall have been delivered subsequently to the signature of the present treaty and previously to the entry into possession on the part of the French State, and to the actuarial reserves of pension rights which have been acquired by the employees of the mines and their accessories and dependencies, which rights the French Government takes over the obligation to maintain.

Article IV.

Railroad Rates.

No differential tariff shall be established on the German railways and canals to the prejudice of the transport of persons and products of the mines and their accessories and dependencies or of the material necessary for their working. Such transportation shall enjoy all the rights and privileges which any international railway convention might guarantee to similar products of French origin.

The French State shall have the right to demand the establishment of workmen's trains in the coal basin and the adjacent districts on such sections of the lines and according to such timetables as it shall judge necessary for the workmen and employees of the mines under the most favorable conditions established by the German tariff for similar transportation.

Article V.

Railroad Facilities.

Germany engages to place no obstacle in the way of such ameliorations of railways or waterways as the French Government shall judge necessary to assure the clearing of the transportation of the products of the mines, such as double trackage, enlargement of stations, construction of railway yards. The distribution of expense in such cases will be subject to arbitration. It engages also to provide within a reasonable time the personnel and the equipment necessary to insure the clearing and the transportation of these products.

Article VI.

Right of developing Means of Communication on the part of France.

The French State shall be substituted for the German, Prussian, and Bavarian Governments, under the legislation in force 11 November 1918, as regards measures of reparation for damage caused by the exploitation of the mines, and as regards the acquisition of such land as it may judge necessary for the exploitation of the mines and their subsidiaries and accessories. Thus it may in particular establish the means of communication which it shall judge necessary, such as railroads, canals, highways, electric lines and telephonic connections. Under the same conditions it may exploit freely without any restriction the means of communication of which it is the owner, particularly those connecting the mines and their subsidiaries and accessories with the means of communication situated in France.

Article VII.

Rights of Subrogation.

Every person whom the French State shall put in its place as regards the whole or a part of its rights to the exploitation of the mines shall have the benefit of the rights and privileges concerted in the present Treaty.

Article VIII.

Exemption of Personnel and Property from all Requisition.

The mines and other real estate which become the property of the French State may never be made the subject of measures of derogation, forced sale, expropriation, or requisition, nor of any other measure affecting the right of property.

The personnel and the plant and material associated with the exploitation of these mines, their accessories and subsidiaries, as well as the product extracted from the mines or manufactured in their accessories and subsidiaries may never be made the subject of any measure of requisition.

Article IX.

Rights of Workmen.

Germany may not take any measure for regulating the recruiting, dismissal, or wages of those employed by the French State or regarding the internal regulation of the mines.

Germany may not impede in any way the introduction or employment in the mines, their accessories, and subsidiaries, of French or foreign labor.

None the less those employed in the mines, their accessories and subsidiaries, shall have the right to take advantage of the guarantees of French law as these may affect workmen of the same category in France.

Article X.

Schools.

The French State shall always have the right of organizing as an incident of its ownership of the mines primary or technical schools *for its employees or their children*[2] and of causing instruction therein to be given in the French language in accordance with such programmes and by such teachers as it may select.

Article XI.

Protection of Labour and Property.

In case of disorder or conflict the German Government shall have the obligation to assure protection to the employees and the property of the French State. *If it fails in that duty* Reparation for damage to the one or the other shall be at the cost of the German Government.

Article XII.

Private Watchmen.

The French State shall have the right to appoint private watchmen at its own selection to assure within and about its own property the surveillance and protection of its property whether moveable or immoveable. These watchmen who shall be paid by the French Government and under its orders will have the same powers as those assigned to the German public police.

Article XIII.

Exemption from all Mining, Industrial or Social Regulations.

No mining, industrial or social regulations and in particular no regulation as to the exploitation of the mines, the conditions of labour, labour unions, accidents and pensions, may be imposed on the working of the mines or the personnel employed by the French Government in their working without the consent of the latter. Officials charged with the supervision of the execution of such regulations may not be appointed except with the approval of the French Government.

The workmen may belong to the French Labour Unions.

Article XIV.

Exemption from Taxation.

No tax, contribution, or royalty for the benefit of the State, whatever its nature, object or kind, shall be imposed upon the French Government, either as regards their property, the working of their mines, their accessories and subsidiaries, or as regards the direct or indirect product of this working nor under any other title whatsoever. The French Government will thus be free from all State

---

[2] Words in italics here and in the second sentence of the following article added by Wilson. Wilson probably made these additions after he had read David Hunter Miller's "Corrections in Articles on the Saar Basin," printed as Enclosure I with D. H. Miller to EMH, April 8, 1919.

taxes and contributions imposed upon other properties and work-ings situated within the territory defined under Article 1.

This exemption shall not apply to taxes imposed with the object of providing for local needs within the Saar basin, on condition that the amount paid by the mines toward the local contribution in any commune shall not exceed in any year the proportion paid during the year ending 11 November 1918. This exemption shall not apply to the general taxes affecting the individual property of the per-sonnel connected with the explaoitation [exploitation] of the mines, their subsidiaries and accessories. At the same time the taxes to which this personnel may be subject shall be identical with those imposed upon similar personnel connected with other mines in Germany. No French citizen shall be subject to special taxes re-sulting from the reparations imposed upon Germany by the Allied and Associated Powers.

Article XV
Freedom of Commerce
The French government shall enjoy complete liberty with respect to the distribution, despatch, and prices of sale of the products of the mines and their subsidiaries and accessories.

Article XVI
Customs Union
The territory above defined shall form part of the French customs system. It will have the advantage of the temporary exemption from import duties into Germany which is granted to Alsace-Lorraine.

No export tax shall be levied by France upon the metallurgical products of the Saar basin sent into Germany.

No customs dues shall be levied on products of this region in transit through German territory.

Article XVII
Money
No prohibition or restriction shall be imposed upon the circulation of French money in the Saar basin, and the French government shall have the right to use French money in all purchases, pay-ments, and contracts connected with the exploitation of the mines, their subsidiaries, and accessories.

T MS (WP, DLC).

Cary Travers Grayson to Joseph Patrick Tumulty

Paris. April 6, 1919.

The President says the situation here is extremely complex and intricate, but seems to be improving and he expects to have it in hand this week, but if necessary will act according to your suggestions.[1] The President is confined to bed but steadily improving. Thanks for your telegram.

Love to Mrs. Grayson.   Grayson.

T telegram (J. P. Tumulty Papers, DLC).
  [1] See JPT to C. T. Grayson, April 5, 1919.

Jessie Woodrow Wilson Sayre to Edith Bolling Galt Wilson

Dearest Edith,   Cambridge. April 6th, 1919.

I was so distressed to hear of Father's illness. I feel sure he had been worn down by those pig-headed old-timers that are blocking every thing. I do hope the papers are truthful and that he really is to be up again soon.

We are safely home again, the little boy[1] and I. We both caught colds at once in this very damp and changeable Cambridge weather and I was really quite frenetically anxious about him for a while. He seemed to be strangling all the time. Now, at last, he is better but not yet quite well.

I am going to trouble dear Father through you about a matter connected with the Y.W.C.A. because he asked me so sincerely to be sure to do so if the occasion should arise.

The case is this as briefly as I can state it. Our Y.W.C.A. secretaries have been in Russia since the war started and when our soldiers came there they were able to open a Hostess House and to initiate all their work for the soldiers as in other places. The commanding officer, Stewart,[2] was at first hesitant about letting them begin but their work has made him an enthusiastic convert.

Now they want to go to Siberia. The work is urgent there. American women under the Red Cross are going there in numbers and we are needed badly.

A group of 15 were ready to start. Secretary Lansing approved heartily and Keppel[3] of the War Department was favorable but advised them to send only six at first in order to win over General Graves before starting the work on a large scale. General Graves has he said a "No in his constitution" and to cable him would bring a No with certainty. So he promised to put it through. Passage was engaged and the six were to sail when suddenly a telegram came informing us that Secretary Baker says "No," until he has arrived in France and consulted Father. This seems so absurd and without reason. Why is it such a deeply important question that Father should be troubled with it. Indeed we consider that in view of the great problems to the fore this little business will be entirely overlooked by Baker when he arrives and we shall be held up indefinitely.

So my plea is that it may not be overlooked and that our work can go on uninterrupted. I am enclosing letters about it, from Stewart at Archangel and Ambassador Francis.[4]

Dear me, all my letter has been filled with this! What a bore!

We have the nicest house here and the children were so adorable when I came home that I haven't gotten over it yet. They were particularly delighted that Woodrow was "alive" and are never tired of watching him tucking him in and "helping" in many ways some of which are calculated to add a few gray hairs to an anxious mother's head! But they are so sweet about it.

Tell Margaret if you see her that I will write her again when I have a little more strength and time. I would that she could spare the time to send me even a "postley card" as the children say.

With dearest love to Father and yourself

Lovingly yours   Jessie.

ALS (WP, DLC).
[1] That is, Woodrow Wilson Sayre.
[2] Col. George E. Stewart, commander of the American forces in North Russia.
[3] Frederick Paul Keppel, Third Assistant Secretary of War.
[4] G. E. Stewart to Marcia O. Dunham, Jan. 20, 1919, TCL, and D. R. Francis to B. Miles, n.d., TCL, both in WP, DLC.

William Shepherd Benson to Naval Operations[1]

750-am 4-7-19

From: Knapp, London.
To: Opnav, Washington.

DOUBLE PRIORITY 8343 Mission number 389 For Opnav. What is earliest possible date USS GEORGE WASHINGTON can sail for Brest, France, and what is probable earliest date of arrival Brest. President desires movements of this vessel expedited. Carefully conceal fact that any communication on this subject has been received No distribution for this dispatch except officers actually concerned. 21106 Benson 8343.   Knapp.

T telegram (R. S. Baker Papers, NjP).
[1] Benson actually sent the following telegram at around 10:20 p.m. on April 6 from Paris via the London office of the Naval Communication Service. However, it was held

up in London for ten and a half hours and, consequently, did not reach Washington until the early hours of April 7. See W. S. Benson to H. S. Knapp, April 7, 1919, and H. S. Knapp to W. S. Benson, April 9, 1919, T telegrams (WP, DLC).

From the Diary of Dr. Grayson

Monday, April 7, 1919.

The President's temperature this morning is normal and he had a good night's rest. After my morning treatment he said: "I really feel first-rate." Then the President asked me: "Do you see any change in House; I don't mean a physical change; he does not show the same free and easy spirit; he seems to act distant with me as if he has something on his conscience." I replied: "I don't think it is so much in the Colonel himself as it is a case of too much son-in-law. The son-in-law, to be perfectly frank with you, Mr. President, has the air and attitude as if he and Colonel House were the prime movers in the Peace Commission. I don't like to take the matter seriously because it is such a joke. There are some people who do not grow up to their job; they swell up to it. Some people assert that if Auchincloss continues to swell at the rate he has been swelling since his arrival in Paris, should he remain here much longer, he will bust."

A peculiar development today indicated that Colonel House was not entirely frank in his various statements to the President. He told the President a story dealing with alleged French duplicity, yet when the President repeated the same thing to Ray Stannard Baker, the American Commission's press representative, Colonel House modified the story and told Baker it was not as serious as it seemed. The matter came about in this wise:

Colonel House came over to the President's room after attending the meeting of the Council of Four and appeared to be very mad and disgusted with the proceedings of the meeting, saying that he had got so mad that he left the meeting. He gave the impression that nothing was doing, and that Clemenceau had actually lied because he stated at the meeting that he had not seen the draft covering the indemnity program, when the Colonel said that he (Clemenceau) had told him several days ago that he had read it and that it was all right. Today, however, at the meeting Clemenceau emphatically stated that he had not seen this before.

I then asked Ray Stannard Baker to come to the temporary White House. The President told him of the conversation with Colonel House and how disgusted House was with the meeting. Then the President gave his views to Mr. Baker. He expressed himself along the lines of a suggested editorial to Mr. Grasty of the New York TIMES. When Baker returned to the Commission headquarters this evening, Colonel House told him (Baker) not to make the picture too dark; that it was not as bad as the President had painted it to him. The Colonel told Baker that as a matter of fact everything was agreed to in the afternoon except a few minor details. Baker asked him: "Do you consider Fiume a minor detail to the Italians?" He said: "No, I don't." It was impossible for me to reconcile this statement with the Colonel's self-reported action in leaving the meeting.

Sunday evening a message was sent by Admiral Benson to Captain McCauley directing him to take the GEORGE WASHINGTON out of the dry-dock and to bring her to Brest as soon as possible. No information regarding this move was made public to the newspaper correspondents at the time. However, it leaked out and of course furnished the basis for much comment and speculation.[1] Of course,

[1] News about Wilson's orders for the return of the *George Washington* leaked out so fast that it seems highly likely that Grayson himself had revealed the information to Richard V. Oulahan of the *New York Times*, who was known to be sympathetic to Wilson's views. Oulahan immediately wired his report to New York, where it was received even before Wilson's instructions had reached the Navy Department in Washington. Thus, the *New York Times* of April 7 was the first paper to carry the news, beating even the French afternoon papers of that date. Under the six-column headline "Wilson Summons His Ship, The 'George Washington,'" Oulahan's report, dated "Paris, April 6," summarized Benson's cable and speculated on the meaning of Wilson's order. According to Oulahan, it implied either that Wilson had decided to go home without making further efforts to harmonize the differences between the United States and the Allies or that Wilson believed that a complete agreement was virtually assured by the time the *George Washington* would reach Brest. In any event, Oulahan concluded: "It is understood to mean that he is preparing for possible unpleasant eventualities, but with the hope that they will not occur."

In the afternoon of April 7, the New York *Evening Post*, too, reported the recall of the *George Washington* but, in contrast to the *Times*, carried only an inconspicuous little notice about the incident. Moreover, the *Evening Post* concluded that Wilson's orders did not mean that the President was contemplating a "premature departure" from Paris. "They are thought rather to reflect a belief," the *Evening Post* stated, "that the Peace Conference will be able to effect an adjustment of outstanding problems at a comparatively early date."

However, once Ray Stannard Baker had briefed the Paris correspondents in the morning of April 7 and other American officials had left no doubt as to the significance of Wilson's orders, the American press treated the episode as a major sensation. In their editions of April 8, the leading papers carried headlines such as: "PEACE CONFERENCE AT CRISIS. EARLY RESULTS EXPECTED. WILSON'S PLANS FOR RETURN INTERPRETED AS WARNING" (*New York Times*); "WILSON SERVES ALLIES ULTIMATUM; MAY RETURN TO MAKE DIRECT PEACE; WEARIES OF DELAY" (New York *Sun*); and "ELEVENTH HOUR CRISIS AT PARIS; AMERICANS TALK OF ULTIMATUM AS WILSON SENDS FOR HIS SHIP" (*New York Tribune*). Most American papers then printed one of two Associated Press reports from Paris. One of these reports cited "one of the most responsible authorities associated with President Wilson" to the effect that he would not be surprised if the American delegation would leave the conference in the event of further delays over details. "Some of the President's closest intimates . . . ," the report continued, "were of the opinion that the summoning of the steamer would be accepted as an intimation by the allied leaders that delays must be brought to a speedy conclusion." See, for example, the *New York Times*, the New York *World*, and the *Washington Post*, April 8, 1919.

A second Associated Press report, printed, for example, in the New York *Sun* and the *New York Tribune* of April 8, stated that, according to "some officials," Wilson's orders had to be seen as "preliminary to a determined move to force an agreement at an early date by the Peace Conference." Although "those close to the President" denied the rumor that Wilson had delivered an ultimatum of forty-eight hours to the Allies, there was a general belief that he would take "definite action" if a deadlock was actually reached.

Reports from the staff correspondents of major American papers affirmed that Wilson "really" intended to return to the United States if no agreement was in sight by the

there was only one object, and that was simply the President's emphatic way of preparing every detail. In case it was necessary for him to go home he would have the boat here and would not be obliged to wait. During the morning I was bombarded with tele-phonic inquiries from newspapermen of all stripes who wanted to know the reason. This reached its climax when one French cor-respondent called me up to ask whether the GEORGE WASHINGTON

time of the arrival of the *George Washington*. Citing "officials close to Mr. Wilson," Truman H. Talley of the *New York Herald* stated that the President was determined either to force an equitable peace or quit the conference. Laurence Hills of the New York *Sun* reported that Wilson had served a "virtual ultimatum" to his associates in the Council of Four that they must speedily agree upon peace terms or the American delegation would leave Paris and negotiate a separate peace with Germany. And Frank H. Simonds wrote in the *New York Tribune* that Wilson's orders had precipitated the "final crisis" of the conference, that the President had in his possession a sketch of a separate treaty with Germany, and that "all dreams and illusions of world settlement" had vanished. *New York Herald* and New York *Sun*, April 8, 1919; *New York Tribune*, April 9, 1919.

In marked contrast to the sensational coverage of the *George Washington* episode in the leading American papers, the heavily censored French press minimized the signif-icance of the incident. For the most part, the Paris papers reported nothing but the bare facts of Wilson's announcement without drawing any inferences and, at best, printed brief comments from the Anglo-American press in Paris. For example, on April 8, *Le Temps* carried short excerpts from the Paris editions of the London *Daily Mail* and the *New York Herald* which suggested, respectively, that Wilson anticipated a rapid con-clusion of the negotiations and that Wilson might leave the conference in fifteen days, even though an agreement might not have been reached. See George Bernard Noble, *Policies and Opinions at Paris, 1919: Wilsonian Diplomacy, the Versailles Peace, and French Public Opinion* (New York, 1935), pp. 325-26.

Those Paris papers which discussed the incident at all mostly denied that it had any significant implications. For instance, *Le Journal* of April 7 reported "great excitement . . . among the American clan" over Wilson's orders, and it asked how the President could possibly consider leaving when so many questions still had to be decided. It continued: "The wildest deductions have been made, but no one believed that President Wilson wished merely to advertise his haste to get done with it. That is too simple." Cited, e.g., in the New York *Sun*, April 9, 1919.

An editorial in *Le Matin* of April 9 went still further in condemning those—"perhaps of the Hearst Press"—who had spread the "ridiculous rumors" that Wilson might not ratify the French demands and leave the conference. Indeed, the editorial stated, Paris had witnessed a "curious thing" the other day: "American propagandists, or newspaper men, knowing that President Wilson had summoned to Brest the ship which is to take him back to America, saw in this natural order an opportunity for blackmail. They made . . . a bold-faced attempt at intimidation. 'If you are not more accommodating,' they went all over the city saying, 'our President will return home, and you can extricate yourself from your difficulties by yourself.' " See, e.g., the *New York Times*, April 10, 1919, and Noble, pp. 326-27.

However, the fact that the *George Washington* incident alarmed the French govern-ment was clearly reflected in the Paris press. In the wake of Wilson's announcement, the Paris papers, which, in the past weeks, had emphasized the differences between the French and the American positions and had painted a pessimistic picture about the fate of the conference, suddenly denied emphatically that any real disagreements existed and predicted that the negotiations would be completed within "several days." See the New York *Sun*, April 9, 1919. Moreover, the French authorities also realized immediately the importance of minimizing France's annexationist aims. Thus, in the afternoon of April 7, shortly after the news about the *George Washington* had been given out, a semiofficial statement in *Le Temps* declared that France had no "annexationist claim . . . to any territory inhabited by Germans." In an obvious allusion to the Saar Valley, the statement further pointed out that this pertained "particularly to the regions lying between the boundaries of 1871 and 1814." See the *New York Times*, April 8, 1919, and Noble, p. 324. See also the extract from the Diary of Dr. Grayson printed at April 8, 1919.

was coming because of the state of the President's health or other-wise. I took great pleasure in telling him it was "otherwise."

It developed as a result of the newspaper discussion over the GEORGE WASHINGTON that there was a distinct and decided lack of team work among the members of the Commission. In the morning Secretary of State Lansing very frankly stated that it was true that the GEORGE WASHINGTON had been ordered to Brest. In the evening, however, Colonel House, for some unknown reason, saw fit to be-little the suggestion, and in effect told the newspapermen who conferred with him that very often orders were written for public consumption when there was no intention of carrying them out.[2] This rather angered some of the newspaper correspondents and resulted in the cognomen being coined for the benefit of the Colo-nel, which characterized him as "The Great American Acquiescor." It was a fact that so far as I have been able to find out since I have been in Paris, no one has yet heard Colonel House say NO. When he doesn't say YES, he half-heartedly consents, and in any event he never refuses.

I discouraged one newspaperman from writing an article which was to have been captioned—The Great American Acquiescor— and was designed to show that whenever some one said YES to the Colonel he agreed; when they said NO to the Colonel he agreed; and when they tried to disagree regardless of what the subject was the Colonel maneuvered so that at no time was he placed in a position of opposition to whoever he happened to be talking with. After persuading one correspondent not to write such an article in the morning, I was compelled to tell another to "hold his horses" when he called me on the phone after the Colonel House conference to inquire why this lack of teamwork and why a man was so anxious to rob the GEORGE WASHINGTON incident of a significance that was extremely necessary at the present time.

As a matter of fact, it did not appear that it was entirely Colonel House's fault. I talked the thing over with a number of people and got the opinion of several—one Nevin[3] summed the thing up in this way:

[2] There is no doubt that House had tried to belittle the significance of Wilson's orders. For example, Frederick Moore observed in the *New York Tribune* of April 9, 1919, that it was "unmistakably evident" that House deplored Wilson's "drastic action" and was "endeavoring to reconcile the conflicting elements and save the situation from calamity." Similarly, Laurence Hills remarked in the New York *Sun* of April 9, 1919, that "strange inconsistencies" appeared in the various statements issued by "those supposedly close to the President." As Hills pointed out: "From Col. E. M. House's menage came vigorous denial that the situation had become as desperate as some followers of the President had pictured it coincident with the George Washington announcement." See also André Tardieu, *The Truth About the Treaty* (London, 1921), p. 185, which states that, "in spite of Mr. House, the mendacious news" was published that the *George Washington* had been hurriedly summoned to Brest.

[3] That is, John Edwin Nevin.

"Colonel House's greatest success was when he was known as the sphinx. In the early days when the President utilized him for special investigations and other matters he was able to absorb the situation, return with it and explain it to the President and decline to talk for publication at all. The result was that his reputation for wisdom grew, as it always does when a man is known to be silent. However, when the war progressed and the Colonel came to France at a time when it was apparent that the Allies were winning, he was given much publicity by the French, who are the cleverest publicity workers in the entire world. The Colonel had his son-in-law, Mr. Gordon Auchincloss, with him. Auchincloss is young and has not had the opportunity of realizing that promises and performances do not always run hand in hand. His head was completely turned. Naturally his influence with the Colonel was great, and he reflected to the Colonel the views that were presented to him at the various social functions he attended, and at which he was more or less lionized. Then the Peace Conference came on and the Colonel, who heretofore had shunned newspapermen, began to warm up to them. He saw his name in print. It had the same effect upon him that it has had upon Henry Ford, who for twenty years was believed to be one of the greatest men who ever lived, but after he began talking for publication, he began gathering to himself enemies. Colonel House naturally was putty in the hands of the newspapermen when they could get him to talk. And as time went on he talked more and more freely and the sphinx reputation disappeared. His son-in-law, of course, feted by persons who are desirous of using him, swelled up to the occasion, and the result was that neither the Colonel nor his acquired relative were as useful as they could have been."

The fact, however, remains that whether Nevin's opinion actually summarized the case or not, it was true that Colonel House's YES, YES and NO, NO to Lloyd-George and Clemenceau and Orlando had had a very serious effect in handicapping the President in dealing with these gentlemen. Colonel House had apparently been very friendly to Clemenceau, yet as a matter of fact it was peculiar that some of the statements which he (House) made regarding Clemenceau did not develop when they were actually investigated by the President. I once asked the President what he thought of Colonel House's estimates of Clemenceau as communicated to him, and the President replied that he had found Clemenceau to be exactly the opposite of everything that House had said he was.[4] The President added that House had certainly missed his diagnosis in sizing up the French Premier.

[4] See, for example, EMH to WW, Nov. 9, 1918 (first telegram of that date), Vol. 53.

The President was able to sit up today for the first time since his seizure. I had lunch on a little table with the President and Mrs. Wilson by the fire in the President's bedroom. Notwithstanding the discouraging news in connection with international affairs, the President maintained as good spirits as one would in the midst of normal proceedings.

Mr. Charles H. Grasty, of the New York TIMES, came to me and told me he would like to have some suggestions for an editorial comment which he was cabling to the TIMES, and which he knew I could give him inasmuch as I was perfectly familiar with the President's viewpoint and also with the President's general plans. I gave him the following:

"I (the President) came over here believing that they meant what they had authorized me to say to Germany in arranging for the armistice and for the peace terms. The time is at hand now to demand whether they mean business or not. Before taking any decided action I had made up my mind patiently to wait so that I could hear what all had to say. After having heard them I found what the most cynical had predicted before I came here—that it was only a contest of selfish interests."

On the basis of this Mr. Grasty wrote a most forceful editorial for the TIMES.[5]

The Council of Four had two sessions today, the second in Lloyd-George's bed room, he having a slight cold. Afterwards it was frankly admitted that absolutely no progress had been made.

[5] Actually, an article, entitled "Wilson for Lasting Peace," which appeared under the dateline of "Paris, April 6" in the *New York Times* on April 8, 1919. Grasty stated that, contrary to common assertions, neither the secrecy surrounding the peace conference nor its delay and present deadlock could be attributed to anything that Wilson had done. For one thing, Wilson would have probably preferred complete publicity, but he had had to concede that "European conditions" did not permit open diplomacy. Thus, he had been forced to go along with the strong Allied demands for secret negotiations in order to prevent an otherwise almost certain collapse of the Allied governments. As for the delay of the conference, Grasty maintained that it was solely due to the repeated refusal of the Allied, and particularly the French, leaders to negotiate peace terms on the basis of the Fourteen Points and the principles of the Armistice agreement. Whereas America desired nothing but a durable peace, each of the Allies was attempting to have its particular point of view written into the treaty. As Grasty continued: "President Wilson has taken the shock of all these demands. He has stood his ground. With patience and amiability, and without a trace of arbitrariness, he has maintained himself against the persistence which only European diplomats know how to bring to bear. The President has examined and re-examined the whole situation day after day for the purpose of making every concession consistent with a sound peace. At every stage he has felt himself honorably bound by the armistice agreement, and in this position he has been supported by his conviction that European interests and world interests would be best subserved by carrying out that agreement. To make a scrap of paper out of it was unthinkable, both for America and her allies.

"There matters rest today. The armistice agreement, with its twelve points accepted and two reserved, is the rock on which the President stands. In all essentials it must be the basis of peace. . . . President Wilson has met every demand with sympathy and open-mindedness, but has steadfastly refused to abandon the underlying principles of the armistice agreement. . . . His has been the spirit of disinterested helpfulness, which is America's spirit, and he has pursued a consistent, wise, and steady course."

From the Diary of Ray Stannard Baker

Monday the 7th [April 1919]

This has been a great day—and we are now upon the very crisis of events. We shall know in a day or so whether the Peace Conference is going to pieces or not. This morning Admiral Grayson sent me word that the President had ordered the *George Washington* to sail immediately for Brest. She is in dry-dock & was not expected out until the 14th, so that the order has peculiar significance. In giving it out to the press I took pains to make no interpretations—stating the fact & leaving the correspondents to place upon it such interpretation as they chose. The implication, however, is perfectly clear—that the President has grown tired of the delay & is determined to make an end of it.

I went up to see Mr. Wilson at 6:30—the first time since he fell ill—and had a long talk. I found him fully dressed, in his study, looking still thin & pale. A slight hollowness of the eyes emphasized a characteristic I had often noted before—the size & luminosity of his eyes. They are extraordinarily clear, & he looks at one with a piercing intentness.

What he said put new courage into me. He is going to fight, & fight to the end. He is going to fight for his principles. It was really no news—yet his reaffirmation was great news. He has reached the point where he will give no further. He will win for the principles though he lose the peace & lose his own prestige—& this is what matters. When I talk with Col. House (he was to-day as smoothly optimistic as ever) I am half persuaded that he can win peace—a peace that doesn't much matter—but when I talk with this man— this tremendous, grim, rock-like man, I think he can die for faith, that he can bring down the world around him before giving over his convictions, and everything that is strong & sure within me rejoices—this is *victory*.

I had suggested to Grayson that I was confused by the diverse counsels I got from House & Lansing & when I came in the President said:

"What about this difference between Lansing & House?"

"They do not agree at all," I said, "as to the present situation in the Conference. Colonel House is strongly optimistic, Mr. Lansing is pessimistic."

"Lansing is much nearer right," said the President.

(In passing, Close told me that only half an hour before I saw the President, Col. House, coming over from the meeting of the Big Four at Lloyd-George's, had talked with the President & had then come rushing out, saying that everything was going to pieces, that there was no agreement anywhere. He was evidently at his wit's end. Yet half an hour later, on his return to the Crillon he was giving the correspondents the usual soothing dose of hopefulness, saying that there was only differences in details &c &c. In a time like this what matters but the truth!)

I told the President about the effect of his announcement regarding the George Washington.

"Well, the time has come to bring this thing to a head," he said. "House was just here & told me that Clemenceau & Klotz had talked away another day. They brought in a report which Clemenceau said he had not seen. There is the best of evidence that he had seen it. The unspeakable Klotz was called to explain it. One mass of tergiversations! I will not discuss anything with them any more."

I then urged, as I have done before, that a statement be issued at once—and with specific applications of his principles. This we discussed, he being doubtful about too detailed a statement upon the specific issues. He said, if he had not fallen ill, the time for meeting the situation would have been to-day.

He proposed to stand upon his principles.

"Then Italy will not get Fiume."

"Absolutely not—so long as I am here," he said sharply.

"Nor France the Saar."

"No. We agreed among ourselves & we agreed with Germany upon certain general principles. The whole course of the conference has been made up of a series of attempts, especially by France, to break over this agreement, to get territory, to impose crushing indemnities. The only real interest of France in Poland is in weakening Germany by giving Poland territory to which she has no right."

He said that a League of Nations founded upon an unjust peace could have no future.

I told him of the remark of the Italian who came to see me the other day. When I asked him whether or not he was for the L. of N. he replied naively:

"Yes, but we want Fiume first." I observed that this seemed typical of the position of all the allies, that they wanted first to be sure of their 'grabs' & 'indemnities' & then to have a L. of N. to protect them in their possession. I told him how I had answered the Italians who declared they were going home if they did not get Fiume.

"That is interesting," I said. "It would relieve us of a great responsibility."

"How is that," they said.

"Well, we are now stabilizing your lira at 6.32. Of course, if you withdraw from the Conference, you cannot expect us to go forward doing that." Their faces fell. "And," I said, "our merchants are now shipping much wheat & other food to Italy. I presume they will not care to do this unless they are well assured of their pay." The two Italians (who are aides of Orlandos) went off, as I said, with a new angle of the case in mind.

"That was exactly what you should have said," the President remarked.

We had some talk of Lloyd-George's position—& the clear intimation that he is preparing to throw the blame for delay upon Wilson.

"Well," said the President sadly, "I suppose I shall have to stand alone."

I told him that I believed the great masses of people were still strongly with him, but were confused & puzzled by hearing every case in the world but ours & that they would rally again strongly to his support if he told them exactly what the situation was, & the nature of his opposition.

"I believe so too," he said.

I asked him what I could say to the correspondents, & he told me to tell them to read again our agreements with the other allies & with Germany & to assure them that he would not surrender on these principles—which I did, gladly.

He is not "bluffing" in ordering the George Washington—he is not the kind of man who bluffs.

When I got back Col. House sent for me & said that some of the correspondents told him that I was putting a dark interpretation on the situation & he expostulated. He had actually *not known* until evening that the President had sent for the G.W. Nor did he know that I had seen the President until I told him.

"The President does not seem cheerful," I said.

"No," he admitted.

"And if he wants to show that his patience is exhausted," I argued, "by so extreme a step as the ordering of the G.W. I do not see why we should try to smooth over the situation & imply that everything is all right."

"We are together on everything but certain small details."

"Have you decided the question of Fiume?"

"Not yet."

"Or that of Poland."

"No."

—And there you are! Details, of course, cause all the trouble. In settling an estate it is often not the money nor the old home over

which the heirs quarrel, but the family Bible & grandmother's al-
paca shawl.

Nearly all the trouble in the world comes from trying to apply
excellent general principles to difficult specific cases—where
[whether] the general principles are the 14 points or the 10 com-
mandments or the Golden Rule. One was crucified by trying to
apply the latter.

Wilson will get *something* out of it, but will disappoint most of
the world, now dreaming of ideal results & doubtful whether Wil-
sonism or Bolshevism is the remedy.

From the Diary of Colonel House

April 7, 1919.

Lloyd George sent word this morning that he was ill and wished
to postpone the morning meeting of the Council of Four until the
afternoon at three o'clock. I agreed with the substitution of half-
past three for three o'clock.

It was the most footless of many footless meetings. We had agreed
absolutely upon the terms of reparations. Loucheur, after a draft
of the terms had been prepared, told Davis that Clemenceau had
read and approved it *in toto*. This was in response to my endeavor
to have the draft approved without the crossing of a t or the dotting
of an i. I had difficulty in persuading George to agree to this. I sent
word to him by both Kerr, Wiseman and Hankey, and as a last
resort, saw him myself five minutes before the meeting and finally
got him to agree that he would make no amendments.

He had in the first line of Article One, "and the German Government accepts." The President cut this out. I got George to consent to allow it to remain out, and when he did consent to do so, I
offered myself to put it back because he seemed so reluctant and
seemed to attach so much importance to it.

When Clemenceau and Orlando came this is what happened:
Clemenceau declared it was the first time he had seen the draft.
This, of course, was not true, because most of it was read and
thoroughly discussed at our Saturday meeting. The old man was
in an ugly and belligerent mood and for the first time showed
evidence and signs of mental weariness. He got everything wrong
and would agree to nothing. Loucheur told me time and again, after
we had accepted and voted over a few verbal and unimportant
changes, that it was the last, and yet when the very next sentence
was read, both he and Klotz would again make suggestions for
changes. This was done many times and the final upshot of our

discussion was that I refused to take part in it and at six o'clock I left the meeting in order to show my displeasure.

I crossed the street to tell the President about the meeting and he thoroughly approved what I had done. We wasted the entire afternoon, accomplishing nothing, for the text when finished was practically what it was when we went into the meeting. Any drafting committee could have done it better. This is what makes me so impatient at the whole procedure of the Conference. Instead of drawing the picture with big lines, they are drawing it like an etching. If the world was not aflame, this would be permissible, but it is almost suicidal to to [sic] try to write a treaty of peace, embracing so many varied and intricate subjects, with such methods in times like these.

Lloyd George acted splendidly. He lived up to his promise and whispered to me time and again, "what is the matter with the old man today?" "Is he trying to delay us for any reason?" I do not believe he was and I think the trouble was largely due to the bad advice of his Minister of Finance.

The President and I were thoroughly discouraged when we talked the matter over and we wondered what the outcome was to be.

After leaving the President, I went to the Crillon for an interview with Montagu, Secretary of State for India. He, too, sees the tragedy of this waste of time. He is returning home thoroughly disgusted.

Philip Kerr called after dinner to tell me that tomorrow at eleven they would take up the question of "Responsibility for the War." I did not wish to attend this meeting and asked the President to send Lansing in his place and in mine. When Lloyd George heard this was to be done he sent me word that it would be no use to hold the meeting and he preferred that we hold our meeting as usual to take up some other matters, and in the afternoon, if the President was well enough, they would take up the question of "Responsibility." This was finally agreed upon.

Orlando came at noon to present a new plan for the settlement of the Adriatic question. It was a perfectly foolish suggestion. He desired to make a free city to the west of Fiume and give the Jugo-Slavs a chance to develop a flat and sandy beach as a port. He pledged me to great secrecy, saying his people had not authorized him to offer this compromise, and he hoped I would protect him and let it come from me, provided I thought it might solve the problem. I promised to take it up with the President, which I did, and which he turned down as quickly as I did myself.

Hankey's and Mantoux's Notes of a Meeting of the Council of Four[1]

I.C.-170J.   Prime Minister's Flat, 23 Rue Nitot, Paris,
                                         April 7, 1919, 3:30 p.m.

1. It was agreed that the Council of Foreign Ministers should be requested to examine the questions in Appendix I.

2. MR. LLOYD GEORGE distributed a paraphrase of a telegram from General Smuts to Mr. Balfour. (Appendix II.)

§Mantoux's notes:

Lloyd George. . . . I will apprise you of telegram which we have just received from General Smuts. He has failed. He declares that the Hungarian government, which he was supposed to visit, has no authority beyond the limits of the region of Budapest. He asks to return. I suggest that he visit the French headquarters on the way in order to be able to make a complete report to us on the situation.

Clemenceau. There could only be advantages in doing that.

Lloyd George. He could also go to Rumania, so that he could report to us as many facts as possible. We will undoubtedly have to take some decisions.

Clemenceau. We agree. §

It was agreed:

That Mr. Lloyd George should inform General Smuts that his telegram had been considered by the Supreme Council, and that it had been agreed that he should visit the French and Roumanian Headquarters, and ascertain the whole situation in all aspects before returning.

3. MR. LLOYD GEORGE communicated the gist of a message he had received from the British Military Agents at Berlin who reported a great increase in Spartacism.

M. CLEMENCEAU said that his information corresponded to this.

§Mantoux's Notes:

Lloyd George. We have also received a report from our military representative in Berlin. He thinks that the Spartacists are making progress, and he proposes an Allied occupation; that is always the solution of the military.

Clemenceau. The information we have received is very similar.

Lloyd George. According to the same report, the organized troops that the German government has at its disposal are not more than 80,000 men, that is, 25,000 in Berlin, 6,000 in Halle, 6,800 in the Ruhr basin, between 8,000 and 10,000 in Silesia, and the remainder

[1] The complete text of Hankey's minutes is printed in *PPC*, V, 39-43.

on the Polish frontier. Berlin is thought to be able to hold out for a month.

Do these figures correspond to those of Marshal Foch?

Foch. We do not have the exact figures; but these do not contradict what we know.

Lloyd George. A Spartacist coup is expected this week.§

4. MARSHALL FOCH made a short statement of the results of his negotiations at Spa in regard to the transport of General Haller's Army to Poland.[2] He handed round the three following documents:

(1) A Report on the negotiations of April 3rd and 4th at Spa.[3]

(2) An Appendix to the above.[4]

(3) A protocol with Annexes.[5]

MR. LLOYD GEORGE congratulated Marshal Foch on the remarkable skill and ability he had shown in the conduct of these negotiations.

COLONEL HOUSE strongly supported this expression of opinion, which was generally agreed to.

§Mantoux's notes:

Marshal Foch presents his report on the negotiations at Spa concerning the transport of Polish troops.

Clemenceau. Mr. Lloyd George can read at his leisure the report of the negotiations.

[2] For the discussion leading to the decision to send Marshal Foch to Spa, see the minutes of the meetings of the Council of Four, April 1, 1919, 11 a.m. and April 2, 1919, 11 a.m., both printed in Vol. 56.

[3] "REPORT ON THE NEGOCIATIONS OF APRIL 3RD AND 4TH 1919 AT SPA," CC MS (WP, DLC). This "report" actually consisted of the minutes of the meetings between Foch and the German delegate, Matthias Erzberger. According to Erzberger, the German government acknowledged the "absolute necessity" of sending Haller's army to Poland. However, as the Council of Four had anticipated, Erzberger then brought up the suggestion which he had already unofficially conveyed to Wilson (see Enclosure II printed with T. H. Bliss to WW, April 1, 1919, Vol. 56): instead of shipping Haller's forces to Poland via Danzig, where the German government could not guarantee the absence of disturbances, the troops could be transported safely from the Rhine bridgeheads across Germany by rail. Foch immediately accepted the proposal, but he insisted that the German government explicitly recognize the legal right of the Allies, according to the Armistice agreement, to have their troops disembark at Danzig. The remainder of the negotiations was taken up almost entirely with the question of whether Haller's troops were, in fact, Allied troops and as such had the theoretical right to pass through Danzig.

[4] "ANNEXED APPENDIX TO THE REPORT OF THE NEGOCIATIONS OF APRIL 3rd and 4th at SPA," CC MS (WP, DLC). It included the correspondence between Foch and Erzberger of April 3 and 4, 1919, and various drafts of the "Protocol" described in the following note.

[5] F. Foch and M. Erzberger, "PROTOCOL," April 4, 1919, CC MS (WP, DLC). This agreement stipulated the general terms which would govern the transport of General Haller's army to Poland. On the question of whether these troops could, in principle, pass through Danzig, Foch and Erzberger reached a compromise: the Allies affirmed this right, but the German government did not explicitly acknowledge it. Thus, the first paragraph of the "Protocol" read as follows: "By Article XVI of the Armistice Convention of 11th November 1918, Germany is bound to authorize the passage via Danzig of allied troops, and consequently (according to the Allies' understanding of the matter) that of General Haller's troops also."

An attached "ANNEX to the Protocol of 4th April, 1919," CC MS (WP, DLC) spelled out in detail the arrangements for the implementation of the agreement.

Foch. I believe that it would be worthwhile because it shows the present temperature of the German government.

Lloyd George. This document is too interesting not to be read attentively.

(Perusing it) They want the French to occupy Budapest! And Vienna! They want everyplace occupied, except Germany.[6] Naturally, Erzberger is very hostile toward the Bolsheviks; he is a Catholic. . . . Ah! But he is very friendly!

Very interesting; I believe that Marshal Foch has established his qualifications as a great diplomat. We should congratulate him for his skill and success.

Foch. Several practical matters remain to be settled.§

5. GENERAL WEYGAND asked that the Governments which had troops in the area of occupation on the Western bank of the Rhine should provide the Allied Officers to accompany trains carrying General Haller's troops across Germany.

GENERAL WILSON said that the number of British Officers required was 83. We should have no difficulty in supplying these.

COLONEL HOUSE said he must consult the American Military Authorities.

(Subject to Colonel House's reservation, General Weygand's proposal was agreed to.)

6. GENERAL WEYGAND said that the whole plan of transportation would require eight days to get into working order. It would therefore commence on the 15th, and would continue until June 15th. He asked if the Polish Government had been officially informed.

M. CLEMENCEAU said he had seen M. Paderewski today, and he had knowledge of the position.

(It was agreed that Marshal Foch should pay an official visit to M. Paderewski, and give him an an official notification on behalf of the Allied and Associated Powers.)

7. GENERAL WEYGAND said that the American, British, and French

---

[6] In his private conversation with Foch on April 3 before the opening of the official negotiations, Erzberger stated that, if the Allies "really" intended to establish a barrier against Bolshevism by sending Haller's army to Poland, the German government would do all it could to assist in this endeavor. However, the German government believed that the danger of the spread of Bolshevism was greatest in South Central Europe. Whereas in the Baltic region and in Poland, anti-Bolshevik forces were effectively holding the line, the "southern wing of the forces opposed to Bolshevism" in Rumania, Bessarabia, and Hungary was not capable of fulfilling its mission. In Hungary, Bolshevism was already victorious; in Bessarabia, a country of great landowners, the ground was favorable for the outbreak of Bolshevism. Erzberger concluded: "The German Government thinks that, if the Marshal wants to defeat Bolshevism, it is necessary for the French Authorities to settle in BUDAPEST. There is in that direction a great danger lest Bolshevism should spread through VIENNA and BAVARIA, and reach the RHINE and ITALY. The German Government is convinced that the southern wing of the forces actually opposed to Bolshevism are unemployable." "REPORT ON THE NEGOCIATIONS . . . ," cited in n. 1.

Generals were in agreement that the German Government ought to be allowed to send back Russian prisoners to Russia, provided that they were not sent against their will.

M. CLEMENCEAU said that he had 120,000 Russian prisoners in France.

(It was agreed that the German Government should be permitted to return Russian prisoners, provided it was not against their will.)

§Mantoux's notes:

Lloyd George. I believe that these Russians are equally dangerous in Germany and in Russia.

Clemenceau. I also have many Russians to send back; it is not a small problem.§

Marshal Foch, General Weygand, and General Wilson withdrew, and financial experts were introduced. The Meeting with the financial experts is recorded separately.

SECRET

APPENDIX I.

The Council of Foreign Ministers is requested to examine the following questions:

1. Preparation of an Article in the Treaty of Peace terminating the state of War.
2. Preparation of Articles in the Treaty of Peace in regard to the restriction of opium traffic.
3. The question of arms traffic.
4. A minor amendment of the military terms proposed by the British Delegation.
5. The question of Morocco as soon as reported on by the Moroccan Commission.
6. The preparation of Articles in the Treaty of Peace in regard to the recognition of the British Protectorate of Egypt and the renunciation of territorial privileges and the recognition of the transfer to his Majesty's Government of the Sultan's right under the Suez Canal Convention.
7. Preparation of Articles in the Treaty of Peace with Germany by which Germany undertakes to be bound down by the terms of the Treaty of Peace with Turkey, Austria-Hungary and Bulgaria.
8. Preparation of Articles in the Treaty of Peace whereby Germany binds herself to recognise a new regime replacing the Treaty of 1839 as to Belgium.
9. Preparation of Articles in the Treaty of Peace providing for the

acceptance by the enemy of all Allied prize court decisions and orders.

10. Preparation of Articles in the Treaty of Peace providing for the recognition in advance by Germany of any arrangements made by the Allied and Associated Governments with reference to previous Russian territory, including special arrangements with new States.

11. Waiver of German claims in the Antarctic region.

Paris, April 7th, 1919.

APPENDIX II.

TELEGRAM FROM GENERAL SMUTS, BUDA PESTH.

TO MR. BALFOUR, *April 4th, 1919.*

In consequence of the change which took place yesterday in the Hungarian Government, BELA KUHN is now Chief Commissary for Foreign Affairs as well as for War, and probably the most important member of the administration. I had a long conversation with him on my arrival here this morning, and explained that the line notified to the Hungarian Government by Colonel Vix was not intended to be a permanent political frontier and therefore that the withdrawal of the Hungarian troops behind it and the creation of a neutral zone occupied by Allied troops, which was necessary if peace and good order were to be maintained, would in no way prejudice the Hungarian case. I pressed him to order the withdrawal of the Hungarian troops behind that line. BELA KUHN replied that there were two chief reasons why the withdrawal was impossible. These were:

Firstly, that compliance with Colonel Vix' orders would involve the immediate fall of the Government, because large sections of the population attach great importance to territorial boundaries although the Government itself did not. He observed that the mere demand to withdraw had sealed the fate of the Government of Count Karolyi.

Secondly, if the Government ordered such a withdrawal it would not be obeyed and it was not willing to undertake an obligation which it knew that it could not fulfil. The reason of this was that the hold of the Government over the troops who were defending the territory in question was very slight. Those troops were local forces, mostly Szeklers.[7] This plea is probably valid, since information from many trustworthy sources has reached me to the effect

---

[7] A people of Magyar or Magyarized Turki origin, who were settled in the Middle Ages in eastern Transylvania to serve, as their Magyar name *Székely* implies, as "frontier guards." They regularly supplied some of Hungary's best soldiers and, at this time, comprised a significant part of Béla Kun's Red Army.

that the Government has but slight authority over the Provinces and that it is in the main effective only in the capital.

BELA KUHN said that if the Government resigned, which it would do if the withdrawal of the troops were insisted on, there was no party capable of assuming power and that chaos would therefore ensue. If, therefore, the Entente carried out its present policy, it must be prepared to run Hungary on its own responsibility and to occupy the capital and other districts as well as the neutral zone. In reply to observations from me to the effect that great advantages would accrue to Hungary from the removal of the blockade and the establishment of friendly relations with the Powers of the Entente which would enable the country to recover its prosperity, BELA KUHN said that he wished for such relations but that, for the reasons above given, evacuation could not be carried out at present. He proved insensible to the argument that the Armistice had to be carried out and that political frontiers could be finally settled later, though he said that the Hungarian Government adhered to the Armistice. The Hungarian Government recognised the principles of nationality laid down by Mr. Wilson and considered that the situation should be governed by popular self-determination. The Hungarian Government renounced the ideals of territorial integrity formerly prevalent, but rather than yield to the demand for evacuation which was constantly growing stronger, it preferred the definite settlement of the whole question of frontiers to be arrived at at meetings between representatives of the Hungarian, German, Austrian, Bohemian, Serbian and Roumanian Governments. He suggested that I might preside at these meetings, to which the Hungarian Government would bring an accommodating spirit and willingness to make concessions from the territorial point of view. Count Karolyi suggested that these meetings might be held at Vienna or Prague.

BELA KUHN further observed that the question of food and others of a similar nature were more important to the Hungarian Government than that of frontiers. The economic position of the New States might therefore also be dealt with at these meetings and it would probably be necessary to come to some arrangement such as that advocated by Masaryk,[8] among the Danubian States.

It appears to me that BELA KUHN's suggestion might at once be

[8] That is, the convocation, under the aegis and the presidency of the Great Powers, of a conference of the successor states to the former Austro-Hungarian Empire to settle their most urgent economic problems and to reestablish economic relations among them. See the memorandum by J. C. Smuts printed at April 9, 1919. For a brief discussion of Masaryk's proposal and the differences between his and Smuts' plan, see D. Perman, *The Shaping of the Czechoslovak State: Diplomatic History of the Boundaries of Czechoslovakia, 1914-1920* (Leiden, 1962), pp. 189-90.

adopted, as it will in any case be necessary to invite the Germans, Austrians and Hungarians to send representatives to Paris before the signature of the Preliminaries of Peace. All parties interested in the fate of the former Austro-Hungarian Monarchy could be called together in order to settle at least principles on which definite boundaries could be ultimately drawn, if not to decide the boundaries themselves. On this basis it would be possible to sign Preliminaries of Peace. I would accordingly suggest that, as all other interested parties already have representatives at Paris, the meetings should be at once held there and that the attendance of German and Austrian representatives should be invited. If objection is felt to a more detailed invitation to Austria and Hungary, the summons might merely ask them to state their case before the Conference. The signature of this Preliminary Peace might take place at the same time as or even before the conclusion of the Preliminary Peace with Germany, if proceedings are as far as possible expedited.

I request leave to return to Paris as there appears to be no further object in my remaining here.

T MS (SDR, RG 256, 180.03401/104, DNA); Mantoux, I, 166-68.

Hankey's and Mantoux's Notes of a Meeting of the Council of Four[1]

I.C.-170K.   Prime Minister's Flat, 23 Rue Nitot, Paris, April 7, 1919, 4 p.m.

1. The Supreme Council had before them a revised edition of the clauses on reparation prepared by Mr. Lamont, Mr. Keynes and M. Loucheur as a result of the Meeting held on Saturday, April 5th. (Appendix I.)[2]

This Article [1] was accepted subject to the addition in line 1, after the word "affirm" of the following words: "and the Enemy States accept." This addition had been agreed to at the Meeting on April 5th, but had been dropped out in the drafting.

Clause 1, as finally approved, reads as follows:

"The Allied and Associated Governments affirm and the Enemy States accept the responsibility of the Enemy States for causing all the loss and damage to which the Allied and Associated Governments and their nationals have been subjected as a consequence of the war imposed upon them by the aggression of the Enemy States."

[1] The complete text of Hankey's minutes is printed in PPC, V, 44-55.
[2] It is printed in ibid., pp. 55-56. See also n. 1 to the extract from the Diary of Colonel House printed at April 6, 1919.

(As a matter of accuracy the above amendment to Clause 1 was introduced as the result of the discussion on Clause 2)

There was a prolonged discussion on various points in Clause 2.

M. KLOTZ took exception to two points in the draft of this clause. First, the statement that "The financial resources of the Enemy States are not unlimited." He agreed that this might be expressed somewhere in the Treaty, for example, in a preamble, but he considered it would have a bad political effect on the population if stated in the Treaty.

Second, the phrase "To the extent of her utmost capacity," the wording of which, he pointed out, in a previous draft had been "At whatever cost to themselves."[3]

In the course of the discussion, Mr. Lloyd George pointed out that it was necessary somewhere in the document for the reasons to appear why the Allies could accept less then the whole cost of the war. This phrase had not been put in for the benefit of the Germans but to enable M. Clemenceau and himself to justify to the French and British peoples their acceptance of less than the whole cost of the war.

§Mantoux's notes:

Lloyd George. I do not favor removing from this text the indication of the enemy's inability to pay all that he owes. It is surely necessary to justify in some way the action of the British and French governments, which find themselves obliged to accept less than complete compensation for the expenses of the war. We must clearly establish that it is not because it would be unjust to claim it, but because it is impossible to obtain it, that we have adopted a limiting formula.

Clemenceau. It must be said in a preamble, but not in the financial clauses of the treaty.

Klotz. Likewise the enemy must be required to acknowledge not only what he can pay, but what he owes. I share Mr. Lloyd George's opinion on the benefit of explaining the attitude of the governments; but like M. Clemenceau, I think that this should be done in a preamble.

Lloyd George. I agree with you on the second point. I have already said that Germany must acknowledge her entire debt. But I would observe that the second sentence no longer makes sense if we omit the first.

Klotz. In any case the wording is poor. To say that the enemy states do not have unlimited resources is to state a truism. No state has unlimited resources. It is better to say that the enormity of the debt surpasses all possibilities of payment.

---

[3] See the first draft of an Anglo-American accord on reparations printed at April 1, 1919, Vol. 56.

Lloyd George. The best thing is simply to omit the words "up to the very limit of their capacity." What remains is sufficient, and agrees with the precise commitment already undertaken at the time of the Armistice.§

In the course of a prolonged discussion M. Klotz put forward the following alternative draft:

"The Allied and Associated Governments, recognising that financial resources of the Enemy States in the situation in which they are left at the conclusion of Peace, will not be adequate to make complete reparation for all the losses and damages mentioned in Article 1, demand that the German Government shall compensate all the losses enumerated in the annexed text."

MR. LLOYD GEORGE considered this draft would be bad from the point of view of public opinion which, both in France and Great Britain, desired very heavy damages. Public opinion would say: "Why do you take the situation at the time Peace is signed." The facts that ought to be taken into consideration were not the ephemeral conditions existing on the signature of Peace, but the permanent diminutions of Germany, such as the loss of their coalfields, iron-fields, ships and Colonies.

§Mantoux's notes:

Lloyd George. I regret that we have spent so much time on a simple question of wording. But permit me to say to you that from the point of view of public opinion, that draft does not seem a good one to me. Our public opinion, like yours, insists on reparation as complete as possible. Think about the effect of this formula: to take into consideration the enemy's situation at the time of the conclusion of the peace, that is a phrase more vague and less satisfactory than that with which we had been presented. The public will say: "It is not the enemy's situation on the day after the peace, but a rather long period of time, ten years, twenty years, that must be envisaged in order to know what he should pay us."

The only thing which we must take into account, because it is a permanent fact, is the loss by the enemy of his iron mines, of part of his coal mines, of his colonies, of his merchant marine. All that has a direct influence upon his capacity to pay.

I earnestly beg you not to let us be held up on questions of wording. With what the Americans accept, that is, the omission of the words "up to the very limit of his capacity" and the addition, further on, of the statement that resources are not adequate—emphasizing this—to compensate damages, I believe that this text would be reasonably satisfactory.

House. We favor neither one nor the other of these two clauses. If you wish to delete one or both, the Americans will not object.§

[After an adjournment, the council agreed to Articles 2 and 3 in the form shown in the full text ("Reparations") printed below as part of this document. Klotz referred to the last sentence of Article 3 and asked whether the Allied and Associated Governments would have to be unanimous in giving their instructions to the commission.]

MR. DAVIS said that the experts had not attempted to settle that. This sentence had only been inserted to meet M. Clemenceau's point raised on Saturday that the Commission, as a Commission, should not have too much power and that the Governments should retain power.

M. KLOTZ considered it important to settle the question of unanimity.

MR. DAVIS said that on this question of power it had throughout the discussion of the Reparation Commission been agreed by the American, British, French and Italian experts that the Commission should have powers to postpone the dates of payment.

M. KLOTZ insisted that the Commission's question was as to whether the vote was to be a unanimous one or a majority vote.

MR. LAMONT said this was a point to be covered in the constitution of the Commission which had not yet been dealt with.

M. CLEMENCEAU urged that if the Governments were agreed on the principle, it would be better to settle it here and now.

MR. LLOYD GEORGE said that if, while principles were being discussed, details such as the composition and constitution of the Commission and how it was to vote had to be settled, the Supreme Council would never get to the end of its task.

M. CLEMENCEAU did not wish to insert anything in the clause now under consideration, but thought it would be as well to settle the question. He said that so far as France was concerned, the French Government considered unanimity essential.

M. ORLANDO agreed.

MR. LLOYD GEORGE said he was prepared to agree.

M. KLOTZ said that the question of sovereignty was raised by this. No Government could afford to cede its rights in this manner. The fate of the nation was in the hands of each Government which could not yield its responsibility to anyone. If the matter were handed over to a majority, the Government would be ceding its authority and its sovereignty.

(The principle of unanimity in the instructions by the Allied and Associated Governments to the Commission in regard to the manner in which any balance remaining unpaid by the enemy should be dealt with was accepted, subject to a reservation by Colonel House who said he had no authority from the President to settle the matter.)

§Mantoux's notes:

House. Without raising opposition, I am obliged to reserve the judgment of President Wilson.§

[After further discussion, and House's withdrawal, the council adopted Articles 4, 5, and 6.]

Article 7 was adopted subject to a reservation on the part of M. Clemenceau, who reserved the right to speak to President Wilson about the deletion of a passage of the original text concerning the restitution of cattle.

[A new Article 8 was adopted, and the question of means of payment was discussed.]

It was agreed:

(1) That the Raw Materials Committee of the Supreme Economic Council engaged on the examination of transitory matters should relinquish its enquiries into the question of payment in kind by means of coal, etc.

[It was further agreed that a small expert committee should consider the question of form of payment (e.g., payment in kind, coal, etc.), that another committee should consider the question of utilizing German labor for the restoration of the devastated areas, and that a third committee should consider the constitution of the commission to be set up under the articles of the peace treaty.]

The text of the Articles, as finally adopted, is as follows:

REPARATION.

1. The Allied and Associated Governments affirm and the enemy States accept the responsibility of the Enemy States for causing all the loss and damage to which the Allied and Associated Governments and their nationals have been subjected as a consequence of the war imposed upon them by the aggression of the enemy States.

2. The Allied and Associated Governments recognise that the financial resources of the enemy States are not adequate after taking into account permanent diminutions of such resources which will result from other treaty clauses to make complete reparation for all such loss and damage. The Allied and Associated Governments however, require, and the German Government undertakes that she will make compensation for all damage done to the civilian population of the Allied or Associated Powers and to their property by her aggression by land, by sea and from the air, as defined in the annexed Schedule.

3. The amount of such damage (as set forth under the specific categories attached hereto) for which compensation is to be made by the enemy States, shall be determined by an Inter-Allied Com-

mission, to be constituted in such form as the Allied and Associated Governments shall forthwith determine. This Commission shall examine into the claims and give to the enemy States a just opportunity to be heard. The findings of the Commission as to the amount of damage defined as above shall be concluded and notified to Germany on or before May 1st, 1921, as representing the extent of their obligations. The Commission shall concurrently draw up a schedule of payments prescribing the time and manner for securing and discharging the entire obligation within a period of 30 years from May 1, 1921. In the event, however, that within the period mentioned, Germany shall have failed to discharge her obligation, then any balance remaining unpaid may, within the discretion of the Commission, be postponed for settlement in subsequent years: or may be handled otherwise in such manner as the Allied and Associated Governments, acting through the Commission, shall determine.

4. The Inter-Allied Commission shall thereafter, from time to time, consider the resources and capacity of Germany and, after giving her representative a just opportunity to be heard, shall have discretion to extend the date, and to modify the form of payments, such as are to be provided for in Clause 3: but not to cancel any part, except with the specific authority of the several Governments represented upon the Commission.

5. In order to enable the Allied and Associated Powers to proceed at once to the restoration of their industrial and economic life, pending the full determination of their claim, Germany shall pay in such instalments and in such manner (whether in gold, commodities, ships, securities or otherwise) as the Inter-Allied Commission may fix, in 1919 and 1920, the equivalent of $5,000,000,000 gold towards the liquidation of the above claims, out of which the expenses of the army of occupation subsequent to the Armistice shall first be met, provided that such supplies of food and raw materials as may be judged by the Allied and Associated Governments to be essential to enable Germany to meet her obligations for reparation may, with the approval of the Allied and Associated Governments, be paid for out of the above sum.

6. The successive instalments paid over by the enemy States in satisfaction of the above claims shall be divided by the Allied and Associated Governments in proportions which have been determined upon by them in advance, on a basis of general equity, and of the rights of each.

7. The payments mentioned above do not include restitution in kind of cash taken away, seized or sequestrated, nor the res-

titution in kind of animals, objects of every nature and securities taken away, seized or sequestrated, in the cases in which it proves possible to identify them in enemy territory.

8. The German Government undertakes to make forthwith the restitution contemplated by Article 7 and to make the payments contemplated by Articles 3, 4 and 5.

The German Government recognises the Commission provided for by Article 3 as the same may be constituted by the Allied and Associated Governments, and agrees irrevocably to the possession and exercise by such Commission of the power and authority given it by Articles 3, 4 and 5. The German Government will supply to the Commission all the information which the Commission may require relative to the financial situation and operations of the German Government, its States, Municipalities and other governmental sub-divisions, and accords to the members of the Commission and its authorized agents the same rights and immunities as are enjoyed in Germany by duly accredited diplomatic agents of friendly Powers. The German Government further agrees to provide for the compensation and expenses of the Commission and of such staff as it may employ.

THE SUPREME COUNCIL next examined the text in regard to Categories of Damage, which had been prepared since the last meeting. (Appendix 2.)[4]

Article 1 was adopted subject to the addition in (g) of the following words: (French scale to be adopted.)

§Mantoux's notes:

Lloyd George. I read in Chapter II, paragraph e, that pensions will be calculated on the basis of the French scale. I would like to have this examined again. I do not propose that the nation which pays the most generous pensions would receive more. The question is to know if we should not take the English scale for pensions as the uniform basis. That seems to me worth considering.

You will certainly have in France, as we have in England, a movement to increase pensions. If you accept from now on compensation on the most modest basis, any increase will be at your own expense. That is the reason why I propose to take the British scale as the identical basis for all nations concerned.

McCormick. When this article was discussed in our commission, we thought we understood that the Prime Ministers agreed on the formula adopted. In fact, Italy and Serbia have pensions lower than the French pensions. That is why the French figures were adopted as the average.

---

[4] It is printed in PPC, V, 57-58.

Lloyd George. If President Wilson has the impression that the principle was agreed upon, I do not insist.

McCormick. I note that the French have already raised the scale of their pensions, and it is the new scale that will be taken as the basis.§

MR. LLOYD GEORGE suggested that Article 2b⁵ was too wide: a million Belgians might say that they had refused to accept wages from the Germans for 4 years and might claim compensation for the work they had abstained from. A very large sum might then be run up.

M. ORLANDO agreed.

M. KLOTZ gave the following illustration of the reason for inserting this clause:

Supposing works existed within an area occupied by the enemy and the enemy wished to use them for making shells. The proprietor might have refused. While the factory was out of work the owners might have done their best to give an allowance to the workers. Surely it was justifiable that recompense should be given to the employers who had paid the employment benefit in these conditions. Of course, however, it would be necessary to be very sure of the facts.

M. CLEMENCEAU agreed with Mr. Lloyd George that it opened the gates to abuses.

M. KLOTZ agreed to drop Article 2(b).

Article 2(a) was retained.

Clause 3 was adopted subject to some re-drafting required as a consequence of the omission of Article 4, see below.

MR. LLOYD GEORGE said that he had been given to understand the meaning of this Article [4],⁶ to be that reparation would not only have to be paid for the actual destruction of non-military property but also for the consequent loss of business. The instance of a farm had been given to him. If a farm was destroyed, not only would the farmer get the value of the destruction inflicted but also the loss incurred owing to the farm not being in operation. He himself was very familiar with farmers' accounts. When it was a question of preparing an Income Tax Return their profits were very low, (M. Clemenceau interjected that this is the case in France also) but for a claim in this connection their profits would be very high. Consider the case of shipping. The British Government pro-

---

⁵ It read as follows: "Damage caused to civilians by being compelled to abstain from all work as the only alternative to doing military work for the enemy or employing themselves on his armaments."

⁶ It read as follows: "Interference with non-military property directly caused by acts of war on land, on sea and from the air or illegal acts of the enemy or war measures in the nature of requisitions or sequestrations taken by the enemy."

posed to put in a claim for the many millions of tons lost, but they had not hitherto proposed to put in a claim for compensation for all the consequential loss owing to the stoppage of business due to the loss of ships, loss of wages to the crews, loss of wages at the docks, etc., etc. These could be claimed under this clause. Consider yet another instance. The enemy had bombarded the East Coast of England and destroyed many lodging houses. Under this could be claimed not only the damage to the lodging houses but equally the loss of business. Yet another case. The colonial trade has been greatly interfered with by the submarine warfare. Australia had suffered greatly. Under this clause Australia could claim compensation for all the grain eaten by rats. If this clause was to stand we should have to revise our claims and he himself had understood that both he and M. Clemenceau had agreed not to include demands for loss of trade and business, but only compensation for life and property.

M. CLEMENCEAU agreed.

M. LOUCHEUR suggested that at least we ought to permit interest to be paid between the date of the Armistice and the date of payment.

MR. LLOYD GEORGE said that if this was applied to ships also, it would be very favourable to us. Personally, however, he was opposed to these small claims that could be so easily forced up to a big bill.

M. LOUCHEUR pointed out that it would be 10 years before the mines in North France would be fully repaired. Surely interest ought to be provided for these.

MR. LLOYD GEORGE admitted that large claims like this were on a different footing.

It was agreed:

1. To omit Clause 4.
2. That M. Loucheur and Lord Sumner should prepare a new draft covering only large items such as the French mines referred to by M. Loucheur.

MR. MCCORMICK on behalf of the United States of America made a reservation that Belgium must be properly provided for.

The Supreme Council next considered the two alternative draft paragraphs in regard to the compensation for Belgium.[7]

---

[7] "*Draft No. 1*. Nothing contained in or omitted from, the foregoing schedule shall restrict the restoration of Belgium contemplated by point 7 of the address of the President of the United States to Congress, made January 7 [8], 1918, and concurred in by the Allied and Associated Governments."

"*Draft No. 2*. Nothing contained in, or omitted from, the foregoing schedule shall operate to limit the making of such reparation for that damage done to Belgium as will serve to restore confidence among the nations in the laws which they have themselves set and determined for the Government of their relations with one another, and without which the whole structure and validity of international law is for ever impaired."

MR. LLOYD GEORGE opposed any special articles in regard to Belgium. If these were adopted, there would be a suggestion that Belgium was getting something that was left out in the case of France.

M. CLEMENCEAU agreed that there ought to be equal treatment for Belgium and France.

MR. MCCORMICK said that on behalf of the United States of America, he reserved the right to see that Belgium was protected as promised in Point 7 of the address of the President of the United States at the Congress made on January 7th [8th], 1918, and concurred in by the Allied and Associated Governments.

MR. LLOYD GEORGE agreed that Belgium must be protected but objected to the suggestion in this clause that there was something special being provided for Belgium and not for France. The proper course was when all the clauses had been provided to let Belgium see them and state her case.

[After some discussion the council agreed to refer to a committee the question of reparation in regard to the redemption of depreciated German marks held by prisoners of war and by persons in Belgium and in the occupied portions of France. Lloyd George pointed out that the current holders of the marks in many cases were not the persons who had suffered the losses involved.]

The list of categories of damage as finally agreed to was as follows:

COMPENSATION may be claimed under Clause 2 under the following categories of DAMAGE.

I. (a) Damage to injured persons and to surviving independents [dependents] by personal injury to or death of civilians caused by acts of war (including bombardments or other attacks on land, on sea or from the air, and all the direct consequences thereof, and of all operations of war by the two groups of belligerents wherever arising).

(b) Damage caused to civilian victims of acts of cruelty, violence or maltreatment, (including injuries to life or health as a consequence of imprisonment, deportation, internment or evacuation, of exposure at sea or of being forced to labour by the enemy) committed or ordered by the enemy wherever arising and to the surviving independence [dependents] of such victims.

(c) Damage caused to civilian victims of all acts of the enemy in occupied, invaded or enemy territory injurious to health or capacity to work, or to honour, and to the surviving dependence [dependents] of such victims.

(d) Damage caused by any kind of maltreatment of prisoners of war.

(e) As damage caused to the peoples of the Allied and Associated Powers all pensions and compensations in the nature of pensions to naval and military victims of war, whether mutilated, wounded, sick or invalided, and to the dependence [dependents] of such victims, the French scale to be adopted.

(f) Cost of assistance by the State to prisoners of war and to their families and dependents.

(g) Allowance by the state to the families and dependents of mobilised persons or persons serving with the forces. (The French scale to be adopted.)

II. Damage caused to civilians by being forced by the enemy to labour without just remuneration.

III. Damage in respect of all property wherever situated belonging to any of the Allied or Associated States or to any of their peoples, with the exception of military works or materials, which has been carried off, seized, injured or destroyed by the acts of the enemy on land, on sea or from the air, or damage directly in consequence of hostilities or of any operation of war.[8]

IV. Damage in the form of levies, fines and other similar exactions imposed by the enemy upon the civilian population.

(The Meeting then adjourned.)

T MS (SDR, RG 256, 180.03401/105, DNA); Mantoux, I, 169, 170, 171, 174.

[8] T marginal note: "To be redrafted."

Tasker Howard Bliss to Eleanora Anderson Bliss

My dear Nellie: [Paris] April 7, 1919.

. . . In the afternoon[1] the American Commission had a two hours' conference with President Wilson at his house. We all agreed that there should be no more secret conferences of the "Big Four" but that the President should tell his colleagues that they must at once come to time [terms?], or to insist on having all points of difference openly discussed in the Plenary Conference. I think things will come to a crisis this week. We have said that often before, but now I do not see how it can be postponed. . . .

TCL (T. H. Bliss Papers, DLC).
[1] That is, on April 6, 1919.

To Edward Mandell House

My dear House,   [Paris, c. April 7, 1919]

You are doing such fine, patient work to help smoothe out difficulties, that it is very hard not to go the full length with you in
concessions, but I am sorry to say that I do not agree with Orlando
that the enclosed map furnishes a satisfactory basis for discussion.[1]
I cannot in conscience concur in conceding Fiume to Italy (though
I am still willing to consider the policy of making it in the full sense
a free city), and I think the memoranda[2] attached to the other maps[3]
absolutely unanswerable. I must stick by them. Perhaps you will
think it best to break this to our friend,—of whom I am really fond
and whom I long to help.   Affectionately,   W.W.

WWTLI (E. M. House Papers, CtY).
  [1] The Editors have been unable to find this map. Perhaps it was the map described
in the memorandum printed at April 14, 1919. About House's meeting with Orlando,
see the extract from the House Diary printed at April. 7, 1919.
  [2] W. E. Lunt *et al.* to WW, April 4, 1919, and its Enclosure, Vol. 56.
  [3] About these maps, see the Enclosure just cited.

A Memorandum by Gilbert Fairchild Close

MEMORANDUM for the President.   [Paris] April 7, 1919.

Mr. Baruch who has seen the attached report on the Saar Basin[1]
says that this seems to him unfair to Germany from the facts that
he has. He would like to get first of all the reasons why the coal
mines of the Saar Valley should be given to France, and then if the
reasons are sound we should consider the method of their transfer.   GFC

TI MS (WP, DLC).
  [1] See the memorandum by Charles H. Haskins and Others printed at April 6, 1919.

From the Diary of David Hunter Miller

Monday, April 7th [1919]

Colonel House sent for me to go over to see him about one o'clock.
He handed me some papers regarding the Saar which consisted of
a memorandum to the President regarding Baruch's view, signed
G.F.C.,[1] a letter from Mr. Close to Mr. Auchincloss and a memorandum enclosed in that letter, from Professor Haskins.[2] The memorandum had one or two changes in it in the President's hand-
writing. Colonel House told me that the President was willing to
take this and to agree to it if I possibly could. The President said
that there was a great deal in it that was legal and he wanted me

to look it over and see what I thought. I told him that Haskins had explained to me about it in general, although I had not seen the paper, and I approved of his scheme. Colonel House said I could get in touch with Haskins and accordingly he came to the office in the afternoon and I had a long talk with him. I went over the paper and made certain suggestions as to minor changes.[3] I also drafted certain additional articles.[4] (Among the papers are) the French text of the articles[5] which Mr. Haskins handed me and his memorandum as to whether the Saar Basin should go to France.[6] I was to see Colonel House about the matter in the evening but he got back so late that it was put over.

David Hunter Miller, *My Diary at the Conference of Paris,* I, 227-28.
    [1] That is, the preceding document.
    [2] That is, the memorandum by C. H. Haskins and Others printed at April 6, 1919.
    [3] See Enclosure I printed with D. H. Miller to EMH, April 8, 1919.
    [4] See Enclosure II printed with *ibid.*
    [5] Printed in Miller, *My Diary at the Conference of Paris,* VIII, 34-40.
    [6] An "unofficial memo.," entitled "The Saar Basin" and dated March 30, 1919. It is printed in *ibid.*, pp. 41-43. See also Harold I. Nelson, *Land and Power: British and Allied Policy on Germany's Frontiers, 1916-19* (London and Toronto, 1963), pp. 259-60.

A Memorandum by Josephus Daniels

Paris, 7 April, 1919.
Memorandum for the President from the Secretary of the Navy.

Admiral Benson feels strongly that we should go on building until our Navy is as strong as Great Britain's, which of course would mean that we would have to ask for a big appropriation for new ships in the next Congress. Lloyd George is very earnest and very strong in saying that he would not give a snap of his finger for the League of Nations if we keep on building. I explained to him that the programme that we were working on was enacted by Congress in 1916 and that much of the material was fabricated, the machinery under contract, and the armor ordered, and that Congressional direction to build these ships could not be changed except by Congressional action, and that even when they were built Great Britain would have 33 battle ships to our 23; 13 battle cruisers to our six; 79 light cruisers to our ten; 535 destroyers to our 370; and 219 submarines to our 98. He replied that that was true, but that he was concerned about nothing except capital ships, and that their 46 capital ships as compared with our 29 would look as if we had a large disparity in comparison with Great Britain, but in gun power and modern firing our later ships would be much superior and their older ships would be outclassed.

Mr. Long[1] put it plainly afterwards that he wished us to agree to stop the 1916 programme, which we are now building and which was authorized by Congress, which would of course leave us much inferior to Great Britain. It is upon that line that he wishes to talk with me, and I have wished to have the President's views before having a further conference.

It is my judgment that if any agreement is to be made at all, it ought not to be between Great Britain and America, but ought to be between all the Allied nations, and that it is very questionable whether a conference between Mr. Long and myself could reach any result that will be satisfactory to Mr. Lloyd George. From his very strong expressions the other morning, there is no doubt that he feels that when Great Britain sinks the ships that she will get and quits building battle cruisers, we should stop construction of capital ships. I do not think the American people would stand for this or that Congress would authorize it. It would raise another argument against the League of Nations that in America would be so strong that we could not defend it successfully.

T MS (WP, DLC).
¹ That is, Walter Hume Long, First Lord of the Admiralty.

From the Diary of Josephus Daniels

1919   Monday 7   April

Reached Paris 10 am. Long talk with Benson who feels B— [Britain] is trying to dictate naval matters in order to control commerce. Suggested I do not talk with them unless he or someone else present as I might be misunderstood or misquoted to my great injury at home. When Benson met me (1/2 hour late because train was ahead of time) he said Admiral Wemyss had been inquiring when I would arrive, as he wished to meet me at the train. Benson thought it cheeky. I did not wish to see him or Long until I could communicate with the President. He said "Please say you have seen the President and have found him deeply concerned about the whole method with which the whole peace program is being handled and that you have been instructed by the President to say that he cannot make any sort of agreement until he sees what the outcome is going to be." I made appmt to see Long. Talked about my visit to G.B. and he thought it best to go to Scapa Flow and Rosyth & Scotland first and then come back to London when members of Parliament had returned from Easter holiday. He thought we might make agreements on principle to stop building and get together on details when I reached England. I then gave him the views of the President, & of course the matter was not pressed further. He will see L.G. Later I talked to the President & told him of conversation with Long. L.G. & WW will now take it up. WW's position greatly relieved me.

Hw bound diary (J. Daniels Papers, DLC).

A Draft of a Letter to Fridtjof Nansen[1]

Dear Sir: Paris, April 7, 1919.

The misery and suffering in Russia described in your letter of April 3d[2] appeals to the sympathies of all peoples. It is shocking to humanity that millions of men, women and children lack the food and the necessities, which make life endurable.

The governments and peoples whom we represent, would be glad to cooperate, without thought of political, military or financial advantage, in any proposal which would relieve this situation in Russia. It seems to us that such a Commission as you propose would offer a practical means of achieving the beneficent results you have in view, and could not, either in its conception or its operation, be considered as having any other aim than the "humanitarian purpose of saving life."

There are great difficulties to be overcome, political difficulties, owing to the existing situation in Russia, and difficulties of supply and transport. But if the existing local[3] governments of Russia are as willing as the governments and peoples whom we represent to see succor and relief given to the stricken peoples of Russia, no political obstacle will remain. There will remain, however, the difficulties of supply and transport, which we have mentioned, and also the problem of distribution in Russia itself. The problem of suppy we can ourselves[4] hope to solve, in connection with the advice and cooperation of such a commission as you propose. The problem of transport of supplies to Russia we can hope to meet with the assistance of your own and other neutral governments. The problems of transport in Russia and of distribution can be solved only by the people of Russia themselves, with the assistance, advice and supervision of your Commission.

Subject to such supervision, the problem of distribution should be solely under the control of the people of Russia themselves. The people in each locality should be given, as under the regime of the Belgian Relief Commission, the fullest opportunity to advise your Commission upon the methods and the personnel by which their community is to be relieved. In no other circumstances could it be believed that the purpose of this relief was humanitarian, and not political, under no other conditions could it be certain that the hungry would be fed.

That such a course would involve cessation of all hostilities within the territory of ⟨the former Russian Empire⟩ *Russia* is obvious.[5] And the cessation of hostilities would, necessarily,[6] involve a complete suspension of the transfer of troops and military material of all sorts to and within ⟨these territories⟩ *Russian territory*. Indeed, relief to Russia which did not mean a return to a state of peace would be futile, and would be impossible to consider.

Under such conditions as we have outlined, we believe that your plan could be successfully carried into effect, and we should be prepared to give it our full support.   Woodrow Wilson

TLS (E. M. House Papers, CtY).
  [1] About the earlier struggle between Gordon Auchincloss and David Hunter Miller, on the one side, and William C. Bullitt, on the other side, to determine the text of this letter, see John M. Thompson, *Russia, Bolshevism, and the Versailles Peace* (Princeton, N. J., 1966), pp. 251-54. Bullitt prepared the original draft (T MS, SDR, RG 256, 861.5018/9, DNA). Bullitt's draft was then retyped, and it is this second version which we print. Significant changes in Bullitt's draft are indicated in footnotes. Wilson, with the approval of the other American commissioners, signed the revised letter on April 6 and promised to submit it to the other members of the Council of Four for their signatures. For the letter sent, see the Enclosure printed with F. Nansen to WW, April 17, 1919.
  [2] F. Nansen to WW, April 3, 1919, Vol. 56.
  [3] "de facto" in Bullitt's draft.
  [4] "safely" deleted here.
  [5] Words in angle brackets deleted by Lansing; words in italics added by him.
  [6] "of course" in Bullitt's draft.

Two Letters from Robert Lansing

Dear Mr. President: Paris, April 7, 1919.

In reply to the Mission's telegram of April 1st, four p.m.,[1] a copy of which is attached for reference, the Department of State sends the accompanying message 1431 of April 4th intended for yourself and signed by Secretary Baker.[2]

As will be noted, Secretary Baker objects to the establishment of a zone within which General Graves is to exercise definite police powers fearing it might lead to a large increase of Japanese forces and possibly to the assumption by Japan of civil control within the proposed zone. He proposes that the State Department take up with the Allied Nations represented in Siberia the declaration of a policy limiting the objectives of our military forces to the preservation of order about the railroad, its stations and trains.

You will recall that immediately after the agreement with Japan respecting the reorganization of the railways in Siberia,[3] General Graves was instructed to cooperate with the military forces of the Allied Governments in protecting the railway communications and that the additional instruction of April 1st was called out by the request of the Department for more definite instructions. It was, therefore, proposed by delimiting a zone to restrict the movements of his forces: it was not intended to enlarge the field of their operations. Mr. Phillips in a telegram to the Mission, #1432 of April 4th,[4] concurs in Secretary Baker's recommendations. This, therefore, leaves the situation just as it was prior to April 1st. I see no objection to the narrowing of the field of operations to the immediate vicinity of the railway, if that will suffice for the protection of the lines and the men operating them, and provided that the Allied Governments will agree so to restrict the movements of their troops. If you approve Secretary Baker's suggestion, I shall so inform the Department of State and request the Acting-Secretary of State to seek the concurrence of the other interested governments in the policy proposed.   Faithfully yours,   Robert Lansing

TLS (SDR, RG 256, 861.00/473, DNA).
   [1] RL to FLP, April 1, 1919, Vol. 56.
   [2] NDB to WW, April 4 [3], 1919, *ibid.*
   [3] See FLP to RL, Dec. 30, 1918, n. 4, Vol. 53.
   [4] W. Phillips to the American Commission, April 4, 1919, Vol. 56.

My dear Mr. President: Paris, April 7th, 1919.

   Mr. Wallace Young,[1] who has been assigned as Consul to Prague, is now in Paris awaiting instructions to proceed to his post. In the event that a Minister is soon to be appointed to the Czecho-Slovak Republic, it is believed that it would be better for our diplomatic and consular representatives to proceed to Prague together. If it does not seem practicable to appoint the Minister at an early date, then it might be desirable for Mr. Young to proceed at once to his new post so that we might have some representative there pending the opening of the Legation. The latter course, however, would not tend to better the present feeling that the interests of the United States are being prejudiced owing to the fact that Great Britain, France and Italy have diplomatic representatives at Prague while our Legation has not yet been established.

   I shall be very much obliged if you will indicate to me what you desire in the premises.   Faithfully yours,   Robert Lansing

TLS (R. Lansing Papers, DLC).
   [1] Wallace Jesse Young, at this time American Consul in Göteborg, Sweden.

Archibald Cary Coolidge to the American Commissioners

Sirs: Vienna, Austria, April 7, 1919.

I have the honor to report that I beg to call attention to certain aspects of the question of the future of the German-speaking region of the Tyrol south of the Brenner Pass now held by the Italians and claimed by them.

In no question of boundary at present under discussion have we more clearly the principles of history, nationality and self-determination on the one side and strategic and imperialistic considerations on the other. For this reason although the size of the territory itself and the number of people concerned are relatively small, the case might be regarded as a test one under the Fourteen Points.

It may be conceded that geographically German South Tyrol is a part of Italy, as is the Swiss canton of the Ticino, but, whereas the Ticino represents the result of a comparatively recent foreign conquest, is inhabited by an Italian-speaking population, and is separated by no good natural frontiers from the kingdom of Italy, German South Tyrol has a perfectly satisfactory southern frontier, and it is and has been inhabited for many centuries by a German-speaking population, which has come in by a process of peaceful colonization and by a gradual absorption of the earlier Ladin elements.[1] In no question now before the Conference does the linguistic frontier coincide more exactly and satisfactorily with an excellent geographical one, and its application means hardship to smaller minorities. The proper solution for the small Ladin districts is more open to doubt although the sympathies of the inhabitants are for the most part on the side of Austria.

The Italians have maintained that for the protection of Italy against future attack they need to hold the territory up to the Brenner Pass which forms a good first line of defense. This argument of an advanced first line of defense is a strategic one that can be pushed to great lengths. It is no truer of the Brenner Pass than it is of the Lower Rhine as between France and Germany, and it belongs to an order of ideas which we trust will soon begin to be obsolete. We may hope that after the constitution of the League of Nations purely strategic considerations may be accorded less weight than they have been in the past, particularly when they sacrifice the happiness of peoples. With the acquisition of the Italian-speaking region of the Trentino Italy will have a much better and more defensible frontier than she has had up till now, but even the old one she was able to hold against all the offensive efforts of the Austrians during the present war. It was not there that the Italian armies gave way.

Historically, the district of German South Tyrol has been inhab-

ited by people of German speech, race, sympathies and characteristics for many hundred years. During much the greater part of
that time they have been connected politically with Germany, and
the apparent barrier of the Alps has not interfered with Tyrolese
unity except during one of the ephemeral arrangements made by
the great Napoleon. The people of the whole Tyrol, both north and
south of the Alps, in order to maintain their cherished unity are
willing to make almost any sacrifice—to set themselves up as an
independent republic or do whatever else is demanded of them.

Economically too, it should be remembered that German South
Tyrol profits by its connection with the north. Its fruits have a great
advantage in their easy access to the Austrian and German markets,
where they are likely to have tariff protection. On the other hand,
once within the Italian customs line, they will have to face the
competition of similar products grown on more fertile soil and at
less cost.

A last point worth taking into consideration is the extremely
strong feeling on the part not only of German-Austrians but of all
German peoples for this territory, small in area, population, and
economic value but endeared to them by its beauty and its romance,
the one bit of Germany in a southern clime, a land of legend and
of history, the home of the Minnesingers in the Middle Ages, and
of Andreas Hofer, who led the heroic struggle for independence
against the French. Every year it is visited by hundreds of thousands, and its loss would produce far deeper resentment than would
the cutting off of an equal number of people from some other part
of Germany.

But the strongest argument of all is the one first mentioned, that
to give the German South Tyrol to Italy would be as frank a departure from the principle of national self-determination as it is
easy to conceive, and would be judged accordingly.

I have the honor to be, Sirs,

Your obedient servant,   Archibald Cary Coolidge[2]

TCL (WP, DLC).
   [1] The Ladine are people whose mother tongue is Ladin, a dialect belonging to the
Rhaetian group of Romance languages.
   [2] See also A. C. Coolidge to the A.C.N.P., April 28, 1919, TCL (WP, DLC), and its
enclosure, a printed petition of "German South Tyrol" to WW, "Dated, in German South
Tyrol, February 1919" and a mimeographed list, dated March 30, 1919, of the towns
endorsing the petition, both in WP, DLC.

From the Very Reverend Hardwicke Drummond Rawnsley

Dear Mr. President   Grasmere. April 7 [1919].

This is very generous of you,[1] & in the name of the fund I thank you sincerely. We have now reached a sum of £2100, & many appeals have gone to his American friends, which will I am sure receive cordial answers. We are all troubled to hear of your being in bed with a temperature & who can wonder if flesh & blood cannot stand the terrific strain that you are bearing for us all at this time. God bless & keep you,   Yours truly   H D Rawnsley

ALS (WP, DLC).
[1] See WW to H. D. Rawnsley, March 22, 1919; H. D. Rawnsley to WW, March 26, 1919; and WW to H. D. Rawnsley, April 2, 1919, all in Vol. 56.

From the Diary of Dr. Grayson

Tuesday, April 8, 1919.

I went into the President's bedroom this morning and prescribed a bath for him—after which he had a ten-o'clock breakfast. He was feeling better but was a little "wabbly" on his feet, markedly showing the effects of the infection from which he had been suffering. His temperature was sub-normal. I am taking every precaution to prevent a recurrence, paying special attention to avoiding drafts and having the room properly heated with wood fires. I am trying to keep the President in an even temperature. As an added precaution, I advised him not to attend any meetings outside of his residence for a few days.

The President had his lunch today in the dining-room for the first time since his illness.

John Edwin Nevin, of the International News Service, wrote me a confidential letter suggesting that in view of the mixed state of opinion in the United States, and of the fact that partisan newspapers were making capital out of the secrecy in connection with the Conference it would be wise if the President could enlighten the American people as to exactly what was being done. What Nevin wanted was that the President keep in mind that when the time came for him to make a public statement, should that time come soon, it would be unfair to him (the President) not to explain the real reasons why it had been necessary to hold star chamber sessions of the Peace Conference. The reasons were obvious but the President very frequently overlooks placing himself in the broadest possible light in his desire to be extremely just to men who are none too fair to him. I conferred with the President about the matter and he was much impressed with the force of Nevin's suggestions. He remarked to me: "Nevin is a man of fine judgment; he is an excellent newspaperman, and, above all, he is a very loyal and staunch American citizen." "And," he added: "he is a good friend of mine." The President gave Nevin's suggestions his closest attention and valued them.

Today I sent the following message to Secretary Tumulty at the White House in Washington:

"The President is sitting up today. Am taking every precaution with him. Have no fear of his taking the bold step if necessary at the psychological moment. Your aid and presence were never needed more."

The President was able to have the other members of the Big Four gather with him in his bedroom, and they held a conference that admittedly was extremely interesting. Incidentally, for the first time since the Peace Conference began, the seriousness of the existing situation seemed to have impressed itself upon the various members of the Peace Commissions who were stationed in this city.

Last night Lloyd-George had let the British correspondents understand that he was preparing a statement which he would make to them in lieu of an address to the members of the House of Commons who were importuning him to stand pat on England's enormous indemnity demands. He said he would make this statement at three o'clock, but when three o'clock came he was in conference with the President, and after the conference adjourned he announced that he would not "make it for the present."

Speaking on behalf of the French Government, M. Aubert[1] told the American newspaper correspondents that France had reduced her demands to a complete minimum. He said that he had authority to say that they had no territorial aspirations but were perfectly willing that the frontier of 1871 should be the frontier fixed by the present Peace Conference. This would give them what the President has all along insisted they should have—Alsace-Lorraine. Aubert said that he did not believe that France had ever seriously pressed any claims for additional territory, which caused distinct amusement among the American newspaper correspondents, inasmuch as it was only a week ago when Aubert declared that under no circumstances would France consent to any treaty which did not give her complete ownership of the Saar Basin, and also created a Rhinish Republic to be utilized as a buffer state.

After the conference adjourned in the afternoon it was admitted that very material progress had been made along certain lines. In fact were it not that the President has gone through on several occasions with a similar experience only to find that the next day Clemenceau and his associates had gone back where they started from overnight, the outlook would have been more or less promising.

We had another splendid example of the "thrift" of the French Government as at present constituted. They had sent us a bill some days ago for nearly $7,000 for transportation for the President and his party on the special train.[2] As a matter of fact, the American party on all of these trains has always been the minority party. Many of the cars on the train have been filled exclusively with French officers of high and low degree, and with French diplomats of various qualifications. To cap the climax, however, along came today a bill for 8,000 francs for food, which had been served on board this special train. Of course, the French attachés of the train had a very large share of the food that was consumed. The contrast in this and the manner in which the United States had handled the visits of Marshal Joffre, Viviani and the French High Commission[3] was very striking. They were met at New York by representatives of the United States Government, were taken wherever they wanted to go on special trains, fully guarded and protected, were housed and all of their wants taken care of by the United States Government, and no bill of any kind was ever presented to France. As a matter of fact, Joffre himself was taken all the way to San Francisco and returned, while Viviani and other members of the Commission were taken as far West as Springfield, Illinois. It was rather curious, as I figured this out, to remember that the only "hospitality" which was being extended to the United States in Paris was the housing of President Wilson in the temporary White House. When the President left to go back to Washington on his hurried trip, he issued strict instructions to Colonel House to see that a suitable residence was leased for him and to have it ready for his return, the house to be equipped with American servants which he would bring back from the White House in Washington—the house to be entirely American in all of its functions. The President found, however, on his return that Colonel House, whose specialty had been saying YES, not only had not insisted upon this course but had accepted the French Government's offer of the present quarters. The very fact that we found one man among the attendants who had first claimed not to understand English, and then developed an ability to converse entirely in that language, showed that the motive of the French Government was hardly one of hospitality but rather one of espionage. However, I may say that they were welcome to anything they could gather in the temporary White House.

I found the President very tired after the conference and took especial precautions to see that he did not suffer from the severe exertion in view of his weakened state. He said, however, that he felt very much better in mind, because he had been able personally to participate in the things for which he was responsible and had not been compelled longer to submit to trying to do business through an agent. I asked him to retire early, which he did. He went to bed about 9:30.

I had a good opportunity during this afternoon to get a line on the actual sentiment of the people of France. Jean Decrais, the son of the former French Ambassador to London,[4] a man of about fifty years of age, came to see me. He told me that he had been lying awake nights simply appalled over his realization that the French Government did not represent the French people, and that Clemenceau and his little coterie of politicians did not realize that the best friend France had was President Wilson. He asked me to tell the President that he, speaking for both the rich and the poor people of France, whom he knew intimately and well, realized that the President was the true friend of France, and that it was the President who realized more than anything else just what France should have in order to retain her position and maintain her friendship. Decrais spoke English perfectly and was very plainly a man who had thoroughly investigated French public opinion. Therefore, this statement which he especially gave me for the President meant a great deal more than had it come from some other source.

[1] That is, Louis Aubert, about whom see n. 1 to the extract from the Diary of Colonel House printed at Dec. 17, 1918, Vol. 53.

[2] See the extract from the Diary of Edith Benham printed at March 31, 1919; WW to RL, April 1, 1919 (second letter of that date); and RL to WW, April 2, 1919 (first letter of that date), all in Vol. 56.

[3] About the visit of the French mission to the United States in April and May 1917, see the numerous index references under "France and the United States" in Vol. 42.

[4] Louis-Jean Decrais, Counselor of the French Revenue Court; son of Pierre-Louis-Albert Decrais, former French Ambassador to various European countries, including Great Britain (1893-1894), member of the Chamber of Deputies (1897-1899) and the Senate (1903-1915), and Minister of Colonies (1899-1902).

Hankey's and Mantoux's Notes of a Meeting of the Council of Four[1]

I.C.-170.L.   Prime Minister's Residence, 23 Rue Nitot, Paris,
                                               April 8, 1919, 11 a.m.

1. Mr. Lloyd George read General Smuts' telegram, No. 3 received on April 7th.

[1] The complete text of Hankey's minutes is printed in *PPC*, V, 59-70.

SIR MAURICE HANKEY stated that a paraphrase of this telegram (Appendix 1) was being prepared and would be circulated in the afternoon.

MR. LLOYD GEORGE said that he hoped that General Smuts would by this time have received the telegram sent on the previous afternoon,[2] and would alter his plans so as to proceed to French and Roumanian Headquarters.

§Mantoux's notes:

Mr. Lloyd George reads a dispatch from General Smuts. The General was not able to induce the Hungarian government to accept a modified line of demarcation, which would have allowed its troops to be moved toward the east, while respecting the frontier foreseen by the Commission on Rumanian Affairs. It does not seem possible to satisfy the Hungarians without breaking our word to the Rumanians.§

M. ORLANDO read the telegram he had received from Switzerland. The Swiss Government had informed the Italian Government that a Soviet would be declared in Vienna on May 14, and suggested that the best way to avert trouble there was for the Allied and Associated Powers to occupy Vienna.

§Mantoux's notes:

Clemenceau (to Orlando). Your government proposes that we occupy Vienna. We received a formal letter on this subject from the Italian Ambassador.

Orlando. We received a telegram from our legation in Switzerland informing us that the proclamation of a republic of soviets in Vienna is probable for the 14th of this month, unless Vienna be occupied by the Allies.

Lloyd George. Whom do they propose to send to occupy Vienna? If we followed these suggestions, why should we not occupy all of Europe? Our representatives in Berlin speak the same language to us; there would be no reason to stop.§

2. MR. LLOYD GEORGE produced a list prepared by Sir Maurice Hankey under his instructions of the subjects awaiting consideration by the Supreme Council (Appendix 2). He suggested that it was desirable if possible to bring the Germans soon to Versailles. For this it had not seemed to him necessary that the whole of the boundaries of the whole of the new states, for example, Poland and Czecho-Slovakia, should be fixed, so long as the boundaries of the enemy states were clearly fixed.

§Mantoux's notes:

Lloyd George. I wish to present to you a list of questions which absolutely must be settled before inviting the Germans to come to

[2] See the minutes of the Council of Four printed at April 7, 1919, 3:30 p.m.

negotiate with us. I wonder if we are not trying to settle too many questions before meeting the Germans. After all, we have time to determine the frontiers between the Czechs and the Poles or between the Rumanians and the Serbs. As for the Germans, we only have to inform them about what we are taking from them. We will dispose of them in due course as we judge best. If we do not proceed in this way, we shall be here forever.§

COLONEL HOUSE suggested that the enemy states should be invited now to come to Versailles some few weeks hence. He did not wish to deprive the Peace Conference of sufficient time to complete this work, but he thought that ample notice should be given to the enemy, and that this might be given now.

M. CLEMENCEAU said it would not alter the situation to get the Germans here now. There was revolution all through Central Europe. We were sending food to Germany, but so far it had made no difference. It must not be hoped that because you induced the Germans here now, you could get people who would still represent Germany later on.

MR. LLOYD GEORGE agreed. He read a telegram he had received from the Secretary of State for War to the effect that all his military advisers reported that the situation in Germany was fast approaching a catastrophe for lack of food and raw material. To-day came the news that Hungary [Bavaria] had declared a Soviet.[3] It would be necessary when the Germans came to Versailles to ask whom they represented; for example, did they represent Bavaria?

§Mantoux's notes:

Lloyd George. I have received a telegram from the War Office informing me that the situation in Germany is worsening and that a catastrophe is feared. We have an interesting report about this subject from General Haking.[4] General Wilson, who collects this information, thinks that everything is falling apart there. Today, we learn of the proclamation of a republic of soviets in Bavaria. The danger is that when we ask the German delegates: "Whom do you represent?", they will not know what to answer. Time is working against us. That is why we must move ahead without too much attention to detail.

Clemenceau. I agree with you; but I do not think that advancing the date when the Germans will be summoned here will change the situation much. They told us that the solution of the question of victualing would greatly improve Germany's condition; food is

---

[3] See n. 1 to the extract from the Diary of Ray Stannard Baker printed at April 5, 1919.

[4] Lt. Gen. Sir Richard Cyril Byrne Haking, chief British representative on the Allied Armistice Commission.

beginning to arrive, and things are going from bad to worse. All that we can do is to move ahead as quickly as possible.§

COLONEL HOUSE asked what ought to be done if the Germans refused to sign.

MR. LLOYD GEORGE said that this was a matter in its military aspects for Marshal Foch, who should be asked to consider it with General Wilson, General Diaz, and General Bliss, and in its naval aspects for Admiral Wemyss, who should consider it with the Allied Admirals in Paris.

(This proposal was agreed to and Sir Maurice Hankey was instructed to draft letters to Marshal Foch and Admiral Wemyss respectively.)

The letters attached (Appendix 3) were approved.[5] The letter to Admiral Wemyss was signed by M. Clemenceau. M. Mantoux undertook to communicate the letter to Marshal Foch to the Ministry of War in order that a French translation might be prepared and signed by M. Clemenceau and transmitted to Marshal Foch. (A copy of the letter actually addressed to Marshal Foch is attached herewith.)

§Mantoux's notes:

House. If people who represent no one come before us to negotiate, what shall we do?

Lloyd George. We must think about that. General Wilson correctly tells me that it is up to Marshal Foch to consider how we must answer that question. It is also necessary to ask that of our admirals. Assuredly, we must begin to think about it immediately.

Must we proceed to an occupation? Will it be necessary to renew the blockade? In any case, we must have a plan at the ready so that we have only to take a decision. I suggest that we ask our generals and admirals to prepare these plans, based on different hypotheses: (1) if we have no one before us with whom to sign; (2) if the Germans refuse to sign.

House. What will you do?

Lloyd George. We might be led to occupy Berlin. But I do not know whether that will serve any purpose.

Clemenceau. I think it will; the Germans are a servile race.

---

[5] For the text of these letters, see *PPC*, V, 65-66. The letters called for reports, as soon as possible, as to what action Foch and Wemyss would advise, from a military or a naval point of view, in each of the following contingencies:

"(1) In the event of a refusal by the enemy powers (Germany, Austria, Bulgaria and Turkey) to sign the Treaty of Peace.

"(2) In the event of such a state of chaos in any of the enemy's countries that there is no Government in existence to sign the Treaty of Peace.

"(3) In the event of the German Government being able to sign the Treaty of Peace on behalf of the whole of Germany except Bavaria owing to the fact that its jurisdiction is not recognised in and does not in fact extend to that country."

Orlando. Personally I do not favor occupations, whatever the opinion of certain representatives of Italy. But if it comes to that, I will remind you of what Erzberger told Marshal Foch,[6] drawing attention to the weakness of our right wing: it is useless to be very strong on the side facing Germany, if Bolshevism turns our Austrian flank. If we want to do something in that direction, it must be done with a certain symmetry and not to leave one of our flanks exposed.

Lloyd George. We agree to consider what we must do not only if Germany falls apart, but also if the situation worsens in Austria and in neighboring countries.

Clemenceau. I am not much worried about the symmetry from the strategic point of view; but I am very much concerned about the necessity of maintaining our military and political situation. It is not necessary to ask Marshal Foch: "Do you favor the occupation of Berlin or Vienna?" but: "From the military point of view, what measures would you advise if we have no one before us to sign the peace treaty, or if the enemy refuses to sign it, or if Germany can sign but not Bavaria, supposing that she does not recognize the authority of the central German government?"

House. Can we not now set a date for meeting the Germans?

Clemenceau. We would risk having them wait, if we are not prepared.

House. I think that even the summons could help the present government.

Lloyd George. Let us wait until Thursday to take a decision.

Clemenceau. I fear very strongly that we have enough to do for this entire week. Are there not still points to be decided concerning the military conditions to impose on Germany?

Lloyd George. Nothing very important. There are only a few questions of first order: that of reparations first, that of responsibilities, to which the English public attaches a very great importance. For it would not for an instant permit that the crimes of submarines, the bad treatment of prisoners, the violence committed against civilians, the abominable treatment of women and girls in invaded countries, the use of asphyxiating gas and other methods of warfare contrary to international law, go unpunished.

The questions that the Economic Commission is studying are of primary importance; since the members of that commission are far from an agreement, things must be taken in hand and settled promptly. §

3. It was agreed that the Economic Commission should be asked to send in its report at once.

---

[6] See n. 6 to the minutes of the Council of Four printed at April 7, 1919, 3:30 p.m.

4. MR. LLOYD GEORGE said that the report prepared by M. Tardieu, Dr. Haskins, and Mr. Headlam-Morley on the Saar Valley was to the effect that no really workable scheme could be drawn up on the basis that they had been given.[7]

He thought therefore that it would be necessary to adopt some other scheme. He then read extracts from three alternative schemes which had been submitted to him at an earlier stage by Mr. Headlam-Morley.[8] The scheme which attracted him most was scheme C. which would create a new state in the Saar Valley, somewhat larger than had hitherto been proposed, in customs union with France and for which France would have a mandate from the League of Nations. He handed copies of these schemes to Mr. Clemenceau (who undertook to consult M. Tardieu about it) and Col. House. He promised to send a copy to M. Orlando. (Appendix IV.)

(The Meeting then adjourned).

§Mantoux's notes:

Lloyd George. On the question of the Saar, the report that I have received from one of my advisers concludes that the plan submitted to us is not practicable; that was my conviction, but I did not wish to prevent examination of this plan. We must return to the plan of which I have already spoken. You cannot grant ownership of the mines to France, with very extensive powers over the avenues of communication, etc., if, on the other hand, sovereignty remains with Germany. This would be a perpetual source of friction, with very serious risks of war.

I myself favor a system which would establish a sort of Luxembourg in that region. The advantage of that combination is that you do not make the inhabitants French against their will, which we would not accept. You leave them their language, their legislation, the right to govern themselves. I would apply this regime to a region more extended than the Saar Valley strictly speaking. We must include the entire industrial region whose economic life depends upon the mines and even go as far as the Moselle; for the question of navigable waterways and canals to be built between the coal basin and the Moselle is a vital question.

I would grant this country independence, under the authority of the League of Nations. A customs union would attach it to France. In fact, there are no natural economic ties between this region and Germany; all its relations are with Alsace and Lorraine. If one says to the inhabitants: "You will not be French, and you will govern

---

[7] Again, see the memorandum by C. H. Haskins and others printed at April 6, 1919.
[8] There are carbon copies of these memoranda, which Wilson entitled "British Substitutes," in WP, DLC.

yourselves freely," no injustice is done them; and we must not forget that this country was mostly French up until the beginning of the nineteenth century, that it was taken from France by force and despite the opposition of English statesmen at the time.

Mr. Haskins was no less impressed than our own representatives by the advantages of this system. Our expert, Mr. Headlam-Morley, is very hostile to annexation to France but does not think that we can make this region viable, if we do not constitute it as a political entity. Another advantage would be to have there a sort of buffer state larger than Luxembourg, with a population of at least 600,000 inhabitants.

It is essential to make it part of the French customs system. Without Alsace and Briey, this country cannot live. I am persuaded that, if a plebiscite should take place in a few years from now, that population would not ask to return to Germany.

House. That statement seems to me very reasonable, and I wish to inform President Wilson about it immediately.

Clemenceau. I must remind you that President Wilson admitted in the plan which he communicated to us[9] that there was reason for studying an administration and political solution permitting the functioning of the economic regime envisaged by him.

Lloyd George. There is a strong analogy between this case and that of Danzig, and I think that the same system, or a similar one, will succeed in both cases. The life of Danzig depends entirely upon its commercial relations with Poland, just as the life of the Saar depends upon its economic relations with France, including Alsace and Lorraine. I would like to be able to extend this solution to Fiume as well.

Orlando. That—it is impossible!

Lloyd George. Three different plans have been submitted to me. The first assumes that sovereignty remains with Germany, economic administration being in the hands of France. I reject that solution, for the reason I stated.

The second solution is the one which I have just explained; local sovereignty under the authority of the League of Nations, with a local parliament, and a mandate given to France, which would appoint a governor, while respecting local institutions. The country would be attached to France by a customs union. It would be completely disarmed and its inhabitants could not perform any military service. Ownership of the coal mines would belong to France, which would deduct from the yield of these mines what would be necessary for the administrative costs of the country. §

[9] See the Enclosure printed with C. H. Haskins to WW, March 29, 1919, and the minutes of the Council of Four, March 31, 1919, 11 a.m., both printed in Vol. 56.

APPENDIX I.

Paraphrase of telegram from General Smuts to Mr. Balfour. Despatched: Buda-Pest, 6.45 p.m. April 6th, 1919. Received: 10 a.m. April 7th, 1919.

Reference my telegram of April 4th.[10]

I spent April 5th also in consultation with Hungarian Government; two important members of Government—the Prime Minister, Garbai, and the Commissary for Education, Kunfy[11]—assisted at the Conferences. As regards the limit to which they should withdraw Hungarian troops I had one time practically succeeded in securing acceptance of a new armistice line, running further east than Colonel Vix's line, but nevertheless well to the west of the territory which the Roumanian Committee of the Conference assigned to Roumania in their Report. Draft of agreement was drawn up and ready to be signed, but Hungarian Ministers then consulted their other colleagues again and refused to sign, saying that if they did so civil war would break out in neutral zone and Government would fall at once. They produced an alternative proposal, to the effect that if the Roumanians withdrew their forces behind the line of the Maros river (i.e. the line laid down on November 13 by General Franchet d'Esperey) and the Great Powers occupied the whole of the neutral zone, Hungarian Government would accept the new armistice lines mentioned above. I rejected this proposal as trouble with Roumania would immediately ensue. Attitude of Hungarian Government is as follows: there is no state of war between the Great Powers and Hungary, who wishes to remain at peace with them, to secure removal of blockade and obtain facilities for importation of commodities most urgently needed such as fats and coal; I had undertaken by the lapsed draft of agreement to recommend this course to the Great Powers; Hungary still adheres to the terms fixed on November 3, 1918, by the Armistice and to those of the Military Convention concluded on November 13; she has hitherto complied with all demands for further withdrawal to the west, but cannot carry out withdrawal either to the line fixed by Colonel Vix, or even to that which I had proposed as being the only means of satisfying the fair territorial claims of Roumania— the reason being that their Szekler troops on the frontier were opposed to it; if they did accept there would certainly be a nationalist reaction and the Government would fall. Hungarian Government however still declare that as (passage undecypherable) stable Gov-

[10] Printed as Appendix II to the minutes of the Council of Four, April 7, 1919, 3:30 p.m.
[11] That is, Sándor Garbai and Zsigmond Kunfi.

ernment, territorial questions are of less interest to them than economic questions; they are ready to lay their case, previous to final decision being taken, before any Conference of States bordering on Hungary to be convened and presided over by the Great Powers, and to discuss matters in an accommodating spirit. My conviction is that there is no hostility towards the Great Powers, in the Hungarian attitude. The Government however are weak, they have internal divisions which are likely to lead to their fall at an early date while, except on conditions which would be of an insulting character as regards Roumania they are too frightened to accept line. If we can handle Hungary wisely, I do not think that she is by any means lost to the Allies and I adhere to the view, after consideration of the whole case, that the wisest course for us to take is not to provoke a conflict over the armistice terms which may be unnecessary, but, after hearing the Hungarians' statement in Paris or some other place, to settle the final political frontiers. Economic questions are of such importance to the future of Hungary that, in my opinion, the Great Powers should, as an earnest of their benevolent intentions, at once allow the trainload of fats which, though bought and paid for with the consent of the Allies, are now held up by the Allied authorities at Agram[12], to proceed to Buda-Pest, without however raising the blockade for the present. I am starting for Prague today in order to exchange ideas there with Professor Masaryk and shall leave for Paris as soon as possible from Vienna.

APPENDIX 2.
LIST OF SUBJECTS FOR CONSIDERATION BY THE COUNCIL OF FOUR.

Subject.	Present Position.
(a) GENERAL QUESTIONS.	
Reparations:	To approval final revise of clause agreed to yesterday. Mr. Lamont and Mr. Keynes are working on this.
"Categories."	The British draft is being examined by experts.
Means of Payment.	Mr. Loucheur is preparing a draft to be examined by experts.
The Composition of and Instructions to the Commission.	

[12] That is, Zagreb.

The Names of the Powers to be allowed to claim on Germany.	
The Division of sums obtained for reparation.	
Breaches of Laws of War.	Final report agreed, but not yet issued pending the receipt of reservations by the United States and Japanese Delegations.
Ports, Railways and Waterways.	Report complete.
Economic Commission.	Report is in draft but has not yet been passed by the Commission.
Financial Commission.	Articles for inclusion in the Peace Treaty with Germany are ready.
Aeronautical Commission.	Report should be ready to-morrow, Monday, April 7th.

(b) QUESTIONS AFFECTING PEACE WITH GERMANY.

The question of a temporary army of occupation West of the Rhine.	
Western Frontier of Germany.	The Saar Valley scheme, based on Mr. Wilson's proposal is ready.
Dantzig.	The scheme now being worked out is ready.
Luxemburg (future status).	It is understood that no action has been initiated in regard to this.
Method of conducting the Negotiations with the Enemy at Versailles.	An early decision on this is desirable. The Secretary-General has put forward a short memorandum on the subject. (Attached)[13]

[13] It is missing.

Heligoland.

Reserved from the Naval Terms. No reason is seen why this should not be taken up at once unless it is preferred to remit it to the Foreign Ministers.

Northern Frontiers of Germany. (Schleswig)

Reports of Commission and of coordinating Commission have been considered by Committee of Foreign Ministers to March 28th, and approved in principle ad referendum to the Council of Four and subject to reservations by Mr. Balfour. This is ready for consideration.

Boundaries of Belgium.

Reports of Belgium Commission and of Coordinating Commission complete and ready for consideration.

(c) QUESTIONS AFFECTING PEACE WITH AUSTRIA.

The Italian claims as regards the Tyrol, the Adriatic, including Dalmatia and Fiume Montenegro.

No action has been initiated on this.

Czecho-Slovak Frontiers.

Only the German portion of these frontiers have been settled. The remainder of the report has been before the Council of Foreign Ministers but further consideration is postponed pending a joint meeting between experts from the Czecho-Slovak and Polish Boundary Commissions in regard to Teschen. This

	might come before the Foreign Ministers before being considered by the Council of Four.
Roumanian Boundaries.	Final report of the Commission is not yet ready though nearly finished.
Yugo-Slav Boundaries.	Final report of the Commission is not yet ready though nearly finished.
Albania.	Report of the Greek Commission on Southern Albania is available but not unanimous. The report on the remainder of the Albanian frontiers is not yet ready.

(d) QUESTIONS AFFECTING
      PEACE WITH BULGARIA.

Boundary between Bulgaria and Roumania.	Awaits the report of the Roumanian Commission which is nearly ready.
Boundaries between Bulgaria and Serbia.	Awaits the report of the same Commission as above which also deals with Yugo-Slav boundaries outside the Italian claims. A report is nearly ready.
Boundaries between Bulgaria and Greece.	Report of the Greek Commission is ready
Boundaries between Bulgaria and Turkey.	Report of the Greek Commission is ready.

(e) QUESTIONS AFFECTING
      PEACE *with* TURKEY

Greek claims in Turkey.	Report of the Greek Commission on this subject is ready.
	Note: The first step towards the settlement of the Turkish Question is the

(f) MISCELLANEOUS.

nomination of the members of the Syrian Commission.

No action has yet been taken with regard to the allocation of mandates and the drafting of the B and C Mandates for the German Colonies.

Financial and economic questions in regard to Peace with the above countries are under consideration by the Financial and Economic Commissions.

There are a few questions which might usefully be referred to the Foreign Ministers and on this I attach a draft resolution.

Japanese questions as regards Kiauchou and Shantung.

APPENDIX IV.

Attached are copies of three schemes for the establishment of a new régime in the Saar Valley:

(a) Leaves the sovereignty of Germany but transfers the administration to France.

(b) which is almost identical, transfers the sovereignty to the League of Nations, but gives the administration to France.

(c) Establishes a separate State which will be under the protectorate of France, which controls the foreign relations and has complete administrative control of the administration, together with the ownership and right of exploitation of the mines.

J.W.H.-M. 31.3.19.

A. & B.

SAAR BASIN.

1. Germany renounces in favour of the Allied and Associated Powers, as trustees of the League of Nations, all rights of administration and exploitation over the territory as described in Annex I, and herein referred to as the "Saar Basin":

1. (Alternative) Germany renounces in favour of the Allied and Associated Powers, as trustees of the League of Nations, all her rights and title over the territory as described in Annex I, and herein referred to as the "Saar Basin":

2. The Allied and Associated Powers confer upon the French Government a mandate to administer the Saar Basin on behalf of the League of Nations.

3. The French Government accepts the mandate to administer the Saar Basin and makes itself responsible for peace, order and good government therein. It will carry out the mandate in accordance with the provisions of this treaty.

4. The French Government will appoint a Governor of the Saar Basin who will be responsible to it for the government of the territory and for the due execution of the provisions of this treaty.

In organising the administration of the territory the Governor will continue, so far as may be possible, the existing system to which the inhabitants of the country are accustomed.

5. There shall be a legislative assembly for the Saar Basin elected by the (male) inhabitants. In all debates in the legislative assembly the members shall be entitled to use their own language.

6. A complete customs union shall be established between France and the Saar Basin.

7. The Governor shall organize a gendarmerie for the policing of the Saar Basin, but subject thereto the inhabitants of the Basin will not be permitted to bear arms or receive any military training or to be incorporated in any military organisation either on a voluntary or compulsory basis, and no fortifications, depots, establishments, railway construction or works of any kind adapted to military purposes will be permitted to exist within the territory.

(Nor will the territory be allowed to contribute directly or indirectly in men, money or in material of any description towards the armies of Germany.)

8. The control of the educational system in the Saar Basin will be vested in the Governor in accordance with such laws as may be enacted by the Legislative Assembly.

Facilities shall be afforded for the education of children in the language of their parents.

9. The freedom and outward exercise of all forms of worship shall be assured to all persons in the Saar Basin, and no hindrance shall be offered either to the hierarchical organisation of the different communions, or to their relations with their spiritual chiefs.

10. The property in the Saar Basin formerly belonging to the Imperial German Government, or the Government of any German State will pass to the Administration of the Saar Basin.

11. An exclusive right to the exploitation of the mines in the Saar Basin which were formerly the property of the Imperial German Government or of any German State shall pass to the Government of the French Republic, which will make such arrangements as it may deem necessary for exercising the rights so conferred.

In the exploitation of the mines no distinction will be made in the pay or conditions of employment of the workmen, whatever their nationality.

A fixed sum per ton of coal raised will be paid to the Administration by the French Government as a contribution towards the expenses of the administration.

12. The French Government shall be entitled to the exclusive right of operating the railways and waterways of the Saar Basin. For this purpose it shall be entitled to purchase or lease them from the Administration at such price or rent as may be agreed, or failing agreement, may be decided by arbitration under the supervision of the League of Nations.

The rights conferred by this article shall extend also to the development and improvement of the existing railways and waterways and to the purchase of such land as may be necessary for the purpose.

13. No obstacle shall at any time be placed in the way of any inhabitant of the Saar Basin who wishes to withdraw from the territory.

14. (German nationals inhabiting the Saar Basin will *ipso facto* lose their German nationality and when outside the Saar Basin will be entitled to French diplomatic protection.)

15. All questions other than those dealt with above arising out of the arrangements now made relating to the Saar Basin, including the amount of the payment per ton of coal raised referred to in article 11, will be made the subject of subsequent agreements between the parties concerned.

C.
SAAR BASIN.

1. The territory comprised within the following limits is hereby constituted an independent state under the name of the Saar Republic (geographical boundaries).

Germany renounces all rights and title over the said territory.

2. Pending the convocation of a constituent assembly charged with the duty of preparing and enacting an organic law for the Saar Republic the League of Nations will appoint a Governor of the Saar Basin who will be responsible to it for the government of the territory

until the coming into force of the organic law and the establishment of the administration of the Republic.

In organising the administration of the territory the Governor will continue so far as may be possible the existing system to which the inhabitants of the country are accustomed.

The Governor will also be responsible for the due execution of the provisions of the Treaty.

3. The organic law shall provide for a legislative assembly elected by the (male) inhabitants of the Republic for the establishment of a judicial system, and for the organisation of the administration.

4. A complete customs union shall be established between France and the Saar Republic, and shall not be terminated without the consent of the French Government.

5. There shall be a gendarmerie for the policing of the territory of the Saar Republic, but subject thereto the inhabitants of the Republic will not be permitted to bear arms or receive any military training or to be incorporated in any military organisation either on a voluntary or compulsory basis. No fortifications, depots, establishments, railway construction or works of any kind adapted to military purposes will be permitted to exist.

6. The freedom and outward exercise of all forms of worship shall be assured to all persons belonging to the Saar Republic, as well as to foreigners in its territory and no hindrance shall be offered either to the hierarchical organisation of the different communions or to their relations with their spiritual chiefs.

7. The property in the territory of the Saar Republic which belonged to the Imperial German Government, or the Government of any German State, will pass to the Government of the Saar Republic.

8. The French Government shall enjoy an exclusive right to the exploitation of the mines within the territory of the Saar Republic which were formerly the property of the Imperial German Government or of any German State. The French Government will make such arrangements as it may deem necessary for exercising the rights so conferred.

In the exploitation of the mines no distinction will be made in the pay or conditions of employment of the workmen whatever their nationality.

A fixed sum per ton of coal raised will be paid to the Republic by the French Government as a contribution towards the expenses of the administration.

9. The French Government shall be entitled to the exclusive right of operating the railways and waterways in the Saar Republic. For this purpose it shall be entitled to purchase or lease them from the Administration of the Republic at such price or rent as may be

agreed, or failing agreement may be decided by arbitration under the supervision of the League of Nations.

The rights conferred by this article shall extend also to the development and improvement of the existing railways and waterways and to the purchase of such land as may be necessary for the purpose.

10. German nationals habitually resident in the territories described in Article I will ipso facto become citizens of the Saar Republic and will lose their German nationality.

Within a period of (   ) from the coming into effect of the present Treaty, German nationals not less than 18 years old and habitually resident in the Saar Republic will be entitled to opt for German nationality. Option by a husband will cover his wife, and option by parents will cover that of their children less than 18 years old.

All persons who have exercised the above right to opt must within the succeeding twelve months transfer their place of residence to Germany.

They will be entitled to retain their landed property in the Saar Republic. They may carry with them their moveable property of every description. No export or import duties or charges may be imposed upon them in connection with the removal of such property.

11. The control of the foreign relations of the Saar Republic will be entrusted to the French Government and all citizens of the Republic will be entitled when outside the limits of the Republic to French diplomatic protection.

12. All questions other than those dealt with above arising out of the arrangements now made relating to the Saar Basin, including the amount of payment per ton of coal raised referred to in Article 8, will be made the subject of subsequent agreements between the parties concerned.

T MS (SDR, RG 256, 180.03401/106, DNA); Mantoux, I, 179-83.

David Hunter Miller to Edward Mandell House, with Enclosures

Paris 8 April, 1919.

MEMORANDUM FOR COLONEL HOUSE

After consultation with Doctor Haskins,[1] he and I agree upon certain changes in the text of the articles on the Saar Basin which you have.[2] A list of these changes is annexed.

With these changes, which are minor, I agree with the proposal subject to additions, ONE, the creation of a permanent arbitration commission in order to solve quickly the difficulties which will arise in the area and TWO, the fixing of a period at which the situation of a division of rights between Germany and France would end according to the wishes of the population.

Articles relating to these two points and giving broad powers to the League of Nations have been drafted and are transmitted herewith.

I am of the opinion that such provisions regarding the Saar Basin as are indicated in the papers submitted are in accordance with the principles of the President and in particular in accordance with those stated in the fourteen points and that these provisions would be so generally regarded.   David Hunter Miller

TS MS (WP, DLC).
  [1] See the extract from the Diary of D. H. Miller printed at April 7, 1919.
  [2] That is, the memorandum by C. H. Haskins and Others printed at April 6, 1919.

E N C L O S U R E   I

CORRECTIONS IN ARTICLES ON THE SAAR BASIN

Article I—for "Existing French legislation" read: "German law in force 11 November 1918."

Article III—After "customers" insert "whose rights therein the French Government will respect."

Article IV—Amend first two lines so as to read "no tariff shall be established on the German railways and canals which directly or indirectly discriminates to the prejudice, etc."

ARTICLE VIII—For "derogation" read "forfeiture."

Article IX—Last paragraph to read as follows: "None the less, those employed in the mines, their accessories and assiduaries, shall have all the rights and privileges of French law as this may affect workmen in the same category in France."

Article X—After "technical schools" insert "for its employees and their children."

Article XI—Insert at the beginning of the second sentence "if it fails in that duty, reparation, etc."

Article XVI—Insert at the close of the first paragraph "during the same period it may import freely from Germany articles destined for local consumption and use."

E N C L O S U R E   I I

I.

Nothing in these articles shall be deemed to impair the political or civil rights of German subjects, and subject to the provisions of these articles the sovereignty of Germany over the said territory is recognized as continuing.

II.

A permanent Commission of Arbitration shall be appointed to decide all questions and differences which may arise in regard to the construction, interpretation or operation of these articles. In all cases the Commission shall have power to decide by majority vote and its decisions shall be accepted as final and conclusive by both the French and German Governments who agree in all good faith to carry them in all respects into effect. The Commission shall have power to interpret these articles and shall also have power to make any necessary supplementary regulations in accordance therewith.

The Commission shall consist of five members, of whome one shall be appointed by the Government of France, one by the Government of Germany and three by the League of Nations and all of the last three named shall be citizens or subjects of different countries and of countries other than France and Germany. The members of the Commission shall be subject at any time to removal by those appointing them who shall fill any vacancies.

A vacancy or failure to appoint shall not affect competence of the Commission.

The compensation and expenses of the Commission shall be paid equally by the French and German Governments.

France and Germany agree that any dispute whatsoever, not only arising under these articles but any dispute that decision of which may be affected by the terms of these articles, shall be referred to the said Arbitration Commission for final hearing and determination and they agree to carry into effect in full good faith any award or decision which the said Commission or a majority thereof shall make.

III.

At the expiration of fifteen years a plebiscite shall be held on the said territory under the supervision of the League of Nations. The vote may be taken by communes or districts and the qualifications of the voters, method and time of the vote shall be determined by the *Council of the*[1] League of Nations which shall make all regulations which are deemed necessary, in order to ensure a free and secret vote. In the voting there shall be no discrimination on the ground of sex. The powers of the League of Nations, in respect of the said plebiscite, and matters connected therewith or arising therefrom, shall include not only power to make all necessary decisions and regulations, but shall in all respects be plenary.

IV.

The League of Nations, in accordance with the wishes of the inhabitants, as expressed by the plebiscite, shall decide as to the sovereignty of the territory in question, and Germany undertakes to cede to France the whole or any part of the territory in question in accordance with such decision of the League of Nations.

V.

On such of the said territory as shall remain German under the result of the decision of the League of Nations, the property rights of the Government of France under these articles shall be taken over as a whole by Germany at a price payable in gold which shall be determined by three appraisers or a majority of them, one of whom shall be appointed by Germany, one by France and one who shall be neither a German nor a French citizen by the League of Nations.

VI.

The price so fixed shall be payable within [blank] after the determination thereof and unless the said price so fixed shall be then paid by Germany to the Government of France, the territory which would otherwise remain German shall thereafter be occupied and administered by France as an integral portion of French territory.

VII.

As soon after the plebiscite as possible, the League of Nations shall make regulations for bringing to an end all provisions for a special regime in the territory in question, having due regard to personal and property rights.

Accepted at capitalized value as part of indemnity.[2]

T MSS (WP, DLC).
[1] Words in italics added by Wilson.
[2] This sentence added by Wilson.

Mantoux's Notes of a Meeting of the Council of Four

April 8, 1919, 3 p.m.

Clemenceau. Must we not hear M. Paderewski on the question of the Polish frontiers?

Wilson. If we transform these conversations into interviews as we have done several times, I fear that we will fall back into all the disadvantages of the procedures which we wished to change by meeting as the four.

Clemenceau. It seems to me difficult not to hear M. Paderewski. I have seen him, and I think that he will agree to the regime we have in mind for Danzig; but he is making strong objections to the assignment of Marienwerder to Germany because of the railway line, which would be cut by the German frontier.

Wilson. I think it is better that each of us hear M. Paderewski. As for the question of Marienwerder, I would remark that the use of the railway must be in any case guaranteed to Poland, just as we will guarantee it to Germany to cross the territory of Danzig from the East to the West.

Wilson. Shall we discuss the report [about responsibilities][1] article by article?

Lloyd George. It is better to proceed more broadly and to distinguish clearly between two categories of punishable acts. First, criminal acts properly speaking; second, general orders contrary to international law, for example, the order given to submarines instituted veritable piracy. Two hundred years ago, our corsairs did not sink ships without warning and did not abandon crews to their fate.

Wilson. I think you agree with me that the author of a purely negative action, for example the officer who, by refusing to obey an order, would have been able to prevent a criminal act, and who did not do so, committed a crime from a moral point of view, but not a crime from a legal point of view.

Lloyd George. We could begin with submarines. With regard to all established laws, their activity is nothing other than piracy. According to the laws of war, we would have had the right to shoot all enemy sailors who took part in the submarine war. But we considered that they had obeyed orders, and we preferred to make them prisoners, and to await the power to punish those who had given the criminal orders. The man, or the two or three men, who ordered the submarine campaign are obviously guilty, which does not make certain crimes disappear, like the one of the commanders of submarines who fired upon shipwrecked crews.

Wilson. There is general responsibility, that of Admiral Tirpitz[2] if you will, and responsibilities in the execution, such as that of the officers who gave the inhuman orders you refer to.

Lloyd George. In short, all those who initiated criminal action are responsible.

[1] About which, see n. 4 to the minutes of the Council of Four printed at April 2, 1919, 4 p.m., Vol. 56.
[2] That is, Grand Admiral Alfred Peter Friedrich von Tirpitz, father of the Imperial German navy.

It should be the same concerning the bad treatment inflicted upon prisoners. If an order came from Berlin, the one who gave it must be punished. But given the unequal treatment of prisoners in the different camps, I am persuaded that most often it is the head of the region or of the camp who was responsible.

Wilson. Mr. Lansing does not disagree with his colleagues concerning criminal acts properly speaking;[3] what he finds difficult is to know how to judge them and according to what law. Shall we institute a tribunal which will make its own law, by choosing among national laws? Mr. Lansing says that we have established courts martial in each country, which judge crimes of this type; we might conceive of the convocation of these courts martial—an international court martial—on which French, English, Belgians, Italians, etc. would sit, this tribunal applying laws in force either in the place where the crime took place, or in the victims' country of origin. But I fear that it would be difficult to catch the true culprits, because nothing is easier than to destroy the trail of orders given. I fear that we lack evidence.

Lloyd George. The one who committed the crime is responsible if he cannot show the order of execution.

A more difficult case is that of the violation of treaties. Here it is a matter of a crime against international law. In actuality, the treaty of 1839 created a league of four nations which guaranteed the neutrality of Belgium. The man who broke the pact and thereby caused the unspeakable sufferings of the entire world is the worst of criminals. We can treat him in two ways: either order his internment as a political measure, as the Allies did in 1815 to Napoleon, or put him on trial. The method does not much matter to me, provided that the man be punished and placed where he cannot harm anyone; at the same time we must prevent intrigues which might enable him to regain a dangerous power and set an example. Send him to the Falkland Islands or Devil's Island,[4] do whatever you wish, that does not much matter to me.

Clemenceau. A solemn judgment is what will make the greatest impression.

Wilson. What I wish is to dishonor the Kaiser and to avoid creating any kind of sympathy in his favor. If you refuse, according to the conclusions of the commission, to try him as the author of the war, which is to say as the author of the decision which led immediately to the invasion of Belgium, you incriminate him only for the means that he used to carry out his policy of violence. Unfortunately there are many precedents in past wars.

[3] In the "Memorandum of Reservations" printed at April 4, 1919, Vol. 56.
[4] The notorious French penal colony off the coast of French Guiana.

Lloyd George. Not so; there is nothing which resembles the invasion of Belgium in the War of 1870, nor in the wars which we have witnessed between Japan and Russia, between the United States and Spain. Those were open conflicts which were resolved by the appeal to arms, but without violation of an international treaty by those who themselves had guaranteed it.

Clemenceau. The German Emperor must be tried. The violation of law in the case of Belgium was so flagrant that the conscience of the peoples would not be satisfied if that act was treated in any other way than as a crime against the public law.

Wilson. It is indeed a crime, but one for which no sanction has been provided, because there is no legal precedent. Today we are founding the regime of the League of Nations from which will emerge new rules and new formulas of international law. But today we are obliged to create the principle and the penalty.

Clemenceau. The violation of a treaty calls for a sanction against the nation which is judged guilty of it. But if one man is responsible for what that nation did, will it satisfy us to know that three or four million Germans were killed and to allow the guilty one to go free?

Lloyd George. Suppose that the Kaiser alone, in peacetime, had crossed the frontier of Belgium with gun in hand and that he had fired on the inhabitants: the first Belgian policeman arriving had the right to arrest him and to have him hanged; and because, instead of doing it himself, he sent a million men into Belgium, he would go unscathed?

Clemenceau. That is what our peoples would never understand.

Wilson. Perhaps it would not be understood in the United States either; but I can only do what I believe is just, regardless of whether public sentiment is for or against the judgment of my conscience.

Lloyd George. War between nations is justifiable according to precedents. But aggression without provocation, without any grievance against the nation attacked, because it was advantageous to cross its territory and despite a solemn commitment treated like a scrap of paper, is indisputably a crime.

Wilson. What I seek is the severest lesson. I say: this is an unspeakable crime; but we did not wish to lower ourselves to the level of the criminal by abandoning principles of law, and we have treated him so as to spare him nothing of the universal contempt which should overwhelm him. We might have the right to take political precautions against a political danger; but we must not exalt the culprit by summoning him before the highest tribunal we can conceive. The worst punishment will be that of public opinion.

Clemenceau. Don't count on it.

Lloyd George. I also have my doubts on this subject. No sovereign was more despicable than James II, whom we chased out in order to replace him by a Dutchman. But James II in exile became the symbol of legitimacy, and he had partisans who later sought to create disorder in England.

William II was the greatest commercial traveler of Germany and of the world. We remember his speeches on the merchant marine and all that he did for the economic development of his country. The industrialists and businessmen in Germany will remember him with regret; they will think: "In his time, Germany was great and wealthy," and who knows what feelings and what actions might follow? What we do must be a lesson for kings and for all those who have responsibility for government.

Wilson. What would you propose to do?

Lloyd George. I would bring him to trial solely for violation of the treaty of 1839. The tribunal would hear witnesses who would explain how the treaty was violated, who would recall the atrocities committed in Dinant, in Louvain, and I would then say to the Court: "Judge!"

Wilson. How would you conceive of the composition of this tribunal?

Lloyd George. Members must be taken from the highest jurisdictions of our different countries, from the French, Belgian, and Italian courts of cassation, from the Supreme Court of Appeal of Great Britain, from the American Supreme Court. But, in my opinion, Belgium must be the public prosecutor. As for us, we only came to Belgium as defenders of law, and I can guarantee you that, if we take judges from our courts, they will act with perfect impartiality. They are men of high conscience, without any responsibility toward Parliament or public opinion.

Wilson. This tribunal would be too large if each great power had three representatives.

Clemenceau. We must limit ourselves to the great powers, which would each have one representative. Belgium could play the role of public prosecutor.

Wilson. In this case, I would add Serbia to it. Another question is whether the verdict must be by unanimous vote.

Clemenceau. In tribunals a majority is sufficient.

Lloyd George. In our country, the jury must decide unanimously.

Clemenceau. In our country, the jury renders its verdict by majority.

Orlando. In Italy, the same.

Wilson. In all international transactions, it is the rule to require unanimity.

Lloyd George. Yes, for deciding on questions of interest. But the problem that we are examining is completely different. Think about the effect that would be produced by the acquittal of the Emperor of Germany by one voice against four, and I would not completely trust our Japanese friends. If we gave to a single vote—that of Japan—the right of pronouncing the acquittal of the Kaiser, it would have a very bad effect in Europe.

Wilson. It seems to me that we have sorted out this question in its large outline. I would like to hear M. Orlando's opinion.

Orlando. I appointed two delegates to the commission: one a professor of law in the University of Rome, the other a counselor to our court of cassation,[5] both jurists of great ability. I left them entirely free. They accepted the conclusions of the majority; hence I go along with them. But if I must express my personal opinion, I think that we have no right to punish. I repeat that I leave the matter to the considered opinion of my jurists, and that is why I did not think I should take part in your discussion until now. But, in my opinion, crime is essentially a violation of the internal law of each national entity, a violation of a subject's obligation toward his sovereign. To create a different precedent is a grave thing.

One can say that practical necessity forces us to create law. Undoubtedly! But we should fear the consequences of a violation of established principles. We could find ourselves faced with difficulties which we will not know how to resolve because we are no longer sure of our principle. The Italian government supports the commission's conclusions. But since you ask my personal opinion, I give it to you frankly.

Wilson. I asked M. Orlando to answer us as a jurist. We have distinguished between two clearly different cases. The first is the violation of recognized laws of war, with penalties provided when those guilty of such acts are captured during hostilities. For crimes of this type, I suggested the formation of a military tribunal to apply the established rules. Here we can base ourselves upon known principle and procedure. The second question is that of the responsibility of heads of state, and the Kaiser in particular; here, we are entering into completely unexplored territory.

But what does M. Orlando think about the first point?

Orlando. I heard Mr. Lloyd George's observation when he said, speaking of the crews of submarines: "We were within the law to hang those men as pirates." According to the law of war, that would have been justified. But can we apply in peacetime a law which assumes war and a state of present hostilities? Moreover, we will have the greatest difficulty in determining responsibility. A general

[5] Vittorio Scialoja and Mariano D'Amelio.

who takes prisoners can discover their orders on the battlefield, if they are carrying any. But we are no longer at war; will we be able to trace these orders to their source?

What we have the right to do is to require that the Germans themselves judge those who are rendered guilty of certain crimes. But I cannot begin to conceive of an international court established in peacetime to judge by applying a wartime principle.

As for the heads of state, it seems to me that there would be less hypocrisy in imposing upon them a punishment by the peace treaty, on whatever grounds you wish; but I cannot begin to understand how we can summon them before a tribunal. Until now heads of state have been considered in all they do as representatives of collectivities. It is the collectivity which is in fact responsible for their errors; it is the people who pay for them, and it must be said that, in the case which concerns us, that of Germany, the people and the sovereign are surely one. But we would be establishing a completely new principle if we wished to punish as an individual a man who was acting as the instrument of the collectivity.

Clemenceau. We have examples: Louis XVI in France, Charles I in England.

Orlando. In both cases, the question was an internal one for the state. In the international domain, the law which you are trying to establish cannot be based upon any precedent.

Clemenceau. Was there a precedent on the day when liberty was given to men for the first time? Each one must assume his own responsibility, and I assume mine.

I do not understand M. Orlando's argument. He asks: are we going to apply in peacetime the law of war? For me, one law dominates all others: that of responsibility. Civilization is the organization of human responsibilities. M. Orlando says: "Yes, within each nation." I say: "In the international domain." I say this along with President Wilson who, by establishing the foundations of the League of Nations, has had the honor of transferring into international law the essential principles of national law.

What we want to do today is essential, if we want to see international law established. None of us doubts that William II bears responsibility for the war. I agree with M. Orlando on the solidarity of the German people with its sovereign. However, there is one man who gave the order, while the others followed it. It is said: "It is better to exile him and to expose him to the scorn of the world, without convicting him." It is a sanction which can be defended; it is not the one I prefer. Today we have a perfect occasion to carry into international law the principle of responsibility which is at the basis of national law.

There is no precedent? There is never a precedent. What is a precedent? I will tell you. A man comes; he acts, for good or evil. Out of the good he does, we create a precedent. Out of the evil he does, criminals, individuals or heads of state, create the precedent for their crimes. We have no precedent? But that is our best argument. Was there in recent generations a precedent for the atrocities committed by the Germans during the present war, for the systematic destruction of wealth in order to end competition, for the torture of prisoners, for submarine piracy, for the abominable treatment of women in occupied countries? To those precedents, we will oppose a precedent of justice.

Our judges, who will meet in the tribunal which we propose to establish, will be accustomed to applying different laws. We will ask them to unite their consciences in a concept of equity. We will assemble the greatest judges in England, France, America, and Italy. We will tell them: "Seek among yourselves the principles upon which you must depend in order to judge the greatest crime of history."

I will resign myself to a solution which is not mine, if necessary. But I beg the heads of state to reflect that, if they follow my advice, they will create to their own glory an unprecedented thing—I admit it—in establishing international justice, which until now has existed only in books, and which we will at last make a reality.

Wilson. A practical question arises. We do not have the legal means to compel Holland to deliver the Kaiser to us.

Lloyd George. No, but we can tell Holland that if she refuses, she will not be admitted to the League of Nations.

Wilson. Referring to crimes committed by individuals, M. Orlando said: "Beware of applying in peacetime a principle of wartime against the violation of the laws of war." In his capacity as a jurist, what does he think it possible to impose upon the Germans in the peace treaty? Can we project, so to speak, the procedure of wartime in the period which follows the war?

Clemenceau. It would be too easy for criminals if peace annulled all responsibilities. Believe me: among peoples who have suffered for these five years, nothing would sow so many real seeds of hatred than an amnesty granted to all the criminals.

Lloyd George. We have the right to say that, for us, war will not be ended so long as the enemy has not delivered to us those who are rendered guilty of certain crimes. Along with the question of reparations, this question is the one of most concern to English opinion, and we could not sign a peace treaty which left it unresolved.

Wilson. Ideas are beginning to become clearer about this. Nevertheless, you will permit me, because of the special competence of Mr. Lansing in the field of international law, not to take a final decision without speaking with him.

Lloyd George. We have called together, in England, six or seven of our greatest authorities on matters of international law, including Sir Frederick Pollock.[6] They concluded unanimously in favor of charging the Kaiser, as well as all those who committed crimes against international law. It is on the conclusions of these jurists that the British government bases its opinion.

Orlando. I must add that, after having read the commission's report, I discussed the conclusions with the Italian delegates whom I just mentioned. We had a serious, even stormy discussion. But they maintained their point of view, and I did not want to impose mine upon them.

In my opinion, the only principle which justifies our action is the one of M. Clemenceau. I accept M. Clemenceau's views, because they raise us above legal technicalities; it is history that is taking place here, it is no longer law. If we consult the code, we shall have great difficulty in finding there what we seek. If we speak only about international morality, it is different.

I still insist that Italy has as much to say about this subject of crimes committed as the other Allied nations. The number of Italian ships sunk by submarines on the open seas constitutes a higher proportion of our commercial fleet than do the losses suffered by the English merchant marine. One hundred thousand Italians died in the enemy's prisoner of war camps, victims of the bad treatment they suffered.

Question of the Saar

Wilson. Since we seem to be agreeing about this question of responsibilities, I would like to speak to you about another question which we have to resolve; that of the Saar Basin.

I have received a new report from my experts. It seems to them, and to me, very difficult to establish a semi-independent state in that region. It would be a mistake to create a new political entity there unless absolutely necessary.

I have received M. Tardieu's plan[7] concerning the economic aspect of the question. It seems very practical to me; but certain elements are missing, as indicated in the document which I now submit to you.[8]

[6] One of the foremost British legal experts; former Corpus Professor of Jurisprudence at Oxford University, bencher at Lincoln's Inn, editor of the *Law Quarterly Review*, at this time Judge of the Admiralty Court of Cinque Ports.

[7] Again, see the memorandum by C. H. Haskins and others printed at April 6, 1919, and n. 1 thereto.

[8] That is, Enclosure II printed with the preceding document.

I would propose not to end German sovereignty over the territory of the Saar, but to establish there—in order to settle all the litigious questions which could arise from the economic point of view on account of the special situation granted to France—a permanent arbitration commission charged with interpreting the treaty and making the regulations necessary for its proper execution. That commission would be composed of five members, a Frenchman, a German, and three members appointed by the League of Nations. The expenses of the commission would be shared between France and Germany. Upon the expiration of a period of fifteen years, the population would be consulted about its future political status by means of a plebiscite, this plebiscite taking place by district and by commune, according to a method of voting determined by the League of Nations. It is this consultation which would decide finally the territorial sovereignty over the whole and over all the parts composing that region. If certain districts should return definitively to Germany, that power could repurchase ownership of the mines through payment in gold.

Clemenceau. The main thing is to make the exploitation possible. I do not think that this system would give us the necessary security.

Wilson. Its great advantage is to eliminate the political difficulty raised by an immediate transfer of sovereignty.

Lloyd George. My advisers are clearly of opinion that the functioning of the economic regime proposed by M. Tardieu is incompatible with German sovereignty.

Wilson. According to M. Tardieu, France would have the police in the region.

Lloyd George. It is almost annexation to France. But Germany would retain title to sovereignty and could intervene, no longer to do there anything positive or useful, but in order to disorganize and disturb everything.

Wilson. I continue to repeat that I am opposed to the arbitrary creation of an independent state in the Saar Valley. This case cannot be compared with that of Luxembourg, which is a small historical entity. Rather, I would compare it to the Pittsburgh region, if this same problem could arise there. There you have a large industrial district, with a floating population, Italian workers for example, who are only transient. No common political tradition, nothing upon which an independent society could be established.

The difficulties that seem to be feared seem to me to be largely imaginary. In certain industrial districts of the United States, large private companies have their own police, which operate in the factory and in the coal basin, without any conflict with local or federal authorities. The arbitration commission which I propose to establish will prevent or settle disputes on questions of ownership or of exploitation; and in the end, the plebiscite will decide the fate of the country.

Clemenceau. Would a customs union with France be established?

Wilson. All industrial operations would be carried out under the French customs systems.

Clemenceau. We shall study that; but I fear that such a system could only lead to endless disputes.

Wilson. I ask you now not to let world peace be hung up on this question of the Saar.

Clemenceau. No, but world peace requires that we first establish justice among ourselves.

Wilson. In my opinion, we have spent too much time discussing questions which concern exclusively the four powers represented here.

Lloyd George. They are, after all, the ones which together carried the burden of the war.

Mantoux, I, 184-94.

A Memorandum

Paris, 8 April, 1919.

Memorandum on the Amendments proposed by France[1] to the Agreement suggested by President Wilson regarding the Rhine Frontier.[2]

(1) I think it would be a great mistake to go further than the military terms already provisionally agreed upon in the matter of obliging Germany to withdraw all fortifications on the east bank of the Rhine. It is my clear judgment that we should adhere to the fifty kilometers stipulated in the military terms.

(2) There is a serious objection to stipulating that there shall be maintained in the region in question only a maximum force of local gendarmerie. It is this: in order to enforce such a provision, inspection would be necessary from time to time; and inspection would breed friction and would promote not safety but antagonism.

(3) I am sorry to say I cannot at all agree to include in the third paragraph the military, naval and air clauses of the Treaty of Peace with regard to the added paragraph concerning the right of the signatory powers to notify the Executive Council of the League of any violations of these regulations which might have been observed. It is clear that that right already exists on the part of members of the League if any action is taken anywhere which threatens to

disturb the peace of the world, and that it would be unwise to connect it with this special agreement and treaty.

(4) I have no objection to the introduction in the fourth paragraph of the words "by the contracting powers."

I am sorry to be obliged to say that Marshal Foch's arguments recently addressed to us respecting the necessity for taking special precautions with regard to the Rhine have been by no means convincing to me.[3]

I beg very respectfully to urge upon the French Government this reflection: The proposals that I made jointly with Mr. Lloyd George with regard to assuring the safety of France on her eastern frontier were made after mature reflection, after full consideration of all other plans suggested, and necessarily represent the maximum of what I myself deem necessary or possible on the part of the United States.[4]

T MS (WP, DLC).
  [1] Tardieu's memorandum is printed as Enclosure I with WW to EMH, April 12, 1919.
  [2] Printed at March 28, 1919, Vol. 56.
  [3] See the memorandum by Marshal Foch printed at March 31, 1919, *ibid.*
  [4] This version of the memorandum was not submitted to the French delegation. Its substitute is printed as Enclosure II with WW to EMH, April 12, 1919.

From Robert Lansing, with Enclosure

My dear Mr. President: Paris, April 8, 1919.

I have given very careful consideration to the proposal to bring the ex-Kaiser to some sort of trial for violation of the neutrality of Belgium, and I have the following observations:

First: That the offense is one which cannot be described as a violation of criminal law and, therefore, the offender is not subject to condemnation by a judicial tribunal.

Second: That the offense is, however, so utterly violative of international morality and the sanctity of treaties that it may be a wise policy to demand that the culpability of the ex-Kaiser, the one most responsible for this heinous act of the German armies, should be determined by an extraordinary tribunal with authority to decide an appropriate punishment as an example for the future and as a menace to those who would by committing a similar act plunge the world into war.

Third: that the offense should be recognized as a political one and not one to which legal criminality attaches; that the extraordinary tribunal is of political origin though adopting a procedure similar to judicial tribunals; and that the punishment, penalty or sanction is determined upon as a political measure, dictated by the highest motives of international policy in order to deter those who in future would invade the sanctity of treaties for personal ends. Napoleon was exiled by the political power as a matter of high international policy. The difference in this case would be that a form of trial intervenes to determine the extent of culpability in order that the extraordinary tribunal, the agent of the political power, should not impose a penalty without full and accurate knowledge.

The foregoing points I believe to be sound, and offer a way to meet the views of your colleagues, but I think that in the event that an extraordinary tribunal is decided upon it should be made clear beyond question that the constitution, authority and decision are political and not legal, and that high international policy requires that an offense like the invasion of Belgian neutrality cannot be passed over without registering in the most solemn and effective way the condemnation of the nations.

Personally I hope that the Council upon further reflection will determine that action of this sort is inadvisable and will resort to the means of a public condemnation without a political trial.

If, however, you advise me that the final determination is otherwise, and give me roughly its terms I will be very glad to prepare definitive articles for the treaty, but I do hope that you can impress the provisions with a political and not a legal character, since that will avoid criticisms which I think we would find very difficult to meet.

I am also enclosing for your consideration a translation of the Japanese memorandum. As I said, I do not believe that Japan would be willing to participate in the proceeding proposed even if it is given a political foundation.

Faithfully yours,   Robert Lansing.

TLS (WP, DLC).

E N C L O S U R E[1]

MEMORANDUM PRESENTED BY THE JAPANESE DELEGATION TO THE COMMISSION ON THE RESPONSIBILITY OF THE AUTHORS OF THE WAR AND ON ENFORCEMENT ON PENALTIES.

The Delegates of Japan to the Commission on Responsibilities for the War being convinced that many crimes have been committed by the enemy in the course of the present war in violation of the fundamental principles of international law and recognizing that the responsibility for these crimes falls chiefly on individuals of high rank belonging to enemy states, consider that in order to restore for the future the authority of these principles which have been thus disregarded, it is incumbent upon them to find practical means to chastise the persons who are responsible for the violations in question.

The question might be raised as to whether it is admitted as a principle of international law that a High Tribunal established by belligerents may, after the war has terminated, judge every individual belonging to the enemy who is presumed guilty of a crime against the laws or customs of war.[2] Likewise, it might be asked if international law provides what penal law should be applied to those who are found guilty.

At any rate it seems to us advisable to consider the consequences of the precedent which would be established in the history of international law by the prosecution before a tribunal established by one group of belligerents of the heads of States belonging to the enemy for infractions of the laws and customs of war. Our scruples would be still greater if the question should arise of bringing before a tribunal, established along the lines indicated above, enemies of high rank solely because they may have abstained from preventing, putting an end to or repressing acts in violation of the laws or customs of war as is provided in Section C, Paragraph B, Chapter IV.

It will be observed that, in order to impress upon public opinion the fairness of the judgment of the appropriate tribunal, it would be preferable to adhere to the strict interpretation of the principles of penal responsibility and consequently to refrain from making cases of abstention the basis of this responsibility.

Under these conditions the Japanese Delegates adhered to the proposal presented by the Greek Delegate to eliminate from Section C, Paragraph B, Chapter IV, the words "including the heads of States," as well as the provision concerning cases of abstention. Furthermore, they experience a certain hesitation in accepting the amendment which admits criminal responsibility in the case where the accused with knowledge thereof and with power to intervene, abstained from preventing or taking measures to prevent, putting an end to, or repressing violations of the laws or customs of war.

The Japaneses Delegates declare that with the exception of the reserves mentioned above, they are disposed to examine with the greatest alacrity any suggestion tending to bring about unanimity in the Commission.

T MS (WP, DLC).
    [1] The following was a memorandum of reservations by the Japanese delegation to the report of the Commission on the Responsibility of the Authors of the War and on Enforcement of Penalties. A slightly differently translated version is included as Annex III in the commission's *Report Presented to the Preliminary Peace Conference* (about which, see n. 4 to the minutes of the Council of Four printed at April 2, 1919, 4 p.m., Vol. 56).

[2] That is, the commission's recommendation of a trial by a high tribunal of "all authorities, civil or military, belonging to enemy countries, however high their position may have been, without distinction of rank, including the heads of States, who ordered, or with knowledge thereof and with power to intervene, abstained from preventing or taking measures to prevent, putting an end to or repressing, violations of the laws or customs of war."

From Robert Lansing

Dear Mr. President: [Paris] April 8, 1919.

Adverting to my letter of the 7th instant to you, relating to Secretary Baker's telegram of April 4th, I am glad to call attention to the enclosed cable message from Ambassador Morris in which he asks authority to make to the Minister of Foreign Affairs certain representations concerning the policy to be pursued in regard to the Siberian Railways.

Inasmuch as Secretary Baker is disposed to limit the work of our troops to the protection of the railway and its stations and since General Tanaka[1] now is also of opinion that military activities should hereafter be confined simply to guarding the railway, Mr. Morris' suggestion does not appear to be altogether appropriate. The defense of the population in a "protected area" as he proposes and "in the cities and towns where the Allied troops are quartered" is similar to the policy proposed last week of the exercise of police powers in a zone along the railway.

Secretary Baker's objections to that policy would apply in a measure to Mr. Morris' proposal also. General Tanaka's willingness to limit military activities to the guarding of the railway seems to make Secretary Baker's suggestion entirely practicable and I feel that we ought to lose no time in an effort to have the Japanese Foreign Office adopt General Tanaka's advice.

                        Very sincerely yours,   Robert Lansing

Dear Mr. Sec'y

Morris's telegram was *not* enclosed,[2] but I hope that you will immediately take the steps necessary to urge upon the Japanese Foreign Office Baker's and Tanaka's advice.   W.W.

TLS (SDR, RG 256, 861.00/474, DNA).
  [1] Lt. Gen. Giichi Tanaka, Japanese Minister of War.
  [2] See RL to WW, April 12, 1919 (second letter of that date).

From Tasker Howard Bliss

My dear Mr. President: Paris, April 8th, 1919.

I learned by telephone from General Pershing's Headquarters this afternoon, of the receipt there of the request contained in the attached document from Marshal Foch's Headuarters.[1] At General Pershing's Headquarters they knew nothing of the matter nor of the authority under which the request was made. I myself knew nothing of it and on visiting Marshal Foch's Headquarters late in the afternoon of to-day I received the document attached.

The Marshal informed me that it was desired to place one American, one British, and one French officer on each train conveying the Polish divisions through Germany to Poland, for the reason set forth in the first paragraph of the attached document. It calls for a detail of eighty-three officers and a certain number of orderlies and clerks to be in Paris on the four different dates mentioned, in order to receive their instructions from the Marshal and then proceed to the points at which the Polish divisions will entrain for Poland.

As I have said, I knew nothing whatever of the matter until to-day. The Marshal assures me that it is the result of a formal agreement arrived at by the heads of the Allied and Associated Governments.

I recommend that you authorize me to inform General Pershing that you approve the request of Marshal Foch, bearing in mind that the first detachment of American officers must report here in Paris on the eleventh instant.

The last sentence of the attached document says that the duration of the mission of these American officers "*is for two months at least.*" This contemplates an unknown future use of this American personnel. The document of Marshal Foch states that their sole duty is to prevent any untoward incident occurring between the Polish troops and the German population on their journey through Germany. I can see no reason for the necessity of their continuance on this duty after the Polish troops arrive at their destination in Poland.

I therefore recommend that you instruct me to say to General Pershing that on the termination of the journey to Poland these American officers will return to their proper stations in France.

I think that it is of the utmost necessity that an immediate determination be arrived at as to the purpose for which the American troops were placed under the orders of Marshal Foch at the time that you consented to have him made the Allied Commander-in-Chief on the Western Front. At the time that you did this, that purpose was to secure unity of command of the Allied troops operating on the Western Front in the war against Germany. I think, therefore, that you should have a distinct understanding with your colleagues on the following line:

That the American troops now in France and on the Rhine are

under the command of Marshal Foch for the purpose of any possible further resumption of hostilities by Germany against the Allied and Associated Powers or by the latter against Germany, which resumption of hostilities will only occur after an agreement between yourself and your colleagues; that Marshal Foch has no power to order any American officer or enlisted man to any point not on the present German front without your specific authority; and that your authority will be communicated to General Pershing by yourself or by whatever American agent you choose to designate; in short, that no orders shall be given involving the use of American troops or money or material except on the present German front, without your specific authority.   Very sincerely,   Tasker H. Bliss[2]

TLS (WP, DLC).
    [1] F. Foch to J. J. Pershing, April 7, 1919, TCL (WP, DLC). Bliss summarizes its contents well.
    [2] For some unknown reason, this letter ended up in House's hands before Wilson saw it. House, who then had it delivered to Wilson by courier, wrote on the top of the letter: "Dear Governor, it is urgent that you send Gen. Bliss a reply at once." House also instructed the courier to wait for Wilson's answer. For Wilson's reply, see WW to T. H. Bliss, April 9, 1919.

A Memorandum by Henry White

MEMORANDUM   [Paris] 8 April 1919

Mr. Bratiano[1] has been to see me today, by appointment, to lay certain grievances before the American Delegation. He is much exercised in his mind because he fears that decisions are being arrived at in respect to Roumania without consulting the Delegates of that country. He complains that ever since he has been here, he and his colleagues have had no knowledge of what has been going on in the Conference and that they are still completely in the dark as to whether any conclusions have been arrived at or not.

He intimated, furthermore, that he could not but consider it as verging upon discourtesy on the part of the Conference to have sent General Smuts to Roumania to make investigations in its behalf without having previously notified the representatives of that country in Paris; the fact being that he himself had no knowledge of General Smuts' mission to Roumania until he saw in the newspapers that he had arrived at Budapest.

Mr. Bratiano, having asked for a map of that part of Europe, pointed out what, in his opinion, should be the portions of Hungary assigned to Roumania in order to render her existence possible as a state and to prevent the possibility of wars in the future, the boundary line being practically that of the new so-called temporary Armistice line, which has caused the revolution in Hungary.

His opinion is that the Conference should at once order the Bulgarians, Hungarians and German-Austrians to lay down their arms and cease fighting; otherwise he feels sure that there will be an explosion before long in the part of Europe—a period of weeks, he emphasized—which will bring about a renewed state of war throughout that whole region. He made a point of the importance on the part of the Allies of notifying the countries previously mentioned that, unless they should obey the directions of the Conference and cease fighting Roumania, an Allied expedition would be sent against them which would compel them to do so.

In the course of his conversation, which lasted for more than half an hour, he expressed himself as of the opinion that the affairs of the Conference had been conducted in a manner not likely to promote the furtherance of business, and that it would have been very much better if there had been regular plenary sessions of the Conference once or twice a week, before which the views of his own country and that of the other new nations in course of formation could have been laid.

He added, also, that, as far as he was concerned, for the last four months he had been endeavoring to obtain an audience with the President of the United States, but unsuccessfully, and he seems to consider that circumstance a considerable hardship. He wound up by expressing the earnest hope and requesting me to convey this view to the President, that no decisions be taken relative to his country without allowing its representatives to state their case fully.

Mr. Bratiano said, on leaving, that he desired to express his sincere thanks for the great assistance rendered by the United States and by it alone to his country in supplying the latter with food, a much needed work of benevolence which had been and is still admirably performed by Mr. Hoover.

T MS (WP, DLC).
  ¹ That is, the Rumanian Prime Minister, Ionel (or Ion I. C.) Brătianu.

Robert Howard Lord to Joseph Clark Grew

From: R. H. Lord,   [Paris] April 8, 1919.
To: Mr. Grew.
Subject: Baltic Commission.

RECOMMENDATION.

It is recommended that the Council of Four appoint a Commission to investigate and report on all questions properly coming before the Peace Conference relating to the Baltic countries of Esthonia, Latvia, Lithuania, and Finland.

DISCUSSION.

Since the armistice of November, there have been established in Esthonia, Latvia and Lithuania, provisional republican governments which with more or less success have been waging war against the Russian Bolshevist invaders of their respective countries.

The Peace Conference has adopted no definite attitude toward these governments, which have received only occasional and limited assistance from individual powers of the Entente. Germany, on the contrary, has sent armed forces into Latvia and Lithuania, ostensibly to aid the governments of those countries against the Bolshevists.

The provisional governments of Esthonia, Latvia and Lithuania have for several months maintained at Paris, official delegates, who have not even been given a hearing by the Peace Conference. Recently all three delegations have presented in writing the statement that without aid, or at least encouragement from the Conference, they cannot much longer continue the struggle against the Bolshevists. German and Bolshevist propaganda is taking advantage of their physical and economic exhaustion, and of the Entente's neglect, to spread among the Baltic peoples the idea that they will be handed over by the Peace Conference to Russia, to Poland, or to Germany; thus undermining the support of the provisional governments and destroying the prestige of the Peace Conference.

The Supreme Council will eventually have to decide whether or not to recognize the independence of Esthonia, Latvia and Lithuania, and to fix their frontiers. It must decide what sort of support, if any, to grant these peoples in their struggle for freedom; it must be ready to oversee the evacuation of the German armies of occupation, to delimit a frontier between Lithuania and Poland; and to envisage numerous other questions in relation to this border region.

The advantage of appointing a commission to investigate these matters without further delay, and present its conclusions to the Supreme Council, is obvious. The mere creation of such a body will be highly gratifying to the hitherto neglected delegates of Esthonia, Latvia and Lithuania; will afford them an opportunity to be heard officially, and convince their peoples that the Peace Conference does not intend to pass them by. The commission should be able to work out a definite Baltic policy to be presented to the Supreme Council as soon as the preliminary peace treaty is disposed of.

Certain questions relating to Finland are hardly less urgent. In

Finland, a new government based on a free election is in process of construction. But the country is still seething with political animosities and social unrest. It is doubtful whether the new government can maintain itself against violent opposition from the left and the right, without recognition and moral support from the Entente. There are also Finnish territorial questions that can hardly be avoided by the Conference. The inhabitants of the Aland Islands demand reunion with Sweden, which the Finnish government refuses to consider; and Finland demands an outlet on the Arctic ocean, and the annexation of Eastern Karelia. These questions could logically be assigned for investigation and report to the same Baltic Commission.

A possible argument against the prompt consideration of these questions might be their connection with a general supposed Russian policy. But the Conference Politique at Paris[1] (MM. Lvov, Maklakov, Savinkov, etc.) on March 8th urged the Peace Conference to recognize these governments de facto, and to satisfy their immediate economic, financial and military needs.[2] I believe that the peoples in question, being distinct and non-Russian races, are as much entitled as Poland to separate consideration; and that, furthermore, events in the Baltic region will not wait upon such time as the Supreme Council may resume consideration of Great Russia.

T MS (WP, DLC).
[1] That is, the so-called Russian Political Conference, a group of anti-Bolshevik Russian political leaders and diplomats which had been organized in late 1918 by Boris Aleksandrovich Bakhmet'ev and Vasilii Alekseevich Maklakov, a founding member of the Constitutional Democratic (Cadet) party in 1905 and the Ambassador of the Provisional Government to France. The membership of the conference covered a wide political spectrum and ranged from members of the Socialist Revolutionary party, such as Boris Viktorovich Savinkov, to the Foreign Minister of the last czarist government, Sergei Dmitrievich Sazonov. Its purpose was threefold: to represent the interests of Russia before the peace conference; to help direct the foreign policies of the White Russian governments and to promote the unification of these governments; and to organize and coordinate the efforts by Russian émigrés for increased Allied aid to the anti-Bolshevik movement. The directing organ of the conference was the so-called Russian Political Delegation Abroad, which consisted of Prince L'vov, the chairman of the conference, Sazonov, Maklakov, and Nikolai Vasil'evich Chaikovskii. For a detailed discussion, see Thompson, *Russia, Bolshevism and the Versailles Peace*, pp. 66-81.
[2] S. D. Sazonov *et al.* to G. Clemenceau, March 9 (not 8), 1919, TCL (SDR, RG 256, 861.00/336, DNA).

From the Diary of Colonel House

April 8, 1919.

Lloyd George was so determined not to have a meeting on the question of "Responsibility for the War" without either the President or me being present that it was agreed to postpone the conference until this afternoon and in the meantime constitute the morning meeting at his home into one to expedite business.

Clemenceau was in a much more amenable frame of mind than yesterday. He was unusually affectionate toward me and several times put his arms around my shoulders when we were standing together. I do not know that we accomplished much, but the *Proces Verbal* which Gordon and Hankey made will tell its own story.

George wished to read several plans which he said he had in mind for the settlement of the Sarre Basin. He started in to read them, but since they were of no earthly value, I asked to be excused, alleging that I had an urgent engagement with the President. I went across the street and was with the President for a half hour or more, going over what he and I thought would be the best means of settling the various questions to come up within the next few days.

The President met with the three Prime Ministers in the afternoon and, much to my delight, they came to a tentative settlement of the question of reparations.[1] The President yielded more than I thought he would, but not more I think than the occasion required. We had a long talk over the telephone about it tonight.

[1] Undoubtedly a mistake in transcription by Miss Denton. House certainly dictated "responsibilities." The Big Four did not discuss reparations at their meeting in the afternoon of April 8.

From the Diary of Ray Stannard Baker

Tuesday [April 8, 1919]

I saw Wilson this evening: he is much more hopeful. His gesture in ordering the G.W. was effective. He is driving toward a settlement: but he will say nothing!

I have had to take on a big new piece of work—the press side of the Supreme Economic Council, which is almost a government in itself.

From the Diary of Edith Benham

April 8, 1919

I have had so little to write about these last two days and a G.P.[1] coming tomorrow and a bad headache yesterday that I have left our friend the "Diary" alone. The President has been ill and Mrs. W. has been with him all the time, and so I don't hear from her much of what is going on. I don't know whether this move of his in calling for the George Washington will bring these people to time or not. She told me today of one of the many exasperations. The "Four" agreed to leave to a committee of experts the question of reparations, and they, the "Four," agreed to abide by their decision (these experts are, of course, in constant touch with their heads of the "Four"). They put in their report. Mr. Lloyd George said the thing was not satisfactory in every respect to him, but it could not be expected to be so in every respect to everyone, but he would sign it. It was given to Clemenceau to sign. He said he had never heard of such a thing and never seen any report. Dr. G. says that people are saying around here that when Clemenceau doesn't obstruct some measure, Lloyd George does, and that there is a deal between the two to do this. Colonel House, Mrs. Wilson says, who was representing the President at these meetings, was so mad after this last one that he was perfectly white with rage and said he was so mad he couldn't come this morning and could Lansing take his place, and the Colonel is a most quiet little person.

Apropos of the Lansings, I stopped to see her this morning. She has been ill but is all right, but she rather broke down in talking to me. She says she has no one here or at home to whom she can talk without seeming to be disloyal to the P. She always meant to be that, and she knew I would know and understand. I do perfectly, and I know how she feels. She says Mr. Lansing knows nothing of anything that is going on, that he is left out of everything and the French and the British just leave him alone because they know this. She has begged him to say to the P. that he is of no use and can he return and take up his duties as Secretary of State. Mr. L. says he won't do that for it would mean his resignation and he won't make any trouble for the P. now. It is humiliating to have Col. House doing all of his work here and work which the Prime Ministers of other countries are doing. All I could do was to give her the comfort of listening and letting her feel she was talking to someone who loved her and to whom she could speak safely. I knew how true her feeling is for I think the P. heartily dislikes Mr. L. and I am sorry to say he seems to show it in rather a petty way, for he speaks of letters he has written admonishing him like a school boy, and he seems glad when any one mentions anything to his discredit. Of course, that you and I are the only ones to know. Everything Mr. L. does seems to irritate him. The fact that they go out to dinner so much, accept invitations from people he (the P.) doesn't like. He is simply intolerant of any form of life save the one he leads. The Lansings are a very devoted and happy pair and I think that is almost a wrong because they don't live as he lives for his great happiness. All through this I think the Lansings have conducted themselves with great dignity under terribly trying circumstances.

T MS (Edith B. Helm Papers, DLC).
[1] That is, Grand Party.

From the Diary of Lord Robert Cecil

Tuesday. April 8[-10] [1919].

Breakfasted with the P.M. at his request—no one there but Philip [Kerr]. He worked very hard to fascinate me, or perhaps I should say to soothe my temper. On many points there was no difficulty, but we rather came to an issue over the League of Nations and the Navy. He is anxious to use his assent to the League of Nations as a lever to compel Wilson to give up increased naval construction.[1] I quite agree that it is unreasonable for Wilson to build a large Navy and insist on everybody else joining the League of Nations; but I am sure that any attempt to combine the two will only irritate the Americans without securing any advantage. Unfortunately the matter has now got into a mess. The P.M. has entrusted Walter Long with the negociation, and he has got across the United States naval authorities, with the result that neither can retreat without a certain amount of loss of face. At breakfast the P.M. showed some consciousness that he was in a mess, and suggested that I should take the matter up with House, which I agreed to do. I accordingly saw Wiseman, and after talking the matter over with him, wrote to House the annexed letter,[2] to which I received the annexed reply.[3] To finish the story, I took the two letters to the P.M. this morning (April 10), when he said that House's letter was unsatisfactory because it left him still able, by building his accepted programme, to build a fleet nearly equal in numbers and superior in armament to the British Fleet. I urged that even so the better tactical course was to agree to the Monroe Doctrine amendment, which is the principal difficulty of the moment with the League of Nations, keeping that question entirely separate from that of the Navy. However, the little man was obdurate, and I saw House, with the result recorded in the annexed memorandum.[4] What will be the upshot of it I don't know, but it is very harrassing and provoking.

T MS (R. Cecil Papers, Add. MSS 51071-51157, PRO).

[1] An Anglo-American controversy of potentially very serious proportions had been brewing since March 27, when Lloyd George informed Wilson, through Lord Robert Cecil and Colonel House, that he, Lloyd George, "had no intention" of signing a peace treaty which included the Covenant of the League of Nations until he had had a "complete understanding" with Wilson concerning the naval building program of the United States. See the entry from the House Diary printed at March 27, 1919, Vol. 56.

In the present volume, we print the correspondence between Cecil and House that led to the solution that enabled Cecil to stand down Lloyd George and other British leaders. The best (because based upon British as well as American sources) discussion of this matter is George W. Egerton, *Great Britain and the Creation of the League of Nations: Strategy, Politics, and International Organization, 1914-1919* (Chapel Hill, N. C., 1978), pp. 157-63. But see also Seth P. Tillman, *Anglo-American Relations at the Paris Peace Conference of 1919* (Princeton, N. J., 1961), pp. 280-94. Harold and Margaret Sprout, *Toward a New Order of Sea Power: American Naval Policy and the World Scene, 1918-1922* (Princeton, N. J., 1940), pp. 35-59, is particularly good on the state of the United States Navy at the end of the war and on American naval building plans in 1919 and their potential threat to British naval supremacy; but see also their account of the "naval battle of Paris" in *ibid.*, pp. 59-69.

2 It is printed as the next document.
3 See EMH to R. Cecil, April 9, 1919.
4 It is printed at April 10, 1919.

Lord Robert Cecil to Edward Mandell House

Confidential

My dear Colonel House,   Paris. April 8, 1919

I have found in exalted quarters that some of the recent utter-
ances by high officials connected with the United States Navy have
produced a very unfortunate impression. Very possibly they have
been misunderstood, but they have in fact conveyed the idea that
the naval policy of America is one of expansion; that the American
ambition is to have a navy at least as strong or stronger than that
of the British Empire, and so on. It is urged with some force that
such an attitude is wholly inconsistent with the conception of the
League of Nations, and that if it really represents the settled policy
of the United States it could only lead sooner or later to a competition
in arms between us and them. To inaugurate the League of Nations
by a competition in armaments between its two chief supporters
would doom it to complete sterility or worse. I cannot help feeling
that there is a great deal of force in this contention, and I do believe
that in some way or another the impression I have tried to describe
ought to be removed if the League is to have a fair start. The position
is undoubtedly complicated by the British sentiment about sea power.
It has been now for centuries past an article of faith with every
British statesman that the safety of the country depends upon her
ability to maintain her sea defence, and like all deep-rooted popular
sentiments it is founded in truth. Not only have we dominions
scattered over the face of the world, each of which requires protection from the sea, but the teeming population of the islands of
the United Kingdom can only be fed and clothed provided the
avenues of sea traffic are safe. We import four-fifths of our cereals,
two-thirds of our meat, the whole of our cotton and almost the
whole of our wool. If we were blockaded for a month or less we
should have to surrender at discretion. That is not true of any other
country in the world to the same extent. Least of all is it true of
the United States, which could, as far as necessaries of life are
concerned, laugh at any blockade.

I think you will believe me when I say that I am passionately
desirous of Anglo-American friendship, and a convinced believer
in its existence and durability, but I must freely admit that if I were
British Minister of the Navy and I saw that British naval safety was
being threatened, even by America, I should have to recommend

to my fellowcountrymen to spend their last shilling in bringing our fleet up to the point which I was advised was necessary for safety. I do not of course ask you to accept these views, but I do ask you to recognise their existence. I do not know whether in your country you have any traditional policy around which popular sentiment has crystallized in a similar way, but if you have you will be able to appreciate the kind of British feeling that exists on this point.

You have sometimes been good enough to invite me to speak to you as frankly as I would to one of my own countrymen, and in that spirit I venture to ask you whether you could do anything to reassure us on this point. Would it be possible, for instance, for you to say that when the Treaty of Peace containing the League of Nations has been signed you would abandon or modify your new naval programme? I am sure that the British Government would be only too ready to give corresponding assurances. That would be what the French call a "beau geste" with which to inaugurate the League; and if you could also intimate, however informally, that the two governments would consult together from year to year as to their naval programmes, and that the British sentiment on the matter would not be disregarded I feel confident that the present very genuine anxieties on the point could be completely removed.

Yours very sincerely,   Robert Cecil

TLS (E. M. House Papers, CtY).

From Herbert Clark Hoover

Dear Mr. President: Paris, France. April 8, 1919.

I now hear from Mr. Barnes that he will accept the formal invitation of yourself to undertake the administration of the Government guaranty of the 1919 crop and, in order to advance the matter a step further, I have prepared the attached draft telegram,[1] which, if you could see your way to dispatch, will procure the necessary response from Mr. Barnes.

You will recollect that his staff is composed of volunteers of considerable substances and at a great deal of sacrifice and I have taken the liberty of attaching to this telegram a direct appreciation of their services as I feel that it may help Mr. Barnes in securing their continuation in service for a further period.

Faithfully yours,   Herbert Hoover

TLS (WP, DLC).
[1] It is missing in WP, DLC. However, see WW to J. H. Barnes, April 15, 1919.

From the Diary of Dr. Grayson

Wednesday, April 9, 1919.

The President stayed in bed until 10:00 o'clock this morning. He had breakfast in his bedroom, and at 11:00 o'clock he was ready for the meeting of the Council of Four. At the conclusion of the meeting the President told me that they had made progress.

The President had withstood the fatigue of the morning session better than yesterday, which showed that the improvement in his condition continued. I had been extremely fortunate in treating the President in having the complete and active cooperation of Mrs. Wilson, whose devotion to the President had enabled her to nurse him in a way that made unnecessary the securing of a professional nurse. She was a perfect angel. She was most attentive, her only thought being for the President's comfort. Mrs. Wilson frequently attended Red Cross meetings, attended Y.M.C.A. functions, visited various places for crippled children, went to hospitals almost every afternoon. But she forsook all of this work and everything else, and gave all of her time to the President, remaining constantly at his side and cheering him and keeping his mind diverted from the fact that he was unable purely through physical reasons from continuing the work that he had started.

After the morning conference the President, Mrs. Wilson and I lunched together. The President showed a decided effect of the fatigue of the morning. He sent for me before he went to lunch and said: "I feel a little chilly and am tired, but I am extremely anxious to proceed with the afternoon conference. But I want your advice before doing so." I told him he could go through with it if he was extremely careful and rested as much as possible before the conference.

Deviating from our usual rule not to discuss business at the table, the conversation during the lunch turned to an article in the morning's London Daily Mail, which stated that 300 members of the British Parliament had united in an urgent joint telegram to the British Premier demanding a renewed assurance that he (Lloyd-George) had not departed from his pledge to the British Empire that he would present a complete war bill to Germany.[1] The President said that Lloyd-George had told him it was his intention to send a curt reply to this joint telegram informing the British Parliament that if they persisted in their wild demand it would be better for them to send some one here who could handle the thing better than he could, as he was not in sympathy with this position. The President smilingly remarked that while Lloyd-George had told him that this was his intention, he (the President) had his "doots."

After luncheon the President sat by the fire and read a paper dealing with the program that was to be considered at the afternoon conference. When the time came for the conference he was somewhat rested and was able to sit in as usual.

As a result of the editorial prepared and sent by Mr. Grasty to the New York TIMES,[2] the following message was today received from Secretary Tumulty: "Grasty has written a wonderful article; the President ought to keep close to him."[3] Mr. Tumulty was not aware of my conference with Mr. Grasty in connection with the editorial in question.

The Big Four session in the afternoon brought about the first written agreement between the conferees. It was the decision on the responsibilities and punishment of the authors of the war. It was agreed that while the Kaiser could not be placed upon trial on a charge of having directly caused the war, he was answerable to a charge of violation of the sanctity of treaties and international morality. The four members signed the report and it was to be submitted later to Japan for signature. This marked a real stepping-stone in the progress of the treaty making. The other members of the Big Four evinced a desire to wait and sign it when Japan's representative would be present, but the President insisted that the matter should be disposed of immediately, which was done. The President passed the paper around the table himself, handing it first to Clemenceau to sign, then to Lloyd-George, to Orlando, and then he affixed his own signature. The method proposed for the trial of those responsible will be through the creation of a High Court composed of one representative of each of the big five nations.

I attended Mrs. Wilson's tea in the afternoon and about the time it was over the President sent for me and he and I went for a drive despite the fact that it was raining outside. We made the run through the Bois, and the President enjoyed it very much, the rain being a spring rain, the air being warm, and he being well wrapped up to prevent catching any additional cold.

During the drive the President said to me: "We made progress today, not through the match of wits, but simply through my hammering and forcing them to decisions. It appears to me that the GEORGE WASHINGTON incident has had a beneficial effect on the French. They wanted to know when I was going back and I told them in very plain language that the results would be the determining factor."[4]

Returning to the house we had dinner and then the President went to his study, where he worked at very important business, sitting before an open-fire.

It developed tonight that the President's judgment on Lloyd-

George's "defiant" telegram, which the Premier had declared he would send, was in every way correct. The actual telegram sent was far from being forceful.[5]

[1] After Bonar Law, in his speech in the House of Commons of April 2, 1919, had failed to quell the virulent criticism by members of his own Conservative party of the government's willingness to settle for less than a full indemnity from Germany (see n. 7 to the minutes of the Council of Four printed at April 5, 1919, 11 a.m.), the attacks against Lloyd George's reparation policy culminated in a virtual parliamentary revolt on April 8. At the instigation of Kennedy Jones, 233 Conservative members of Lloyd George's coalition sent a minatory telegram to the Prime Minister, claiming that "the greatest anxiety" existed throughout Great Britain at the persistent reports from Paris that the British delegation, rather than formulating "the complete financial claim of the Empire," was merely considering what amount could be exacted from Germany. The telegram, which was eventually signed by 370 Unionist M.P.s, continued: "Our constituents have always expected—and still expect—that the first action of the Peace Delegates would be, as you repeatedly stated in your election speeches, to present the Bill in full, to make Germany acknowledge the debt and then to discuss ways and means of obtaining payment.

"Although we have the utmost confidence in your intention to fulfil your pledges to the country, may we, as we have to meet innumerable inquiries from our constituents, have your assurance that you have in no way departed from your original intention."

See David Lloyd George, *The Truth about the Peace Treaties* (2 vols., London, 1938), I, 563. For a brief discussion, see also Mayer, *Politics and Diplomacy of Peacemaking*, pp. 630-31.

[2] About which, see n. 5 to the extract from the Grayson Diary printed at April 7, 1919.

[3] JPT to C. T. Grayson, April 8, 1919, T telegram (WP, DLC).

[4] This brings up the question to which we adverted in n. 2 to the entry from the Grayson Diary printed at April 3, 1919, Volume 56—whether, as Dr. Weinstein has conjectured (Edwin A. Weinstein, *Woodrow Wilson: A Medical and Psychological Biography* [Princeton, N. J., 1981], pp. 338-44), Wilson was in a state of euphoria at this time caused by the encephalitis which was a sequela of Wilson's attack of "influenza" on April 3. As evidence to support this diagnosis, Weinstein (pp. 339-40) points to a number of concessions which Wilson made during his confinement and immediately afterward. In fact, Wilson made no concessions at all during this period. "Probably the most startling political expression of the changes in Wilson's behavior," Weinstein writes (pp. 342-43), "was the reversal of his attitudes on German war guilt and the trial of the ex-Kaiser." Weinstein reviews the debate on this subject in the Council of Four on April 2 and April 8 and then points to Wilson's formula for responsibilities which Wilson presented to the Council of Four on April 9 as evidence that Wilson, in a state of euphoria, had reversed himself by providing for William's trial.

The facts are as follows. There had never been any controversy in the Commission on Responsibilities about the right of the Allied and Associated Governments to try members of the armed forces of the enemy for acts already, that is, before the war, deemed to be criminal during wartime, although opinions varied as to how to apprehend enemy war criminals, how to try them, and whether it would be possible to apprehend them. The single issue in controversy was whether to try and punish the former German Emperor for war crimes. As the discussions in the Council of Four during the afternoon of April 8 clearly and vividly reveal, Lloyd George and Clemenceau insisted, not only upon trying William, but also upon inflicting some kind of condign punishment upon him *for criminal acts*. As is well known, the Unionist party had recently run on the slogan, "Hang the Kaiser and make Germany pay!"

In preparing the protocol on responsibilities, printed below, Wilson was responding to the minority report of Lansing and James Brown Scott in the report of the Commission on Responsibilities (printed at April 4, 1919, Vol. 56) and, most specifically, to the recommendations in Lansing's letter to Wilson of April 8, 1919, just printed. What Wilson proposed was perhaps in the nature of a compromise, but it held fast to the position that Wilson had consistently taken heretofore: the former Kaiser should be tried and held up to the execration of mankind for violations of international law and morality, *but not for criminal offenses*, provided that Holland would cooperate by extraditing him. Wilson almost certainly doubted that Holland would ever extradite William.

Wilson was certainly pleased, if not euphoric, over his achievement in the Council of Four during the morning of April 9. And well he might have been. He had personally written the protocol, brought an end (so it then seemed) to an important controversy, and, most important, had succeeded in persuading a united Council of Four to take the first firm decision that it had taken to this point.

⁵ The telegram, drafted in conjunction with Bonar Law, who had immediately gone to Paris for a consultation with Lloyd George, read as follows: "My colleagues and I mean to stand faithfully by all the pledges we gave to the constituencies. We are prepared at any moment to submit to the judgment of Parliament and if necessary of the Country our efforts loyally to redeem our promises." Lloyd George, *Truth about the Peace Treaties*, I, 564.

From the Diary of Ray Stannard Baker

Wednesday [April 9, 1919]

I get no time even to write here—these whirly days.

High politics are being played   a desperate effort is being made to separate Wilson & Lloyd George. Northcliffe & his press are attacking George bitterly for his "kindness" to the Germans & his effort to work with the Russians

Here is the Northcliffe indictment of both George & Wilson

Tenderness for the enemy;

Charity towards Bolshevism;

Love of moneylenders;

Stern impartiality towards friendly peoples;

Anxiety to raise the stricken foe and readiness
   to forgive his sins;

Fidelity to principle and, in particular,
   to the principle of relativity.¹

When Wilson was ill L.G.—the inconstant—began to play with the French: gave loving interviews to the *Matin* & *Petit Parisien*.² When Wilson got up again & made his defiance with the calling of the George Washington L.G. came to heel again. It is a struggle between Northcliffe & Wilson for the soul of Lloyd-George—who has no soul.

Italy is falling apart. I doubt whether peace arrives before anarchy after all. All the forces are working against Wilson.

¹ Clipping pasted on the page of the diary.
² In a statement printed in the *Petit Parisien* of April 4, 1919, Lloyd George had emphatically denied that he was opposed to the guarantees demanded by France against a renewed German attack. He had claimed that, on the contrary, there was a "complete and absolute" understanding between France and Great Britain on the question of French security. While there had been some discussions about the nature of the final agreement, no dissensions could ever exist between the two countries, and England was prepared to make any sacrifices necessary to guarantee the peace and independence of France. See the *New York Times*, April 5, 1919.

Similarly, in an interview with Stéphane Lauzanne, editor of *Le Matin*, on April 6, 1919, Lloyd George had stated that, although the technical reports of the various delegations disagreed on certain details, there was no divergence among the negotiators about the principal questions of the peace treaty. Some of the technical difficulties could only be settled after close study, and the public, instead of believing all kinds of rumors, should be patient and "wait a few days" for the final outcome of the negotiations before passing judgment on the work of the conference. "No day passes," Lloyd George claimed, "but that we in silent deliberation feel approaching nearer the great aim, and experience for each other more esteem, confidence, and affection." As a result, Lloyd George concluded, the preliminary peace treaty would be ready by Easter, and the Germans would be asked to sign it by the end of April or the beginning of May. *Ibid*, April 7, 1919.

To Robert Lansing

My dear Lansing: [Paris] 9 April, 1919.

Here is the formula which I drew up about criminal responsibility. I have a copy of it signed by all of the four conferrees, and I have undertaken to see Baron Makino about it. I sincerely hope that this concludes a very difficult business.

Cordially and faithfully yours,   [Woodrow Wilson]

CCL (WP, DLC).

Mantoux's Notes of a Meeting of the Council of Four

April 9, 1919, 11 a.m.

President Wilson reads aloud a text on the question of responsibilities.

"1. All persons guilty of crimes against the laws of war will be tried before military tribunals, according to customary procedure, and, if they are found guilty, will be sentenced to the usual penalties. If the crime was committed against the nationals of a single belligerent nation, the case will be tried by the military tribunals of that nation. If the crime was committed against the nationals of several of the belligerents, the case will come before a military tribunal composed of judges taken from the military courts of the belligerents concerned. In all cases, the accused will have the right to choose his legal counsel.

"2. Holland will be requested to deliver the ex-Kaiser to the Allied and Associated Powers, in order to be tried by a special tribunal. This tribunal will be composed of five judges designated respectively by the following five powers: the United States of America, Great Britain, France, Italy, and Japan.

"The crime for which it is proposed to bring the ex-Kaiser to trial will not be defined as a violation of the criminal law, but as a supreme offense against international morality and the sanctity of treaties.

"The penalty to be pronounced is left to the discretion of the court, which must follow the highest principles of international policy, with a view to vindicating the solemn obligations of international agreements and the inviolability of international morality."[1]

President Wilson adds: I remind you of the objections which were made by the Japanese delegation; but, it seems to me, they do not exactly run counter to this text.

Lloyd George. Although it has not been expressly stated, at the root of the Japanese objections is the idea of divine right; it is a notion that Europe has abandoned forever.

Wilson. In any case, it is necessary that the Japanese representatives take part in our decision. Should they not be summoned?

Lloyd George. I think it is better to wait, in order to present them at the same time with all questions of a general nature in which Japan is interested.

I think that the formulas which are proposed to us by the President cover all cases of violation of international law that we want to punish. It will be easy for us to prove that these crimes are not, as the Germans alleged, merely reprisals against our actions, nor are they justified as new methods of war. Concerning poisonous gases, for example, I could show you in indisputable documents that during the Crimean War the British government rejected a proposal suggesting the use of sulphurous gas. That proposal, made again at the beginning of the war of 1914 by Mr. Winston Churchill, was rejected a second time as contrary to principles which we did not wish to abandon.

Hence the Germans do not have the right to say that they introduced a new element into the war, by means of an invention which we would be sorry not to have made before them; we had the invention, and we refused to use it ourselves.

Question of the Saar

Lloyd George. We have all received a copy of M. Tardieu's memorandum[2] in response to the proposal made yesterday by the President of the United States.[3] It is a document whose argument has much force, and merits attentive reading.

Wilson. What makes difficult the solution of this problem is that the only certain justification for all that we can do in the Saar Basin is France's right to reparation for her economic losses; that does not justify a change of territorial sovereignty.

Lloyd George. In this problem there is something in addition to the simple question of reparation: there is the past. I recall yet again the English government's repugnance in 1815 to permit Prussia to

[1] Wilson's own draft of this protocol, recently discovered, is printed as an addendum in this volume.
[2] It is printed as the next document.
[3] That is, Enclosure II printed with D. H. Miller to EMH, April 8, 1919.

annex this territory. There is the fact that part of the population of this district has retained anti-Prussian sentiments.

I note that M. Tardieu in his memorandum accepts the plebiscite; it is a great concession, which must allow you to accept for your part that the Saar Valley be placed under a special political regime.

The question is postponed until the afternoon session.

Lloyd George. We have received information about the work of the small special committee which last studied the question of the Polish frontier. I see that in the small state which we propose to create around Danzig, there will be 324,000 inhabitants, of whom only 16,000 will be Poles. In the region of Marienwerder, whose fate will be settled by a plebiscite and which can, if the population decides in this sense, be joined to East Prussia, there are 169,000 inhabitants, the number of Poles being no more than 26,000. This justifies the policy which we have defended.

Wilson. This text gives the Poles the necessary guarantees for their communications with the sea.

Lloyd George. We are devising equivalent guarantees for German communications between West Prussia and East Prussia and, for the Poles, between Danzig and Warsaw.

Orlando. How many Germans would remain on Polish territory after the modification of the frontier proposed by the commission?

Wilson. There are more than two million.

Orlando. Let us say 2,200,000. If you subtract 450,000 around Danzig, and from Marienwerder, nearly 1,800,000 will still remain in Poland.

Wilson. I recognize that it cannot be otherwise, since these German populations are scattered, and their presence is due in large measure to a systematic colonization.

Lloyd George. That is inevitable. What we want to avoid is taking from Germany territories which have always been part of East Prussia, even while Poland was independent.

Reading of the text concerning Danzig: the city, with the surrounding territory, will be made into an autonomous state, under the authority of the League of Nations. It will be attached by a customs union to Poland, which will in addition have ownership of the railways, free use of the port of Danzig, and the control of foreign relations of the state thus constituted.

Reading of the text concerning the region of Marienwerder: the fate of this region will be settled by a plebiscite, which will take place by universal suffrage, including women, and by commune, the country being first evacuated by German and Polish armies and placed under the provisional administration of an inter-Allied commission.

M. Paderewski is introduced.

Wilson. At this time, we are doing our best to arrive at a settlement of Polish affairs in such a way as not to provoke grave dangers in the future. We are striving to follow lines indicated by ethnography and to assure to Poland indispensable communications with the sea without including any more Germans than necessary in the Polish state. Our wish is to establish the Polish state on a foundation which will give it as few enemies as possible.

The plan that we have prepared can be summarized as follows— and I assure you that there is no question which has been studied more conscientiously; Danzig will cease to belong to Germany and will form along with the adjacent territory a distinct and autonomous political entity. It will be included in the Polish customs union and subordinated to Poland for all its foreign relations. We have provided sure guarantees for Poland's free communication with the port of Danzig. Polish sovereignty will be established over the course of the Vistula, over the railway parallel to this river, and over the territory lying on its left bank. The free use of the railway from Danzig to Mlawa will be assured to the Poles, as the railway crossing the territory of Danzig will be assured to the Germans, permitting East Prussia to communicate with Germany proper.

Concerning the concentrated German group which is located to the southeast of Danzig, we propose to apply the same principle as in the southern part of East Prussia: a plebiscite will permit the population to decide for itself its own fate.

Our concern is to avoid in Poland the dangers which would bring about the existence of a *Germania irredenta*. We know from past experience that there is no more serious and lasting cause of international conflict. We ask you for your observations on the advantages and disadvantages of this plan.

Paderewski. I am not very well prepared for this discussion; I did not expect to be called today. But I am authorized to express the sentiment of my country. The Polish Diet, which is probably the most democratic assembly in existence today in the world, conveys to you its respect and its complete confidence. It begs me to transmit its best wishes.

It wishes first of all a complete alliance with the Entente; it also wishes to have the territorial guarantees necessary for our own existence. Unfortunately, we know the Germans better than you; we have been their neighbors and their victims for seven centuries. Please believe me: however little is taken from Germany, there will always be a *Germania irredenta*.

The Germans are at the moment playing a rather crafty diplomatic game, and we are in danger of being its first victims. Danzig is indispensable to Poland, which cannot breathe without this window on the sea. It is patriotic sentiment which has permitted the Polish government to maintain order in Poland. Our country is surrounded by a furious assault of disorder and violence; it stands as the fortress of political order in eastern Europe. But our situation is only maintained thanks to our confidence in you. If that confidence proved false, the disappointment, the despair which would result could lead to a catastrophe and open the doors to Bolshevism.

Poland must be strong, and she cannot be strong without Danzig.

If we study the districts inhabited by German peoples, along the length of the Mlawa line, we see that, according to the statistics, the district of Stuhm has a Polish population of 47 percent. But if one takes as a basis the number of Polish-speaking children in the schools—a more honest figure—that proportion rises to 59 percent. In the district of Marienwerder, Polish children form 47 percent of the school population.

Lloyd George. Is that not an argument in favor of the plebiscite?

Paderewski. That population is still frightened; it does not feel strongly enough that we are victorious over the Germans.

Lloyd George. There would be assured guarantees of the freedom of the vote; we are providing for the evacuation of these territories by all military forces, the temporary establishment of an inter-Allied administration. If your figures are correct—and I have no intention of contesting them—the plebiscite would be in your favor.

Paderewski. In that entire region, German civil servants and soldiers comprise 11.45 percent of the population. In the district of Rosenberg, the most Germanized, the Polish population forms only 17 percent of the total; but on the other hand, there are 19 percent of officials and soldiers.

With regard to the city of Danzig, if it is interrogated not by German officials but under conditions which would permit it to express itself freely, I am persuaded that it would vote for annexation to Poland; that is in its economic interest.

Lloyd George. If it is impossible for you purely and simply to annex Danzig, would you accept a popular referendum as a last resort?

Paderewski. Our Diet, which is an assembly of peasants and workers, with a small number of representatives from the petite bourgeoisie, has very democratic sentiments and does not want conquests. But it unanimously demands Danzig; it is the voice of the Polish people, of which I am the servant. The representatives of Poland are making the incorporation of Danzig into the Polish

State a condition *sine qua non*, like the reunion of Upper Silesia to our territory, like the reintegration of Lemberg. They also want federation with Lithuania.

Lloyd George. On this last question, I believe there has been no report presented.

Paderewski. For us the question of Danzig is a question of life or of death.

Wilson. Our intention is to place Danzig entirely at the disposal of Poland. We would like to make it a free city, such as it was in the Middle Ages, within the customs frontier of Poland, which will have in every respect the same economic rights in the port of Danzig as if she had sovereignty there.

Lloyd George. It is a sort of Home Rule for Danzig. Foreign relations being in your hands, Danzig has less autonomy vis-à-vis Poland than Canada has vis-à-vis England.

Paderewski. But Danzig would remain between the hands of the Germans, and consequently of Germany, to which it would return in the end.

Wilson. Did you not say—and we also believe it on the basis of our information—that the economic interest of Danzig's population must lead it to the side of Poland?

Paderewski. We must take into account national sentiment; Germany is not yet *hors de combat*.

Lloyd George. Really?

Paderewski. She challenges you over the passage through Danzig; she uses revolution and Bolshevism as means toward her ends.

Wilson. Do you believe that Germany can for long employ toward a political goal a means which is ruining her?

Paderewski. The instinct for obedience among the Germans is an amazing thing; they are capable of making or of stopping revolutions on order. In eastern Poland, we see German troops as they withdraw, themselves preparing quarters for the Bolshevists.

Germany can give up Danzig; she has an entire series of great ports, Emden, Bremen, Hamburg, Stettin, Königsberg; that is enough for her 60 million inhabitants. And are the 25 million Poles not to have a single port?

Wilson. On the contrary, we want to assure you use of the port of Danzig, while establishing a system of government there which creates the least possible danger for the future.

Paderewski. We are prepared to treat well the Germans who will reside on Polish territory; we will not imitate their persecutions.

Wilson. Our desire is not to leave Germany any pretext to seek a quarrel with you.

Clemenceau. Would you not consent to a plebiscite?

Paderewski. I am prepared for all the plebiscites that one might wish in order to settle the difficulties that we have with our friends, on the side of Lithuania, or on the side of Bohemia, but not with our enemies.

The question would not be resolved, moreover, even if we had Danzig, in case you should not give us at the same time the territory through which passes the route which links Danzig to Poland; is it not better, if we must choose, to sacrifice 300,000 Germans than 25 million Poles?

Lloyd George. If Danzig would prefer to be Polish, or if, fearing the creation of a port at a neighboring point on the coast, she turned voluntarily to you, that would be the best solution. What we do not want is to create in Danzig an Alsace-Lorraine question, in which Germany could assume the posture of a victim.

Wilson. Will you not be satisfied if you have special guarantees for the use of the railways?

Paderewski. We know the Germans too well to rely on any guarantees that they will accept. We have seen them be always the same ever since the tenth century; for a long time we have been familiar with their scraps of paper. I could remind you of the story of this grand master of the Teutonic Order who, having signed a treaty with several Pomeranian and Polish princes of the coastal region, invited them all to a banquet during which he had them assassinated. That is the kind of treaties we have made with Germany in the past.

I ask you to take into consideration what I have told you and to inform me of your conclusions.

Wilson. We were anxious to hear you, and I thank you for having responded to our appeal.

Mantoux, I, 195-202.

A Translation of a Memorandum by André Tardieu

April 9, 1919.

REPLY TO THE NOTE OF PRESIDENT WILSON,
of April 8th.

I. PRELIMINARY OBSERVATIONS

The note delivered by President Wilson to Mr. Clemenceau on the 31st of March[1] was worded as follows:

---

[1] Wilson's note to Clemenceau is missing; however, he sent him a copy of the proposed agreement on the Saar question, printed as an Enclosure with C. H. Haskins to WW, March 29, 1919. Tardieu here repeats Haskins' memorandum verbatim.

"It is agreed in principle:

"1st—That full ownership of the coal mines of the Saar Basin should pass to France to be credited on her claims against Germany for reparation.

"2nd—That for the exploitation of these mines the fullest economic facilities shall be accorded to France, including particularly:

a)—Exemption from taxation on the part of Germany including import and export dues.

b)—Full mobility of labour, foreign and native.

c)—Freedom for the development of adequate means of communication by rail and water.

"3rd—That the political and administrative arrangements necessary to secure the foregoing results be enquired into."

In reference to this note, the three designated experts have established a plan of economic clauses which they recognize as just and necessary, not only in the interest of development but also for the general prosperity of the valley and for the inhabitants.[2]

The experts have also drawn attention to the fact that, in their opinion, certain of these clauses (Nos. 9 to 17) would cause, in their application, inevitable friction and conflict if a special political and administrative form of government were not established.

The note delivered the 8th of April[3] accepts, with the exception of certain amendments, the plan of economic clauses, but it does not include any political or administrative clauses.

In effect, it creates a court with full powers which will decide conflicting questions, but it does not arrange in any way to prevent these difficulties. In other words, the note of the 8th of April recognizes that differences will arise and restricts itself to the establishment of a jurisdiction which, in each case, will decide between France and Germany.

In this way the Valley of the Saar will be, in the last analysis, administered by a court.

Such administration of perpetual suits seems inacceptable, not only for France and for Germany, but also in the interest of the inhabitants of the Saar and in that of the peace of the world.

II. EXAMPLES OF DISPUTED POINTS THAT ARE CERTAIN TO ARISE.

That disputes are certain to arise is proved by an examination of the articles. For example:[4]

Article IX. If the sovereignty and administration of Germany remain in full, how would it be possible to apply French law in the

---

[2] That is, the memorandum by Haskins and others printed at April 6, 1919.
[3] That is, Enclosure II printed with D. H. Miller to EMH, April 8, 1919.
[4] Here Tardieu begins to comment on articles in the memorandum of April 6, 1919.

matter of labor, recruiting, salaries, etc., to a portion of the workmen in the valley?

Article XII. How will it be possible to bring into accord the police powers of the guards named by the French State with the German administration of police and the law?

Article XIII. How will France be able to exercise its right of visa in connection with mining, industrial and social regulations if she is not delegated any rights of sovereignty or administration? Let us suppose that the laws of Weimar reduces the working day to six hours for a central electric power station supplying the mines; how will it be possible for the mines to work eight hours under the administration of the French law?

Article XVI. How will it be possible to put the territory of the Czar [Saar] under French custom regulations if France possesses no administrative personell nor any other right than the ownership of the mines? There can be no customs without people to administer them.

All these articles are necessary and economically just, but they require an administrative and political complement, which the experts have asked for, and which the note of April 8th does not take into consideration. Many more examples can be found.

III. GENERAL CONSEQUENCES OF THE PROPOSED SYSTEM

According to the terms of the suggested solution the situation will be as follows:

1st—The inhabitants will be represented in the Reichstag where incidents could be artificially provoked.

2nd—The entire administrative organization of Germany and Prussia, which has oppressed this region for a hundred years, will be maintained.

3rd—Every economic measure taken by the French Government, no matter how indispensable it might be, could be indefinitely retarded by the German authorities, for whom, in order to bring this about, it would only be necessary to introduce an action before the court of arbitration.

4th—If the 72,000 workmen subject to the French labor laws go on strike what legislation will be applicable in the valley?

The result arrived at will be to multiply Franco-German friction in this region, which will react on the relations of the two countries as a whole. It is not a special and local tribunal which will be able to repair the harm thus brought about.

The Valley of the Saar will become, under such an administration, a European Morocco, with all the faults of the Algesiras action still further aggravated. It will be a field and source of a continual Franco-German conflict.

IV. THE BLOCKING OF TWO INTERESTS ESSENTIAL TO FRANCE.

Still further the suggested combination does not give satisfaction to either of the two essential interests which the French Government must safeguard.

1. In regard to that which concerns underground (rights).

The property of the mines has been confirmed in perpetual title by the note of President Wilson to Mr. Clemenceau of the 31st of March. France has established that the coal to which she has the right as a reparation is indispensable for herself and for Alsace Lorraine; moreover, the note of the 8th of April considers the cession of this right of property in whole or in part after 15 years. France cannot subscribe to this, for coal cannot be replaced by gold.

2. In regard to that which concerns the surface.

To the first French demand, the President of the United States made the objection that there were in this territory, in large part formerly French, too many German elements (immigrants) for an immediate union with France to be acceptable. The French Government consented on the 28th of March to study out another solution. But it has constantly declared that in this same territory there were too many French elements now turned towards it for France to be able to give up safeguarding in the future their rights to union.

Therefore, in order that this union may result in 15 years as the result of a free vote of the population, the minimum condition is that from now on it be removed from oppression of Prussian administration, to which it has submitted for 100 years.

This administration (elections officials, etc) for the continuation of which the note of the 8th of April provides, assures in fact, to the Germans, the benefit of that terror by which they have always reigned and will deprive the inhabitants of that *fair chance* for liberation which France wishes to bring about for them.

France agrees that all guarantees, even those of nationality, be given to the inhabitants as individuals. But she cannot admit that the economic and social powers which may be of interest to her should be hypothecated at every moment by the exercise of Prussian sovereignty and administration.

V. CONCLUSION.

To sum up, the French Government, after a careful study of the note of the 8th of April, believes that this note:

1st—Does not contain the administrative and political caluses [clauses] which the report of the experts of the 5th [6th] of April judges indispensable to avoid conflict.

2nd—Entailing, for this reason, great risk of complications, both local and general.

3rd—It furnishes to Germany a permanent method of obstruction against French exploitation of the mines of the valley.

4th—It reopens the question at the end of fifteen years of the right of property by France to the mines, confirmed by the note of President Wilson of the 31st of March.

5th—It does not assure to the inhabitants, in view of the proposed plebiscite, the guarantees indispensable after a hundred years of Prussian oppression.

The French Government wishes, therefore, to restrict itself to one of the three propositions of Mr. Lloyd George.[5]

It is ready to carry them out in conformity with the suggestions of President Wilson.

a) By a plebiscite at the end of fifteen years,

b) By a court of arbitration empowered to decide possible differences in the application of one or the other of these three solutions.

T MS (WP, DLC).
[5] They are printed in Appendix IV to the minutes of the Council of Four printed at April 8, 1919, 11 a.m.

From Bernard Mannes Baruch

My dear Mr. President: Paris April 9, 1919

The proposed arrangment by which the French would own the coal mines in the Sarre Valley, while the territory itself would remain German, would, in my opinion, be a constant source of turmoil and unending friction. A solution is possible through making a distribution of the product of the Sarre Valley as one item in the general allocation of coal from Germany to France, as a part of the reparation adjustment.

So long as the Sarre mines exist, the French are entitled to the delivery of that quantity of coal from the Sarre Basin that has been used in Alsace-Lorraine, and as much more as they desire to use which can be produced from the Sarre mines without interference with the present German industrial and civil life, which is now dependent upon this coal. The French are now asking for twenty-seven millions additional tons of coal in substitution for that which was produced from the Lens and Pas de Calais fields, and are quite willing to accept that solution. There seems to be no reason why the same thing should not be done in the case of the Sarre Valley. The following is my recommendation:

1. Germany should be required to deliver to France seven million tons a year, the amount which France imported annually before the war.

2. Germany should be required to supply to France an amount of coal sufficient to make up the deficit in the normal production of the Lens and Pas de Calais fields during the period of their restoration. The complete restoration of the mines should require not to exceed five years.

3. During the life of the Sarre mines Germany should be required to sell the same amount of coal she has heretofore sold to territories that have now become French, France having the option to receive a percentage of the increased production of the Sarre, which its present demands bear to the total production.

It is well to note that the German metallurgical industries in the Sarre Valley, as well as many of the gas works of Southern Germany, are dependent upon the coal of the Valley of the Sarre. Therefore, the ownership of these mines by the French could be used to handicap these industries and greatly disturb the economic life. It should also be noted that the steel mills in the Sarre Valley and the adjacent German territory are dependent upon the iron ores from Lorraine, which is now French territory. This furnishes the French with a powerful weapon for trading.

The Germans might, with equal justice, demand an ownership in the iron mines of Lorraine for the protection of their industries which have heretofore been supplied from this source, and from which a large amount must come for reparational purposes.

A solution of the Sarre Valley-Lorraine problem would be a reciprocal arrangement, whereby Germany would be required to furnish the same percentage of the coal output that has heretofore been used in Lorraine; and the French, in turn, be required to furnish to Germany the same percentage of the iron ore output that had previously been distributed to the territory that still remains in Germany.   Very sincerely yours,   Bernard M Baruch

TLS (WP, DLC).

From Herbert Clark Hoover

Confidential

Dear Mr. President: Paris, France. April 9, 1919.

The most difficult point in relief of Russia is shipping. On this, in case neutral tonnage proves deficient, I feel you must take some pledge from the three Premiers to make sacrifices to this end, particularly Mr. Lloyd George. The deficiencies of shipping for France, Italy, Belgium and the General Relief (after deducting available German tonnage) in food and coal seem to me to be a burden upon the United States and United Kingdom as being the two Governments with surplus shipping over their own food & supply import needs. This burden ought to fall upon each in proportion to their available mercantile tonnage. I enclose a recent statement[1] showing that today we are furnishing 31% of our ships to these purposes and the British 18%. If they took 31% of the burden the Russian relief would be solved. If you could get Mr. Lloyd George to agree that we and they should carry these dificiency [deficiency] burdens (i.e., France, Italy, Belgium and Relief) in proportion to our resources in shipping, this problem for Russia would be solved.

Faithfully yours,   Herbert Hoover.

TLS (WP, DLC).
  [1] T MS (WP, DLC).

Mantoux's Notes of a Meeting of the Council of Four

April 9, 1919, 3:30 p.m.

Wilson. I have read the three plans presented by the British delegation on the question of the Saar. All three entail Germany's renunciation of sovereignty over the Saar basin. In my opinion, this would prejudice the result of the popular consultation which must take place fifteen years after the signing of the peace. I consulted Professor Haskins about this subject, and it seems to me that any plan which would eliminate German sovereignty and substitute that of the League of Nations, with a mandate conferred upon France, would give only an ambiguous solution to the problem.

Moreover, as I have already said very frankly, I am afraid of a solution of this type for reasons of principle. However, I do not want to hold inflexibly to the letter of the principle, if a reasonable solution can be reached. What I would reject is a system which would prejudice the result of the plebiscite.

I propose to require Germany to leave, for fifteen years, this land under the administration of a commission appointed by the League of Nations and responsible to it. The population would keep its laws, its present institutions, the commission having power to institute modifications made necessary by the special economic regime established by the treaty. At the same time I would give to this commission the functions of a court of arbitration to settle all the disputes arising from the application of the treaty, at the same time that it would have legislative and executive power over the entire region.

Fundamental rules would be established to assure the population complete religious freedom, respect for its educational institutions, etc. In short, the sovereignty of Germany would be suspended for a period of fifteen years, and, at the end of that period, the population would decide for itself its fate by a plebiscite.

The other solutions proposed remove the country from German sovereignty without placing it under French sovereignty, and give it a French governor appointed by the League of Nations. I prefer the regime which I have just explained, which places the country under a provisional regime while awaiting the result of the plebiscite.

Lloyd George. It seems to me that this plan responds to the objections raised by M. Tardieu in the memorandum which he presented to us about the earlier plan.

Clemenceau. I understand that German sovereignty would be suspended and administration assigned to the League of Nations. But in this case, why would the League of Nations not give a mandate to France?

Lloyd George. I would point out to you that the entire economic life of the country would already be in the hands of France.

Wilson. I am seeking with all my abilities a solution which would satisfy you and satisfy me; I see no acceptable one with the abolition of German sovereignty. The declarations that we have made, the commitments which I have undertaken, promise France reparation for the wrong done her in 1871. Perhaps it would have been better to have said: "The wrong done to France in Alsace-Lorraine," or any other formula which would have included the violation of the rights of France in 1815. But only the Treaty of Frankfurt[1] was mentioned, and we are bound by what we have said.

I cannot return to the United States and say to the American people: "After examination, we found it easy to go back on our word." They would answer that we had committed ourselves by the terms of the Armistice and by the declarations that we made at the time it was signed.

I asked you to help me find a path in your direction. I have taken

---

[1] That is, the treaty between France and the German Empire signed at Frankfurt on May 10, 1871. It concluded the Franco-Prussian War.

many steps to meet you; do not make it impossible for me to help you as much as I can.

Lloyd George. The most important thing for France is to have the coal of the Saar.

Clemenceau. That depends upon which public you are thinking of; obviously it is true of the French industrialists. But the rest of France attaches another importance to the Saar region.

Lloyd George. A solution must be reached which gives France the coal of the Saar without creating new causes for conflict in the future. The document criticized by M. Tardieu did not fulfill that condition, and M. Tardieu's criticisms were just. But the same objections do not apply to what President Wilson has just proposed. The sovereignty of Germany would be suspended for the period of fifteen years which must precede the plebiscite. During these fifteen years, France will have time to recover economically and, at the end of that period, the Saar region will be so closely tied to France by its interests that it will go voluntarily toward her.

Clemenceau. I make no objection to this plan. I would only like to have it carefully examined by my advisers.

Lloyd George. It could be interesting to see immediately the impressions of the experts.

Messrs. Tardieu and Headlam-Morley are introduced.

Clemenceau. President Wilson is going to explain a new solution to the problem of the Saar.

Wilson. The decision that we have to take must be based upon our public commitments. We declared that "the wrong done to France in 1871"—and not "in 1815"—must be redressed. I want to act scrupulously toward Germany, for the very reason of her own lack of scruple.

The last solution proposed would actually give the country to France, with a plebiscite which would be hardly more than a formality. To that there is an objection that is for me insurmountable, and here is what I propose.

German sovereignty would be suspended for fifteen years and transferred, in fact, to the League of Nations, which would be represented in the Saar region by a commission which would receive a clearly defined mandate. Except for the economic administration, conferred on France under conditions which you know, the population would keep its laws, of which the commission could make necessary changes in order to accommodate them to the necessities of French economic control. At the same time it would play the role of a court of arbitration. At the end of the fifteen-year period, a plebiscite would take place to settle in a definitive manner the question of sovereignty.

I said to M. Clemenceau that I am obliged to remain faithful to my Fourteen Points, but without inflexibility, and going as far as possible to meet your legitimate wishes. We are not prejudging the question of sovereignty; we are leaving it in suspense.

Tardieu. Would the commission have administrative power?

Wilson. And legislative.

Tardieu. How does this plan differ from one of Mr. Lloyd George's proposals, which would transfer administration to the League of Nations?

Lloyd George. One of our hypotheses did in fact envisage the administration of the country by the League of Nations, with Germany theoretically retaining sovereignty.

Clemenceau. The difference is that here sovereignty is transferred to the League of Nations for fifteen years.

Wilson. It is not necessary to use the word "sovereignty." We would only say that the administration of the country passes into the hands of the League of Nations for the contemplated period.

Lloyd George. Is it not necessary to have M. Tardieu and Mr. Headlam-Morley study your text?

Wilson. What I bring you is only an outline. I asked Professor Haskins to formulate the plan with all the required precision. It is preferable to discuss a well-defined text. As I see it, the essential point is to leave open the question of sovereignty and to assure respect for local institutions, except as it might perhaps be necessary to accommodate them to the necessities of the new economic regime.

Clemenceau. In your system, will it be possible to remove Prussian civil servants?

Wilson. The commission will have all powers.

Headlam-Morley. But would not the population be under a dictatorial regime? Would it have a voice concerning education and all its local interests?

Lloyd George. There would be a great advantage in giving it the beginnings of local autonomy on local questions; nothing will assist it more in detaching itself from Prussia. A population which has acquired these kinds of rights does not want to be deprived of them.

Wilson. It is very difficult for us to decide here, in this room, what will best suit this population. Let us give the commission the power to organize a system of local government agreeable to the population itself. Would it like an assembly? Would it be content to have organizations to deal with educational questions or other questions of local interest? It is to that population itself that belongs the right to make it known.

Tardieu. It will not be represented in the Reichstag?

Wilson. No, no more than in the French Chambers.

Tardieu. We will confer, Mr. Headlam-Morley and I, and we will come back to present our report to you.

Clemenceau. I foresee a satisfactory agreement on these terms.

Wilson. The most important thing is to adjust this plan to the economic conditions upon which we have already agreed.

Messrs. Tardieu and Headlam-Morley withdraw.

President Wilson reads aloud the report which has been submitted about M. Nansen's proposal,[2] suggesting the organization of the victualing of Russia by neutral nations.

The greatest difficulty appears to be that of tonnage.

Lloyd George. From the political point of view, the most important question is the one of distribution in the interior of Russia. I do not see any organization which can take charge of this distribution, except the Bolshevist government. Does M. Nansen care nothing for giving Lenin the power that would be conferred upon him by distribution of hundreds of thousands of tons of wheat to the Russian peoples?

Wilson. I think that an essential condition is that the distribution be made by a neutral organization.

Lloyd George. We should draw our inspiration from the one which functioned in Belgium under the direction of Mr. Hoover.

Wilson. I do not think that the Russians will oppose that. Lenin will be only too happy to find someone to take on this responsibility. M. Nansen thinks that it is possible to establish an organization of this type. He only asks us to accept the principle and to assist him in the measure as much as we can. I can understand the interest of the neutrals in that matter: they can establish very interesting commercial relations with Russia for the future.

Lloyd George. Another point which we must think about inserting into the treaty is the interdependence of debts. Germany must know to what countries she owes reparation.

Wilson. Since we will ask Germany to pay everything which she is materially capable of paying, I think that the problem of distribution can remain among ourselves.

Orlando. As far as Italy is concerned, I would comment that German submarines sank our ships in the Mediterranean, that a great number of our prisoners died in German camps, that the bomber planes which devastated our cities were German planes. At the beginning of the war, the Emperor of Austria had given the order not to bomb open cities; from the moment of their appearance, the German aviators showed zeal in doing just that. The Austrian high command having forbidden them to do it, they protested violently; it is a German prisoner who boastingly recounted it.

[2] That is, the following document.

After the disaster of Caporetto, the Germans took half the plunder.

I recognize that, by right, the question of interdependence of debts should be debated among ourselves. The Germans will certainly have no right whatever to protest; we will consider that interdependence in crime entails interdependence in obligations.

Lloyd George. I do not wish to make an objection; I would simply like to suggest a question which the Germans could ask. Italy suffered losses before declaring war on Germany; must Germany be held responsible for them?

Orlando. Even if this question is answered in the way the Germans may wish, the matter is of no great importance. The war was so long that that makes no great difference.

Lloyd George. What is the date of your declaration of war against Germany?

Orlando. June 1916.

Lloyd George. Germany could repudiate all responsibility for the thirteen first months, from the end of May 1915.

Wilson. This question must be definitively settled among ourselves.

Reading and approval of the text on responsibilities studied during the previous session.

Mantoux, I, 203-208.

From Herbert Clark Hoover

Dear Mr. President: [Paris] 9 April 1919.

I have had a very brief discussion of Dr. Nansen's proposition for relief of Russia with Lord Robert Cecil, Mr. Clementel, and Signor Crespi. My understanding of their views is as follows:

(a) They express themselves as in agreement in principle with the proposals.

(b) They point out that the finance of this relief must be settled. The only immediate method is for the Russian authorities to pay from their own resources.

(c) The shipping required must be found. Possibly neutral governments could be persuaded by Dr. Nansen to undertake the transport as their interest in the project is of large moral and political order. In any event, proposals should not go forward unless the Associated Governments are prepared to make the necessary sacrifice of shipping as a last resort.

(d) The exact boundaries of Bolshevik Russia would need be determined, if fighting is to be stopped.

To save time, I have amended the proposed reply to Dr. Nansen,[1] which was handed me so as to include these points and I am transmitting this note to each of the above gentlemen, and no doubt if I do not correctly express their views they will notify their Premiers.   Faithfully yours,   Herbert Hoover.

TLS (WP, DLC).
[1] It is missing in both the Hoover Archives, CSt-H, and WP, DLC.

A Memorandum by Jan Christiaan Smuts

SECRET.   *Paris, April 9th, 1919.*

THE MISSION TO AUSTRIA-HUNGARY.
(Report by General Smuts.)

The mandate which I had from the Great Powers was principally concerned with the working of the two Austro-Hungarian armistices of the 3rd and 13th November, 1918, and the regulation of a neutral zone between the Hungarian and Roumanian forces. It was, however, impossible to enquire into these subjects without hearing and seeing much about other matters more or less closely connected with them. The advance of Bolshevism into the territories of former Austria-Hungary, the position and attitude of the new Governments, and the urgent economic questions arising out of the carving up of the old Empire and the drawing of new economic and political frontiers,—all these and similar matters were continually pressed on my attention. As I was asked to report generally I shall, therefore, in this report deal as briefly as possible with all the matters which are of special interest to the Great Powers or which call for urgent action.

I left Paris on the 1st April, spent the 3rd April in Vienna, mostly in discussions with the Allied Military Missions, and spent the 4th and 5th April in Buda-Pesth, holding five meetings with members of the Hungarian Government, besides seeing the Allied representatives still remaining in the Hungarian capital, and many other people. On the 6th April I was again in Vienna making further enquiries, during which the Chancellor, Dr. Renner,[1] and the Foreign Secretary, Dr. Bauer,[2] came to see me; on April 7th I saw President Masaryk at Prague and had a very helpful exchange of ideas with him; and on the evening of that day I left Vienna for Paris, after having an interesting conversation with Dr. Schumpeter, the Finance Minister of the Austrian Government.[3] All my

[1] That is, Karl Renner.
[2] That is, Otto Bauer, prominent Austrian Social-Democratic leader.
[3] Joseph Alois Schumpeter (1883-1950), already by this time a world-renowned economist. He was Professor of Economics at Harvard from 1932 until his death.

time was thus fully occupied, mostly in conference by day and travelling by night.

I. *The Armistices and the Neutral Zone.*

When I left Paris it was not quite certain what had become of the Allied Missions at Buda-Pesth after the accession to power of the Communist or Sovyet Government, and whether the new Government was at war with the Allies or still adhered to the Armistices of 3rd and 13th November. On these questions I was soon reassured. Our Missions had mostly left Buda-Pesth and those members who had remained behind were quite safe and still in communication with the new Government. A memorandum on the treatment of the Allied Missions prepared by the members of my staff from information collected at Buda-Pesth, as also a memorandum regarding the political conditions in Hungary is annexed hereto. (See Enclosures V and VI.)[4] The Government considered itself as still at peace with the Allies and professed to adhere to the two Armistices, but was in considerable doubt and fear as to the future attitude of the Allies towards the Sovyet Government and whether war would not be declared against them. They were, therefore, very much elated and even amazed that an emissary of the Great Powers had come to speak to them, and as the fact was obviously of great significance to the new Government they have in their numerous press communiques exploited it to the full. This risk was, however, well worth running, as it is certain that an important change has been brought about in the attitude of the new Government.

Before my arrival they were seriously apprehensive of the attitude of the Great Powers towards them, and although they had concluded no alliance with the Moscow Government, they were leaning heavily towards Russia for support against a possible hostile movement by the Great Powers. Now that this fear has been removed from their minds they are obviously more inclined to stand well with the Great Powers, and the danger of their joining with the Russians in an attack upon Roumania has not only been minimised but probably definitely removed.

The Hungarian Government are anxious to attend conferences with us, and to work out their future relations under our aegis, and have probably by our wise and conciliatory attitude been definitely deflected from any pro-Russian course. It is also certain that we could by wise counsel considerably modify the excesses of their communist policy, and thus prevent them from doing too much harm during the more or less short period of their power in Hun-

---

[4] *"Memorandum regarding treatment of Allied Missions and Subjects, by Hungarian Authorities"* and "OBSERVATION ON GENERAL SITUATION IN HUNGARY" T MSS (WP, DLC).

gary. For there is no doubt that they will have to go. As a Government they are very weak. They consist entirely of Jews and do not represent more than the large Jewish proletariat of Buda-Pesth. Outside the capital their authority is very small, if not practically non-existent, and in Buda-Pesth itself they represent only a minority.

Hungary is not a Bolshevist country, and with wise handling on the part of the Great Powers will not long persist in a Bolshevist policy. The Government is sharply divided into a moderate socialist element and an aggressive Communist section, of which Bela Kun, at present Chief Commissary both for War and Foreign Affairs, and a personal friend of Lenin, appears to be the leader. The Communists are in the ascendant for the moment, but the excesses of their confiscatory policy in Buda-Pesth are already leading to a change of feeling, and a re-action is certain to follow, although perhaps not before the Communists have tried their hands at some more disastrous social experiments. In spite of these temporary aberrations and excesses, however, it seems to me clear that the wise course for the Great Powers to pursue is to keep Hungary in hand and away from Russia, and this can best be done by the steady following of the policy initiated by my Mission.

The bourgeoisie and moderate elements are cowed today, but they are sure to revive; and if we remain on the spot this revival will come all the sooner and be all the healthier.

After these general remarks I proceed to deal with the Armistice negotiations. As I have said, the Hungarian Government appear to adhere to the two Armistices, and more particularly to that of the 13th November which especially concerns them. Indeed they assumed throughout the discussion that they were bound by the Armistices, and the only difficulty with them was as to the extent of our constantly growing demands for further withdrawals of the Hungarian forces, culminating in the final request of Colonel Vyx which precipitated the fall of Count Karolyi. The Vyx line had been settled by the Military Representatives at Versailles after hearing the Roumanian case. But it was drawn so far back in Hungarian national territory, and included so much more than the Powers are ever likely to demand from Hungary, that I was prepared to curtail it considerably in order to arrive at a fair and reasonable settlement.

I therefore took as my basis the future political frontier between Hungary and Roumania which had been agreed upon in the Territorial Sub-Committee of the Peace Conference dealing with these questions, and drew a line well to the West of this frontier, and thus covering all the Hungarian territory which the powers are likely to demand for cession to Roumania. To this line I induced the Hungarian Government to agree, and I also agreed to their insistent request that the neutral zone thus created should be occupied not by Roumanian but by French, Italian, British and, if possible, American contingents. On this basis an agreement was drafted and ready for signature. At the last moment, however, the three Ministers negotiating with me (Garbai, Prime Minister, Kunfi, Commissary for Education and Bela Kun) asked for time to consult the remainder of their colleagues.

The result of this consultation was that on the evening of the 5th April they returned to me with a document, which, while agreeing to the proposed line and neutral zone, made it a condition of their withdrawal that the Roumanians should also withdraw to the line of the River Maros which had been provided for in the Armistice of 13th November. The Roumanians had, as a matter of fact, advanced far beyond this line, and my acceptance of this condition would have meant trouble with the Roumanians. I could not possibly agree to it; and I declined therefore to accept the document proferred by these Ministers. They have since published it and I annex a copy together with a copy of my draft agreement which was not agreed to (see Enclosures I and II).[5] I also annex copies of my telegrams of the 4th and 6th April (see Enclosures III and IV)[6] which explain the course of my negotiations with the Hungarian Government.

Although no agreement was thus reached in regard to the central zone, it is clear that the Hungarians agreed to it, but attached an irrelevant condition which I could not accept as being insulting to the Roumanians.

It is, therefore, probable that if the ultimate political frontiers were fixed along the lines advised by the territorial sub-committee, which follow the ethnological line as closely as possible, we shall have no great difficulty in inducing the Hungarians to accept it.

They are, however, very much upset at our continually increasing demands under the Armistice which, while thoroughly antagonising their people, appear at no stage to approach finality anf [and] therefore combine all possible disadvantages. They prefer a definite and final settlement once for all of political boundaries, so that they may know the worst and adjust themselves to it.

I consider this attitude in all the circumstances justified and

[5] "Draft Agreement submitted to Hungarian Government," and "Note handed in by Hungarian Government, but returned to them by General Smuts," T MSS (WP, DLC).

[6] "TELEGRAM FROM GENERAL SMUTS, BUDA PESTH. TO MR. BALFOUR. April 4th, 1919," T MS (WP, DLC), printed as Appendix II to the minutes of the Council of Four printed at April 7, 1919, 3:30 p.m.; and "Paraphrase of telegram from General Smuts to Mr. Balfour," April 6, 1919, T MS (WP, DLC), printed as Appendix I to the minutes of the Council of Four printed at April 8, 1919, 11 a.m.

would recommend that steps be immediately taken for the settlement of the future political frontiers between Hungary and Roumania.

In order that what has happened may not appear like a rebuff to the Great Powers I would—subject to the reservation mentioned below—be in favour of the policy embodied in my draft agreement being carried out, in spite of the refusal of the Hungarian representatives to sign it. That is to say, I would favour the occupation of the zone adopted by me by troops of the Great Powers, but not by Roumanian troops, and the raising of the blockade as soon as the zone has been occupied. The trainload of fats now held up at Agram should be allowed to proceed to Buda-Pest as an earnest of our benevolent intentions. The Hungarian Government in that case to be notified that the draft agreement is being carried out as an Armistice measure, but that political boundaries will be settled by the Peace Conference at Paris. If it could be added that the Hungarian case would first be heard, so much the better.

I am, however, loth definitely to recommend the execution of the draft agreement and the occupation of the new neutral zone because I am not conversant with the local military situation, nor do I know what troops would be required for the operation and whether, apart from the Roumanian forces, the Great Powers have sufficient troops left on that front to undertake the operation with safety. I, therefore, make the reservation that this question should first be submitted for the advice of the Allied High Command at Constantinople.

II. An Economic and Territorial Conference.

The Hungarian Government were at great pains to explain to me that, as a Soviet Government, they were not so much interested in territorial questions. Hungary had had an imperialist policy in the past which was one of the causes of its present downfall, and the national sentiment among the people was still strong. The present Government, however, occupied a somewhat different standpoint, and would prove more accommodating on the question of territorial boundaries than a Government inclining more to the Right could be expected to be. They were, however, profoundly interested in the economic questions which were arising from the great territorial re-adjustments. As it was now proposed to cut up Hungary, the country would cease to be an economic entity and would, indeed, become economically impossible, unless its position was safeguarded by economic arrangements with the neighbouring States. They were completely cut off from the territories occupied by the Czecho-Slovak, Jugo-Slav, and Roumanian forces, and both from a food and an industrial point of view the position was becoming impossible.

They, therefore, pressed very strongly that the settlement of political frontiers should be accompanied by a simultaneous arrangement of urgent economic questions, and they pointed out that an economic settlement would help to render the territorial settlement palatable. This view was so obviously reasonable and sound that I was not surprised to find the members of the German-Austrian Government who saw me also strongly pressing for it. I, therefore, decided to go to Prague in order to ascertain the views of President Masaryk. He agreed that a settlement of urgent economic questions would be most necessary, and that a conference of the neighbouring States, comprising the former territories of Austria-Hungary, should be called immediately for the purpose. President Masaryk considered it, however, essential that his Conference should meet under the aegis and presidency of the Great Powers.

In view of this general agreement, the necessity for such a Conference needs no further argument from me. It is, indeed, not only Hungary's position which will become economically impossible under the new territorial arrangements. German-Austria is in as difficult a plight, and unless she can obtain suitable economic arrangements with her neighbours, she must inevitably be driven into the arms of Germany. Besides, the drawing of new lines across the old Austria-Hungary and the prevention of intercourse and communications in which the various States are freely indulging, destroy all chance of the resumption of normal industrial and commercial life, strangle the economic life of these large areas, and by rendering impossible all production and industry, are making it a sure bredding [breeding] place for Bolshevism and anarchy. As it is both the duty and interest of the Great Powers without any further delay to put an end to this intolerable situation, it is incumbent upon them to call the economic Conference for which these States are clamouring.

By assuming their proper rôle of guidance and help in this grave emergency the Great Powers will not only contribute to the salvation of the suffering peoples of this part of Europe, but they will establish their moral authority and enhance the prestige of the League of Nations, which will in its early stages, be mostly an expression of the joint action of the Great Powers.

The question is what form this Conference should take. As I have said, the Hungarian Government were most anxious that economic arrangements should be settled and announced *pari passu* with territorial frontiers, and they therefore asked that the neighbouring States should be called together under the presidency of a representative of the Great Powers to discuss both boundary and economic questions. They suggested Vienna or Prague as the place of meeting.

The Great Powers will have to decide whether and where such a Conference should be held. To my mind, the balance of convenience is in favour of Paris as the meeting place. In the first place, the Hungarian and Austrian representatives will, in any case, have to be invited there for the signature of the Peace Treaty. In the second place, the Prime Ministers of Czecho-Slovakia and Roumania, as well as the representatives of Yugo-Slavia are delegates to the Peace Conference, and it would in many respects be inadvisable to call them away from their duties at Paris in order to attend a Conference at, say, Vienna. In the third place, this meeting should be held not only under the presidency of a representative of the Great Powers, but also under their influence and general control, and for that purpose Paris is obviously the only suitable place.

If the Conference idea is accepted I would suggest that business be expedited by the parties being called together not in a general debating conference but in pairs (Roumania and Hungary, Hungary and Czecho-Slovakia, German-Austria and Czecho-Slovakia, etc. etc.) with the representative of the Great Powers as chairman and umpire, and that all questions be rapidly disposed of. The countries represented would state their respective territorial cases, and in the absence of agreement between them, the chairman or the Great Powers on reference from him could finally decide on all points of difference. The economic question could, at the same time, be agreed upon between the parties and could probably be announced simultaneously with the signature of the Peace Treaty. The economic questions to be dealt with should be those of most urgent necessity, such as freedom of inter-communication and exchange of necessary raw materials and urgent currency questions.

III. *A Mandatory of the Great Powers for Austria-Hungary.*

I have said enough to show that a sufficient community of interests will remain among the new States arising from the old Austro-Hungarian Empire to call for a common handling of them by the Great Powers. The new Governments are mostly weak, and some of them are sadly deficient in administrative experience. The peoples are actuated by old historic feelings of hostility towards each other. Without the helping hand and the wise guidance of the Great Powers, I am doubtful whether any of them would achieve success in the immediate future, and their failure will involve grave dangers to the peace of Europe. I, therefore, consider it advisable that for the present, and for some time to come, the Great Powers should, in addition to their individual representatives with the several States, have a common representative of high standing, under whom all the Missions of the Great Powers should work, and who would be responsible for advising the Great Powers, and later on the Executive Council of the League of Nations, on all important questions involving the common interests of the new States. Such an official would not only represent the Great Powers, but also be the symbol of the surviving unity and the common interests which would continue to bind together the new States. His experience and authority would be necessary to help them to solve the very difficult questions of common concern which otherwise might well prove beyond their powers. He would inaugurate a policy of Conferences between them to discuss common interests which while teaching them new habits of co-operation, would help to allay the old historic bitternesses which still survive.

In that way German Austria might be kept away from union with Germany, and Czecho-Slovakia might thus be secured from the danger of being outflanked by such a union. Co-operation among the new States under the beneficent unifying guidance of the Great Powers would raise a happier temper among the peoples, and in this new atmosphere the load of despair, which is now one of the most fruitful sources of Bolshevism, would be lifted from the minds of the peoples. Nothing has impressed me more in all my enquiries on this Mission than the urgent need of common action by the Powers in all these countries and of their joint representation through a mandatory of wide experience and authority.

On a number of special points brought to my attention in the course of my enquiries, I shall circulate separate notes.

I summarise the foregoing report by making the following recommendations:

I. (1) That subject to (2) a force representative of the four Great Powers should at once be sent to occupy a neutral zone as defined in the draft agreement with the Hungarian Government.

 (2) That the military question whether, apart from Roumania, the forces of the Great Powers available on that front are sufficient for the purpose, should first be submitted to the advice of the High Command at Constantinople.

 (3) That the Hungarian Government should be notified that this occupation is being carried out as an Armistice measure without prejudice to the future political frontiers. It should, if possible, be added that the Hungarian Government will be given an opportunity of stating their case to a Conference before their frontiers are finally laid down by the Great Powers.

(4) That as an earnest of our good intentions, the train-load of fats now held up at Agram should at once be sent to Buda-Pesth.

(5) That so soon as the occupation of the neutral zone has been pacifically accomplished, the blockade against Hungary should be raised by the Allied Powers.

II.   That a Conference should at once be summoned to meet, preferably in Paris, under the direction and guidance of the Allied Powers, at which the component States of the former Austro-Hungarian Empire should meet together to discuss territorial adjustments and to arrive at an agreement regarding mutual economic and financial problems.

III.   That apart from their respective representatives in the several component States of the late Austro-Hungarian Empire, the Allied Powers should be represented by a joint representative of high position and experience under whom all the Missions of the Great Powers would work. This representative to advise the Great Powers and later on the Executive Council of the League of Nations on all important questions involving the common interests of the new States, and to assist the States themselves in reaching and maintaining agreement on questions of mutual interest and necessity.

(signed) J. C. Smuts.

T MS (WP, DLC).

William Graves Sharp to Frank Lyon Polk

[Paris] April 9th, 1919.

URGENT. 8075.

The following is confidential. An interest amounting almost to a sensation was caused by the announcement appearing in all the morning papers that President Wilson had ordered the GEORGE WASHINGTON to proceed to Brest with a view to returning to the United States at the end of another two weeks. Both the NEW YORK HERALD and the DAILY MAIL (Paris Editions) have contained each morning in their editorial columns the most ungenerous kind of criticism, while not much less severe has been that of several of the French Papers. This announcement comes as the culmination of a series of unusually vindictive criticism on the part of a number of the prominent journals in Paris directed against the work of the Peace Conference. Only the virulence and the puerility of some of these criticisms deprive them of the force they might otherwise have. Those in the DAILY MAIL in particular are so violent in their tone as to, in my judgment, presage a positive reaction. All this criticism had tended greatly to discredit the Conference in the

minds of that class of people who let the newspapers do their thinking for them.

I am sure that among a good many people there is a just indignation over the occasional criticisms of President Wilson and America in general that are indulged in through the columns of these
papers.

Calling at the Embassy today, Madame Ribot[1] said that her husband, the former Premier, has declared that, upon the occasion of
President Wilson's visit to England last winter, instead of the arms
of France which ought to have received him in cordial welcome,
he would be taken in by the arms of Great Britain.

One is, however, encouraged to find frequently an expression
from the more conservative men in high places to the effect that
the Allies must not use their victory in such a way as to ensure
another war, notwithstanding this wide-spread dissatisfaction over
the doings of the Conference.

It would be worth knowing to be able to uncover the actuating
motives of some of these journals which have sought in every way
to discredit the work of the Conference in advance. I do not think
such motives would stand the light of the day, as an observer of
the happening of unusual events over here during the past four
years.

At the Hotel Ritz today, the Ministers of the South and Central
American Republics gave me a farewell luncheon. The Brazilian
Minister[2] voiced an expression of hearty goodwill toward America,
which all those present greatly applauded. In the next pouch, I
shall send a copy of his remarks. I felicitated them upon the fact
that their countries were united with ours in the bonds of common
sympathy and aspirations as never before and urged them to trust
President Wilson in my reply, which was warmly greeted. The fact
is that these ministers have always manifested the greatest confidence in the intentions of America in the war, both in private conversation and in public utterance. They seem to recognize that our
interests are identical in every respect. Directly or indirectly, I have
never heard of any one of my South and Central American Colleagues uttering anything but the most friendly sentiments for the
President and the policies which he champions.

I believe no particular importance should be attached to the big
parade of working men and socialist followers on last Sunday in
protesting over the verdict of the Jaures case.[3] It was simply an
ebullition of the hour and will not have any lasting effect. The very
fact that it was allowed full freedom of action deprived the movement of any untoward consequences. It is, however, undeniable
that the Premier is not as strong as heretofore among his own party

followers. I think he undoubtedly has in mind to leave the Ministry upon the signing of peace, and he intimated to me within the last few days that his time for retirement would soon come.

Sharp.

T telegram (WP, DLC).
    [1] Mary Burch (Mme. Alexandre) Ribot; daughter of Isaac N. Burch, at one time one of the leading bankers of Chicago.
    [2] Olyntho de Magalhaes, Brazilian Minister to France.
    [3] A jury had just acquitted Raoul Villain, a deranged nationalist, of the murder of Jean Jaurès, the preeminent French Socialist leader, on July 31, 1914.

Joseph Patrick Tumulty to Cary Travers Grayson

The White House, April 9, 1919.

#53. The ordering of the GEORGE WASHINGTON to return to France looked upon here as an act of impatience and petulance on the President's part and not accepted here in good grace either by friends or foes. It is considered as evidence that the President intends to leave the conference if his views are not accepted. I think this method of withdrawal most unwise and fraught with the most dangerous possibilities here and abroad, because it puts upon the President the responsibility of withdrawing when the President should by his own act place the responsibility for a break of the Conference where it properly belongs. The President should not put himself in the position of being the first to withdraw if his 14 points are not accepted. Rather he should put himself in the position of being the one who remained at the Conference until the very last demanding an acceptance of his 14 principles. Nothing should be said about his leaving France, but he ought when the time and occasion arrive re-state his views in terms of the deepest solemnity and yet without any ultimatum attached and then await a response from his associates. In other words let him by his acts and words place his associates in the position of those who refuse to continue the Conference because of their unwillingness to live up to the terms of the armistice. Then the President can return to this country and justify his withdrawal. He cannot justify his withdrawal any other way. Up to this time the world has been living on stories coming out of Paris that there was to be an agreement on the League of Nations. Suddenly out of the clear sky comes an order for the GEORGE WASHINGTON and unofficial statements of the President's withdrawal. A withdrawal at this time would be a desertion.

Tumulty.

T telegram (WP, DLC).

To Tasker Howard Bliss

My dear General Bliss: Paris, 9 April, 1919.

Marshal Foch overstates the matter when he says that the detail of officers requested was *formally* agreed to,[1] but he is right in substance, for it was informally agreed to, and I authorize you to inform General Pershing that I approve Marshal Foch's request, the officers to serve for the specific purpose named and only so long as the movement of General Haller's troops by rail from the Rhine to Poland continues.

I note what you say about the general relation of our troops to the Allied Commander-in-Chief and shall try to act upon your advice, which is in every way sound.

Cordially and faithfully yours, Woodrow Wilson

TLS (T. H. Bliss Papers, DLC).
[1] See T. H. Bliss to WW, April 8, 1919.

From the Diary of Colonel House

April 9, 1919.

Orlando desired to see me again today but I put him off until Friday. It is a mere waste of time since I cannot come to his way of thinking. The whole interest centers around Fiume. It seems quite clear that they do not care for Fiume itself or for its Italian population, but the purpose is to strangle it in order to make a greater Trieste. I am told that a majority of the Adriatic tonnage is other than Itlaian [Italian], and that if the Jugo-Slavs have a port of their own, Trieste is bound to suffer.

I have the usual consultations today with the experts, particularly, the financial and economic sections.

Last night General Bliss was much excited over what he termed the casual way in which the President was deciding military matters. He thought if he were not careful, he would have impeachment proceedings. He showed great excitement and it was with difficulty I calmed him. I am sorry to see him getting as garrulous by word of mouth as on paper.

Lord Robert Cecil and I have been exchanging notes[1] on the question of naval armaments. My letter to him of today, which I sent to the President for his approval before sending it to Lord Robert, is an important part of the diary.[2] It is to be noted that I promise nothing whatsoever. It is merely the spirit of his suggestion that I am accepting. I particularly reserve and insist upon the completion of our past naval program. It is only the future with which we deal.

I sent Gordon to the President with the letter. He seemed to think it was a little stiff and that the British would not like it. However, he made no suggestions as to change. Lord Robert Cecil thought well of it, but said he would have to take it up with the Prime Minister in the morning. I prophesy that the P.M. will catch the point and will disapprove it.

[1] See R. Cecil to EMH, April 8, 1919.
[2] It is printed as the following document.

From Edward Mandell House, with Enclosure

Dear Governor—   [Paris] April 9 [1919].

This is about the kind of letter Cecil wants. He may object because I made clear that we intend carrying out the old programme. Both Gregory and Miller have read the letter and approve it.
                              Affectionately,   E.M.H.

Quick action is necessary because of our League of Nations meeting tomorrow night. This letter is of course in lieu of the one I was to send Lloyd George.

ALI (E. M. House Papers, CtY).

E N C L O S U R E

Edward Mandell House to Lord Robert Cecil[1]

Dear Lord Robert: Paris, April 9th, 1919.

Thank you for your letter of April eighth with the spirit of which I am in cordial agreement. If the kind of peace is made for which we are working and which will include a League of Nations it will surely be necessary for us to live up to its intentions, and in order to do this I am sure you will find the United States ready to "abandon or modify our new naval programme," *by which I understand you to mean our programme not yet provided for by law, as our naval bill for the next fiscal year has not yet passed.*[2] I am also certain that you will find us ready and willing to consult with the British Government from year to year regarding the naval programmes of the two Governments. The President himself has, I think, made our intentions in this matter quite clear in a statement which he made to the London Times on December twenty-first[3] in which he said: "It is essential to the future peace of the world that there should be the frankest possible cooperation, and the most generous understanding between the two English-speaking Democracies. We comprehend and appreciate, I believe, the grave problems which the war has brought to the British people, and fully understand the special international questions which arise from the fact of your peculiar position as an Island Empire."

I am sending this letter with the President's approval.

I am, my dear Lord Robert,

Yours very sincerely,   E. M. House.

CCL (E. M. House Papers, CtY).
  [1] The following letter was partly based on a draft by Cecil: Hw MS, dated c. April 8, 1919, E. M. House Papers, CtY. About the drafting of House's letter, see Miller, *My Diary at the Conference of Paris*, I, 229-30, and VIII, 138-47. See also the Diary of Gordon Auchincloss, April 9, 1919, T MS (G. Auchincloss Papers, CtY).
  [2] Words in italics added at the suggestion of David Hunter Miller.
  [3] Wilson's interview is printed at Dec. 18, 1918, Vol. 53.

From William Shepherd Benson, with Enclosure

My dear Mr. President: Paris, April 9, 1919.

I am sending you herewith a paper which we have prepared after much thought and study.

If I may presume to say so, I urge you to read it, as it will undoubtedly assist you in forming definite conclusions on this most important subject without consuming the time that would otherwise be necessary for independent investigation.

My own opinion is that the necessity for at least two approximately equal naval powers is absolute in order to stabilize the League of Nations. This fact should be recognized, and the United States should give it as a reason for building up and maintaining its Navy.

Sincerely yours,   W. S. Benson.

TLS (WP, DLC).

E N C L O S U R E

CONFIDENTIAL.

U. S. NAVAL ADVISORY STAFF, PARIS.

MEMORANDUM NO. XXV. 7 APRIL 1919

SUBJECT: UNITED STATES NAVAL POLICY.

There is no subject in connection with the League of Nations that has caused so much perplexity, both at home and abroad, as the apparent inconsistency of the United States in advocating a general reduction of armaments, while itself undertaking an intensified Naval Building programme.

It is natural that a hostile foreign press should seize upon this apparent inconsistency as an evidence of hypocrisy on the part of the American Government, which is accused of aiming to obtain an advantage over other Powers by inducing them to trust in the ideal strength of an unarmed League, while continuing itself to rely on the practical strength of an armed nation. We hope that the following examination of the subject will make clear to all that American aims are legitimate aims, and that the step America is taking is one demanded by world interest, and one that menaces the just aspirations of no Power whatever.

Every great change in world conditions makes it incumbent on each of the several States of the world to re-examine its special situation, and to determine from this examination the policies that will enable it best to fulfil its duties to the world and to itself. Such a change in world conditions has come and such a duty now falls upon us as Americans. There are many inter-related external policies which America must detemine, but this paper deals with naval policy only. Naval policy is a means to an end, a means designed to assist the State in the attainment of its international mission. This mission for the United States is two-fold—a duty to itself and a duty to the world.

   I. To promote and guard the interests of the United States in every way consonant with justice.

   II. To assist in promoting the welfare of the world.

We can make no progress in promoting our international interests, or in promoting the welfare of the world, except through international relations. Whenever we enter into such relations we meet with other national aims, with other national desires for the advancement of the interests of other nations. The result is in part a system of exchange of advantages between States. If all international relations were but systems of exchange of advantages and concessions, and if no advantages were sought by any State except on the basis of equal exchange, there might be no occasion for the use of force in international relations, but such is not the case.

The growth of populations, the developments of national character, changes in national life, all introduce at times insistent demands on other nations that are not consonant with the interests of those nations. As our principle is the promotion of national interests and world interests in harmony with justice, we have to consider how extra-ordinary international demands may be resisted where they are not just.

Just and friendly relations are stimulated when national aims may be attained through the reciprocal granting of advantages on an equitable basis. The aim, of course, on either side of a negociation is *profit* in some form or other. The natural aim is towards the maximum profit. This is as true in international negociation as in private negociation, so there is a constant tendency for nations to devise means for obtaining by negociation advantages as great as possible. The negociations of individuals and of corporations are governed by written law, which has a distinctly limiting influence on attempts to obtain unjust profits. When States negociate, they are free from the restraining influence of law and may exact every advantage which their position makes it possible for them to exact. On minor questions we expect them to apply equitable principles in their negociations, but when questions of great national importance are at issue, expediency rather than principle governs.

The question then becomes not so much a question of exchange of *advantages* as the acceptance by the weaker State of demands made, rather than submission to the penalties that otherwise would be inflicted by the more powerful State. In other words, the attention of the negociators is shifted from the principle of exchange to the principle of power, and decisions are arrived at by an estimate of relative power, and this whether force be used or not.

If Liberia cannot prevent occasional crimes within her borders, she is compelled to yield territory to neighbouring colonies as compensation, the alternative being still more drastic action.

If Japan cannot get from China the concessions she desires, she presents China with twenty-one demands and intimates that the exchange China has to make is the granting of those demands in return for the non-infliction on her of the alternative penalties of war measures. Potential military force slips in and closes the bargain that China maintains is an unjust bargain.

If England cannot get by the mild terms of diplomatic notes the decisions she desires regarding equal rights in the use of the Panama Canal, she presents a note that uncovers the idea of a military superiority sufficient to enforce what she considers a just decision.

When we examine our own world situation in the new order of things, we realise that all of our important international relations and all of our important international questions hinge upon matters relating to the sea and sea communications. We cannot advance our external interests, nor can we influence world policy, except by way of the sea. Practically all of our great commerce is sea commerce. If any foreign State desires to bring military pressure to bear upon us, it must be a pressure based upon possible operations by way of the sea. The attack of our Colonies, of our commerce, of our frontiers, depends first of all upon what happens at sea. Conversely if we desire to retaliate or to exert opposing military pressure, we must base our efforts upon our sea power.

In the past our naval position has derived great strength from the potential hostility of the British and German fleets. Neither the German nor the British fleet could venture abroad without grave risk that the other would seize the opportunity thus presented to crush a rival. This condition gave to America a position of special strength both in council and in decision, because her Navy was so strong that no other Navy could neglect its influence. All that is now changed. The German fleet has ceased to exist, with the result that we suddenly find the British Navy in a position of unparalleled strength. No navy is left in Europe capable of offering any real resistance to the British Navy.

Under present conditions the British Navy, with its world wide supporting organisation, is strong enough to dominate the seas in whatever quarter of the globe that domination may be required. We do not consider this a condition calculated to advance either our own just interests or the welfare of the world. A power so absolute that it may disregard other powers with impunity, is less apt to act with justice than if there be a balancing influence of force as well as of world opinion to oppose it. This is true within a league of nations as well as without a league of nations.

Even when force is not applied, the knowledge of its readiness is always an asset in negociation. The smooth and leisurely phrases of diplomacy derive their pungency from a vision of the force in readiness that lies beind them. Governments are influenced less by words than by material facts. We are conscious of this in every phase of the proceedings of the Peace Conference now in progress. Everyone, except ourselves, looks to British Naval Representatives for suggestions in naval matters and to French Military Representatives for suggestions in military matters. This phenomenon is the unavoidable tendency of the strong to dominate, and of the weak to accept domination.

Since we are considering naval policy as affecting American interests, and since the British Navy is the only Navy in existence that can threaten the American Navy, British policies have a peculiar interest for us.

Every great commercial rival of the British Empire has eventually found itself at war with Great Britain—and has been defeated. Every such defeat has strengthened the commercial position of Great Britain.

The constant effort of Great Britain through centuries has been to acquire control of the focii of the sea commerce of the world.

A present governing policy of Great Britain is the control and monopoly, so far as possible, of international communications. These include—

Submarine Telegraph Cables,
Radio Systems,
Commercial Aircraft,
Merchant shipping,
Fuelling facilities,
Fuel deposits.

The British negociations at the Peace Conference are conducted with these objects frankly in view. Their attainment is possible largely through British strength at sea. No-one can contend that such monopolies represent the promotion of interests that are just to all the world.

The possibility of future war is never absent from the minds of statesmen, so we see in the British negociations a very careful attention to the preservation of their present military domination of the sea. Among the measures they contend for are—

1. *The distribution of the German and Austrian Fleets.*
   COMMENT. Great Britain now has more than half of all the dreadnoughts of the world; if the German and Austrian ships are distributed on the most probable basis of *losses during the present war*, the United States would have to add to its Navy double the number of dreadnoughts it already possesses, or else remain an inferior naval power. In any case this perfectly logical policy of Great Britain, if carried out, will place her in a position of supremacy for many years to come.

2. *The razing of fortifications commanding waterways that Great Britain does not control.*
   COMMENT. This is a natural policy of a great sea power. Its object is to give, in time of war, the maximum possible freedom to that Power whose navy controls the sea. It is put forward as being a policy in the interest of freedom of the seas, but the true object is that given above.

3. *The most liberal possible interpretation of belligerent rights on the High Seas.*
   COMMENT. Very few people realise how reluctant the British are to codify maritime international law. They naturally prefer the absence of law in order that during war their Navy may have complete freedom of action. The absence of Maritime Law during the present war has led to an expansion of so-called belligerent rights that certainly would never be accepted by an International Congress. As an example, if Canada should attempt to gain her independence from Great Britain by force,

and if the United States remained neutral, it is the British contention that Great Britain could blockade every port of the United States and could so regulate our imports that we could spare none for exportation to Canada. This is not International Law, but an application of the law of force to neutrals. The only reply is the presence of a potential force that will secure the abandonment of the contention.

These proposals take on a special significance because of a recent pronouncement. At a time when all the world is seeking to form a League of Nations that will secure justice to great and small nations alike, the British Prime Minister announces that the British alliance with France will continue for ever.[1] In the Far East, Japan remains within the British alliance. We look in vain for any provision of the League Covenant that forbids such alliances. Such combinations seem to us to contain elements of grave danger and to demand of us extraordinary measures.

Our own present and prospective world position needs special consideration. We are setting out to be the greatest commercial rival of Great Britain on the seas. We know that increase of population, the development of our great national resources, and our lack of real dependence on the rest of the world, spread before us the promise of a greater future than any other Power may expect. The gradual realisation of this promise is bound to excite enmity and to cause unjust opposition to our expanding world interests. Heretofore we have lived apart, but now we are to live in constant and intimate relation with the rest of the world. We must be able to enter every world conference with the confidence of equality. We can have this confidence in but one way and that is by actually being equal to the greatest. The equality that counts in conferences as well as in conflicts is the equality of power, and specially for us the equality of sea power. Given that equality, our superiority of motive will attract to us a following that will mean better days in the world. But while we are weak we may expect the powers of the world to group themselves about strength rather than about the promise of a distant justice.

So far we have been considering the questions of naval policy more particularly from the standpoint of our just interests, but there is a higher standpoint still—the promotion of the welfare of the world, that demands with special insistence that the American Navy equal the most powerful navy in the world. At present the great international ideal is the League of Nations for the maintenance of international justice. The League is to operate through the asso-

[1] See n. 2 to the extract from the Diary of Ray Stannard Baker printed at April 9, 1919.

ciation of the Powers. Its decisions are to be arrived at by conferences of representatives of the Powers. It is unavoidable that in those conferences military and naval power will speak with a special authority. America stands for high ideals and desires above all to promote those ideals. The possession of power, and especially of the kind of power that is most effective in our international relations, sea power, will give to her proposals an importance and a probability of acceptance far greater than we could expect otherwise.

Whatever may be the eventual form of the Covenant of the League of Nations as adopted, it will undoubtedly contain as a fundamental idea of the duty of the League to restrain, if necessary, by the use of armed force, any recalcitrant member that endangers the peace of the world. It is obvious that the Covenant cannot be accepted as just, even in principle, unless it contemplates that the will of the League shall be imposed upon the strong as well as upon the weak. When we think of a recalcitrant member, we are too apt to think of Albania instead of one of the Great Powers, but the soundness of the League as a practicable working scheme must stand the test of its ability to restrain, if necessary, its strongest member. This cannot be done by a heteroge[e]nous combination of naval craft assembled by the nations of the League, unless in that assemblage there is one group of a single nationality that is equal in strength to the strongest navy. It happens now that that navy is the British Navy, but the principle does not depend upon nationality. Given that single groups of vessels, that navy of a single nationality equal in strength to the strongest, and we may be sure that the minor Powers of the League will furnish the additional force to swing the League to the side of justice against the efforts of a navy as powerful as any, whether that Navy be our own or the British Navy.[2]

We want the world League to be secure, to endure, and to establish a new order—the reign of law among nations. This cannot be brought about if some one Power is to dominate the decisions of the League by a world wide predominance of naval strength. We do not need to argue that whoever dominates the sea exercises more control over world policies than any other Power may do. As the interdependence of nations increases this dominance of sea power over world policies will become more and more complete. It is contrary to human experience to expect small weak nations, whose own immediate interests are not vitally concerned, to place themselves in military opposition to a strong power, even within a League of Nations, for the sake of principle, unless by so doing they find themselves ranged with another strong Power. If they

[2] This sentence *sic*.

depend upon sea communications to a special extent they will be governed by interests and side with the Power that can crush them the easiest.

As long as Great Britain insists on retaining her overwhelming naval force, the only answer for the purposes of the League is the building of an equal force by some nation capable of constructing and maintaining a fleet of equal strength and efficiency. The United States is the only power that is to-day financially and physically capable of building such a fleet, or of undertaking a future building competition with Great Britain.

It is not believed, however, that any competition in armaments is necessary. Once the principle of two equal naval Powers within the League is made clear to our own people and to the British public, a means will be found to maintain a parity of the two fleets with the minimum of burden to the taxpayer. Equality of the two fleets can be brought about by the destruction of the German fleet, the bulk of which would go to Great Britain on any probable scheme of distribution, and by a further reduction of the British fleet that, while leaving Great Britain ample strength to protect her world commerce and colonies, would still make it possible for the United States with a reasonable increase of its fleet, to equal the size of the British fleet.

It may be asked what would happen if the United States and Great Britain combined against the League. We need not be disturbed by this question. With satisfied ambitions the future interests of the United States demand only the continuation of world peace. Should we forget our ideals and attempt some day to support with arms the cause of injustice, it is highly improbable that our interests would march with those of Great Britain, and there would remain an equal force within the League to bring us to our senses.

The example of the United States in this war, and its present attitude towards nations dependent upon us for financial and economic support, can be relied upon to absolve us in the eyes of the world from the charge of Pharisaism when we assert our confident belief that the League of Nations will never have anything to fear from the United States.

With two navies of equal strength, the world would breathe free from the fear of a naval domination that has the power at any moment of threatening the economic life of any nation. The resulting mutual respect of Great Britain and the United States would go farther than anything else toward the establishment of just maritime law upon the high seas both in peace and in war.

The success of the League of Nations will rest in large part on the honesty, integrity and strength of the United States. The political and economic weakness of Europe as a result of the world war have thrust upon us the burden of imparting vital force to a Covenant that attempts to reconcile the conflicting interests of the world.

Our ability to sustain the League in its formative period and establish it eventually on a secure foundation will depend chiefly on the strength we give it to *resist the domination of any single Power*. We ourselves have no desire to dominate the League, but we believe it to be our duty to the world to make our counsels heard as attentively as the counsels of any other Power.

CONCLUSION

As one of an unorganised society of nations we need a navy equal to the greatest—

1. To guard our great and greatly growing interests.
2. To give our voice in the councils of the world the weight our world position warrants.
3. To give our ideals full expression and to obtain for them a just recognition in the development of the world organisation that is about to be undertaken.

As a member of the League of Nations we need a Navy equal to the greatest—

1. So that there may be within the League a power strong enough to restrain any Power whatever seeking unjust advantage by force.
2. So that the League may be relieved from the dominance of any single Power, and thereby ensure to it a greater stability and a greater probability of just administration.

We believe that a better way in which to obtain two equal navies in the world is for the British Navy to be reduced in strength, and for Great Britain and America to determine jointly from time to time what the strength of the two fleets shall be.

T MS (WP, DLC).

From Joseph Patrick Tumulty

[The White House] April 9 [1919]

No. 55. A great number of your friends here feel that the position of the United States in matter of indemnity and reparation, which is a paramount question with European nations and only of indirect interest to us, will solidify the opposition of England, France, Italy and Belgium to a League of Nations. Our friends believe that any necessary sacrifice to assure a League of Nations should be made.

Your supporters would be happy if you could throw upon the other nations the burden of exacting indemnities and at the same time win their support to a League of Nations.   Tumulty.

T telegram (WP, DLC).

From Vance Criswell McCormick

My dear Mr. President: Paris. April 9, 1919.

I have just received a letter from my newspaper manager in Harrisburg, in which he has written me an account of a meeting in Philadelphia, which I thought might interest you. Senator Medill McCormick spoke at a Saint Patrick's Day meeting there, and made a vicious partisan attack, and had considerable difficulty in being heard on account of the attitude of many of those present who resented his attack. When your name was mentioned, there was tremendous enthusiasm, and the crowd cheered for many minutes. A number of the Philadelphia papers carried the story. This, coming from Philadelphia, is an indication of the sentiment in the states. I have been watching the press closely from a distance, and I am convinced that the sentiment of our people is with you.

Very sincerely yours,   Vance C. McCormick

TLS (WP, DLC).

From Tasker Howard Bliss, with Enclosure

My dear Mr. President: Paris, April 9th, 1919.

I enclose herewith a telegram received this afternoon in the cipher of the Secretary of War (Mr. Baker).

Sincerely yours,   Tasker H. Bliss.

TLS (WP, DLC).

E N C L O S U R E

April 8th [1919]. CONFIDENTIAL.

NDB 11. For the President.

Paragraph 1. The Philippine Mission now in Washington bearing a message of goodwill, respect, and gratitude from all the inhabitants of the Philippine Islands to the Government and people of the United States, regret their inability to convey this message to you in person, but are happy and gratified at the reassuring statement(s) you left in the hands of the Secretary of War which was (were) delivered to them on the occasion of their official visit to the Secretary of War.[1]

Subparagraph A. The Filipino people are gratefully conscious of what you have done and are doing in their behalf and of your efforts to secure for them as for the rest of mankind the blessings of liberty, justice, and democracy. The avowed policy of the United States to grant the Philippines their independence which has brought friendly and affectionate relations between the American and Filipino peoples and won for the United States the unqualified support and loyal cooperation of the Philippines during the war is not only a positive evidence of the faith of the American people in the principle(s) of self determination, but it is also an object lesson to the world.

Subparagraph B. In the name of the Filipino people as well as in our own, we beg to express to you our cordial and respectful greetings wishing you success in the noble task you have before you in helping to bring about a lasting peace to the world based upon the rights of every people, whether great or small, to have an independent existence and enjoy free and unhampered self development.

Subparagraph C. It will be a pleasure to the Mission to communicate to the people of the Philippine Islands your message as transmitted by the Secretary of War and your own feelings as translated by him, which, we are sure, will instill in them fresh hopes and will evoke in their hearts feelings of deep gratitude.

For the Mission, Manuel L. Queson, Chairman.

T MS (WP, DLC).
[1] See WW to NDB, March 3, 1919, Vol. 55.

From the Diary of Dr. Grayson

Thursday, April 10, 1919.

The President and Mrs. Wilson and I called on the Queen of Roumania[1] in her suite at the Ritz Hotel at 9:30 this morning. The President was obliged to make an early visit owing to the big business which faced him during the day, beginning with a conference with the Council of Four at 11:00 o'clock at the temporary White House.

We were introduced to the Queen by her lady-in-waiting,[2] after which the lady-in-waiting withdrew, and there was no one present

[1] That is, Marie.
[2] She cannot be identified.

except the Queen, the President and Mrs. Wilson, and myself. The Queen, who is an English woman, greeted the President by saying: "I appreciate this honor so much. I am delighted to see that you have recovered from your illness." The Queen is a tall, well-proportioned, very handsome lady. She is of the blonde type. She was dressed in excellent taste, wearing a gray gown with slippers to match. She wore a beautiful string of pearls, and two beautiful earring pearls, and a pearl ring.

The Queen said: "Mr. President, you know that I am not a constitutional Queen. I was married at the age of seventeen and was taken to Roumania; and, incidentally, I had to work like a man. But I have the advantage of being able to do things and say things, and not to be held responsible by the constitution of Roumania. This, you know, gives an advantage over most Queens." She said this in a more or less humorous fashion. The Queen said: "I told this to Mr. Orlando of Italy and he seemed to think that it was not only amusing but a very convenient thing, not to be a constitutional Queen." She was a very free talker and said to the President: "You are here in a very perplexing and complicated situation, because I realize that everybody wants the impossible, and they look to you to give it to them. And you certainly have my sympathy. Not only do they expect you to settle all of the indemnity questions, annexations, but they even want you to draw the boundary lines, which I know is a very unpleasant and unpopular task. I am extremely interested in your propositions concerning the League of Nations, and coming from a small country I am wondering what effect it will have upon the small countries." The President told her that they would be benefitted by it from the fact that they would have the support and cooperation of the large countries.

The Queen said: "Mr. President, you are doing wonderful things for the world, and I hope you will not think that it is not being appreciated by the people of the world, notwithstanding the fact that the Paris papers are blaming you for all the delays." She continued: "While the Conference may not consider it a question of great importance at this moment, to my mind the determination of the boundary lines is one of tremendous importance to the people concerned, because they want to know what is theirs and under what government they are going to be. They will be very unrestful until they know under whom and where they are living. I think the people are paying you a great tribute because it is almost universally accepted that whatever you determine they will be satisfied with because they have the supreme confidence that you will do the just and right thing. These boundary lines are of particular interest to the smaller countries." The President thanked her for her generous expressions, and said: "As a matter of fact, I feel sometimes now that in helping to determine the boundary lines of the states of Europe, I am getting my revenge for the difficulty which attended my study of geography while I was a boy." The President thus very cleverly edged away from a discussion of boundaries which it was very plain to be seen the Queen had hoped to bring about, probably with an idea in her mind of bringing up the Roumanian situation, and especially the extension of Roumania towards Bulgaria.

The Queen made another attempt to get back to the boundary question with the President, when she brought up the subject of Bolshevism and its spread. She told the President that in her opinion Bolshevism would be hard to check, unless the boundaries of the several states were so adjusted as to satisfy the people themselves. The President asked the Queen whether she did not believe that one of the compelling reasons for the spread of Bolshevism was the old system of hoarded property and unworked land. The Queen said in reply that while this undoubtedly was one of the reasons and the big reason, yet Bolshevism was a most horrible thing inasmuch as it constituted nearly everything unlawful. As an instance of this, the Queen said that she knew that one of the Bolshevist doctrines was that all women under forty years of age were to be made the common property of the state and could remain with their husbands only two days in each week. The Queen was going into detail in her denunciation of this system when the President skillfully changed her train of thought by saying: "May I ask you to give me a little history of your Prime Minister?"[3] The Queen said: "I am glad you mentioned that because I am going to ask that you give him a private audience because it would mean much to his prestige politically in Roumania to have an audience with you. He is a good man but you will find him a tiresome, sticky and tedious individual. But a man of much ability. He is frequently attacked by the opposition party in Roumania, who claim that he fails to perform and to carry out promises which have been made. However, when they raise this point I always tell them that Roumania is a country of opportunity and if they themselves can perform the duties of the government better than the Premier they are welcome to take his place." To this the President replied: "Well, to reduce it to American slang, you say to them either put up or shut up." The Queen again made it plain that she would appreciate very much an audience for the Prime Minister. The President said he would very gladly receive him but, he pointed out to her, that his slate was very much filled

[3] That is, Ionel (or Ion I. C.) Brătianu.

these days and it was hard to get a moment of leisure. He commented on the fact that one of the reasons for his calling so early this morning was because he could not find any other time to do so. Turning to me the President said: "And, in addition, my doctor here demands some of my time."

At the end of about twenty minutes Mrs. Wilson showed evidence of being ready to depart and the Queen turned to her and said. "I am looking forward with very much pleasure to coming to luncheon with you tomorrow. How many shall I bring with me?" Inasmuch as it had been expected the Queen would come alone there was a slight pause while the President and Mrs. Wilson looked at each other, and then both of them said: "Why, bring whoever is agreeable to you from your party." The Queen then said: "Well, I will bring with me my two daughters[4] and my lady-in-waiting and the gentleman-in-waiting,[5] and if I may also my relative [blank] of Spain,[6] who has just arrived in Paris today."

As a parting thrust, showing that she realized that she had been sidetracked in her earlier conversation, the Queen said to the President: "I hope that you will talk international affairs and let me speak of Roumania all during the lunch."[7]

Enroute back home, I asked the President what he thought of the Queen, to which he replied: "She is a brilliant woman; in conversation a rapid repeater, and she is traveling in high gear this morning."

At eleven o'clock the President attended a meeting of the Big Four. He lunched with Mrs. Wilson and myself at 1:00 o'clock, and attended another meeting of the Council of Four in the afternoon. Good progress was made at these meetings.

In the evening the President attended a meeting of the League of Nations committee at the Hotel Crillon. The President moved the insertion in the covenant of an article which safeguarded the Monroe Doctrine and provided that nothing in connection with the League of Nations could affect it. The President made what was termed by those who heard it to be the greatest speech he had ever made in his career. Unfortunately, no one of the President's staff of stenographers was present to take it, and the copy as finally submitted could not be characterized as official. However, I secured a copy of it, which is as follows:[blank]

[4] Princesses Elisabeth and Marie.
[5] Probably Gen. E. Ballif, the Queen's longtime aide-de-camp, whose given names are unknown to the Editors.
[6] Beatrice, Marie's youngest sister, wife of Alfonso, Infante of Orleans-Bourbon.
[7] For a brief account of this conversation by the Queen, see Terence Elsberry, *Marie of Romania: The Intimate Life of a Twentieth Century Queen* (New York, 1972), p. 161.

The President made a second speech when the question of the seat of the League of Nations came up for consideration. The Belgian representatives had asked that the League be permanently located at Brussels. The President, however, favored Geneva, and in a strong speech declared that it would be a big mistake to have the seat of the League in the devastated section of Belgium, whereby there would always be a constant incentive to hatred and it would be impossible to forget the enmities that the war had engendered.

The President did not return home until after 12:00 o'clock.

Today I sent the following message to Secretary Tumulty at the White House in Washington as explanatory of the conditions which had developed over here and which apparently Secretary Tumulty misunderstood because of the distance he was away from us:

Paris, 10 April, 1919.

Tumulty,
    White House,
      Washington.

Have shown your message to the President.[8] From your side of the water your points are well taken but he has formed his ideas through immediate contact with actual conditions on this side. The French are the champion time killers of the world. The George Washington incident has had a castor oil effect on them all. More progress has been made in the last two days than has been made for the last two weeks. Am spending all the time I can in guiding correspondents and showing them every attention. I confer with Grasty every day. The President is working too hard following his recent illness. To know that things are going on and not properly handled and yet be responsible for them makes him feel that the worry and anxiety thus caused does him more harm than actual participation. This is a matter that worries me. If his health can hold out I am still confident that he will win handsomely. Am keeping as cheerful a front as possible over here.

Grayson.[9]

[8] That is, JPT to C. T. Grayson, April 9, 1919.
[9] The "original" of this telegram is in the J. P. Tumulty Papers, DLC.

From the Diary of Ray Stannard Baker

Thursday April 10 [1919]

Today to Versailles to decide on press arrangements for the signing of the treaty—which may never be signed. They propose rubbing salt in the Germans' wounds in the same Hall of Mirrors in which the Peace of 1870[1] was signed. I talked with Mr. Wilson this evening. He looks very old & worn. Things are not going well. He is working too hard—2 conferences of the Big Four to-day & the League of Nations Commission this evening until midnight.

[1] Actually, the proclamation of the German Empire on January 18, 1871.

From the Diary of David Hunter Miller

Thursday, April 10th [1919]

At 11 o'clock I went up with Dr. Haskins to the President's House, to attend a meeting of the Four. The President and Mr. Lloyd George were there when we arrived, and shortly afterwards M. Clemenceau and Orlando came in. While waiting, Dr. Haskins and I had some talk with Tardieu, who said that the last clause regarding the re-purchase of the coal mines by Germany at the end of the fifteen years was not agreed to and the French experts were against it. We told him that this was a serious difficulty, but that the other questions which he mentioned as to sovereignty, etc., could be fixed. The President then came out and asked us into the meeting. Those present besides the Four, were Headlam-Morley for the British, Dr. Haskins and myself for the Americans, Tardieu of the French, and Prof. Mantoux, an interpreter. Mantoux did not interpret much, except for Orlando, beside whom he sat. I sat between Orlando and Tardieu. The paper which the British had gotten up[1] was sent to us this morning, was gone through in detail and the pencil notes on it are the changes made at the meeting, except that the separate article which is to come after 5 is not in the text. I handed my copy to the President, and he suggested that it be changed from a mixed commission to the Reparation Commission. This was adopted. Clemenceau reserved until tomorrow on Articles 3, 4, and 5, of Annex III, as he said he wanted to talk to his experts. The question of the extent of the territory then came up and Haskins' map was produced and discussed. My understanding of the agreement was that the coal area was to be included, with such changes as might be needed for local arrangements.

I told the President that the formula of the principles of boundary which he had discussed could be prepared, which would be sufficient and which would be necessary in any event. He said that this was to be done.

Miller, *My Diary at the Conference of Paris*, I, 233-34.
[1] Printed as the following document.

A Memorandum[1]

SECRET.   Paris, 9th April, 1919.

THE SAAR BASIN.
Draft Proposals.

A. In order to award to France compensation for the destruction of the coal-mines in the north of France and as a part payment of the amount due for reparation from Germany to France, the full ownership and exclusive right to the exploitation of the coal-mines in the Saar Basin is ceded to France.

B. In order to assure the rights and welfare of the population and to secure to France the necessary freedom of exploitation of the mines, Germany agrees to the clauses set out in Annex I and II.

C. In order to make in due time permanent provision for the government of the Saar Basin in accordance with the wishes of the population, France and Germany agree to the clauses set out in Annex III.

ANNEX I.

This is identical with the Economic and Administrative articles already communicated. They will be subject to such changes as will be necessary if Annex II is approved.

ANNEX II.

1. Germany, ⟨while preserving her sovereignty,⟩[2] renounces in favour of ⟨the Allied and Associated Powers as trustees of⟩ the League of Nations *as trustee* all her rights of ⟨administration⟩ *government* over the territory defined in Article I.

2. The League of Nations shall appoint a Commission to administer the district.

3. The Commission will consist of five members chosen by the Council of the League of Nations, of whom one shall be a citizen of France, one ⟨a German subject, the latter⟩ a⟨n⟩ *native* inhabitant of the Basin of the Saar *who is not a French subject*, and the others chosen from three countries other than France or Germany. The members of the Commission shall be appointed for one year; they can be removed and replaced by the Council of the League of Nations.

4. The Chairman of the Commission shall be appointed for one year from its members by the League of Nations; he can be re-appointed; he will be the executive of the Commission.

5. The Commission shall have all those powers of ⟨administration and police⟩ *government* hitherto belonging to Germany, Prussia or Bavaria, including the appointment and dismissal of all functionaries and the creation of such administrative bodies as it deems

necessary. In particular, it will have full control of the administration of railways and canals. The decision will be given by a majority vote.

The use of the property in the Saar Basin belonging to the Imperial German Government, or the Government of any German State will pass to the Administration of the Saar Basin, subject to reasonable compensation.

6. The territory shall be governed subject to the provisions of Annex I. in conformity with the existing law; amendments necessary, whether for general reasons or for bringing the said laws into accord with the said provisions, shall be decided and put into effect by the Commission after consultation with the local representatives in such a manner as the Commission shall determine. No law or amendment thereto can affect or limit the provisions of Annex I.

7. The local civil and criminal courts of the territory will continue. Civil and criminal courts will be appointed by the Commission to judge appeals against the decisions of the said local courts and to decide all matters which cannot be determined by the local courts. The Commission will determine the competence of this last named jurisdiction.

8. The Commission will alone have the power of levying taxes in the district; these taxes will be exclusively applied to the local needs of the district. The present fiscal system will be maintained as far as possible. No new tax will be imposed without consulting the elected representatives.

9. The inhabitants will retain their present nationality, but no hindrance shall be placed in the way of those who wish to acquire a different nationality. They will preserve under the control of the Commission their local assemblies, their religious liberties, their schools, their language. The right of voting for local assemblies will belong without distinction of sex to every inhabitant above the age of 20 years. On the other hand there will be no right of voting for a representative whether in the Reichstag or in the Prussian or Bavarian Chambers or in the French Chamber.

10. Those of the inhabitants who desire to leave the district will have every facility for retaining their real estate or for selling it at a fair price and for freely taking their moveable property with them.

11. There will be no compulsory military service or voluntary recruiting or fortifications. A local gendarmerie for the maintenance of order may alone be established.

12. The Commission shall have power to arrange under conditions which it shall determine for the ⟨representation⟩ *protection* abroad of the interests of the inhabitants of the territory.

13. The Commission shall have power to decide all questions which may arise regarding the interpretation of these articles.

ANNEX III.

1. At the termination of a period of fifteen years, there shall be held a plebiscite in the above defined territory under the control of the Commission. The vote shall be held by communes or districts. In the vote there shall be no discrimination on the ground of sex. None shall be admitted to the vote except inhabitants domiciled in the territory at the time of the signing of the present peace. The regulations as well as the date for the voting shall be fixed by the Executive Council of the League of Nations in such a way as to secure the liberty and secrecy of the vote.

2. The League of Nations shall decide on the sovereignty of the territory in conformity with the wishes of the inhabitants thus expressed. Germany agrees to cede to France, in accordance with the decision of the League, all that territory to which the decision of the League applies.

3. On such of the said territory as shall remain German under the result of the decision of the League of Nations, the property rights of the Government of France under these articles shall be taken over as a whole by Germany at a price payable in gold which shall be determined by three appraisers or a majority of them, one of whom shall be appointed by Germany, one by France, and one who shall be neither a German nor a French citizen by the League of Nations.

4. The price so fixed shall be payable within [blank] after the determination thereof and unless the said price so fixed shall be then paid by Germany to the Government of France, the territory which would otherwise remain German shall thereafter be occupied and administered by France as an integral portion of French territory.

5. The provisions of the foregoing article shall be subject to any agreement which may have been reached between France and Germany with regard to the rights of France before the time fixed for the payment above mentioned.

6. As soon after the plebiscite as possible the League of Nations shall make regulations for bringing to an end all provisions for a special regime in the territory in question, having due regard to personal and property rights.

The value of the property ceded to France under these articles shall be credited as a part payment of the amount due for reparation from Germany to France. This value shall be determined by ⟨a mixed⟩ *the Reparation* Commission appointed by the Council of the League of Nations, on which both France and Germany shall be represented and which shall make its decisions by majority vote.

T MS (WP, DLC).
  ¹ This document is printed at April 10, 1919, because this is the date on which Wilson emended it.
  ² Words in angle brackets deleted by Wilson; words in italics added by him.

Mantoux's Notes of a Meeting of the Council of Four

April 10, 1919, 11 a.m.

Wilson. The text which was to detail the suggestions which I made yesterday is in our hands, and, for my part, I give my approval to it.

Clemenceau. I read in Article 1 that sovereignty remains with Germany. I would like to replace this sentence by another which would indicate that sovereignty is transferred to the League of Nations.

I would like you to well understand my feelings, as I am doing my utmost to understand yours. I have no hatred against the Germans as individuals, and I hope that in the future it will be possible for the two nations to be reconciled, if the Germans behave decently. But we cannot abolish our memories. For us this question is not simply one of interest. Sarrelouis was established by Louis XIV and Landau suffered a historic siege in the epoch of the Revolution during a German invasion. Your point of departure is the principle of reparation. Mine is reparation—and something else. That matters little, provided that we arrive at the same end.

Lloyd George. As was said yesterday, the simplest thing is not to place the word "sovereignty" here and to write simply: "Germany surrenders the administration of that region to the Allied and Associated Powers as trustees of the League of Nations."

Wilson. I would observe that the Allied and Associated Powers do not constitute a legal personality, while the League of Nations will be one. I would prefer to write that Germany renounces the administration of that region in favor of the League of Nations.

Clemenceau. Would this not seem to leave sovereignty to Germany?

Lloyd George. It seems to me that the formula is satisfactory.

Clemenceau. Not to me.

Orlando. It is a question of words. The word "administration" in French and in Italian has too narrow a sense, which corresponds to that of the German word "Verwaltung." If we wish to avoid an ambiguity, which M. Clemenceau fears, "administration" must be replaced by "government."

This proposal is adopted.

Messrs. Haskins, Headlam-Morley and Tardieu are introduced.

Wilson. Our desire is to avoid raising the question of sovereignty. Do you see any drawback in eliminating this word, and in replacing "administration" by "government"?

Haskins. I see no objection.

Reading of the text by M. Tardieu (summary):

The League of Nations appoints a commission charged with the government of the region. This commission is composed of five members, one of whom is French and one a native of the region. These five members are appointed for one year and eligible for reappointment. The League of Nations designates the president.

The commission possesses all the rights of government. It appoints and dismisses officials. It can create all the administrative and representative bodies judged necessary. The use of property of the state other than the mines is transferred to the League of Nations, *in return for compensation.* (After an exchange of views, this last phrase is deleted.)

Except for the clauses relating to the mines and means of communication, the local laws will be maintained. The commission can permit the formation of local assemblies elected by universal suffrage, women included. The inhabitants cannot be represented in any assembly outside the territory under discussion. The commission will be charged with the protection of the interests of the inhabitants in foreign countries.

At the end of a period of fifteen years, a plebiscite by commune or by district, by universal suffrage, for both sexes, will decide the final fate of the country.

Clemenceau. It is a question here of giving the right to vote, at the time of the plebiscite, to the "inhabitants": there could be foreigners among them.

Tardieu. The vote is reserved to persons domiciled in the region of the Saar at the time of the signing of the peace.

Lloyd George. I would favor specifying a shorter period of residence. You have every advantage in permitting Italian or Slavic workers (who are numerous in all the great German industrial regions) to take part in the plebiscite. Many will vote in your favor.

Tardieu. The work force in the region of the Saar is overwhelmingly of local origin. I do not see why foreign elements which have come to work temporarily in the mines should have the right to vote, and I would fear that Germany would take advantage of this clause to introduce into the country elements which would be hostile to us.

Orlando. I agree with M. Tardieu; the right to vote must belong to citizens, not to immigrants; the latter are not qualified to decide the fate of a country to which they have only recently come to settle. On the basis of such an arrangement, Germany could use all the corrupt means of which she is a past master.

Lloyd George. I am not of that opinion. I remember that a question of this kind was raised in the Transvaal, before the South African War. That war could not be avoided because President Krüger demanded a residence of fourteen years—instead of seven, the figure demanded by the British government—to grant newcomers the right to vote.

Tardieu. If the period of obligatory residence is reduced to five or seven years, I believe there will be a systematic invasion of German elements.

Reading of the article providing, in the case of a return of part of the territory to Germany after the plebiscite, for the repurchase of ownership of the mines by payment in gold.

Clemenceau. France must have the right to keep ownership of the mines and to sell only if she wishes.

Lloyd George. One of our main reasons for supporting M. Tardieu's arguments and objections to the preceding plan is the desire not to separate ownership and sovereignty; we have recognized that that could lead to frictions and continual dangers. If government was restored to Germany and ownership remained with you, these dangers could not be avoided.

Tardieu. That is a very strong argument. But in fifteen years, the relations between France and Germany might be very different from what they are today. Moreover, if it is true that recognition of our right to sell preserves, by the same token, our right to ownership, I must inform you that the coal of the Saar is necessary for us as coal and cannot be replaced by gold. If this necessity is acknowledged, we must be assured of a supply of coal; and a stipulation to this effect must be part of the treaty.

Wilson. I hope that relations between France and Germany can improve. But the reasons for conflict, if sovereignty and ownership are not linked, will remain the very ones which you have explained to us.

As for furnishing coal, we are told that the coal of the Saar was consumed entirely in the region or in the factories of Lorraine. There is no reason to assume that that will change.

Lloyd George. This coal seems to be of such quality that it transports poorly and can only be used in a rather limited area. The coal mines of the Saar can find their market only in Lorraine. Further north, they would meet the crushing competition of coal from Westphalia. Moreover, in fifteen years France will have recovered use of her mines in the Nord. I do not see the usefulness of a stipulation such as M. Tardieu suggests.

Tardieu. We could impose upon Germany the obligation to continue to furnish coal.

Haskins. Those supplies will take place by the force of events. Exchange between the iron ore of Lorraine and the coal of the Saar will continue, whatever be the stipulations of the treaty.

Tardieu. But meanwhile, I take the liberty of insisting on the guarantee which to me seems necessary.

Wilson. The strongest obligation is the economic obligation, and it exists in this case. It would be an error to transform it into a political obligation which would last for fifty years or more. What would you do if Germany made an agreement and then refused to keep it? Would you declare war on her for that?

Clemenceau. I do not know in advance, in the event that the plebiscite should divide this region, what proportion of coal would return to Germany. My opinion depends upon concrete facts, about which I would still like to consult my experts. I ask you for twenty-four or forty-eight hours in which to respond to you definitively. I am sure that we will reach an agreement.

Lloyd George. Think also about what I have said concerning the right to vote. As a friend of France, I advise you to require only a residence of five years. There will be Italian workers, for example, coming in great numbers to work in the region; do you not think that they could be a favorable electoral element?

Orlando. May I take the liberty of declaring myself against the right of Italians to vote in that region. They are Italian citizens; why should they participate in the exercise of a right which should be reserved to the true inhabitants?

Before breaking up, the meeting examines the map of the Saar Basin. It is agreed that the frontier of that region will be drawn around the limit of the present coal basin, with the modifications necessary to allow it to include established administrative units.

Mantoux, I, 209-13.

From the Diary of Vance Criswell McCormick

April 10 (Thursday) [1919]

After lunch we went to President's house to discuss with him question we had been discussing all morning, namely, should the United States be represented on the Commission of Reparations of the Allies to collect the debt and estimate claims against Germany. Baruch and I took the negative; Davis trimming but the President had previously made up his mind that we were committed to looking after interests of weak nations and in keeping a hand on the financial situation in Europe as well as protecting our own interests in the question of international exchange, etc., and our own only real reason for pulling out would be a selfish one in looking out for our own interests alone. I am not yet sure he is right and Baruch was not convinced.

At 4.00 P.M. we went to sessions in the larger room with Lloyd George, Clemenceau, Orlando, Bonar Law and other advisers. The above gentlemen were delighted when the President announced we would join the Commission if desired. The Chiefs were all in good humor and spirits, much better than at last meeting, which was rather strained. They discussed whether the vote of the proposed Reparation Commission should be unanimous in the event of the cancellation of the amount Germany was to pay and on the amount of the first installment of bonds to be issued by Germany as a guarantee. President agreed to both, the latter, however, to be fixed in the instructions to Commission before Peace Treaty signed and sub-committee instructed to fix amount at once.

Printed copy (V. C. McCormick Papers, CtY).

Hankey's and Mantoux's Notes of a Meeting of the Council of Four[1]

I.C.-170Q   President Wilson's House, April 10, 1919,
4 p.m.

1. M. KLOTZ, at the request of President Wilson, explained the reason of the Meeting being held. As a result of a Meeting held on the previous Monday,[2] a Committee had been formed to consider a Memorandum by Lord Sumner[3] in regard to the constitution of

---

[1] The complete text of Hankey's minutes is printed in *PPC*, V, 71-79.
[2] See the minutes of the Council of Four printed at April 7, 1919, 4 p.m.
[3] This memorandum is printed in Philip M. Burnett, *Reparation at the Paris Peace Conference from the Standpoint of the American Delegation* (2 vols., New York, 1940), I, 822-24. For its discussion by the committee, see *ibid.*, pp. 870-71.

the proposed Inter-Allied Commission, which was to determine the amount of damage for which compensation is to be made by enemy States under Article 3 of the Articles already agreed to.

LORD SUMNER had proposed a text which he said was open to amendment. The French Delegation wished to raise three points of principle.

PRESIDENT WILSON suggested that it was premature to bring points even of principle before the Supreme War Council before the full report of the Committee was available, and a final effort had been made by the Committee to settle the points themselves.

MR. LLOYD GEORGE suggested that there was some advantage in considering points of principle even before the Commission had reported. It had always been agreed that if the experts could not reach unanimous conclusions the Supreme Council should take the matter up. He understood that the following two points of principle were raised; one, as to whether the United States of America could participate in the Commission at all; two, question of a bond issue.

M. KLOTZ added, three, the question of unanimity by the Commission in regard to the manner in which any balance remaining unpaid by the enemy should be dealt with.

2. PRESIDENT WILSON said that the first point was not one of principle at all, and he could accept it at once. If the arrangements for the Commission were sound, the United States of America would participate. Otherwise, they would not.

3. MR. LLOYD GEORGE said that this settled the first point. As regards the question of unanimity, he reminded the Supreme Council that this had been agreed to at the meeting held at the Rue Nitot on Monday afternoon, April 7th. He confirmed his recollection of what occurred by reading the following extract from the Secretary's notes of that Meeting:

"The principle of unanimity in the instructions by the Allied and Associated Governments to the Commission in regard to the manner in which any balance remaining unpaid by the enemy should be dealt with, was accepted subject to a reservation by Colonel House, who said that he had no authority from the President to settle the matter."

PRESIDENT WILSON suggested it was premature to try and settle questions of this kind before the report of the Committee on the whole subject was available. Already the Supreme Council were being brought into the work for which the Committee had been appointed. He did not consider this a right or wise procedure. On the question of unanimity, what he had previously agreed in consultation with his own experts, although he had not finally decided the point until the report on the whole subject was available, was that unanimity was essential in regard to the cancellation of any part of the enemy debt.

§Mantoux's notes:

Wilson. The constitution of the commission is still being examined by our delegates. I just said that, if this constitution seems to me established upon an acceptable foundation, the United States will participate in the work of that commission. But the subcommission's report is not yet ready, and our participation will depend upon the merits of the plan that it offers us. That is why I am not yet in a position to tell you whether or not the decision in the case you mention must be or must not be taken unanimously.

My opinion is that the decisions must be taken by majority, except in the case of a complete cancellation of part of the debt. What surprises me, because this appears to be your own desire as well, is that our experts have not seen to what extent we have agreed.§

(President Wilson read from a document prepared by the United States experts as a draft for his consideration, but which had not been circulated.)[4]

MR LLOYD GEORGE AND MR BONAR LAW said that if this was his view, there was no more to be said, since all were in agreement.

MR LLOYD GEORGE pointed out that two of M. Klotz's points had now virtually been settled.

M. LOUCHEUR asked if this decision meant that a majority vote would suffice to decide the means of payment. Supposing for example a majority of the Commission were to decide that half the amount for reparation was to be paid in marks, would a majority vote suffice in such a case?

MR. BONAR LAW explained that M. Loucheur's suggestion was that in fact by some such decision as he had quoted as an example, the Commission might by a majority remit part of the payment although by their constitution they would be prevented from doing so directly.

PRESIDENT WILSON pointed out that the raising of this point illustrated his whole objection to the present discussion. An isolated question of this kind was brought forward and was at once found to possess many ramifications. To a member of the Commission who was fully conversant with all aspects of the subject, these ramifications were familiar. He, himself, however, not being so conversant with the subject was unwilling to express an opinion on an incomplete document. He was prepared to say, however, that

---

[4] Five such drafts are printed in *ibid.*, pp. 877-79, 893-95, 896-98, 903-905, and 919-21. However, the context indicates that Wilson read from either the second or the third of these drafts.

with regard to any remission of part of the enemy's debt there must be unanimity. He was not prepared, however, to agree in an incomplete scheme, and as yet, no complete report had been presented.

M. CLEMENCEAU said he had had doubts as to whether the question could be settled this afternoon, but he had brought it up because there had been a general desire that it should be raised. As the report was not complete, however, he was prepared to postpone further discussion.

MR. LLOYD GEORGE pointed out the advantages of hearing the Experts and deciding in their presence if possible. The Experts he pointed out had been arguing about these questions for months. Eventually, however, they always came up against big questions which they could not take the responsibility of deciding. In the present instance there were one or two such points—for example—the question of a bond issue. If you remit it to the Experts they would be bound to come back and say that questions of principle were raised which they could not decide. He would like the Supreme Council to reach an agreement on points of principle and then give their instructions to the Experts.

PRESIDENT WILSON said he had no objection to discussing the Bonds scheme if one was ready to be discussed.

M. CLEMENCEAU agreed that the attempt should be made to discuss it.

§Mantoux's notes:

Lloyd George. We did not say that it was better to hear the arguments presented on each side by our experts, who have debated for months. But if they are not given guidance by decisions of principle taken by the heads of government, they will not manage to find a way out of their controversies. It is up to us to assume the responsibility for certain decisions. If we send the experts back to their work without having given them any guidance, they will not agree, because they will clash, as before, on questions of principle which they cannot possibly resolve themselves. It would be best to give them instructions, after a short conversation among ourselves.

Wilson. I see no objection to discussing immediately the question of bonds if we have a chance of reaching a conclusion. I did not hear it said that the subcommission is in such disagreement on this subject that it despairs of finding a way out.§

4. MR. LLOYD GEORGE repeated the suggestion he had made in personal conversation with President Wilson in the morning. His proposal was that instead of fixing in the Treaty of Peace a sum which Germany was to pay, the Commission itself should be instructed, after seeing all the claims, to fix the amount of the Bond

issue which should be made by the enemy. The British and French point of view in this matter was identical. If, for example, it was laid down now that there should be a first Bond issue of six thousand millions sterling, critics in Parliament would at once say "this is all they are to pay." If the amount was left to the Commission to fix, they could be given an indication not of the actual amount but of the principles on which the amount should be assessed. This would surmount some of the parliamentary difficulties which he and M. Clemenceau would have to face. Mr. Bonar Law who had already been confronted with this question in Parliament, was in full agreement with him.

M. KLOTZ said it was not so much a question of making provision for a certain amount as of fixing the first installment of what would have to be paid later. From a public point of view the Governments would be asked for guarantees. What were their guarantees? At the meeting on Monday at Rue Nitot he had suggested a lien on customs, ports, shipping etc. Mr. Lloyd George had replied "no not that." The Commission it was now proposed should agree on a figure. What guarantees had we that after two years the enemy would pay? How could Governments prepare their Budgets for 1920 and 1921? The inclusion of a figure of 150 billions of francs (6,000 million Pounds) would give great satisfaction to public opinion. In private transactions where there was no land or other property that could be mortgaged a bond was usually given; similarly that would be an advantage in this public transaction; if no figure was quoted public opinion would say "You have constructed a wonderful machine but you have no coal for it." An issue of bonds would give great satisfaction both to the public and to Parliament.

MR. LLOYD GEORGE said that his suggestion was that the Commission should immediately, after examining the claim, announce the amount of an immediate issue of bonds to be made by the enemy. He did not think that M. Klotz could have apprehended his proposal.

M. KLOTZ asked whether Mr. Lloyd George considered that a Commission could be constituted soon enough to meet immediately and to announce the amount at the very moment of the signature by the enemy of the Treaty of Peace.

MR. LLOYD GEORGE replied that this depended on how soon the Nations had their claims ready.

PRESIDENT WILSON asked what use it was proposed to make of the bonds.

M. KLOTZ said that the Commission would retain the bonds. It must carefully avoid distributing quantities of bonds at once to different nations. This would lead to great dangers. Each Nation, however, under his scheme, would know how much it would get and could issue the bonds retained by the Commission as a sort of collateral for a part of its financial operations during the next two years. At the end of the two years a distribution of the bonds would be made. On the date of the signature of the Treaty of Peace Germany would hand over bonds for Six thousand Million Pounds. Although the Commission would not make a distribution Nations could raise credit on the bonds. In a word, the Nations would not receive the bonds to sell but would issue them as collateral for the purpose of getting credit.

MR LAMONT said that this question had been discussed by a special Committee, which had been very largely in accord on all points except as to M. Klotz's proposed amount, namely 30 milliards of dollars (6,000 million pounds). He (M. Klotz) had said that this was only a suggestion as a basis for consideration. The only difference that he could see between M. Klotz and Mr Lloyd George was that the former wanted to name the sum now, and Mr Lloyd George did not.

PRESIDENT WILSON said that his understanding of his conversation with Mr. Lloyd George was that he had not doubted for a moment the desirability, if not the necessity, of an issue of sufficient bonds to sustain the credit of the nations concerned. What they doubted was the advisability of stating the sum arbitrarily, for it was only arbitrarily that they could do it at the present time. He agreed, however, that the Commission should be empowered to determine the sums of the bonds to be immediately issued by the German Government.

MR LAMONT said that the United States Delegates had intended to propose that the Commission should meet within a week of the signature of the Treaty of Peace.

M. CLEMENCEAU asked if they would meet and decide?

PRESIDENT WILSON said it would decide if it had the data in its hands.

M. ORLANDO suggested it would take six months to collect the claims.

MR LLOYD GEORGE said that it would not take so long to collect provisional claims.

PRESIDENT WILSON said he was informed that France was the only country that had not yet put in its figures.

M. CLEMENCEAU said the reason of this was partly the extent of the figures, and partly because of the earnest desire of France not to exaggerate.

M. KLOTZ said that France would give a figure very carefully drawn up and without any exaggeration.

§Mantoux's notes:

Klotz. In short, it is only a matter of fixing a down payment for the total sum to be collected. From the parliamentary point of view, what we must fear is being asked this question: "Where are your guarantees?" When I proposed to you to take the customs, ports, and railways as guarantees, Mr. Lloyd George said that he did not want such kinds of guarantees. Do we have others? The commission will fix a figure. But what guarantee do we have that, when this figure is transmitted to Germany in two years, Germany will not reject it? In the interval, how, by what means, shall we prepare our budgets of 1920 and 1921? We must be able to base them on something other than promises.

If we announce the figure of 150 billion francs, we satisfy public opinion; for we are taking care to say that it is only a down payment. Between private persons, in the absence of mortgages, the creditor asks the debtor to give him an acknowledgement of debt, a document which bears a signature and which is negotiable. We need a guarantee of that kind. From this point of view, a promise to pay 150 billions imposed upon Germany will satisfy public opinion immediately. If we announce no figure, we shall be blamed for having built a fine machine without putting coal in it.

Lloyd George. You are not exactly responding to my observation. Like you, I am a partisan of the issue of bonds; I feel as strongly about this as you do, and I am of the opinion that a figure must be announced. I am only proposing to reserve this task for the commission, which must carry it out, not at the end of its work, but from the moment of its constitution, or, more exactly, as soon as it has received all the claims, and before examining them in detail. I agree completely with you on the necessity of that issue to give us the guarantee that we need.

Clemenceau. In your opinion, should not our commission of experts have completed its work by the time the preliminaries of peace are signed?

Lloyd George. That depends upon the promptness with which all parties can submit their documents.

Wilson. What shall be done with the bonds once issued?

Klotz. Our proposal is that these bonds remain in the treasury of the commission. It would be very dangerous to place, within a limited time, an exorbitant sum at the disposal of any one of us. But each nation will know nevertheless what it has the right to, and can use the bonds as collateral for the credits it seeks to obtain during the first two years. On the day of the signing, Germany will give us bonds for 150 billions. The commission will not distribute them but will reserve for each of us the quantities necessary to permit him to get credit. In short, these bonds will not be negotiated, but the commission will permit them to be pledged in part.

Lamont. Our subcommission is not in disagreement about that. We are divided on the figure; but M. Klotz recognizes that 150 billions was simply a figure submitted for discussion. The only difference of opinion between us is that, according to M. Klotz, the figure must be announced immediately, while Mr. Lloyd George proposes that it be the commission which announces it.

Wilson. I do not doubt, any more than Mr. Lloyd George does, the necessity of an issue of bonds to support the credit indispensable to the reconstruction of the countries which have suffered from the war. But there is a great disadvantage in including in the text of the peace treaty an arbitrary figure, since we do not yet have all the claims before us.

In the peace treaty, the Germans will have to accept the power of the commission with all its consequences. If we demand that the sum be set in the preliminaries of peace, we will only appreciably delay the signing.

Mr. Lamont, who just spoke to me, adds that the commission could be required to meet one week after the signing of the preliminaries.

Clemenceau. But when will it make its decision known? The study of the documents might make us wait six months.

Wilson. At this time, France is the only country which has not provided us with its complete figures.§

M. CLEMENCEAU said that France desired to state a figure that was less than the total amount to be claimed. Because they were doing this, however, they did not wish to disappoint public opinion. If, however, no figure was mentioned, public opinion would not only be disappointed, but would think that Germany was being spared. What inconvenience, he asked, would result from saying that there would be an issue of such and such an amount of bonds? As regards Mr. Lloyd George's remark on the parliamentary point of view, he was not sure, since opinion in the two countries was very different. If, however, no figure should be named, perhaps a date could be given. He was very anxious to reach an agreement, and to do so he would make a concession, provided a date were given by which the Commission should report. To agree without either a figure or a date was further than he could go.

MR LLOYD GEORGE did not see why the Commission should not be brought together, as Mr. Lamont had suggested, immediately after the signature of the Treaty of Peace, provided that the claims could be put in at once. Many of the figures could be reached by a mere process of addition. For example, pensions, which alone came to thousands of millions, could be established at once. The Commission could then name a sum, so to speak, on account and decide that Germany should issue bonds for this amount. He did not see why more than 48 hours should be required for this.

PRESIDENT WILSON said he was somewhat mystified by this discussion. Months had been spent to trying to reach a figure, then it had been decided to drop the attempt. Now it was proposed to ask the Commission to name it right away. Were we not agreed, he asked, that the amount of the bonds issued by Germany should be determined by the Commission at the earliest possible date?

MR LLOYD GEORGE suggested that the date should be a fortnight after the claims had been put in.

M. CLEMENCEAU said he might accept Mr Lloyd George's proposal, although he found it difficult. Supposing someone were to steal his watches, his pictures, his statues, his furniture, etc., and the thief was caught. He would not know the value immediately, but he could give an approximate figure for temporary settlement. However, he would agree, provided that President Wilson would agree.

PRESIDENT WILSON said he had already expressed his agreement.

§Mantoux's notes:

Clemenceau. France suffered losses so heavy and so varied that it is perhaps less easy for her than for others to know the extent immediately. On the other hand, we want to examine our estimates closely, so that no one can reproach us for having exaggerated them. In short, it is only a matter of fixing a figure which will obviously be less than the total which we are entitled to claim. If we hesitate to announce this figure, it will be a great disappointment to public opinion. It will believe that we wish to spare the Germans. I see no valid reason for not declaring this figure. I fear the deplorable effect which, in France certainly, would result from this silence. However, if at least a date was set on which this figure would be known, opinion could be appeased. But no figure and no date: that I cannot accept.

Lloyd George. Concerning your claims, you can furnish provisional figures rapidly. That would suffice for the immediate work that one could ask of the commission. I do not see what would prevent the commission from being provided with all the necessary figures within one week after its constitution, and it could take an immediate decision. There are figures which can be established by simple addition, such as those of the pensions included in our different budgets. The commission could then in a very short time determine the total amount of the down-payment demanded.

Clemenceau. You do not intend that the Germans discuss the amount of the issue?

Lloyd George. No, that concerns the commission alone.

Wilson. I must confess that I do not know where I am. After long discussions, we had arrived at the conclusion that it was better not to try for the moment to fix the figures; whatever they are, they may indeed cause disappointment. Today, we are absolutely insistent on returning to the figures.

Lloyd George. This time it is not a matter of fixing the figure of what Germany must or can pay us, but only the amount of a down payment.

Wilson. I think we agree now in thinking that the amount of the issue would have to be determined by the commission at the earliest possible date. But how can we fix this date now without knowing when the commission will have in its hands the documents necessary to take its decision?

Lloyd George. I would give it two weeks from the time of its constitution.

Clemenceau. I could accept this. But I do not understand the difficulty there could be in fixing the amount of a down payment. They steal from me my watch, my paintings, my furniture. The thief is apprehended; it is not difficult to fix a sum before an appraisal; that happens every day, it is the practice of the courts. In a spirit of conciliation, I would go as far as accepting what Mr. Lloyd George has just proposed, if President Wilson agrees with him on this.

Wilson. I have already said that I agree. But another question arises: will the amount of the issue be determined by a majority of the commission? §

M. CLEMENCEAU asked whether the amount was to be decided unanimously, or by a majority of the Commission.

MR LLOYD GEORGE said, surely by a majority.

M. CLEMENCEAU said he would accept.

PRESIDENT WILSON said he could not accept a majority, and must insist on unanimity.

M. CLEMENCEAU made two observations in regard to this. First, it was always possible to take an unanimous decision in a small meeting of statesmen. This, however, was much harder in a large technical Commission. Consequently, if unanimity was essential, the period of a fortnight proposed by Mr Lloyd George was an illusion, because the Commission would never agree within that time. Second, it had been suggested by United States experts in the course of the discussion that part of the payment could be allowed to be made in paper marks. This would be disastrous from the point of view of public opinion.

MR LLOYD GEORGE, on the question of unanimity, said that if this was demanded as essential, it would be fatal to the whole scheme, and there would be no alternative but to fix the figure now. He understood that the Commission would consist of representatives of the United States, the British Empire, France, Italy and Belgium. If any of these powers declined to agree, they could hold the Commission up indefinitely. Belgium, for example, might say: "We won't agree unless you will agree to so and so." They might say they would not agree unless they themselves were given one or two thousand million bonds. He was only quoting Belgium as an example, but the same might apply to any of the states involved.

PRESIDENT WILSON said that the object of the bonds was to provide collateral for borrowing purposes, and some of this borrowing would have to be done in the United States of America. If there was an extravagant issue of bonds, it would upset the credit of the world. Bankers would not lend on a depreciated security. He did not want to be obstructive, but he must state that if this question was to be decided by a majority, it would not be wise for the United States of America to participate.

MR LLOYD GEORGE said it was most important for the United States to participate, because they were the only really impartial power in the matter.

PRESIDENT WILSON said that the United States would be more than willing to participate, but they must have this safeguard. The initial steps would affect the whole structure of credit of which the United States were a part. Consequently, they could not afford to be outvoted.

MR LLOYD GEORGE agreed that the United States was a country to which the other Powers would all have to resort for credit. The British Empire, however, was also affected. Some of the things which Belgium and France needed most come from the British Empire, for example—wool and machinery, which the United States of America would not alone be able to supply. He was unable, however, to see how American or British credit would be affected by too many marks being put on the market. It would merely affect the value of the marks themselves.

PRESIDENT WILSON pointed out that any country that accepted marks as collateral would be affected.

MR LLOYD GEORGE said that the United States would use its own judgment as to the value of the marks. If bankers were not satisfied that their value as collateral was sufficient, they would not lend. They would only give credit to the extent to which they believed the collateral to be sound.

PRESIDENT WILSON said Mr. Lloyd George had overlooked one

point. It was not to the interest of the world that the credit of France or Great Britain should be depressed. If a beginning were made by the issue of a huge sum in bonds, and Great Britain and France sought to borrow, the bankers would say that they were borrowing on the strength of a collateral that had been issued too profusely, and thus the whole structure of credit would be affected.

MR BONAR LAW agreed, but said that this was exactly what the Commission would have to bear in mind as regards fixing the amount to be issued. If unanimity was insisted on, any State could hold up the Commission either way, whether the amount was not regarded as big enough or as too big.

MR LLOYD GEORGE suggested that the Commission should have powers to decide how much of the paper could be put on the market at one time, in order to counter the risk of the market being flooded.

PRESIDENT WILSON agreed that this should be part of the scheme.

MR DAVIS said that the Commission should not put loose on the market a larger amount than that for which Germany was in a position to meet the coupons.

MR LLOYD GEORGE recalled that in previous discussions on fixing the amount that Germany could pay, it had always been assumed that she would not be able to pay for the first two years and that the greater part of the payment would have to begin in the third year. There was no reason why bonds should not be issued to be payable later on.

MR BONAR LAW pointed out that bonds would be available as credit as long as people thought that ultimately they would be paid. Otherwise they would not be available.

PRESIDENT WILSON suggested that a non-essential subject was now being discussed. If the question were to be decided by a majority vote but nevertheless the United States of America did not agree and issued a minority report, they would really kill the whole scheme of credit. Consequently, the scheme had to be acceptable to the United States of America. The same applied to Great Britain.

M. CLEMENCEAU suggested that the United States of America was a country where there were great varieties of opinion and was not certain that everyone would accept the decision of the Government.

PRESIDENT WILSON pointed out that the Secretary of the Treasury would have a good deal to say.

MR LAMONT suggested that the Committee might fix a minimum sum for the bond issue to be adopted by the Commission.

MR DAVIS suggested that the Committee might come together again to consider this question.

MR LLOYD GEORGE agreed and proposed that, after this preliminary discussion, the experts should resume their meetings and endeavour to fix on a minimum sum.
           (This proposal was adopted and the
           Supreme Council adjourned.)

T MS (SDR, RG 256, 180.03401/107, DNA); Mantoux, I, 214-19.

From the Diary of Colonel House

April 10, 1919.

The most important matter I have dealt with today has been the naval building program. *Cecil came to see me and I declined to discuss it in connection with the Monroe Doctrine. I told him we would offer the amendment tonight at the meeting of the League of Nations Committee and if the British wanted to turn it down they were privileged to do so. Our public opinion demanded our making the attempt to have it in the Covenant and if Lloyd George objected, he might take the responsibility if he so desired. My letter of last night,[1] I told Cecil, stood on its own merits, and I did not send it with the idea of bargaining with them as to the Monroe Doctrine.*

Lloyd George, as I anticipated, objected to my letter and wanted it to include ships still not under construction but provided for by law.[2] Cecil had written me a letter covering this which he said he would deliver if I thought worth while, otherwise we could consider that it had never been offered. I declined to accept the letter and he took it back with him. He then wished to know if I would be willing to have him write a memorandum of our conversation this morning which he would send to me for verification before sending it to the Prime Minister.

Shortly after Cecil left, he sent me the memorandum of our conversation and it is attached. I accepted it as being correct other than the mentioning of Admiral Benson by name. I insisted that in the two places where Benson's name is used that *"American naval officers"* should be substituted. I am curious to hear what the Prime Minister will say in the circumstances now that he knows we are going ahead with our Monroe Doctrine amendment regardless of his wishes.

[1] EMH to R. Cecil, April 9, 1919.
[2] See the extract from the Cecil Diary printed at April 8, 1919.

Lord Robert Cecil to Edward Mandell House, with Enclosures

My dear Colonel House   Paris. 10 April 19.

Here is the memorandum. If you approve it & could let me know that you approve by telephone or otherwise I will send it on to the Prime Minister   yours very truly   Robert Cecil[1]

ALS (E. M. House Papers, CtY).

[1] At the bottom of a typed copy of this letter, also in the House Papers, House wrote: "I read this letter & memo to the President tonight and he approved. E.M.H. April 10/19."

E N C L O S U R E   I

Paris. April 10, 1919.

Memorandum

I saw Colonel House this morning and showed him the draft letter a copy of which is annexed. He said to me that the difficulty was that the programme which the United States Government were now working on was one sanctioned some little time ago, and its execution had been postponed by reason of the diversion of all the energies of the United States authorities towards building the quantities of small craft which they had been constructing for the anti-submarine campaign. But for that it would have been completed, or nearly completed, some time ago. As it was, contracts had been made for the whole of it, and almost all of it was either begun or on the point of being begun. As all this had been done under the authority of Congress he was himself doubtful whether the President could interfere with it.

I asked him whether it would not be possible for the President to postpone the commencement of those ships which had not been actually begun until after the Treaty of Peace had been signed, so that we might have time to discuss and consider the matter together.

He said he thought that might be possible, and would see what could be done in that direction. At the same time he repeated more than once that there was no idea in the mind of the President of building a fleet in competition with that of Great Britain. That was entirely foreign to his purpose. Nor did he believe that anyone, save possibly Admiral Benson, harboured any such idea.

I told him that I thought things that had been said by Admiral Benson in private had added to the difficulties of the situation. He admitted that that was possible, and added that some things our sailors were saying were not calculated to produce a good international atmosphere. For instance many of them said quite openly that now was the time for Great Britain to go to war with the United States, when her fleet was superior to theirs, so that they could finish them once and for all. They said this to American sailors.

We agreed that the point of view of the fighting services made any accommodation between nations very difficult. He then urged that it really would be much better to leave the thing as it was left by his letter to me:[1] that we might fully rely on the intention of the President not to build in competition with us; and that he thought that some arrangement as to the relative strengths of the fleets ought to be arrived at; and that conversations with that object might well be begun as soon as the Treaty of Peace was signed. But he added that he was very much afraid that if the matter were stirred in public at all now national spirit on both sides would be aroused and no accommodation would be possible. I assured him that it was far from our purpose to have any public controversy on the subject, and that all that had passed between us was strictly confidential.   Robert Cecil

TS MS (E. M. House Papers, CtY).
[1] That is, EMH to R. Cecil, April 9, 1919, printed as an Enclosure with EMH to WW, April 9, 1919.

E N C L O S U R E   I I

Paris.

Many thanks for your letter with the spirit of which I am in hearty agreement. Indeed, I have already written to Mr Lloyd George who had spoken to me on the subject that once the League of Nations was part of the treaty of peace it will be necessary for all of us to live up to its spirit & to do this it will be inconsistent to continue to increase armaments either by land or sea. That is as I have ascertained also the view of the President. In the same way it will be part of our duty under the Covenant to interchange information as to our naval programmes & I should hope that in the case of America & England that obligation will be carried out in cordial cooperation. You will not forget in this connection the recognition by the President of Great Britain's special position as to sea power.

RChw MS (E. M. House Papers, CtY).

A British Amendment to the Covenant

[c. April 10, 1919]

Nothing in this Covenant shall be deemed to affect any international engagement or understanding for securing the peace of the world such as treaties of arbitration and the Monroe Doctrine.[1]

T MS (WP, DLC).
[1] House wrote the following comment on this page: "Balfour & Cecil have worked this out as a feasible article to cover the point you have in mind. If you approve please let me know.   E.M.H."

Minutes of a Meeting of the League of Nations Commission

FOURTEENTH MEETING, APRIL 10, 1919, AT 8 P.M.
PRESIDENT WILSON *in the Chair.*

A delegation representing the International Council of Women and the Suffragist Conference of the Allied countries and the United States was received by the Commission at 8 o'clock. The delegation was led by Lady Aberdeen, and consisted of:

Mrs. Fanny Fern Andrews.	Mrs. Grimberg.
Mrs. Corbett Ashby.	Mrs. Puesch.
Mrs. Bratianu.	Mrs. George Rublee.
Mrs. Brunschwieg.	Mrs. Schivioni.
Mrs. Brigode.	Mrs. Schlumberger.
Mrs. d'Amelio.	Mrs. Jules Siegfried.
Miss Margery Fry.	Mrs. Avril de Ste. Croix.
Major Girard-Mangin.	Mrs. Marie Verone.[1]

[1] Those persons who have not heretofore been identified and who can be readily identified were: Fannie Fern Phillips (Mrs. Edwin G.) Andrews, social and educational worker, lecturer, and author of Boston, involved in school reform and the promotion of international peace, founder of the American School Peace League, vice-president of the League to Enforce Peace, and a member of the executive committee of the Central Organization for a Durable Peace; at this time also the representative of the United States Bureau of Education at the peace conference; Margery Corbett (Mrs. A. B.) Ashby, prominent speaker and organizer for the British woman suffrage movement, former secretary of the National Union of Women's Suffrage Societies and later secretary and president, respectively, of the International Alliance of Women; Cécile Kahn (Mrs. Léon) Brunschvicg, French feminist leader, at various times secretary and president, respectively, of the Union Française pour le Suffrage des Femmes; Jane Brigode, president of the Fédération Belge pour le Suffrage des Femmes; Sara Margery Fry, secretary of the Penal Reform League of Great Britain; Suzanne Grinberg, lecturer and author of books on women's rights and an attorney at the Paris Court of Appeal; Alice Schiavoni Bosio, a leader of the moderate wing of the Italian woman suffrage movement and head of the Associazione per la Donna; Julie Puaux (Mrs. Jules) Siegfried, president of the Conseil National des Femmes Françaises; Eugénie Avril de Sainte Croix, French feminist leader, journalist, lecturer, and philanthropist, involved particularly in the fight against prostitution; later president of the Conseil National des Femmes Françaises and a French delegate to the League of Nations; Maria Vérone (Mrs. Georges Lhermitte), prominent French suffragist, author, lecturer, and one of the leading attorneys of France; at various times secretary-general and president of the radical Ligue Française pour le Droit des Femmes.

Lady Aberdeen, in introducing the delegation, said that she was ready to place the experience of the organisations which she represented at the service of the League. She asked the President to give his earnest attention to the points which the Delegates would bring before the Commission.

Mrs. Corbett Ashby requested the members of the Commission to see to it that their Governments did in effect nominate women to positions under the League, and that the women were democratically chosen.

Mrs. Rublee supported Mrs. Corbett Ashby.

Mrs. Grimberg, dealing with moral questions, pleaded for the abolition of the traffic in women and children. The League should only admit nations which allowed women complete liberty of life.

Mrs. Avril de Ste. Croix supported Mrs. Grimberg, and urged that State-recognised prostitution should be abolished.

Mrs. Schlumberger pleaded for universal women's suffrage.

Miss Margery Fry urged that whenever a referendum was resorted to women should vote in the same way as men.

Mrs. Schivioni asked that the League should establish an international education bureau.

Mrs. Fanny Fern Andrews supported her.

Major Girard-Mangin pleaded for an international health organisation.

Mrs. Jules Siegfried thanked the Commission for the welcome it had extended to the delegation and appealed to it to call upon women to help in the great task of building a temple of peace.

President Wilson said that it had been a pleasure to hear the speeches, and that if it were not possible to accede to all requests it was only because the League could not begin by arranging all the affairs of mankind, not because the Commission did not agree that the demands were excellent.[2]

The Women's delegation then withdrew.

Lord Robert Cecil presented the draft Convention[3] as amended by the Drafting Committee.

ARTICLE I.

With reference to the words "within two months of the coming into force of the Covenant," *General Smuts* asked when the Covenant would come into force. *Lord Robert Cecil* replied that this would be at the same time as the first Treaty of Peace.

[2] A more detailed exposition of these demands can be found in International Council of Women and Conferences of Women Suffragists of the Allied Countries and of the United States to the President and Members of the League of Nations Commission of the Peace Conference, c. April 9, 1919, T MS, enclosed in Lady Aberdeen to WW, April 9, 1919, ALS (WP, DLC).

[3] For the draft of the Covenant before its amendment by the Drafting Committee, see Wilson's address to the Third Plenary Session of the peace conference printed at Feb. 14, 1919, Vol. 55.

Mr. Larnaude asked whether notice would be sent to neutral States inviting them to become members of the League.

Lord Robert Cecil replied in the affirmative.

In reply to a question by *Mr. Larnaude* as to whether "signatories" meant signatories of the Treaty of Peace, *Lord Robert Cecil* said that this was so.

Mr. Vesnitch asked whether the two months started only from the date of the exchange of the ratifications; *President Wilson* replied in the affirmative.

ARTICLE 2.

Lord Robert Cecil regretted that he was unable to accept the French text as an accurate account of what took place at the Drafting Committee.

Mr. Larnaude asked whether there would be one text or two, or several. He urged that translation should be carried out independently, since anything approaching literal translation was impossible.

Mr. Hymans entirely agreed with Lord Robert Cecil that it was most important that the two texts should be identical.

Lord Robert Cecil thought that the matter was one for the Conference to decide, but he wished to point out that the work throughout had been carried out on the basis of the English text, and that therefore the English text represented the views of the members of the Committee.

President Wilson said that it was not within the competence of the Commission to settle the language question, but the English text was at present now the correct one.

Mr. Orlando thought that if there were differences between the English and the French texts, the French text should be altered. He asked that if more than one official text were adopted, an Italian text should also be recognised.

Lord Robert Cecil said that it was useless to discuss the question since the Commission could not settle it.

Mr. Bourgeois said he thought it would be helpful at least to discuss the question of the official language of the League of Nations.

President Wilson said that he thought that any discussion of this matter would be out of order.

Mr. Bourgeois persisted in his opinion and asked for the privilege of making a statement.

Mr. Bourgeois then read proposed Article 26, which was as follows:

Proposition de la Délégation française.	*French Amendment.*
ARTICLE 26.	ARTICLE 26.
Les membres de la Société conviennent d'accepter comme faisant foi entre elles le texte français de la présente Convention.	The members of the League agree to accept as binding the French text of the present Covenant.
La langue française sera également acceptée dans les mêmes conditions pour la rédaction des actes officiels des divers organes de la Société des Nations.	French shall similarly be the official language used in all acts of the various organs of the League of Nations.

President Wilson said that though he had allowed the matter to be discussed, he was compelled to rule the resolution out of order since a decision was beyond the competence of the Commission.

Mr. Larnaude said that it would be necessary to decide which meaning should be adopted in cases where the French and English texts did not agree. There were cases, as in Article 1, where the English draft should be changed, for it provided that States merely invited but not having accepted might become members of the League.

Lord Robert Cecil said that the French text had never even been presented to the Drafting Committee.

Mr. Veniselos said that he thought it would be necessary to appoint a Committee to go into the question; and if the two texts did not agree, the French text should be the one altered.

It was agreed that Mr. Larnaude and Mr. D. H. Miller should undertake this work.

ARTICLE 3.

General Smuts asked whether the Assembly would have the right to deal with general questions of international law.

President Wilson replied in the affirmative.

Mr. Larnaude reserved judgment.

ARTICLE 4.

General Smuts asked whether States summoned to meetings of the Council would have the right to vote.

Lord Robert Cecil said that he thought it would be no satisfaction to States to be summoned as non-effective members. The League should not be able to dispose of the rights of any State or to order about its soldiers without the consent of that State. The State affected by a decision should have the power of voting on that decision.

Mr. Reis asked why the words about "binding" had been abandoned. *Lord Robert Cecil* replied that it was a principle of the League that no State should be forced into a decision against its will.

ARTICLE 5.

Mr. Reis moved that the order of the first two paragraphs should be reversed.

This change was accepted.

Mr. Larnaude agreed. He thought that the word "Assembly" should not occur before the word "Council."

ARTICLE 6.

Was passed without discussion.

ARTICLE 7.

Mr. Orlando, representing the Committee appointed at the last meeting to enquire into the question of the seat of the League, proposed Geneva. Switzerland was a quiet country, had long been neutral and would probably continue to be neutral. The Swiss Government had been unofficially approached on the matter and had given a satisfactory reply.

Mr. Hymans said that Mr. Orlando had only given two reasons in favour of Geneva, the first of which was that Switzerland would provide an atmosphere of tranquility. He thought that Belgium had during the war given proof that she too could be calm. The other was that Switzerland was a neutral country. Belgium also had long been neutral. The League demanded sacrifices from its members; what country had given better proof of willingness to make sacrifices than Belgium? He complained that Mr. Orlando had not so much as referred to Brussels.

If some great city had been selected he would have raised no objection, but he thought that if a small city were selected it should be Brussels. It was true that Belgium bore traces of the war, but would it be possible to escape from recollections of the war at Geneva? He thought that it would be wrong to try to efface these memories, they should rather be carefully preserved. England had taken up arms because Belgium had been violated. This was the kind of thing which we should teach our children; the kind of thing which should be remembered at the seat of the League.

Mr. Hymans then made the following speech:

"Belgium has long been one of the most active centres of international life, intellectual, judicial, and economic.

"Since 1847 Brussels has been the seat of a long series of international congresses and meetings. There have been 425 in 65 years.

111 international associations have made their home in the city. Out of 22 international exhibitions which took place between 1851 and 1915, 6 were organised in Belgium. It was in Belgium that the Institute of International Law was born.

"Belgium is situated at the junction of several great currents of civilisation and of culture, and is fitted by her geographical situation and her ethnical conditions to be a rallying point.

"Belgium enjoys thoroughly liberal and democratic institutions. Her Constitution has always been considered a model. Thanks to the wisdom of her people and her institutions she has avoided all revolutionary contagion.

"She has an intellectual past and an artistic heritage which shine in the history of the world and reveal noble ideals of beauty, of justice, and of liberty.

"Why then should a country which has taken no part in the war be preferred to Belgium?

"The violation of Belgium's neutrality aroused the conscience of the world. To-day, Germany is compelled to admit the crime which was committed. What better means could be found of giving this confession its full value than to set the capital of the League of Nations on the very soil on which the crime was committed? Belgium was the symbol during the war of violated right. Should she not become the symbol of right restored?

"The Covenant of the League of Nations imposes international obligations on the States which sign it. Belgium accepts them and is ready to collaborate in the great institution which is to ensure the reign of justice and to protect the little nations against the machinations of force.

"Why then should Belgium be set on one side? Is it because she took part in the war? The fact of having been unjustly attacked, brutally invaded and oppressed, in defiance of Treaties, is thus made a reason for exclusion.

"We refuse to believe that the Commission can come to a conclusion of this kind."

Mr. Orlando explained that he had meant no disrespect to Brussels by not mentioning it; on the contrary, it was respect for Belgium and the sacrifices which she had made that had induced him to preserve silence.

He had the utmost respect for Belgium. She had been the standard-bearer of honour and the symbol of faith. She had more than done her duty in opposing with arms the violation of international law. Thus he felt that as a matter of delicacy, it would have been preferable not to have had this discussion. The choice of Geneva was merely based upon practical considerations.

Mr. Kramar said that the League would direct the world; therefore it would be unwise to select an out-of-the-way place for its seat. A centre of politics and of affairs should be chosen.

Lord Robert Cecil said that if it were a question of conferring honours or rewards on a city, no one would hesitate between Geneva and Brussels. It would be an impertinence to do so. He implored members to set aside every other consideration, but that of giving this experiment the best chance of success.

He was in favour of Geneva, first because he thought that the seat of the League should not be situated in the capital city of any country. There could be no doubt that the country selected would have a considerable advantage, and it was important that the world should be inspired with a belief in the absolute impartiality of the League. Second, because impartiality and not the preservation of the glorious memories of the war was the object of the League.

Switzerland, on the other hand, had not only been a neutral country for a long time, it was also the most cosmopolitan country in the world. Switzerland, and Geneva especially, had international traditions. Switzerland, moreover, was more central than Brussels.

Mr. Larnaude observed that in any case the League could always change its seat.

Mr. Vesnitch permitted himself to say that Serbia also had made great sacrifices, but he did not insist upon this aspect of the question. He thought, however, that the Commission should know the reasons which had induced the Committee to select Geneva, and that a vote should then be taken.

Mr. Veniselos agreed with President Wilson that past antagonisms should be avoided. Belgium, however, did not come into the war on account of past antagonisms, but because she was cynically violated by Germany.

Mr. Bourgeois said that Paris and Versailles were ready to give the League a brilliant reception, but he did not insist on urging their claims. If it was decided that the Seat of the League should be in a small country, the Hague would offer great advantages; it would recall the permanent Arbitral Court of the Conference, in the name of which the crimes of Germany were to be punished. But if Holland were set aside, he thought that Belgium should be chosen. In the first place, Belgium had agreed to accept the obligations of the League, whereas Switzerland asked to preserve its permanent neutrality. Moreover, it was the Allied and Associated Powers which had formed the nucleus of the League. Would it not be setting a good example to request one of those Allied peoples which had suffered the most to give its hospitality to the institution which was to represent right in the world? He believed that such a course would be a profound moral lesson for humanity. We were inspired, not by hatred of any people, but by hatred of the violation of Treaties and solemn engagements.

Mr. Larnaude thought that it would be a great mistake to install the League in a town which was not a political centre. Geneva, in this respect, seemed to be less well-placed than Brussels, the natural meeting-place of the political currents of several continents. Brussels, moreover, represented imperishable memories which we should not wish to dim, since but for the resistance of Belgium the League of Nations would probably never have come about.

Mr. Kramar drew attention to the shortcomings of a town like Geneva where there were no diplomatic representatives. It was a matter not of setting up a mere Court of Arbitration, but of creating a centre of political life.

President Wilson yielded to none in his admiration for Belgium, but the present question was one not of awarding honours but of finding the best surroundings for international deliberation. The antipathies of the war should be set aside; otherwise it might be thought that the League was a mere coalition of Allies moved by the hatreds born of the war. Our object was to bring about friendly relations between all peoples. We wished to rid the world of the sufferings of war. We should not obtain this result if we chose a town where the memory of this war would prevent impartial discussion. The peace of the world could not be secured by perpetuating international hatreds. Geneva was already the seat of the International Red Cross, which had placed itself at the service of both groups of belligerents, and which, so far as possible, had remained unaffected by the antipathies provoked by the war. Moreover, Switzerland was a people vowed to absolute neutrality by its constitution and its blend of races and languages. It was marked out to be the meeting-place of other peoples desiring to undertake a work of peace and co-operation. The choice of Geneva did not mean that we did not recognise the eminent merits of Belgium and of Brussels. There could be no comparison between the two peoples from the point of view of their conduct during the war. The capitals of other neutral nations might have been proposed, but none had behaved so impartially as Switzerland. Switzerland had always acted with dignity; she had suffered from the war and she had gained the respect of both groups of belligerents.

Mr. Vesnitch: No change in roneoed [duplicated] text.

Mr. Veniselos: No change in roneoed text.

Mr. Bourgeois doubted if the proposed decision came within the functions of the Commission. The question of the Seat of the League was a political question of great importance, and it seemed to him outside the scope of the work of the Commission.

Mr. Hymans thanked the Commission for the tributes which had been paid to Belgium, but he maintained that the foundation of the League of Nations was intimately connected with the war. We should not therefore seek to blot out its memories, but, on the contrary, to uphold them as an example of value to the cause of right and of humanity.

After further discussion a vote was taken, and twelve members of the Commission voted in favour of the Report.

ARTICLES 8 AND 9.

Mr. Larnaude asked whether the Commission was to draw up any plan of disarmament. Could States which refused to accept the plans for reduction of armaments proposed by the Council remain in the League?

Lord Robert Cecil replied that refusing States might certainly remain in the League. There would be no obligation to carry out recommendations, which would be formulated merely for the consideration of the several Governments.

Mr. Larnaude said that he made all possible reserves.

Mr. Bourgeois said that in this case the obligation implied no obligation at all and that the refusal of a single State could prevent general disarmament. He reserved the right to bring forward his amendments to Articles 7 and 9 at the Plenary Conference. Mr. Clemenceau had received Lord Robert Cecil's proposals, and they had been rejected by the French Government.

ARTICLE 10.

Mr. Larnaude remarked that this Article implied a formal guarantee of the territorial integrity and independence of each member of the League, and consequently bound the League to take the military measures necessary to make this guarantee effective. He asked that this interpretation of the Article should be maintained.

President Wilson proposed the following amendment, to appear at the end of Article 10:

> "Nothing in this Covenant shall be deemed to affect the validity of international engagements such as Treaties of arbitration or regional understandings like the Monroe Doctrine for securing the maintenance of peace."

Mr. Koo did not wish to be understood to be opposing the amendment, of which he approved in principle. He wished, however, to suggest that the Monroe Doctrine should be named specifically and alone in this Article, and not made one of a class of regional understandings.

Mr. Larnaude was anxious to have a clear definition of the Monroe Doctrine. Every time liberty had been threatened, either in America or in Europe, the United States had either acted upon the Doctrine or had reserved the right to intervene. If an European war occurred in which the interests of the United States were imperilled, the Monroe Doctrine would not prevent her from taking part. Did President Wilson's amendment consecrate or change this policy?

Mr. Reis said that he knew of no text in which the Monroe Doctrine was clearly defined. He was therefore unable to pledge his Government in this matter.

Lord Robert Cecil did not wish to oppose the amendment, but to explain its meaning. He understood it to mean, oddly enough, exactly what it said: "Nothing in this Covenant shall be deemed to affect the validity of * * *" various international engagements. It gave to these engagements no sanction or validity which they had not previously enjoyed. It accepted them as they were. In particular it accepted the Monroe Doctrine as it was—a Doctrine which had never been clearly defined. It was well to leave it undefined and as an example, for any attempt at definition might extend or limit its application. In spite of the fact that it never had been definitely formulated, it would not be common sense to deny that such a doctrine had existed, had been acted upon, and had been accepted by other States.

The amendment had been inserted in order to quiet doubts, and to calm misunderstandings. It did not make the substance of the Doctrine more or less valid. He understood this amendment to say what he believed to be implicit in the Covenant, what he believed to be true—that there was nothing in the Monroe Doctrine which conflicted with the Covenant, and therefore nothing in the Covenant which interfered with international understandings like the Monroe Doctrine.

Mr. Reis asked whether the Monroe Doctrine would prevent League action in American affairs.

President Wilson replied in the negative. The Covenant provided that the members of the League should mutually defend one another in respect of their political and territorial integrity. The Covenant was therefore the highest possible tribute to the Monroe Doctrine. It adopted the principle of the Monroe Doctrine as a world doctrine. It was an international acceptance of the principle by which the United States had said that it would protect the political independence and territorial integrity of other American States. The Commission should study, not theoretical interpretations which had been placed upon the Monroe Doctrine, but actions of the United States which had been taken thereunder.

His colleagues in America had asked him whether the Covenant would destroy the Monroe Doctrine. He had replied that the Covenant was nothing but a confirmation and extension of the doctrine. He had then been asked whether, if this were so, there would be any objection to making a specific statement to that effect in the text. It was by way of concession to this reasonable request that he was asking the Commission to state definitely something which was already implied.

Mr. Koo observed that the word "understandings" was in the plural. It appeared to him to be too broad. It would cover all kinds of undertakings [understandings], good, bad, and indifferent. If there were no serious objection he would like to have the words "regional understandings like" struck out, and the word "of" substituted.

Mr. Larnaude said that the serious thing about this amendment was that it was the only one which concerned a particular country. It was therefore out of harmony with the rest of the document. Article 20 provided that all States which entered the League were bound to make their international engagements conform to the spirit of the League. If they were not inconsistent they could stand. If, therefore, there was nothing in the Monroe Doctrine inconsistent with the Covenant it would not be affected. He regretted that he felt compelled to join Lord Robert Cecil against the President.

Lord Robert Cecil explained that he was far from disagreeing with the President. He disapproved of Mr. Koo's amendment because it made the amendment to apply to America only. In the President's amendment the Monroe Doctrine was given only as an example.

Mr. Larnaude asked that his observations might appear in the Minutes. He considered that the amendment was inconsistent with Article 20.

Mr. Orlando thought that the amendment was not inconsistent with Article 20.

Mr. Reis was anxious to add at the end of President Wilson's amendment the words: "So far as the Monroe Doctrine is not inconsistent with the League."

Mr. Larnaude thought that it would certainly be very unfortunate if the Monroe Doctrine should be interpreted to mean that the United States could not participate in any settlement of European affairs decided upon by the League.

Mr. Orlando said that Mr. Larnaude would remember that the United States came to participate in this war, and that if they did so under the principles of the Monroe Doctrine, then the more so would they come in similar circumstances if they were members of the League.

President Wilson said that should the Monroe Doctrine in future be interpreted in a manner prejudicial to the peace of the world, the League of Nations would be there to deal with it. He was prepared, if necessary, to delete the word "regional": it was perhaps hardly applicable to so large a territory as the western hemisphere.

Lord Robert Cecil said that perhaps Mr. Bourgeois would permit him to explain again what he thought had been made quite clear. The amendment simply proposed to emphasise an implicit principle: that the validity of the Monroe Doctrine was not affected by anything in the Covenant. The amendment did not give validity to anything which did not already possess validity. Defensive alliances, so long as they were really defensive, were not affected.

Mr. Koo was in complete agreement with President Wilson and Lord Robert Cecil in wishing to have the Monroe Doctrine mentioned in the Covenant. The Doctrine had been tested for a century, and it had contributed greatly to the development of liberty and peace throughout the world. He would therefore be glad to see the words "regional understandings" or even "understandings" omitted unless Lord Robert Cecil had some other similar understandings in mind. As the amendment stood it might uphold understandings which might become obsolete, and might also include future understandings. If Lord Robert Cecil wished to retain the word "understandings" he would like to add after it the words "hitherto commonly accepted."

Lord Robert Cecil explained that there were other understandings such as those concerning the tribes of Arabia, whereby these tribes carried out their negotiations with the outside world through Great Britain only. The words "hitherto commonly accepted" might raise difficulties as to what had or had not been commonly accepted. It might extend or limit the validity of existing understandings. As the Article now read, it did neither. It created nothing which did not already exist.

Mr. Koo persisted in his wish to avoid the use of so broad a word as "understandings." He wished to see the Monroe Doctrine alone specified.

Lord Robert Cecil thought that it would be a very unfortunate thing to state it singly. The French Delegation had already formally entered an objection on this score.

President Wilson again explained that any understanding which infringed upon the territorial integrity or political independence of any State would be inconsistent with the Covenant. Any State which signed the Covenant obliged itself immediately to abrogate such an understanding. The inclusion of this reference to the Monroe Doctrine was in effect nothing but a recognition of the *fact* that it was not inconsistent with the terms of the Covenant.

Mr. Larnaude thought that if it was not inconsistent with the terms of the Covenant, it was unnecessary to refer to it. What was unnecessary might be dangerous. Relying on the special mention of the Monroe Doctrine in the Covenant, the United States might some day assert that this doctrine forbade some act of intervention decided upon by the other members of the League.

President Wilson again assured Mr. Larnaude that if the United States signed this document they would be solemnly obliged to render aid to European affairs, when the territorial integrity of any European State was threatened by external aggression.

Mr. Orlando again reminded Mr. Larnaude that the Monroe Doctrine had not prevented the United States from intervening in this war. They would be more ready to do so when they had accepted the additional obligations of membership of the League. He could not understand Mr. Larnaude's doubts.

Mr. Larnaude said that the United States came in because they felt inclined to. For the future it was a question of imposing an obligation in the name of the Covenant and not of allowing States to intervene or not according to the caprice of the moment.

President Wilson asked Mr. Larnaude to explain whether he really doubted that the United States would live up to its obligations if it became a signatory to the Covenant of the League.

Mr. Larnaude thought that it could not honourably escape them, but that it would not be legally bound. He did not think that the Americans would avail themselves of the avenue of escape which they would have, but he thought that the matter should be settled. There should be a formal explanation of the Monroe Doctrine.

President Wilson thought that it had been completely explained.

Mr. Bourgeois feared that if the amendment was accepted there would be two groups of States under the Covenant: The United States on the one hand, and the European States on the other.

President Wilson said that it was anticipated that other States on the American Continent, such as Brazil, would enter the League at once. It was hoped that practically all the States in the world would become members. In such a world-League it seemed out of place to talk about two groups.

Lord Robert Cecil thought that the anxiety of the French Delegates was caused partly by the fact that the amendment had been introduced as an addition to Article 10, the Article which was of the greatest importance to France. They feared that the amendment might limit the protection which was afforded by Article 10. He suggested that the amendment should be placed under Article 20.

President Wilson agreed.

Mr. Larnaude said that the amendment should be put at the end of Article 20, and that an explanation in the form of a footnote, which should be part of the Covenant, should state exactly what the Monroe Doctrine was.

Mr. Vesnitch urged that the amendment should be accepted. He explained that the Monroe Doctrine had two parts: the object of the first part was to protect America from aggression at the hands of autocratic Powers. Monroe and his successors had said to the world "we cannot allow you to intervene in our affairs but in return we will not intervene in yours." The second part, the non-intervention of America in Europe, was thus only a corollary of the first. But experience had shown that neither of these principles prevented the intervention of America in Europe when the liberty of the world or great interests were at stake.

Mr. Larnaude still objected. He wished to have an obligation imposed on America to take part in European affairs.

President Wilson thought it might help the discussion if he explained the history of the Monroe Doctrine. At a time when the world was in the grip of absolutism, one of the two or three then free States of Europe suggested to the United States that they should take some political step to guard against the spread of absolutism to the American Continent. Among these States was England. Acting upon this suggestion the principles of the Monroe Doctrine were laid down, and from that day to this, they had proved a successful barrier against the entrance of absolutism into North and South America. Now that a document was being drafted which was the logical extension of the Monroe Doctrine to the whole world, was the United States to be penalised for her early adoption of this policy? A hundred years ago the Americans had said that the absolutism of Europe should not come to the American Continent. When there had come a time when the liberty of Europe was threatened by the spectre of a new absolutism, America came gladly to help in the preservation of European liberty. Was this issue going to be debated, was the Commission going to scruple on words at a time when the United States was ready to sign a Covenant which made her for ever part of the movement for liberty? Was this the way in which America's early service to liberty was to be rewarded? The Commission could not afford to deprive America of the privilege of joining in this movement.

Mr. Larnaude said that he had no doubt that the United States would come again to the help of Europe if it were threatened by absolutism. Future wars might not, however, be wars of liberation. They might be economic in origin. The question was, therefore, whether the United States would come to the help of France should she be engaged in a struggle with a country which happened to be quite as liberal as herself.

Lord Robert Cecil said that Mr. Larnaude was clearly wrong in his interpretation of the way in which the Monroe Doctrine had been applied. If he would consult history he would find that the Monroe Doctrine had never in a single instance been applied to American policy with regard to American participation in Europe, but always with regard to European participation in American affairs. When American statesmen or international lawyers made objection to the interference of America in European affairs, they never did so on the basis of the Monroe Doctrine, but always on the basis of Washington's farewell address.

President Wilson asked why Mr. Larnaude asked this question when America promised to come to the rescue of France, as she did by signing the Covenant. Was it conceivable that he wanted the United States alone of the signatories of the Covenant to say that she would not repudiate her obligations under that Covenant? Did she wish to stop her signing the Covenant?

Mr. Reis said that after this discussion he accepted the clause absolutely.

President Wilson said that if the clause was accepted by the Commission a logical place should be found for it in the text.

The amendment was then adopted.

Baron Makino reserved the right to raise other questions under Article 10 at the next meeting of the Commission.

(The Commission then adjourned.)

Printed copy (WP, DLC).

From Vittorio Emanuele Orlando

[Paris] 10 Aprile '19

Never were such noble ideas expressed in such a noble way!

Orlando

ALS (WP, DLC).

From William Howard Taft and Abbott Lawrence Lowell

New York, N. Y., April 10th, 1919.

Friends of Covenant are seriously alarmed over report that no amendment will be made more specifically safeguarding Monroe Doctrine. At full meeting of Executive Committee of League to Enforce Peace, with thirty members from eighteen States present, unanimous opinion that without such amendment, Republican Senators will certainly defeat ratification of treaty because public opinion will sustain them. With such amendment, treaty will be promptly ratified.

William H Taft   A. Lawrence Lowell.

T telegram (WP, DLC).

From Walker Downer Hines

Washington Apl 10 1919

Number fifty six Following is sent at request of Director General Hines Quote I have given the most careful consideration to the question whether the Railroad Administration would be justified in giving its approval to the steel and iron prices which were fixed and announced by the Industrial Board of the Department of Commerce as being appropriate prices for the rest of this calendar year Stop My purchasing advisers unanimously advised that the prices were unreasonably high Stop Afterwards the matter was discussed at length with Messrs Glass Baker Lane Burleson Redfield and others and as a result there was a further conference between the Industrial Board and my representatives who were R S Lovett[1] Henry Walters Interstate Commerce Commissioner C C McChord and my staff representatives T C Powell and H B Spencer[2] Stop Again my advisers unanimously advised that the prices were too high Stop A further conference was then arranged between representatives of the steel interests and Messrs Lovett Walters and Spencer representing me and my advisers remained of the same opinion Stop Public uncertain and speculation as to the Railroad Administrations attitude have indicated the importance of prompt definition of that attitude Stop I have announced today that I cannot approve the prices Stop I am advised that all the members of the Interstate Commerce Commission heartily concur in this view Stop I believe the question involved is much broader than the mere question of the Railroad Administration paying an unreasonably high price for its own materials Stop I think if excessive prices should be officially endorsed by the Railroad Administration the result would be that the prices so endorsed would then become the standard peace prices for the steel industry and therefore it would be able to keep future prices higher than if such endorsement is withheld Stop I therefore believe that my action is distinctly in the interest of the consuming public not only for the immediate present but for a long period in the future Stop My action ought to aid in creating a presumption against these high prices whereas official approval would create a very strong presumption in their favor Stop A further question may be presented to you as to the future activities of the Industrial Board Stop The Railroad Administration will be glad in the absence of other instructions from you to avail of the service of the Industrial Board as a mediator with respect to prices on commodities which seem to admit of that method of treatment Stop But I am very doubtful whether there are many commodities which can be handled in that way to the advantage of the public Stop I sent you a letter on Saturday April fifth[3] fully presenting the reasons why in my opinion it would be highly detrimental to the public interest as well as to the interest of the Railroad Administration to establish through any governmental agency uniform prices on coal since such uniform prices would be unnecessarily high and result in the imposition of a very serious burden upon the consumers of coal throughout the country and I am satisfied no such action is necessary for the protection of the labor situation Stop The Attorney General tells me he has just given an opinion as to the legal limitations on the Industrial Board Signed Walker D Hines Unquote   Tumulty

T telegram (WP, DLC).
    [1] That is, Robert Scott Lovett.
    [2] That is, Thomas Carr Powell and Henry Benning Spencer.
    [3] W. D. Hines to WW, April 5, 1919.

From Frank J. Hayes

New York Apl 10 1919

Leaving for Paris tomorrow Desire conference with you on situation in coal mining industry.
            Frank J Hayes,   President United Mine Workers
                                                of America.

T telegram (WP, DLC).

Cary Travers Grayson to Joseph Patrick Tumulty

Personal and Confidential.

Dear Mr. Tumulty: Paris, 10 April, 1919.

While the contents of this letter may possibly be somewhat out of date by the time it reaches you, nevertheless you may find something in it of interest.

This has been one of the most complexing and trying weeks of my existence over here. The President was taken violently sick last Thursday. The attack was very sudden. At three o'clock he was apparently all right; at six he was seized with violent paroxysms of coughing, which were so severe and frequent that it interfered with his breathing. He had a fever of over 103 and a profuse diarrhoea. I was at first suspicious that his food had been tampered with, but it turned out to be the beginning of an attack of influenza. That night was one of the worst through which I have ever passed. I was able to control the spasms of coughing but his condition looked very serious. Since that time he has been gradually improving every day so that he is now back at work,—he went out for the first time yesterday. This disease is so treacherous, especially in this climate, that I am perhaps over-anxious for fear of a flare-back—and a flare-back in a case of this kind often results in pneumonia. I have [been] spending every minute of my time with him, not only as physician but as nurse. Mrs. Wilson was a perfect angel through it all.

In addition to these anxieties and worries, the workings of the Peace Conference have been very discouraging. The President was more or less depressed, just before he became sick, because of his inability to bring about results. While he would not admit it, he must have felt undoubtedly the lack of needed support from the American peace delegates. Colonel House has the reputation over here as being the "Great American Acquiescor,"—the champion Yes, Yes man with Lloyd-George, and Yes, Yes with Clemenceau. Correspondents have told me that this attitude has embarrassed the President very much when he had to make bold and fearless decisions. One hears these things constantly over here. I have had great difficulty in restraining some of the most important newspapermen from writing articles on the Colonel. One had an article prepared called "The Great American Acquiescor"; another had prepared one, "The Champion Yes, Yes Man of the Peace Conference"; another, "The Modest Colonel House"; but I persuaded these men to withhold the articles, telling them how it would embarrass the President.

I shall not go into the GEORGE WASHINGTON matter, as that will be a dead issue by the time this letter reaches you. But the news of its coming has had the desired effect on the French. It caused them to get a move on themselves, and they were very much alarmed for fear the President would go off and leave them high and dry. The French are the champion time-killers of the world.

I wired you yesterday that the President is making progress now by his force and by hammering them along.[1]

Publicity matters are hard to handle over here. Colonel House, Secretary Lansing and others are constantly giving out statements that do not agree with the President's viewpoint. The Colonel, while meaning good, gives out statements telling the correspondents not to take things too seriously, that a compromise can be made—and this news, or rather news of this kind, is very harmful to the President, as it gives the French the impression that the Colonel is speaking for the President, and then the French say the President is simply bluffing. It also gives encouragement to those who are unfriendly to the President, such as the correspondents of the SUN, TRIBUNE and other papers.

I cannot thank you enough for your thoughtfulness in sending a word from Mrs. Grayson and the boys. You can't imagine how comforting this is to me.

There's lots more I would like to write, but I am hastening to get this off to you by the courier, who is leaving in a few minutes.

Of course, if the President knew I were writing he would join in affectionate regards.

Please convey my kindest regards to Mrs. Tumulty and the family, and with all good wishes for yourself, believe me,

Faithfully yours,   Cary T. Grayson

TLS (J. P. Tumulty Papers, DLC).
  [1] C. T. Grayson to JPT, April 9, 1919, T transcript (WP, DLC).

From the Diary of Colonel House

April 11, 1919.

One of the most important meetings of the Committee for the League of Nations was held last night at eight o'clock. We heard the women present their claims in a series of admirable short speeches. Five minutes was as much as any one used, but each speech was crowded with a wealth of argument and statement within the time limit. I think the entire Committee was impressed.

Then followed one of the stormiest meetings we have had at all. There was a row with Bourgeois at the beginning over the question of the use of French for the official text of the League. After that, we fought for another hour over the insertion of a clause covering the Monroe Doctrine. Here, again, it was the French. Everyone else was willing. It seems the irony of fate that France, who has more at stake in the League of Nations than any other country, should have tried to keep us from putting in a clause which will practically make certain the acceptance of the League by the American people and the Senate. Of all the stupid performances I have ever witnessed, this was the worst. The President finally lost patience and made an impassioned speech on the subject. He did not speak longer than ten minutes, but what he said was full of eloquence and good sense. It convinced everybody but the French Delegates at whom it was directed. We finally passed the clause or thought we had. I learn today that the French Delegates believe that it was not passed and that they will renew the fight tonight.

Then came a contest over the seat of the League. Hymans made a foolish protest against Geneva and urged the selection of Brussels. Everything he said tended to make a fair-minded person feel that Brussels was the last place for a league for peace to go. The Portueguese Delegate, Reis, is another stupid gentleman.

Cecil bears the brunt of explanation, and his patience is marvellous. When twelve o'clock came I expressed the hope that he would not become Prime Minister of England before the League was in working order, for I was certain that he would undertake to fight the French and shake the Portueguese from the English embrace. France has done herself infinite harm by having these two old though worthy gentlemen to represent her. Bourgeois, I believe, is a fine character, but something appears to have gone wrong with his thinking apparatus. Cecil and some of the others desired to quit around eleven o'clock, but the President and I held on until 12.15, and even then we had but half finished. Another meeting is on for tonight, a meeting that bids fair to be as stormy as the other.

From the Diary of Dr. Grayson

Friday, April 11, 1919.

At 10:00 o'clock this morning the President received two Galacian Peasants, who were accompanied by a Polish priest and a Polish astronomer,[1] who had taken them in charge. The two men were goat-herds and came from a small mountain community in Galacia, south of the Polish border. They represented two little colonies of Poles, who were desirous of having the boundary line of Galacia changed so that their homes would be in the new Republic of Poland. These two men were picturesquely garbed in a native mountain costume, which had not been washed since they first put it on, and they smelled very strongly of their herds of goats that they had left in their native hills. They deserved a great deal of credit. They had heard that the President was in Paris, so they set out each separately from his own little village and met on the highway. They were walking toward Warsaw and they met the astronomer, who accompanied them and who showed them the way by the stars at night in their long walk. At Warsaw the Polish authorities took them up and arranged for them to come to Paris, but they defrayed the cost of their trip from their own savings. The Bishop[2] interpreted their remarks for the President, and the President thanked them for coming so far to see him. Their meeting with the President was one of the most touching scenes I have ever witnessed. They said they had come to ask the President—the biggest man in all the world—to see that they were turned over to Poland and not Cheko-Slovia.

At 11:00 o'clock the Big Four meeting was resumed in the temporary White House. It was understood that material progress was made along several lines.

At 1:00 o'clock the Queen of Roumania came for lunch. She was twenty minutes late. She was accompanied by her two daughters, her sister, her lady-in-waiting and her gentleman-in-waiting. She wanted to talk business all through the lunch, and immediately began on the Bolsheviki question, which seemed uppermost in her mind. She started out along this line and said that the King of Roumania[3] had decided to divide his land and not keep such large estates. It was very apparent that this was not voluntary but a matter of necessity. The President was most charming and gracious to her but she asked very pointed questions at times, which he always diplomatically evaded. One of the questions she asked was: "What one individual is causing the greatest obstruction in the Peace Conference?" The President replied by telling her the many complications that had arisen, and that he was sure that she would realize that it was impossible to establish a just peace that would be pleasing to every one. Each section and each country had some special claim they wished granted, which often was incompatible with the principles of justice for all Europe. She said: "But don't you think that the League of Nations will cause a lot of weeping and gnashing of teeth by those who are not satisfied with it?" He said: "That reminds me of a sermon I once heard by a negro preacher in America. He chose as his text: 'And there shall be weeping and gnashing of teeth.' During his discourse he frequently repeated the words of his text, and finally, at a very excited moment, and with great emphasis of voice, he said: 'And there shall be weeping and gnashing of teeth and them that hasn't teeth will have to gum it.' "

The Queen did not seem to understand many of his stories, but she got this one.

At the luncheon the Queen reiterated a number of requests for information which she had made at the time the President called on her at the Ritz. The President handled her not only as a gentleman but with diplomatic care.

It developed that the Queen was a pronounced advocate of monarchies. She referred to the magnanimity with which the King of Roumania had decided to give up certain of his lands and then she exclaimed that in her opinion monarchies were less liable to breed Bolshevism than were democracies. However, the President told her that in his opinion the proposition of planting a King on a country where he did not originate was fraught with very serious danger, not only to the King but to the country itself. The President said to me afterward: "Perhaps I went a little too far in saying what I did as to the transplanting of Kings." I said to the President: "I think not. You did just right. She started it. And after you spoke she changed the subject." The President told the Queen my Haig and Haig story.[4]

At 3:00 o'clock, the President, accompanied by Mrs. Wilson and myself, went to the Quai d'Orsay, where he attended the fourth meeting of the Plenary Session. Mrs. Wilson remained in the car and returned to the house, while the President and I entered the building. The Plenary Session approved the labor convention.[5]

After the meeting had adjourned the President and I took a short motor ride, during which I asked him what progress was being made by the Big Four, and he said: "We are making progress, but it is not straight-forward as it should be. The French cannot make straight-forward progress. If they make any progress it has to be made by a spiral route."

On our return the President was so fatigued that I persuaded him to take a nap. He slept for an hour, which refreshed him greatly. He then had dinner, and at 8:30 o'clock he went to the Crillon Hotel, where he attended a session of the League of Nations committee. He did not return to the house until after 1:00 o'clock, and did not retire until 2:00 o'clock.

This session of the League of Nations committee completed the reconsideration of the constitution so that it was in readiness to be called up whenever a Plenary Session was deemed advisable. The French suggestion that the League create a general military staff failed of adoption, as did the Japanese demand that the preamble of the League declare for equality between nations. Concealed in the Japanese apparently simple request was the nucleus for serious trouble in the United States should it be adopted, inasmuch as it would allow the Asiatics to demand the repeal of the Asiatic Exclusion Law of the United States. However, it was not necessary for the United States openly to oppose the suggested amendment because Australia and New Zealand through the British representatives had taken the position of positive opposition.

[1] About this delegation, see the extract from the Diary of Ray Stannard Baker printed at March 31, 1919, Vol. 56.

[2] Presumably the same person as the "priest" mentioned above.

[3] That is, King Ferdinand, the grandson of Prince Charles (or Carol) of Hohenzollern-Sigmaringen, the first King of Rumania.

[4] For which, see the extract from the Diary of Dr. Grayson printed at Dec. 27, 1918, Vol. 53.

[5] The session was held from 3 to 5:30 p.m. The sole business was the presentation and adoption of the report, draft convention, and clauses proposed for insertion in the treaty of peace by the Commission on International Labor Legislation. George Nicoll Barnes of Great Britain presented these documents on behalf of the commission and spoke in explanation and support of their contents. Plenipotentiary delegates of several nations spoke in favor of the documents, although they occasionally made reservations in regard to some clauses. Wilson twice spoke very briefly: once expressing pleasure at the proposal that the first international labor conference be held in Washington, again, indicating his regret that Samuel Gompers, the chairman of the Commission on International Labor Legislation, could not be present at the plenary session. The minutes of the session are printed in *PPC*, III, 240-60, and in James T. Shotwell, *The Origins of the International Labor Organization* (2 vols., New York, 1934), II, 387-409. Wilson's remarks appear in *PPC*, III, 247 and 260, and in Shotwell, II, 396 and 408. The report of the commission, the draft convention creating the International Labour Organization, and the clauses relating to labor proposed for insertion in the treaty of peace are printed in *PPC*, III, 261-84, and in Shotwell, II, 368-78; I, 373-423; and II, 412; respectively. The clauses proposed for insertion in the treaty are also printed as an Enclosure with H. M. Robinson to WW, March 24, 1919, Vol. 56.

From the Diary of Ray Stannard Baker

Friday the 11th [April 1919].

The President is toiling terribly. Besides two meetings of the Big Four to-day he sat as Chairman of the L. of N. Commission at 8:30 until 1:30 in the morning. They met in Col. House's rooms on this floor of the hotel & I sat up in my room until it was over & then had a short talk with the Colonel. They have finished the Covenant except final touches on the Monroe Doctrine article & the Japanese question.

The President is evidently being required to give ground, for the political exigencies of Lloyd-George & Clemenceau. It is either that or invite at once the explosion of the world. News to-day indicates that Italy is tottering into the abyss:[1] and word from Germany gives little hope that the Germans will sign the treaty when they really get it.

The President when ill—irritable C _____[2] thought him, but he did not raise voice or show anger—, only he trembled when he came away (not having got the document) for the P. ordered all docs. from P. C. sent at once into his library.

Puts off seeing all press correspondents because of his dislike of M. & H.[3]—aloofness & aloneness—a man of consuming mind, hard, predetermined, it is fortunate as Miss T.[4] says that he is for right things, not wrong. He would be terrible if he were evil. In him John Knox—Calvin—on too large a scale.

[1] The Italian Socialist party and the Rome Labor Council staged a general strike and mass march in Rome on April 11. Numerous right-wing and ultranationalistic groups held counterdemonstrations. Although there were some skirmishes between rightists and leftists, there was no serious bloodshed. The Rome security forces arrested many Socialist leaders. See Mayer, *Politics and Diplomacy of Peacemaking*, pp. 683-84.

[2] Gilbert F. Close. On April 5, Close and Charles L. Swem had driven to Versailles in one of the White House automobiles. Wilson learned about their excursion and issued an order which forbade members of his staff to use automobiles except for official business. Weinstein, *Woodrow Wilson*, p. 340, n. 41.

[3] There are numerous possibilities for "M. & H." among the correspondents accredited to the peace conference. Among the most likely are James Jackson Montague of the *New York American*, Frederick Moore and Bampton Hunt of the *New York Tribune*, Frank Morse of the *Washington Post*, Merle Farmer Murphy and Percy Hammond of the *Chicago Tribune*, and Laurence Hills and J. B. Hirsch of the New York *Sun*. See A.C.N.P., "LIST OF PRESS CORRESPONDENTS, HOLDING PERMANENT PASSES . . . ," Jan. 13, 1919, mimeograph copy (WP, DLC).

[4] Ida Minerva Tarbell, in Paris at this time as correspondent for the *Red Cross Magazine*.

From the Diary of Edith Benham

April 11, 1919

I am rather putting the cart before the horse, for I didn't write yesterday, and while today's memories are fresh I thought I would put them down. The great event, of course, was the Queen of Roumania's coming for luncheon. After saying she would bring four from her own household, yesterday morning when the P. and Mrs. W. went to call, she said she would like to bring her sister, the Infanta Eulalia.[1] Great consternation for we thought it was the disreputable Eulalia who toured America several years ago, at the World's Fair time I think,[2] and has had many husbands and near husbands. However, we found that it was her sister or sister-in-law who turned out to be a very attractive person—not as good looking as the Queen but far more genuine and clever. I think the Queen is rather a spectacular person. She enjoys being at the head of her troops and standing in every way in the limelight.

She was invited at one and the P. arranged to meet her upstairs. Harts and Grayson met her at the door and conducted her and her party upstairs. Of course, the P. and Mrs. W. were ready promptly, and we all went upstairs to wait, looking out of the windows of the drawing room so the P. and Mrs. W. would have time to go out to the head of the stairs to meet her. Nothing infuriates the P. like waiting or being late. The Queen had come to establish a propaganda for Roumania, a Greater Roumania, and she did the worst thing she could in being nearly twenty-five minutes late. Every moment we waited I could see from the cut of the P.'s jaw that a slice of the Dobrudja, or Roumania, was being lopped off. At one time he threatened to go on and begin luncheon without her, and asked me to telephone the Ritz to find out if she was coming. By the time she did arrive he would scarcely go out into the hall to meet her and it required all Mrs. W.'s powers to persuade him.

[1] As mentioned in n. 6 to the extract from the Diary of Dr. Grayson printed at April 10, 1919, the sister of Queen Marie who visited Wilson was the Infanta Beatrice. Miss Benham has somehow confused her with the Infanta Eulalia (1864-1958), a daughter of Queen Isabella II of Spain, wife of Prince Antoine of Bourbon-Orleans, and no relation to Queen Marie. For some details of her controversial life, see the obituary notice in the *New York Times*, March 9, 1958.
[2] Eulalia had visited the World's Columbian Exposition in Chicago in 1893.

Mantoux's Notes of a Meeting of the Council of Four

April 11, 1919, 11 a.m.

Mr. Lloyd George explains the reasons why he must go to England next week: he must answer those who are offering criticism, and who are expressing concern about the settlement of indemnities, and to ask for a vote of confidence from them.

Orlando. Placing myself in the same point of view as Mr. Lloyd George, I would call your attention to the interest that exists in no longer delaying any further the examination of the questions which interest Italy. I have to face the same difficulties in my country as you. Yesterday, there was a Bolshevik demonstration in the streets of Rome which, it is true, turned against its organizers and ended as a great patriotic demonstration. But that shows the unrest among the people. The inevitable postponement of the discussion of Italian questions is creating an unfortunate impression in Italy, and we must avoid prolonging it.

I wish to have a conversation with President Wilson as soon as possible. I would like to know, if Mr. Lloyd George is leaving Paris, when he will return. I myself must attend the opening session of the Italian Chamber on April 23, which has already once been postponed by royal decree and which cannot possibly be postponed a second time. I cannot go to Rome without the Italian questions having been tackled.

Lloyd George. I plan to leave on Tuesday, Monday if I can, and I hope to be able to return on Friday. But these discussions must not be interrupted. Mr. Balfour will represent me here, and he has studied the questions concerning Italy with particular care.

I will return on Friday, unless the House of Commons refuses me its confidence—in which case it will be with Lord Northcliffe or with Horatio Bottomley[1] that you will continue these discussions.

* * *

Wilson. I know better than anyone how little time we have had to examine the questions which concern M. Orlando; for I sat with him on the League of Nations Commission yesterday until midnight. However, I did have a conversation with him, and I promised him to prepare a memorandum, to discuss it with him, and to bring the results of our conversation before you. Perhaps the best time to do it would be in a few days, during Mr. Lloyd George's absence.

Lloyd George. This question must first be settled between the President of the United States and M. Orlando; for, concerning the frontier of the Adriatic, France and England are bound by the treaty they have signed with Italy.[2]

Loucheur. If, after a period of fifteen years, a part of the coal basin of the Saar should return to Germany, France would ask for guarantees to receive the coal necessary for Alsace and Lorraine and for the industries of the East. Will it be said that she can obtain it by the mere action of free competition? Here is what prevents us from believing it.

During the ten years preceding the war, we submitted to German blackmail each year, made possible by the need which our industries had of coal from the Saar. English coal, which could only arrive in Lorraine by way of the Seine and by long and slow navigable routes, cost the metallurgical industries four or five francs more per ton than German coal. The Germans played on that difference and used it to impose conditions upon our steel mills which placed them in an inferior position in relation to their own establishments. We do *not* want that to happen again.

Furthermore, Alsace and Lorraine consume, beyond what is produced on their own soil, around 8 million tons of coal coming from the Saar basin. Without Alsace and Lorraine, France already had a deficit in coal consumption; if in fifteen years she is deprived of the coal necessary for the industries of Alsace and Lorraine, the situation will be more difficult than ever and will tempt the Germans to exert distressing pressure on her.

What we are asking is the right of option for the average annual quantity consumed in the three years which will precede the plebiscite, at the same price as on the German domestic market.

Lloyd George. You are fixing no time limit. Can the same ar-

---

[1] Horatio William Bottomley, M.P. 1906-1912, reelected December 14, 1918. He was a journalist and financier of very dubious reputation, made and lost several fortunes, was several times bankrupt, and was frequently charged with fraud.

[2] That is, the Treaty of London.

rangement be made in perpetuity based on the price of the three last years?

Loucheur. That is not right; it is not the price but the quantity which will be fixed according to the average of the three last years. As for the price, we only ask that it be the same for the French consumer as for the German consumer.

Wilson. What seems to me difficult is the enforcement of such a clause; I see a danger of frictions and conflicts there.

Loucheur. I think that Germany will execute that clause without difficulty. What would be more serious than the conflict which you foresee would be the halting of the activity of our industries of the East. We are not asking anything except the continuation, after the contemplated period of fifteen years, of a *de facto* situation which will have existed during that period. We only wish to protect our industries against what Germany might do in a spirit of revenge. That will do no great harm to Germany, because it is a matter— assuming that the entire Saar Basin returns to Germany—of 13 million tons out of a production of 240 million tons.

Lloyd George. It is an arrangement analogous to that which we are making in England when we obtain water for a large city; we provide what is called "water of compensation." It seems to me that that clause contains nothing which can be called humiliating or abusive. The danger would be great if ownership of the mines belonged to France and sovereignty to Germany: we all agree to avoid that. But if Germany recognizes her obligation to furnish France a certain quantity of coal and if she finds herself not in a position to do so for reasons beyond her control, as a result of strikes for example, nothing will be easier than for her to explain that to the representatives of the League of Nations. If she should refuse without any justification, she would show by this her spirit of revenge and her desire to ruin the industries of eastern France; this would be a serious sign which we would have to worry about.

Wilson. What is the opinion of our experts on M. Loucheur's plan?

Loucheur. I have not consulted the American experts about this subject.

Wilson. Mr. Lloyd George called to our attention the other day that the coal of the Saar does not lend itself to transport over a long distance and can only be consumed in a rather limited area. If that is so, why not simply stipulate that the coal will be sold at the same price in France and on the domestic market? The means of pressure employed by the Germans, if I understand M. Loucheur, has been the difference in price between the coal of the Saar and English coal. Thus it is from this angle that a solution must be sought.

Loucheur. I think that it is indispensable to mention the quantity to be delivered.

Wilson. Do you not think that the usual commercial motives will continue to operate? What we wish to avoid is allowing the Germans to raise prices arbitrarily. We are preventing that by obliging them to sell this coal to France at the same price as to consumers in their own domestic market. If we fix a quantity and if that quantity is not delivered, must not the League of Nations intervene?

I see a serious danger in obliging any country, for an unlimited period, to give another country any kind of service. Suppose that the French government proves itself too demanding in the execution of a clause of this kind; suppose that Germany shows bad faith: I see difficulties on all sides as a consequence of that stipulation imposed without time limit.

Lloyd George. This problem does not arise only in the Saar Valley. There are other countries in Europe where we are obliged to provide arrangements of this nature, for example in the basin of Teschen. It would seem to me unjust to take that region from Poland, the population being Polish and passionately Polish. But the coal is necessary for the industries of Bohemia, which it has always supplied. M. Paderewski makes no objection to a clause like that suggested by M. Loucheur. He recognizes that the coal of Teschen is indispensable to Bohemia, and he is prepared to accept, without considering it any humiliation, the obligation to furnish coal to the Czechoslovak Republic, the Polish population of Teschen not being forced to separate itself from the Polish nation.

When the mines necessary to the existence of one country are located in a neighboring country, that situation imposes a sort of obligation upon the latter. The sole objection which I have to make concerns the duration of the period which must serve as the basis for determining the required quantity. We only wish to be just, and we believe we are being scrupulous in giving the population of the Saar the right to become German again at the end of fifteen years. But that does not mean that Germany will be able to deprive France of the coal she needs. That would be as if, in deciding that a mountain will cease to be part of a country inside whose frontiers it was formerly included, one would give to the new owner the right to divert the river which created the wealth of an entire region.

Clemenceau. Will the difficulties foreseen not be the same whether it is the price which is fixed obligatorily or whether it is the quantity to be delivered?

Wilson. I do not see any principle at stake here, and what I fear is not injustice. I am seeking only the system which can function best and with the least danger of future conflicts.

I am not a prophet, and I would hesitate in a case of this type to impose a regime whose operation could be delicate for an indeterminate time. I ask you to draft a text which satisfies you and to do this in agreement with our experts.

Lloyd George. Could we not at the same time instruct them to modify the article relating to the plebiscite? Instead of asking the inhabitants only if they wish to become French or return to being German, can they not be asked a third question, that is, if they wish to remain constituted as a separate state? Born myself in a small country, I believe in the advantages of small societies and the services they can render. I think they are often capable of taking initiatives useful to humanity which would be more difficult for large countries.

Wilson. You were born in a small country; I was born in a conquered and devastated country and that has helped me, believe it, to understand the questions which are asked here. What I fear is giving the League of Nations too much to do, imposing upon it too many duties at the same time, and multiplying the number of its officials. Are you sure that we will find them?

Lloyd George. We find men to administer, in a torrid climate, with low salaries, the most backward regions of the Indies. I do not see why you would fail to find persons to represent the League of Nations in the Saar Basin.

Wilson. Your officials have one of the most powerful motives which act on men: they are serving their country. That motive does not yet exist for the League of Nations.

Lloyd George. I am convinced that the men who will come to the Saar Basin to represent the League of Nations there will be aware of their authority and will never regret having accepted this post.

It is decided that M. Loucheur will draw up a definitive text along with Messrs. Tardieu, Haskins, Bennett, Cornwall,[3] and Headlam-Morley.

Wilson. Have you appointed your representatives to the commission of inquiry which must ascertain the attitudes of the different populations of the Ottoman Empire? Mine are appointed and ready to leave.

Lloyd George. We have not yet appointed ours, and I believe there must be a conversation on the subject between M. Clemenceau and myself.

[3] The Editors have been unable to identify anyone named "Bennett" connected with the Paris Peace Conference. Mantoux undoubtedly meant Bernard M. Baruch, who did attend the meeting of this committee. See David Hunter Miller, *My Diary at the Conference of Paris*, I, 241-42. Cornwall was Lt. Col. James Handyside Marshall Cornwall, a British technical expert on military questions relating to Austria, Czechoslovakia, and Hungary.

Wilson. We have taken a formal decision about this, and I do not see how an agreement between France and England could release us from sending that commission to Asia. It is a matter of knowing, not whether France and England agree, but what is the sentiment of the populations.

Clemenceau. Undoubtedly; but it would be useful to know in advance how France and England can agree on the question of mandates, in order to be able to submit proposals that the populations can accept.

Lloyd George. The opinions of our representatives differ. You have heard General Alby. Mr. Wilson,[4] who represents us in Mesopotamia, and who knows much better than General Alby the mentality of the Eastern populations, is of opinion contrary to his, especially concerning the sentiments of the Arabs of Damascus toward France.

After a short discussion, it is decided that a conversation will take place between the French and English governments on the subject of Syria, Mr. Lloyd George declaring that he dissociates himself from that question, and that he wishes the Emir Faisal to understand that he must not rely on a disagreement between France and England.

Mantoux, I, 223-29.

[4] Capt. Arnold Talbot Wilson, British Political Resident in the Persian Gulf and Civil Commissioner in Mesopotamia.

From the Diary of Lord Robert Cecil

April 11 [1919]

That evening League of Nations Commission. The Japs brought forward their "equality of nations" amendment in an extremely effective paper, read by Makino. Smuts, without giving me any adequate warning, had fled, and as I did not realise he was not going to be there I had got no one else to take his place, and had to grapple with the Japanese as best I could, which was not very well. The result of a long and rather incoherent discussion was that eleven of those present voted for the Japanese amendment, and only Dmowski the Pole besides myself voted against it. The President however ruled that it could not be inserted in the Covenant as it had not been carried unanimously. But he did not show quite as much courage as I could have hoped in resisting the amendment. He is a very curious mixture of the politician and the idealist, reminding me more and more in his point of view of Gladstone. He is not to me very attractive.

Minutes of a Meeting of the League of Nations Commission

FIFTEENTH MEETING, APRIL 11, 1919, AT 8:30 P.M.
President WILSON *in the Chair.*

ARTICLE 11.

The Commission continued its examination of the Covenant beginning with Article 11. There were no observations.

ARTICLE 12.

Lord Robert Cecil called the attention of the Commission to the difficulties which would arise if the Japanese amendment, which had been presented as Article 12A, should be adopted (Annex 1).[1]

Such a provision would give an important advantage to such States as maintained their military establishment in a highly developed state. Should a crisis arise, the small and peaceful nations with a low military establishment would find themselves at a serious disadvantage if they could not make use of the period of three months in order to prepare a better defence against a nation with superior armaments and effectives.

Baron Makino observed that the whole spirit of the Covenant was opposed to the principle that nations might make military preparations in a crisis. If they should undertake warlike measures, a tense and anxious atmosphere would be created which would hardly conduce to a peaceful settlement. Moreover, if the nation whose military preparations were inadequate should augment them, the better armed nation would do the same and the discrepancy between the two military forces would remain the same.

The Committee had raised the objection that the Japanese amendment would result in forcing nations into a military programme of serious dimensions. In answer, it might be said that the purpose of Article 8 was to lay down limits of armaments which might not be exceeded.

President Wilson said that he understood the provisions of Article 8 as they had been interpreted by Baron Makino. Nevertheless, without violating the obligations imposed by this Article, the States members of the League might increase their armaments up to the permitted maximum even during the period of time which would follow recourse to arbitration.

Lord Robert Cecil imagined the following hypothetical case. Sup-

---

[1] It is missing from all versions of the minutes. However, its text is as follows: "From the time a dispute is submitted to arbitration or to inquiry by the Council, and until the lapse of the aforesaid term of three months, the parties to the dispute shall refrain from making any military preparations." David Hunter Miller, *The Drafting of the Covenant* (2 vols., New York, 1928), II, 676.

pose that an unscrupulous nation should be considering an attack against a neighbouring State. She mobilizes all her troops, masses them on the frontier, and thereupon starts a dispute of a nature calculated to lead to a rupture. The dispute would then be submitted to arbitration, and while the case was being examined the aggressor State would have all its forces ready for action. On the other hand, the State which was threatened would not be able to take any preparatory measures. As far as Naval Power was concerned, a State might quite easily without violating Article 8 mobilize its fleet with a view to aggression. The Japanese amendment would therefore seem to impose obligations too great for human nature and to put tremendous advantages into the hands of unscrupulous States.

Mr. Larnaude supported these observations of Lord Robert Cecil, which had previously been discussed by the Drafting Committee. He himself thought that the Japanese amendment would compel states to increase the number of their effectives. On the other hand, if they knew that they might take advantage of the period of three months, they would not maintain in time of peace forces equal to the maximum allowed them.

Viscount Chinda asked whether it was the idea of the Drafting Committee that military preparations might be made during the period of three months.

Lord Robert Cecil replied that if the forces of any State were less than the maximum fixed by the programme of reduction they might be increased up to the maximum, but not beyond this point. Moreover he recognised the force of the argument made by Mr. Larnaude: if the amendment were adopted it would compel each State to maintain its forces at the maximum in order that it might be sure of defending itself against any aggressive act.

Mr. Bourgeois remarked that in this matter as in many other matters the whole difficulty lay in the fact that a control of armaments such as he advocated would not exist.

Mr. Orlando said that the Japanese amendment was unquestionably in harmony with the spirit of the Covenant. If the three months period were to be considered as a period of military preparation, the first thing which every State would do in case of dispute would be to mobilize its armies on the frontier and increase its output of material. Could anyone imagine a state of things less favourable to a peaceful settlement? It would be a kind of invitation to war.

Mr. Vesnitch thought that the States who were to become members of the League would be uneasy if they were not able to make military preparations in case they thought themselves threatened by a more or less open aggression. For this reason he thought that it would be better not to adopt the Japanese amendment.

Mr. Koo said that he only wished to add a few words to what had already been said. The spirit of the proposed amendment pleased him, inasmuch as it had unquestionably been conceived in the interests of peace. He thought however that it would not achieve the desired object inasmuch as it would encourage certain States, as Mr. Larnaude had just said, to maintain throughout a period of peace the maximum military force. Finally such a situation would turn the world into a veritable armed camp just as it had been before the war. Military preparations were contagious. Should one nation maintain its forces at the maximum, another nation would do the same and still another nation would follow the example set by the two. Moreover, the possibility of taking military steps during the moratorium would make it possible for nations to pay less attention to military preparations and would not compel such nations as were favourably disposed toward a programme of disarmament to keep their establishment up to the maximum permitted. A peaceful atmosphere would conduce to peace. Therefore, Mr. Koo thought that the amendment should be rejected.

Lord Robert Cecil said that the League of Nations looked toward a programme of complete disarmament, and that the Japanese amendment would tend to force nations into maintaining the maximum of armaments in order to avoid finding themselves at a military disadvantage.

Mr. Reis, as a representative of a small Power, was opposed to the amendment. The Great Powers always could impose their will upon the small Powers, and the only salvation of the latter lay in their being able to arm themselves as well as possible in case of need in order to re-establish the balance as well as they might.

President Wilson explained why he had welcomed the adoption of the Japanese amendment at an earlier meeting. In a Treaty concluded by the United States with twenty-six other States, an unsuccessful attempt had been made to introduce a provision like the one before the Commission.[2] In other words, he had a sentimental interest in the Japanese amendment inasmuch as it had given him a momentary feeling that he was taking a friendly revenge upon those who had opposed the insertion of a similar clause in these other Treaties. He admitted, however, that he had perhaps not given sufficient consideration to all the consequences which a provision of this sort might lead to. Every member of the Commission must be in sympathy with the generous impulse which had inspired the Japanese amendment, but he thought that a majority now felt the inconveniences which would arise if it were incorporated.

[2] That is, Bryan's "cooling-off treaties," about which see n. 1 to the Enclosure printed with WJB to JPT, April 8, 1913, Vol. 27.

Baron Makino did not insist upon the retention of his amendment, but expressed the desire that the Council would strictly supervise the performance of the programme of reduction laid down for various States.

Thereupon the amendment was withdrawn.

ARTICLE 13.

President Wilson observed that the list of cases capable of solution by arbitration given in the Article was for the purpose of indicating the general character of such cases, and was not intended to limit them.

In answer to a question of *Mr. Bourgeois, Lord Robert Cecil* said that the Hague Conventions were included in the Treaties referred to in Article 13.

Mr. Reis said that the word "generally," which did not appear in the French translation, seemed objectionable. To enumerate cases "generally" susceptible of arbitration implied that in certain particular cases recourse to arbitration was not possible. The word "generally" was contrary to the spirit of the English text which enumerated questions to be solved by arbitration. He reminded the Commission of the reservations made in the past with such harmful results in Treaties of arbitration.

Lord Robert Cecil replied that it was difficult to lay down a strict rule. For example, one could not say that the question of the interpretation of a Treaty should be submitted to arbitration in every instance. It might happen that such an interpretation would involve the honour or the essential interests of a country. In such a case the question should rather be submitted to examination by the Council of the League. It would be dangerous for the future of the principle of arbitration to impose it too strictly in a great number of cases.

Mr. Larnaude called the attention of the Commission to a letter addressed to the Chairman by the Swedish Delegation[3] (Annex 2),[4] in which the request was made that a Court of Justice might be established by the Assembly rather than by the Council, in order to give it a legal rather than a political character. It seemed to him very desirable that the members of the Court should be men versed in the science of law, but he did not think it necessary to have them nominated by a large assembly. The selection of the judges of the Court would probably be made in a more rational way if they were selected by a small number of competent persons such as the members of the Council would be. The thing which seemed essential

---

[3] Count Johan Jacob Albert Ehrensvärd, Swedish Minister to France, and Count Anton Magnus Hermann Wrangel, Swedish Minister to Great Britain.

[4] Missing in all versions, but Larnaude explains it well.

to Mr. Larnaude was that certain qualifications of ability and fitness should be required of the members of the Court of Justice. If such conditions of selection were laid down, the anxiety of the neutral Powers would be relieved and the choice of the Council would not fall upon mere politicians. Still, if necessary, the President of the Court might be a statesman who was possessed of considerable knowledge of law.

Mr. Kramar remarked that the permanent court provided for in Article 14 would have to decide not only questions of law, but political questions as well.

Lord Robert Cecil thought that it would be unfortunate if the Covenant attempted to define the conditions under which the members of the Court should be appointed. This Court would have to command the respect of the world, and such a result would best be obtained if the selection were left to the judgment of those who appointed its members. According to Article 14, the Council was to submit its plan for a Court of Justice to the members of the League. In reality, therefore, the Assembly would establish the Court.

Mr. Bourgeois asked what authority would nominate the judges themselves.

Lord Robert Cecil thought that the Council should make recommendations in this matter to the Members of the League.

ARTICLE 15.

Lord Robert Cecil stated the two amendments to this Article which had been proposed by the Drafting Committee. First, to add at the end of paragraph 5 of the English text, the following sentence:

"In the event of any party to the dispute failing to comply with these recommendations, the Council shall consider what steps, if any, should be taken to give effect to them."

Such an amendment would empower the Council to execute its decisions whenever they had been adopted unanimously.

President Wilson reminded the Commission that a similar clause had been struck out in the course of the first reading. At all events, he preferred "may consider" to "shall consider," inasmuch as provisions of this sort had given rise to criticism within the United States based upon the feeling that it would too deeply involve the signatories to the Covenant.

Baron Makino said that the provision would lose all its force if it were amended to read "may consider."

Lord Robert Cecil did not wish to insist upon the insertion of this amendment, since the Council would always be in a position to act as it thought fit if one of the parties should not accept its recommendations.

Mr. Bourgeois said that if the Commission were not prepared to say that the Council should consider measures to be taken in order to give effect to its recommendations, the whole strength of the organisation of the League would disappear.

President Wilson said that a similar provision had been eliminated from the first text, since a satisfactory formula could not be found.

The first amendment proposed by the Drafting Committee to this Article was thereupon withdrawn.

Lord Robert Cecil read the second amendment of the Drafting Committee—to add the following sentence as a new paragraph after paragraph 5 of the English text:

"If the Council fails to reach a report which is unanimously agreed to by the members thereof, other than the representatives of one or more parties to the dispute, the Members of the League reserve to themselves the right to take such action as they shall consider necessary for the maintenance of right and justice."

Mr. Bourgeois expressed the conviction that the whole idea of obligation had now disappeared. It would, therefore, be necessary to continue and to conclude separate alliances, inasmuch as the League admitted its inability to offer a formal guarantee of protection to its own members.

Lord Robert Cecil said that defensive alliances would not be incompatible with the object of the League, if they were entered into in accordance with the provisions of Article 15.

Mr. Orlando pointed out the difficulties which might arise from the provision that representatives of all parties to the dispute were to be excluded from the deliberations. There were certain cases where the exclusion of interested parties would lead to most unfortunate results. Suppose a dispute relating to the use of an international canal; if the parties to the dispute were debarred from voting, it might happen that small Powers not directly interested would settle a question upon which the Great Powers were divided.

Lord Robert Cecil explained the relation of this Article to such an issue. If a dispute were submitted to the Council, the parties to the dispute would participate in the discussion together with the other members of the Council. If all the States participating in the discussion should agree upon an unanimous report, no difficulty would arise. On the other hand, should the decision not be unanimous, it would be necessary to exclude the interested parties who were not willing to support the opinion of the majority.

President Wilson said that a State would have to declare either that it was a party to the dispute, in which case it could not vote; or that it was *not* a party to the dispute, and in that case it could vote.

ARTICLE 16.

Lord Robert Cecil stated that the Drafting Committee had slightly amplified this Article in so far as the question of passage of troops was concerned. The new draft now read:

"Upon the request of the Council they will take the necessary steps to afford passage through their territory to the forces of any of the Members of the League which are co-operating to protect the Covenants of the League."

President Wilson remarked that the passage of troops raised a very serious question, a question more important than the severance of economic and financial relations, a question calculated to give rise to discussions and controversies which might delay the military action of the League.

Mr. Bourgeois said that the obligation to permit the passage of troops applied to States Members of the League who were confronted with an unanimous decision of the Council. If this provision were struck out there would be a danger of isolating a State which was forced to resist an aggressive State more powerful than itself.

Lord Robert Cecil stated that the Drafting Committee had been equally divided over the question of the right of passage. The Committee had finally proposed that this right should be accorded to the interested parties "at the request of the Council" and not *ipso facto* as was provided in the case of economic measures.

President Wilson believed that a number of the members of the Commission were opposed to the insertion of this provision relative to the right of passage of troops.

The amendment was withdrawn.

ARTICLE 17.

No remarks.

ARTICLE 18.

No remarks.

ARTICLE 19.

No remarks.

ARTICLE 20.

Mr. Larnaude presented a new form of words, of the nature of a compromise, with regard to the Monroe Doctrine, which had been discussed at the last meeting; it had been agreed that the provisions relating to this doctrine should be inserted under Article 20. He thought that the Commission was not wholly in agreement on this question; so, in order to obtain unanimity, he proposed the following text:

"International understandings intended to assure the maintenance of peace, such as Treaties of arbitration, are not considered as incompatible with the provisions of this Covenant. Likewise with regard to understandings or doctrines pertaining to certain regions, such as the Monroe Doctrine, in so far as they do not in any way prevent the signatory States from executing their obligations under this Covenant."

This wording indicated that the Monroe Doctrine must not create obstacles to the fulfilment of obligations arising out of the present Covenant, and stated in so many words what President Wilson had said at the previous meeting. The President's statements, however, would only appear in the Minutes. If they should be included in the Covenant they would relieve the apprehension suggested by the present form of words. President Wilson had said the day before that the Monroe Doctrine was compatible with obligations arising out of the Covenant; it was the intention of Mr. Larnaude's amendment to state this fact rather than leave it unstated. Furthermore, in mentioning the Monroe Doctrine a special and privileged place had been given to the United States.

President Wilson feared that the proposed text would create the impression that there was an incompatibility between the Monroe Doctrine and the obligations of the Covenant and that an unwarranted suspicion would thus be cast upon the Doctrine.

Mr. Larnaude protested against this interpretation. He said that the proposed text was intended to clarify the situation by correcting the ill-informed opinion that the Monroe Doctrine prevented Europe from taking a hand in American affairs, and America from participating in the settlement of European questions. This misapprehension would be corrected if it were specifically stated that the Doctrine was not incompatible with the obligations arising out of the Covenant.

Lord Robert Cecil said that he did not desire either to support or to oppose the amendment. He merely wished to inquire whether this amendment would be likely to satisfy the criticisms and the fears which had arisen in the United States.

President Wilson remarked that there was no fear in America that the Monroe Doctrine was contrary to the obligations of the Covenant. There was, however, a fear that the Covenant might to some extent invalidate the Monroe Doctrine. If there were anything in the Doctrine inconsistent with the Covenant, the Covenant would take precedence over the Monroe Doctrine not only because it was subsequent to it, but because it constituted a body of definite international engagements. No one could doubt that if the United States subscribed to these engagements, they would carry them out.

Mr. Larnaude was of opinion that his amendment would satisfy French anxieties and would not cause any dissatisfaction in the United States. What objection could there be to stating explicitly something which was known the world over? If there were the least implication of suspicion in his amendment another formula might be found which would eliminate the suspicion and still preserve the principle of his amendment. He thought that it was necessary to do this in order to secure the unanimous approval of the Commission.

Mr. Bourgeois remarked that the French amendment was based upon two different ideas: First, it was intended to state that there was no incompatibility between the Covenant and the Monroe Doctrine. Second, it associated with this Doctrine a group of ideas and understandings which likewise were intended to secure peace and which, consequently, were to be considered as understandings compatible with the Covenant. In this way a general principle was laid down and the Monroe Doctrine was made a particular application of this principle.

Mr. Kramar asked whether in case of a dispute between Paraguay and Uruguay the League of Nations would have the right to come to the aid of whichever of the two States was supported by the decision of the Executive Council.

President Wilson replied in the affirmative.

Lord Robert Cecil believed that the Monroe Doctrine would in no wise prevent the forces of an European State from going to America in order to defend the rights of the oppressed. The sole object of the Monroe Doctrine was to prevent any European Power from acquiring any influence, territory, or political supremacy on the American continent. The idea that the Monroe Doctrine would prevent the Executive Council, in the execution of an unanimous decision, from acting in Europe, America, Africa, or Asia, was a perversion of the Monroe Doctrine, and citizens of the United States would be the first to disclaim it.

President Wilson agreed.

Mr. Koo said that he was reluctant to prolong discussion of this amendment inasmuch as the Commission had discussed it for a long time on the previous day. Nevertheless, he thought that if the amendment which he had proposed at the previous meeting were adopted, the objections of the French and Czecho-Slovak Delegations as well as his own would be met. He had suggested adding after the word "understanding" the following clause:

"Which are not incompatible with the terms of this Covenant and which are intended to assure the maintenance of peace, such as the Monroe Doctrine."

President Wilson made the same objections to this amendment which he had made to the French.

Mr. Koo proposed to add the words "or understandings" after the word "obligations" in the second line of the first paragraph of Article 20.

This amendment was adopted.

Mr. Larnaude proposed a new draft which was intended to correct the impression of suspicion in his first draft. The second sentence of his amendment was now to read as follows:

"Similarly with regard to all other arrangements, particularly those pertaining to certain regions, such as arise out of the Monroe Doctrine, in so far as they conduce to the maintenance of the peace which it is the object of this Covenant to assure."

President Wilson thought that this draft was not satisfactory. Moreover a provision with regard to the Monroe Doctrine had been accepted the day before and the Commission had decided to make a separate Article of it.

Mr. Larnaude declared that if this were the case the French Delegation would be obliged to make a reservation.

President Wilson asked whether this reservation indicated that the French Delegation would publicly oppose the American amendment. He thought that such a situation would create a most unfortunate impression on the other side of the water.

Mr. Bourgeois had no intention of creating such an impression in the United States, but he wanted to avoid discussions which might take place before the Plenary Conference and in the press. He thought that this result would be secured if the draft proposed by Mr. Larnaude were adopted.

President Wilson declared that the amendment was not adopted.

ARTICLE 21.

Lord Robert Cecil stated that a change had been made in this Article by the Drafting Committee, who had decided to add after the word "responsibility" in the second paragraph the words "and who are willing to accept it."

This amendment was adopted.

Viscount Chinda asked for an interpretation of the paragraph which referred to the administration of the South Pacific Islands.

President Wilson replied that this was a provision which had been adopted by the Council of Ten and that the Commission was not competent to change it.

Mr. Bourgeois proposed an amendment to Article 21 relating to the protection of historic monuments and antiquities found in Turkey. This amendment was proposed in a form which had been drawn for him by the French Minister of Public Education (Annex 3).[5]

President Wilson said that the Council of the League of Nations would doubtless accept with pleasure such a provision, which was completely in accord with the functions entrusted to it. It seemed unnecessary, however, to insert in the Covenant itself any provision with regard to this question.

Mr. Bourgeois made note of this statement which he considered satisfactory.

ARTICLE 22.

No remarks.

ARTICLE 23.

No remarks.

ARTICLE 24.

Mr. Bourgeois said that Article 24 seemed to him to give an exclusive position to the Red Cross without any reference to a great number of like associations which equally merited the support of the League of Nations, such as the International Society for the Prevention of Tuberculosis.

Lord Robert Cecil replied that Paragraph (f) of Article 22 was sufficiently broad to satisfy the anxieties of Mr. Bourgeois.

ARTICLE 25.

Mr. Pessoa stated that, according to the Brazilian Constitution, Brazil could not accept any Treaty before ratification by its legislative body. It therefore followed that if Brazil were not a member of the Executive Council, or were not included in the majority of the Assembly which ratified an amendment, it could not be bound by a provision which had not been ratified by its Congress.

Mr. Reis made the same observation with regard to his own country. He asked whether a State would have the right to withdraw from the League if its Parliament failed to ratify an amendment to the Covenant.

Lord Robert Cecil admitted that such a possibility might occur, but said that the idea of amending the Covenant could not be given up because of the opposition of a small number of States.

Mr. Orlando thought that the situation was not a difficult one. No State could be compelled to act against its will. On the other

---

[5] This annex is also missing in all versions. However, a full text is printed in Miller, *Drafting of the Covenant*, II, 385-86.

hand no Treaty could be made rigid and unchangeable for centuries. He thought that the proper solution therefore was to permit a State to withdraw immediately from the League if it refused to accept an amendment to the Covenant.

After this discussion the Commission adopted the following Amendment:

"Provided that no such amendment shall bind any Member of the League which signifies its dissent therefrom, but in that case it shall cease to be a Member of the League."

Preamble.

Mr. Bourgeois inquired whether the idea of "the peaceful settlement of international disputes" had been intentionally left out of the Preamble. This phraseology was very widely understood, it summarised the objects of the Covenant, and public opinion would not be able to understand why it had been omitted.

Lord Robert Cecil thought that the Convention to which Mr. Bourgeois referred was implied in the terms of the Preamble and that it would be unwise to change the text since every addition would give rise to hopes which it would be difficult to satisfy.

Baron Makino made the following statement:

"I have already had occasion to bring up this subject before the committee, but it was in another form and with a different meaning. The subject is a matter of such great moment and concern for a considerable part of mankind and especially to the nation I represent, that I deem it my duty to present it again for your consideration. My reasons having already been set forth on a previous occasion, I shall now be as brief as possible.

"This League is intended to be a world instrument for enforcing righteousness and defeating force. It is to be the highest Court of Justice. It will, besides providing for social reforms, also look after the welfare and interests of the less advanced peoples by entrusting their government to mandatory States. It is an attempt to regulate the conduct of nations and peoples towards one another according to a higher moral standard than has obtained in the past, and to administer fairer justice throughout the world. These ideas have touched the inmost human soul and have quickened the common feelings of different peoples scattered over the five continents. It has given birth to hopes and aspirations, and strengthened the sense of legitimate claims they consider as their due.

"The sentiment of nationality, one of the strongest human feelings, has been aroused by the present world-wide moral renaissance, and is at present receiving just recognition in adjusting international affairs. In close connection with the grievances of the oppressed nationalities, there exist the wrongs of racial discrimination which was, and is, the subject of deep resentment on the part of a large portion of the human race. The feeling of being slighted has long been a standing grievance with certain peoples. And the announcement of the principle of justice for peoples and nationalities as the basis of the future international relationship has so heightened their legitimate aspirations, that they consider it their right that this wrong should be redressed.

"It must be admitted that it has been possible to bring this work to this advanced stage, because the prevailing world opinion has backed the different Governments in working it out, and that the enduring success of this undertaking will depend much more on the adherence to (and espousal of) the noble ideals, set forth in the Preamble, of the various peoples concerned than on the support of acts of respective Governments that may change from time to time. The peoples constituting the States Members must be the future trustees of this work, and their close harmony and mutual confidence are necessary for insuring such success.

"Believing these conditions to be indispensable, I think it only reasonable that the principle of the equality of nations and the just treatment of their nationals should be laid down as a fundamental basis of future relations in this world organisation. If this reasonable and just claim is now denied, it will, in the eyes of those peoples with reason to be keenly interested, have the significance of a reflection on their quality and status. Their faith in the justice and righteousness, which are to be the guiding spirit of the Covenant, may be shaken.

"Such a frame of mind may, it is to be gravely feared, lead to their unwillingness and reluctance to carry out obligations, such as military contribution, which certain emergencies, foreseen in different articles, may require. A most deplorable situation may thus be created, now that the world is to move on a higher plane of international political life. It will not be easy for people to reconcile themselves to the idea of submitting to a call for heavy and serious obligations, perchance in defence of those at whose hands they are refused a just treatment. Such a contingency must be borne in mind, for pride is one of the most forceful and sometimes uncontrollable causes of human action.

"I state in all seriousness, that although at this particular centre of political life the practical bearing of such a dangerous development of the question may not at this moment be properly realised, I, for one, entertain much anxiety about the possible future outcome of this question.

"My amendment to the Preamble is simply to lay down a general principle as regards the relations between at least the nationalities forming the League, just as it prescribes the rules of conduct to be observed between the Governments of the States Members.

"It is not intended that the amendment should encroach on the internal affairs of any nation. It simply sets forth a guiding principle for future international intercourse. The work of carrying out this principle comes within the indisputable competence of the proper authorities. This amendment does not fully meet our wishes, but it is an attempt to conciliate the view points of different peoples, the result arrived at after a thorough and mature consideration of various aspects and realities of present international relations."

Baron Makino asked therefore that, after the words "relations between Nations" in the Preamble, the following clause should be inserted: "by the endorsement of the principle of the equality of Nations and the just treatment of their nationals."

Lord Robert Cecil regretted that he was not in a position to vote for this amendment although he was personally entirely in accord with the idea advanced by the Japanese Delegation. The British Government realised the importance of the racial question, but its solution could not be attempted by the Commission without encroaching upon the sovereignty of States members of the League. One of two things must be true: either the points which the Japanese Delegation proposed to add to the Preamble were vague and ineffective, or else they were of practical significance. In the latter case, they opened the door to serious controversy and to interference in the domestic affairs of States members of the League. There were a great many things which the States themselves ought to do: but these were not included in the Preamble. For example, it had been found impossible to include in the text, matters so unquestionably right as those of religious liberty, the claims of the International Council of Women, and a great many other principles of this sort because they would result in infringements of the sovereignty of States. Furthermore, Japan would be permanently represented on the Executive Council and this fact would place her in a situation of complete equality with the other Great Powers. This being so, it would always be possible for her to raise the question of equality of races and of nations before the Council itself.

Viscount Chinda replied to the objections raised by Lord Robert Cecil. He pointed out that the Japanese Delegate had not broached the question of race or of immigration. He asked for nothing more than the principle of equality of nations and the just treatment of their nationals. These words might have a broad significance, but they meant that all the members of the League should be treated with equality and justice. He thought it quite as important to introduce this principle into the Covenant as it was to introduce such other questions as the supervision of labour conditions, public health, traffic in arms, &c. Acceptance of the Japanese amendment would mean nothing except that the League of Nations was to be founded upon justice. Japanese public opinion was so strongly behind this amendment that he asked the Commission to put it to the vote. If the amendment were rejected, it would be an indication to Japan that the equality of members of the League was not recognised and, as a consequence, the new organisation would be most un-popular. The formula which he proposed was of great importance, and the national aspirations of Japan were depending upon its adop-tion. Public opinion in Japan was very much concerned over this question and certain people had even gone so far as to say that Japan would not become a member of the League of Nations unless she were satisfied on this point.

Mr. Orlando supported the Japanese amendment. Originally the Commission had been inclined to adopt an Article proclaiming the most important of all liberties, that of religion. He himself would have been glad if this Article had been retained in a Covenant which was intended to bind together nations of a democratic character. The equality of nations was a question which perhaps ought not to have been raised; but once having been raised, there was no other solution except that of adopting the amendment. Lord Robert Cecil had spoken of the practical reasons why its application would be difficult. Such an argument would carry weight if the Commis-sion were considering the adoption of an Article in the Covenant which put the members of the League under a definite obligation. All that was now asked, however, was the insertion of a principle in the Preamble. If this principle were rejected, it would give rise to feelings which were hardly in harmony with the new organi-sation.

Mr. Bourgeois agreed with Mr. Orlando. He felt that it was im-possible to vote for the rejection of an amendment which embodied an indisputable principle of justice.

Mr. Larnaude remarked that the Japanese amendment had now reappeared in an entirely different form and that it would be difficult not to adopt the principle of equality of nations as it was now proposed. Moreover, it was intended that this declaration should appear in the Preamble, and preambles ordinarily laid down broad declarations of principle which did not impose obligations so strict as those of subsequent articles. For these two reasons he thought that the Commission could not avoid voting for the amendment.

Mr. Veniselos reminded the Commission that he had been largely responsible for the disappearance of the religious liberty clause from the Covenant. He had thought that if this clause were cut out the difficulty relative to the racial question would likewise be eliminated. To-day, however, the question had appeared in a different light and Japan had taken her stand upon another ground; they were talking not of the equality of races, but of the equality of nations themselves and of just treatment of their nationals. It would be very difficult to reject such a proposal especially since Baron Makino had carefully pointed out that his proposal did not involve any State in the obligation to pass any measures whatever with respect to immigration. If the Japanese amendment were accepted and were written into the Preamble, a clause relative to religious liberty might also be introduced.

Mr. Kramar could not see how any danger could arise out of the Japanese amendment. He himself was pretty well acquainted with a State where a certain Article 19[6] provided for the equality of nations and where these nations had been cruelly oppressed over a long period of time. He thought that the words of the Japanese amendment were entirely in harmony with the rest of the Preamble and particularly with the expression "open, just, and honourable relations."

Mr. Dmowski expressed himself as in entire sympathy with the Japanese Delegates, but he did not see how a general declaration could be included in the Preamble when it was not to be enforced by particular provisions in subsequent Articles.

Mr. Koo read the following statement:

"I believe that the principle contained in the Japanese amendment involves a number of questions to which time alone can give an universally satisfactory solution. Nevertheless I should be very glad indeed to see the principle itself given recognition in the Covenant, and I hope that the Commission will not find serious difficulties in the way of its acceptance. I should like to have my statement appear in the Minutes."

President Wilson felt that the greatest difficulty lay in controversies which would be bound to take place outside the Commission over the Japanese proposal, and that in order to avoid these discussions it would perhaps be wise not to insert such a provision in

[6] That is, Article 19 of Statute 142 enacted by the Austrian Parliament in 1867 which declared that all ethnic groups within the Austrian state had equal rights and that each ethnic group had the inviolable right to preserve and cultivate its own nationality and language. The same article recognized the equality of all languages customarily spoken in the crownlands in schools, governmental agencies, and public life and stated that the public schools should be so organized that each ethnic group would receive the necessary funds for training in its own language without being compelled to learn a second language. For a translation of and a commentary on this famous article, see Robert A. Kann, *A History of the Habsburg Empire, 1526-1918* (Berkeley and Los Angeles, 1974), pp. 339-40.

the Preamble. The equality of nations was a fundamental principle of the League of Nations. It was the spirit of the Covenant to make a faithful attempt to place all nations upon a footing of equality, in the hope that the greater nations might aid the lesser in advantageous ways. Not only did the Covenant recognise the equality of States, but it laid down provisions for defending this equality in case it should be threatened.

Baron Makino said that he did not wish to continue an unprofitable discussion, but in these matters he was representing the unqualified opinion of the Government of Japan. Therefore he could not avoid the necessity of asking the Commission to make a definite decision in this matter and he had the honour of asking his fellow-members to vote upon the question of the insertion of his amendment in the Preamble.

A vote was taken and eleven votes out of seventeen were recorded in favour of the amendment.

President Wilson declared that the amendment was not adopted inasmuch as it had not received the unanimous approval of the Commission.

Mr. Larnaude called attention to the fact that a majority had voted in its favour.

President Wilson admitted that a majority had so voted, but stated that decisions of the Commission were not valid unless unanimous, and the Japanese amendment had not received unanimous support. There was only one case where a decision of the majority had prevailed, and that was in the case of determining the Seat of the League. In that case it had been necessary to accept the opinion of the majority inasmuch as no other procedure was possible if the question was to be decided at all. In the present instance there was, certainly, a majority, but strong opposition had manifested itself against the amendment and under these circumstances the resolution could not be considered as adopted.

Mr. Vesnitch said that he had voted for the amendment because it laid down a principle of international law, that of the equality of nations. As for the question of "just treatment of their nationals," one could depend upon the honour of self-respecting nations to respect the citizens of other States. No one could deny these principles, and the vote taken by the Commission must have given satisfaction on this point to Baron Makino and to Japanese opinion at large.

Lord Robert Cecil thought it better that the Covenant should be silent on these questions of right. Silence would avoid much discussion.

President Wilson said that no one could dream of interpreting the vote which had just been taken as condemnation of the principle proposed by the Japanese Delegation.

Baron Makino said that he was sorry to insist upon the point, but asked that the number of votes which had been cast in favour of the Japanese amendment should appear in the Minutes. He would take the question up again on the first appropriate occasion.

Mr. Larnaude reminded the Commission that he had proposed, by way of compromise, a clause which should recognise the Monroe Doctrine in the Covenant and at the same time preserve the integrities of the principles upon which the Covenant was based.

President Wilson said that the proposed clause would raise objections in the United States and thought it would be better not to insist upon it.

Mr. Larnaude said that in these circumstances he would make a reservation on the matter and that the French Delegation would consult with its Government.

After an exchange of views between *Mr. Bourgeois, Lord Robert Cecil,* and *Mr. Larnaude,* it was decided that an agreement between the English and French texts should be reached by a small Drafting Committee composed of both French and English speaking members.

Lord Robert Cecil proposed that the Chairman should be entrusted with the duty of naming the four States to be represented on the Council in addition to the Five Great Powers.

Mr. Larnaude thought that this choice might be left to the representatives of the Five Great Powers who were to be members of the Council.

Mr. Orlando asked whether any neutrals would be included among these four States.

Lord Robert Cecil thought that three Allied Powers and one neutral might be named.

Mr. Veniselos asked how the representatives of a neutral State which was not yet a member of the League could become a member of the Council.

Lord Robert Cecil answered that neutral States would be admitted at once. Spain in particular had already indicated a desire to become a member of the League of Nations.

Mr. Bourgeois thought that the nomination of the four members of the Council who were to represent States with special interests was a political act of the greatest importance. Such a question could not be decided casually and it would be necessary that the Governments should be consulted on this matter.

Mr. Orlando said that the Commission had not the competence to decide this question.

Mr. Larnaude said that the Five Great Powers had been named by the Conference and asked how the four others could possibly be named by the Commission.

Lord Robert Cecil said that a similar question arose with regard to Article 1, namely, what neutral States should be invited to accede to the Covenant. Would the Plenary Conference have to undertake to draw up this list of invitations? He thought this list might fairly include the thirteen neutral States who had stated their views before the Commission. Last of all, there was the question of the provisional organisation of the League which might be entrusted to a committee of representatives of seven States (including two neutrals) who might be named by the Chairman.

Mr. Bourgeois inquired whether the Commission had the power to create such an organisation. At all events, the Commission ought to agree upon the names to be proposed as members of the Committee of Organisation and report them to the Plenary Conference for its approval.

Lord Robert Cecil replied that, if any work was to be done, an organisation would have to be provided as quickly as possible.

President Wilson said that the suggestion had been made that a Committee of Seven be nominated to report upon the provisional organisation of the League of Nations.

Lord Robert Cecil said that if there were any matters still undecided, each Delegation might send its observations on them to the President. Furthermore, the members of the Commission might present these views at the Plenary Conference.

The meeting adjourned at 12:50 A.M.

Printed copy (WP, DLC).

Remarks on the Monroe Doctrine[1]

[April 11, 1919]

I do not think there is a thing, and if there is something or may be something in the Monroe Doctrine which is inconsistent with these obligations, and if there is, and I do not think there is—I am clear that there is not—but if there is, of course the obligations of the United States under this Covenant take precedence of anything that might stand in the way. There can be no doubt as to what the United States binds itself to in this Covenant, and I would urge that I don't like that suspicion cast upon the Monroe Doctrine.

◇

May I say this? There is no thought in America that the Monroe Doctrine interferes with the full performance of the obligations of the United States under the Covenant. There is in some quarters what I consider an unfounded impression that the Covenant to some extent may invalidate the Monroe Doctrine. There is no thought in my mind that the Monroe Doctrine invalidates the Covenant, but there is in some minds the thought that the Covenant invalidates the Doctrine, so that we are seeking to remove that, as I believe, erroneous impression by distinctly saying, there is nothing in this Covenant inconsistent with the Monroe Doctrine. Now, if there is anything in the Monroe Doctrine inconsistent with the Covenant, the Covenant takes precedence of the Monroe Doctrine, not only because it is subsequent to it, but because it is a body of definite obligations which the United States cannot explain away even if it wanted to explain. Anybody reading the Covenant and seeing the assent of the United States appended cannot [doubt that it will] bring its forces to Europe whenever it is obligated to do so by the terms of this Covenant. That is the only thing, that until this time, the United States never did. It is one thing that it never wanted to do, but it is one thing that it is consciously consenting to in becoming a member of this League; so that it is reversing its whole historic [policy] in assenting to this Covenant, and it needs to be assured that in doing that it is not invalidating long-continuing understandings on the other side of the water. And, therefore, I earnestly hope that the suggestion will not be pressed that the original language be altered.

I respectfully urge that in phraseology of that sort we are casting suspicion upon the good faith of the United States in signing this Doctrine [document]. I mean that any language of that sort is susceptible of that interpretation. How could the United States consciously sign this Doctrine [document] if the Monroe Doctrine was incompatible with it. It is inconceivable. You see, the whole object of this mentioning of the Monroe Doctrine is to relieve a state of mind and misapprehension on the other side of the water; relieve the mind of certain consciencious public men in the United States who want to be assured that there is no intention in this League to interfere with the Doctrine, which if they all knew to be inconsistent with the Covenant, they would not in the same breath ask for an explanation like this and ask to be admitted to a League which was inconsistent with a situation like this.

T MS (WP, DLC).

¹ The following transcript was prepared by Whitney Hart Shepardson, secretary for the League of Nations in the A.C.N.P. At an unknown date, Shepardson gave the document to Ray Stannard Baker, who deposited it in WP, DLC. It is entitled "VERBATIM COPY OF REMARKS MADE BY PRESIDENT WILSON ON THE MONROE DOCTRINE AT THE MEETING OF THE LEAGUE OF NATIONS COMMISSION IN PARIS."

It is of course possible that this document represents a "verbatim" record of what Wilson said. If this is true, then fatigue and embarrassment, and not dementia (general deterioration of mental power), were responsible for this very un-Wilsonian prose. It seems to us that Shepardson might possibly have been a poor stenographer and transcriber. For example, Wilson almost certainly said "document" instead of "Doctrine." The outlines for these words in Gregg shorthand are almost identical, and it would have been easy for Shepardson to have made a mistake in writing or transcribing them. In addition, the verbatim transcripts of Wilson's remarks in the Council of Four at this time show that Wilson still retained his remarkable powers of speech and language.

In fairness to Shepardson, we should point out the possibility that he was not in a position to hear Wilson well when he took down in shorthand the transcripts printed above. He must have moved close to Wilson when he took down the notes for the transcript which follows. Therein, Wilson displays his characteristic mastery of the English language.

Remarks upon the Clause for Racial Equality¹

[April 11, 1919]

Regarding Japanese Proposal.

Gentlemen, it seems to me that it is wisest that we should be perfectly candid with one another in a matter of deep importance like this. The trouble is not that any one of us wishes to deny the equality of nations or wishes to deny the principle of just treatment of nationals in any nation. The trouble is not with our decisions here, but with the discussions which would certainly be raised in the Plenary Council if the words suggested were introduced into this Covenant. My own interest, let me say, is to quiet discussion that raises national differences and racial prejudices. I would wish them, particularly at this juncture in the history of the relations with one another, to be forced as much as possible into the background. We here have no choice as to the part that is to be played by others of our colleagues of the Conference of Peace in the discussion of matters of this sort. It is not only in this room, but elsewhere, that attention has been drawn to this and similar suggestions, and those very suggestions have set burning flames of prejudice, which it would be very unwise to allow to flare out in the public view in the Plenary Conference. It is in my own mind for the purpose of quieting these prejudices, of letting them play no part in the discussions connected with the establishment of this League, that I am looking at this whole matter. How can you treat on its merits in this quiet room a question which will not be treated on its merits when it gets out of this room. It is a question altogether of the wisest thing to do, not a question of our sentiments towards each other or of our position with regard to the abstract statement of the equality of nations. This League is obviously based on the principle of equality of nations. Nobody can read anything connected with its institution or read any of the articles in the Covenant itself, without realizing that it is an attempt—that [the] first serious and systematic attempt made in the world to put nations on a footing of equality with each other in their international relations. It is recognized everywhere that this is an attempt, a most hopeful attempt, to secure for those nations which could not successfully protect themselves if attacked by the stronger nations of the world, the support of strong nations of the world in their defence. It is a combination of moral and physical strength of nations for the benefit of the smallest as well as the greatest. That is not only a recognition of the equality of nations, it is a vindication of the equality of nations. No one could question, therefore, the principle upon which this Covenant is based, and I think we ought to approach the present question which has been raised, in what I must call the very impressive [remarks] by Baron Makino, from the point of view of what it is wisest to do in connection with the discussion which will attend the institution of this great League. I know from my knowledge of their attitude and character that these considerations apply strongly to the very thoughtful men who represent Japan at this table. In presenting this matter they are doing their duty; they are doing it with conscious solemnity. But, I am saying what I have just said with a view to avoiding the very embarrassments which I think they have in mind. I offer these suggestions with the utmost friendship, as I need not assure my Japanese colleagues, and with a view to the eventual discussion of these articles.

I will put the question to a vote. All in favor of incorporating this phrase will be kind enough to raise their hand.

I have counted eleven.

It has been our practice to make the vote unanimous when incorporating a provision unless those who have entered are willing to let a provision be incorporated as a reservation on their part.

I think there are two serious objections on the part of some of us to make that possible.

◇

I think that M. Larnaude is mistaken. I follow the course of saying that then the proposition was adopted if there was no objection. In several cases, the French delegates have merely made a reservation; have stated that they would not insist upon their objection. Whenever an objection has been insisted upon, I felt obliged to say that it has not been adopted. At least one objection is insisted upon by one of the governments concerned.

I am obliged to say that it is not adopted.

◇

I have gone on the principle that any objection insisted upon was an obstacle to the adoption.

I do not think that anybody will ever interpret the result of this evening's discussion as a rejection on our part of the principle of equality of nations.

T MS (WP, DLC).
    ¹ The following document is, in fact, a continuation of Shephardson's transcript beginning with Wilson's remarks upon the Monroe Doctrine.

Isaiah Bowman to Edward Mandell House

[Paris] April 11, 1919

To: Colonel House
From: Isaiah Bowman
Re: Map of Northern Italy

Olinto Marinelli is the author of the attached map,¹ which was published in the March number of the *Geographical Review*. There are but two copies in France.

Marinelli is a teacher of physical geography in the High School at Florence. His work is well known to me, and I know him personally, having traveled with him in America in 1912. He is the leading Italian geographer. There are others who occupy a higher place, but there is none other so capable.

As a proof of his standing among Italian scholars may be cited the fact that when the Italian Touring Club decided to get out a general atlas of the world under Italian editorship and raised the sum of a half million lira to back the plan, they selected Olinto Marinelli as the scientific editor.

It seems to me that the map should not only receive the closest scrutiny on the part of yourself and the President, but that the President should have it at hand when the Italian questions are discussed, in order that there should be no question about the ethnographical facts as presented on American maps. I have asked Major Johnson for comment upon the map, and he states, "I think you will be interested in the substantial accord between the conclusions of the Italian authority and the conclusions of our own specialists,² especially as regards the eastern frontier region."

T MS (SDR, RG 256, 186.3411/369, DNA).
¹ "ETHNOGRAPHIC MAP OF THE FRONTIER ZONE OF NORTHERN ITALY," printed map
(SDR, RG 256, 186.3411/369, DNA).
² See W. E. Lunt *et al.* to WW, April 4, 1919, Vol. 56.

A Memorandum

[c. April 11, 1919]
Italy (Map etc)

At the very outset we shall have followed the fatal error of making
Italy's nearest neighbors on her east her enemies, nursing just such
a sense of injustice as has disturbed the peace of Europe for generations together with playing no small part in bringing on the
dreadful conflict through which we have just passed.

T transcript of WWsh (WC, NjP), written on the verso of the preceding document.

From Herbert Clark Hoover

Dear Mr. President: [Paris] 11 April 1919.

Your economic group has had before it the question of whether
the United States should continue membership in the various commissions set up under the peace treaty. I should like to lay before
you my own views on this subject.

I feel strongly that any continuation of the United States in such
an Allied relationship can only lead to vast difficulty and would
militate against the efficiency of the League of Nations. My reasons
are as follows:

I. These commissions are primarily to secure the enforcement of
reparation and other conditions imposed upon the Central Empires.
As the United States is not calling for any form of reparation that
requires continued enforcement, our presence on these commissions would appear to be for one of the following purposes.

(a) To give moral and political support to the Allied Governments
in measures generally for their benefit. It cannot be conceived that
in the prostrate condition of the enemy that the Allies will require
any physical assistance to the enforcement of their demands. In
this event, the United States will be lending itself to the political
and financial interests of other governments during peace, a situation that must be entirely repulsive to our national interests, traditions and ideals.

(b) Another objective might be that we should remain in these
commissions with a view to securing justice and moderation in the
demands of the Allies against the Central Empires. We would thus

be thrust into the repulsive position of the defender of our late enemy, in order to secure what we would conceive to be constructive and statesmanlike rehabilitation in Europe. Our experience during the last three months has shown us bitterly that we thus subject ourselves to complaint and attack from the Allied Governments and such a continued relationship should only breed the most acute international friction.

II. If our experience in the last four months counts for anything, the practical result always is that the Allied Governments, knowing our disposition, necessarily ask for more than they expect to get, and that we find ourselves psychologically and, in fact, politically on the side of the enemy in these negotiations, and in a constant desire to find practical working formula we are frequently forced to abandon some measure of what we consider sane statesmanship. The continuation of this relationship will bind us for a long period of years to a succession of compromises fundamentally at variance with our national convictions. I am not attempting to dispute the righteousness of any Allied demand, but merely to set up the fact that our viewpoint is so essentially different. One other practical result of our experience already is that the Americans who sit on such commissions, if they don't acquiesce and assist in enforcing any propositions from various government officials, become immediately and personally subject to attack as being inimical to their interests and with the powerful engines of propaganda which they employ in Europe and our own country no such man can endure for long. These governments, if they were faced with the sole responsibility for their actions, would not attempt the measures which they seek under our protection. Therefore, for all reasons, I do not see that we can effect any real justice in these matters.

III. If we continue to sit in the enforcement of this peace, we will be in effect participating in an armed alliance in Europe, where every change in the political wind will affect the action of these commissions. We will be obliged to participate in all European questions and we will be firmly tied definitely to one side, unless we precipitate a break and lend ourselves to the charge that we have been traitors to the "common cause."

IV. This whole matter has a very practical relationship to the League of Nations. If we can bring to an early end our whole relationship to these political combinations in Europe, which grew up before and during the war and can lend our strength to the League of Nations, that body will gain a stability and importance which it could not otherwise attain. As the Central Empires and Russia will not be for some years admitted to the League, and if we continue in what is in effect an armed alliance in Europe dominating these empires, the League will become simply a few neutrals gyrating around this armed alliance. It will tend to drive the Central Empires and Russia into an independent League. If, on the other hand, we can again secure our independence, we can make of the League that strong and independent Court of Appeal that will have authority.

V. I am convinced that there has grown up since the Armistice the policy, perhaps unconscious but nevertheless effective, of dragging the United States into every political and economic question in Europe and constantly endeavoring to secure pledges of economic and political support from us in return for our agreeing to matters which we consider for their common good, where we have no interest, and constantly using us as a stocking [stalking] horse economically and politically, solely in the interests of internal political groups within the Allied governments. These objectives and interests may be perfectly justified from their point of view, but it forces us into violations of our every instinct and into situations that our own people will never stand. For instance, I don't see how we can remain in these enforcement commissions unless we participate in the military enforcement with its enormous cost and risk, and the tendency will always be to exact the political objectives with the military strength of the United States as a background.

VI. I have the feeling that revolution in Europe is by no means over. The social wrongs in these countries are far from solution and the tempest must blow itself out, probably with enormous violence. Our people are not prepared for us to undertake the military policing of Europe while it boils out its social wrongs. I have no doubt that if we could undertake to police the world and had the wisdom of statesmanship to see its gradual social evolution, that we would be making a great contribution to civilization, but I am certain that the American people are not prepared for any such a measure and I am also sure that if we remain in Europe with military force, tied in an alliance which we have never undertaken, we should be forced into this storm of repression of revolution, and forced in under terms of co-ordination with other people that would make our independence of action wholly impossible.

VII. It grows upon me daily that the United States is the one great moral reserve in the world today and that we cannot maintain that independence of action through which this reserve is to be maintained if we allow ourselves to be dragged into detailed European entanglements over a period of years. In my view, if the Allies can be brought to adopt peace on the basis of the 14 points, we should retire from Europe lock, stock and barrel, and we should lend to the whole world our economic and moral strength, or the world will swim in a sea of misery and disaster worse than the dark ages. If they cannot be brought to accept peace on this basis, our national honor is at stake and we should have to make peace independently and retire. I know of nothing in letter or spirit of any statement of your own, or in the 14 points, that directly or indirectly ties the United States to carry on this war through the phase of enforcement or [of] the multitudinous demands and intrigues of a great number of other governments and their officials. It does appear to me that your conception of the League of Nations was with view to the provision of a dominant Court, where these difficulties could be thrashed out and if we sit as one of the prosecutors, the Court will have no judge.

Faithfully yours,   Herbert Hoover

TLS (WP, DLC).

From Tasker Howard Bliss

My dear Mr. President: Paris, April 11, 1919.

I have received today an "Outline of Recommendations of General Smuts as a result of his trip to Budapest, Vienna and Prague."[1]

I note that he recommends that "a military force representing the four Great Powers shall occupy the neutral zone in Transylvania." The Eastern boundary of this neutral zone would require the Roumanians to keep about forty kilometers east of the former zone and the one which brought on the revolution in Hungary.

Knowing the confidence that you have in General Smuts (a confidence which I share), I hope that you will allow me to invite your especial attention to this recommendation because I think that it would be unwise to accede to it.

You already have my views as to the undesirability of the United States becoming a party to any of these military adventures in Europe until we have signed peace with Germany and until the United States can then have an opportunity to calmly consider the situation in Europe and determine to what extent it will further assist in the military and financial solution of problems growing out of the war but not having any necessary connection with our peace with Germany.

If we accept General Smuts' recommendation, I think that we will find ourselves in a rather absurd position. The Allies are now contributing to the support of an enlarged Roumanian army. They have asked us to contribute a large quantity of supplies, although I do not know what your final decision has been. This Roumanian army threatens, and probably will continue to threaten, the peace by invading Hungary in order to secure a boundary line which has not yet been given it by the Peace Conference. At the same time, if we act on General Smuts' recommendation, we would send an Allied army into Hungary to occupy the neutral zone and keep the Roumanians back. Thus, on the one hand we would be supporting a Roumanian army that is attacking Hungary, and at the same time would be sending an Allied army to protect the Hungarians from the Roumanians.

I believe that if you were to *demand* from the Allies that none of these things be done; that we say to Roumania that unless she stops on the line indicated by General Smuts she will get no assistance whatever from the Allies, Roumania will obey.

Mr. Lansing tells me to-night that he will at once send to you General Kernan's report of his observations in Eastern Europe. I hope that you will particularly notice what he says under the heads of BOLSHEVISM and MILITARISM.

I suppose that General Smuts' recommendations may come up for action by the Council at any moment, and for that reason have permitted myself to make the foregoing suggestions.

Very sincerely,   Tasker H. Bliss.

TLS (WP, DLC).
[1] See the memorandum by J. C. Smuts printed at April 9, 1919.

A Memorandum by Francis Joseph Kernan

Confidential   *Robert Lansing*

Paris, France 11 April, 1919.

Confidential Memorandum for The American Commission to Negotiate Peace.
Subject: Suspension of Arms between Poles and Ukrainians in Eastern Galicia, and some general observations on conditions in Poland.

On March 20th, last, the Great Powers sent identical telegrams to the Ukrainian and Polish Commanders in Eastern Galicia requesting, in substance, that a suspension of arms should be forthwith effected, following the lines of the former one, dated Feb. 24th, 1919, this to be followed by a formal armistice to be arranged preferably in Paris under the direct supervision of the Peace Commission.[1] A copy of this identical telegram was furnished the undersigned with instructions to see that it reached the hands of each

[1] See n. 2 to the extract from the Diary of Dr. Grayson printed at March 21, 1919, Vol. 56.

of the Commanding Generals in Eastern Galicia, together with a second explanatory telegram. As directed I delivered these telegrams personally to General Jwaszkiewricz,[2] Polish Commander at Przemysl on March 24th, and on March 25th I met General Pavlenko,[3] the Ukrainian Commander, at Sambor and delivered the same messages to him. These had already been received directly by wireless and both parties had, so I was informed, accepted the proposition of the Great Powers and the two Commanding Generals were in communication with each other for the purpose of arranging a meeting between delegates. Both parties requested me to be present at this meeting and left me to designate the place. Pursuant to this arrangement five delegates from each side met on the afternoon of March 27th at Chyrow, just within the Polish lines.

I had suggested to each party the advisability of going to the Conference with a prepared draft for the convention and this course was followed. Before the actual meeting of the delegates, each side read to me their propositions. The Polish proposition contained an article providing that the Poles should have the right to denounce the suspension of arms at the end of three days unless, within that period, the Ukrainian authorities had accepted en toto the armistice terms drawn up Feb. 28th, 1919, by Dr. Lord, General Berthelemy[4] and General DeWiatt[5] of the Inter-Allied Mission to Poland. This armistice had been rejected by the Ukrainian authorities and it was practically certain that their injection into the new effort to bring about a cessation of hostilities meant the failure of that effort. I told the Polish delegates this, and also pointed out that the procedure they were following did not conform to the request of the Great Powers, as accepted by them; that is to say, instead of attempting to make a simple suspension of arms, leaving the formal armistice for subsequent arrangement, they were tacking the one to the other and so defeating both. They replied that their instructions had come from their Government and that they had no power to abate the conditions respecting the armistice as written in their draft. The Ukrainians had drawn up a simple plan for a suspension of arms, each party remaining on the ground occupied, and with the necessary stipulations for securing its execution. When the delegates met and the Polish terms were unfolded, the Ukrainians at once stated that they had come to make a suspension of arms merely, in agreement with their promise to Paris, and not an armistice such as the Poles were proposing. They added that they were willing to

[2] Gen. Waclaw Teodor Iwaszkiewicz-Rudoszanski.
[3] Gen. Mykhailo Omelianovych-Pavlenko, commander of the Ukrainian Galician Army.
[4] That is, Gen. Marie Joseph Raoul Léon Barthélemy.
[5] That is, Maj. Gen. Adrian Carton de Wiart.

abide by whatever armistice terms their delegates agreed to in Paris. Since the Polish delegation was without authority to modify their demands the meeting broke up.

Before leaving the Polish Headquarters at Przemysl the following day I addressed to the Polish Commander a letter outlining what I thought should be the substance and nature of a brief convention establishing a suspension of arms. On arrival in Warsaw I enclosed a copy of this letter to Mr. Paderewski, the Secretary of Foreign Affairs, indicating my views of what the Polish Government should do in order to comply with the clear and earnest desire of the Great Powers. Copies of these letters are attached hereto, marked "A."[6]

While en route to Paris with the other members of the Inter-Allied Commission, I received a message from the Peace Commission directing me to proceed again to the Ukrainian front and to make a further effort to bring about a suspension of arms. I did so and found that the Polish Commanding General was powerless to make a truce except upon the terms already stated above. He told me that the matter was not in his hands but in the hands of higher authority and that he could do nothing. In this state of affairs, and knowing that the head of the Polish Government was en route to Paris, I left Przemysl and proceeded to this city where I arrived yesterday April 10th.

The distinct impression I brought away from Eastern Galicia was that the Ukrainians were exceedingly anxious for a truce and that their leaders were intelligent men by no means Bolshevik and sincerely desirous of building up a great Ukrainian Republic. General Pavlenko was quite frank and stated that the Russian Soviet forces were pressing the Ukrainians on the East and that his Government was anxious to secure a truce on the Polish side in order to bring as strong a Ukrainian force as possible into action against the Russian Soviets. Besides my own observations I talked with quite a number of disinterested observers who had been travelling through The Ukraine quite recently and as a result I am convinced that the present Ukrainian Government and the Ukrainians in the mass are by no means Bolshevik. It must, however, be realized that some of that spirit has penetrated at least into the eastern fringe of The Ukraine and that the failure of the present Government might result in Soviet ascendency. The Ukrainians are wholly isolated from Europe and they have, I believe, been misrepresented in a large degree

---

[6] [F. J. Kernan to W. T. Iwaszkiewicz-Rudoszanski], March 28, 1919, and F. J. Kernan to [I. J. Paderewski], March 30, 1919, both TCL (WP, DLC). As indicated above, the letter to the Polish commander outlined the terms of an agreement for a suspension of arms between the Polish and Ukrainian armies in Galicia. This suspension was the "clear and earnest desire of the Great Powers," which Kernan discussed briefly in his covering letter to Paderewski.

to the world, it being the policy of their enemies to denounce them as bandits and Bolsheviks. Reiterated statements of this kind have their effect however groundless they may be.

I travelled more than two thousand miles in Poland by automobile, from Posen on the West to Slonim on the East, southward through Brest Litovsk to a point beyond Lemberg and back by way of Cracow to Warsaw. I was approximately two months in Poland and talked with a great many people. From this experience I have drawn the following conclusions:

(A) Food and Economic conditions.

Want of the extremest character prevails in the large cities, in the industrial centers, and in the territory lying between Grodno and Brest Litovsk. There is, I believe, enough food in Poland to tide the population over until the next harvest, assuming the American food supplies to continue flowing into Poland at the present rate. The supply is not evenly distributed but an effort is being made by the Polish authorities in connection with our Food Mission to overcome this difficulty. If raw materials go into Poland and public works are started by the Government so that employment can be given to those not engaged in agriculture, much of the dire distress will be done away with. When the Russians made their great retreat they drove the people out of a vast area of agricultural land which remains practically without population today and which for several years has been a solitude outside of the larger towns. No acre of ground has been plowed, no seed planted, no domestic animals are there, and practically no population. It is a vast area and it is nearly a desert today. Manifestly no crops can be sowed there this year, but the wretched inhabitants are straggling back slowly, many on foot, shoeless, clothed in rags, their whole worldly possessions carried on their backs. The agricultural villages show here and there a sign of life, and undoubtedly more of the former inhabitants will return as the summer goes on. Since they can raise no crops this year, manifestly they must be fed from outside. It is in this region that the greatest desolation and extremest want prevail. This was Russian Poland. In their best days the lives of this agricultural population must have approximated that of the animals which they worked. These squalid villages explain the spread of Bolshevism better than any other thing which has fallen under my observation.

(B) Bolshevism.

Although the common report and the common talk in Poland constantly spoke of Bolshevik aggression against Poland, I could get no evidence to that effect whatever. On the contrary, I am satisfied that the desultory skirmishing along the Eastern frontiers of Poland represents an aggressive effort of the Poles to extend their military occupation as far as possible and as quickly as possible into Russia. The ease with which they have done this proves conclusively that no strong organized Soviet force has been opposing the Poles. My belief is that as an aggressive military crusade, undertaking to spread its propaganda by violence from Russia as a center, the Bolshevik or Soviet movement has come to a halt. It may be stirred into life again by aggressive action directed against it from without, a danger to be feared from Poland or from other States. This view may seem to be contradicted by recent happenings about Archangel and in the region of Odessa. But it must be remembered that the Soviet Government claims sovereignty over those areas and its military operations there can be accounted for on the ground of national defense and wholly apart from any schemes of forcible propaganda. Communistic views are not a new thing. The terrific outburst in Russia and the more recent happenings in other parts of Central Europe signify an extraordinary condition of the masses brought about by generations of misgovernment and suddenly intensified beyond further endurance by nearly five years of war. In this view, the great cause of the apparent spread of Bolshevism in Europe is to be found in the despairing and wretched condition of its masses. It is not progressing in these days by force of arms but through propaganda falling upon ground prepared by long years of misery and culminating in the hardships of the great war. Therefore, if the normal life of the world can be restored, accompanied by such bettered living conditions as will enable the masses to have not merely enough bread to keep body and soul together, but some little share in the ordinary happiness of humankind, Bolshevism will be stopped.

(C) Militarism.

In Central Europe the French uniform is everywhere in evidence, officers and men. There is a concerted, distinct effort being made by these agents to foster the military spirit in Poland, Czecho-Slovakia, and, I Believe, in Roumania. The imperi[a]listic idea has seized upon the French mind like a kind of madness and the obvious effort is to create a chain of States, highly militarized, organized as far as possible under French guidance, and intended to be future Allies of France. I have no doubt whatever of this general plan and it is apparently meeting with great success. Poland is endeavoring to raise an army of approximately 600,000; the Czechs are striving to raise an army of about 250,000, and Roumania is struggling under a very extensive military burden. All of this means that these people have no belief in the efficacy of the League of Nations to protect them and that under the guidance of the French a strong military combination is being built up capable, perhaps, of dominating Europe. This purpose of course is not avowed. The claim is that this chain of strong military states is essential to hold back the tide of Russian Bolshevism. I regard this largely as camouflage. Each of the three States named has aggressive designs upon the surrounding territory and each is determined to get by force, if need be, as large an area as possible. Nobody is attacking Poland today. Quite the contrary; and it seems deplorable that in a country where so much distress prevails and where the energies of the Government and its resources should be devoted to bettering the conditions of its people and to organizing an efficient state administration, this rampant military spirit should have taken possession. It presents today more danger to the future of Poland than Bolshevism does. Bolshevism can be eradicated by good Government and equal opportunity for all citizens, but the military disease, once fastened upon the State, is going to be difficult to eradicate. With the arrival of Haller's Army it is to be feared that aggressive military action will be taken against the Russian, The Lithuanian, and the Ukrainian fronts unless the Great Powers can find effective means of checking the outburst of intoxicated nationalism already existent and becomming stronger every day.

I advise strongly against Inter Allied Missions where information or concrete results are sought. Send Americans alone upon such tasks.

F. J. Kernan
Major General, U. S. Army

TS MS (WP, DLC).

From William Cox Redfield

Washington, April 11, 1919.

1535. URGENT. For President from Redfield.

Director General Hines publicly announces refusal accept steel prices recommended by Industrial Board, stating in his opinion prices are too high. Against his opinion stands the unanimous conviction of the Industrial Board, except railroad member, based upon analyses of costs from Federal Trade Commission from producers themselves and checked by experts specially invited by Board and known to Baruch. Facts respecting costs placed before Railroad Administration who were repeatedly asked to furnish any facts and data tending to modify them. They have expressed their belief, but have presented no facts or figures relating to costs under existing conditions. No other government purchasing department or service has objected but action of the Railroad Administration suspends activities of Board. As to reasonableness of rail prices, attention is directed to fact that figures presented by Steel Corporation show an increase in its direct labor cost alone per ton of product since 1913 of $19.48. Assuming old rail price $30.00 per ton was fair, new price of $47.00 does not take care of actual increase in direct labor cost alone, exclusive of increase in cost of transportation and other elements of cost. Quite apart from prices, however, Railroad Administration definitely opposes policy represented by Industrial Board. In published statement April 5th, Hines expresses himself regarding policy in connection with coal, i.e.; "I have therefore been unwilling to comply with the suggestion which has come from the National Coal Association to the Railroad Administration *withdraw your communication* bids and instead undertake to buy its coal at uniform prices for the various districts fixed by some government agency." Matters therefore between Railroad Administration and Industrial Board at deadlock. Palmer has rendered opinion to me stating "that the proposed plan of the Industrial Board of the Department of Commerce viewed in any aspect is unauthorized by law." This opinion refers to action of Board in recommending fair price for steel. Board has repeatedly expressed *comma* its willingness to change form of procedure to meet view of (?). This opinion not published but general tenor known to Railroad Administration. Palmer personally friendly to work of Board and to purposes sought to be accomplished, appreciating serious industrial and political effects probable. Thinks situation such that method might be found accomplish results if your wishes clearly known. Steel industry state immediate effect of Board's announcement of the stabilized prices resulted in revival orders, in some cases as much as forty per cent, but when Railroad Administration did not promptly accept prices and failed to place orders, business immediately sagged to point of stagnation and so remains. Board desires your decision, through me, whether should abandon work in view of Hines' attitude and Palmer's opinion or whether matter should remain quiescent until your return. This latter course satisfactory to Palmer. I, however, recommend immediate decision. Instructions awaited. Redfield.

Polk,   Acting.

T telegram (WP, DLC).

Two Telegrams from George Nelson Peek to Bernard Mannes Baruch

Washington, April 11, 1919.

1529. Baruch from Peek.

Your 1501, April 7th and 1520, April 8th.[1]

Please read carefully my cable number 1255, March 22nd, number 1329, March 27th, number 1455 April 5th.[2] Corporation reports that for 1913 the cost of direct labor from ore, coal and stone through to the finished product, all steel products manufactured by it, exclusive of cost of labor and transportation $15.13 per ton, and at present on basis of March wage scale $34.61, an increase of $19.48 per ton. Considering old rail price of $30.00 and adding additional direct labor cost alone $19.48 would make price $49.48 as against $47.00 approved by board. Cable number 1455 April 5th, explains Hines' position, i.e., that it is the policy he now objects to rather than the price of rails. This, notwithstanding the fact that he was personally present and concurred in plan at Cabinet meeting when plan was conceived before I undertook work. Prices not determined for any particular period but board announced that it believed its prices were as low as public could reasonably expect this year. There is nothing in any of our negotiations or understandings which prevents any producer from selling at either a higher or lower price. Or limiting any buyer to these prices. Have just returned from Hines' office. Situation at this moment is, he confirms his position declining to accept steel prices but has submitted no data at any time, expresses once for all opinion that prices are too high, contrasted to which is our analysis of federal trade figures, advice of industry and independent investigation by Seiferty[3] and others. It is clear, therefore, that it is the policy he objects to and drags in the Sherman law. Judge Lovett told me yesterday in New York that it was not a question of the price of rails but solely one of policy, Mr. Hines would have to determine.

Hines has publicly stated that he is now opposed to any Governmental agency fixing prices on coal for the Railroad Administration, and intends to rely on concentrating bids for coal. People claim railroads resorting to old time practices in coal purchases.

Am taking entire matter up with Secretary Redfield, who will cable President for instructions regarding the dismissal of our Board. I cannot refrain from adding that in my opinion the effect upon the country of this action will be serious if not dangerous.

Polk,   Acting.

[1] B. M. Baruch to G. N. Peek, April 7 and 8, 1919, T telegrams (WP, DLC).

[2] G. N. Peek to B. M. Baruch, March 24 (not 22), 27, and April 5, 1919, T telegrams (WP, DLC).

[3] The Editors have been unable to identify him.

Washington. April 11th, 1919.

URGENT. 1536. Baruch from Peek.

It is obvious that the position taken by the Railroad Administration will but add to the feeling of unrest and uncertainty which already permeates labor and industry in this country. The spectacle of a single governmental agency refusing to conform to a policy designed to further the interests of the entire country must inevitably lead to a loss of confidence in the ability of the government to assist in the restoration of normal conditions. Reduced to the simplest terms the point at issue is—are the interests of labor and the entire commercial structure of the United States to be subordinated to the claimed interests of a single governmental agency? The policy of the Department of Commerce affects so vitally the people of this country as a whole that it must be referred to the President for final approval or rejection. Supplementing earlier cable today on street prices number 1529 no time limit determined for steel prices. In making our public announcement we did say that on account of high cost of living conditions, the public could not reasonably expect to buy at lower prices during the current year. We have repeatedly stated both publicly and privately to governmental departments including Attorney General that if there is any suggestion objectionable in the form of our announcement we will gladly correct it.   Polk,   Acting.

T telegrams (WP, DLC).

From Carter Glass

Washington, April 11th, 1919.

1532. PERSONAL AND CONFIDENTIAL.

For the President from Glass.

Subject to your approval, I have decided to issue four and one-half billion dollars gold notes of the U. S. Treasury Liberty Loan, dated May 20th, maturing in four years redeemable at the option of the United States in three years, in two series, one series bearing four and three-quarters percent interest and exempt from normal income tax and the other series bearing three and three-quarters percent interest and exempt from all taxes. I hope this may meet with your approval and that I may have your reply by cable at the earliest possible date. As already announced, the popular campaign will extend from April 21st to May 10th. May I ask that you give such instructions that the contents of this cable will be held as strictly confidential. 1532.   Polk,   Acting.

T telegram (WP, DLC).

From the Right Reverend Charles Henry Brent

Dear Mr. President: [Chaumont] April 11, 1919.

A friend, writing from the United States, has put into my mind a proposition which I would like to present to you for consideration.

If, in the proposed draft of the League of Nations, there is no clause indicating God's purpose to bind all Nations into one, could not something of the sort be inserted, even if it were only a sentence? The more I have thought of the attempt which we are making to create world order, the more I have concluded its hopelessness without looking to God to do that work above and beyond as well as through us which is necessary for anything permanent.

I merely throw this out as a suggestion, and believe that it would tend to stabilize our idealism if the first mention of unity were referred to as the product and purpose of God's mind.

Yours very faithfully,   C. H. Brent
Senior Chaplain, A.E.F.

TLS (WP, DLC).

From the Diary of Dr. Grayson

Saturday, April 12, 1919.

The President had breakfast at 9:45 o'clock this morning. I had a conference with him concerning his health. At 11:00 o'clock the Big Four meeting was held here in the temporary White House. The President was determined to hurry things along as fast as possible. The arrangements dealing with the Saar Valley situation were brought enough to a head to warrant the conclusion that this knotty problem had at last been solved.

At one o'clock the President and Mrs. Wilson lunched together, after which the President went for a short ride. Upon his return he resumed the Big Four conference.

The President, Mrs. Wilson and I had dinner, and after dinner the President told me that things had brightened up considerably, and that they had really gotten into working action. The President retired at a late hour.

From the Diary of Colonel House

April 12, 1919.

Last night we did not adjourn the meeting of the Committee for the League of Nations until a quarter past one o'clock. Again Cecil and the others wished to quit and again the President and I held them to the task until they had finished. Long experience in such matters teaches me that it is the last quarter of an hour that does the work. Everybody practically gave up and we passed matters almost as fast as we could read them during the last fifteen minutes. This is a game I have played all my life, and I felt so much at home that when it was over I was not even tired. Around half past twelve Cecil asked how long the meeting was to continue. I told him until daylight or until we had finished.

The French Delegates brought up again the question of the Monroe Doctrine just as blithely as if it had not been passed and settled last night. They repeatedly submitted amendments which the President would hand to me and which I would advise against accepting. Cecil would try to improve on the French amendment, and David Miller would make suggestions, but we were not in a humor to take anything except what we wanted and what we wanted was finally passed.

It was an exhibition of Anglo Saxon tenacity. The President, Cecil and I were alone with about fifteen of the others against us, and yet in some way we always carried our point.

The Japanese brought up their amendment to the Preamble. The President was for accepting it, but Cecil, under instructions from his Government, could not, and since I knew that Hughes would fight it and make an inflammatory speech in the Plenary [Plenary] Session, I urged the President to stay with the British, which he did, and in a speech made the argument I gave him.

It was a fine fight from start to finish and since we won I went to bed at two o'clock quite content. . . .

Not long ago, the President asked me to submit someone for Minister to Poland. Hugh Gibson's name was at the top of the list and last night the President said he would appoint him. I sent for Gibson while Paderewski was here and introduced him.

At the request of the President, I asked Tardieu to call in order to read the riot act to Clemenceau, through him, regarding the left bank of the Rhine and the protection of France. We discussed the Sarre Basin which has now come back to the plan Tardieu and I approved some two weeks ago and which the President rejected.[1] I took occasion to tell Tardieu of the action of Bourgeois and Larnaude concerning the Monroe Doctrine.

And this reminds me that last night I re-wrote the resolution which I gave Lord Robert Cecil to introduce, and which was passed in the hasty moments of closing. This resolution will place the direction of the organization, the preparation of the Agenda for the first meeting of the League, and the place of the meeting largely in my hands. I am attaching a copy of this resolution.

Among my other activities today was a meeting of the Economic Council. I had prepared a summary of what the League of Nations Commission had done at the last two meetings so as to give it to the Press, and had Whitney Shepardson prepare a statement concerning the Japanese question.[2] Before giving this out, I sent it to the Japanese Delegates for their approval. They were pleased with the substance of it. I also sent it to the President for his approval, and then warned the correspondents against any sensational or inflammatory statements.

[1] See the extract from the Diary of Colonel House printed at March 29, 1919, Vol. 56.
[2] Shephardson's statement is printed in Miller, *Drafting of the Covenant*, I, 465-66. Wilson and Baker, in preparing the statement that was issued (see n. 1 to the following document), used most of Shephardson's draft; they omitted the two paragraphs preceding the last paragraph. Miller, *ibid.*, p. 465, is of course incorrect in intimating that the statement was never published.

From the Diary of Ray Stannard Baker

Friday [Saturday] the 12th [April 1919]

I had quite a talk with the President this evening, after his long session with the Big Four & the financial experts (Lamont & Davis). They spent the day trying to settle the final details of the Reparations clauses of the treaty. This morning, they had up the very confidential matters of the time of inviting the Germans to Versailles: & also discussed how to keep secret the details of the treaty. I found the President pretty tired, & looking worn, and I thought not hopeful. We had prepared a statement on the Japanese clause in the Covenant, explaining why it was not accepted & had submitted it to Baron Makino for his approval. I wanted, if possible, to have the President sign it but he said he thought he had no right, as Chairman of the L. of N. Commission, to put out a statement of what took place in the meetings. But he approved the substance of it & I put it out for publication this evening, after reading it aloud to the correspondents.[1] The President discussed with me the method he thought the Conference must pursue in presenting the treaty to the Germans, & the need of preserving secrecy.

[1] The statement read as follows: "At a meeting of the League of Nations Commission on Friday, April 11, the Japanese delegation proposed an amendment to the preamble

of the covenant, as follows: To insert after the words 'by the prescription of open, just and honorable relations between nations,' an additional clause to read: 'By the indorsement of the principle of equality of nations and just treatment of their nationals.'

"The amendment was admirably presented by Baron Makino. In the course of his speech he emphasized the great desire of the Japanese government and of the Japanese people that such a principle be recognized in the covenant. His argument was supported with great force by Viscount Chinda.

"A discussion followed, in which practically all of the members of the commission participated. The discussion was marked by breadth of thought, free and sympathetic exchange of opinion and a complete appreciation by the members of the commission of the difficulties which lay in the way of either accepting or rejecting the amendment.

"The commission was impressed by the justice of the Japanese claim and by the spirit in which it was presented. Mention was frequently made in the course of the discussion of the fact that the covenant provided for the representation of Japan on the Executive Council as one of the five Great Powers, and that a rejection of the proposed amendment could not, therefore, be construed as diminishing the prestige of Japan.

"Various members of the commission, however, felt that they could not vote for its specific inclusion in the covenant. Therefore, the commission was reluctantly unable to give to the amendment that unanimous approval which is necessary for its adoption."
New York Times, April 13, 1919.

From the Peace Conference Diary of Thomas William Lamont

April Saturday 12 1919

At Pres't's house at 11. Mistake, did not need us. I said to him: "Mr. Pres't, we can handle this High Comn. matter on Reparation O.K. if you will only tell us that you instruct us to follow the schedule which we shall propose to you." He replied—"Mr. L., I agree in advance to endorse any program that you 4 agree on, & you may work on that basis." An hour's meeting w. Sumner & Cunliffe re releasing bonds & voting. NHD & I not in entire accord.

Hw bound diary (T. W. Lamont Papers, MH-BA).

From the Peace Conference Diary of Bernard Mannes Baruch

April 12, 1919

The President authorized me to make such an agreement upon the clause affecting the amount and prices of coal that France would need at the expiration of fifteen years, if the coal mines of the Sarre Basin go back to Germany. The following is the clause which I reported to Dr. Haskins as agreeable to me, and which met with the approval of Summers and Legge.[1]

If the ownership of the mines, or a part thereof, passes to Germany, it is understood that France or French nationals will have a just claim to the use of such coal of the Sarre Valley as their industrial and domestic needs will be found at that time to require. An equitable arrangement regarding amounts, time of contract and prices will be fixed at that time by the Council of the League of Nations.

I informed the President and Dr. Haskins that I was reporting only on this clause, and not upon the general arrangement, which did not seem to me to be the wisest thing to do.

Dr. Haskins asked me what should be done to protect the metallurgical works in the Sarre Basin, and if it would be satisfactory to leave it to the Commission to be set up. I told him that that was probably the best thing that could be done, and further, that the commission should control the distribution of the entire products of the Sarre Basin, and should be the one to decide the questions regarding the further opening up of mines, workmen's trains, schools, and the other matters with reference to the conduct of the Sarre Valley coal mines; in other words, to have the commissioners sitting on top of the whole thing, and having the final say in all matters.
. . .

I informed the President that I was not passing upon, and had not been asked to pass upon, the Sarre Valley coal matter, other than the particular clause referred to.

T MS (B. M. Baruch Papers, NjP).
    [1] That is, Leland Laflin Summers and Alexander Legge. Both were at this time economic advisers in the A.C.N.P.

Mantoux's Notes of a Meeting of the Council of Four

April 12, 1919, 11 a.m.

Lloyd George. I wish to speak to you about the publication of the preliminaries of peace. Before leaving for London, I will ask you if we agree about the question of whether that publication should take place before or after the time when we will meet the German plenipotentiaries.

Wilson. In my opinion, it would be very unwise to publish this text before the beginning of the negotiations. I would do everything possible to prevent any disclosure.

Lloyd George. In England, we can issue an order under the powers granted to the government by the Defence of the Realm Act.

Wilson. I do not have corresponding powers. But I believe I can get the press to abstain from any disclosure of this kind.

Lloyd George. Do you have this influence over the Hearst press?

Wilson. Its representative in Paris[1] is perhaps the best of the

    [1] John Edwin Nevin, who represented William Randolph Hearst's International News Service.

American correspondents and one of the most public spirited. I believe it is possible to lean upon him.

Clemenceau. What does M. Orlando think?

Orlando. From my point of view, any publication before the start of the negotiations could only have very regrettable effects.

Lloyd George. Do you not think that we should have a conversation about this with the Ministers of Foreign Affairs? We could see them this very morning.

It would be madness to publish the articles of the treaty before the arrival of the German plenipotentiaries. It would make it impossible for them to accept our conditions, if German public opinion flares up even a little.

I have another question to pose: for what date will we summon the Germans? Since nearly all the provisions are ready, I would favor summoning them Friday week, April 25.

Orlando. Unfortunately, it is the time when I must be in Rome for the opening of Parliament.

Lloyd George. I had forgotten that. When will you return from Italy?

Orlando. I hope that the questions which most concern Italy will have been settled in their main outlines before my departure for Rome. That is of particular importance for Italian opinion; it would not understand why talks with the Germans were beginning before the problems especially concerning us had been taken up.

Once that is done, it is not essential that I be present at the exact moment when negotiations with the Germans begin. M. Sonnino can represent the Italian government here if I arrive two or three days later. The important thing as far as I am concerned is that, when the Germans arrive at Versailles, Italian opinion has the impression that our questions have received a satisfactory solution in principle.

Clemenceau. Before summoning the Germans, the question of Danzig must also be settled.

Lloyd George. Are we not agreed on its solution?

Clemenceau. Undoubtedly; but you have seen M. Paderewski's opposition. If the region of Marienwerder were not left to Germany, I believe the Poles might resign themselves to the independence of Danzig.

Lloyd George. It would be contrary to all our ideas to leave within the Polish State a territory so obviously German, and which has always been part of ancient Prussia.

Clemenceau. You cannot imagine Paderewski's emotion; it went even to tears.

Wilson. Yes, but you must take account of his sensitivity, which is very lively.

Lloyd George. After all, the Poles are assured of independence after a century and a half of servitude. If they do not believe themselves capable of surviving because we refuse them a small territory which contains 150,000 Germans! * * *

Wilson. I would favor giving M. Paderewski a declaration signed by us, explaining our motives, in order to make the Poles understand that we have acted without any desire to favor their enemies, but on the contrary, in order to preserve them from future danger.

Lloyd George. On the question of Teschen, I lean toward the side of the Poles. The population of that region seems to be Polish by a large majority. On the other hand, it is just to assure Bohemia a right to the use of the coal under conditions analogous to those provided for France in case the Saar Basin should become German again. M. Paderewski understands that and recognizes the vital importance of those coal mines for the industries of Bohemia.

Wilson. I must tell you how moved I was yesterday by a visit of a group of Polish peasants who came from their country, having traveled 60 kilometers on foot to the nearest station, and whose villages had furnished them the funds necessary for the trip. They begged me to see to it that the line of the frontier unites them to Poland, their country, and not to make them subjects of the Czechoslovak Republic. Their simplicity and passion were touching. This is a case of one of those indentations in the drawing of the frontiers about which it is so difficult for us to decide.

Lloyd George. We wanted to maintain the frontier between Bohemia and Germany such as it existed before the war. But concerning the frontiers between friendly states such as Bohemia and Poland, or Rumania and Serbia, I do not see why it would not be possible, in cases where several doubtful points remain, to give some commissions the mandate to settle these difficulties after the conclusion of the preliminaries of peace.

Marshal Foch and General Weygand are introduced.

Foch. I asked to see you to inform you of a telegram which I just received from our headquarters in Mainz. They tell me that one of our agents in Weimar makes known that Dr. Heim,[2] head of the Bavarian Peasants' League in the German National Assembly, asks for a safe conduct to be able to enter into contact with a representative of Marshal Foch, to whom he has an important communication to make. I ask for your instructions.

Lloyd George. It probably concerns some movement against the soviets.

Wilson. Why does this Dr. Heim address himself to the military authority?

[2] Dr. Georg Heim.

Clemenceau. He thinks that Marshal Foch will communicate to us what he will say.

Lloyd George. That could mean that, if the soviets are holding the Bavarian cities, the peasants are hostile to them. It can be interesting to hear what a representative of the peasants has to say.

About our attitudes toward the German parties, we have several questions to ask ourselves. Do we wish to intervene in the internal quarrels of Germany? Do we wish to prevent Bavaria from separating from the rest of Germany, if such is her desire? If Austria joined a Bavaria separated from the rest of Germany, would that not be a situation altogether different from the one created by the union of Austria with a unified Germany?

Foch. I conclude then that I should respond to our headquarters in Mainz to give a safe conduct to Dr. Heim and to arrange an interview with him, either in Mainz or in Kreuznach.

Marshal Foch and General Weygand withdraw.

Messrs. Lansing, Balfour, Pichon, and Sonnino are introduced.

President Wilson explains to the Ministers of Foreign Affairs the question already, examined by the heads of government, of publicity concerning the preliminaries of peace. The heads of government agree in thinking that all publicity must be avoided before the opening of the negotiations with the Germans; but they were eager to hear the Ministers of Foreign Affairs on this subject.

Mr. Balfour says that, after a first conversation with Mr. Lloyd George, he believes with him that this publicity would have very dangerous effects, as much in Germany, where it could provoke a movement which could make negotiations difficult, as in our different countries, where it might cause more or less violent discussions.

Lloyd George. There are two ways to avoid publicity. The first is to try to prevent indiscretions, which is very difficult. The second is to prevent publication. We can do this in England, in France, and in Italy. The President of the United States believes that he can, in using his influence over the press, obtain the same result. There is still the question of knowing if we can communicate the text to the Germans before having communicated it to all the powers represented at the conference. In any case, those who took direct part in the war against Germany must be summoned.

Mr. Lansing thinks that all the powers which declared war on Germany must sign the treaty and, consequently, have the right to know the proposed text in advance.

Lloyd George. A distinction should be made between the countries which are directly affected by certain clauses of the treaty and those which only have a general interest in it. To Belgium, to Bohemia, to Poland, we are obviously obliged to submit the clauses which involve them.

Mr. Lansing insists on the same right for all the powers at war with Germany, who cannot accept being informed at the same time as the enemy, or after him.

Mr. Balfour proposes, in the first place, an examination of the clauses of special interest to certain powers, such as Belgium, with the representatives of these powers, and, in the second place, a plenary and secret session of the representatives of all the Allied and Associated Powers, to which the preliminaries would be explained in their main outlines, without the text in all its details being communicated to them.

After an exchange of views, that proposal is provisionally adopted.

Mantoux, I, 230-34.

From Robert Lansing

My dear Mr. President: Paris, April 12, 1919.

I have been thinking over the meeting which took place this noon at your house in regard to publicity of the terms of peace, and the more I think of it the more I am convinced that it would be a mistake to follow the course suggested by Mr. Lloyd-George and apparently approved by Mr. Clemenceau.

The reasons for this opinion are that no matter what precautions are taken the substance if not the text of the articles will become known and will find their way into the press; that to attempt to suppress them will increase the irritation of the press and public as to secret agreements; and that the smaller belligerents will deeply resent this manifest distrust in their discretion and may adopt a course which would be embarrassing.

The attitude taken by Mr. Lloyd-George in regard to the other belligerents would be most impolitic. We cannot treat them as we treat the Germans and demand that they sign the treaty without considering its terms. No delegates of self-respecting governments will consent, unless compelled to do so, to obey without question dictation of that sort. They represent free and independent nations, which voluntarily entered the war. They have a right certainly to consider the terms on which they are to make peace. I do not think that they can be treated as vassals, which is apparently their status in Mr. Lloyd-George's eyes.

There is undoubtedly a wide-spread irritation among the lesser belligerent states as to the way that they have been ignored and generally excluded from the deliberations as to the terms of the treaty. If this exclusion is carried up to the day when the treaty is laid before the German representatives there will be great irritation and possibly actual rebellion against the dictatorship by the Five Powers.

Personally I am strongly opposed to continued secrecy after the Germans have started for the Peace Conference. In fact I think that the secrecy which has been so strongly advocated by the British and French has made a very bad impression. I know that Mr. Lloyd-George and Mr. Clemenceau are trying to save their political skins by avoiding criticism until the peace is signed by Germany, when they can claim that it is too late to change the terms, but as a matter of policy, even if it were on the face possible to prevent publicity, I think that the people of the various countries would be more generous in opinion if they knew the truth and did not feel that attempts were being made to deceive them. I do not think that secrecy thus far has been very successful while it has unquestionably aroused resentment in all the countries involved and among the delegates of the smaller states represented in the Peace Conference.

In my judgment the best way is to lay a completed draft of the treaty before the Conference and ask its approval; the second best way is the oral statement suggested by Mr. Balfour; and the poorest way is the one indicated by Mr. Lloyd-George, which amounts to the dictation of an oligarchy composed of the Five Powers.

As I have no confidence in the ability to prevent the substance, if not the text, of the treaty from becoming known after it is drafted, I believe that an open and frank statement is the most expedient course to avoid criticism of an effort at secrecy which I am sure will be unavailing.

As to the position of yourself and the United States with the smaller states and with the peoples of all states I need say nothing as the advantage to be gained by publicity which insures terms "openly arrived at" is manifest.

Faithfully yours,   Robert Lansing

TLS (WP, DLC).

Mantoux's Notes of a Meeting of the Council of Four

April 12, 1919, 5 p.m.

M. Loucheur explains the state of the question of bonds to be issued by Germany. The American delegate, Mr. Norman Davis, thinks that Germany could not pay the interest on an amount of bonds over 15 billion dollars before a certain number of years; he does not deny that Germany must pay in gold, but says that if one emits so many bonds that Germany cannot pay the interest on them, these bonds will have no value, whatever the quantity. Mr. Davis' view is correct from the financial point of view, but difficult to explain to the public.

Mr. Davis suggests the issue of 10 billion dollars in paper marks. That solution seems dangerous to us. We would prefer that Germany, while issuing bonds for only 15 billion dollars in gold, must give us in addition an acknowledgment of a debt of 10 billion dollars, the means and time of the issue being left to the judgment of the commission. Thus we would arrive at a total guarantee of 25 billion dollars in gold, without risking an excessive issue.

Mr. Davis would prefer to leave to the commission complete liberty to determine the time and method of future payments, without announcing now the amount in gold.

Mr. Lloyd George fears that the solution proposed by M. Loucheur would be dangerous from the political point of view. The public, ascertaining that Germany is issuing bonds for only 15 billion dollars and is merely signing an acknowledgment of debt for the rest, would conclude, wrongly no doubt, that this is all we are proposing to ask of her. It is an impression that could not be avoided.

M. Clemenceau insists strongly that no issue of bonds in paper marks be provided for in the peace treaty. If ultimately Germany cannot pay, it is preferable to cancel part of her debt at that time rather than to declare in advance that paper without assured value will be accepted from her in payment or in guarantee.

Mr. Davis observes that if Germany proves capable of paying the interest on an issue of 15 billion dollars, that will prove that her affairs are sufficiently restored to raise her exchange rate. From that time, the paper mark will rise in value. Thus the bonds will be more easily negotiable than if we had tried to set the issue at an excessive figure.

Lord Sumner presents a text which, after discussion, is adopted and which provides for an issue of bearer bonds for 100 billion marks in gold, in three periods, namely:

(1) Twenty billion marks issued immediately, corresponding to the down payment which will be demanded of Germany at the time of the signature of the preliminaries;

(2) Forty billions which will be issued after the signing of the peace and which will bear 2½ per cent interest until 1921, then 5 per cent, and, beginning in 1926, 1 per cent for amortization;

(3) A bond for 40 billion marks which will be transformed into

an issue of negotiable bonds only when the Reparation Commission judges that Germany is in a condition to pay the interest.

The commission will be able subsequently to prescribe other issues according to the financial means of Germany, up to the amount of the acknowledged debt. The times and the means of these issues will be left to the judgment of the commission.

Mantoux, I, 235-36.

To Edward Mandell House, with Enclosures

My dear House: Paris, 12 April, 1919.

Since I received at your hands from Mr. Tardieu the memorandum which is herewith returned, I am going to ask you if you will not hand this reply to Mr. Tardieu with the very solemn warning that it is necessary for him to induce his chief to accept these terms as drawn, pointing out to him that this is an extraordinary step for the United States to take, and that there will be no possible hope of my obtaining the proposed treaty, if the additions he suggested were made.

It would be well for him to understand that this is the only obtainable solution of the problem of the protection for France of her eastern frontier.

Affectionately yours,   Woodrow Wilson

TLS (E. M. House Papers, CtY).

E N C L O S U R E   I
A Translation of a Memorandum by André Tardieu

April 2, 1919

AMENDMENTS PROPOSED BY FRANCE[1]

1. No fortifications to the west of a line drawn to the east of the Rhine (*conforming to the enclosed map*) *at a distance from this river palpably equal to the distance between the Rhine and the Belgian and French frontiers.*[2]

2. The maintenance or assembling of armed forces, either permanently or temporarily, will be forbidden in that zone, as well as all maneuvers and the maintenance of physical facilities for mobilization. *A force of local policemen to an effective maximum of* [blank] *only will be authorized.*

3. Violations of these conditions *or of the military, naval, and aerial clauses of the peace treaty* will be regarded as a hostile act

against the signatories of this treaty and as calculated to disturb the peace of the world.*

If one of the signatory powers determines that Germany has violated one of the above clauses, it will have the right to refer the matter to the Executive Council of the League, which will immediately proceed to a verification of the facts set forth. Germany agrees to accept the said verification made in the interest of peace and its maintenance.

4. A pledge by the United States (and of Great Britain), subject to the approval of the Executive Council of the League of Nations, to come immediately to the assistance of France so soon as any unprovoked movement of aggression, *as it has been defined by Art. 3*, against her is made by Germany,—this pledge to remain in force until the *contracting powers agree that* the League provides, by itself, sufficient protection.**5

* The note of the Marshal of March 31 has established that Germany, once it advanced to the Rhine, could renew, against France and Belgium—inferiors in number—the invasion of 1914. That is evident. He has replied, it is true, that the treaty of peace would disarm Germany and that, consequently, the aggression of 1914 would be to him impossible. That is true. But, by the same token, we recognize that, if Germany ceases to respect the military clauses which disarm her, the danger pointed out by the Marshal would exist. It is therefore necessary that the guarantee given be applicable not only to a violation by Germany of her engagements in the neutralized zone, but also to all the military terms of the peace treaty.
It is therefore proposed to modify in this sense Art. 3 and to create a means to verify the occurrence of the said violation.
** The note of Marshal Foch of March 31 has shown the gravity of the risk to which France, in certain eventualities, could be exposed. It is thus of the highest necessity that the guarantee which one has suggested to substitute for the permanent occupation of the Rhine have an absolute precision and that no doubt could arise about the nature of the events which will cause the agreement to be put into operation.

T MS (WC, NjP) of T MS (E. M. House Papers, CtY).
1 House wrote at the top of this document: "This is the plan Tardieu brought me & with one exception I consider satisfactory. The French do not insist on no. 1. E.M.H."
2 Italics indicate text added by Tardieu to Wilson's proposal printed at March 28, 1919, Vol. 56.
3 EMHhw.
4 EMHhw.
5 Here House wrote: "The League should decide. E.M.H."

E N C L O S U R E   I I

A Memorandum

Paris, 12 April, 1919.

Memorandum on the Amendments proposed by France
to the Agreement suggested by President Wilson
regarding the Rhine Frontier.

In commenting upon this memorandum, may I not very earnestly and respectfully call attention once more to the proposals which I made, proposals of a very definite and constructive kind, made after the most mature consideration of all the circumstances involved.

I proposed that the following stipulations should be embodied in the Treaty of Peace with Germany: (a) That no fortifications of any kind were to be maintained by Germany west of a line drawn fifty kilometers to the east of the Rhine (as in the military terms already provisionally agreed upon); (b) That the maintenance or assembling of armed forces within that area, either permanently or temporarily, should be explicitly forbidden, as well as all military maneuvers of every kind, and the maintenance of any physical facilities for mobilization; (c) That I should lay before the Senate of the United States and urge for adoption a treaty with France containing a pledge by the United States, subject to the approval of the Executive Council of the League of Nations, to come immediately to the assistance of France so soon as any unprovoked movement of aggression against her is made by Germany, this agreement to remain in force until it shall be recognized by the contracting powers that the League of Nations itself gives sufficient guarantee in these matters.

It will be recalled that these proposals were made jointly with Mr. Lloyd George, who made practically identical proposals with regard to the action of Great Britain. Both Mr. Lloyd George's proposals and my own were made after repeated consideration of all other plans suggested, and they represent the maximum of what I myself deem necessary for the safety of France or possible on the part of the United States.

(1) I think it would be a great mistake to go further than the military terms already provisionally agreed upon in the matter of obliging Germany to withdraw all fortifications on the east bank of the Rhine. It is my clear judgment that we should adhere to the fifty kilometers stipulated in the military terms.

(2) The provision with regard to a maximum force of local gendarmerie is unnecessary, because it is already contained in a more general form with regard to the whole of Germany in the military terms already provisionally agreed upon.

(3) I am sorry to say I cannot at all agree to include in the third paragraph the military, naval, and air clauses of the Treaty of Peace. With regard to the added paragraph concerning the right of the signatory powers to notify the Executive Council of the League of any violations of these regulations which might have been observed, it is clear that that right already exists on the part of members of the League if any action is taken anywhere which threatens to disturb the peace of the world, and that it would be unwise to connect it with this special agreement and treaty.

(4) I have embodied in the fourth paragraph the words "by the contracting powers," which were suggested.

Woodrow Wilson

TS MS (E. M. House Papers, CtY).

From Robert Lansing, with Enclosure

Dear Mr. President: Paris, April 12, 1919.

At the request of Dr. Wellington Koo,[1] I am sending you herewith an aide-memoire relating to the Shantung question in which he sets forth very clearly the international importance of Tsaingtao, whose railway connections will make it the chief port of north China, and the injury to European and American trade already wrought by the temporary occupation of the port by Japan. That injury appears to be due to the unfair methods employed by Japan.

I am, my dear Mr. President,

Faithfully yours,   Robert Lansing

TLS (SDR, RG 256, 185.1158/64A, DNA).
  [1] V. K. Wellington Koo to RL, April 8, 1919, TLS (SDR, RG 256, 185.1158/60, DNA).

E N C L O S U R E

A Memorandum by Vi Kyuin Wellington Koo

Hotel Lutetia, Paris, April 8, 1919.

With reference to China's claim for direct restitution to herself of the leased territory of Kiaochow, the Tsingtao-Chinan Railway and other German rights in respect of Shantung Province, the Chinese Government are desirous to have it settled as early as possible and venture to hope that President Wilson will see his way to bring it before the Conference of the Four Chiefs of Government for a decision.

In communicating this desire on their part, the Chinese Government wish earnestly to solicit the firm support of the United States whose traditional friendship for China has contributed, in no small measure, to the hope and inspiration of the Chinese people.

That denial of China's claim would jeopardize her political independence, territorial integrity and economic welfare,[1] has been dwelt upon at length in the memorandum submitted to the Council of Ten.[2] That such denial would equally prejudice the interests of foreign powers in China has not perhaps been made so apparent, though it is none the less true.

Tsingtao, being the best harbor on the coast of China and connected, as it is, by a system of railways, with the principal centres of production and distribution, is destined to control, in a very large measure, the entire trade of North China. To leave the port or the Tsingtao-Chinan Railway in the hands of any foreign power is, therefore, to place in its hands the most powerful weapon for securing trade domination and for jeopardizing the principle of equal opportunity for the commerce of all nations. Even a temporary occupation of Tsingtao of less than three years has secured for Japan a preponderant share of its trade. Whereas,[3] for example, in 1913, Japan's share of the import trade of Tsingtao was less than 35 per cent; in 1917, it was more than 57 per cent. Similarly as regards exports. In 1913, Japan's share of the export trade was 7.9 per cent; in 1917, it was 59 per cent.

The change in the course of the shipping trade of the port in the last three years is even more striking. During 1913 the total tonnage of all vessels clearing from the port was 1,300,442, of which the share of Japan was 222,693 tons; in 1917, it was 1,600,459, of which the Japanese share was 1,114,159 tons.

To return the leased territory of Tsingtao to China and at the same time permit Japan to have an exclusive Japanese Concession therein would appear likewise inexpedient. The part of Tsingtao which the Japanese propose should be designated as their exclusive concession includes all the revenue-producing areas. It is the business section of Tsingtao. According to a map which they have prepared, the customs, harbor, wharf, and railway terminus would be all in the Japanese Concession, which would be still further extended by a reclamation from the sea. For purposes of trade, this section virtually constitutes the whole emporium, the remaining part being used and adapted only as a residential quarter.

The Chinese Government request that restitution to China of German rights in Shantung be effected directly by the Conference. Indirect restitution through Japan may carry implications of meaning which the Chinese Government deem it most desirable to avoid. For one thing, such indirect restitution might be claimed to imply a recognition and confirmation of the Treaties and Notes which Japan compelled China to accept in the Spring of 1915 by an ultimatum following the delivery of the 21 Demands.[4] One of these treaties is that in relation to Shantung Province which purports to bind China "to give full assent" to any agreement which the Japanese Government may make with the German Government relating to the disposal of German rights in Shantung Province. To recognize this arrangement as valid would be, in the view of the

Chinese Government, to countenance infringement of China's right of conducting and controlling her own foreign relations. It would mean, furthermore, an acknowledgement, however unintentional, of Japan's claim that she has a special position in China,—a claim which China cannot and does not admit.

The procedure of direct negotiations between Japan and Germany as contemplated in the said treaty, appears all the more objectionable, since China has been a co-belligerent in the war and, being represented at the Conference, is competent to accept restitution of her rights directly from the Conference; and since the subject-matter of the proposed negotiations is one which has arisen from the war and therefore should be settled only in concert with the Allied and Associated Powers at the Peace Conference.

Complete and direct restitution to China is requested, also, because of its desirable effect on public opinion in China. The claim of China for direct restitution represents the united hope and aspiration of the Chinese people. It is endorsed by them without exception, as evidenced in the great number of cable communications received from the Chinese Parliament and from the Legislature[s], Educational Associations and Chambers of Commerce of every Province in China. They, in full harmony with the attitude of the Chinese Government, look to the United States and other Great Powers for friendly support to China's claim, knowing that these powers are disposed to accord just treatment to China, and that they can render effective support to China, if they are only willing.

The people of China rely on the support of these friendly powers all the more, because they believe that the brightest future of China lies along the path of intimate cooperation with America and Europe as well as with her neighbour in Asia. They are now at the cross roads. If they are unable to win support for their just cause this time, the consequences of a change of attitude on their part vis-à-vis the Occident, once it is effected, may endure for decades before they can be checked or removed.

In urging the support of the United States, the Chinese Government are not unaware of the fact that France, Great Britain and Italy have each previously given Japan an assurance to support her claim in regard to the disposal of German rights in Shantung. It is submitted, however, that the situation has since so far changed that those assurances would seem to have entirely ceased to be applicable. China was then still a neutral; she is now a co-belligerent duly represented at the Peace Conference. Even apart from this view, the validity of these assurances would seem to have been negatived by President Wilson's fourteen principles, which were subsequently pronounced, and which France, Great Britain, Italy and Japan have all accepted as the basis of the peace now about to be made with Germany.

The Chinese Government sincerely hope, therefore, that the Government of the United States will use its good offices to induce the four Powers not to permit the said assurances to stand in the way of their extending a helping hand to China when their help is so much needed to obtain for her a just recognition of her rights.

It is, moreover, the belief of the Chinese Government that Japan herself, if she views the situation in all its aspects, will see that her highest interest lies in according full justice to China on this Shantung question. Japan has repeatedly assured the Chinese people of her friendly desire to help China and if she seizes the present opportunity arising from the Shantung question to give a concrete proof of her friendship, the Chinese Government have every reason to feel confident that it will produce in China that salutary effect on the feelings of the two peoples toward each other which China as much as Japan desires to see produced in the interest of cordial neighbourhood, and which the Powers of America and Europe will surely welcome in the interest of permanent peace in the Far East.

V. K. Wellington Koo

TS MS (SDR, RG 256, 185.1158/64A, DNA).
¹ Wilson's underlining here and below.
² That is, THE CLAIM *of China* . . . , about which see V.K.W. Koo to WW, April 17, 1919, n. 1.
³ Beginning here and to the end of the following paragraph, Wilson drew a line down the right side of the page.
⁴ About which, see the index entries "China," "China and the United States," "Japan," and "Japan and the United States" in Vols. 32 and 33, and the secondary works cited in n. 4 to the minutes of the Council of Four printed at April 18, 1919, 11 a.m.

From Henry White

Personal & Private

Dear Mr President,   [Paris] April 12. 1919

I have been thinking about your reply to my inquiry yesterday afternoon as to the progress which you are making towards a settlement of the important questions still at issue in the Council of Four, and, in the event of a continuation of the tendency to prolong the discussions with a view to further delay, I venture once more to urge upon you the importance of insisting that secret sessions of the Four or of the Ten be discontinued and that plenary sessions of the Conference be held hereafter.

Believe me, the secrecy of the proceedings of the Council of Ten and still more of the Four, is being used in this country and in

England as well as at home, to discredit you; and unless an end is put thereto either by a prompt agreement enabling the German delegates to be brought to Paris or by plenary sessions, at which the real difficulties and your own views relative to a proper Peace can be made known to the Conference and to the World, the position you occupy in the opinion of the latter will be materially, if not irreparably, compromised.

In view of the determination, apparent in certain quarters to retain at all hazards our military and financial assistance indefinitely in Europe—even by so arranging matters that Germany will refuse to sign the Peace Treaty—I would offer the following suggestion:

that you make known to the Council of Four as soon as possible that not one American soldier, dollar, or pound of supplies for military purposes, will be furnished until Peace is made.

General Kernan's report, particularly the section on "militarism," confirms my opinion that such a definite warning from you will not only hasten Peace but will also ward off entanglements which are not unlikely to become exceedingly embarrassing.

I am enclosing for your information a telegram from the Daily News' correspondent at New York[1] showing how generally public opinion is supporting you in the maintenance of the fourteen points and what a favorable impression has been produced by the "George Washington's" having been sent for.

Believe me, dear Mr President,
Very Sincerely Yours   Henry White

Pray do not take a moment even of your valuable time to answer this letter which really needs no reply.

ALS (WP, DLC).
[1] It is missing.

From Boghos Nubar

Mr. President,   Paris, le April 12th 1919

Circumstances did not allow you to grant to me the honour of being received by you during your first sojourn in Paris. I shall, though, never forget your very kind letter expressing your deep sympathy for the Armenians. I now hope that you will not return to the States without granting to me, as president of the Armenian National Delegation, a few minutes in your presence.

Since your return from Washington, I have abstained from troubling you, knowing well how you were already overburdened with work as long as the Covenant of the League of Nations was not definitely arranged, and I was waiting for a favourable opportunity, which was unfortunately delayed by your recent indisposition, of which thanks [thank] God you have completely recovered.

I therefore hope that you will have the kindness, before your departure, of receiving me as well as my colleague Mr. Aharonian,[1] the Representative of the Armenian Republic in the Caucasus and Prof. A. Der-Hagopian,[2] of Robert College, Constantinople, Vice-President of our Delegation, to whom you have already granted an audience sometime ago.

We would be deeply grateful to you, as we know that it would be a great disappointment to the entire Armenian Nation if we, their representatives in Paris, were deprived of the honour of at least shaking hands with you, whom they consider as their best friend and protector.

I am, Mr. President
yours most respectfully　Boghos Nubar

TLS (WP, DLC).
[1] That is, Avetis Aharonian.
[2] Actually, Abraham Ter-Hakobian.

From Samuel Gompers

Washington April 12, 1919

1552. For the President from Gompers.

"I feel impelled to enter protest against any change[1] at this time in the convention of protocol adopted by the Commission on International Labor Legislation which sat at Paris. Any amendment may menace the entire project.["]　　　Polk　Acting

T telegram (WP, DLC).
[1] See R. L. Borden to W. T. White, April 12, 1919.

From Vance Criswell McCormick

My dear Mr. President:　　　　　　　　Paris. April 12, 1919.

I am enclosing a newspaper clipping from Le Journal,[1] which raises the query in my mind as to whether the time has not come for you to restate the position of the United States in regard to Peace terms, particularly along the lines of our claims. It would clear up many doubts, relieve a strained situation, and place the responsibility for delays where it belongs.

Very sincerely yours,　Vance C. McCormick

TLS (WP, DLC).
[1] It is missing.

Cary Travers Grayson to William Gibbs McAdoo

Personal and Confidential.

My dear Mr. Secretary: Paris, 12 April, 1919.

My silence is not indicative of the fact that my thoughts fail to turn to you, for I can assure you that a day does not pass but that I wish you were here. There is so much that I would like to tell you, and so little I can put in a letter. But when I get home I will have a store of things to unload on you.

There has never been a time that the President has needed you as badly as he has since he has been over here. Your cooperation, vision, and more than all else, your boldness and your courage and good common-sense are just what the President needs in this crisis. Some of those who are close to him and are supposed to represent him have hurt the situation materially by attempting to compromise or soft-pedal the issue, when by doing so it was contrary to the President's principles. Then when the President would take a bold stand for his principles, this false representation led the French to believe that the President was merely bluffing and caused the loss of valuable time. You cannot imagine what a terrific handicap this has been. And what a strain it has been on the President. He has never worked as hard nor has he ever put in as many working hours in a day. The situation has been so complex and trying that he has had very little time for recreation. He is within fifteen minutes of a golf course and has only played two games since his arrival in France on the 13th of December.

About ten days ago the President was taken violently sick with the influenza, but by promptly going to bed, and with prompt treatment, he was only laid up one week. As you know, the influenza is weakening and even treacherous, and I have had to guard him very carefully for fear of a relapse and complications. He is working beyond his endurance. Yesterday, for instance, he received a delegation immediately after breakfast. The Council of Four met at eleven o'clock and did not adjourn until the lunch hour. He had the Queen of Roumania and party for lunch, and at three o'clock he attended the Plenary Session of the Peace Conference, which adjourned just before dinner. After dinner, at eight o'clock, he went to the League of Nations meeting and did not get to bed until this morning after 1:00 o'clock. Every night he is up until after 11:00 o'clock. You must remember that in addition to his duties here at the Peace Conference, he has a lot of work to attend to from Washington. The strain he is going through is almost beyond superhuman endurance. But he is at a stage where he cannot let up. When I tell him that he needs rest and relaxation, he answers me by saying that in the midst of this imminent crisis he feels that he should participate in the things for which he is responsible; if he were away from these meetings and did not know what was going on, he would worry. He feels that a mess would be made of things in his absence. I agree that worry would do him more harm than physical fatigue. Confidentially, one cannot blame the President for worrying under the conditions which exist here. As you know, I am loyal to the President first and above all, and I am his doctor and friend; but when I see the way some of the others are trading on him, not only acting as weaklings, but blaming him for the delays and errors, for which they themselves are responsible, it simply makes my blood boil. If you were here behind the scenes and could see and hear what I do, your vocabulary of cuss-words would not last ten minutes.

Of course, I don't know anything about finances, but this is an illustration of what has happened: A prominent member of the American Delegation[1] undertook to handle one of the financial problems, but he got so hopelessly entangled that he was compelled to call on a fellow-American who was not a delegate to help him out of the swamp!

You must excuse me for writing such a "blue" letter. I feel I would give anything if I could have a confidential talk and could explode without reserve. That I have wished for your presence over here a hundred times but feebly expresses it. With the President's great brain and courage I am confident that everything ultimately is going to come out all right. But I feel that he is going through a lot of unnecessary strain by not having the proper help.

I suppose you have heard the good news from Gertrude as to the new son. The following cable which I received tells the story:

"I salute you. I weigh seven pounds, seven ounces, but am slightly bald. Mother, Gordon and I are well and send dearest love. Please write to me.

(Signed) Lieutenant Cary T. Grayson, Jr."

When a fellow receives such a wonderful message as this, and has such a true-blue partner as Gertrude, the other things of life for the moment—peace or war, revolutions or Bolshevism—seem of little consequence.

I was deeply distressed to hear of the death of Nona's husband and of her illness.[2] I sent you a telegram and wrote you a letter just before sailing, which I hope you received.

Not knowing your address, I am sending this letter in care of the White House, with the request that it be forwarded to you. It goes forward to you from here in the diplomatic pouch.

I hope you are enjoying good health and that everything is going all right with you. I hear many complimentary things about you in this part of the world.

If the President and Mrs. Wilson knew I were writing I know they would send their love to both Miss Eleanor and yourself.

With warmest regards to you both, believe me,

Affectionately yours,   Cary T. Grayson

TLS (W. G. McAdoo Papers, DLC).
   [1] Norman H. Davis, who had been outwitted by the British financial experts on the issue of categories of reparations. The fellow American referred to below was Vance C. McCormick. About this episode, see the extracts from the Diary of Vance C. McCormick printed at April 2 and 3, 1919, Vol. 56.
   [2] That is Nona Hazlehurst McAdoo de Mohrenschildt and Ferdinand de Mohrenschildt. See n. 1 to the extract from the Grayson Diary printed at March 5, 1919, Vol. 55, and WW to E. de Mohrenschildt, March 20, 1919, Vol. 56.

Sir Robert Borden to Sir Thomas White[1]

SECRET.   Paris, April 12th, 1919.

GENERAL MEMORANDUM NO. 16.

1. This memorandum covers the period from Monday evening, 7th April, to Saturday evening, 12th April.

2. During the present week there has been much discussion in the British Empire Delegations with regard to the proposed Labour Convention. Its provisions were canvassed very fully at these discussions and there was not complete unanimity with respect thereto. Eventually, however, such amendments were made or agreed upon as induced its acceptance, although the Ministers for the Dominions were not disposed to accept the view that this Convention should be linked up so closely with the Covenant of the League of Nations. There was a distinct agreement that Article 35 should be modified so that the provisions of the Convention would conform to those of the Covenant in respect to the character of the membership and the method of adherence. Through some mistake this understanding was not carried out in the copy circulated at the Plenary Conference held on Friday. As a result, Sir Robert Borden moved and carried an amendment to Mr. Barnes'[2] motion. That motion was as follows:

"THAT the Conference approves the Draft Convention creating a permanent organisation for the promotion of the international regulation of labour conditions which has been submitted by the Labour Commission, with the amendments proposed by the British Delegation; instructs the Secretariat to request the govern-

   [1] William Thomas White, Minister of Finance and Acting Prime Minister of Canada.
   [2] That is, George N. Barnes.

ments concerned to nominate forthwith their representatives on the Organising Committee for the October Conference, and authorises that Committee to proceed at once with its work."

Sir Robert Borden's amendment added the following clause thereto: "The Conference authorizes the Drafting Committee to make such amendments as may be necessary to have the Convention conform to the Covenant of the League of Nations in the character of its membership and in the method of adherence."

3. The report of the Labour Commission included the submission of certain clauses proposed for inclusion in the Treaty of Peace, copy of which is annexed.[3] At the meeting of the British Delegations on Wednesday, 9th April, it was distinctly agreed that these clauses were not to be discussed or approved at the Plenary Conference on Friday. The 8th Clause[4] was particularly objectionable from the standpoint of several Dominions. For example, in Canada it would conflict with provincial legislation in Saskatchewan and British Columbia which imposes restrictions on Oriental labour in certain trades or occupations. Much to their surprise the delegates from the Dominions were told while present in the Plenary Conference that this arrangement could not be carried out, and that a resolution must be passed approving these clauses for insertion in the Treaty of Peace. The Prime Ministers from the Dominions took very firm ground against this in which they were strongly supported by Mr. Balfour, who had given the promise alluded to. Mr. Lloyd George who was not familiar with the difficulties of the case, asked Sir Robert Borden to confer with Mr. Wilson and Mr. Clemenceau, which he did. Mr. Wilson admitted the dangerous character of Clause 8 but was apprehensive that any failure to pass the clauses as a whole would have bad results in Europe. Sir Robert Borden pointed out that Clause 8 might lead to great disorder, and possibly rebellion, on the Pacific Coast of the United States and of Canada. Eventually it was arranged that no motion should be made with regard to these clauses, and they therefore remain for the present upon the table of the Plenary Conference.

4. On Saturday, the 12th instant, there was a meeting of the British Delegations at which the proposals of the Aerial Commission were under consideration. A copy of those proposals, as submitted, is sent herewith.[5] Various amendments were found to be necessary of which only a few involved any question of principle. A further

[3] This enclosure is missing. However, these clauses are printed as the Enclosure with H. M. Robinson to WW, March 24, 1919, Vol. 56.

[4] It reads as follows: "In all matters concerning their status as workers and social insurance foreign workers lawfully admitted to any country and their families should be ensured the same treatment as the nationals of that country." *Ibid.*

[5] This enclosure is also missing.

draft is being prepared and a copy thereof will be forwarded. As to representation of the Dominions, under Article 34, Sir Robert Borden proposed that there should be a Committee, or, better still, a panel comprising representatives of the United Kingdom and of the Dominions, including India, and that the British representatives upon the International Commission for Air Navigation should be selected from this panel. It was pointed out by the representatives of the Dominions that the proposed Council has certain very important powers which inter alia enable it to make regulations having the force of law. The Dominions would not be satisfied to entrust such a power to the proposed International Commission for Air Navigation unless they were directly represented in some effective way.

5. On Thursday morning there was a long Conference at Mr. Lloyd George's apartments which lasted from nine till twelve, and at which he reported to the Prime Ministers of the Dominions the proceedings and conclusions of the Council of Four to date. The chief points touched upon were the following:

(a). The frontier between France and Germany. The French Government have finally agreed to withdraw their extreme proposals which involved the annexation to France of a considerable territory west of the Rhine, the population of which is almost exclusively German. There has been much discussion on this subject and it is now regarded as practically concluded.

(b). The coal fields in the Saar Valley. It is proposed to place this territory under the League of Nations for fifteen years, during which period the French shall be entitled to the coal produced. At the end of fifteen years a plebi[s]cite will be taken and according to its result the territory in question will revert to Germany or be annexed to France. The coal acquired by the French in this way will be taken into account in considering their claims for reparation.

(c). Practically, an agreement has been reached with respect to the Eastern Frontier of Germany, in which the chief difficulty arose as to the Port of Danzig. This city will be created into an independent international entity under the protection and direction of the League of Nations. Both Germany and Poland will be granted special facilities in connection therewith.

(d). Responsibility for the war. It is not proposed to try the Kaiser for his general responsibility in precipitating the war but only for his responsibility in attacking a state the neutrality of which was guaranteed by Germany itself. For this purpose a tribunal will be erected and a demand will be made upon Holland to deliver up the Kaiser. President Wilson was very pronounced against any such course at first, but eventually changed his opinion. He has also agreed to the establishment of tribunals for the trial of persons who have violated the ordinary rules and conventions of warfare; but he desires that such persons shall be tried by Courts Martial to be established by the Allied Nations.

(e). Reparation and indemnity. This has proved, perhaps, the most difficult subject and has occupied very extensively the time of the four statesmen who were dealing with it. The fourteen points propounded by President Wilson and expressly relied upon by the Germans in proposing the Armistice did not, apparently, contemplate indemnity at all. For this reason President Wilson cannot agree that the costs of the war shall be included in the demand for indemnity or that they shall constitute a basis upon which indemnity shall be exacted. In this respect, as well as with regard to responsibility for the war, he has very materially modified his point of view; and in both cases against the advice of his experts. In order to meet the difficult situation in which he finds himself, it has been agreed that the provision made by way of pensions, allowances, etc., for loss or injury to human life during the war, shall be taken as a basis of reparation. The situation of the negotiations with respect to this matter has been at times very acute and possibly it is not yet thoroughly settled. According to estimates submitted to the Dominion Ministers by Mr. Lloyd George, the total claims of the various allies, estimated in millions of pounds sterling, upon this basis will be as follows:

France,—	5,100
British Empire,—	2,200
Belgium,—	1,500
Italy,—	1,000
Other nations,—	500
TOTAL,—	10,300

Between France on the one hand and the United States on the other hand, the situation of the British Empire was both difficult and embarrassing. The United States desired to reduce the demand for indemnity to a minimum, having regard to the principles laid down in the fourteen points. On the other hand, France demanded that an absolute preference should be accorded to her claims for reparation in respect of the devastated areas; and those claims, which are based on extraordinarily high estimates, would have left little or nothing for any claims of the British Empire. To obtain an absolute preference France was willing to reduce her claims materially and that proposal obviously harmonized with the point of view originally insisted on by President Wilson. However, unless there is some unexpected development the arrangement above outlined will probably be carried out. Doubtless it will encounter fierce criticism not only in France but in many other allied nations. It is understood that the United States will not participate in any indemnity but may present certain relatively small claims for destruction of shipping.

6. The proposals as to reparation and indemnity submitted by Mr. Lloyd George[6] commanded the approval of all the Dominions' Prime Ministers except Mr. Hughes,[7] who was rather vague in defining what he would be prepared to accept. About an hour and a half was taken up with him in discussing the subject.

7. One disadvantage of this proposal would have been obviated by another arrangement outlined in a previous memorandum.[8] The claims of the allied nations must be submitted to a commission which will report upon the amount properly allowable. This commission will probably have power to give a hearing to the Germans and may permit them to offer evidence. It should be added that the claim of the British Empire, estimated at 2,200 in millions of pounds sterling, comprises (a). the capitalized value of pensions throughout the Empire, estimated at 1,200, and (b). the destruction of shipping and other property estimated at 1,000. In capitalizing pensions it will be necessary to adopt (purely for this purpose) an arbitrary scale applicable to all countries, in order to arrive at a just and uniform result.

8. In accepting the proposals submitted by Mr. Lloyd George, and upon which it was necessary to reach a quick determination, the Prime Ministers of the Dominions were largely influenced by their belief, which was shared by Mr. Lloyd George, that if this proposal could not be carried out the situation likely to develope in view of the attitude assumed by France and by the United States would result in the British Empire receiving nothing by way of indemnity and little by way of reparation.

9. Sir Robert Borden was also influenced by his belief that the terms thus proposed fixed the outside limit of what Germany will be able to pay. He expressed doubt as to whether Germany would not regard an acceptance of the Bolshevist Regime as preferable to even these terms. That possibility was freely admitted by Mr. Lloyd George and by other Dominions' Prime Ministers; but it was felt that the risk must be taken. In France there are eight million men engaged in agriculture and four million in industrial pursuits. In Germany the number of workmen is more than double that of the

[6] See Appendix III to the minutes of the Council of Four printed at March 29, 1919, Vol. 56.

[7] That is, William Morris Hughes.

[8] That is, Klotz's memorandum, an abstract of which is printed in n. 1 to the minutes of the Council of Four printed at March 28, 1919, Vol. 56.

farmers. Some millions of them are receiving unemployement wages; and a very considerable proportion are infected with the Bolshevist propaganda. Even a manufacturer on a large scale might reach the conclusion that while he would at present lose everything by such a policy, yet Germany's future would be endowed with such wonderful possibilities by an economic and military alliance with Russia that he would be prepared to accept for the moment the principles of Bolshevism, which Germany could greatly modify, and through which she would obtain an absolute domination of Russia's enormous resources. The Germans may imagine with some reason that in carrying out such a policy they can snatch out of defeat a greater victory than they ever anticipated. In other words they may hope to exploit and develop Bolshevism to their own vast advantage, to the ruin of other countries and to the accomplishment of their ideal of world domination. The Allies of course have great odds in their favour for defeating any such policy; but those odds are by no means so great as they were four months ago and probably they are growing less every day.

10. Sir Robert Borden recently discussed conditions in Russia and Poland with Mr. Paderewski, who impressed him as a really able man with a wide outlook. Paderewski describes the conditions in Russia as terrible and he believes that Europe is only at the beginning of its troubles. One startling statement which he made related to the probability that Europe would be scourged by epidemics of terrible diseases. He asserts with great positiveness that the disease of glanders[9] has broken out among human beings in Russia upon a considerable scale; and he attributes this to the consumption of the flesh of horses afflicted with the disease. According to his statement the Russians shoot all persons in whom the disease manifests itself. Mr. Paderewski believes that this course is quite justifiable as every case is absolutely hopeless and the danger of infection can only be removed in that way. He states that in a Polish Legion which has been fighting in Lithuania two officers, personal friends of the commandant, contracted the disease and were immediately shot by his orders. Spotted Typhus is ravaging the population of Poland at present.

11. Sir George Foster, Mr. Sifton and Mr. Doherty[10] have been very actively engaged in attendance upon the committees of which they are members, in attending meetings of the British Empire

---

[9] A contagious and usually fatal bacterial disease especially affecting horses, mules, and donkeys. It can also be transmitted to cats, dogs, goats, sheep, and human beings.
[10] Sir George [Eulas] Foster, Canadian Minister of Trade and Commerce; Arthur Lewis Sifton, Minister of Customs; and Charles Joseph Doherty, Minister of Justice. They, together with Sir Robert Borden, were all plenipotentiary delegates to the peace conference.

Delegation and of its committees and in the conferences of the Canadian Ministers respecting messages from Ottawa and from London touching the general affairs of the Dominion and especially the progress of demobilization and parliamentary matters. The work of the Committees with which Mr. Doherty and Mr. Sifton were concerned has been practically concluded; but Sir George Foster has been working very actively throughout the week in the Economic Committee, the sittings of which have sometimes lasted until half past eight o'clock in the evening.

T MS (R. L. Borden Papers, CaOOA).

From the Peace Conference Diary of William Linn Westermann

Saturday, April 12, 1919

Sweetzer,[1] who is with Ray Stannard Baker in publicity in our organization, told me today that none of the Commissioners (I judge that Col. House is to be excepted) had seen the President since his return until last Sunday. Last week he told Commissioner White that there was to be a Plenary Session of the Peace Delegates the next day. Mr. White said "Impossible. I have not heard a word about it." Then when Sweetzer insisted, Mr. White blustered into Lansing's office with the news. It proved that Mr. Lansing did not know anything about it. He called up Leland Harrison who said it was true. Lansing was sore and said that this was an astounding state of affairs etc., that an American Commissioner should have no announcement of plenary sessions. On Sunday the Commissioners, who had not seen hide or hair of the President, called upon him at his house. He was in bed, sick with the influenza. They had intended to have it out with him. The actual situation is that the Four, Wilson, Clemenceau, Lloyd-George and Orlando, decide things in closed Committee and nobody ever hears of them. The rest of the Am. Commissioners are as ill-informed as any of us. So Sweetzer avers, at least.

The President pulled on them a characteristic Wilsonian coup. He said: "Gentlemen, this is not a meeting of the American Commissioners. It is a war council. I have ordered the George Washington to sail to Brest." Evidently then the sending for the G.W. *was* caused by the political situation here, and the President is using it as a political threat.

Then the Commissioners began to condone with him, commiserate him upon his illness etc.; and the great protest and revolt was ended.

It seems tonight that the Interallied Commission to Syria is going. But Sec. Lansing said today that he did not know—said it to me—and said that we seemed to be the only ones who favored it. I told him that that was true. Lansing may be sore about the calling off of the other Commission under Leon Dominian.[2]

T MS (W. L. Westermann Papers, NNC).
[1] Arthur Sweetser (not Sweetzer), former war correspondent and State Department correspondent for the Associated Press, most recently a captain in the Aviation Section of the Signal Corps, U.S.A.
[2] In February and March 1919, Lansing and other members of the A.C.N.P. had discussed the sending of a mission to investigate conditions throughout the Middle East, this mission to be headed by the Rev. Dr. James Levi Barton and Leon Dominian. Dominian, born and educated in Constantinople, was a naturalized citizen of the United States. He had been a geographer and editorial writer for the American Geographical Society and had investigated boundary problems for the State Department. The proposed Barton-Dominian mission was dropped in early March on the ground that the A.C.N.P. did not really need extensive information covering a large area of the Middle East. See Harry Nicholas Howard, *The King-Crane Commission; An American Inquiry in the Middle East* (Beirut, 1963), p. 24.

From Robert Lansing, with Enclosures

Dear Mr. President: [Paris] April 12, 1919.

I regret exceedingly the inadvertence which led to the omission from my letter of April 8th[1] of the telegram from Ambassador Morris to which the letter referred. I am sending a copy of it herein, together with a copy of the message of April 11th sent by the Commission to the Department in accordance with your instructions of the 9th instant.[2]

I am, my dear Mr. President,
                    Faithfully yours,   Robert Lansing

TLS (WP, DLC).
[1] RL to WW, April 8, 1919 (second letter of that date).
[2] That is, Wilson's instructions written on the bottom of the letter just cited.

E N C L O S U R E   I

Washington April 5, 1919

1463. Department is in receipt of a telegram dated March 31st from the Embassy at Tokyo which is transmitted for your information. Telegram reads as follows:

"The discussions in government circles, referred to in the last paragraph of my March 23, 4 p.m.,[1] have apparently reached a conclusion and the silence of the past two weeks was broken this afternoon when General Tanaka, Minister of War, called upon me. He referred to the conflict of policy between our respective forces in Siberia and the embarrassing position in which he was placed, being held responsible for the activities of the Japanese troops and yet being without any agreed policy to guide him. He admitted that the Cossack military commanders were oppressing the population and this oppression had led to unrest and disorder. He stated that the Japanese troops were being changed and new divisions substituted for the old ones and that now was the time to define our joint policy for the future. He expressed his personal conviction that military activities should be confined hereafter simply to the guarding of the railway. This, however, was a diplomatic question and his only reason seeking this confidential talk with me was to urge upon me the importance of a frank exchange of views with Viscount Uchida[2] and of a speedy understanding with our governments.

In reply I briefly reviewed the causes which led to the joint expedition and explained the policy which General Graves had pursued. I concluded by expressing my willingness to discuss the question with the Foreign Minister if he so desired. General Tanaka then explained that he proposed to submit to the cabinet tomorrow the views which he had expressed to me and that I would probably hear from the Foreign Minister.

This interview indicates to me that the dominant influences in the general staff have compromised in Siberia; are prepared to cooperate with General Graves, and to modify their previous policy of supporting local Cossack leaders. This interview is supported by a letter received this morning from General Graves in which he states that Ivanoff-Rinoff[3] has sought a meeting with him with a view to a better understanding, and had recently stated that the public abuse of Americans had not succeeded and they were now going to try other tactics; that Colonel Butenko[4] is showing a more conciliatory spirit; that his only serious difficulty is with the representatives of Japan and he continues 'To be perfectly frank I was very much pleased with the outburst from the War Department in Tokyo as it gave me an indication that they think they are losing.'

Should the Foreign Minister consult with me on this question of policy, would the Department approve of my suggesting as my personal view, the policy I submitted for consideration in the last paragraph of my telegram of March 8, 10 a.m. referred to above, reads as follows: 'I suggest for the consideration of the Department that in carrying out the agreement for the military protection of the railroad, our government should insist that in the protected area, and in the cities and towns along the railway where Allied troops are quartered, the population should be protected from the arbitrary action of any group. I believe that this position will be guaranteed by our European associates, but I fear it will not be acceptable to the Japanese Military Authorities. I feel, however, that now is the time frankly to discuss the question with our associates and reach a clear understanding in regard to it?' "   Polk,   Acting.

T telegram (WP, DLC).
    [1] The date of this telegram seems to be incorrect. There is no telegram in the State Department files from Morris dated March 23, 1919, 4 p.m. Morris probably referred to the telegram conveyed in FLP to RL and V. C. McCormick printed at March 13, 1919, Vol. 55.
    [2] That is, Viscount Yasuya Uchida, Japanese Minister of Foreign Affairs.
    [3] That is, Pavel Pavlovich Ivanov-Rinov.
    [4] Commander of the fortress at Vladivostok. The Editors have been unable to find his given names.

ENCLOSURE II

[Paris] April 11, 1919.

1557. Your 1431, April 4, noon, 1432, April 4 and 1463, April 5, 5 p.m.

Now that General Tanaka is convinced that military activities should be confined hereafter to the guarding of the railway, the President desires you to instruct Ambassador Morris to urge upon the Japanese Foreign Office the desirability of adopting General Tanaka's advice. This frank expression of opinion by General Tanaka seems to make Secretary Baker's proposals entirely feasible and it is suggested that the Department take up with the Governments having military forces in Siberia the formulation of the policy which Secretary Baker suggests, that is to say, to limit the use of the military forces to the preservation of order in the immediate vicinity of the railway, its stations and trains when those in charge so request, and to use interallied forces to suppress local violence by conflicting Russian forces only when such conflicts affect the despatch of trains or operation of the railway and even then only to the extent necessary to protect the railway and those engaged in its operation.   Ammission.

T telegram (WP, DLC).

From William Howard Taft and Abbott Lawrence Lowell

Washington, April 12th, 1919.

1555, CONFIDENTIAL. For President.

"Thirty members of Executive Committee of our league[1] from 18 states unanimous of opinion that unless Monroe Doctrine amendment is inserted in League constitution, Republican Senators will defeat treaty and public opinion will sustain them. Urge vital need of insisting on amendment. Taft. Lowell."

Polk,   Acting.

T telegram (WP, DLC).
  ¹ That is, the League to Enforce Peace.

From the Diary of Dr. Grayson

Sunday, April 13, 1919.

The President remained in bed until noon. I persuaded him to take a much-needed rest, as he showed marked signs of fatigue from the trying and strenuous week through which he had passed.

At 1:00 o'clock the President had lunch with Mrs. Wilson and myself. In the afternoon the President and Mrs. Wilson went out motoring. Upon his return he sent me out to see some newspaper correspondents, among them Mr. Swope of the New York WORLD.

At six o'clock the President saw Lloyd-George, Clemenceau and Orlando, the conference lasting until eight o'clock. He told me that Lloyd-George was leaving the next morning for London, where he would go before Parliament to explain his position here at the Peace Conference, and that he (Lloyd-George) was also going to inform the British Parliament that the Germans would be invited to the Peace Conference on April 25th. It was the understanding that the President was to give out this notice on Monday evening and prepare the invitation to the Germans, but the British gave it to the press without the President's knowledge and in violation of the understanding.

At eight o'clock the President, Mrs. Wilson and I had dinner. After dinner the President talked to Mrs. Wilson and myself about the happenings of the Conference, and he asked me to go on a confidential mission to see Mr. Bernard M. Baruch at the Ritz Hotel. The President retired about 11:00 o'clock.

From the Diary of Ray Stannard Baker

Sunday the 13th [April 1919]

A fine spring day. I took a couple of long walks.

The Big Four met at 6 o'clock at the President's House & sat over the dinner hour, to 8:15. I saw the President for a moment after the meeting was over. They have now settled all the important points, & April 25 has been set as the time when the Germans are to come—though the President asked me not to announce the date until to-morrow. He will receive Orlando Monday & try to get at some solution of the Italian question—the French & British leaving it to him. Lloyd-George goes home tomorrow to present his case to the British parliament. It looks now as though he would "stay hitched," although Northcliffe is still after him. Clemenceau will be explaining to his government & Orlando will go home the last of next week to meet his parliament.

The President seemed quite cheery this evening for he evidently feels that real progress has been made. He may talk to the correspondents to-morrow.

From Vittorio Emanuele Orlando[1]

Confidential.

My dear President: Paris, April 13th, 1919.

I fear my urgency may seem importunate, but I know you well enough to be sure that you will excuse me.

A rapid solution of the Italian question is essential to a rapid conclusion of peace, as you yourself have admitted; but it is also absolutely essential to calm the anxiety of the Italian people, an anxiety which many symptoms clearly show me is growing more and more intense.

It is undoubtedly true that the assiduous labors of these last four weeks have been entirely taken up by the examination of the French questions; and it cannot reasonably be said that the Italian questions have been intentionally neglected. But reason and feeling do not always coincide, especially in the mind of a people; and, as I have pointed out to you, the impression that the peace conditions for France are now settled, while those of Italy are still trembling in the balance has led to the most acute nervous tension in my country.

I therefore earnestly request you to arrange for a conference with me either to-day (Sunday) in the afternoon or evening, or tomorrow (Monday) at a time which will not interfere with the meeting of the Council of Four.

I am expecting the Memorandum[2] which you promised me, but, in any case, I would still request you to arrange for the proposed conference between us, as it would afford me the opportunity of explaining to you the necessity for Italy to insist on a certain minimum of her aspirations, of the justice of which she is convinced.

I must again apologise for my urgency in insisting on this matter, but I assure you once again that it is a case of absolute necessity.

Please accept, my dear President, the assurance of my cordial friendship, and believe me,

Sincerely yours   V. E. Orlando

TLS (WP, DLC).

[1] House, in his diary entry of April 13, 1919, says: "I dictated a note which I advised Orlando to send to the President and told him that I, in turn, would get in touch with the President myself."

[2] It is printed at April 14, 1919.

Mantoux's Notes of a Meeting of the Council of Four

April 13, 1919, 6 p.m.

Wilson. We must know if we can now set the date for summoning the German plenipotentiaries. M. Orlando, to whom I have just spoken, wishes that no definite decision be taken on this subject so long as we have not agreed in principle on the Italian questions.

Orlando. It would indeed be impossible for me to accept it. The impression would be disastrous in Italy if I told my compatriots that five months after the conclusion of the Armistice, all the French questions are settled, while there is not even an agreement in principle on the Italian questions. I am very reasonable, and I am not asking that the latter be completely settled before the summoning of the German plenipotentiaries; I am only asking that decisions of principle be arrived at. If there is no serious disagreement among us, that could be done in forty-eight hours. It would be sufficient to set down the bases of the agreement and, between the time when the Germans are summoned and the moment when they arrive in Versailles, we will have time to pursue the matter. I would observe that until now Italian affairs have never been discussed in this Council of Four.

Clemenceau. That is because in everyone's opinion, the most pressing matter was to settle German affairs. However I do not wish to argue against what you are saying.

Orlando. Four or five days must be devoted to the study of Italian questions.

Clemenceau. Do you mean all the questions that interest Italy, or only the one of Fiume and Dalmatia?

Orlando. It is that which is the most important.

Lloyd George. Like you, I think that examination of these questions must not be delayed. But before my departure, which takes place tomorrow, I am anxious that we set the date for summoning the Germans.

Clemenceau. We must not set this date before we are sure we will be ready.

Wilson. Will we be if we provide for a postponement of ten days?

Lloyd George. I was just visited by two Belgian ministers, MM. Hymans and Vandervelde.[1] I found the latter very open and very reasonable.

They wished to discuss with me the question of Luxembourg. I told them that we were not ready, and I informed them of the outlines of the treaty we have prepared. They seemed satisfied about what I told them regarding reparations, as well as about our resolution regarding the responsibilities and trial of the Kaiser; they are especially happy about our proposal to reserve for Belgium the role of prosecutor. I proposed to submit to their financial experts the final draft of the text relative to reparations, on which they have, after all, collaborated in the commission.

Wilson. What do they say about the territorial questions?

Lloyd George. They would like to receive a letter from us telling them that we are happy to know that they have undertaken negotiations with Luxembourg looking toward a rapprochement of the two countries.

Clemenceau. I am prepared to do everything to assist them, except to appear to give them Luxembourg as a gift.

Lloyd George. The Belgians view with displeasure the plebiscite in Luxembourg, which, I think, must settle, at the same time, the political regime of the country and its customs system. They would like at this time for us to assist them with a letter expressing our good will toward their negotiations with Luxembourg. Mr. Lansing, it seems, has shown himself favorable. But I told them that I could promise them nothing before bringing the question before the Four.

Wilson. Mr. Lansing was only expressing a personal opinion. Naturally, any decision must be taken in common.

Clemenceau. I am not against the union of Belgium and Luxembourg; but it must be done properly. For my part, I cannot throw Luxembourg into the arms of Belgium. I want more information about the state of the question before replying to you.

Wilson. Let us return to the question raised by M. Orlando. Would he see any objection to summoning the Germans now, to appear within ten days, while committing ourselves to spending this week the time necessary to examine among ourselves the Italian question before the time when he himself must return to Italy? When the Germans arrive, they will need several days to examine the text we submit to them, and that will give us time to complete, if necessary, our examination of the problems which interest Italy particularly.

[1] Émile Vandervelde, Minister of State and delegate to the peace conference.

Orlando. I have the greatest desire to reach agreement with you. But I have two observations to make. First and foremost, it is necessary to present again the impression that such a decision would create in Italy. My compatriots know that at the present time the questions which concern us are not resolved. If we now announce that the Germans are summoned for a date in the near future, that will cause the Italians to believe that the questions they consider vital are seen by the Allies as being outside the general peace. So much the better if that impression is consequently contradicted by events; but at the outset it will be disastrous.

In the second place, I believe that our questions can be settled in principle this week, and I hope that they will be; they can receive a simple solution. But in what situation would I find myself and in what situation would you place the conference itself if the Germans arrived here before the Italian question was settled? The Italian government would then be in a very perilous situation; the effect would be nearly the same as that of a separate peace, and that would create dangers so grave that I prefer not to explain myself further.

Clemenceau. Can you be precise about what you are asking?

Orlando. I am asking that the summons of the Germans not be issued before the Italian questions are settled in grand outlines; that can be done in forty-eight hours and, in that case, the summons could follow immediately, the Germans could still be here in ten days. But I would not like them to be summoned before our agreement in principle had been reached.

Lloyd George. It is absolutely impossible. I would comment that the first request for the Armistice came from Germany. Afterward, we received the news that Austria wished to negotiate. Then we examined the situation, and in spite of our particular interest, which was to stop hostilities with Germany as soon as possible, given the heavy losses which the British, French, and American armies were suffering, we decided in the general interest to conclude first an armistice with Austria.

Today, the terms of the problem are reversed: if it is impossible to lead two horses abreast, one must be allowed to move in front of the other, and there is no doubt that it is with Germany that we must treat with first. Do not forget that Italy is also interested in the conclusion of the preliminaries with Germany, if only in the chapter on reparations.

We have spent weeks and months preparing the preliminaries of peace with Germany because we all agreed on the necessity of negotiating first with that power. You are not proposing to summon here the Austrians, the Turks, the Bulgarians, to discuss with them at the same time as with the Germans. We could say about Turkey what you are saying about Austria. We still have hundreds of thousands of British soldiers on Ottoman territory, and we would like to be able to demobilize them. In delaying, however little, direct negotiations with Germany, we run the risk of prolonging the anxiety and uneasiness of the entire world, in which Italy has her part. From the political point of view, what interests Italy the most is the settlement of the Austrian questions. But from the economic point of view, Italy is interested in the settlement of German affairs.

We cannot further delay summoning the German plenipotentiaries. They will need some time to examine the document which we will hand them, not only because this document will be long and complicated, but also because it affects the entire life of their people for a period of perhaps half a century. While they proceed with that examination, we could examine the Austrian questions and even summon here the Austrian delegates. I hope that the summoning of the Germans will not be delayed until we have completely settled our determinations on Fiume and Dalmatia, questions which have absolutely nothing to do with Germany.

Wilson. Would M. Orlando be satisfied if we announced at the same time that we are summoning the Germans and that we are actively continuing the examination of the other questions, that the Italian question has priority over all the others? We could add that we have every hope of a prompt solution of the problems that concern Italy.

Orlando. I would reply to Mr. Lloyd George that there is no relationship between the question raised today about the peace and that which was raised last November about the subject of the Armistice. At the basis of our decision on the date of the Armistice there was a question of fact. I truly believe that we received a definite request for an armistice from Austria before receiving one from Germany. But in any case, the problem of the peace is completely different. Now it is a matter of reestablishing law and normal conditions.

Mr. Lloyd George says: "The questions concerning Italy and those which govern the German peace are separate." Perhaps they are legally; but politically, they are linked. If we get down to the concrete and not to the abstract, I would ask you this question: what would happen if the peace was signed with Germany while a state of war continued in the Adriatic? England, France, the United States would be at peace, and there would be no peace for Italy.

I appeal to Mr. Lloyd George's sense of justice and to the friendship between us during several years of collaboration. Five months have passed since the conclusion of the Armistice; weeks have been devoted to difficult and admittedly necessary discussions about problems such as the one of reparations. The representatives of Italy have waited patiently; during this delay they did not ask for priority for the questions which particularly interest them. At the end of these five months, I ask you for a few days to know at least in what sauce you intend to cook me, and you refuse?

To President Wilson, I would reply: are we certain that we can arrive at a general agreement on the Italian questions between the time the Germans are summoned and their arrival? I hope so. But are we sure of it?

Clemenceau. No.

Orlando. I thank M. Clemenceau for this word. We have still not deliberated on the questions which interest me; I am in the dark, and I cannot say if the conversation among the four of us will permit me to be in time [*sic*].

Clemenceau. Do not misunderstand what I just said. I agree with President Wilson to ask for the immediate summoning of the Germans; in the interval, we must, without losing a moment, do what is necessary to be ready when the Germans arrive. Between the moment of their arrival and the beginning of the negotiations, I am ready to examine the Italian questions. But I repeat that we have not a moment to lose if we wish to be prepared to talk with the Germans within ten days.

Orlando. I renew my objection. When we are prepared to sign the preliminaries with the Germans, will the Italian questions have received a satisfactory solution at least in principle? In the contrary case you would be placing me in an extremely difficult situation. From the Italian point of view, it is dangerous that the summoning of the Germans be announced when we know nothing about the solutions which concern us. What I am asking you for is an effort of two or three days.

Clemenceau. Why will you not agree that our discussion take place from the time when the Germans arrive, during the period they need to examine the text of the preliminaries? Do not forget that we still have very important points to settle before meeting the German plenipotentiaries: the text relating to Alsace-Lorraine, the text relating to direct reconstruction of the devastated regions.

Orlando. The proposal that President Wilson made a short time ago differs from that which M. Clemenceau is now making. President Wilson said: "We shall study the Italian questions during the interval between the time when we summon the Germans and the time of their arrival." M. Clemenceau proposes to examine them after the arrival of the Germans: that proposal is still more unfavorable to me.

Wilson. May I say aloud the thoughts which come to my mind? The difficulty M. Orlando is struggling with is real; it is the same one which worries Mr. Lloyd George in England and M. Clemenceau in France. It is a matter of satisfying a public opinion which is ill informed and worried. This problem is not foreign to me. In America also we are asked: "What are you doing? What is your attitude? What is happening in those meetings between you and the three statesmen who visit you every day?" Without any doubt, it is time to respond. I will also be obliged myself to do it, and in writing, while you have the advantage of being able to speak directly to your assemblies.

Would M. Orlando be satisfied if we should announce now that all the questions relating to Germany have arrived at a point of maturity, which permits us to summon the German plenipotentiaries within ten days, but that we have decided to delay that summons until we have arrived at an agreement with Italy on the questions concerning her? This manner of proceeding would have the advantage of informing our public that we are prepared, and announcing at the same time that we have thought it reasonable to acknowledge to our Italian colleague that the Italian questions must be settled urgently.

Lloyd George. How will this system work? At the time of the final draft of the treaty, certain lacunae will obviously be found which we will have to fill in. There are still certain questions of principle about which we have not yet arrived at a definitive formula. Do you mean that we shall only summon the Germans after having resolved in detail all the questions of wording, and after having solved the Italian question? I am very sorry, but I cannot agree with that view. I am persuaded that it is in the general interest to summon the Germans immediately and thus to prepare ourselves to negotiate with the only enemy state which is still standing.

Orlando. I thank President Wilson. He has understood that my feeling is sincere and profound. Since I have always shown myself to be very conciliatory, you will understand that I must have very serious reasons for speaking as I do. I do not believe that what I am asking can cause a considerable delay. I am only asking of you a very short time to permit study of our questions. If, in three days, we succeed in outlining the solution, we could then summon the Germans for the following week. We are not keeping a transcript, and my memory may deceive me; but I believe I remember that we always thought not to summon the Germans before having general ideas about the solution of all important questions. I believe I even remember that President Wilson spoke of the interest that he had in not delaying the solution of eastern questions.

I am asking you to place me at least in a position to announce that our questions have been examined by the Allies. Otherwise, the impression in Italy would be terrible. It will be said that problems vital to the Italian people were relegated to the same rank as those of Teschen or Mesopotamia. Italian opinion is very nervous. I am doing everything possible to calm it; but the consequences of a disappointment of this kind would be very grave. When, on April 23, I appear before the Italian Parliament, the least that can happen is the fall of the cabinet, the effect of which would certainly not be to hasten the conclusion of the peace. I beg you to accept what President Wilson has proposed.

Wilson. In any case, you could tell the Italian Parliament that the Italian questions have been and will continue to be examined without losing a moment during the ten-day period from now. By announcing that we have summoned the Germans at the end of that period of ten days, we would be announcing that this will not at all delay the examination of questions outside the preliminaries of peace with Germany, and that first on the list is the Italian question.

It is possible that we will not arrive at a solution of the Italian problems before April 23. In this case, would it not be advantageous for M. Orlando to be able to explain to his Parliament his own view as well as that of the other associated governments in order to inform Italy that what is delaying the solution is only the exchange of views necessary among friends who wish to do nothing except in a spirit of friendship for the Italian people? I hope that it will be possible now to set a date for the Germans and to declare that the Italian question is the first item on our agenda.

I was just going to propose not to meet among ourselves tomorrow, in order to allow me time to examine these problems at length with M. Orlando. By announcing only the day after tomorrow that we are summoning the Germans, we shall have the right to say that the discussion of the Italian questions has begun.

Orlando. I hope that our conversation tomorrow can clarify the situation. If the Germans are not summoned before Tuesday, I can wait. But that only allows me to suspend my judgment for twenty-four hours more.

Lloyd George. This means that if tomorrow there is not the prospect of an immediate agreement on the question of the Adriatic, the German treaty will remain in the air; that is what is impossible for me to accept. To indicate my feelings regarding Italy, I add that I am ready to accept in advance any solution on which President Wilson and M. Orlando manage to agree.

M. Orlando appeals to our sentiments of friendship. I ask him to consider our situation. France and Great Britain made war longer than Italy; their losses were heavier: England had twice as many dead and France at least three times. Without speaking of the general interest, we have the right to stress to Italy those considerations which particularly concern us.

There is also the matter of permitting world commerce to revive; as long as we have no treaty with Germany, the economic life of the entire world will remain at a standstill.

Orlando. I do not wish to compare our sacrifices, and I accept Mr. Lloyd George's comment, while recalling that, if the number of dead is compared to the population, I believe Italy's losses were heavier than those of England.

I understand as well as anyone the interest we all have in promptly making peace with Germany. That is why I have consented for weeks to allow priority to the German questions. I gave you weeks, and I am only asking for a few days: I hope that this proportion of time is consistent with that of our sacrifices.

Wilson. Tomorrow we shall spend the day discussing the Italian questions tête à tête. I would be very happy to be able to announce on Tuesday that the examination has been pursued actively and even, if our conversation permits it, that we glimpse the solution. We shall say that the Germans are summoned for April 25 because the preliminaries of peace with Germany are ready and that that very fact even facilitates the discussion of other important questions, of which the first is the Italian question. I do not see how we could give you a clearer priority, and I hope that this will permit you to face the difficulties that you foresee.

Clemenceau. I agree to summon the Germans for April 25.

Wilson. We must do what is necessary to press actively the examination of the Italian question, without neglecting the finishing touches to the preliminaries of peace with Germany.

Orlando. I insist on repeating that I can only suspend my judgment until after our conversation tomorrow. I do not know if it will be possible for me to say anything tomorrow evening other than what I am saying today.

Lloyd George. If that is so, you are placing everything in question again. As for myself, I am obliged to leave tomorrow morning.

Orlando. I will try to inform you about my position before your departure.

Messrs. Haskins, Headlam-Morley, and Tardieu are introduced. They show on the map the last modifications in the delimitation of the territory of the Saar, to bring the frontier into conformity with administrative divisions.

Mantoux, I, 237-45.

Two Letters from Robert Lansing

My dear Mr. President: Paris, April 13, 1919.

At a meeting held yesterday morning by your colleagues on the Commission a telegram dated Washington, March 4th,[1] containing a statement purporting to have been made by you regarding your attitude on the Jewish Commonwealth[2]—which was published in the Egyptian Press as an official American communiqué emanating from the American Diplomatic Agency at Cairo was brought to their attention; and I was requested to forward a copy of this telegram to you and to ask you whether the quotation contained therein is correct, because if not it is the belief of your colleagues that the matter should be denied promptly.[3]

I am, my dear Mr. President,

Faithfully yours,   Robert Lansing.

TCL (WP, DLC).

[1] Embodied in W. L. Westermann to W. C. Bullitt, April 11, 1919, T MS (WP, DLC).
[2] For Wilson's remarks to American Jewish leaders, see the news report printed at March 2, 1919, Vol. 55.
[3] Westermann, in the above-mentioned memorandum to Bullitt, said that Wilson's remarks had been published in the Egyptian press as an official American communiqué emanating from the American diplomatic agency in Cairo. Westermann added:

"The last sentence of this telegram as published in Egypt, which states in part that 'the American Government were agreed that the foundations of a Jewish Commonwealth should be laid in Palestine' grants much more to the Zionists than the Balfour declaration. The latter promises the establishment in Palestine of a National Home for the Jewish people. The statement accredited to President Wilson implies that the Allies and the United States will support the laying of the foundations of a future Jewish State in Palestine.

"We are not aware that such a promise had been given by the President to the Zionists, and if it be possible we should like to be fully informed on this point, as such a declaration would of necessity affect both the Palestinian and Syrian Question.

"We are under the impression that President Wilson does not wish to commit the American Government for anything more than the Balfour Declaration. We point out that the statement of the President as published in the Egyptian papers does further commit the United States and is so being interpreted in the Near East.

"The situation in Palestine is very acute. The Arabs have become very bitter against Zionism. We are receiving vigorous protests addressed to President Wilson against Jewish immigration and the establishment of a Jewish State, and demanding that Palestine be included in a Syrian State. In view of this delicate situation, the statement concerning a Jewish Commonwealth should, if not true, be at once officially denied through Mr. Gary, the Diplomatic Agent at Cairo, who should be requested to inquire how it appeared in this distorted form in the Egyptian papers."

My dear Mr. President: Paris, April 13, 1919.

Yesterday afternoon Mr. Paderewski called to see me and we discussed Poland and Polish affairs.

In connection with the Teschen situation I suggested that Poland and Bohemia should attempt to reach a friendly settlement between themselves if possible as it would leave a much better feeling than if it was settled by others. He agreed with this view and said that the two countries must be friends because of their common dangers.

I suggested to him that it might be possible for Poland to select two commissioners and Bohemia to select two, the four to meet here in Paris at once independently of the Conference, and consider an agreement. If they failed to agree, they could reduce their differences to the smallest compass and then call in a third person, mutually acceptable, to settle the question.

Mr. Paderewski seemed really enthusiastic over this suggestion and said that he would endeavor to arrange such a joint commission with the Czechs. I told him that I thought both sides should assume, on entering the negotiation, that neither would be satisfied. He replied that he understood and quite agreed that that should be the basis.

I suggested this course because I feel that if the parties to a territorial dispute can reach an amicable settlement independently it will not leave the feeling of resentment which will be aroused if an international commission dictates the terms, a resentment which may develop future wars.

Another reason for this method is that it removes the impression that France is the ultimate arbiter between the new states of Eastern Europe, an impression which is being industriously spread by the French military clique who are making all sorts of promises to the various nationalities as to political and economic as well as military matters.

Until, therefore, I have heard again from Mr. Paderewski I hope that nothing will be done with the report of the territorial commission dealing with Teschen, which I understand is practically completed.

If the French learn of this proposed method of independent settlement, I am afraid that they will attempt to block it as it does not offer an opportunity for them to claim credit through intrigue. This, I believe, is the chief danger, because Paderewski and Beneš are both reasonable men and will, I think, be disposed to an amicable adjustment.   Faithfully yours,   Robert Lansing

TLS (WP, DLC).

From Robert Lansing, with Enclosure

My Dear Mr. President: Paris, April 13, 1919.

At a meeting held yesterday morning by your colleagues on the Commission, the appended memorandum by Dr. Lord, dated April 10th, on the subject of the suspension of arms in Eastern Galicia, was considered; and I was requested to transmit this memorandum to you and to invite your attention to the fact that the Council of Four definitely committed itself on this question by its telegram of March 19th and that the present action of the Poles appears to be a direct violation of the desires of the four Chiefs of State as indicated in that telegram.

I am, my dear Mr. President,

Faithfully yours,   Robert Lansing

TLS (T. H. Bliss Papers, DLC).

E N C L O S U R E

Suggestion by Mr. Lord[1]

The Allied and Associated Governments, deeply concerned over the conflict which has been going on for many months between Poles and Ukrainians in Galicia, address themselves again to the Polish Government with the earnest desire to bring about a suspension of hostilities. In all the efforts which they have made to terminate this conflict, the Allied and Associated Governments have been moved solely by their desire to end the misery and suffering inflicted by this struggle upon a region already sorely tried by four years of warfare; and to end it upon terms which would assure the rights and vital interests of both the contending parties during the period that must elapse until the definitive settlement of the political questions affecting Eastern Galicia.

This final settlement is now close at hand; but in beginning their deliberations upon the future political status of Eastern Galicia, the Allied and Associated Governments more than ever feel it necessary that the present hostilities should cease. For they cannot permit the interested parties to attempt to anticipate their decision by creating *faits accomplis*, and they cannot but point out that military successes won by aggressive operations are more likely to injure than advance the interests of the aggressor.

In order to facilitate the end of this conflict, the Allied and Associated Governments have already had preliminary negotiations conducted with the two belligerents by an Inter-Allied Commission at Paris. In order to afford every guarantee of fairness and of thorough consideration, the four Chiefs of States are prepared to give their personal attention to the final formulation of the armistice terms which they propose to offer by way of mediation; and before deciding upon the formulation of those terms, they are ready to discuss their content with representatives of the Polish Government and to make every effort to meet the justifiable wishes and the needs of Poland.

As a condition of this mediation, however, the Allied and Associated Governments must insist that the Polish High Command should at once agree to confine itself henceforth to a purely defensive attitude pending the conclusion of an armistice.

The Allied and Associated Governments feel themselves the more entitled to make this request because, at the moment when the peace with Germany approaches its completion, they are confident that the Polish Government and the Polish people will not fail to recognize both the sincere regard for the rights and interests of Poland of which this treaty gives proof, and the importance, particularly at such a moment, of maintaining the utmost harmony between Poland and the Allied Powers.

T MS (WP, DLC).
[1] WWhw.

A Translation of a Letter from Gustave Ador

Mr. President, Berne, April 13, 1919.

It is at your suggestion and thanks to your powerful influence that the Committee of the League of Nations has just designated Geneva as the seat of the League.

Permit me, Mr. President, in my double capacity of a citizen of Geneva and of President of the Confederation, to express to you my profound gratitude for the great honor done to Switzerland and to my native city.

The city of Calvin, of J. J. Rousseau and of the Red Cross will be proud and happy to be able to collaborate in the great work of peace and union among the nations, the prompt realization of which will be the just recompense of your generous initiative and of your persevering efforts. The Swiss nation, which has already received so many tokens of sympathy from you, will remember that the designation of Geneva is a new proof of a kindness and friendship which are infinitely precious to it.

I am sure I am its faithful interpreter in expressing to you all its gratitude.

Please receive, I beg you, the assurances of my high and respectful consideration. Ador.

T MS (WP, DLC).

From Henry Pomeroy Davison

Dear Mr. President: Cannes, April 13, 1919.

Unfortunately conditions seem not to permit the postponement of any movement which may contribute in any degree to the betterment of the world, which fact is my only excuse for bothering you at this time.

Our Red Cross plans have proceeded most satisfactorily and we are now at the point of completing our organization for operation. As you too well know, this involves the necessity of securing qualified men. We are to adopt the name of "The League of Red Cross Societies," and our organization will be formulated along the lines of the organization of the League of Nations. I have consented to accept the Chairmanship of the Council and we are now looking for the right man for Director General. Out of consideration for your time I shall not write you at length of the duties involved in this position, but will sum them up by saying the responsibilities and opportunities in connection with this work are so great as to command the talent of a very efficient, broad man of character and experience. Certainly there is no position which will afford an opportunity to an individual to render greater humanitarian service to the peoples of the world than that of the Director General of the League of Red Cross Societies.

I have canvassed the field with my associates here, and we have all reached the opinion that no man is better qualified to undertake this work than Secretary Lane, but naturally I would not want to make any suggestion that would cause you the slightest unnecessary inconvenience. If you should have no objection and Secretary Lane should conclude to accept this position, it would be unnecessary for him to leave his office for several months, and certainly he would not consider leaving without due regard to his responsibilities to you.

I am sure, my dear Mr. President, that you will realize that I greatly regret troubling you, but in view of all the circumstances, I feel justified in bringing this to you in this manner and shall await your reply before considering any other name.

Hoping you are now quite well, I am

Cordially yours,   H. P. Davison

TLS (WP, DLC).

From Josephus Daniels

My Dear Mr. President: [Paris] April 13, 1919

I cannot leave the city without a word which is the result of my impressions after seeing people from half a dozen countries. In Paris one is apt to forget that the people of the world are as sincere and as eager for a settlement [that] will prevent future wars as they showed their feeling when you first came over. But back home, though now unexpressed, they are looking to you with a dumb faith. I have felt this atmosphere though sometimes enveloped in an atmosphere of doubt, grab and hoping to hold on to [the] old order. I know your devotion to the ideal that brought you over cannot waver, but thought you would like to know that I have sensed the feelings of hope in you—a hope not of today only but of all the future. That knowledge must give you comfort and strength for the last days of the ordeal. Our people at home, in spite of lack of vision and small politics and junkerism, are in accord and grateful for your righteous leadership.

With my warm regards to Mrs. Wilson.

Sincerely,   Josephus Daniels

Admiral Benson has my address and you can reach me any time before I sail if desired.

I hope a high court will try the Kaiser and let it fix the punishment JD

ALS (WP, DLC).

From the Diary of Dr. Grayson

Monday, April 14, 1919.

The President had breakfast this morning at 8:30 o'clock, after which he immediately withdrew to his study to dispose of an accumulated correspondence. At 11:00 o'clock he conferred with Mr. Orlando and other members of the Italian delegation, which conference lasted until lunch time. Mrs. Wilson was indisposed, and the President had lunch with her in her bed-room.

At 2:00 o'clock the President received a telephone message saying that ex-President Taft and President Lowell of Harvard University were keenly disappointed in the language used in including the Monroe Doctrine in the League of Nations covenant.

A few minutes after two o'clock he received Frank H. Hitchcock, who was Postmaster General under President Taft and Manager of the first Taft campaign. When he greeted Mr. Hitchcock he said:

"Mr. Hitchcock, I am glad to have this opportunity to shake your hand, and to thank you, as a patriotic American, for your cooperation in helping to secure support for the League of Nations not only here but at home, and particularly for the inclusion of the Monroe Doctrine." Mr. Hitchcock replied: "It is very generous of you to receive me and speak in this manner. I deeply appreciate it. It is the first time I have had the pleasure of shaking hands with the President for a long time (not since President Taft left the White House six years ago), and, as an American, I want to say that we are very proud of your achievements for the world. I am glad to tell you that the cause which you have so earnestly advocated is one resting on high grounds. I regret that there was partisan opposition to your plans at home. It is a matter in which partisanship should not enter; it should be handled on higher grounds. I have little patience with those who are trying to make partisan capital out of it." The President then said: "It will be of interest to you to know that I have just received word that ex-President Taft and Mr. Lowell object to the wording of the Monroe Doctrine clause in the League of Nations covenant." Mr. Hitchcock said: "I do not see how they could object to it, and I do not believe that when they read the exact wording and study it they can object; I think that a big majority of the American people will back you up in the stand you have taken." Mr. Hitchcock added: "I must not take any more of your valuable time. I do hope that your strength and health will hold out so that you may win out with this big undertaking handsomely, which I feel sure you will do. When I realize what a fine Doctor you have, I have entire confidence that your health will bear up under the strain." The President said: "I agree to all that you say about the Doctor." Mr. Hitchcock said: "I speak from experience because I had the opportunity to know him before you did." The President was most generous in his remarks about me, which was distinctly embarrassing to me.

At 2:30 o'clock Secretary Lansing and ex-Ambassador White and General Bliss called for the purpose of conferring with the President.

At noon today I asked the President whether he expected to have the Big Four meeting this evening, and he said: "No. Clemenceau always goes to bed at about seven o'clock and gets up at three." I asked the President whether he had noticed any difference in Clemenceau physically. He said that recently he had noticed a very marked difference; that his memory was much affected, and that when he wanted to discuss a question, he would say: "I cannot do that; I have to call for my experts." This would refer to matters in connection with which it should not be necessary for him to call for outside assistance.

I was called upon today to investigate the circumstances under which H. B. Swope of the New York WORLD had obtained the exact text of the [proposals of the?] American Reparation Commissioners.[1] Swope had telegraphed this text to London to the Freemen's Journal, which was to relay it on to New York, but it was held up by the British censor and referred back to the President for investigation as to the manner in which Swope had obtained it. I took the matter up with Mr. Baruch as chief of the American experts. Incidentally, it developed as a bit of poetic justice that Swope in an effort to cover the manner in which he had obtained it had furnished it to Hills of the New York SUN, who had filed it by direct cable to New York, with the result that it was published in the SUN[2] although it was never published in the WORLD.

The President had been urged to make a public statement dealing with the work of the Commission. Yesterday Clemenceau had talked freely to a committee of the Radical French members of the Chamber on the entire subject of the work of the treaty and had told them that a satisfactory arrangement seemed in sight and that France's claims would be honorably disposed of. The President was urged by me to prepare a statement for the press of the world, setting forth his position and to give it immediate publicity in order that it would be disposed of prior to Lloyd-George's speech in the House of Commons on Wednesday. The President had a crowded day and it was not until late in the evening that he was able to prepare the statement. However, he did so, and its publication was received with much enthusiasm by the newspapermen, who wanted to be fair inasmuch as it showed that the danger of deadlock so far as the German situation was concerned apparently had been passed. The statement is as follows:[3]

Today I sent the following message to Admiral Braisted:[4]

"It has come to my knowledge that you have recommended me for a Distinguished Service medal. If my information is correct, I hope you will withdraw your recommendation. Your action is a distinction and honor which I deeply appreciate, coming from you as Surgeon General of the Navy, and this is sufficient for me. Am sorry I am not at home to make this request in person."

The President dined with Mrs. Wilson in her bed-room. The President worked in his study and retired early.

[1] That is, Bernard M. Baruch, Norman H. Davis, and Vance C. McCormick.

[2] The text of the reparation clauses of the treaty of peace, published under Laurence Hills' byline in the New York *Sun*, April 12, 1919, was, with a few minor changes in wording, the one adopted by the Council of Four on April 7, 1919, 4 p.m., and embodied in the notes of that meeting printed at that date and time. Hills accompanied this text with various speculations regarding the reparation clauses. Most notable was his assertion that "experts" had settled on $45,000,000,000 as the sum of reparations to be demanded of Germany.

[3] This statement is printed as an Enclosure with WW to RSB, April 14, 1919.

[4] That is, Rear Adm. William Clarence Braisted.

From the Diary of Colonel House

April 14, 1919.

I had a talk with the President this morning regarding Luxembourg which I am insisting that the French allow to go to Belgium if it is desired. We discussed the Adriatic situation and he is to meet Orlando at eleven. The date for calling in the Germans has been tentatively fixed for the 25th of April. This is as early and a little earlier than I expected after the decision was reached to include all the treaties in one, or at least having them all ready for signature at the same time and making them final.

I spoke of Greece and suggested that he come to no settlement of that question until I had a chance to talk with him further. I reminded him to send in the names of Hugh Gibson for Poland, Norman Hapgood for Denmark and Richard Crane for Czecho-Slovakia as interim appointments.

It has been a fruitful day. By far the most interesting visitor was Clemenceau. He asked to come this afternoon and I made the appointment for five. He remained for nearly an hour. On Friday at the Plenary Conference, he told me that in a few days he wanted to give me a warning. The President heard him and we both wondered what was on the old man's mind. He had evidently forgotten whatever grievances he had, for matters have been going fairly well with him since. Instead of a warning, or anything disagreeable, it was more in the nature of a love-feast.

He wished to discuss Syria among other things. He brought his matter[1] and told me of a conference he and Lloyd George had yesterday or the day before. He also told of a conference he had with Prince Feisal. He and Feisal came to an agreement, but after Feisal had talked with Col. Lawrence, his British Aide, he withdrew from what he had said to Clemenceau. They had agreed that the French should pay the sum which the British have been paying to the Royal House. This, Clemenceau said, at one time amounted to two million, five hundred thousand francs a year. The French were to have an army of occupation and only the army was to use the French Colors. The Arab Flag was to be flown otherwise.

Clemenceau asked me to tell the President about these conversations and to say that although the French had been promised Cilicia, which takes in the seacoast of what should be Armenia, he was willing to give it up provided the United States would take the Mandatory for Armenia. He wished France to retian [retain], however, Alexandretta and a small valley which he pointed out on the map. He was willing to send the mission the President had suggested but he advised against its going at once. He had heard that a massacre of Christians is contemplated soon in Syria and the East generally.

He said Orlando was threatening to go home and to withdraw Italy from the Conference and largely upon the ground that a peace with Germany was to be made before and not simultaneously with a peace with the A[u]stro-Hungarian Empires. He blamed the President for this—foolishly Clemenceau said—for he and Lloyd George were at one with the President in the matter. He spoke of Orlando's threatened action as stupid beyond conception.

He said he would agree to the President's terms for the protection of France and the west bank of the Rhine. It was not what he wanted but with the guarnatee [guarantee] of the United States he thought it sufficient. He would have to fight Foch and his other Marshals but he was willing to make the fight provided the President would agree to let the French occupy three stratas of German territory. The first strata for five years, the second for ten years, and the third for fifteen years. The first strata to include Coblentz, the second Maintz and the third would come closer to the French frontier. He said in the Treaty of '71 Germany insisted upon occupying France for five years or until the indemnity was paid. The indemnity was paid sooner, therefore the troops were withdrawn sooner, nevertheless, it set a precedent for his demand.

If the President would consent to it he, Clemenceau, could beat his Marshals in the Chamber of Deputies and the Senate, and he would also take occasion to state the generous action of the President toward France in the Peace Conference.

I talked to Clemenceau about Russia and I got him to agree to the feeding of Russia by the Neutrals. He declared he was perfectly willing to do what I had in mind and he agreed that if Russia could be opened up in some way to give the people a chance to look at conditions there, no one would desire to bring about similar conditions in their own countries.

The reason I get along with Clemenceau better than the President does is that in talking of such matters as this Russian question, the President talks to him as he would to me, while I never think of using the same argument with Clemenceau as I use with the President. One is an idealist, the other a practical old-line statesman. When I told him about Russia and the good it would do France and the rest of us to open it up, he saw at once and was willing. If I had told him it was to save life in Russia and to make things easier there for the sick, for the weak and for the helpless, it would have had no effect.

[1] *Sic.*

To Ray Stannard Baker, with Enclosure

My dear Baker: Paris, 14 April, 1919

At the request of my colleagues of the so-called Council of Four, I have formulated the enclosed statement of the reasons for advising that the German plenipotentiaries be summoned, and the effect which this will have upon the rest of the business of the Peace Conference.

Will you not be kind enough to see that this statement is immediately put in the hands of all the press representatives of all the countries? It is official, and I am merely acting as the spokesman of the conferences that have been held at the Place des Etats Unis.

Faithfully yours,   W.W.

TCL (R. S. Baker Papers, DLC).

ENCLOSURE

OFFICIAL STATEMENT TO BE GIVEN TO ALL REPRESENTATIVES
OF THE PRESS OF THE SEVERAL COUNTRIES

In view of the fact that the questions which must be settled in the peace with Germany have been brought so near complete solution that they can now quickly be put through the final process of drafting, those who have been most constantly in conference about them have decided to advise that the German plenipotentiaries be invited to meet representatives of the associated belligerent nations at Versailles on the twenty-fifth of April.

This does not mean that the many other questions connected with the general peace settlement will be interrupted or that their consideration, which has long been under way, will be retarded. On the contrary it is expected that rapid progress will now be made with those questions, so that they may also presently be expected to be ready for final settlement. It is hoped that the questions most directly affecting Italy, especially the Adriatic question, can now be brought to a speedy agreement. The Adriatic question will be given for the time precedence over other questions and pressed by continual study to its final stage.

The settlements that belong especially to the treaty with Germany will in this way be got out of the way at the same time that all other settlements are being brought to a complete formulation. It is realized that though this process must be followed, all the questions of the present great settlement are parts of a single whole.[1]

T MS (R. S. Baker Papers, DLC).
[1] There is a WWsh draft of this statement in the C. L. Swem Coll., NjP.

A Memorandum

REPORT OF THE CONFERENCE BETWEEN PRESIDENT WILSON AND THE
DEPUTY OSSOINACH[1] HELD IN THE PRESENCE OF PRESIDENT ORLANDO
APRIL 14TH 1919. PARIS.

Deputy Ossoinach, after being introduced to President Wilson by Signor Orlando, made the following statement:

Mr. President: as the unanimously elected deputy of Fiume, and as plenipotentiary of Fiume to the Peace Conference, I take the liberty of explaining to you the special case of Fiume.

First of all (pointing to the map) it must be stated that Fiume and its territory have well defined, historical frontiers, traced on the map for hundreds of years past, thus constituting a definitely bounded territory which has always been respected by successive governments, even by the last, the Hungarian, in spite of its well-known chauvinism. This special circumstance differentiates the territory of Fiume from the territories of all the other States now under discussion, such as Czeco-Slovackia and Jugo-Slavia, which are only now going to define their frontiers in a more or less justifiable way. In this way Fiume and its adjoining territory always constituted a *corpus separatum.* History proves the legal rights of this *corpus separatum* dating back to remote periods. One of the first important documents on the subject dates back to 1530, the Statute of Ferdinand, but the legal and historical basis of this right is set forth in the Diploma of Maria Theresa of 1779, of which a legalised photographic copy has been submitted to the Peace Conference.

How strong was the Italian nationality of the population of Fiume even at that time can be shown by the fact that when court intrigues at Vienna induced Maria Theresa to annex this *corpus separatum* to Croatia in 1776, the population of Fiume protested so vigorously that Maria Theresa was compelled to rescind this decision and to issue the one above referred to in 1779 in force of which Fiume was recognized as a *corpus separatum* and attached direct to Hungary without having any connection with Croatia.

In this connection, I must state that the diploma above referred to has nothing whatsoever to do with those documents which the Jugo-Slavs pretend have been falsified. The diploma of 1779 is the one of historical importance.

If the statistical data which show that out of 50,000 inhabitants in 1910 only 15,000 were Jugo-Slavs, and on 31st Dec. 1918 only 10,000 Jugo-Slavs, are not sufficient evidence of the Italian nationality of this population, I will make a description of the spirit which was ruling there even during the war and armistice.

[1] That is, Andrea Ossoinack.

First of all Fiume holds the second place among the "irredente" towns for the number of soldiers and officers who deserted from the Austro-Hungarian army in order to join the Italians and fight against Austria-Hungary, while those who remained at home tried by all means to help the Entente cause against Hungary. It was a great relief to this population, and aroused the greatest enthusiasm among them when all President Wilson's terms were made known, for they strengthened their hope that if the Entente won the war that they too would be freed from the oppression of a foreign government. This conviction grew to such an extent that I felt the absolute necessity that the Deputy of Fiume should make a clear, categorical declaration, in accordance with the Wilson principles, in the very chauvinistic Hungarian Parliament. Therefore on the 18th of October, before anyone knew that the war would be so soon over, I made the following declaration:

(Mr. Ossoinach then read from the stenographic report)

"The world war has upset the world, and it looks as if the world peace will upset it still more. For while at home the Croatians are claiming the city of Fiume, according to telegrams from abroad there is a wish to sacrifice Fiume to Jugoslavia. In the face of this tendency I deem it my duty to protest in this House and before the whole world against anybody who wishes to give Fiume to the Croatians. Not only was Fiume never Croatian, on the contrary, it has been Italian in the past, and it should remain Italian in the future."

Juriga[2] (Slovak) turning to the deputies of the labor party: now you should applaud!

Mr. Ossoinach continuing:

"For these reasons, and also for the fact that Fiume owing to its position in public law constitutes a *corpus separatum*, and because such an arbitrary solution of the destinies of Fiume would be contradictory to the right of self-determination of peoples I take the liberty to make the following declaration: (interruptions from the labor benches 'in whose behalf are you speaking?')

"I will tell you that also! It is, however, ridiculous! We have not yet reached the point to make such enquiries!

"With reference to the ideas set forth above, as Deputy of Fiume, unanimously elected, (turns towards the labor benches: 'Do you understand that?') I take the liberty to make the following declaration: (reads)

"As Austria-Hungary in the peace proposals has accepted the right of self-determination of the peoples proclaimed by Wilson,

[2] Father Ferdiš Juriga, the only Slovak member of the Hungarian Parliament at that time.

Fiume, as a *corpus separatum*, claims this right for itself. In conformity therewith it demands to exercise this right without restrictions of any kind.

["]I have taken the liberty of stating before this House this simple but clear point of view: Fiume stands by the right of self-determination." (Loud protests)

(Mr. Ossoinach, continuing)

This declaration of mine was received by the House with loud protests and abusive words, for instance, the Minister of Commerce,[3] making the gesture of placing a halter round the throat, shouted at me that I was a traitor.

In conformity with this declaration of mine in favor of self-determination, when the Hungarian government authorities ran away from Fiume on the 29th October and the Croat soldiers, the very best soldiers of Austria-Hungary, occupied the town, the population of Fiume in sign of protest, regardless of the consequences, constituted the National Council which, on the 30th of October, made the following proclamation: before anyone knew that the battle of Vittorio Veneto had begun:

(reads)

"The National Italian Council of Fiume, assembled this day in plenary session, declares that, in virtue of the right by which the peoples have risen to national independence and to liberty, the city of Fiume, which till now has been a 'separate body' forming a free national Italian commune, claims also for itself the right of self-determination common to all peoples. Basing itself on this right the National Council of Fiume proclaims the union of Fiume with the Mother Country, Italy.

"The Italian National Council considers as temporary the state of things brought about on October 29th, 1918, and places its right under the protection of America, mother of liberty and of universal democracy, and awaits the recognition of this right by the Peace Conference."

(Ossoinach emphasising this last paragraph, says)

The fact that Fiume appeals to America proves how deeply the population of Fiume was impressed by Wilson's terms. The Italian population of Fiume, being in an overwhelming majority, has the incontestable right of deciding in favor of union with Italy, and the Peace Conference cannot fail to ratify this decision, especially as the territory of Fiume now adjoins to that of Italy on the western border.

President Wilson (interrupting): The Peace Conference has not

[3] József, Baron Szterényi, Hungarian Minister of Commerce, January 25 to October 31, 1919.

yet decided that this territory will be Italian, and therefore we cannot yet speak of territorial continuity.

Ossoinach: But those territories are Italian territories. This coast, the Istrian coast, and the whole of Dalmatia with the islands are Italian lands which have been artificially denationalised in part. Fiume has been able to preserve its Italian nationality by reason of its special rights, and the injustice perpetrated on the other territories by the policy of artificial denationalisation largely carried out by depriving them of all their schools, cannot be recognised as constituting a right to prove that those territories were and should be Jugo-Slav. All the monuments, all the centres of culture in the towns and villages prove their Italian culture. Jugo-Slavia begins on the mountains and not on the coast. I am proud of being born in Fiume and not on the mountains.

From the economical standpoint the population dwelling in the *corpus separatum* of Fiume lives on the trade passing through the port from and to the hinterland, and therefore it is absurd to assert that they would bottle-up the hinterland, for if they did so they would starve. It is quite right that all economic advantages should be guaranteed to the hinterland, and to prove how firmly convinced Fiume is of this I may say that Fiume itself wishes to be a free port, by which means all economic advantages would be secured to the hinterland, because practically by making Fiume a free port the first custom boundary line will be that of Jugo-Slavia.

Jugo-Slavia does not need Fiume as a port as their trade is of no importance to that port. To prove that I need only point out that their greatest article of export is lumber and that along the railway line all the big forests are more or less used up, so that we see that since 1899 until 1908 this export trade has fallen 30%, and it is certain that in the next ten years it will suffer a further very sensible decline. The great forestry, mineral, and agricultural wealth is situated in the centre of Jugo-Slavia and therefore the trade is gravitating towards the southern ports of Dalmatia.

President Wilson (interrupting): Those railway lines meet with enormous difficulties in reaching the coast on account of the very high mountains.

Ossoinach: My dear Sir, you are wrong. First of all, these railways are already connected up with the ports, and the connections can be extended to the other ports also, so that the whole railway system would be placed in touch with the coast. Anyhow, however, the whole railway system of Jugo-Slavia is a narrow gauge system and therefore they cannot connect up with the normal gauge railways of the Fiume lines. It is therefore a technical absurdity to claim that the narrow gauge Jugo-Slav railway system must be connected up with the Fiume broad gauge system for all the lumber, minerals, and other goods would have to be trans[s]hipped in order to pass from the narrow-gauge to the broad gauge tracks, thus entailing very great delay and heavy expense, therefore this could not be economical. The fact of this difference of gauge disunites the whole Jugoslav railway system from the Port of Fiume, and therefore Fiume cannot be the natural and economical outlet of Jugoslavia.

President Wilson. (pointing on the map) It is not a question of Fiume belonging to Jugo-Slavia; it is a question of a port necessary to the whole of the hinterland, especially to that above Jugo-Slavia, and therefore it must be left open for this trade.

Ossoinach: I am very pleased to hear that, because it is my opinion too that Fiume should serve the whole hinterland, and that is the reason why it should become Italian, because Italy will have every interest to serve impartially Jugoslavia and Hungary and all the hinterland.

President Wilson: Fiume should be a free city, for in this way it would surely be open for the whole hinterland.

Ossoinach: I understand that there is a wish that Fiume should become a free city in order to guarantee the economic interests of the hinterland, but for this purpose it is not necessary that Fiume be a free city; the same results can be attained by the proposed *free port*. Moreover, the free city could not sustain itself. We see now that Fiume being independently governed is working with millions of deficit. And then who will invest the money required for the port?

President Wilson (interrupting): The interested hinterland countries will support the expenses and will make all the necessary investments.

Ossoinach: That means that Fiume would be dependent on that country to which it would be most heavily indebted, and what sort of a free city would Fiume be? No, my dear Sir, you will not solve the question of Fiume by making it a free city. Such a decision would only increase the hopes of both sides, of Jugo-Slavia and of Italy, and would make this city the apple of discord between those two countries, and will give rise to very fierce national struggles even between inhabitants of Fiume.

President Wilson (interrupting): But the Fiumani themselves wish to be a free city, so I have been told by them.

Ossoinach: No, Sir, that must be a mistake, a misunderstanding between free city and free port, or some Jugo-Slav masked as a Fiuman told you that, because the Fiumani solemnly declared against any other solution than that of being united to the Kingdom of Italy.

President Wilson: You mean that Fiume should belong politically to Italy as a free port; but in this case the Jugo-Slavs would not be well accepted in Fiume.

President Orlando: On this point I must remind you of the national guarantees I offered you once, when you were kind enough to say that Italy is such a chivalrous nation that it is superfluous for her to give such guarantees. Well, I renew the offer, and I am prepared to give the maximum national guarantees for all the different nationalities which will live in Italy.

Ossoinach: There is another very strong argument why Fiume should be Italian, and this is the regular navigation lines (pointing to the map). The three northern ports, Venice, Trieste, and Fiume, can only work rationally in cooperation one with the other, that is to say that at least the two ports of Trieste and Fiume must work together, and the regular cargo service must touch all three ports, because we must remember that these ports are not so important, especially so the port of Fiume which is only a moderate sized complementary port. * * *

President Wilson (interrupting): That is the point; they should not work together, but there should be competition between the two ports.

Ossoinach: Nobody will be able to prevent competition, and especially when Fiume is a free port; but I was saying that Fiume by itself cannot feed regular lines in such a way as to guarantee a rational service and freights, without which it is not possible to have a sound economical development of the hinterland. To prove this I need only remind you that the Hungarian government was giving millions in subsidies to regular navigation lines from Fiume just for the sake of ensuring a regular service of its own, and yet with all these government subsidies the Hungarian government had to allow these lines to charge rates 50 per cent higher than they should have been as compared to world freight market. For instance, from Odessa to England the freight was 9/, from Fiume to England these companies demanded 14/.

It is my irremovable opinion that the only equitable solution which will definitely settle the Fiume question, not only for itself but also guaranteeing all economic benefits to the hinterland is for Fiume to be annexed to the Kingdom of Italy. Should that settlement not be made, even if Fiume should be a free city, I wish to state that while I do not wish to make any kind of threats—for I am a very moderate man—but very thoroughly informed of the general opinion prevailing in Fiume, I am obliged to say without hesitation that Fiume will not accept any other solution, and I for my part decline all responsibility for the results which may ensure [ensue] on any decision other than that of uniting Fiume to Italy.

The people of Fiume expect justice from the Peace Conference, and I am confident that you, Mr. President, the man of justice, will see that justice is done in this case.

I beg to thank you, Mr. President, for the kind attention you have given to my statements.

CC MS (H. White Papers, DLC).

A Memorandum[1]

[April 14, 1919]

MEMORANDUM CONCERNING THE QUESTION OF ITALIAN CLAIMS ON THE ADRIATIC

There is no question to which I have given more careful or anxious thought than I have given to this, because in common with all my colleagues it is my earnest desire to see the utmost justice done to Italy. Throughout my consideration of it, however, I have felt that there was one matter in which I had no choice and could wish to have none. I felt bound to square every conclusion that I should reach as accurately as possible with the fourteen principles of peace which I set forth in my address to the Congress of the United States on the eighth of January, 1918 and in subsequent addresses. These fourteen points and the principles laid down in the subsequent addresses were formally adopted, with only a single reservation, by the Powers associated against Germany and will consitute the basis of peace with Germany. I do not feel at liberty to suggest one basis for peace with Germany and another for peace with Austria.

It will be remembered that in reply to a communication from the Austrian Government offering to enter into negotiations for an armistice and peace on the basis of the fourteen points to which I have alluded, I said that there was one matter to which those points no longer applied. They had demanded autonomy for the several states which had constituted parts of the Austro-Hungarian empire, and I pointed out that it must now be left to the choice of the people of those several countries what their destiny and political relations should be. They have chosen, with the sympathy of the whole world, to be set up as independent states. Their complete separation from Austria and the consequent complete dissolution of the Austro-Hungarian empire has given a new aspect and significance to the settlements which must be effected with regard at any rate to the Eastern boundaries of Italy. Personally, I am quite willing that Italy should be accorded along the whole length of her Nothern frontier and wherever she comes into contact with Austrian territory all that was accorded her in the so-called Pact of London, but I am of the clear opinion that the pact of London can no longer apply to the settlement of her Eastern boundaries. The line drawn in the Pact of London was conceived for the purpose of establishing an absolutely adequate frontier of safety for Italy against any possible hostility or aggression on the part of Austro-Hungary. But Austro-Hungary no longer exists. These Eastern frontiers will touch countries stripped of the military and naval power of Austria, set up in entire independence of Austria, and organized for the purpose of satisfying legitimate national aspirations, and created states not hostile to the new European order but arising out of it, interested in its maintenance, dependent upon the cultivation of friendships, and bound to a common policy of peace and accommodation by the covenants of the League of Nations.

It is with these facts in mind that I have approached the Adriatic question. It is commonly agreed, and I very heartily adhere to the agreement, that the ports of Trieste and Pola and with them the greater part of the Istrian Peninsula should be ceded to Italy, her Eastern frontier running along the natural strategic line established by the physical conformation of the country, a line which it has been attempted to draw with some degree of accuracy on the attached map. Within this line on the Italian side will lie considerable bodies of non-Italian population, but their fortunes are so naturally linked by the nature of the country itself with the fortunes of the Italian people that I think their inclusion is fully justified.

There would be no such justification, in my judgment, in including Fiume or any part of the coast lying to the South of Fiume within the boundaries of the Italian kingdom.

Fiume is by situation and by all the circumstances of its development, not an Italian but an international port, serving the countries to the East and North of the Gulf of Fiume. Just because it is an international port and cannot with justice be subordinated to any one sovereignty, it is my clear judgment that it should enjoy a very considerable degree of genuine autonomy and that, while it should be included no doubt within the customs system of the new Jugo-Slavic state, it should nevertheless be left free in its own interest and in the interest of the states lying about it to devote itself to the service of the commerce which naturally and inevitably seeks an outlet or inlet at its port. The states which it serves will be new states. They will need to have complete confidence in their access to an outlet on the sea. The friendships and the connections of the future will largely depend upon such an arrangement as I have suggested; and friendship, cooperation, freedom of action must underlie every arrangement of peace, if peace is to be lasting.

I believe that there will be common agreement that the Island of Lissa[2] should be ceded to Italy and that she should retain the port of Valona.[3] I believe that it will be generally agreed that the fortifications which the Austrian government established upon the islands near the eastern coast of the Adriatic should be permanently dismantled under international guarantees, and that the disarmament which is to be arranged under the League of Nations should limit the states on the eastern coast of the Adriatic to only such minor naval forces as are necessary for policing the waters of the islands and the coast.

These are the conclusions to which I am forced by the compulsion of the understandings which underlay the whole initiation of the present peace. No other conclusions seem to me susceptible of being rendered consistent with those understandings. They were understandings accepted by the whole world, and bear with peculiar compulsion upon the United States because the privilege was accorded her of taking the initiative in bringing about the negotiations for peace and her pledges underlie the whole business.

And certainly Italy obtains under such a settlement the great historic objects which her people have so long had in mind. The historical wrongs inflicted upon her by Austro-Hungary and by a long series of unjust transactions which I hope will before long sink out of the memory of men, are completely redressed. Nothing is denied her which will complete her national unity.

Here and there upon the islands of the Adriatic and upon the Eastern coast of that sea there are settlements containing large Italian elements of population, but the pledges under which the new states enter the family of nations will abundantly safeguard the liberty, the development, and all the just rights of national or racial minorities, and back of those safeguards will always lie the watchful and sufficient authority of the League of Nations. And at the very outset we shall have avoided the fatal error of making Italy's nearest neighbors on the East her enemies and nursing just such a sense of injustice as has disturbed the peace of Europe for generations together and played no small part in bringing on the terrible conflict through which we have just passed.

CC MS (WP, DLC).
    [1] Wilson presented this memorandum to Orlando during their conversation on April 14 and told Orlando that he could make it public in Italy. However, Orlando chose not to make the document public until April 29. On that date, he distributed copies to all members of the Italian Parliament and to the press as part of his defense of his conduct at the peace conference. On that date also, the American delegation in Paris gave the statement to the press. See the *New York Times*, April 30, 1919.
    [2] Vis Island, now part of Yugoslavia, thirty-three miles south southwest of Split.
    [3] Valona is now in Albania.

Three Letters to Robert Lansing

My dear Mr. Secretary: [Paris] 14 April, 1919.

This is an interesting difficulty which you state about the last part of the formula adopted.[1] How would it do to embody the agreement as a protocol attached to the Treaty, because I have the instinctive feeling that Germany ought to be apprised of the whole thing at the time of signing the treaty and in some direct or indirect way give her assent.

Cordially and sincerely yours,   [Woodrow Wilson]

[1] Lansing's letter is missing. However, it undoubtedly referred to WW to RL, April 9, 1919, enclosing Wilson's formula concerning responsibilities.

My dear Mr. Secretary: [Paris] 14 April, 1919.

I find myself in general accord with these suggestions.[1] I wonder if you have had any means of judging what the attitude of the other governments towards them would be.

Cordially and sincerely yours,   [Woodrow Wilson]

CCL (WP, DLC).
[1] Lansing's letter, to which this was a reply, is missing; however, for its subject matter, see RL to WW, April 17, 1919.

My dear Lansing: Paris, 14 April, 1919.

Pardon my delay in replying to this letter.[1] I entirely approve of Secretary Baker's recommendation, in which Mr. Phillips appears to concur.[2]

Cordially and faithfully yours,   Woodrow Wilson

TLS (SDR, RG 256, 861.00/506, DNA).
[1] RL to WW, April 7, 1919 (first letter of that date).
[2] See NDB to WW, April 3, 1919, and W. Phillips to the A.C.N.P., April 4, 1919, both in Vol. 56.

To Herbert Clark Hoover

My dear Mr. Hoover: [Paris] 14 April, 1919.

I have been very glad to sign the enclosed cable[1] and hope that you will have it dispatched.

Cordially and faithfully yours,   [Woodrow Wilson]

CCL (WP, DLC).
[1] WW to J. H. Barnes, April 15, 1919.

From Herbert Clark Hoover, with Enclosure

Dear Mr. President: Paris, France. 14 April 1919.

I hope that you will have time to at least glance over the attached report, which will show what the Americans are doing in the Relief.[1]
                    Faithfully yours,   Herbert Hoover

TLS (WP, DLC).
[1] Report of the Director General of Relief, T MS dated April 10, 1919. This long and detailed report, replete with statistical data, covered the activities of the relief administration during the month of March 1919. It is printed in Suda L. Bane and Ralph H. Lutz, eds., *Organization of American Relief in Europe, 1918-1919* (Stanford, Calif., 1943), pp. 390-95.

From Josephus Daniels

My dear Mr. President: [Paris] Apr. 14. 1919.

If its finally determined to sink or beach the German Navy I earnestly hope it may be agreed that the action will be joint and that there will be no division of the spoil, leaving one nation to sink or the others to keep as may be decided. The moral lesson, much more than Lloyd George's "ostentatious sinking" will be of tremendous significance to the whole world. I happen to know that able French naval leaders believe the ships that would fall to France would be a liability instead of an assett. To divide and then debate whether to sink or not, or for some to hold and some to sink, loses the object lesson of the Peace Conferences resolve to reduce armament. The more spectacular it is made the better.

Division is bad. Unified action is the answer.
                    Sincerely yours,   Josephus Daniels

ALS (WP, DLC).

From Carter Glass

                    Washington. April 15 [14], 1919.[1]

1584, VERY URGENT. President from Glass. I have read the further statements of Secretary Redfield and the Industrial Board and Director General Hines, and I have reluctantly come to the following conclusions:

(1) That the Industrial Board allowed themselves to be unduly impressed by steel interests' talk of reduction in wages and fixed prices at rather a high level which will not stimulate industry but on the whole will tend to prevent a revival of business and therefore to increase unemployment.

(2) That the Industrial Board have not proceeded along lines recommended to and approved by you which contemplated not price fixing but mediation between the industries and governmental buying agencies and on the contrary have allowed themselves to be put in the position of sanctioning the practices which were first initiated at the famous Gary dinners[2] and have given governmental approval to a minimum price fixing plan effective for a year.

(3) That the sworn officers of the government should not be ordered to make purchases at prices which in their judgment are too high and which have been fixed by men who are not sworn officers of the government but are themselves interested in productive industry and whose natural even if unconscious bias is towards the side of the producers.

(4) That notwithstanding every effort to bring the Industrial Board to a realization of their mistakes they are disposed to persist in a policy which is fundamentally unsound economically and politically and that therefore the sooner the Board is dissolved the better.

(5) That you should not allow yourself to be drawn into this controversial matter and that the best solution is for the Attorney General promptly to announce the opinion, which he informs me he has reached, that the lines on which the Industrial Board has been proceeding are contrary to law.   Polk   Acting

T telegram (WP, DLC).
    [1] This, a corrected copy, was received in Paris on April 18, 1919.
    [2] A series of dinners and other meetings of leaders of the iron and steel industry initiated by Elbert Henry Gary of the United States Steel Corporation on November 20, 1907. They continued intermittently until May 29, 1911. Their objective was to bring about informal agreements to stabilize the prices of various iron and steel products without running afoul of the laws against collusion and price-fixing. See Maurice H. Robinson, "The Gary Dinner System: An Experiment in Cooperative Price Stabilization," *Southwestern Political and Social Science Quarterly*, VII (Sept. 1926), 137-61, and Melvin I. Urofsky, *Big Steel and the Wilson Administration: A Study in Business-Government Relations* (Columbus, Ohio, 1969), pp. 14-16.

From Charles Mills Galloway

My dear Mr. President: Washington, D. C. April 14, 1919.

I am today in receipt of your very considerate letter of March the 25th,[1] and heartily appreciate all that you have said. I can not, however, feel otherwise than that if I leave the Civil Service Commission under a demand for my resignation it will follow as a reflection on me through life; and my confidence in your sense of justice is so absolute that I am sure you would not inflict that kind of injustice on any man not guilty of misconduct. If I felt that my further service on the Commission would interfere with its harmonious work, or if I thought I was in any way responsible for the friction which heretofore had marred the harmony of the Commission, I would neither ask nor desire to remain a member of it. But knowing that I was in nowise responsible for the factional differences which have heretofore existed, and finding myself working in full and complete accord with my present colleagues on the Commission, I can not but feel that, with all the facts fairly laid before you, you will most cheerfully reconsider your request for my resignation.

I am all the more fully convinced of that belief by the fact that Mr. McIlhenny, who was a Roosevelt appointee and who was wholly responsible for the divisions which made harmonious work with him impossible, has been given an appointment, through the State Department, which I am informed pays him $10,000 a year. In view of that favor bestowed upon him it does not seem possible that you will permit the only undisputed Democrat on the Commission to be dismissed without public recognition of any kind, and especially since that Democrat held his commission by your favor and has done nothing to forfeit the good will which called him to his present position.

In this connection I feel it proper to say that I enjoy the full confidence and esteem of practically the entire force of the Civil Service Commission, and I earnestly request that you make inquiry as to my standing with my present associates and the subordinates of this office before insisting upon my resignation.

I have the honor to be,
          Respectfully and sincerely yours,   Chas M Galloway

TLS (WP, DLC).
    ¹ WW to C. M. Galloway, March 25, 1919, Vol. 56.

From the Diary of Dr. Grayson

Tuesday, April 15, 1919.

The President arose early and was ready for work at 8:30 o'clock. The Council of Four met here at the temporary White House at 11:00 o'clock. They discussed the question of bringing the German delegation to Versailles. Mr. Balfour sat in as the British representative in place of Lloyd-George, who was in London.

In the afternoon the Big Four had Admiral Benson and other experts in to discuss the dismantlement of Heligoland and the disposition of the German province of Schleswig-Holstein. The report of the naval experts on Heligoland was unanimously approved, but the status of Schleswig-Holstein was not passed upon.

As a result of today's meeting the Big Four official invitation to the German delegates to proceed to Versailles was completed and sent forward. It was sent direct to Weimar, Germany, in an automobile, which was manned by two expert chauffeurs and two despatch bearers. The orders to the chauffeurs were that they were to relieve each other and not halt until they had delivered the message.

At lunch today I was one of the guests of Tay Pay O'Connor[1] in honor of Venizelos of Greece. There were about twenty guests present, representing nearly every nationality, with the result that it was a wearisome affair as one could not understand his neighbor.

After lunch I took Frank H. Hitchcock over to see Field Marshal Foch at his office in the War Ministry. I was deeply impressed with the democratic manner in which I found the Marshal, and in which he received us. There was no over-plus of uniformed aides. He simply had one with him. He told me that he was very glad to receive us, saying that my face was very familiar to him, he having seen me so much with the President, and that he was very glad to receive my friend. Mr. Hitchcock told the Field Marshal that he deeply appreciated the opportunity of meeting him; that he had followed his career as a general officer with great interest and that in America the fame of the Marshal as a great General was well-known. I explained to the Marshal that while Mr. Hitchcock was in no sense a military man, he had experience in managing campaigns in that he had led the Republican party in a successful Presidential fight and had gathered delegates for national conventions on many occasions. The Marshal smiled and bowed and told me he was glad to meet the "Civilian General." He also added, very seriously however, that had it not been for the wonderful bravery of the American soldiers, the war might not have been won.

Following the Big Four conference the President went to the Crillon Hotel, where he held conferences individually with each of the American delegates. Heretofore the President had been in the habit of having the entire American delegation assembled in the offices of Colonel House, where he could talk with them more conveniently. However, it had developed that some of Mr. House's associates, notably Mr. Auchincloss, had been making capital of the fact that these meetings were held in the Colonel's office, he holding that it indicated House's supremacy in the commission, and boasting that they had put the others out of business, so the President decided that he would hereafter individually confer with the Commissioners except when a general meeting was held, at which time they would of course assemble in the main meeting parlor on the second floor of the Crillon Hotel.

The President returned to the house at 6:30 o'clock. I was going to send a cablegram to Secretary Tumulty and I asked the President whether I should tell Tumulty that he was making progress. He said: "Tell him we are making distinct progress."

The President, Mrs. Wilson, Miss Benham and I had dinner together. After dinner during our conversation I asked the President about the recurring attacks on him in the inspired French press, especially that portion of it which was recognized as the mouthpiece of the government. He said that I should pay no attention to that because it was simply the echoing of the voluble members of the Ministry, especially Clemenceau and Klotz. The President said he could not conceive why Klotz ever had been appointed as a member of the French Peace Commission, because he was the greatest waster of time of all of them, and it was very hard to understand why he should have been picked, especially as he displayed practically no knowledge of the big financial questions that were involved, although he was the French Minister of Finance. The President said that he had asked Clemenceau how he had happened to choose Klotz as a financier. Clemenceau did not reply directly, simply saying that Klotz was the only Jew he ever saw who did not know anything about finance. The President said that Klotz was so trying in a number of meetings at which he was present, especially through his volubility of expression, that "I had thought several times I would have to send for you to treat me for '*clots* on the brain.'" The President then added that he would hate to have to contract any disease from a person of the Klotz type.

The President said that Clemenceau was losing a lot of time lately by insisting that it was necessary for him to call to his assistance members of his Ministry, although whenever they were sent for it was found entirely unnecessary inasmuch as the facts had been reduced to writing beforehand. They had also been thoroughly thrashed out from time to time at the several meetings. However, it was the President's opinion that the real reason for this was that Clemenceau was beginning to understand that he was weakening before the people, and especially with the majority in the Chamber of Deputies, and he was, therefore, calling in the various members of the Ministry, who knew nothing about the matters, in order that they would share equally with him responsibility for all decisions. By pursuing this course Clemenceau would be able to forestall a vote of confidence inasmuch as each Minister had his individual following and the combined total was a majority of the Chamber of Deputies at all times.

I went over to the American Embassy tonight to visit briefly my friend, the Ambassador, Mr. Hugh C. Wallace, of Washington, D. C., and Washington State. Mr. and Mrs. Wallace[2] brought me the latest news from home.

[1] That is, Thomas Power O'Connor.
[2] Mildred Fuller Wallace.

From the Diary of Colonel House

April 15, 1919.

Some of the guests at our dinner last night were Venizelos, Orlando and Marechal Joffre. After dinner, Paderewski and I had a talk about Poland and conditions there. He told among other things complimentary to me, that I had exercised the greatest influence on his life of anyone he had known. He tried to explain why, but it was not very clear to me.

I talked with Orlando and found him exceedingly bitter toward Lloyd George. He feels that both Lloyd George and Clemenceau have "thrown him," not only regarding the Italian frontier but because of their desire to make peace with Germany before settling the question between Italy and the former Austrian Empire. What he said about Lloyd George was "scarcely fit to print." He spoke of him as a slippery prestid[i]gitator; that he did not keep his word, and he summed it all up by saying that unfortunately England had a Prime Minister who was not a gentleman.

He asked to come around this morning at ten and he was with me for a half hour. I undertook to try to get the questions between Italy and the former Austro-Hungarian Empire settled simultaneously with the Peace Treaty with Germany. I begged him not to be discouraged about the settlement of their frontier. The questions between France on the one side and the United States and England on the other, were much more difficult and had seemed insoluable. However, we have been working upon them for several months with Clemenceau, on the one hand, and with Lloyd George, on the other, and now they were being settled to the satisfaction of all parties concerned. I thought the Italian questions could also be settled, provided there was a disposition to yield a little by all parties, and if there was a continuous discussion of them, which must necessarily bring out new ideas and some compromises. I called his attention to the fact that Fiume was the main difficulty. If we could get over that hurdle, the rest would be settled in a canter.

In talking with the President later, I advised that some solution be reached for the moment, a solution that was not permanent but which would tide over the present and give passion time to cool. Strangely enough, the President said "this might be done by the League of Nations taking over the disputed territory for the time being." This is precisely what I suggested to the President yesterday and which he dismissed as not being feasible. He added, "this thought has just come to me." It leads me to remark that none of us know where our "original ideas" come from. I am sure that I am constantly picking up the thoughts of others and afterward elaborating them as my own. I am sure, too, that I often get a hint in certain directions which while utterly impracticable as hinted, yet lends itself to a train of thought that brings about a practical solution.

I took Hugh Wallace, our new Ambassador, to motor with me this morning and gave him an outline of the situation here. I hope he will make a success, for I feel wholly responsible for him.

This afternoon was one of great accomplishment. The President came in to see me and I obtained his consent to everything that Clemenceau desired me to put through for him. The President made a wry face over some of it, particularly the three five year period[s] of occupation, but he agreed to do it all. I told him we had better do it with a *"beau geste"* rather than grudgingly. I also got him to tentatively consent to the putting of Fiume and the disputed Italian territory under the League of Nations until everything quiets down and becomes more normal than now.

In speaking to Clemenceau about this later, he declared that it was the part of wisdom to delay decisions of that nature until passions cooled.

The President said that only once before had he experienced such an unhappy time as that with Orlando yesterday. Once when he was President of Princeton it was necessary to expel a student. His mother, a delicate woman, called and plead with him for an hour and a half urging that she was about to undergo a capital operation and if the boy was expelled she would die and her death would be due to him. His reply was that his responsibility to the College was greater than his responsibility for her health, and he declined to grant her request. She had the operation but recovered.

I went to the Ministry of War to see Clemenceau immediately after the President left. I said to him "I am the bearer of good news. The President has consented to all that you asked of me yesterday." He grasped both my hands and then embraced me, saying I was his good friend and that he would never forget how much I had done for France. I went into detail regarding the different items and advised him to take them up with the President tomorrow.

Ray Stannard Baker and others of our entourage have been after me for several days concerning attacks in the French Press not only against the President but against the United States. I told Clemenceau about this and said that I cared nothing about it individually, but I did care about the good relations between the United States and France and I hoped he would stop it. He summoned his secretary and told him in French with much emphasis that he was to notify the Temps, Figaro, Petit Journal, Petit Parisian, Liberté, Echo de Paris, and several others of lesser importance, that all attacks of every description on President Wilson and the United States must cease. That our relations were of the very best, and that there was no disagreement between our two countries upon the questions before the Peace Conference. As for the Matin, which is anti-Clemenceau, he could not control it.

I asked him yesterday why he had not signed the Russian memorandum[1] which the President, Lloyd George and Orlando had already signed and which he had agreed to. He again rang for his secretary and said, "tell Pichon to send that document around to me at once. I do not want any of his comments, I want the document." He then turned to me and said, "I will sign it. Is there anything else?"

Before leaving, he told me that Orlando was calling in the morning and he wondered what had passed between him and the President yesterday. I gave him an outline of their conference and suggested that he might tell Orlando that the only way he could see out of the difficulty was for the League of Nations to take over the disputed territory for a given time. He agreed that that was the solution and promised to press it upon Orlando.

During the day I have been able to arrange an understanding about Luxembourg. The President and Balfour having made a direct request of Clemenceau that something tangible be done. The arrangement to which Clemenceau consented is for the President to advise Luxembourg in the name of the Council of Four not to have a plebecite just now. Balfour was to write the communication and the President was to sign it. The Belgians are happy and expressive of the appreciation for what has been done. It takes away the sting of defeat for not securing the League of Nations for Brussels. . . .

Viscount Chinda followed. His trouble this time was Shantung. I promised to arrange a meeting with the President, which I did later, when the President called. I suggested a way out of his difficulties on the racial question but I pledged him to secrecy until I could first sound out the British Delegation. I did not want the Japanese to make another mistake and court certain defeat. The plan suggested and which I afterward explained to the President and obtained his approval, is to disassociate the resolution entirely from the League of Nations, but at some Plenary Session offer the resolution as an evidence of the spirit of brotherhood and goodwill which is hereafter to prevail. I shall write the resolution myself and submit it to the British and then let the Japanese or preferably some other delegate offer it to the Plenary Session. It will have no binding effect whatever but will be in the nature of compensation to the

Japanese. Chinda was delighted and hoped I might be successful in my efforts.

¹ The proposed reply of the Big Four to Fridtjof Nansen's letter of April 3, 1919, printed at that date in Vol. 56. The reply is printed as an Enclosure with F. Nansen to WW, April 17, 1919.

Mantoux's Notes of Two Meetings of the Council of Four

April 15, 1919, 11 a.m.

Balfour. I would like to discuss the question of Luxembourg with you. England does not have a direct interest in that question. But if, when France is regaining Alsace and Lorraine and obtaining the coal mines of the Saar, Belgium, after events which have earned her the sympathy of the entire world, obtains nothing of what she asks, the impression would be deplorable—and even more so if Luxembourg should become French.

Clemenceau. I agree with you. I accept every word you have just said.

Balfour. I saw M. Hymans: he told me that a draft bill is to be introduced next Thursday in the Parliament of Luxembourg, looking toward holding a plebiscite. He would like the great powers to send the Belgian government a letter indicating that they would view with pleasure the success of the negotiations between Belgium and Luxembourg.

Clemenceau. I could not sign that letter, and if you sign it without us, the impression in France will be unfortunate. I am willing to seek a way to attain what the Belgians want. I do not want to leave Luxembourg as it is; I wish it to be united to Belgium. I only ask that the thing be done in such a way as not to shock French public opinion.

Could we not send to Luxembourg an Englishman or an American—not a Frenchman or a Belgian—to seek information and to sound out opinion? There must be nothing in writing; the conference must be involved. But we must attempt to find out what the Luxembourg parties think and want, and to prepare a solution by the expression of Luxembourg opinion, which no doubt must in the final accounting be consulted by means of a plebiscite.

Balfour. Can we not instruct our envoy to express our sympathy for the idea of a union between Luxembourg and Belgium?

Clemenceau. We must act with tact and say simply that we are leaving the door open to a union between the two countries, if

Luxembourg desires it. I ask you to give me twenty-four hours so that I might have time to speak with M. Poincaré, who favors the union of Luxembourg to Belgium, and also with the Minister of Foreign Affairs. Undoubtedly we shall find a solution. In the meantime, you could write M. Hymans that you cannot do what he asks, but that the conference is acting to the best of its ability, with the desire to do nothing against the will of the Luxembourg people.

Balfour. This is what I propose to write to M. Hymans: (1) I did not succeed in the mission he entrusted to me; but (2) I found M. Clemenceau in full sympathy with Belgium and with no objection to her aspirations, if they can be realized without doing violence to the feelings of the Luxemburgers; (3) the question will be examined with the greatest care by the great powers, and we have every hope of arriving at a satisfactory solution.

The question of the plebiscite remains, which must be decided, in principle, next Thursday. M. Hymans objects to this plebiscite. I will note that the first question to be asked of the Luxembourg people is that of maintaining the dynasty. Would we not have an interest in preventing this plebiscite from taking place now?

Clemenceau. Certainly, and I want to hear no talk of maintaining the German dynasty.

Balfour. Then we can add that we wish the plebiscite to be postponed until we know better the state of opinion in that country.

Clemenceau. That's it; you could advise M. Hymans of that and, at the same time, one of our governments, preferably the American government, since it has troops there, would send a telegram to Luxembourg along these lines.

The proposals of Mr. Balfour and M. Clemenceau are adopted.

Wilson. I have received news in which it is revealed that the Poles are not acting correctly in Lemberg.[1] The Ukrainians complain that the representatives of Poland have dragged out the discussions in order to gain military advantages before the moment of the cease fire. I have here a letter from the Ukrainian General Polenko,[2] according to which the Ukrainians accepted the conditions proposed by the Allies for a military truce, while the Poles have insisted on maintaining a line of demarcation which prejudges the solution of the dispute between them and the Ruthenians, so that it is their fault that hostilities have continued.

I believe that that explanation of the facts is true, and that it

---

[1] See the memorandum by F. J. Kernan printed at April 11, 1919.
[2] He referred to M. Omelianovych-Pavlenko to the Supreme Council of the Peace Conference, n.d., T translation of radiogram (WP, DLC). The text reads as follows: "From the bottom of my heart I accept the proposal of the Supreme Council of the Peace Conference dated 20 March, in order once again to give proof and [that] I and the Ukrainian Army are ready at every moment to put an end to the spilling of blood."

would be useful to make representations to the Polish government. Perhaps there is no reason to summon M. Paderewski about this: General Bliss, who is receiving reports from General Kernan, in charge of mediating between the Ruthenians and the Poles, is fully qualified to speak in our name to the Polish delegation.

This proposal is adopted.

After an exchange of views about the attitude to take toward the secondary powers at the time of summoning the Germans to Versailles, it is decided:

(1) That the Ministers of Foreign Affairs of the United States, France, Great Britain, Italy, and Japan will receive separately, in groups of three, the delegates of the fifteen other belligerent powers and will inform them of the conclusion which the heads of government of the Allied and Associated Governments have reached regarding the date of the convocation (April 25);

(2) They will announce to them for April 24, that is before the first contact with the German plenipotentiaries, a secret session of the representatives of all the belligerent powers, during which the complete text of the preliminaries of peace will be given them;

(3) The reports of the commissions which have not yet been presented will be communicated in the same session or earlier if that is possible.

Mr. Balfour enumerates the questions on which final decisions have not yet been taken and which must be settled before April 25. They are the following:

Territorial questions:

—the frontier of Denmark;

—Heligoland;

—the frontier of Belgium;

—Danzig and Marienwerder.

Have we reached a precise draft?

Wilson. I have that draft on my desk.[3]

Clemenceau. I will ask you to examine again the question of the territory of Marienwerder. If it was decided to make it part of East Prussia, the consequence would be to cut the lines of communication vital for Poland. I completely share the point of view of the Poles on that question.

Wilson. In any case, we must delay the examination of that question until Mr. Lloyd George's return; it is he who is above all interested in it.

Mr. Balfour continues:

—reconstruction in kind in devastated regions (that question is

[3] See Appendix 2 to the minutes of the Council of Four printed at April 8, 1919, 11 a.m.

under study and is to be the subject of a report by M. Loucheur);

—guarantee of the payment of indemnities (question of the temporary occupation of the left bank of the Rhine);

—the Kiel Canal: on that question, the commission on waterways should be consulted. If it has not formulated its opinion, the question should be referred back to it;

—report of the commission on ports, waterways, and railways;

—question of the disarmed zone on the right bank of the Rhine;

—disarmament of the left bank of the Rhine.

Wilson. It seems to me that the draft of the military conditions deals with this question.

Mr. Balfour continues:

—economic conditions;

—stipulations regarding commercial aviation.

Clemenceau. The question of Alsace-Lorraine must be added because we have drafted nothing concerning it, and there must be something about it in the treaty, even if it is only two lines.

Balfour. On the question of cables, Japan has something to ask; she wishes to keep the three lines which she has seized. One of these lines belongs to a private company, and Japan would be prepared to purchase it.

Wilson. I have an observation to make. All these lines, as well as other important lines in the Pacific, meet on a small island called Yap. I will ask that this island be internationalised; for if it should belong to the Japanese, they could cut communications between different parts of the Pacific whenever they liked, notably between the United States and the Philippines.

Balfour. There is still the question of Kiaochow.

Wilson. China does not attach only an economic importance to the cancellation of all foreign concessions in Shantung. Since this province is among those which evoke the most sacred memories of its history and its religion, she is particularly anxious to rid it of foreign influence. On the other hand, what the Japanese most want is not Kiaochow, which they themselves have offered to return to China, but the concessions in Shantung.

My sympathies are on the side of China, and we must not forget that, in the future, the greatest dangers for the world can arise in the Pacific.

Balfour. When Japan entered the war, China being at that time a neutral state, the Japanese demanded to keep what they would take from the Germans. We then consented. Since then, a treaty was concluded between Japan and China.[4] We have asked that it

---

[4] See FLP to WW, Feb. 4, 1919, and n. 1 thereto, Vol. 54.

The Inquiry Division Chiefs

Seated, left to right: Charles H. Haskins, Isaiah Bowman, Sidney E. Mezes, James Brown Scott, David Hunter Miller. *Standing, left to right:* Charles Seymour, Robert H. Lord, William L. Westermann, Mark Jefferson, Colonel House, George Louis Beer, Douglas W. Johnson, Clive Day, William E. Lunt, James T. Shotwell, A. A. Young.

André Tardieu

Baron Sidney Sonnino

Baron Nobuaki Makino

Ignace Jan Paderewski

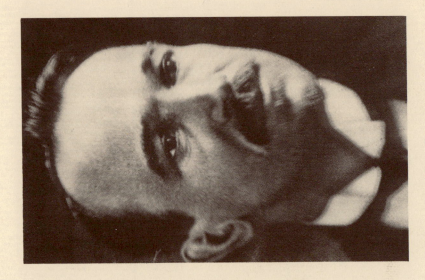

Eduard Beneš

Ion I. C. Brătianu

Ante Trumbić

Nikola Pašić

Viscount Sutemi Chinda

Vi Kyuin Wellington Koo

be communicated to us, and so far we have not received it. The Japanese consent to restore to China what they took from Germany. But they say that, having made the sacrifices which permitted them to retake the territory of Kiaochow, they hold that it must be ceded to them, to be able then to give it back to China. It is here a question of national pride.

Wilson. First we must have the Sino-Japanese treaty under our eyes. The Japanese are rather difficult in affairs. I know by experience that they are very clever in the interpretation of treaties.

Clemenceau. We still have to hear this week the powers which are directly involved in the treaty with Germany: Belgium, Poland, and Bohemia. A morning must be reserved for each of them.

It is agreed that a meeting of the Ministers of Foreign Affairs will be called for 3 o'clock, and that Mr. Balfour will make known there the decisions taken about the communiqué to be given to the secondary powers.

The questions of Schleswig and Heligoland will be studied by the Council of Four at the end of the afternoon.

April 15, 1919, 4 p.m.

Balfour. It is obvious that we cannot leave the island of Heligoland as it was before the war. It constitutes a menace not only for the eastern coasts of England and Scotland, but for all the powers which have interests in the North Sea. In the case where it would be necessary for England and the United States to come to the aid of France under attack by Germany, Heligoland, even deprived of its fortifications, would remain formidable. During the war, it was a powerful station for submarines and mine-layers. It would remain as a spear pointed at the naval communications of the neighboring nations.

Wilson. We all agree about dismantling the island.

Benson. The question which arises is that of knowing if the great port created by the German Admiralty should be destroyed and, in this case, if America should participate in that destruction.

Balfour. About the port, the Admiralty tells us that it was created by the Germans as a naval base and that it never had any other use. Before the construction of this port, there was a small fishing port at Heligoland, which largely served the small resort near the coasts of the island.

Will it be said that by destroying this naval base, we damage some legitimate need of peace time? I am told that ships can seek a refuge there against storms. But the Admiralty assures us that the fishing boats easily found refuge along the island before the port was constructed, and that the disappearance of that naval base will cause them no injury. From the commercial point of view, fishermen have no interest in coming to Heligoland, which is a very small island, at least sixty kilometers from the markets of the mainland.

I conclude that the destruction of the naval base at Heligoland would not harm the population of the island in any way, that it would do little injury to navigation, and that it would free the naval communications of neighboring powers from an indisputable danger. Once destroyed, this naval base could only be rebuilt by major and very lengthy construction. If the port, even disarmed, remains as it is, in a matter of days the Germans, in revenge, can, lacking fortifications, protect it by mines and restore nearly all its offensive and defensive value.

Wilson. Is not the fact that this port only served military uses due to the German government's having reserved it for such uses?

Hope. As a refuge, this port is useless. In time of storm, ships of a certain tonnage can reach the mouth of the Elbe or the gulf of Jade Bay without difficulty, and fishing boats find adequate refuge in the small port which existed before the present construction.

Benson. The reservation I have to make is this: once the island is disarmed, the port can be used for peaceful purposes, and it is better not to allow ourselves pointless destruction.

Wilson. My concern is not to destroy anything unnecessarily, in order not to give the impression of gratuitous violence. Since we are doing what is essential in destroying fortifications, I would not go so far as to destroy works which could be useful in peacetime.

Balfour. Here is the argument of our navy. In time of war, what is most important today is to have a submarine base. To protect it, artillery is necessary, which we will destroy. But in the absence of artillery, one can fall back on minefields, which require only two nights of work to lay, and which would in an instant make the island of Heligoland a redoubtable menace for all maritime powers.

De Bon. When we previously examined this question in the Supreme War Council, we had made the distinction between the fishing port and the naval port artificially created by Germany as an instrument of war. We find it legitimate to destroy the instrument of war, while leaving the fishing port, which is essentially adequate for economic needs. By leaving the artificial port to the Germans, we would be leaving them what really constitutes the first step toward a complete restoration of their naval base. That seems to me pointless and dangerous.

If this port is considered as other than a fishing port, its existence would have to be justified by its commercial utility; but this utility does not exist, the island being only a pebble in the middle of the sea.

Wilson. It is as a refuge that the port can be useful.

Balfour. Does the Admiral think that this port can be very useful as a refuge against storms?

De Bon. No; for small boats, the only ones which would need that kind of refuge, the natural ports suffice. The only two reasons that could be invoked for not destroying the port are the fear of effecting a destruction which is not really necessary and, on the other hand, the difficulty of the work of destruction, which will be considerable.

Balfour. I could invoke another argument, although I only wish to do it with discretion; it is that of public sentiment in England. The island of Heligoland belonged to Great Britain until 1890. We would never have ceded it to Germany if we had known what use she could make of it; but at that time we did not know about submarines, or mines, or aviation. Lord Salisbury, wishing to settle all sorts of questions pending between Great Britain and Germany all over the world, threw this little bit of change into the balance, thinking that Heligoland had little value for us and a certain sentimental value for the Germans.

Since then, bitter reproaches about this cession have been made against that government, of which I was a member, while forgetting the great transaction of which it was part. If today, with the left bank of the Rhine being disarmed despite the forced reduction of the German army, Heligoland keeps even a dismantled military port, English opinion will not forgive us for it.

Clemenceau. If this port is only a naval base, as our admirals think, there is no reason not to destroy it.

Wilson. I could answer Mr. Balfour that, in the United States, opinion will reproach us for having lost our calm, in forgetting that Germany had been, through our actions, reduced to the status of a naval power of third rank.

Hope. The Admiralty has studied closely the question of the possible use of the port of Heligoland for fishing or for commerce; its conclusion is that this port would serve neither. Besides, the proposals that we have presented for its destruction leave enough elements of jetties or piers to allow the island to provide more refuge than it possessed previously.

Wilson. I cannot hold an opinion contrary to that of the naval authorities; but I believe that we are exaggerating the importance of this matter.

Clemenceau. It can become considerable in certain circumstances.

Balfour. Do our naval experts not agree on this point, that during the war Heligoland was the most formidable base of the German fleet?

Benson. On the contrary, I think that the importance of Heligoland has been exaggerated. In the future, its greatest value will undoubtedly be for aviation; in that regard, Heligoland could constitute a danger. But with the naval power of Germany being reduced as it must be, I do not believe that that destruction is justifiable.

Balfour. We are in agreement if Germany, from the naval point of view, remains what we intend to make her by the treaty. But we do not have more certainty in that respect than about the army, and I will call to your attention that, despite the reduction of military forces in Germany, we are stipulating that her land fortifications will be destroyed.

Wilson. Yes, but we do not stipulate the destruction of the railroads on the left bank of the Rhine, although railroads are very important from the military point of view. The question did not even arise, because rail networks are not made solely for war.

Balfour. I wonder if that argument does not turn against you, for on the left bank of the Rhine we want the destruction of the detraining platforms. The port of Heligoland responds to no present commercial need.

Wilson. If you do not believe in the permanence of the dispositions of the treaty, according to which the military and naval forces of Germany must be reduced to limited proportions, you are correct in taking other precautions. But while chemical installations can be converted into factories for asphyxiating gases, I do not believe that it is possible to construct warships, including submarines, without anyone knowing about it.

Benson. It is not impossible for submarines, which can be constructed in sections.

Wilson. I am not convinced of the necessity of this destruction. If it was absolutely necessary, I would not refuse.

Clemenceau. I must declare that I cannot refuse England the destruction which seems to her indispensable.

Balfour. My request does not seem unreasonable to you?

Clemenceau. Not at all; I would act as you do if I were in your place.

Wilson. I continue to believe that your fears are excessive.

Clemenceau. I don't know; I have known the Germans for many years.

De Bon. As long as the Germans keep this port, they will be able to make it into an instrument of war rapidly.

Balfour. I recall yet again that no economic interest is at stake, and I am persuaded that the arguments of the Admiralty are very strong. Moreover, we will be reproached in England for not having gone far enough and for not having asked for the destruction of the entire island.

Besides, the time may come when we are blamed for having been too shortsighted, and for not having foreseen the development of aviation, or of some other such danger in the future. The role of destroyer is not the one I prefer.

The naval experts withdraw.

Balfour. I will explain to you the conclusions on which the commission has agreed with the representatives of Denmark. Northern Schleswig would be divided into three zones. In the first, where the population is purely Danish, a plebiscite would soon take place for that entire region, after its complete evacuation of all German soldiers and officials. The second, the region of Flensburg, is Germanized in part, especially the city of Flensburg itself, where the Germans created a port of some importance and where the majority of the population speaks German. In that zone, the plebiscite would take place later and by communes, instead of for the entire area at once. The third region, further south, which extends as far as the city of Schleswig, would be subject to the same system of plebiscite as the preceding one; but the operation would be delayed there still further. The reason given is that that zone has been completely terrorized by the Germans for a long time. The example of the northern region, followed by that of the intermediate region, might give it the courage necessary to express its sentiments openly.

A natural objection to this plan is the following: why apply different systems to these three zones? The representation of Denmark particularly insisted that these precautions be taken. The Danes do not wish to be open to reproach for having annexed any part of German territory by force.

If the vote by communes yields a result so that the frontier line does not take shape by itself, an international commission will be charged with drawing this frontier.

I fear difficulties in Flensburg; but the Danes seem more assured than I. They believe that the economic interest of that city will lead it to their side. Our experts are of the opinion that, despite its apparent absurdities, this plan can work and will yield good results.

Wilson. The commune which would have voted in favor of return to Denmark and which would then be located inside the German frontiers would find itself in a painful situation. All that I can say is that it is up to Denmark to decide about that, for it is she who suffered in 1864, and if this plan is agreeable to the Danes, I accept it.

There follows a conversation about the agenda; it is decided that the frontier between Belgium and Germany will be examined tomorrow at 11 o'clock, with a view to a definitive solution.

Mantoux, I, 246-56.

A Report by Arthur James Balfour[1]

April 15th, 1919.

President Wilson asked me to come over this morning three-quarters of an hour before the Conference met. I found that what he wished to discuss was the ITALIAN situation. He had had a most painful interview, he told me, with Signor Orlando, but as what Signor Orlando said was exactly on the lines of Imperiali's[2] conversation with me, I need not attempt to reproduce it.

The President read me out a long letter which he had written to Signor Orlando after his conversation.[3] It was most courteous and conciliatory, recapitulating at considerable length, and with great force, the familiar case against making FIUME an Italian city.

The President is seriously alarmed at the position. He thought it not improbable that Sonnino would leave the Conference, and he had little doubt that, if Sonnino took this course, Orlando, rather than quarrel with him, would follow his example. Whether he did or not, the future in this particular quarter looked black enough. Signor Orlando appears to have said the Italian troops would mutiny rather than leave Fiume; that there would certainly be bloodshed, and that it was impossible to foresee what social catastrophe might not occur in Italy. This is, of course, merely repeating (if possible in stronger language) what Imperiali said to me on Sunday, which I have already recorded in a despatch.

I had received an intimation from M. Hymans that President Wilson was going to raise the question of LUXEMBOURG. I found, however, that the President had never even heard of the suggestion, and I therefore carried out the plan agreed upon and raised the matter myself.

M. Clemenceau was strongly averse to the plan which M. Hymans developed to us on Sunday, but expressed his absolute agreement with the case which I made for Belgium, and promised, if possible, to contrive some method by which Belgium's ambitions might in this respect be satisfied. Whatever was done, however, must be done with the assent of the LUXEMBOURG bourgeois, and he (M. Clemenceau) was naturally averse to doing anything which would shock the vocal portion of French opinion which clamoured for the acquisition by France of the little Duchy. M. Poincaré is also anxious for the Belgian solution, and M. Clemenceau promised to consult him upon the subject. He does not often help him, he said, but perhaps he will on this occasion; especially, he added, as there is something rather roundabout and indirect in the policy which it is proposed to be pursued.

It was finally decided that in the meanwhile steps should be taken to delay the plebiscite now being prepared in Luxembourg, and the agent for indicating discreetly and unofficially the wishes of the Conference to the Luxembourg authorities should be General Pershing, acting under instructions from President Wilson.

President Wilson informed us that, while the Ukrainians were playing the game (as he put it) with regard to the Lemberg armistice, the Poles were not. They were making difficulties, and taking undue military advantage of delays which they themselves had caused. It was agreed that General Bliss (who is a man of tact and judgment and knows the military case) should have a friendly and semi-official conference with M. Paderewski on the subject, with a view of getting the matter put right.

The President then raised the question of the procedure to be adopted in the Plenary Conference of the Allies in connection with the German Delegation to discuss terms of Peace at Versailles. It was finally decided that the Foreign Secretaries should personally communicate with a representative from each of the belligerent Delegations, and inform them:

(a). Invitation being sent to Germans for evening of 25th.
(b). A Plenary Conference being summoned for that day on which full terms will be laid before them.
(c). Reports of Commissions to be presented on the same day or previously.

I promised to convey these instructions to the Foreign Ministers, which I did at 3 o'clock in the afternoon, but, with their concurrence, I somewhat modified the formula agreed upon in the morning, which now runs as follows:

FORMULA

(a). Invitation to be sent to Germans for evening of 25th.
(b). Before terms are communicated to Germans we shall take Conference fully into our confidence.
(c). Reports of Commissions to be presented on the same day or previously.

I then expressed my fear lest the Conference was not underrating the amount of work to be done, and begged them to consider the tasks which had yet to be accomplished before the 25th. and the arrival of the German representatives.

Among other things, I pointed out that there were questions raised both as regards German submarine cables in the Far East, and Chinese-Japanese relations over German rights in Shantung, which were of the utmost difficulty and delicacy. The President then made some observations on both of these points, which clearly showed that these problems were going to be at least as troublesome as I had feared. I saw Baron Machimo [Makino] at the Quai d'Orsay in the afternoon, and told him that I had reminded the Conference that there were Japanese questions which had to be settled before the Peace was signed, and he intimated to me that Japan would not be ready to discuss them until some day early next week.

The Council of Prime Ministers was resumed at 4 o'clock. I told them what I had done at the Quai d'Orsay, and of the slight modification which I had introduced into their instructions of the morning. These were agreed to, and we then proceeded to discuss HE-LIGOLAND.

The President declined (and I think from the general point of view quite rightly) to take Heligoland over under the League of Nations, which would no doubt have been the most convenient solution for Great Britain. He was prepared to sanction the destruction of the fortifications, and to introduce a provision in the Treaty against their restoration; but we had a long struggle over the destruction of the Naval harbour. His contention—in which he was backed up by Admiral Benson—was (1). That there was nothing further to be feared from the existence of this harbour since the German fleet was practically eliminated; (2). That, although the harbour had never been used for anything but purposes connected with naval warfare, it might hereafter prove of value in the works of peace, and that there was an element of wanton destruction about the suggested policy which greatly repelled him. I expressed my sympathy with this view, but urged, on the other side, that there was no real work of peace to which this harbour could materially contribute. It was not suited to be a harbour of refuge, nor could the Island itself be turned to any commercial purpose or serve as a base for fishing fleets. If shelter was required it could be obtained either in the old non-naval harbours—which it was not proposed to touch—or else in some of the many safe anchorages which could be found under the lee of the Island.

I also pointed out (though I admitted that the argument was one that should be used with reserve and caution) that there would undoubtedly be a strong feeling in England if this formidable naval base, from which we had greatly suffered, was left substantially uninjured as a potential menace to our sea communications. I further pointed out that the destruction of the fortifications which protected the harbour would only be a half-measure, because in a few nights' work mines could be laid which would be quite as effective in preventing a maritime attack.

I fear I did not convince the President, but he finally yielded, and the arrangement at length come to was that we should introduce into the terms of Peace provisions for destroying both the fortifications and the naval harbour.

After Heligoland had been disposed of, we proceeded to discuss the arrangements for re-arranging the boundaries between DENMARK and GERMANY. I explained the proposals of our Commission at some length, and though they undoubtedly seem over-elaborate and open to criticism from more than one point of view, we were agreed that it was probably wise to accept decisions which had been come to after a careful study, not merely of the problem itself, but of the way in which this problem was regarded by the Danish Government and people. The Report was therefore accepted, and the necessary clauses will be embodied in the Treaty.

The question of the frontier between BELGIUM and GERMANY will be discussed to-morrow.

T MS (Balfour Papers, Add. MSS, 49750, British Library).
    [1] This and the following reports by Balfour were sent to Whitehall during Lloyd George's absence from Paris.
    [2] That is, Marquis Guglielmo Imperiali.
    [3] That is, Wilson's memorandum on Italian claims printed at April 14, 1919.

From Herbert Clark Hoover, with Enclosure

Dear Mr. President: Paris, 15 April 1919.

With respect to the enclosed letter, which represents a matter of extreme urgency and upon which hangs a great deal of life and suffering, I have the benefit of a consultation with Professor Coolidge and Mr. Brown,[1] representing the American Peace Missions in Vienna and Budapest, respectively, together with Colonels Logan,[2] Causey and Gregory[3] of my staff. The latter three, except one, are not soldiers, but are in fact civilians of distinction and I rely greatly on their combined judgment. I may add as to the Hungarian situation that we are maintaining a thin line of food to show that we stick to our engagements.

The following telegram we have received may be of interest to you.

"Trains of food recently held up by the French arrived yesterday Budapest. Created most favorable feeling for Americans as demonstrating their integrity in carrying out their engagements, more particularly among the Anti-Bolshevik labor element in Budapest."

Faithfully yours,   Herbert Hoover

[1] Philip Marshall Brown, Professor of International Law at Princeton University, at this time a member of the Coolidge Mission stationed in Budapest.

[2] That is, Col. James Addison Logan, Jr., U.S.A., at this time Hoover's chief assistant in relief work.

[3] Capt. Thomas Tingey Craven Gregory, U.S.A., a lawyer of San Francisco in civilian life.

E N C L O S U R E

From Herbert Clark Hoover

Dear Mr. President: Paris, 15 April 1919.

I regret the necessity to trouble you to secure the approval of the three premiers to a short statement that I desire to make to the Hungarian Government by way of premise to the completion of certain negotiations with them vital to the relief of Central Europe.

The position is that just prior to the fall of the Hungarian Government I had been made by the Council of Ten the mandatory for the operation of the railways of the old Austrian Empire so far as it related to the movement of vital supplies and I had established a railway control there. In accordance with this, we had arranged a quota of rolling stock under our control from each of these States, together with the regular operation of our 80 food trains. The participation by Hungary in this matter is vital as they control the majority of certain types of cars and locomotives which we wish to use and the operation of our trains over certain Hungarian railways is vital. My representatives have now reopened the matter with the Hungarian Government and find that they are prepared to accede to all the points that we desire to secure, amongst them the handing over to us of a large number of tank cars which are necessary to the distribution of lubricating and other oils from Roumania in exchange for foodstuffs from the Banat and to enable us to maintain railway service generally.

On the other hand, if we put Hungary on precisely the same food basis as the other states, we shall lose our control of the situation in the surrounding states. We have ample indication that the restraining influence that we hold on the overturn of these governments is effective but if the disturbing elements in Austria, Czecho-Slovakia, Jugo-Slavia, etc., consider that they will be as secure as to food supplies after disturbance as before, our present potentiality to maintain the status quo or order is lost. Furthermore, there are no doubt difficulties in the minds of some of the Allied Governments about the recognition of the Hungarian Government. Therefore, in order to avoid these various pitfalls, I propose to complete the negotiations with the Hungarian Government as to transportation and supply of food with the preliminary announcement on the following lines:

"The proposed economic arrangement with the Food Administration as to railway transportation and food supplies for Hungary is provisional and purely humanitarian and has no relationship to the settlement of any political questions.

"That the Associated Governments do not at present intend to accord the same consideration to Hungary as they are according to liberated countries and German Austria today. To these latter countries they are sending a constantly increasing flow of food supplies for the purchase of which the Allied Governments are voluntarily providing the necessary finances. So far as Hungary is concerned, the Associated Governments will for the present only advance food supplies for such services and funds as may be acceptable to the Food Administration on behalf of the Associated Governments."

The matter is of urgent character and it is impossible for anyone to agree [on] the political issue involved except yourself and the three premiers. Any amount of discussion between the members of the bodies in which I sit cannot possibly result in other than a reference to yourself in the end. All of the economic and practical issues involved have long since been settled by our various Inter-Allied arrangements.   Faithfully yours,   Herbert Hoover

TLS (Hoover Archives, CSt-H).

A Memorandum by Arthur Hugh Frazier

Paris, April 15, 1919.

MEMORANDUM FOR THE PRESIDENT

M. Trumbich, Yugo-Slav Delegate, called on Mr. Frazier this morning and informed him that he and his colleagues were anxious to have the question of Dalmatia and Istria submitted to a plebiscite of the inhabitants.

Mr. Frazier reminded M. Trumbich that, when the same suggestion had been brought to the attention of the President some two weeks before, the latter made the comment that he thought the controversy between the Italians and the Yugo-Slavs could be settled in some other way.

M. Trumbich showed some uneasiness concerning the present situation and asked whether it was likely that the Yugo-Slav Delegates would be summoned before the Council of Four again before a final decision was reached.

Mr. Frazier replied that he did not know. He assured M. Trumbich however that he was quite certain that President Wilson would remain faithful to the principles enunciated in his 14 points.

T MS (WP, DLC).

To Herbert Clark Hoover

My dear Mr. Hoover: Paris, 15 April, 1919.

I am very much impressed by your objection to the United States continuing to supply members to the various commissions which are to be set up under the Peace Treaty[1] and am ready to say at once that I agree with you.

I am afraid that we cannot escape membership on the Financial Commission on Reparation because that commission will undoubtedly need an umpire, and I am afraid we must take the necessary risks in that matter. But with regard to most of the others, you may be sure I shall fight shy.

With warm appreciation of your letter,

Cordially and sincerely yours,   Woodrow Wilson

TLS (Hoover Archives, CSt-H).
    [1] See HCH to WW, April 11, 1919.

Two Letters to Josephus Daniels

My dear Daniels: [Paris] 15 April, 1919

How kind it was of you to write me your reassuring letter of April 13th! These are often days of very deep discouragement and anxiety, and it was an instinct of true friendship which led you to write as you did.

I wish I might have seen you once more before you left, so as to give you an affectionate farewell. You understand, but I am none the less disappointed that I could not.

Affectionately yours,   Woodrow Wilson

My dear Daniels: [Paris] 15 April, 1919.

I have your letter of April 14th with its very sound advice about the sinking of the ships, and you may be sure I shall keep it in mind.   Faithfully yours,   Woodrow Wilson

TLS (J. Daniels Papers, DLC).

Gilbert Fairchild Close to Robert Lansing

My dear Mr. Secretary: Paris, 15 April, 1919.

The President has asked me to acknowledge your letter of April 12th enclosing the statement of Dr. Wellington Koo regarding Tsingtao and to thank you for letting him see it. He asks if you will not be kind enough to keep it in the files of the Commission.
                              Sincerely yours,   [Gilbert F. Close]

CCL (WP, DLC).

To Andrew Furuseth

My dear Mr. Furuseth: [Paris] 15 April, 1919.

You may be sure that I was in sympathy with the sentiments contained in your letter of March 26th,[1] and if the objects you have in view are not for the present attainable, I shall hope with you that they may some day not too far distant be attained.
                              Cordially and sincerely yours,   [Woodrow Wilson]

CCL (WP, DLC).
  [1] A. Furuseth to WW, March 26, 1919, Vol. 56.

To the Right Reverend Charles Henry Brent

My dear Bishop Brent: Paris, 15 April, 1919.

Thank you for your letter of April 11th. I need not tell you that the suggestion it contains appeals to my heart, but I am afraid with the peculiar makeup of our Commission on the League of Nations it would be useless to propose such a sentence as you suggest for the Covenant of the League.

In unavoidable haste,
                              Cordially and sincerely yours,   [Woodrow Wilson]

CCL (WP, DLC).

To Porter James McCumber

My dear Senator McCumber: [Paris] 15 April, 1919.

Your generous letter of March 13th[1] gave me the greatest gratification. I have tried in the conferences of the Commission on the
League of Nations to act upon every item of your advice and think
that I have substantially succeeded.

I cannot tell you how much reassurance and added sense of
comradeship in great things such letters as yours give me, and I
thank you most warmly for the guidance the letter has afforded.

In unavoidable haste,
                    Cordially and faithfully yours,   [Woodrow Wilson]

CCL (WP, DLC).
  [1] P. J. McCumber to WW, March 13, 1919, Vol. 55.

A Memorandum by William B. Wallace

                                        Paris, April 15, 1919.

MEMORANDUM FOR GENERAL BLISS:

The President called in person at 5:50 p.m. and handed me the
attached papers.[1] He believed that General Kernan would have
some information later than that of these papers (which are dated
the 28th of March) as to the status of affairs at Lemberg, and that
in view of this later information he desired General Bliss to have a
conference with Mr. Paderewski and lay the matter before him with
the request that the Poles accept and comply with the terms and
conditions of the truce the same as the Ukrainians had done. That
this request was made by the Peace Conference.

The President also stated that he had a communication to make
to the Luxemburg Government with reference to a pending bill[2]
that was coming up before that Government this week. He was
going to send this communication to General Bliss and asked that
the General send it to the Luxemburg Government through the
American officer in charge of civilian affairs at Luxemburg.

                                        W. B. Wallace,
                                Lieut. Colonel, General Staff.

CC MS (T. H. Bliss Papers, DLC).
  [1] See the memorandum by F. J. Kernan printed at April 11, 1919.
  [2] Actually, two proposed plebiscites. In the first, the voters of Luxembourg would
indicate their preference for the existing Grand Duchy, some other unspecified dynasty,
or a republic. In the second, they were to indicate whether they preferred close economic
ties with France or with Belgium. See Sally Marks, *Innocent Abroad: Belgium at the Paris
Peace Conference of 1919* (Chapel Hill, N. C., 1981), pp. 227-33. Wilson sent his "communication" to General Bliss on the evening of April 15. It was delivered to the Luxembourg
government on April 16. See T. H. Bliss to GFC, April 17, 1919. The text of the communication
is embodied in T. H. Bliss to GFC, April 18, 1919.

Sir Robert Borden to Sir Thomas White

Paris April 15, 1919

X.225. Secret. Japanese have been making unceasing and strenuous efforts to amend preamble of League of Nations Covenant. Their first proposal was actively resisted and has been abandoned but they are now willing to accept following amendments: Insert after the word nations where it first occurs in preamble the following begins by the endorsement of the principle of equality between nations and just treatment of their nationals ends. I understand that this has been agreed to by United States and all other nations except British Empire which has not hitherto assented. As Japan is already recognized as one of the Great Powers and as each nation already acts upon the principle of what it conceives to be just treatment the proposed amendment does not seem to alter existing conditions. Immigration and Naturalization are regarded under international law as matters of domestic concern and the new draft of Covenant contains a clause providing that League of Nations shall not interfere in matters of domestic concern. Further the position of Great Britain and the United States as the most important Powers on League of Nations Council and the fact that no action can be taken except by unanimous consent seems to remove absolutely any danger of attempted interference by the League with these domestic questions.   Borden

T telegram (R. L. Borden Papers, CaOOA).

From Robert Lansing

My dear Mr. President: Paris. 15th April, 1919.

I am sending to you under separate cover the Commission appointing Mr. Hugh Gibson, Envoy-Extraordinary and Minister Plenipotentiary of the United States to Poland, together with his letters of Credence, and shall be glad if you would kindly have these documents returned to me after you have affixed the required signatures.   Faithfully yours,   Robert Lansing.

Returned to Secretary Lansing 4/16/19. GFC

TLS (WP, DLC).

Robert Lansing to Frank Lyon Polk

[Paris] April 15th, 1919.

1627. For Richard Crane.

President has authorized me to tender you appointment as Minister to Czecho-Slovak Republic. You have as you know my warmest congratulations and my personal confidence in your success if you accept the appointment to so difficult a post. Please telegraph immediately your acceptance and how soon you can leave to enter upon your duties. The situation demands the presence of an American Minister at the earliest possible date. 1627.

Lansing Ammission.

T telegram (WP, DLC).

Gilbert Fairchild Close to Robert Lansing

My dear Mr. Secretary: Paris, 15 April, 1919.

The President asks me to return to you the enclosed bill from the Director of State Railroads of the French Republic.[1] He is very deeply surprised at this bill, as he was at the other,[2] but he sees no choice but to pay it.

Sincerely yours,   [Gilbert F. Close]

CCL (WP, DLC).
[1] See RL to WW, April 2, 1919 (first letter of that date), Vol. 56.
[2] See the extract from the Diary of Edith Benham printed at March 31, 1919, and WW to RL, April 1, 1919 (second letter of that date), both in Vol. 56.

Two Letters to Vance Criswell McCormick

My dear McCormick: Paris, 15 April, 1919.

I have had quite a large number of cables about the matter to which Mr. Woolley refers[1] and am afraid the case is not quite as simple as would appear on the surface. I was in hopes from the last advices that the Railroad Administration and Mr. Redfield's conferees could come to an understanding, and I would very much like to know the latest phases of the situation before forming a conclusion. The case is not altogether against the Railway Administration, I feel confident.

In haste,   Faithfully yours,   [Woodrow Wilson]

[1] C. M. Woolley to V. C. McCormick, March 28, 1919, TC telegram (WP, DLC). Woolley warned that the refusal of the Railroad Administration to accept the prices for rails agreed upon by the Industrial Board of the Department of Commerce would destroy the usefulness of that board. He urged McCormick to ask Wilson "to authorize the Railroad Administration to lend its hearty support and cooperation to the constructive and helpful work which has been so successfully inaugurated by the Industrial Board."

My dear McCormick: [Paris] 15 April, 1919.

Articles like this which you sent me in your letter of April twelfth are serious enough, I realize, but my trouble is that I cannot work out in my mind any statement which would not either be a defence (which would savor of weakness) or an indirect incrimination of some of my colleagues, which would be more serious still. Had you yourself thought out a line of statement which would be serviceable? I would be heartily obliged to you if you would let me know, if you have.

In haste, Faithfully yours, [Woodrow Wilson]

CCL (WP, DLC).

To Julius Howland Barnes

[Paris] April 15, 1919.

1624. I should be glad to know if you would accept the position as Director of the administration we must create for the execution of the guarantee of the nineteen nineteen wheat crop. Your responsibility will be directly to myself after Mr. Hoover's retirement as Chairman of Grain Corporation on July 1st. The experience which you have gained and the success which you have attained in handling the wheat and cereal crops under the Food Administration has been so generally recognized by expressions from the different sections of the community that I feel it would be a national loss if we could not have your service continued until the completion of this most important national undertaking.

I should like to take this occasion to express the high appreciation and gratitude which I have for the service performed not only by yourself but by the Directors, Vice-Presidents and other members of the Grain Corporation. The sacrifice which these gentlemen have given in a time of national emergency, the skill and integrity with which they have carried out so difficult an economic undertaking is one which I am sure the whole of our people must appreciate. I am in hopes that these gentlemen will remain with you in this service and I would be glad if you would convey to each of them my personal gratitude for that exhibition of sacrifice and willingness to national service which is so promising to the future welfare of our people. Woodrow Wilson. 1624 Ammission.

T telegram (WP, DLC).

From Joseph Patrick Tumulty

[The White House, April 15, 1919]

No. 58. I understand that Hines has recommended immediate action with reference to return of railroads. Our friends in Treasury Department believe that if any public suggestion of immediate return of railroads is made or action taken before Liberty Loan closes May tenth, it would bring about national catastrophe. Think it would be well to consult Glass before any definite action is taken in this matter.   Tumulty.

T telegram (WP, DLC).

From William Cox Redfield

My dear Mr. President: Washington April 15, 1919.

May I confirm my cablegram of April 11[1] by enclosing copy thereof and review as briefly as I can the discussion between the Railroad Administration and the Industrial Board? These bodies are now at a dead-lock and your instructions are awaited.

You, of course, know my relation to the controversy and will make allowance for that fact. Yet I have tried to avoid a controversial spirit and neither to say or write or permit to be said or written anything which would arouse that spirit.

We in this Department are a unit and others intimate with the matter, such as the Fuel Administrator[2] and the Acting Chairman of the War Trade Board,[3] are in accord. Throughout a wish for kindly cooperation has prevailed with us and my feeling is one of sincere regret that this has failed. We have as conscientiously and courteously as we knew how extended every opportunity of which we could think to bring it about.

The idea on which the Industrial Board is based came from Mr. Wm. M. Ritter, of whom you will know as the largest hard wood lumber producer in this country. He discussed it informally with Secretaries Lane and Wilson and a conference resulted on Monday, February 3, at the office of Secretary Glass, who presided. Among those present were Postmaster General Burleson, Secretary Lane, Director General Hines, Mr. R. C. Leffingwell, Mr. May representative of the Treasury Department on the War Trade Board, Mr. Whitmarsh of the Food Administration, Mr. Ritter and myself. The restless social situation was the background of thought, together

[1] WCR to WW, April 11, 1919.
[2] That is, Harry Augustus Garfield.
[3] That is, Clarence Mott Woolley.

with the need of starting soon the wheels of industry to provide employment for those out of work for seasonal reasons, or because of business stagnation, and for the returning soldiers. The problem being how to start industry moving, it was I think evident to all that this could not be done during the hesitation normal to a falling market. It was felt that the period of normal reaction to a stable basis on which the regular law of supply and demand might resume its sway was sure to be long. Mr. Ritter brought forward his plan to accelerate the stabilizing of prices by conference and consent. He explicitly pointed out that the cooperation of the purchasing branches of the government would be required on a liberal scale. The Director General of Railroads accepted this understanding saying (I do not quote him) he would buy liberally. As he has recently said, however, it is true I think that this was based upon the thought that prices were to be such as would justify him in buying. Certainly no one expected him to agree in advance to purchase at prices that would not justify buying.

After our discussion a unanimous understanding was reached to the substantial effect that the matter would be further discussed at a conference in my office two days later, Wednesday, February 5.

The matter came up at the Cabinet meeting of Tuesday, February 4, at which Attorney General Gregory was present. There was no objection made to the purpose sought or to the proposed plan. Some discussion took place respecting its relation to the anti-trust law. It was understood that it was not to be brought formally before the Attorney General but there appeared no doubt that it could be so treated as not to conflict with the anti-trust laws and it was known that the conference already mentioned was to take place the next day.

At the first conference it had also been expressly stated that there seemed no doubt the matter could be so treated as not to fall within the scope of the anti-trust laws.

It is hard for me, a layman, to understand that it is either good ethics or good politics to allege that laws enacted to prohibit combinations in restraint of trade can be construed to prohibit voluntary cooperation in promotion of trade when the government is itself a party and the only moving forces are those of patriotism, facts and sound sense.

On Wednesday, February 5, the conference at my office lasted all day. A list of the parties present is herewith (1).[4] Note that it includes representatives of the Treasury Department, the War Fi-

[4] TC MS (WP, DLC), not printed.

nance Corporation, the Federal Reserve Board, the Post Office Department, the Railroad Administration and a number of representatives of the former War Industries Board, with officers of the Department of Commerce.

The conference ended in unanimously approving my cabling you as I did on February 6. The message was supported by one from Secretary Glass; copies of both are enclosed (2 and 3).[5]

In due time your own dispatch dated February 13, copy attached (4),[6] was received and as promptly as possible the Board was appointed and assembled. On your return you approved my request of February 24,[7] copy enclosed, for a fund of $75,000 to carry the cost of the work, copy attached (5).[8]

Since the Director General has questioned the membership of the Board in his letter to the Secretary of the Treasury (14),[9] it is proper to speak of it. Its membership is as follows:

Mr. Geo. N. Peek, formerly Vice-President, Deere and Company, Moline, Ill., Commissioner of Finished Products, War Industries Board.

Mr. Samuel P[rescott]. Bush, president, Buckeye Steel Casting Company, Columbus, Ohio, Director, Pennsylvania Rail-Road; former Director, Facilities Division, War Industries Board, and Chief, Section of Forgings, Guns, Small Arms, etc., War Industries Board.

Mr. Anthony Caminetti, Commissioner General of Immigration, Department of Labor, Washington, D. C.

Mr. Thomas K[earney]. Glenn, president, Atlantic Steel Co., Atlanta, Georgia.

Mr. George R[oosa]. James, president, Wm. R. Moore Dry Goods Company, Memphis, Tenn. Former Chief, Cotton Linters Section, Textile Division, War Industries Board.

[5] TC of WCR to WW, Feb. 6, 1919, printed at that date in Vol. 54, and C. Glass to WW, Feb. 6, 1919, TC telegram (WP, DLC). In this telegram, Glass did, indeed, strongly support Redfield's proposal for an Industrial Board.
[6] TC of WW to WCR, Feb. 13, 1919, printed at that date in Vol. 55.
[7] WCR to WW, Feb. 24, 1919, TCL (WP, DLC).
[8] *Idem*, with Wilson's signed approval and authorization.
[9] W. D. Hines to C. Glass, April 4, 1919, TCL (WP, DLC). At the end of this letter, Hines wrote: "I have the highest opinion of the integrity, ability and experience of all the gentlemen on the Board, but I can say without the slightest reflection upon them that I do not regard them as being primarily qualified to act as a Board of final authority either to sanction agreements on the part of the manufacturing industries or to fix prices at which the Government must buy."

Mr. T[homas]. C[arr]. Powell, Director, Capital Expenditures, Railroad Administration, Former Vice-President, Southern Railroad Company.

Mr. Wm. M. Ritter, President, W. M. Ritter Lumber Co., West Virginia; former Assistant to Commissioner of Finished Products, War Industries Board.

After over a quarter century of experience in industry I do not know a more thoughtful, sane, better informed, more broad minded, group of men than the five gentlemen who represent industry on this Board. Mr. Caminetti was substituted with Secretary Wilson's approval for Mr. Frayne,[10] who was named in my telegram to you but could not serve. I should mention that Mr. Glenn, who is a steel manufacturer, does not produce rails.

The Board first took up the basic industries whose product forms the materials for other industries and which were directly related to the great building and contracting operations of the country. It was their thought that if substantial reductions could be made in these foundations the rest would follow. It was no easy task to bring the steel industry into line. A personal talk between Mr. Peek and Judge Gary was followed by two long committee conferences in New York and these by a conference of the entire industry. At this it was voted to cooperate with the government. In due time a committee said to have represented ninety per cent. of the entire production came to Washington and here thrashed out the matter in long sessions. Every member of the Board was present.

When Mr. Powell was appointed to the Board for the Railroad Administration, he was asked by its Chairman to represent not only his own Service but the other purchasing branches of the government. He was provided an office in the rooms of the Board and was assisted in some of the conferences by Mr. Spencer,[11] chairman of the Central Advisory Purchasing Committee, and director of the Division of Finance and Purchases, Railroad Administration.

Throughout the steel discussion Mr. Powell took part and was fully aware of what went on. This bears on the matter of the Director General being informed of what took place. His representative was present and participated. When the steel conference began all members of the Board thought it would be possible to obtain without affecting labor, lower steel prices than those finally recommended. Mr. Powell's views at this juncture were no exception to those of the other members of the Board. When the conference closed, however, Mr. Powell dissented as to rails alone. He did not protest

[10] That is, Hugh Frayne.   [11] Henry Benning Spencer.

against the prices for other steel elements. It is, indeed, stated by the Director General that his representative objected to the steel prices generally, but six members of the Board signed, April 1, a statement to the effect that Mr. Powell dissented only to the price of rails. Copy of this statement is attached (6).[12]

On March 21 the recommendations of the Board were made (7).[13] The announcement was in part in the following language:

"In giving its approval to the schedule of prices just decided upon for the principal articles of iron and steel the Industrial Board of the Department of Commerce, carrying out the purpose for which it was created, believes that a level has been reached below which the public should not expect to buy during the current year."

This language has been criticised by the Director General as involving a breach of the anti-trust laws and showing a departure from the original purpose of the Board. He has stated that the Board's original plan was to be a mediatizing Board which should by conference with industry bring about such low prices as to be attractive to the purchasing departments, or, to use his words, "bring together the sellers of steel and iron articles and the governmental buyers of those articles." This result is what the Board has sincerely tried to bring about but the fruit of their work is not satisfactory to the Director General and he does not accept it. So far as my knowledge goes there has been no change in purpose, plan or method from the original basis on which the Board was founded. Neither the Board nor I cares to insist upon the language of the announcement. We are willing to modify the language or to say that it should have been different or to take any and all other steps as regards the form which matters take that are agreeable to the Attorney General. This we have repeatedly indicated. However, the Acting Solicitor of this Department, Mr. E. T. Quigley[14] was present at all the conferences and meetings of the Board to advise them as to procedure. This was done at the request of Mr. Peek and Mr. Ritter, who before the former accepted the chairmanship of the Board, expressly asked that the assistance of counsel be provided.

The original draft quoted above had the words "and the government" inserted after the word "public" in the above quotation but these three words were struck out at the request of Mr. Powell.

Objection has been made by the Director General to the statement respecting the "current year" above quoted. This is a statement of belief. This, too, we shall be glad to alter if it is important.

[12] T MS (WP, DLC).
[13] T press release, March 21, 1919 (WP, DLC).
[14] Edward T. Quigley.

I was in the northwest during the steel discussions here and when the statement was published (on March 21) and did not return until the night of March 26. Mr. Peek and Mr. Ritter called upon me that evening, pointing out the serious effects upon the business of the country that the refusal on the part of the Railroad Administration to cooperate would involve. They told me that other industries, notably coal, were ready to make price concessions if it was understood that the Railroad Administration would be guided by the recommendations made and if the matter could take such form as not to involve the anti-trust laws. The next day, March 27, Mr. Peek prepared before leaving town his telegram to Mr. Baruch,[15] which you have doubtless seen, and sent it to me by Mr. Bush. Dr. Garfield came and in the presence of both my dispatch to you of March 27,[16] copy attached (8), was prepared, both approving. Dr. Garfield later sent his own dispatch to you which I did not see until the following day, copy attached (9).[17] Mr. Woolley, Acting Chairman of the War Trade Board, having learned the situation from me cabled of his own motion to Mr. McCormick a dispatch which I did not see until a day or two later, copy attached (10).[18] I wish to make it plain that the dispatches from Messrs. Garfield and Woolley were their own. Mine to you was sent with Mr. Peek's to Mr. Baruch before me. The Director General was at that time in the west. A copy of my dispatch to you being wired him by Mr. Powell, was followed by his own dispatch to you, copy attached (11).[19]

At my request a conference was called by Secretary Glass at his office on Wednesday afternoon, April 2. At this the statement of the Board was presented to which reference has already been made above and of which copy is enclosed dated April 1, signed by six of the seven members of the Board (6). There were present Secretary Glass, presiding, Secretary Baker, Secretary Burleson, Secretary Lane and myself, the Director General of Railroads, Mr. Powell, Mr. Spencer, all the members of the Industrial Board, Mr. Woolley of the War Trade Board, Mr. Edgar Rickard of the Food Administration, Judge Glasgow, Counsel of the Food Administration, Dr. Garfield, Mr. May, Mr. Eugene Meyer, Jr., Mr. Leffingwell, Mr. Reed,[20] secretary of the Industrial Board, Mr. E. T. Quigley, Acting Solicitor of this Department, Mr. Cooksey[21] and possibly others. The matter was frankly and fully discussed for several hours.

[15] G. N. Peek to BMB, March 27, 1919, T telegram (WP, DLC).
[16] TC of WCR to WW, March 27, 1919, printed at that date in Vol. 56.
[17] TC of H. A. Garfield to WW, March 27, 1919, printed at that date in Vol. 56.
[18] See n. 1 to WW to V. C. McCormick, April 15, 1919 (first letter of that date).
[19] TC of W. D. Hines to WW, March 28, 1919, printed at that date in Vol. 56.
[20] Lewis Balcombe Reed.
[21] George Robert Cooksey, Assistant to the Secretary of the Treasury.

Prior to this meeting I had sent Secretary Glass a copy of my dispatch to you (8) and he had, I am told, wired to you a message which I have not seen.[22]

The discussion ended without agreement save that the matter was referred back to the Board for further consideration and for conference with the Railroad Administration. A number of conferences have since taken place, both between the Director General of Railroads and the Chairman of the Board personally, and on one occasion between the entire Board and Judge Lovett, Mr. Walters, Mr. McChord,[23] of the Interstate Commerce Commission, and Mr. Spencer acting for the Railroad Administration. Mr. Spencer, Judge Lovett and Mr. Walters were also present at a conference between the Chairman of the Board and Judge Gary, Mr. Schwab and other members of the iron and steel industry, in New York.

Finally, on the 10th instant, the Director General of Railroads publicly announced that he would not accept the steel prices and, I am told, cabled you.[24] (See attached Chamber of Commerce of the United States publication,—12—,[25] giving as of April 10 statement by the Railroad Administration and one of the same date by the Board.) I sent you my cablegram on the 11th instant, copy enclosed (13).[26] This was prepared with the knowledge of the Chairman of the Board.

I think the above is a correct statement of the facts.

However, after the meeting at Secretary Glass' office on the 2d instant, the Director General of Railroads wrote on April 4 to the Secretary of the Treasury a letter of which he kindly sent me copy, which is attached (14).[27] I sent Secretary Glass a memorandum respecting this letter, copy attached (15),[28] and Mr. Peek sent a reply, also, copy enclosed (16).[29] These last two statements fairly represent the spirit of the Board and this Department. It is not necessary to amplify them but for your own eye this should be written: No one seeks or has sought to impose anything upon any one save only so far as its essential truth might require assent. Alone among the government services, the Railroad Administration has objected.

A meeting was held on March 25 at the office of the Industrial Board, the minutes of which are attached (17).[30] It will be noted

[22] See C. Glass to WW, March 27, 1919 (second telegram of that date), Vol. 56.
[23] That is, Henry Walters and Charles Caldwell McChord.
[24] W. D. Hines to WW, April 10, 1919.
[25] Chamber of Commerce of the United States of America, War Service Bulletin No. 54, April 11, 1919, Industrial Board of the Department of Commerce (Washington), copy in WP, DLC.
[26] TC (WP, DLC).
[27] W. D. Hines to C. Glass, April 4, 1919, TCL (WP, DLC).
[28] TS MS, April 7, 1919 (WP, DLC).
[29] G. N. Peek to C. Glass, April 7, 1919, TCL (WP, DLC).
[30] T MS, dated March 25, 1919 (WP, DLC).

that the purchasing departments were well represented, that there was not only no dissent but that the Shipping Board and the Navy (and later the Army in writing through Assistant Secretary Crowell) agreed to cooperate. The Railroad Administration was not present and was and is the only active dissenter up to this writing. I should not omit that Secretary Glass has taken the view of the Railroad Administration or that an opinion was rendered by the Attorney General on April 1 to me, in response to my letter outlining the matter following the steel conference which Dr. Garfield also attended, stating, as wired you, that the proposed plan of the Board "is unauthorized by law."

Before stating briefly the principles involved and the practical results to industry that have already taken place, let me say that I appreciate fully the hard conditions bearing upon the Railroad Administration. Their income is insufficient for the fiscal burdens they have to bear. Their task is most difficult, if not impossible, and in his earnest and able efforts to solve the great problems laid upon him the Director General of Railroads has my most cordial sympathy. I have been and shall be glad to aid him in every possible way. I do not question his sincerity in deciding as he has done in the steel matter.

It is also true that the Railroad Administration is run, naturally, by railroad men and it is too much to expect that these men should throw off their mental habit the result of life-long training. For reasons not wholly within their control railroad buyers have had to be for years past very close buyers, sometimes very hard buyers. Industry and coal producers know well what this has meant to them. I have done business in one or another way with railroads for many years and can say from my own experience that this is true. A large car wheel manufacturer told me last week that the present railway purchasing board had forced him to sell on a bare margin of five percent. in order to keep his works moving. Doubtless with sincerity the railroad men think it their duty under the income conditions pressing upon them to purchase at the lowest point at which they can possibly buy. This attitude of mind has been clearly indicated. Yet it is this very mental attitude which has led to the pressing down of coal prices to the point where the public had to bear the burden which the railroads thrust upon the coal producers. It is, in contrast, the principle of "live and let live" in this respect by a reasonable and fair price, just alike to the government, the coal producer and the coal buying public which was urged upon you by Dr. Garfield and approved by you.

Possibly the Railroad Administration may, by the concentration in a few hands of a mighty purchasing power, force steel producers to a price on rails lower than that the Board recommended but it is also true, if this is done, that either the difference must be taken out of wages or must be distributed by the steel producers over their other products in order to make good the loss arising from government purchases at low prices.

As the enclosures herewith say, (15 and 16), the Industrial Board had before it the official figures of the Federal Trade Commission to check against the statements of the steel producers themselves and these were, in their turn, verified by Mr. Reay[31] of the Wisconsin Steel Company, an independent producer not making rails, who was for that purpose made available to the Industrial Board. We have pointed out to the Director General that at the prices recommended by the Board at least two out of the five mills making rails will at present wages produce at a loss, a third will come out barely whole, and but two will make any profit whatever. We have asked that any data which the Railroad Administration might have which bore upon the subject should be shown us and have given assurance that our views would be modified if any facts were developed to warrant it. No data or facts of any nature bearing upon existing conditions have been furnished. At the meeting in Secretary Glass' office, Mr. Woolley in an effort to mediate made the same suggestion but nothing whatever has been shown. Both the Industrial Board and I myself am at this writing in ignorance of the substantial basis on which the opinion of the Railroad Administration is formed. Judge Lovett said in the conference with the Industrial Board that his opinion, which agreed with the Director General's, was based upon knowledge of general conditions. Later he said to Mr. Peek in New York "it was not a question of the price of rails but solely one of policy Mr. Hines would have to determine." This policy or principle is whether prices shall be accepted which will permit the average efficient independent producer to operate on a moderate basis of profit without making a drive against wages in order that industry be kept going and labor be kept employed without any element in the industry having a monopolistic or indeed a preferential part, as against the principle of buying without direct regard to social or industrial or political effect at the extreme lowest figure to which the exertion of the vast buying power of the government can force prices. The Director General will disclaim this latter basis but his disclaimer is not supported by facts or figures, though these have been repeatedly asked.

As to the effects upon industry, the Journal of Commerce of the 14th instant says:

[31] William M. Reay, controller of the International Harvester Co. International Harvester, which had previously controlled the Wisconsin Steel Co., took over its plants in 1917. The Wisconsin Steel Co. at this time acted only as sales agent for steel products.

"The week just closed created a record for market inactivity and an equally unapproachable record for all around unrest. The way the rail price controversy stood on Saturday it was squarely up to President Wilson as to the exact disposition of the opposing forces. The situation from a market point of view is most unsatisfactory. Orders placed last week were reported to be very light. The best of the lot from the angle of demand were steel bars. Sheets and wire products have been coming in for some attention. Outside of this there is practically nothing to report."

I have before me a letter from the Wheeling Steel and Iron Company, producers of sheet and tin plate (not involved in the rail discussion) by Mr. John Duncan, their General Manager of Sales, which reads in part as follows:

"Our tin mills are running only 25% of their capacity and this condition has obtained for the past two and one half months. To give you an illustration of what this steel controversy has done to the business of the country, I want to cite several cases which have come under my personal observation.

["]One of the largest users of tin plate in this country had practically placed an order with us for 100,000 boxes of tin plate when this Railroad controversy was injected into your stabilization plan. These people immediately withdrew from the market, and stated that they would wait until Mr. Hines had gotten the market down where he claimed it ought to be. This concern is one of the largest oil companies in the world, if not the largest, and they stated to me that in their opinion the plan which you suggested with the result in prices, would certainly have a wonderful influence in starting up the wheels of industry. They, like all other good business concerns however, felt that if Mr. Hines' contention was correct and the government supported him in this position, then naturally lower prices would result and they wanted to obtain the benefit of the same. Only yesterday here in Pittsburgh, I had practically closed for 50,000 boxes of tin plate, which I had been negotiating for for the past two weeks, when the same argument was used and the concern said they would wait until the settlement of the steel controversy."

I enclose an editorial and commercial article from the New York Times of April 12 (18 and 19).[32]

The National Association of Manufacturers under date of the 14th instant and the heading "Trade Prospects for 1919" state:

"The production of iron and steel is universally regarded in business circles as the most reliable barometer of trade conditions. With

[32] Two clippings from the New York Times, April 12, 1919 (WP, DLC).

respect to present business in this industry, the replies indicate that these important trade factors are in a comparative state of lethargy, due mainly to market and price conditions, as well as a general lack of buying on the part of the railroads. Similarly, it is found that 67 per cent of the iron and steel manufacturing plants do not regard the trade prospects for 1919 as very bright."

A chart and pamphlet are also enclosed (20 and 21)[33] which show the relation of railroad purchases to general business conditions in a very striking way.

We have in mind also the effect upon labor of the uncertainty shown by the above to exist. Immediately on the recommendation of the steel prices business started. As I wired you there was a spirit of hope and confidence in the central west that was inspiring. It has gone and with its going has come an uncertainty as to labor which is regrettable. In its work the Industrial Board throughout has taken the view that labor should not now be made to take the shock of readjustment and capital has willingly accepted this viewpoint. Doubtless lower prices can and some day will be made but just as doubtless, also, they must be made in greater or less measure at the expense of labor, for capital has been willing to surrender either all profit or all save the most meager profits for the time being and the result is not accepted by the government.

I am orally informed by a manufacturer that in a discussion of prices within a week with the Railroad Administration on a considerable purchase, the officer representing the latter said to the manufacturer that he thought labor was in some directions too high.

As a final exhibit (22)[34] there is attached the original statement of the Board which was approved by all its members, including Mr. Powell, and which is embodied in Bulletin No. 49 of the Chamber of Commerce of the United States.

Finally: It takes at least two people to quarrel and I will not be one of them. Whatever decision you may have made or will make will be accepted in a cordial spirit of good will because I know your thought will be simply to do that which is wisest for the country.

                    Yours very truly,   William C. Redfield

TLS (WP, DLC).

[33] Printed copies, WP, DLC. The pamphlet was Edward Baker Leigh, president, Chicago Railway Equipment Co., *Railway Purchases Measure General Business Prosperity* (New York, 1919).

[34] Chamber of Commerce of the United States of America, War Service Bulletin No. 49, March 10, 1919, *Industrial Board of the Department of Commerce* (Washington), copy in WP, DLC.

From Bernard Mannes Baruch, with Enclosure

My dear Mr. President: Paris, April 15, 1919.

After an examination of the correspondence between the various departments in Washington, frankness necessitates my saying that a good idea was badly handled. The discussion that is taking place now should have taken place, and a decision been made, before action was taken.

It appears from the correspondence that Hines agreed with the plan, but did not like the way it was put into effect, and that some members of the Cabinet who agreed in the beginning now disagree. However, I recommend your sending the inclosed cable directed to the members of the Cabinet and Director General Hines, which should bring results if they really try to get together.

Very truly yours,   B. M. Baruch

CCL (WP, DLC).

ENCLOSURE

Secretary Redfield reported in his cable of February 8th [6th] that quote in consultation, Glass, Burleson, Lane, Wilson, Woolley, Meyer of War Finance Corporation, Miller of Federal Reserve Board, have expressed their approval, in fact no opposition unquote.

It is advisable that trade shall return to the ordinary laws of supply and demand as quickly as possible, yet conditions warranted some temporary co-operation. In view of this and the general consent indicated I approved of the plan.

The evident purpose underlying the scheme was to stabilize industry and to maintain labor in as full employment, with as high wages as possible with a full knowledge that perhaps in some instances higher prices might be paid, but that the general effect would be for the best interests of all. That some particular interest might benefit, or might suffer, should not outweigh the greater consideration of the general benefit to the whole community.

While I appreciate the views of the Railroad Administration, we must avoid the feeling that the vast power concentrated in the hands of the railroads for the purchase of their materials can be unduly exercised to the disadvantage of the producer or of the consuming public at a time like this. It should rather be used as a stabilizing influence.

This discussion might better have taken place before action was taken.

Therefore, may I not ask that the Industrial Board and the Railroad Administration for the common good come to an immediate agreement, but suggest that the time be limited to October 1st.

T MS (WP, DLC).

From the Diary of Dr. Grayson

Wednesday, April 16, 1919.

The President arose early this morning and was through breakfast at 8:30. He worked in his study and later attended a meeting of the Big Four. This was a good day for me inasmuch as I received a number of letters from home and enclosed in one of the letters was a sample of Cary, Jr.'s hair, which Mrs. Grayson instructed me to compare with my own. I did so and found that they were exactly of the same color, although the baby's was a little more silky than mine.

The President had at lunch today Mr. and Mrs. Garrett,[1] our Minister to The Hague; also Mr. Charles R. Crane, who is just going on a mission to Syria, and Mr. Vance McCormick. Mrs. Garrett is an ardent golfer and the President told her during the lunch some of his choice golf stories. Mrs. Garrett asked the President how he managed to keep in health during all the terrific strain he was undergoing, and the President pointed towards me and said: "Get the prescription on the other side—but I will say the Doctor guards me very carefully."

After luncheon there was informal discussion over the coffee of the doings of the individual members of the Peace Conference, and especially of the apparent effort on the part of some of the members, notably Clemenceau, to assume all of the credit for what had been accomplished. The President said it reminded him very much of the story of the Arab, who had arrived at an oasis and was about to draw some water out of the well. The moon was at its full and as he leaned over he saw the reflection of the moon in the water below him, and he exclaimed: "This is no place for the moon." The Arab got a long pole and began to grapple for the moon at the bottom of the well. His stick caught on the side and he threw his whole weight on the end of the pole, which broke, and he fell heavily with his face towards the heavens. Seeing the moon above him, he rose and rubbing his sore head he said: "Well, that's the best job I have ever done in my life." The President said this story aptly represented the various claims for credit that were now being made in certain quarters.

The President was in good spirits and said that even though it had been a trying time, still there were some things in connection with his task here that relieved the monotony, and for which he was thankful. Then in explanation of this he told another story of an Arab wandering through the streets of a village, stopping passers-by and asking whether they had seen his lost donkey. Invariably told that they had not, the Arab would ejaculate in a prayerful manner: "I am so thankful; I am so thankful," and addressed his question to the next comer. Finally, one of the men who could not understand why he should be thankful when he had lost his only possession, asked him what he meant by saying he was so thankful— to which the Arab replied: "I am thankful that I am not on him or I would be lost."

The visitors asked the President whether he had been able to go to the theatres or to any of the demonstrations while he was in Paris, to which he replied: "No, the Doctor does not like for me to go anywhere where there is a crowd, because he is afraid I might pick up some stray germ and contract some infection, although he will not say whether he means the influenza or something of that sort." The President then said this put him in mind of the story of the King who found that his male subjects were very unhappy, and the strength of his state was being endangered because the men were ruled entirely by their wives. The state of mind of the men finally became so serious that the King was compelled to order an inquiry, so he directed that all of his male subjects should appear at a certain place on a certain day. The King had a blue flag displayed on a staff on one side of the field, and another with a red flag on the other. Then he told the assembled subjects that all who were ruled by their wives should go to the side where the blue flag was displayed. A movement toward the blue flag started, and the King called out that those who were not ruled by their wives should go to the red flag. Only one man went to the latter place. He was a small, very skinny runt of a man, who took his place alone under the red flag. The King addressing him said: "My man, I am surprised that you alone are able to avoid being ruled by your wife. How is it that you are able to take such a strong and noble stand?" The man replied in a very weak voice: "It is not that, sir, but before I left home this morning my wife told me I must avoid crowds."

In the afternoon the Big Four continued its discussion of the German boundaries and passed upon the plans for the reception of the German Peace Delegates when they arrive at Versailles next week. They approved the plan of housing the German delegates in a hotel and of holding all of the conferences as far as possible in the hotel. The reason for this was that the Palace at Versailles was entirely unsanitary and it was impossible to heat it sufficiently so that the peace delegates would not be subject to catching cold or even pneumonia.

The President had dinner with Mrs. Wilson and myself. After dinner we generally discussed the various participants in the Peace Conference covering the ground that had been covered individually and recorded previously. The President retired early.

[1] John Work Garrett and Alice Warder Garrett.

From the Diary of Colonel House

April 16, 1919.

The thing that pleased me most today was getting Clemenceau to sign the Russian pact. He told me he would do it yesterday and that Pichon had the document. I found this morning that it was in Hoover's hands and I sent it to the President's house by Gordon, and the President had Clemenceau sign it as soon as he came in to the morning conference. We will now see how the experiment which Hoover, Gordon and I planned will work out.

Another thing that has pleased me is the complete change in the tone of the French Press. Clemenceau sent me around with his card clippings from the morning papers. It is a complete *volte face*. They all praise the President extravagantly. It shows how entirely the matter has been in Clemenceau's hands from the beginning. I am attaching the clippings. The afternoon papers will probably be equally cordial but I shall not bother to preserve them.

From Edward Mandell House

Dear Governor:　　　　　　　　　　　　　Paris, April 16, 1919.

I saw Clemenceau again yesterday after you left. He was perfectly delighted with what I was able to tell him concerning the Syrian-Armenian matters and the period of occupation.

I took occasion to ask him if he had signed the Russian Memorandum. He said he had not but would do so. He thought that Pichon had it. He rang for his secretary giving instructions to have it brought to him. I find, however, that it is in Hoover's hands and I am sending it to you under this cover so you may have Clemenceau sign it this morning.

I spoke to Clemenceau about the attacks in the French press. It made no difference I told him except that it was bringing about strained relations between our two countries—a condition which I was sure he did not wish. He rang for his secretary again and told him to give directions to the Echo de Paris, Le Petit Journal, Le Petit Parisien, Le Figaro, Le Temps, La Liberté and several others which I do not recall, to say that the relations between France and the United States were of the very best and that there was no disagreement between yourself and himself upon any of the great questions before the Conference. I shall await with interest to see what happens.[1]   Affectionately yours,   E. M. House

TLS (WP, DLC).
[1] House enclosed a current intelligence summary which quoted editorials from Paris newspapers of April 16, 1919.

From the Diary of Vance Criswell McCormick

April 16 (Wednesday) [1919]

Lunched at President's house with President and Mrs. Wilson, Garretts, and Charles Crane. Had a nice informal time. President chatted with us for a long time after lunch. Talked freely about Clemenceau's characteristics. Says he seems to depend more upon his ministers for advice since his shooting. He really thinks he is not as vigorous mentally as formerly and has not quite the same confidence in himself. He suggests another reason for having ministers constantly with him at meetings is that he wants them to share his responsibility in the event of a fight in the Chamber of Deputies. President seemed in good spirits and told many stories. Charles Crane was making farewell visit before leaving for Constantinople and Syria to make report on conditions there for the President.

Mantoux's Notes of a Meeting of the Council of Four

April 16, 1919, 11 a.m.

Wilson. There was a question about whether the commission on navigable waterways had presented us with its conclusions about the Kiel Canal.[1] I have the text of those conclusions, to which we can return shortly.

I have to inform you about a request of Mr. Hoover who, in view of the fact that Hungary is making the victualing of central Europe difficult by retaining some of the railroad rolling stock, wishes to be able to inform the Hungarians that their own victualing will

[1] "Recommendations Regarding the Kiel Canal," c. March 11, 1919, T MS (WP, DLC). Wilson quotes the significant portion of the text near the end of these notes.

depend upon the promptness with which they place the equipment at the disposal of our commission.[2]

This proposal is accepted.

Wilson. I received a memorandum from Dr. Lord,[3] our specialist on Polish and Baltic questions, which recommends the formation of a commission to study on site the questions relating to the constitution and future of Finland, Latvia, Estonia, etc.

Balfour. The present situation in that part of Europe is strange. On the coast of the Baltic, there are German troops who fight against the Bolsheviks and who ask us to help them by supplying them with coal and food and even by permitting them to receive reinforcements from Germany. We consented to allow provisions indispensable to them to pass; but we have refused all reinforcements.

Given the chaos now reigning in those regions, the Germans, by preventing the formation of local armies, and by obliging the countries which they occupy to rely entirely upon their aid against the Bolshevik invasion, work for the permanence of their influence and domination.

It is decided to send the commission of inquiry proposed by Dr. Lord to the Baltic countries.

Clemenceau. I have to propose to you the establishment of a committee of five members to oversee the drafting of the clauses of the treaty and to ensure that they will be complete and arrive on time. This committee would report to us on the 23rd of this month.

Balfour. I fear that this committee would duplicate the work of the Drafting Committee.

Clemenceau. I do not insist.

M. Hymans, Sir Eyre Crowe, Mr. Haskins, and M. Tardieu are introduced.

Wilson (to Hymans). We have invited you to come here in order to prepare with you our final decision about the tracing of the German-Belgian border.

Tardieu. The commission's report concludes in favor of the annexation by Belgium of the territory of Moresnet, left in a state of neutrality between Germany and Belgium by the treaty of 1815, as well as the districts of Malmédy and Eupen.

Clemenceau. Would you like to summarize the main points of these conclusions?

Tardieu. These territories are inhabited by a rather sparse population, almost exclusively Walloon, which was once united to Belgium and has always retained a sympathy for her. Economic in-

---

[2] However, compare HCH to WW, with Enclosure, April 15, 1919 (first letter of that date).
[3] R. H. Lord to J. C. Grew, April 8, 1919.

terest draws it toward the neighboring Belgian population. Moreover, the argument of reparation has merit concerning the forest of Hertogenwald, near Eupen, of which the Belgian portion was destroyed during the war.

The figures for the population of these districts are as follows, respectively: Moresnet, 4,600 inhabitants; Eupen, 26,000; Malmédy, 34,000.

Hymans. I must ask you for a slight modification of our first sketch; the commission has already taken it up. The goal of this modification is twofold. It would permit us in the first place to occupy a dominant position near Aix-la-Chapelle, and in the second place, to have on our territory the entire line of the railroad from Eupen to Malmédy, whose passage across two frontiers would be a nuisance for the population. That modification would affect only 4,000 inhabitants, along with a part of the Hertogenwald.

Balfour. Are these 4,000 Germans or 4,000 Flemings?

Hymans. 4,000 Germans. As for the Flemings, there are none on this side; the nearest populations are Walloon.

Balfour. Did the commission not provide for a plebiscite in those districts or, in any case, an opportunity given to the population to make its feeling known? If that is so, it is not in your interest to claim 4,000 more Germans.

Hymans. We are only doing it because of the railroad, which plays an important role in the life of these peasant people. The line unites Eupen and Malmédy, and it would be very inconvenient, in going from one city to the other, to submit to customs twice.

Balfour. We must carefully consider whether the annexation does not offer more disadvantages than advantages. Is not the population of Eupen largely German?

Hymans. They speak a low German dialect.

Clemenceau. It seems to me that you have no interest to annex too many Germans, if there must be a plebiscite.

Hymans. The question of Eupen is linked to that of the forest of Hertogenwald. The Belgian part of that forest was destroyed by the Germans; we are claiming another part of it as compensation. Now the exploitation of it is impossible without possession of the city of Eupen, where all the roads and means of work are concentrated. Besides, Eupen has the same industry as Verviers, that of wool, and is linked to Verviers by its interests.

Balfour. Do you take into account that the commission declared itself in favor of consulting the inhabitants?

Wilson. The commission proposes that, at the end of six months, a register be opened, where the inhabitants can inscribe their protest or their approval. The result of that consultation will be communicated to the League of Nations, whose decision Belgium accepts in advance.

Hymans. We accept that procedure; overall it is a matter of good administration. Aside from the sentiment of some of the Walloons, we know that their interests attach them to Belgium.

Wilson. Mr. Haskins tells me that the value of the forest of Hertogenwald will be deducted from the reparations, like the value of the mines of the Saar from what is due France. You do not object?

Hymans. No.

Balfour. I notice that the railroad that you wish to see pass only over Belgian territory serves the small city of Montjoie, which would remain in Germany. Is that not an objection which might be made against you?

Hymans. We are not claiming Montjoie, because it is a purely German city, despite its name, which is only a corruption of the original name, Mönchau, "the meadow of the monks."

Tardieu. This railway has only a military value for Germany. It served the camp of Elsenborn, near Malmédy.

Wilson. Does it not seem to you that, despite the small number of people concerned, 4,000, we would in their case risk departing from the principle that we seek to apply to much greater problems? Are we not obliged to have as many scruples, when it is a question of 4,000 Germans or four million?

Hymans. We could emphasize the historical argument and, from this point of view, our claims are very moderate, for we are remaining well within the frontier of 1815. For this entire question, I am relying on your judgment.

Wilson. I am looking at it from the point of view of the sentiment of the population and of the interests of Belgium. If you introduce an element of fermentation into these newly united territories, that will do you no good.

Hymans. I agree with you, and we wish to have as few Boches as possible in Belgium.

Wilson. It is necessary to avoid pointless difficulties and also to avoid seeming to pay little heed to our own principles, just because it affects only a small group of people.

Hymans. That is true; but there must also be logic in drawing a frontier. It is rather absurd to see a railroad which serves two cities cross a foreign territory between those two cities.

Wilson. This problem can be compared to that of the railroad from Danzig to Mlawa, which crosses through German populations, then a rather large group of Polish populations, then again a German territory, in order to enter finally into Poland proper. We are seeking the solution of these difficulties in a convention guaranteeing transit. We do not believe that the fate of a people can be linked to that of a railroad, but that rather it is necessary to resolve the problem of the railroad in such a way as not to violate the rights of peoples.

Hymans. We have sought a logical and practical frontier, and we believe it conforms to the interests of the populations.

Balfour. No great economic interest is involved in that modification.

Hymans. No, except in that which concerns the extension of the forest of Hertogenwald, which would be ceded to us.

As for the small modification which we are asking on the side of Aix-la-Chapelle, it is a very small thing; this is only a matter of a hill which gives us a dominant position in relation to the city.

Wilson. I do not see the necessity of that dominant position, since there will be no German fortification between your frontier and a line fifty kilometers beyond the Rhine.

Mr. Haskins calls my attention to Article 8, which provides modifications of the Dutch-German border. That article would obligate Germany to accept in advance a modification of territory which might ultimately be decided by the League of Nations, in case Holland should demand access to the estuary of the Ems, subject to the agreement of the populations.

Balfour. What is the reason for that article?

Tardieu. The discussion between Holland and Belgium has not yet begun. As we are on the point of opening negotiations with Germany, we must try to open the possibility of later exchanges of territories. In this text, the commission has indicated the principle and, at the same time, fixed the maximum of what could eventually be asked of the Germans.

Wilson. It is dangerous to anticipate negotiations which have not yet begun. Is it our business to rectify the frontier of Holland, whom we neither fought against nor alongside? It would seem to me questionable to insert into our treaty with Germany a clause providing a possible settlement of Dutch-Belgian affairs; we would see ourselves mixed up in something which directly concerns neither Germany nor ourselves.

When M. Hymans first informed us of that question, I told him that we had no means of forcing Holland to cede territories, and that the solution of the difference between Belgium and Holland could be sought only by those two powers. It was asserted, it is true, that it was a matter of revising the treaties of 1839, and that this concerns all the powers which signed these treaties. But on the one hand, all the signatories of the treaties of 1839 are not present, since Holland has not yet participated in the discussion;

on the other hand, newcomers are involved in this discussion, such as the United States, which are forced to take a different point of view. I consider the question of the frontier between Holland and Germany to be foreign to those which we are settling at this time.

Hymans. When we came to explain to the conference our position regarding the treaty of 1839, we had thought that it would not be correct not to make this report before all the Allied and Associated Powers, even though, in fact, that question specifically concerns only the signatories of the treaty of 1839. Holland, invited to discuss with us, replied that she agreed to come and inform the conference of her views. We would like this hearing to take place soon. It will be followed by negotiations between Holland and Belgium for the settlement of questions concerning them. The most important question for our country is that of the navigation of the Scheldt. There lies the future of the port of Antwerp, there lies our military and political security. We are not asking that this problem be resolved by annexations; we are asking that it receive a solution; there can be one other than the territorial solution.

Wilson. The proposal that we are examining at this time envisages compensations for Holland at Germany's expense; we cannot take that route.

Hymans. It must be anticipated that Holland will ask us for compensations; we have the means to furnish them; it does not seem to me unjust to ask them from the enemy, on the condition always that the population therein would not suffer. But the inhabitants of German Gelderland and Friesland are closely related to their neighbors of the Netherlands. After what the Germans did in 1914, after these four years of war and what they have cost our country, I do not believe that it is unjust to ask that compensation from Germany.

Balfour. In my opinion, the only argument which could justify this policy would rest on the sympathy of this region's populations for Holland. Then it would be a question analogous to that of Schleswig. Do we have reason to believe that that sympathy exists?

Tardieu. I will recall that our commission had no mandate concerning the negotiations between Holland and Belgium. Our task was to draft articles which would eventually be helpful in negotiations about which we had no information.

Wilson. The commission did what it had to do. But by providing a plebiscite in German Gelderland and Friesland, you have determined in advance the response of the Dutch. They will say: "What will be our compensation, if these populations refuse to be annexed to Holland?"

Hymans. We could make a conditional arrangement with Holland. But if the proposal that you are examining is discarded, even compensation becomes impossible. We are very anxious to establish a friendly agreement with Holland and to preserve the best of relations with that country. For that, we must not allow irritating questions to remain between Belgium and Holland. A solution must be found for them, and I do not know how we will find it if we cannot dispose of any compensation. The proposed solution seems to me good, because it rests on the real affinity of the populations.

Tardieu. All that the commission sought was to leave the door open to a possible negotiation.

M. Hymans and the experts withdraw.

Wilson. I am afraid of this proposal. To make Germany foot the bill in a transaction which has nothing to do with the war seems to me a bit much.

Balfour. I must say that I also dislike that very much. The attitude of the Belgians in this question has always been a bit brazen. For example, when I told the Dutch Minister: "Be assured that none of us is thinking of taking territory from a neutral power against the will of the inhabitants," M. Hymans told me, "That is true, but you should not have said it to the Dutch Minister."

Wilson. I think we agree to discard these new articles and to keep the commission's text as it was before.

I return to the Kiel Canal, about which here are the conclusions of the commission on navigable waterways. It proposes, on the hypothesis that the Kiel Canal would remain in German territory, to insert into the treaty the following clause, without prejudice to the military guarantees which could be stipulated:

"The Kiel Canal will remain under the sovereignty of Germany, subject to the application to this canal and to its banks of rules which will subsequently be formulated for the regime of international navigable waterways, in particular those rules concerning the freedom of navigation for persons, property, and flags of all nations at peace with Germany, no distinction being made between German persons, property, and flags and those of other states at peace with Germany. That arrangement will apply not only to commercial vessels but also to warships."

I will observe that this clause will place the Kiel Canal under the same regime as the Panama Canal. Concerning the fortifications of the canal, I believe that after examination we have decided not to destroy them. It would be rather delicate for us, who have fortified the Panama Canal, to impose a different condition on the Kiel Canal, which crosses exclusively German territories.

Balfour. Without denying the value of that argument, I will remark that there are also contrary arguments. The Kiel Canal doubles the naval power of Germany, a power which she has, moreover, abused. It could be beneficial to examine this question again.

Clemenceau. I am of that opinion, and I will communicate on this subject with the Ministry of the Navy.

Mantoux, I, 257-64.

A Report by Arthur James Balfour

April 16th, 1919.

At the Meeting of the 'Four' this morning I obtained authority for the Drafting Committee to insert, in the clauses dealing with Responsibility and Punishment, such provisions as they might deem necessary in order to carry out the directions for the establishment of TRIBUNALS, etc., given them some time ago by the Prime Ministers. The character of these additional and supplementary provisions is given in Mr. Hurst's paper of the 14th April.[1]

The President laid before the 'Four' for their approval a suggestion by Mr. Hoover with regard to FOOD for HUNGARY. The Hungarians, it seems, have not been behaving well, either economically or politically, and among other things they are retaining for their own use more than their fair share of the available rolling stock. The essence of Mr. Hoover's proposal was that it should be intimated to the Hungarians that on their behaviour on these and other matters depended the amount of food with which the Allies were prepared to supply them. I have not got a copy of Mr. Hoover's Formula, which was read by the President, but no doubt it could be obtained from his Secretary.

It was proposed by the President, apparently on the suggestion of Mr. Lord, that an Inter-Allied Committee or Commission should be sent to the BALTIC to study conditions in Livonia, Esthonia, Finland, etc. I explained to them what I had already done on my own authority with regard to keeping the German troops in these regions who were fighting the Bolshevists supplied from day to day with coal and provisions; and I also touched upon the anomalous situation of our using German troops more or less as Allies while we were still at war with Germany. I pointed out the dangerous position in which the Allied Powers were being placed through Germany, under our very noses and partly with our help, deliberately building up German influence in the Baltic Provinces. As it appeared to me that the proposed International Commission would be of real assistance to us, both in forming a true judgment of the situation, and in co-ordinating our efforts to deal with it, I gave my assent to its formation. It was understood that the other

Powers would as soon as possible send out their representatives, and that we should do the same unless we deemed that our Officers already on the spot provided us with the necessary personnel.

M. Clemenceau proposed that there should be a Committee of DRAFTSMEN to draw up the Treaty of Peace with Germany, but as he was unable to explain in what its functions would differ from those of the Committee already in existence, the proposal was dropped.

We then discussed the Report of the Commission on GERMAN-BELGIAN FRONTIER questions. M. Hymans was present, as well as the experts of the four Great Powers. M. Hymans suggested certain modifications in the Report of the Commission, varying their line in favour of Belgium. The Conference decided, however, to adhere to the Commission's Report.

The Commission, in obedience to its instructions, had made various suggestions with regard to the possible transfer of certain portions of German territory to HOLLAND, in case compensation should ultimately be required for territory ceded by Holland to Belgium. It was, however, decided after some discussion that this was a scheme difficult, if not impossible, to defend; and it was resolved that the clauses embodying it should *not* be inserted in the Treaty of Peace.

It was felt that no such objection existed with regard to a modification of the frontier line between Germany and Holland which divides the ESTUARY of the EMS. This ought by rights to run along the centre of the channel, but the Germans seemingly had used their superior power to push it towards the Dutch coast, in spite of Dutch protests. But although a rectification of this wrong seemed legitimate, no decision was, I think, come to upon the subject, nor is it easy to see how it could be fitted into the Treaty of Peace with Germany in such a way as to make it a useful pawn in future negotiations between Holland and Belgium.

The Conference accepted the proposals of the Waterways Commission on the subject of the KIEL CANAL, which are, indeed, identical with those that obtain on the Panama Canal. The question of fortification was not, however, dealt with by the Commission on Waterways, and M. Clemenceau expressed a desire to have this further examined by the Naval and Military experts. I understood, but am not quite sure, that he has given the necessary orders.

A.J.B.

T MS (Balfour Papers, Add. MSS 49750, British Library).
    [1] C.J.B. Hurst, memorandum for A. J. Balfour dated April 14, 1919, TS MS (D. Lloyd George Papers, F/147/8/9, House of Lords Record Office). For the later discussion of this matter, see the minutes of the Council of Four printed at May 1, 1919, 11 a.m. and n. 2 thereto.

Hankey's Notes of a Meeting of the Council of Four and the Council of Foreign Ministers[1]

BC-58.   Quai d'Orsay, April 16, 1919, 4 p.m.

I. M. CLEMENCEAU said that the Meeting had been called in order to bring together the Council of Four and the Council of Five. It was proposed that the work done separately should be examined in common. His first request, therefore, was that the Council of Five should report what they had accomplished and what still remained to be done. He asked Baron Sonnino if he would make a statement on this subject.

BARON SONNINO said that on the previous day the Council of Foreign Ministers had before them an agenda of some eleven items. The bulk of these had been remitted to the Drafting Committee, which, he understood, was to meet that day at 5 p.m. The Council of Foreign Ministers was to meet again on Thursday, the 17th instant, to deliberate on the drafts submitted by the Drafting Committee. The Drafting Committee were charged with the task of coordinating proposals made by Great Britain and by the United States. In other words, to reconcile the two drafts suggested.

M. CLEMENCEAU enquired on what subjects the discussion had taken place.

BARON SONNINO said that the subjects dealt with were:

Opium.

Belgium.

The Suez Canal and Egypt, and

An Article requiring from Germany a general renunciation of rights outside Europe, which were to be surrendered to the trusteeship of the Five Powers.

Reference had been made to the Drafting Committee with the object of ensuring that the whole ground was being covered.

PRESIDENT WILSON asked whether the impression that a fuller Conference had been desired to decide these points was erroneous.

BARON SONNINO remarked that another question discussed had been the upkeep of the Army of Occupation in Germany. On this subject, General Weygand had made certain explanations revealing a difference of opinion in calculating the expenses involved in maintaining these forces. Two theses had been put forward and these had been referred to the Council of Four.

MR. LANSING said that his impression was that they had been referred to the Economic Council.

[1] The complete text of these minutes is printed in *PPC*, IV, 476-82. The Council of Foreign Ministers (sometimes referred to as the Council of Five) was established on March 27, 1919, to deal with many of the technical subjects, such as boundaries, before the peace conference. See Maurice P. A. Hankey, *The Supreme Control at the Paris Peace Conference 1919: A Commentary* (London, 1963), pp. 108-10.

M. DUTASTA said that the reference had been to the Council of Four.

MR. BALFOUR observed that, if this was so, the matter should be dealt with.

2. BARON SONNINO said that two methods of calculating the cost had been mentioned. One considered only the actual expenses of the moment, food, billetting, etc. The other considered more general expenses. He was not able to specify exactly what the definition was, as he had not taken an active part in the discussion.

PRESIDENT WILSON said that presumably the latter category included expenses of army administration as separate from the cost of the actual maintenance in the occupied districts.

MR. LANSING remarked that on the 8th March, General Pershing had addressed a written enquiry to Marshal Foch. No answer had been returned. The United States of America were, therefore, somewhat embarrassed in giving an opinion on this subject.

M. CLEMENCEAU said that when the documents relating to the subject were before the Meeting, it would be possible to form an opinion or to remit them to some Committee.

BARON SONNINO said that General Weygand was in a position to state the case fully.

PRESIDENT WILSON observed that if General Weygand were called, he could only re-state the question and not offer a solution. He would suggest that the Military Advisers at Versailles be asked to define what was understood by "cost of military occupation."

BARON SONNINO remarked that there were differences of opinion among military authorities.

PRESIDENT WILSON said that it was desirable to have these differences of opinion laid before the Council.

MR. BALFOUR drew attention to the divergent views held by the various delegates at Spa.

PRESIDENT WILSON asked that a digest of these various views should be prepared and laid before the Council.

MR. BALFOUR agreed that what was required was a brief narrative fitted for civilian understanding. The Council of Four would then be able to reach a decision.

BARON SONNINO observed that the whole discussion had been raised by a question put by the German General von Hammerstein asking for a definition of what was the cost of maintaining a man and a horse in occupied territory.

PRESIDENT WILSON suggested that the correspondence that had taken place at Spa should be referred to the Military Advisers at Versailles in order that a digest should be prepared of the various opinions.

BARON SONNINO said that he did not disagree, but he thought it right to warn the Council that military opinion was divided as to what should be reckoned in the account.

(It was then decided to remit to the Military Advisers of the Supreme War Council at Versailles the drafting of the various points of view regarding the estimation of the cost of upkeep of the Forces of Occupation in Germany.)

BARON SONNINO observed that the cost of upkeep of the Armies of Occupation previous to the signature of Peace was distinct from that of a continuance of occupation after Peace.

PRESIDENT WILSON said that should any occupation subsequent to the signature of Peace be provided for, the same definition and the same interpretation could be adhered to as in the case of occupation previous to Peace.

3. MR. BALFOUR drew attention to Item 6 on the Agenda for the Meeting of Foreign Ministers on the previous day. There were two amendments before the Meeting. One had been adopted, and the other had been referred to the Council of Four. He suggested that the matter be explained by someone who had been present at the Meeting on the previous day.

MR. LANSING said that the difficulty had arisen with regard to exacting from the Germans the disclosure of their secret processes for the manufacture of ingredients for the inhuman conduct of war. As the Allies in another provision had prohibited the manufacture of such things, he regarded the suggested amendment as unnecessary. Further he believed that the disclosure of these secrets would add nothing to the military power of the Allies, who already possessed the secret of making even more deleterious gases than Germany. On the other hand, the revelation of these secrets would be of great economic advantage to Allied industries in that the dye making processes would be revealed at the same time. He believed that this motive very likely was not unconnected with the proposal.

MR. BALFOUR said that the Military Authorities attached great importance to this question. Their opinions were based on military considerations, and they were in no manner concerned with any ambition to obtain industrial secrets. In their memorandum on the subject they took care to state that the dye process was quite divorced from the purpose they had in view. What they required was a purely military piece of knowledge. He did not profess himself to understand or to estimate the value of this knowledge but he was convinced that the Military Experts attached great importance to it.

MR. LANSING said that the American Military Experts did not attach any value to it.

BARON SONNINO pointed out that the British proposal demanded the surrender of all chemical processes out of which gases had been or could be made, and for the production of all substances from which gases or other destructive agencies could be produced. This definition was so wide that it was bound to cover the revelation of the secrets of dye making.

PRESIDENT WILSON said that he believed the framers of the proposal had not this object in view.

M. BALFOUR pointed out that an effective gas mask could not be made without knowledge of the gas which it was to contend with.

PRESIDENT WILSON said that whatever weight might be given to the military opinion on this matter it was certain that many people other than military experts were interested in the revelation of these secrets. There was a further difficulty. However much the Allies might demand the revelation of secrets, they would never be certain that they possessed them all. Twenty five years of University experience had made him well aware that the most difficult secrets to obtain were those of inventors. Many researchers were so suspicious of their fellow men that they contrived to keep their formulae in their own heads for years. In no sphere of life was there so intense a competition as among inventors, each of whom wished to be the first in the field with his invention. This was certainly no less true of Germany than of other countries. He had made objections of a similar character to other proposals, as he thought it was a mistake to exact more than could with certainty be obtained. It could serve no useful purpose to expose oneself to be deceived. The Allies must trust their own inventors to cope with their German rivals. There was a whispering gallery connecting not only the Foreign Offices, but also the laboratories of the world.

BARON SONNINO agreed that the Germans might reveal their second best secrets, but would probably succeed in keeping their best ones.

PRESIDENT WILSON said that they would certainly not reveal their new ones.

MR BALFOUR said that though President Wilson's remarks appealed to him, he felt that he was not in possession of military knowledge and did not feel disposed to take a decision before he had heard what the Military Authorities had to say. He understood that both the French and British military authorities were agreed.

PRESIDENT WILSON remarked that the Military experts were doubtless authorities as to what they wanted to obtain, but that he regarded himself as an authority as to what they would get.

MR BALFOUR said that he would nevertheless like to know what their case was.

M. CLEMENCEAU was also of the opinion that the experts should be consulted.

BARON SONNINO said that in any case the formula suggested was too wide.

PRESIDENT WILSON said that he was always prepared to hear military opinion, but that he wished to register his dissent from the proposal put forward.

M. CLEMENCEAU said that if the military experts were unable to answer the objections that had been raised, he would adopt President Wilson's view.

PRESIDENT WILSON then suggested that this question also should be sent to the Military Advisers at Versailles, in order that they should formulate a military opinion on the subject.

MR BALFOUR agreed, but added that the two categories of objection raised should be communicated to them, namely:

(a) That in all probability the secrets would not be obtained;
(b) That if obtained they would confer an unfair advantage to competing industries in Allied countries.

(The following Resolution was then adopted:

"The Military Advisers of the Supreme War Council at Versailles are requested to state the military advantages of exacting from the Germans the revelation of their secret processes for the manufacture of lethal gases.

It is to be observed:

(a) That no means of supervision exist capable of guaranteeing the veracity of the statements the Germans might make on this subject.

(b) That such a demand for the revelation of German secrets of manufacture might give an unfair advantage to rival industries in Allied countries.)"

(4) M. CLEMENCEAU said he wished to raise the question of the Kiel Canal. A document had been submitted to the Council of Four as being a unanimous report of a Commission on this subject. On examination, the report had proved to be an old report, previously dismissed. It had come up again unamended. He had telephoned to the Secretary of the Naval Committee,[2] who had replied that he knew nothing of it.

PRESIDENT WILSON explained that there had been unanimity on this subject in the Waterways Commission, which had referred the report back to the Council.

M. CLEMENCEAU observed that the question had a military side, on which naval authorities should be called upon to state their views.

[2] He referred to the naval section of the Interallied Military and Naval Committee. See *ibid.*, pp. 87-93. The Editors have been unable to determine the name of the Secretary of the Naval Committee at this time.

PRESIDENT WILSON suggested that the naval authorities might sit in combined session with the Waterways Commission. (It was then decided to refer the question of the Kiel Canal to a Joint Session of Naval Experts, and of the Commission on the International Regime of Ports, Waterways & Railways.)

(5) BARON SONNINO said that two drafts had been proposed on the subject of the validity of Prize Court Decisions. The British draft proposed a clause to be inserted in the treaty stipulating that the validity of Allied Prize Court decisions should not be challenged by the enemy. The American draft proposed, in addition, that the Allies should have the power to invalidate similar decisions taken by German Prize Courts. Both these drafts had been remitted to the Drafting Committee to be fused into one clause. The American draft also contained an additional paragraph, on which he understood the American Delegates did not insist.

MR LANSING remarked that the United States did not insist on the form, but wished the substance to be preserved. The reason for this was that Prize Courts in America had ceased to function at the armistice. Nevertheless, the United States wished to maintain certain seizures made subsequently, and therefore without Prize Court decisions.

(6) M. CLEMENCEAU said that he had another point to submit to the meeting. A resolution had been adopted regarding responsibilities, and it had been considered right that Belgium should undertake the prosecution. This had been agreed, he thought, with the consent of M. Hymans. He had heard since that the President of the Belgian Council[3] had come to Paris, and was prepared to refuse his consent to this proposal. As representative of a monarchical State, he held the view that Belgium could not take the lead in prosecuting a monarch.

PRESIDENT WILSON said that he did not think this obstacle unsurmountable. The essential point was that the Kaiser was to be tried for a high misdemeanour, which might not legally amount to a crime, namely: for violating the neutrality of Belgium. If Belgium refused to be prosecutrix she would not refuse to be witness. He further pointed out that in the draft adopted, Belgium had not been specifically set down as prosecutrix.

M. CLEMENCEAU said that if that was so, he did not wish to press the point any further.

(The Meeting then adjourned.)

T MS (SDR, RG 256, 180.03101/65, DNA).
[3] That is, Léon Delacroix.

Two Letters to Robert Lansing

My dear Lansing: Paris, 16 April, 1919.

I realize the seriousness of the situation disclosed in Doctor Lord's memorandum, and only yesterday requested General Bliss to see Mr. Paderewski and represent the whole matter in the most earnest fashion to him.

Cordially and sincerely yours,   Woodrow Wilson

Connect this with my report to the President of my interview with Mr. Paderewsky.   T.H.B.[1]

TLS (T. H. Bliss Papers, DLC).
[1] T. H. Bliss to WW, April 18, 1919 (second letter of that date).

My dear Lansing: Paris, 16 April, 1919.

Of course I did not use any of the words quoted in the enclosed and they do not indeed purport to be my words.[1] But I did in substance say what is quoted, though the expression "foundations of a Jewish Commonwealth" goes a little further than my idea at the time. All that I meant was to corroborate our expressed acquiescence in the position of the British Government with regard to the future of Palestine.[2]

Faithfully yours,   [Woodrow Wilson]

CCL (WP, DLC).
[1] Wilson was replying to RL to WW, April 13, 1919 (first letter of that date).
[2] On April 18, Lansing, White, House, and Bliss adopted the following minute: "At the meeting of the Commissioners this morning the above memorandum was read regarding the authenticity of a statement attributed to President Wilson respecting his attitude towards the Jewish Commonwealth in Palestine. The Commissioners felt that in view of the rather ambiguous phrasing of the President's reply to an enquiry as to the authenticity of the statement in question it would be safer not to make any official denial thereof." T MS (WP, DLC).

Three Letters to Herbert Clark Hoover

My dear Hoover   [Paris, April 16, 1919]

The Four this morning approved the enclosed plan[1] and I beg that you will proceed with it.   W.W.

ALI (Hoover Archives, CST-H).
[1] See HCH to WW, with Enclosure, April 15, 1919.

My dear Hoover: Paris, 16 April, 1919.

The report[1] you have been kind enough to send me showing what the Americans are doing in Relief, is a most extraordinary and striking document. I did not need to have it proved to me that the tasks were immense and various, but this gives me a most striking conspectus of the whole thing.

Cordially and faithfully yours,   Woodrow Wilson

TLS (Hoover Archives, CSt-H).
¹ See HCH to WW, April 14, 1919, n. 1.

My dear Hoover,   Paris, 16 April, 1919.

I would be very much obliged if you would read the enclosed letter from Secretary Redfield¹ and let me know your judgment as to what reply I should make.

Cordially and faithfully yours,   [Woodrow Wilson]

CCL (WP, DLC).
¹ WCR to WW, April 4, 1919 (third letter of that date), Vol. 56.

From Charles Homer Haskins, with Enclosure

Dear President Wilson,   [Paris] April 16, 1919.

Herewith are the articles relating to the Saar Basin, in the form in which I am sending them today to Major Scott for the final work of the Committee on Redaction.

Very truly yours,   Charles H. Haskins

TLS (WP, DLC).

E N C L O S U R E

THE SAAR BASIN.

A. In order to assure to France compensation for the destruction of the coal-mines in the north of France and as a means of part payment of the amount due for reparation from Germany, the full ownership and exclusive right to the exploitation of the coal-mines in the Saar Basin is ceded to France.

B. In order to assure the rights and welfare of the population and to secure to France the necessary freedom of exploitation of the mines, Germany agrees to the clauses set out in Annex I and II.

C. In order to make in due time permanent provision for the government of the Saar Basin in accordance with the wishes of the population, France and Germany agree to the clauses set out in Annex III.

D. The Saar basin is bounded as follows (see the accompanying map 1:100,000):

On the south and southwest:

By the frontier of France as it is fixed by the present Treaty.

On the northwest and north:

By a line which follows successively the northern administrative limits of the cantons of HILBRINGEN, MERZIG, and HAUSTADT which are incorporated in the aforesaid basin of the Saar, then successively the administrative boundaries separating the Circles (Kreise) of SARRELOUIS, OTTWEILER, and ST. WENDEL from the Circles (Kreise) of MERZIG, TREVES, and the Principality of BIRKENFELD, as far as a point situated about 500 metres north of the village of FURSCHWEILER.

On the northeast and east:

By a line which, starting from the last point indicated above, passes east of FURSCHWEILER, west of ROSCHBERG, east of hills 418, 329 (south of ROSCHBERG), west of LEITERSWEILER, northeast of hill 464, and from this last point follows the line of the crest until it joins, at a distance of about 1000 metres to the south, the administrative boundary of the Circle (Kreis) of KUSEL;

It then follows the above indicated boundary of the Circle (Kreis) of KUSEL to the point where it meets the boundary of the Circle (Kreis) of HOMBURG, then follows this boundary toward the south-southeast to a point situated 1000 metres west of DUNZWEILER;

From this last point it passes over the summits of hill 424 (1000 metres southeast of DUNZWEILER), hill 363 (FUCHSBERG), hill 322 (southwest of WALDMOHR), then east of JÄGERSBURG and ERBACH, then including HOMBURG it passes over the summits of hills 361 (two and one-half kilometers northeast of that town), 342 (two kilometers southeast of that town), 357 (SCHREINERSBERG), 356, 350 (two kilometers southeast of SCHWARZENBACH), passes then east of EINÖD southeast of hills 322 and 333, (two kilometers east of WEBENHEIM and MIMBACH), over the summits of hills 363 (two and one-half kilometers southeast of BLICKWEILER), and 396 (GR. KOHLLENBERG); from this point it follows the eastern boundary of the HOCHWALD (west of BUCKWEILER) to the southern point of the wood, then turns toward the east passing south of NEU ALTHEIM, over the summit of hill 304 (1500 metres south of ALTHEIM), passes one kilometer north of BRENSCHELBACH, north of KOHLENBERG (hill 325), and joins the French frontier at the elbow which it forms one kilometer south of HORNBACH.

ANNEX I.

1. From the date of the signing of the present Treaty all the deposits of mineral substances which under German law in force 11 November, 1918 (excepting provisions thereof which are war measures only) are classified under the heading of mines, and

which are situated within the Saar Basin as it is defined below, belong to the French State, which will have the perpetual right of working them or of not working them, or of transferring to a third party the right of working them, without receiving any previous authorization or fulfilling any formalities.

Questions arising respecting the rights of the French State under the preceding provision will be decided according to the German mining law in force 11 November 1918, excepting provisions thereof which are war measures only.

2. The right of ownership of the French State created by Article 1 applies not only to the deposits which are free and for which concessions have not yet been granted, but also to the deposits for which concessions have already been made, whether they belong to Germany, to the Prussian State, to the Bavarian State, to other corporations or to individuals, whether they have been worked or not, that is to say, to all deposits for the working of which there has already been created a right distinct from the right of the owners of the surface of the soil.

The German State will have to indemnify the Prussian State and the Bavarian State, as well as private proprietors of the said mines, the ownership of which is hereby transferred to the French State.

3. As far as concerns the mines which are being worked, the transference to the French State of the ownership of the mines resulting from the preceding clauses applies not only to the ownership of the mines but also to that of their subsidiaries and accessories, that is to say, to all their plant and equipment as well as on as below the surface, in particular their extracting machinery, their plants for transforming coal into electric power, coke, and by-products, their work-shops, means of communication, electric lines, water catchment areas, reservoirs and conduits, land, buildings such as offices, employees' and workmen's dwellings, schools and hospitals, their stocks and supplies, their archives and plans, and in general everything which those who own or exploit the mines possess or enjoy for the purpose of exploiting the mines and their subsidiaries and accessories.

The transference applies moreover to the debts owing for products which shall have been delivered subsequently to the signature of the present Treaty and previously to the entry into possession on the part of the French State; to deposits of money made by customers, whose rights therein the French Government will respect; and to the actuarial reserves of pension rights which have been acquired or are in course of being acquired by the employees of the mines and their subsidiaries and accessories, which rights (including pensions for old age and for disability) the French Government takes over the obligation to maintain inviolate as of the date of transfer of the mines.

4. The value of the property thus ceded to France shall be credited as a part payment of the amount due for reparation from Germany. This value shall be determined by the Reparation Commission.

5. No tariff shall be established on the German railways and canals which may directly or indirectly discriminate to the prejudice of the transport of persons and products of the mines and their subsidiaries and accessories or of the material necessary to their working. Such transportation shall enjoy all the rights and privileges which any international railway convention may guarantee to similar products of French origin.

The French State shall have the right to demand the establishment of workmen's trains in the German territory adjacent to the Saar Basin on such sections of the lines and according to such timetables as it shall judge necessary for the workmen and employees of the mines, under the most favorable conditions established by the German tariff for similar transportation.

6. No obstacle shall be placed in the way of such improvements of railways or waterways as the French Government shall judge necessary to assure the clearing and the transportation of the products of the mines, their subsidiaries and accessories, such as double trackage, enlargements of stations, construction of railway yards. The distribution of expense in such case will be subject to arbitration. There shall also be provided by the said railways within a reasonable time the personnel and the equipment necessary to insure the clearing and the transportation of these products. The distribution of expense in such case will be subject to arbitration.

7. The payment for damage caused to real estate by the working of the mines, their subsidiaries and accessories, shall be made in accordance with the German mining laws and regulations in force 11 November, 1918, excepting provisions thereof which are war measures only. The French State shall have the right in every case to proceed under such laws and regulations with a view to the acquisition of such land as it may judge necessary for the exploitation of the mines and their subsidiaries and accessories. Thus it may in particular establish means of communication which it shall judge necessary, such as railroads, canals, highways, electric lines and telephone connections. Under the same conditions it may exploit freely and without any restrictions the means of communication of which it may become the owner, particularly those connecting the mines and their subsidiaries and accessories with the means of communication situated in France.

8. Every person whom the French State shall put in its place as

regards the whole or a part of its rights to the exploitation of the mines, their subsidiaries and accessories, shall have the benefit of the rights and privileges provided in the present Treaty.

9. The mines and other real estate which become the property of the French State may never be made the subject of measures of forfeiture, forced sale, expropriation, or requisition, nor of any other measure affecting the right of property.

The personnel and the plant and material associated with the exploitation of these mines, their accessories and subsidiaries, as well as the product extracted from the mines or manufactured in their accessories and subsidiaries, may never be made the subject of any measures of requisition.

10. The regime of exploitation established by German laws and regulations in force 11 November, 1918, excepting provisions thereof which are war measures only, is maintained as far as the French State is concerned with regard to the exploitation of the mines, their subsidiaries and accessories. No modification of this regime, except in accordance with the general labor provisions adopted by the League of Nations, shall be made without previous consultation with the French State.

The rights of workmen shall be maintained as the same are established by German law in force 11 November, 1918, excepting provisions thereof which are war measures only.

The wishes of the local labor organizations and the principles approved by the League of Nations with respect to labor shall be taken into consideration by the Commission provided in Annex II in taking any further measures affecting the conditions and hours of labor for men, women and children.

No impediments of any kind shall be placed in the way of the introduction or employment in the mines, their subsidiaries and accessories, of French or of foreign labor.

The French employees and workmen in the mines, their subsidiaries and accessories, shall have the right to belong to French labor unions.

11. The amount contributed by the mines, their subsidiaries and accessories, whether to the local budget of the Saar Basin or to any Commune, by way of taxes shall be determined by the Commission provided for in Annex II, taking into fair consideration the ratio of the value of the mines to the total taxable wealth of the Basin.

12. The French State shall always have the right of organizing as an incident of its ownership of the mines primary or technical schools for its employees or their children and of causing instruction therein to be given in the French language in accordance with such programmes and by such teachers as it may select.

13. The French Government agrees to provide for the maintenance of the proportion existing in 1913 between the aggregate production of coal in the Saar Basin and the amount of coal consumed in the Basin for industrial and domestic purposes.

But otherwise the French Government shall enjoy complete liberty with respect to distribution, dispatch, and sale prices of the products of the mines, their subsidiaries, and accessories.

14. The Saar Basin shall form part of the French customs system.

No export tax shall be imposed by France upon either the metallurgical products or the coal of the Basin consigned to Germany, nor by Germany upon German exports for the use of the industries of the Basin.

Products of the Basin shall be free of all customs duties in transit on German territory, and, similarly, German products shall be free of all customs in transit on the territory of the Basin.

Products of the Basin imported into Germany shall be free of import duties for a period of five years from the date hereof.

For a like period, articles imported from Germany into the Basin for local use or consumption shall be free of import duties.

15. No prohibition or restriction shall be imposed upon the circulation of French money in the Saar Basin, and the French Government shall have the right to use French money in all purchases, payments, and contracts connected with the exploitation of the mines, their subsidiaries and accessories.

ANNEX II.

1. Germany renounces in favor of the League of Nations as trustee all her rights of government over the territory of the Saar Basin, as defined in Article D.

2. The League of Nations shall appoint a Commission to govern the district.

3. The Commission shall consist of five members chosen by the Council of the League of Nations, of whom one shall be a citizen of France, one a native inhabitant of the Basin of the Saar not a citizen of France, and the others chosen from three countries other than France or Germany. The members of the Commission shall be appointed for one year and may be re-appointed; they can be removed and replaced by the Council of the League of Nations.

4. The Chairman of the Commission shall be appointed for one year from its members by the Council of the League of Nations; he can be re-appointed; he will be the executive of the Commission.

5. The Commission shall have all those powers of government hitherto belonging to Germany, Prussia, or Bavaria, including the appointment and dismissal of all functionaries and the creation of

such administrative or respresentative bodies as it deems necessary. Its decisions shall be taken by a majority vote.

6. The Commission shall have full control of the adminstration and operation of railroads and canals.

The Commission shall have the right of user of all property in the Basin belonging to the Imperial Government, or the Government of any German State, other than mines, their subsidiaries and dependencies.

7. The territory shall be governed subject to the provisions hereof in conformity with the existing laws; amendments necessary, whether for general reasons or for bringing the said laws into accord with the said provisions, shall be decided and put into effect by the Commission after consultation with the local representatives in such a manner as the Commission shall determine. No law or amendment thereto can affect or limit the provisions hereof.

8. The local civil and criminal courts shall continue. A Civil and Criminal Court will be appointed by the Commission to judge appeals from the decisions of the said local courts and to decide all matters which cannot be determined by the local courts. The Commission will determine the competence of this last named jurisdiction.

9. The Commission will alone have the power of levying taxes in the Basin.

These taxes will be exclusively applied to the local needs of the Basin.

The present fiscal system will be maintained as far as possible. No new tax will be imposed without consulting the elected representatives.

10. The inhabitants will retain their present nationality, but no hindrance shall be placed in the way of those who wish to acquire a different nationality. They will preserve, under the control of the Commission, their local assemblies, their religious liberties, their schools, and their language. The right of voting for local assemblies will belong to every inhabitant above the age of twenty years, without distinction of sex. On the other hand, there will be no right of voting for any assembly other than local assemblies.

11. Any of the inhabitants who may desire to leave the territory of the Saar Basin may retain their rights in real property with full power of sale and equitable disposition without restriction, and may remove their personal property free of export or other charges or restrictions of any kind.

12. There will be no compulsory military service, or voluntary recruiting, or fortifications. A local gendarmerie for the maintenance of order may alone be established.

13. The Commission shall have the power to arrange, under conditions which it shall determine, for the protection abroad of the interests of the inhabitants of the territory.

14. The salaries of the members of the Commission shall be fixed by the Council of the League of Nations and shall be paid by the Administration of the Saar Basin.

15. The Commission shall have power to decide all questions which may arise regarding the interpretation of these articles.

France and Germany agree that any dispute whatsoever, not only arising under these articles but any dispute the decision of which may be affected by the terms of these articles, shall be referred to the said Commission for final hearing and determination, and they agree to carry into effect in full good faith any award or decision which the said Commission or a majority thereof shall make.

ANNEX III.

1. At the termination of a period of fifteen years, there shall be held under the control of the Commission a plebiscite in the above defined territory. The vote shall be held by communes (Gemeinden) or districts. In the vote there shall be no discrimination on the ground of sex. None shall be admitted to vote except inhabitants resident in the territory at the time of the signing of the present peace. The regulation, method and date of the vote shall be fixed by the Council of the League of Nations in such a way as to secure the liberty and secrecy of the vote. The vote shall be upon the three following alternatives: the maintenance of the regime established by the present Treaty; union with France; union with Germany.

2. The League of Nations shall decide on the sovereignty of the territory taking into account the wishes of the inhabitants thus expressed.

a. If the vote results (for the whole or part of the territory) in the maintenance of the regime established by the present Treaty, Germany agrees to make such renunciation in favor of the League of Nations as the latter shall deem necessary. The League of Nations will take appropriate steps to adapt the new regime to the permanent interest of the Basin and to the general welfare;

b. If the vote results (for the whole or part of the territory) in favor of union with France, Germany agrees to cede to France in accordance with the decision of the League of Nations all that territory covered by this decision;

c. If the vote results (for the whole or part of the territory) in favor of union with Germany, the League of Nations will cause the German Government to be re-established in so much of the territory as the League shall decide.

3. On such of the said territory as shall remain German under the result of the decision of the League of Nations, all rights of the Government of France under these articles in this territory shall be taken over as a whole by Germany at a price payable in gold which shall be determined by three appraisers or a majority of them; one of these shall be appointed by Germany, one by France, and one, who shall be neither a German nor a French citizen, by the Council of the League of Nations.

4. The price so fixed by the experts shall be payable within six months after the determination thereof, and unless the said price so fixed shall be then paid by Germany to the Government of France, the territory which would otherwise remain German shall thereafter be occupied and administered by France as an integral portion of French territory.

5. If the ownership of the mines, or a part thereof, passes to Germany, it is understood that France or French nationals will have a just claim to the use of such coal of the Saar Basin as their industrial and domestic needs will be found at that time to require. An equitable arrangement regarding amounts, time of contract, and prices will be fixed in due time by the Council of the League of Nations.

6. The provisions of the three foregoing articles shall be subject to any agreement which may have been reached between France and Germany before the time fixed for the payment above-mentioned with regard to the rights and property of France.

7. Except as provided in Article 2a of Annex III, as soon after the plebiscite as possible the League of Nations shall take all necessary steps for bringing to an end all provisions for a special regime in the territory in question, having due regard to personal and property rights.

T MS (WP, DLC).

From Tasker Howard Bliss

My dear Mr. President: Paris, April 16, 1919.

On April 3, 1919, the Council of Four approved a proposal of the American Commission for the appointment of an armistice commission, to be convened in this city and to be composed of one civil and one military member from each of the four Great Powers represented on that Council, for the preparation of the terms of an armistice between the Polish and the Ukrainian forces. The American representatives, Dr. Isaiah Bowman and Colonel S. D. Embick,[1] have been designated, but the representatives of the other Powers have not been designated.

The Ukrainian authorities have heretofore indicated their willingness to consent to a suspension of arms pending the negotiation of an armistice, and from the accompanying copy of a telegram signed "Coolidge"[2] it appears that the Polish Government also is now willing to consent to such a suspension. The representatives in Paris of both these governments have expressed informally their readiness to appear before an armistice commission of the character above mentioned.

In view of these facts and of the great desirability of effecting a cessation of hostilities between the Polish and Ukrainian forces at the earliest practicable date, it is recommended that the attention of the Council of Four be called to the importance of the immediate designation and assembly of the personnel of this commission.

Sincerely yours,   Tasker H. Bliss.

TLS (T. H. Bliss Papers, DLC).
[1] Col. Stanley Dunbar Embick, U.S.A., formerly chief of staff of the American section of the Supreme War Council, at this time a technical adviser on military questions in the A.C.N.P.
[2] A. C. Coolidge to Ammission, for Gen. F. J. Kernan, April 11, 1919, TC telegram (WP, DLC).

From Henry White

PERSONAL AND CONFIDENTIAL

Dear Mr. President: Paris 16 April 1919

During my interview this morning with the representatives of the Press, they asked me to give them particulars in respect to "the guarantee" which they said they understood to have been given by you, or by this Delegation, to the effect that the United States would in future come to the immediate assistance of France in the event of her being invaded by Germany.

I asked them, in reply, to explain the nature of the guarantee to which they were referring, and they replied that they had "ascertained" or "had been given to understand," in authoritative quarters, that our French friends have been assured by you that a provision to the foregoing effect is to be inserted in the Treaty of Peace. I replied, of course, that I had heard nothing of any such proposal in respect to the Treaty and did not believe that a clause such as they had suggested is to be inserted therein.

The Press representatives thereupon inquired whether it might not have been possible for you to give, in the Council of Four, an assurance to that effect; to which I answered that, not being of the

Council of Four, I am not usually made aware of the details of the discussions which take place there. They then asked me whether, in my opinion, an assurance to the foregoing effect given by you in the Council of Four to Mr. Clemenceau, could be binding upon the United States, to which I could only reply in the negative; with the further statement that any agreement or promise such as they suggested, whether made in the Council of Four or elsewhere, would, in order to be binding upon the United States, have to be approved by the Senate.

My object in bringing the matter to your attention is that I am afraid telegrams are being—or may even have been last night— sent to our home newspapers on this subject.[1] If so, I fear that there will be a good deal of adverse comment, to put it mildly, both on the part of advocates of the Covenant of the League of Nations, who will feel that the latter is materially weakened by such a guarantee to France; and by those who object to our entering into any so-called "entangling alliances"; to say nothing of objectors on general principles to anything you may do; so that it may be perhaps well for you to be considering whether a situation may not shortly arise in which you may find it desirable to make a statement in the matter, and, if so, what form it shall assume.

If I may venture to make a suggestion in a matter which pertains to the Administration rather than to the Peace Conference and is consequently not within my province, I would say that I cannot but feel, if your promise to the French can be carried out in the form of a separate arrangement between this country and ourselves, leaving the British to negotiate their own agreement with France to the same effect, that much less opposition is likely to be encountered at home than if there should be a joint Treaty of Alliance to which Great Britain is a party.

Yours very sincerely,   Henry White

TLS (WP, DLC).
[1] Herbert Bayard Swope, in a front-page article in the New York *World*, April 17, 1919, declared that the United States had agreed to a "defensive alliance" in which it and Great Britain would come to the aid of France if the latter should be attacked by Germany. "According to the explanation I have received," he wrote, "the American agreement provides that Congress is to be asked to come to the aid of France in the event of an attack by Germany by declaring a state of war to exist."

Richard V. Oulahan, in a lengthy but very cautiously worded article in the *New York Times*, April 19, 1919, suggested that Wilson himself had given "somewhat definite assurances to Premier Clemenceau." "Reports that bear the stamp of reliability," he said, "credit the President with having agreed to enter into an arrangement with France whereby aggressive action on Germany's part will cause the President to lay the situation before Congress, with a recommendation that Germany's course shall be considered a casus belli, calling for the employment of the land and naval forces of the United States to resist a Teutonic invasion of French territory." Oulahan suggested that it was possible that this agreement might be embodied in a treaty between or among France, the United States, and perhaps Great Britain which would oblige the President to lay the matter before Congress in the event of German aggression against France. He stressed that the President was reported to have repeatedly told French leaders that only Congress had the power to declare war.

In a lead article in the New York *Sun*, April 19, 1919, Laurence Hills was quite emphatic about the "alliance." "There can be no doubt," he declared, "that President Wilson has entered into some kind of agreement with France to guarantee her protection in case she should be attacked again, and that his plan now is to submit this agreement to the American Senate as a separate instrument, entirely outside of the League of Nations covenant, and requiring, therefore, separate approval by the Senate to make it binding." "The new agreement," he continued, "is in the nature of an alliance between the United States and Great Britain, each pledging itself to go to the support of France, but not to the aid of each other, as in the old Triple Alliance." Hills argued that this proposed alliance was not only a radical departure from the traditional American stand against entangling alliances but also revealed Wilson's own "lack of faith" in the League of Nations which he himself had created.

A Translation of a Letter from Nikola Pašić to Georges Clemenceau[1]

Mr. President,   Paris April 16, 1919.

Our Delegation has had the honor of receiving a letter from Your Excellency, dated the 3rd of March, advising it that the Royal Italian Delegation does not accept our offer to settle the problem of our future joint frontier through the arbitration of President Wilson.

In regretting this decision, which according to our view eliminates the best way of settling this delicate question in dispute, and always animated by the desire of finding a friendly course so as to assure the best results in the future, we take the liberty of begging you, Mr. President, to inform the Conference of Peace that in case they should adopt this method of settlement we are ready to agree that the problem of our frontiers with Italy be settled by means of a direct consultation of the interested populations. We believe that we see in this method of settlement a method particularly suitable to settle differences between friendly countries and governments, as we have already declared in the sitting of the Conference of the 31st of January in connecton with the delimitation with Roumania in the Banat.

We trust, Mr. President, that our suggestion will receive the favorable consideration of the Council over which you preside with so much distinction, because it is of such a nature as to assure the harmony of the Allies before the world, a precious guarantee of our mutual relations in the future. We trust equally that the Royal Government of Italy will accept this method of settlement, as it represents the continuation of its own political traditions.

Please accept, Mr. President, the assurances of my very high consideration.   Nik. P. Pachitch

T MS (WP, DLC).
[1] Pašić sent a copy of his original letter to Clemenceau (in French) to Wilson in N. Pašić to WW, April 16, 1919, TLS (WP, DLC).

From Francis Patrick Walsh and Others

Dear Mr. President: Paris, France, April 16, 1919.

We beg to advise you that in pursuance of the commission given us by the Irish Race Convention held in the City of Philadelphia on February 22, 1919,[1] we were, among other things, instructed to obtain, if possible, for the delegates selected by the people of Ireland, a hearing at the Peace Conference.

The delegates so selected are Messrs. Eamonn DeValera, Arthur Griffith and Count Plunkett.[2]

If these gentlemen were furnished safe conduct to Paris so that they might present their case, we feel that our mission would be, in the main, if not entirely, accomplished.

May we, therefore, ask you to obtain from Mr. Lloyd George, or whomsoever may be entrusted with the specific details of such matters by the English Government, safe conduct for Messrs. DeValera, Griffith and Plunkett from Dublin to Paris.

If you could see your way clear to do this, we feel sure that it would meet with the grateful appreciation of many millions of our fellow-citizens, would certainly facilitate the object of our mission, and place us under additional great and lasting obligation to you.

It would afford us the utmost pleasure to call upon you in person in order that we might pay our respects as well as make a brief suggestion as to the subject-matter of this letter, provided such course meets with your approval and convenience.

With assurances of our continued high consideration and esteem, as always,

Sincerely yours,   Frank P Walsh Chairman.
Edward F Dunne[3]
Michael J. Ryan[4]

TLS (WP, DLC).
    [1] For further details, see G. Creel to WW, March 31, 1919, n. 1, Vol. 56.
    [2] Eamon de Valera, participant in the Easter Rising of 1916, at this time president of Sinn Fein and President of the Dail Eireann (constituent assembly) of Ireland; Arthur Griffith, long active as an Irish nationalist journalist and politician, at this time a vice-president of Sinn Fein and Minister of Home Affairs under the Dail Eireann; and George Noble, Count Plunkett, Minister for Foreign Affairs under the Dail Eireann.
    [3] Edward Fitzsimons Dunne, Mayor of Chicago, 1905-1907; Governor of Illinois, 1913-1917.
    [4] City Solicitor of Philadelphia, 1911-1916; Public Service Commissioner of Pennsylvania, 1916-1919.

To Roland Sletor Morris

[Paris] April 16, 1919.

1644. Department's 1108 March 13, 1919, 6 PM.[1] The President directs that the following telegram be sent from him to Ambassador Morris as personal and confidential. "I was much gratified and relieved that the negotiations relative to the operating organization of the Siberian Railway were, last month, brought by you to a successful conclusion. I appreciate the high importance as well as the extreme delicacy of the issues involved, and the solution is one which could have been achieved only by conspicuous ability and tact such as you have shown." 1644.   Ammission

T telegram (WP, DLC).
[1] FLP to RL and V. C. McCormick, March 13, 1919, T telegram (SDR, RG 256, 861.77/83, DNA). In this telegram, Polk reported that Morris had gone to Vladivostok in early February and had there organized an inter-Allied committee to supervise all the operations of the Trans-Siberian Railway. Polk also said that Leonid Aleksandrovich Ustrugov, Minister of Communications in the Omsk (Kolchak) government, had been unanimously elected chairman of the new committee. Polk added: "His appointment seems to satisfy all factions. The military board, which is concerned solely with transportation of troops, and might desire supplies, is not yet finally organized, but no difficulties are anticipated in regard to it."

Robert Lansing and Vance Criswell McCormick to Frank Lyon Polk

[Paris] 16th April 1919.

1648. URGENT CONFIDENTIAL
From Lansing and McCormick.

Department's 1232, March 28th, 1 p.m.,[1] Department's 1533, April 11, 3 p.m. and Department's 1345, March 28th, 5 p.m.[2] In reply to the specific questions presented by Department's 1232:

1. The President desires, provided the Treasury Department sees no objection, that Russian assets of cash, railway supplies, clothing, etc., be protected and used for assistance to Russia provided they can be properly applied to some definite constructive plan which does not imply any present recognition of or obvious assistance to any Russian Government;

2. The President desires Russian diplomatic and consular officials to continue to function in this country to the extent that such functioning is materially useful in connection with the liquidation and utilization in accordance with number one of Russian assets in the United States;

3. It is desired that the Department lend its good offices to assist in safeguarding Russian assets provided a plan for their utilization in accordance with number one is agreed upon.

We have been analyzing the figures given by you showing the status of Russian affairs in the United States and have conferred with Bakhmeteff in regard to the same. It appears that provided arrangements can be made to postpone collection of the principal of maturing obligations, approximately six million dollars will suffice to pay maturing interest charges for the next twelve months. Russian cash assets will thus more than suffice to provide this and to care for the current expenses of essential Russian officials in the United States. There would thus be left a balance of approximately $25,000,000 worth of supplies about half of which comprise railway material. We suggest that these assets be turned over to the United States to furnish the $20,000,000 fund immediately required for the operation of the Siberian Railway as set out in Department's 1345. These supplies in so far as suitable could be delivered in kind, and to the extent not suitable could be sold and the proceeds utilized. This plan would have the great advantage of deferring the proposed inter-allied financing of the railway at least until the detailed and more permanent plan of operation can be developed as contemplated by Department's 1345. Securities or obligations of the railway could be issued in exchange for the advances thus made and such securities or obligations might be held by officials of the United States and ultimately might be delivered to a Russian government, should one be recognized or, possibly, utilized in connection with a settlement of Russian obligations maturing in the United States. The plan thus seems advantageous in that—

1. It applies Russian assets in the United States to a constructive plan without political implications;

2. It defers Japanese financial and consequent political participation in the control of the Siberian railway;

3. It postpones the necessity of United States participation in financing the railway at a time when it might be difficult to secure an appropriation;

4. It tends to preserve the integrity and independence of the Trans-Siberian Railway for the benefit of such Russian government as ultimately may be recognized.

We feel that the advantages of this plan justify the United States in deferring collection of the principal of its maturing obligations and using its influence to have the National City Bank and other creditors refrain from attempting by legal processes to collect the principal of their maturing obligations. Unless this is done we fear that all Russian assets in the United States will become the subject of legal proceedings which will tie them up for several years and prevent any possibility of their being utilized during this period when Russia is in so critical a situation.

We have suggested this plan in broad outlines to Bakhmeteff who is, we believe, disposed to accept it.

This entire cable has been shown to and approved by the President. 1648.   Ammission

T telegram (WP, DLC).
  [1] See FLP to RL and V. C. McCormick, March 21 (not 28), 1919, Vol. 56.
  [2] FLP to RL and V. C. McCormick, April 11, 1919, T telegram (SDR, RG 256, 701.61/3, DNA), and W. Phillips to RL and V. C. McCormick, March 28, 1919, T telegram (SDR, RG 256, 861.77/89, DNA). Polk's brief telegram of April 11 stressed that he could take no effective action in regard to Russian assets and liabilities until he had answers to his questions of March 21 and pointed out that $11,000,000 of Russian Treasury notes with interest would become payable on May 1. William Phillips, in his telegram of March 28, stated that $20,000,000 was immediately necessary for the continued operation of the Trans-Siberian Railway and outlined various ways in which either the Allied governments or the Kolchak regime in Omsk might make this sum available. He requested that he be informed as soon as possible how much the United States would contribute to the operation fund and from what source the United States quota should be derived.

To Brand Whitlock

My dear Mr. Whitlock: Paris, 16 April, 1919.

Pray pardon a busy man for not having replied sooner to your letter of April 1st[1] about the medal which was presented one afternoon by a crowd bearing an American flag which marched to the Legation and came to you explaining that they were the men and women who had worked in the Comité National during the war in the clothing department. It touches me very much that incidents of this sort should occur, and I hope you will have an opportunity of sending word to these working people how deeply I appreciate their action and how thoroughly my heart is with them.

In unavoidable haste,

                          Faithfully yours,   [Woodrow Wilson]

CCL (WP, DLC).
  [1] B. Whitlock to GFC, April 1, 1919, Vol. 56.

To Henry Pomeroy Davison

My dear Mr. Davison: Paris, 16 April, 1919.

Of course you are justified in sending me your letter of April 13th, and I recognize the pressing importance of the matter. If Secretary Lane is willing to accept the duties and responsibilities you suggest for him, I am of course entirely willing that he should do so. When asked about this the other day, I replied that I did not want to indicate my assent until I had received some intimation from him that he would wish to accept the connection you are proposing with the Red Cross, because he has been one of the most valued members of my Cabinet, and I would not for the world create even a momentary impression on his mind that I was cooperating in anything that would take him out of the Cabinet. But of course if he desires to accept the position, for which he is undoubtedly most highly qualified, I shall not stand in his way. I have too high an appreciation of the work that lies ahead of the Red Cross and perceive too completely of what great service he can be in that work.   Cordially and sincerely yours,   [Woodrow Wilson]

CCL (WP, DLC).

To Vance Criswell McCormick, with Enclosure

My dear McCormick: Paris, 16 April, 1919.

I believe you know how heartily I concur in the judgment of the enclosed message from Burleson, and I am sure you do too. Unless you think we cannot honorably do so, I shall authorize the complete termination of the cable censorship. In any case I shall authorize it to be lifted on all cables to Latin-America. Do you not think I would be justified in this?

Cordially and faithfully yours,   Woodrow Wilson

TLS (V. C. McCormick Papers, CtY).

E N C L O S U R E

Washington April 10 1919.

Commercial bodies and business men are bitterly resenting the continuance of the cable censorship stop. They insist that this practice is seriously hampering our industries and is unreasonable and indefensible stop. They cannot understand why it is necessary in order to maintain the blockade of Germany that censorship of cables to Cuba Central and South America by United States should be continued[.] In my opinion it is imperative that the United States cable censorship should be terminated at once if it is possible to do so.   Burleson

T telegram (V. C. McCormick Papers, CtY).

To William Cox Redfield

Paris, 16 April, 1919.

The following for Redfield. QUOTE. In the controversy between the Industrial Board and the Railway Administration with regard to steel and other prices my own judgment inclines to the side of the position of the Railway Administration. I therefore request that the Industrial Board undertake a very serious review and reconsideration of the whole question and that the most serious attempt be made to establish a common view and modus vivendi with the Railway Administration. UNQUOTE. Please show copy of this to Hines as at my request.   Woodrow Wilson.

T telegram (WP, DLC).

To Edward Field Goltra

My dear Mr. Goltra: Paris, 16 April, 1919.

It was certainly kind of you to remember your promise to tell me what was happening to Senator Reed in Missouri.[1] You are certainly taking the right course. I was confident from the first that the people in Missouri would not sustain him in the extraordinary course he is taking.

In great haste, with warm regards,
                    Faithfully yours,   [Woodrow Wilson]

CCL (WP, DLC).
[1] See E. F. Goltra to WW, April 5, 1919.

To William Harrison Short

My dear Mr. Short: Paris, 16 April, 1919.

It was certainly most thoughtful of you to send me your letter of March 29th with its enclosure.[1] I am greatly heartened by the report which it contains. I believe that the prospects for the League brighten with every examination of the proposed Covenant itself, and with every debate that occurs concerning it.
                    Sincerely yours,   [Woodrow Wilson]

CCL (WP, DLC).
[1] W. H. Short to WW, March 29, 1919, Vol. 56.

From Gilbert Monell Hitchcock

                    Washington April 16, 1919.

1603. For the President from Senator Hitchcock.
"Congratulations on great success in improving and perfecting constitution of League of Nations.[1] You have done more than seemed possible. Sentiment for League has been much strengthened, op-

position evidently diminished if not defeated. My audiences in many cities have been sympathetic and enthusiastic."

Polk   Acting

T telegram (WP, DLC).
¹ The process of amending the draft Covenant of the League of Nations had been extensively reported in the American press. The amendment regarding the Monroe Doctrine had received the most attention, but others had been noted as well. See, for example, the *New York Times*, March 28 and April 2, 4, 11, and 12, 1919.

The *Providence News* to Joseph Patrick Tumulty

Providence, R. I., April 16, 1918 [1919].

Kindly transmit the following by cable to the President,

Quote

President Woodrow Wilson,
  Paris, France.

We know that you have larger problems in hand, but telephone strike in New England¹ threatens to produce a general strike in all industries. This deserves your personal attention as one of the great questions of the day in the United States. Postmaster General Burleson does not seem to realize the tendency of this movement. Can you not appoint a commission of three citizens in whom the people will have confidence to settle the case.

> A. E. Hohler,² President, Rhode Island State Federation of Labor;
> Ernest E. Elmer, L. U. 516, International Brotherhood of Electrical Workers, President.
> Edgar R. Gill, President, Local Union No. 258, I.B.E.W.
> Henry Eatough, President, Rhode Island Textile Council;
> James H. Coleman, Business Agent, Street Car Men Union.

UNQUOTE.

The PROVIDENCE NEWS is requested by these Rhode Island labor leaders to forward their message and urge that prompt reply be sent to PROVIDENCE NEWS.

The PROVIDENCE NEWS.

T telegram (WP, DLC).
¹ Telephone operators in Maine, New Hampshire, Vermont, Massachusetts, and Rhode Island had gone on strike against the New England Telephone and Telegraph Co. and the Providence Telephone Co. at 7 a.m. on April 15. They sought a wage increase and the opportunity to bargain directly with the companies involved rather than with the

Post Office Department, which still controlled the telephone system as a war emergency measure. The operators charged that Burleson had failed to heed their demands. *New York Times*, April 16, 1919.
[2] Albert E. Hohler.

From the Diary of Dr. Grayson

Thursday, April 17, 1919.

The President had breakfast very early, and today was the busiest day which he has put in since he left Washington, having approximately eighteen engagements, which covered every conceivable problem dealing with the Peace situation. Among those whom he saw were Frank P. Walsh, of Kansas City, who was the representative of a committee consisting of himself, Ex-Governor Edward F. Dunne, of Illinois, and Michael Ryan, of Massachusetts, who had been sent from the United States as a committee of Irish-Americans to ask the President to use his influence for the establishment of an Irish Republic. The President also saw representatives of many of the minor nations and principalities. His complete list of engagements was as follows:

Dr. Wellington Koo, to present Messrs. Chengting Thomas Wang, Alfred S. K. Sze[1] and Suntchou Wei, Chinese delegates to the Peace Conference.

Assyrian-Chaldean Delegation—Messrs. S. Antoine Namik, R. Louis Nedjib, and Dr. Jean Zebouni, with message from the Assyrian-Chaldean Nation.[2]

Dalmatian Delegation (Eunjevic Joakim, Novakovic Teodor, and Matavulj Simo[3]), to present to the President the result of the plebiscite of that part of Dalmatia occupied by the Italians. (Request of Mr. Vesnitch.)

M. Buequet,[4] Chargé d'Affaires of San Marino (to convey action of Grand Council General of San Marino conferring upon the President the title of "Honorary Citizen of the Republic.")

Miss Schneideman[5] and Miss Mary Anderson, representing the Women Workers of America.

The Patriarch of Constantinople[6]—Head of the Orthodox Eastern Churches.

[1] That is Ku Wei-chün (referred to in this series as Vi Kyuin Wellington Koo), Wang Cheng-t'ing, and Shih Chao-chi.
[2] These names cannot be confirmed. The "Assyrian-Chaldean Nation" was apparently a group of people living in what is now Iraq, who claimed descent from the Assyrians and Chaldeans of antiquity.
[3] These names cannot be confirmed.
[4] Maurice Bucquet.
[5] Rose Schneiderman, not Schneideman.
[6] Germanos V.

M. Essad Pasha, President of the Government of Albania[7]—to present the "just claims of Albania."

Mr. L. A. Coromilas,[8] Greek Minister at Rome.

Mr. Bratiano,[9] of the Roumanian Delegation.

Dr. Alfonso Costa,[10] former Portuguese Prime Minister and President of the Portuguese Delegation of the Peace Conference.

M. Boghos Nubar (Armenia).

Mr. Dawson (Manchester Guardian).[11]

M. Pashitch[12] (Servia).

Mr. Frank Walsh—on the matter of Ireland.

The President had Secretary of War Baker as a guest at luncheon. During the luncheon the President asked the Secretary what the sentiment was back home on the League of Nations and the Peace Conference, and the Secretary said: "I had just returned from a trip throughout the West before sailing from New York, and I found the sentiment about ten to one in favor of the League of Nations. The country is strongly back of you."

The President told the Secretary that he (the President) had been given credit for using the expression: "standing on the frontiers of freedom." This expression was used by Secretary Baker when he was over here on a previous occasion. The President said: "I don't want you to feel that I was guilty of plagiarism in appropriating this eloquent phrase, which originated with you. Sometime in a speech when I have an opportunity I will correct this."

Secretary Baker said that Mrs. Baker[13] had been very much gratified by a school teacher writing her and saying that certain letters written from the War Department during the war were composed in such excellent style that they wanted to use them as models in the school. The Secretary said: "Mrs. Baker was extremely chesty and proud over this, but upon making inquiries as to the authorship of these particular letters, I found that I had not written any of them. They had been prepared by my secretaries."

The Secretary said to me that when he noticed in the press that the President was sick he knew that I would not take any chances with him and would keep him in bed.

Secretary Baker asked the President if he felt tired over his work, or if it was such a natural stimulus that it failed to fatigue him.

---

[7] Essad Pasha Toptanii. His claim as "President of the Government of Albania" was dubious indeed.

[8] Lambros A. Coromilas.

[9] That is, Ion I. C. Brătianu.

[10] Afonso (not Alfonso) Augustó da Costa.

[11] William Harbutt Dawson, identified in W. H. Dawson to WW, April 5, 1919.

[12] That is, Nikola Pašić.

[13] That is, Elizabeth Wells Leopold Baker.

The President smiled and said: "After all this ocean of talk has rolled over me, I feel that I would like to return to America and go back into some great forest, amid the silence, and not hear any argument or speeches for a month. I feel somewhat like [blank], who spent several days in going through the Louvre Gallery studying the various paintings. Some one asked him how it felt, and he replied: "I am just longing now to look upon a blank wall."

The President asked Secretary Baker what he thought of Lloyd-George's speech before the Parliament yesterday.[14] The Secretary replied that in his opinion Lloyd-George had acquitted himself very well, although he was not acquainted with the facts enough to judge.

Baker began to talk business at the table and the President changed the subject and wanted to know whether he had noticed how the White House looked, as he understood a new coat of paint was being put on it. Baker replied: "Very white and pretty." The President said: "I hope it will not be too white and too clean looking. I would like for it not to have too fresh an appearance. It ought to show some signs in keeping with its age.["]

Baker said it looked very lonely around the White House. The sheep on the White House lawn appeared lonesome, and he said: "I can see that they are not the only ones that miss their shepherd."

The President said: "I noticed in big headlines in the papers that you were bringing General Pershing's son Warren with you as a surprise to the General.["] Baker said: "While at Camp Upton I selected a sergeant and talked to him, asking him if he liked children, and I saw that he would be a good man to look after the young boy, so I told him what I wanted him to do. He threw his chest out two or three inches, strutted around the Camp, and told some of the newspaper men about it, and in this way it got into the papers."

[14] Lloyd George spoke in the House of Commons upon its adjournment on April 16, 1919. In a bold defense against his critics, he described the perilous state of the world and the enormous difficulties confronting the statesmen at Paris. He agreed that the Bolshevik government had been guilty of heinous crimes against British subjects and its own citizens and could not be recognized. On the other hand, he said, "a gigantic military enterprise in order to improve the conditions in Russia . . . would be the greatest act of stupidity that any Government could possibly commit." He added, however, that it had been and continued to be sound policy to furnish supplies to the Russian enemies of Bolshevism and food and supplies to the new states of eastern Europe. In response to a question about the Bullitt mission, he answered in the manner quoted in W. C. Bullitt to WW, April 18, 1919. Lloyd George denied that there had ever been any significant differences between President Wilson and Allied leaders in Paris and explained why the terms of the preliminary peace treaty had not yet been published. As for reparations, he asserted that the British delegation at Paris had not betrayed his pledges to the British electorate. Finally, he declared that the people of Great Britain wanted only justice, not revenge, and a new world devoid of the fear of militarism and the scourge of hunger. He concluded by paying an indirect tribute to the League of Nations. *Parliamentary Debates*, House of Commons, Fifth Series, Vol. 114, cols. 2936-56.

The subject turned to prohibition, and the President said: "I notice in the papers that the States wanted to confiscate liquors and wines that have been stored in private residences." Baker agreed that it was true and that it was proper where large amounts had been stored. The President said: "I think that is interfering with personal privileges." Then Baker tried to extricate himself to agree with the President by saying that the "spirit of the law intended to search cellars of only the very wealthy, such as Ed McLean, who it was reported had $60,000 worth of wine stored away." This ended the discussion on this topic, as the President showed that he did not care to discuss the subject any further.

It was something of a coincidence that I received in the regular mail a letter today from the Secretary of War, Mr. Baker, who wrote as Chairman of the Council of National Defense an appreciation of my work. The letter was as follows: . . . .[15]

The President had dinner at seven o'clock with Mrs. Wilson. I had a dinner engagement at eight o'clock at the Ritz Hotel with Major John Stuart Hunt,[16] and Mr. and Mrs. S. S. Howland[17] of New York City. However, I sat with the President and Mrs. Wilson during the dinner, and the President told Mrs. Wilson some of the experiences of the fifteen-year-old son[18] of Bernard M. Baruch, who is attending a very exclusive private school in Milton, Massachusetts. The boy had written his father telling him that he had had a fight with another boy who had called the President a "mutton-head," and that he had blacked his opponent's eyes and split his nose, but the boy said that as a result he had "lost his Saturday and Sunday." The President also told Mrs. Wilson some things I had told him which Baruch had told me about the boy. Last Christmas Baruch went up to the school to bring the boy home for the holidays, and he found him pretty well black and blue. He asked him the reason for this, and the boy told him that it was necessary for him to have a great many fights in this school. When Baruch asked his son why fighting was so necessary, he said there were three reasons: First, he was a Southerner; second, he was a Democrat; and third he was a Jew. This rather made a hit with Baruch, and as they were riding down toward home the boy turned to his father and said that he considered his father and his grandfather[19] the two best men he thought were in the world, and he wanted to

[15] Here follows a copy of NDB to C. T. Grayson, April 1, 1919, commending Grayson's contribution to the work of the General Medical Board of the Advisory Commission of the Council of National Defense.

[16] The Editors have been unable further to identify him.

[17] Samuel Shaw Howland and Leslie Mosby Wallace Howland. He was a gentleman of means of New York.

[18] Bernard Mannes Baruch, Jr.

[19] That is Simon Baruch, M.D.

be the same as they—a Jew—although his mother was a Gentile, and he could easily have posed as one if he so desired. Baruch had told me, and I had told the President, that this was the best evidence he had had that there was real merit in the youngster.

To Gustave Ador

My dear Mr. President: Paris, 17 April, 1919.

Your letter of April 13th has given me a great deal of pleasure. You confer upon me praise which I have not earned in ascribing to my influence the choice of Geneva as the seat of the League of Nations. I was earnestly desirous that Geneva should be chosen, but the choice was suggested by a committee of which I was not a member. It is very delightful to look forward to the establishment in Geneva of the home of the great institution upon which center so many of the finest and most substantial hopes of the world, and I am sure that the choice was prompted by the feeling on the part of the members of the Commission charged by the Conference with this work that Geneva was associated with so many of the coop-erative efforts of the peoples of the world that there could be no more suitable place as the home of the permanent offices of the League.

Permit me, Mr. President, to felicitate your native city and the Confederation of Switzerland upon this appropriate choice.

Cordially and sincerely yours,   [Woodrow Wilson]

CCL (WP, DLC).

To Henry White

My dear Mr. White: Paris, 17 April, 1919.

Thank you for your note about your interview with the newspaper men concerning a "guaranty" to France.[1] You are quite right about the whole thing, and I can assure you that I never had in mind the joint arrangement with Great Britain, but only a separate treaty with France, and, as you know, all that I promised is to try to get it.

In haste, with warm regard and appreciation,

Sincerely yours,   [Woodrow Wilson]

CCL (WP, DLC).
    [1] See H. White to WW, April 16, 1919.

From Vi Kyuin Wellington Koo

My dear Mr. President: [Paris] April 17, 1919.

Referring to the conversation which I had the honor to have with you this morning I beg leave to enclose herewith copy of the Chinese Memorandum on the Shantung Question, giving in its appendices the text of the documents which you referred to.[1]

I am, my dear Mr. President,

Yours respectfully, V. K. Wellington Koo

TLS (WP, DLC).

[1] Chinese Delegation, Preliminary Peace Conference, THE CLAIM of China for direct restitution to herself of the leased territory of Kiaochow, the Tsingtao-Chinan railway and other German rights in respect of Shantung province, February 1919, printed copy (WP, DLC); it is reprinted in Miller, My Diary at the Conference of Paris, VI, 115-212. This eighty-seven-page memorandum, drafted by Koo, summarized the history of Germany's leasehold in Shantung Province, described its occupation by Japan, and documented these developments in twenty-three appendices which included the major diplomatic correspondence, treaties, and exchanges concerning Shantung Province from 1898 through 1918. The memorandum also argued forcefully the reasons why Shantung Province should be returned to China with no strings attached. Koo had made these arguments at shorter length in his statement before the Council of Ten on January 28, 1919 (see the minutes of that body printed at Jan. 28, 1919, 11 a.m., Vol. 54) and in his memorandum of April 8, 1919, printed as an Enclosure with RL to WW, April 12, 1919.

From Vittorio Emanuele Orlando

Confidential

Dear Mr. President, Paris, April 17th 1919.

As I shall not have the pleasure of seeing you to-day, I venture to write to you on the subject of our conversation on Monday last.

On that occasion you were good enough to recognise that it is extremely urgent that the Italian questions should be settled within this week, and kindly gave me the assurance that this would be done. Now, the week is drawing to an end, and so far the matter has remained at the same point it was when we had our last conversation. I must, therefore, ask you to consider the absolute necessity to propose that the meeting of the Four on Saturday morning be set aside for the final decisions to be taken on this subject, and that, as it has already been understood, my Colleague for Foreign Affairs, Baron Sonnino, be present at the meeting.

Please accept, dear Mr. President, the assurance of my most cordial regards. Sincerely yours, V E Orlando

TLS (WP, DLC).

A Translation of a Letter from Georges Clemenceau

Mr. President, Paris, April 17, 1919

I have the honor to bring to your attention, for approval, the text of the communication that I propose to send to the Germans by Marshal Foch.[1]

Accept, Mr. President, the assurance of my high regard.

G Clemenceau

TLS (WP, DLC).
[1] Close wrote the following on this letter: "Proposed letter returned M. Clemenceau with Prest's O.K. GFC." See the extract from the Diary of Colonel House printed at April 19, 1919.

From Isaiah Bowman and Others

Dear Mr. President: [Paris] April 17, 1919

En route to France, on the George Washington in December, the President gave the territorial specialists an inspiriting moral direction:

"Tell me what's right and I'll fight for it. Give me a guaranteed position."[1]

We regard this as a noble charter for the new international order. We have been proud to work for that charter. At this critical moment we should like to take advantage of the gracious invitation of the President to address him directly on matters of the gravest importance, and in accordance therewith beg to submit the following observations:

The Italian representatives demand Fiume and part of Dalmatia in order to emerge from the Conference with loot for their people. These districts belong to Jugo-Slavia, not to Italy. In our opinion there is *no* way—no political or economic device, of a free port or otherwise—which can repair to Jugo-Slavia the injury done if any outside Power prevents Fiume from being made an integral part of the Jugo-Slav organization. It would be charged that we had betrayed the rights of small nations. It would be charged that the principle, "There shall be no bartering of peoples" had been publicly and cynically thrown aside.

Italy *entered* the war with a demand for loot. France and England surrendered to her demand. Of all the world's statesmen the President alone repudiated a war for spoils and proclaimed the just principles of an enduring peace. The belligerent nations, including Italy, agreed to make peace on the President's principles. Italy now insists that she must carry home an ample bag of spoils or the government will fall.

If Italy gets even nominal sovereignty over Fiume as the price of supporting the League of Nations, she has brought the League down to her level. It becomes a coalition to maintain an unjust settlement. The world will see that a big Power has profited by the old methods: secret treaties, shameless demands, selfish oppression. The League of Nations will be charged with the acceptance of the doctrines of Talleyrand and Metternich.

If Jugo-Slavia loses Fiume, war will follow. When it comes, the League will be fighting on the wrong side. Ought we to hope that it will be strong enough to win? Will the people of the world send armies and navies and expend billions of dollars to maintain a selfish and aggressive settlement?

Better a League of Nations based on justice than a League based on Italian participation bought at a price. The Italian government may fall, but the Italian people cannot long withstand the opinion of the world.

Never in his career did the President have presented to him such an opportunity to strike a death blow to the discredited methods of old-world diplomacy. Italian claims are typical of the method of making excessive demands in the hope of saving a portion of the spoils in subsequent compromises. To the President is given the rare privilege of going down in history as the statesman who destroyed, by a clean-cut decision against an infamous arrangement, the last vestige of the old order.

Respectfully submitted,

Chief Territorial Specialist
Isaiah Bowman
Chief of the Italian Division
W E Lunt
Chief of the Balkan Division
Clive Day

Chief of the Division of
Boundary Geography
Douglas W. Johnson
Chief of the Austro-Hungarian
Division
Charles Seymour
Chief of the Division of
Economics and Statistics
Allyn A. Young

TLS (WP, DLC).
¹ See the memorandum by Isaiah Bowman printed at Dec. 10, 1918, Vol. 53.

Thomas Nelson Page to Edward Mandell House

Very Confidential

My dear Colonel House: Rome, April 17, 1919.

I would like this letter brought to the attention of the President, because I feel that the matter it treats of is of great importance as helping to inform the President, as well as other members of the American Mission to Negotiate Peace, as to the exact state of conditions here now in Italy.

The situation has undoubtedly changed here markedly in the last six weeks. This change has, with equal certainty, been brought about in considerable part—perhaps mainly—by the tremendous propaganda which has been put forth throughout Italy directed, as I believe, to a considerable extent from Paris, and contributed to by numerous elements here in Italy. Among these are not only the Nationalists and the traditional anti-Jugo-Slavs, but important elements who have been hitherto most moderate, and even those who formerly were strongly against Sonnino's policy, as outlined in the Treaty of London. Three months ago Fiume hardly entered into the consideration of those who were formulating the Italian rights or claims. I mean as an integral part of Italy, for I think that it was quite generally held that it should be a free city, and protected against Jugo-Slav or Austrian tyranny. Even two months ago the demand that Fiume should be given outright to Italy was hardly so universal that it might not have been met by some arrangement which would satisfy Italy that the Italian element there would not be subject to oppression. But to-day few Italians could be found who would not hold about Fiume quite as strong views as the French held about Alsace and Lorraine, or as the Italians held during the latter part of last year about Trieste and the Trentino, and no Italians would be bold enough to say openly that Fiume should not be given to Italy.

To appreciate this position one must know something of the Italian psychology and way of looking at things. These have been used as the foundation for the press and other propaganda to which I have referred, and the success of this propaganda has been to me quite extraordinary and unexpected. It does not matter in weighing the present facts of the newly aroused, but profound Italian feeling on this subject how such feeling has been aroused. It exists, and those who, a short time back, were discussing calmly the question of the provision to be made for the disposition of Fiume, refer to it to-day with as much passion as those who were for it all along. I question very much if Orlando's Government would stand twenty-four hours after the Chamber meets here if he remains in the Peace

Conference after Fiume's status shall be settled, unless it be given to Italy. It is possible that a clear definition of this status with Fiume wholly protected against Jugo-Slav absorption, and with recognition of its relation to Italy, such as to enable Italy to represent a certain guardianship over it, might in time be accepted here. This will depend on how quickly the present flame, which is now burning throughout Italy, is brought down.

The Vice Premier, Colossimo,[1] Minister of Colonies, in a conversation which I had with him yesterday, and which I sought for the purpose of pointing out the danger contained in the violent propaganda which has been going on so long here in the press, and is now taking the form of nasty attacks against the United States, declared that these attacks in the press represent only the editors of the papers and do not represent the feeling of the people of Italy. He expressed the belief also that they would soon die out and that the people of Italy had a profound friendship for America. I believe it to be true that the attacks do not represent the people's views at present, but as I pointed out, they are being now reflected in the cheap comic papers which the people read or see and the result will be to affect the people also. I called his attention to the manifest effort made a few days since to stir up feeling between us and Japan, contained in certain telegrams from Paris, which criticize acridly what was termed the refusal of the American Delegation to recognize the equality of races in the League of Nations. He said simply this came from the outside, and this brings me to a matter to which I have for some time desired to call attention, not that the Minister alluded in any way to the persons I am about to mention.

I heard some time since that Signor d'Martino,[2] who is now in Paris, and who has much to do with Italian political propaganda, has been somewhat active in the propaganda against England, and I suspect that he has had a hand in the initiation of the propaganda against us to which I have alluded above. I heard also two or three days ago that Sonnino's chief personal secretary, Count Aldrobandi,[3] has recently been assigned by Sonnino to act as the interpreter for Signor Orlando in his Conferences with the Committee of Four. Now, this gentleman, like the other mentioned, is a very

---

[1] Gaspare Colosimo.

[2] That is, Giacomo de Martino. Wilson drew a line down the left-hand side of this paragraph.

[3] Luigi Aldrovandi Marescotti, Count of Viano, chief of the office of the Italian Minister of Foreign Affairs and Secretary General of the Italian delegation to the peace conference. His two books, *Guerra Diplomatica: Ricordi e Frammenti di Diario (1914-1919)* (Milan, 1936) and *Nuovi Ricordi e Frammenti de Diario per far Séguito a Guerra Diplomatica (1914-1919)* (Milan, 1938), are standard sources for the history of Italian diplomacy during the war and the peace conference.

active and secret agent of what might be termed representative secret diplomacy of the Consulta.[4] It happens that both of these gentlemen were reported to me during the war as being strongly pro-German. I do not believe that they were this in any sense which could be interpreted as meaning that they were not patriotically pro-Italy, but I think it worth mentioning that this was their reputation among those who, I believe, had means of knowing their sentiments. They were both brought up in a diplomacy which believed absolutely in the Triple Alliance, and I never, in all my dealing with them, had the least idea that they were in sympathy with France, England or America. My feeling about this has been somewhat deepened by suggestions which I have heard in the day or two, that if Fiume is not given to Italy absolutely Orlando and Sonnino will both have to go by the board and Giolitti[5] may be called into power again with a view to re-cementing the old relations between Italy and Germany. I was informed once by a person who I considered knew what he was talking about that the Italian Foreign Office had throughout the war left the door between Italy and Germany a little ajar and from time to time turned its face in that direction. I said I did not believe that Sonnino did this, and his reply was, "Not so much as the others there, but occasionally he also takes a little squint through the door."

I am endeavoring to give as exact a presentation of the situation here as I am capable of giving in order that the President may know precisely how things stand, for I feel that the situation here demands careful handling, and handling that is sympathetic with the people of Italy. Otherwise there may come a situation that will be not only serious but very serious indeed. The best friends of America feel that the situation is critical so far as the friendship between Italy and America is concerned, and the feeling extends also to the relations with France and England. They say, "We have fought, we have suffered more than others, and we have won with our arms a great victory over the enemies not only of Italy, but of the other countries represented at Paris. We fought alone and our victory was that which led to the victory over Germany. We have fought to emancipate our brothers who have looked to us for generations to emancipate them. We have overcome their oppressors and our enemies and the enemies of our Allies. Now, why should our Allies side with our enemies against us and snatch from us the one chance that may ever be had to restore to Italy elements of the Italian race

[4] That is, the Italian Foreign Office, after the name of the building in which it was housed from 1870 to 1922, a palace built at the behest of Pope Clement XII for the Supremo Tribunale Pontificio della Consulta in 1739.

[5] That is, Giovanni Giolitti, Prime Minister of Italy four times before this date.

who have looked to us through the generations and have suffered so much because of their continued demand to be free." This is their argument—the argument which they are now applying towards Fiume, for I do not believe that at present there is much thought of the Dalmatian coast which at least is thought of only with a view to having guarantees given for the protection of the Italian elements there, though Sonnino undoubtedly has certain views about it as a valuable asset to trade with for other concessions.

One other thing came to my notice yesterday which bears on this subject of Fiume. I have heard rumors for some time that Italy would not give up Fiume no matter what the Conference in Paris should decide about it, but yesterday I was informed that a strong movement exists to hold Fiume as Italian against any other power or combination of powers whatsoever, and not to accept any decree to the contrary, even though it should be made by both the Associated powers and by Italy herself. What I heard is, that even should Italy order the troops out of Fiume, it will be held by Italians even if they had to pull the crown from their caps. This may be all mere talk, but I believe that there is enough in it to start a flame in Italy which may sear the friendship between the United States and the people of Italy beyond the power of cure in the lifetime of anyone living to-day.

Always, Most sincerely yours,   Thos. Nelson Page

TLS (WP, DLC).

From Fridtjof Nansen, with Enclosure

Sir: Paris, 17 April 1919.

I am indeed greatly obliged for your letter of the 17th of April in respect to my suggestions as to the provisioning of Russia.

You will please find attached hereto communication which I have asked my government to transmit by the quickest route to its destination.

Believe me, Sir,
                    Yours most respectfully,   Fridtjof Nansen

TLS (WP, DLC).

E N C L O S U R E

Fridtjof Nansen to Vladimir Ilich Lenin

Sir: Paris, 17 April 1919.

On April third I sent the following letter to President Wilson, Clemenceau, Lloyd-George and Orlando:

"Sir,

The present food situation in Russia, where hundreds of thousands of people are dying monthly from sheer starvation and disease, is one of the problems now uppermost in all men's minds. As it appears that no solution of this food and disease question has so far been reached in any direction, I would like to make a suggestion from a neutral point of view for the alleviation of this gigantic misery, on purely humanitarian grounds.

It would appear to me possible to organize a purely humanitarian Commission for the provisioning of Russia, the foodstuffs and medical supplies to be paid for perhaps to some considerable extent by Russia itself, the justice of distribution to be guaranteed by such a Commission, the membership of the Commission to be comprised of Norwegian, Swedish, and possibly Dutch, Danish and Swiss nationalities. It does not appear that the existing authorities in Russia would refuse the intervention of such a Commission of wholly non-political order, devoted solely to the humanitarian purpose of saving life. If thus organized upon the lines of the Belgian Relief Commission, it would raise no question of political recognition or negotiations between the Allies with the existing authorities in Russia.

I recognize keenly the large political issue involved, and I would be glad to know under what conditions you would approve such an enterprise and whether such Commission could look for actual support in finance, shipping and food and medical supplies from the United States Government.

Believe me, Sir,

Yours most respectfully,

SIGNED: Fridtjof Nansen."

Today April seventeenth I have received the following answer:
"Dear Sir:

The misery and suffering in Russia described in your letter of April 3rd appeals to the sympathies of all peoples. It is shocking to humanity that millions of men, women and children lack the food and the necessities which make life endurable.

The Governments and peoples whom we represent would be glad to cooperate, without thought of political, military or financial advantage, in any proposal which would relieve this situation in Russia. It seems to us that such a Commission as you propose would offer a practical means of achieving the beneficent results you have in view, and could not, either in its conception or its operation, be considered as having any other aim than the 'humanitarian purpose of saving life.'

There are great difficulties to be overcome, political difficulties, owing to the existing situation in Russia, and difficulties of supply and transport. But if the existing local governments of Russia are as willing as the Governments and people whom we represent to see succor and relief given to the stricken peoples of Russia, no political obstacle will remain. There will remain, however, the difficulties of supply, finance and transport which we have mentioned, and also the problem of distribution in Russia itself. The problem of supply we can ourselves hope to solve, in connection with the advice and cooperation of such a Commission as you propose. The problem of finance would seem to us to fall upon the Russian authorities. The problem of transport of supplies to Russia we can hope to meet with the assistance of your own and other Neutral Governments whose interest should be as great as our own and whose losses have been far less. The problems of transport in Russia and of distribution can be solved only by the people of Russia themselves, with the assistance, advice and supervision of your Commission.

Subject to such supervision, the problem of distribution should be solely under the control of the people of Russia themselves. The people in each locality should be given, as under the regime of the Belgian Relief Commission, the fullest opportunity to advise your Commission upon the methods and the personnel by which their community is to be relieved. In no other circumstances could it be believed that the purpose of this relief was humanitarian, and not political, under no other conditions could it be certain that the hungry would be fed.

That such a course would involve cessation of all hostilities within definitive lines in the territory of Russia is obvious. And the cessation of hostilities would, necessarily, involve a complete suspension of the transfer of troops and military material of all sorts to and within Russian territory. Indeed, relief to Russia which did not mean a return to a state of peace would be futile, and would be impossible to consider.

Under such conditions as we have outlined, we believe that your plan could be successfully carried into effect, and we should be prepared to give it our full support.

V. E. ORLANDO.

D. LLOYD GEORGE.

WOODROW WILSON.

G. CLEMENCEAU."

I would be glad to hear from you in this matter at your earliest convenience.

I may add that the neutral organization which I propose offers its services in this cause without any remuneration whatever, but of course its expenditures in the purchase and transportation of supplies must be met by the Soviet Government.

Believe me, Sir,

Yours most respectfully,   Fridtjof Nansen

CCLS (WP, DLC).

From Gilbert Fairchild Close

[Paris, c. April 17, 1919]

MEMORANDUM FOR THE PRESIDENT:

Mr. Herbert Hoover telephoned that the British Premier, Mr. Lloyd George, has suggested that for the communication concerning Russia, from Doctor Nanzen to Lenine, to have the proper effect, should not be sent through British wireless station, as had been intended, but should be sent through a neutral wireless station. In order to have a neutral wireless station communicate this message, the consent of the four Powers must be secured. Mr. Hoover asks if the President will not take the matter up before the Council of Four and secure this approval.   G.F.C.

T MS (WP, DLC).

From Robert Lansing, with Enclosure

My dear Mr. President: Paris, April 17, 1919.

I have taken up the question raised in your letter of April 14th,[1] in which you state that you are in general accord with certain recommendations which I made regarding Allied policy towards Austria and Hungary.

General Smuts has, I understand, drawn up a report of his trip to Hungary, with certain specific recommendations. I am enclosing a rough outline of what I understand these recommendations to be. You will note that points 6 and 7 are in line with my recommendations to you, while points 4 and 5 are measures with which I entirely agree and which might advantageously be adopted at the earliest possible moment. The first three recommendations of General Smuts, which are of a military nature, should presumably receive the study of our military authorities and should probably undergo certain alteration in case by "a military force representing the four

Great Powers," General Smuts would desire American participation in a military occupation of Transylvania.

I desire to suggest that General Smuts be allowed to appear before the Council of Four at the earliest possible moment to submit his report, in order that definite action may be taken to outline our policy towards Austria and Hungary. This I feel is highly important before we become involved in a discussion of the treaty with Germany. In case this method is not practicable, I would suggest that the matter be referred to the Council of Foreign Ministers, who could hear General Smuts and present definite recommendations to the Council of Four.

I am, my dear Mr. President,

Faithfully yours,   Robert Lansing

TLS (WP, DLC).
[1] See WW to RL, April 14, 1919 (second letter of that date).

ENCLOSURE

Outline of Recommendations of General Smuts as a result of his trip to Budapest, Vienna, and Prague.

1. A military force representing the four Great Powers shall occupy the neutral zone in Transylvania bounded on the west by a line east of Mako (on the Maros River)—Totkomlos—Bekescaba—east of Debreczen[1]—east of Mateszalka. (Note: This line is some 40 kilometers to the east of the original line and therefore a concession to the Hungarians.)

2. The military questions involved in the occupation of the neutral zone will be submitted to the High Commander of the Allied Forces at Constantinople,[2] who shall determine the force necessary for the occupation and the manner in which it shall be carried out.

3. As soon as the occupation is completed, the Hungarian authorities on the spot shall be notified that the occupation is in no sense political and shall not prejudice the determination of Hungary's frontiers.

4. Train loads of essential commodities for Hungary shall be despatched as soon as possible to show the good-will of the Allies towards Hungary.

5. The blockade shall be raised as soon as the occupation of the neutral zone has been carried out.

6. A conference shall be summoned to Paris under a Chairman to be appointed by the Great Powers, to discuss territorial adjustments and endeavor to reach solutions of the economic and financial problems of the old Austro-Hungarian Monarchy. German-Aus-

tria and Hungary shall each have two representatives at this conference.

7. The work of the Allied and Associated Governments in the Austro-Hungarian countries shall be co-ordinated by the appointment of a single Commissioner to represent the Allies and to advise the Great Powers, and to assist in the maintenance of agreements which may be reached and to facilitate the reaching of further agreements between the states of the old Monarchy.

T MS (WP, DLC).
    [1] The correct forms of the preceding two names are Bekescsaba and Debrecen.
    [2] Gen. Franchet d'Esperey. The spelling "d'Espérey" in Vol. 56 is incorrect.

From William Shepherd Benson

My dear Mr. President,   Paris 17 April 1919

I have just received a report, dated April 11th, 1919, from the officer commanding our Naval forces in the Adriatic,[1] on the subject of deportation of the Jugo Slavs by Italians. Knowing that the ultimate solution of the questions which have arisen incident to the Italian claims along the Eastern Adriatic are being considered by you, I thought perhaps this report would be of interest. It is as follows:

"The following quotation from the weekly report of the Pola Intelligence Committee forwarded by Ensign R. D. Thiery,[2] U.S.N.R.F., is forwarded for your information:

'Deportation of Jugo Slavs by the Italians is in steady progress here and is causing a great resentment among the Slav population. Our notice has been called to the fact that deportations are made among the class of Slavs who are well educated and very intelligent and who could possibly be of any influence among the Slav population. Those who are being deported are Priests, Teachers, Lawyers, business men and other influential people.

'American Officers in Pola have seen such a deportation take place here.

'A list of a few deported Slavs and every possible reason for deportations are herein attached as per Slav statement of same. This list was placed in the hands of U. S. Officers of Pola by a prominent Jugo Slav lawyer who also expects to be deported on account of his possible influence.

'Deportations are reported to have started here about fifteen days after the Italians arrived in Pola, and have since steadily continued. It is stated that these deported Slavs are interned in Sardinia and Cosenza in Calabria, Italy, and possibly other places. They receive 2.5 Lire a day for subsistence and although permitted to work are unable to find any way of earning more. Several letters and cards have been received by their friends in Istria requesting that money be sent. This has been done in some cases but it is not known whether it has been received.' "

Sincerely yours,   [W. S. Benson]

CCL (W. S. Benson Papers, DLC).
  ¹ Rear Adm. Philip Andrews.
  ² Raymond Donlé Thiery.

A Memorandum by William Linn Westermann

From the Division on Western Asia.   [Paris, c. April 17, 1919]

Abstract of Memorandum which accidentally came into our hands, presumably intended for the French Foreign Office, on the Syrian matter.

1. The British Government will be eager to have us come to an agreement with Feisal because it fears the result of the Interallied Commission projected for Syria.

2. Since the intervention of America the assignment of Syria to France is no longer entirely in England's hands. We can now force England to allow us to create a "de facto" situation there that will aid us in meeting the Commission, if it cannot be avoided, or in meeting any other procedure which may be adopted in deciding the mandate question.

3. England must allow British troops in Syria to be replaced by French troops.

4. England and France must support one another in seeing that mandates are given in accord with the Sykes-Picot Agreement of 1916.

5. Feisal must come to an agreement with us when we have agreed with England, because he knows that he cannot rule certain elements in Syria, which are favorable to us, without our help.

Our Analysis of the Document.

1. The French do not want the Interallied Commission to go to Syria.

2. They know that the British fear the results of it in arousing trouble in Mesopotamia.

(It is for this reason that the French insisted on extending its [their] competence over Palestine, Mesopotamia and Armenia.)

3. The French expect to influence our Commissioners to help them obtain Syria.

4. The mandates of the Near East are to be settled on the general lines of the Sykes-Picot Agreement.

(The old formula "zones" and "zones of influence" is to be changed to "mandates.")

Our Conclusion

If the Interallied Commission goes to Syria it will find the cards stacked everywhere. It can do no good and may do much harm.

All the information requisite to the settlement is already here in Paris. Delay only adds to the difficulties.

The Near East is the great loot of the war. The fight on the question of division and mandates must be fought out here in Paris—and the sooner the better.

T MS (WP, DLC).

Tasker Howard Bliss to Gilbert Fairchild Close

Dear Mr. Close: Paris, April 17th, 1919.

Will you kindly convey the following information to the President?

1. The message which was sent to me by the President[1] day before yesterday (in the evening) for delivery "in a most tactful way" to the Luxemburg authorities by our representative there was delivered at 11 a.m. yesterday morning.*

2. This morning I have had an interview with Mr. Paderewski, as directed by the President, on the subject of the acceptance by the Poles of a truce on the same terms and conditions as already accepted by the Ukrainians. The result, as yet, is not satisfactory. Mr. Paderewski expressed himself as desirous of complying in every respect with the wishes of President Wilson and of the Peace Conference. He denies that the Ukrainians have in Paris any real representative of their government, because he claims that there are three or four different governments in Ukrainia and there is no-one who can bind them. Finally, thinking that it was the best that I could secure from him, I asked him whether he would authorize a Polish representative here in Paris to come before the Inter-Allied Armistice Commission (approved for appointment by the Council of Four on April 3, 1919), together with such representative as the Ukrainian Delegation should designate and allow this Commission to work out the terms of a truce and agree upon terms that would be temporarily satisfactory to all parties concerned. I also asked him whether he would accept these terms in behalf of his government, provided the Supreme Council put the necessary pressure upon the Ukrainian Government to enforce compliance by them. I made this proposition because of our general belief that the Ukrainian Government, in which Mr. Paderewski has no faith, will abide by

*General Bliss tells me (2 p.m. April 17) that he has received word from Luxemburg that the Plebiscite has been postponed.   G.F.C.

the conditions agreed upon without any pressure from the Supreme Council.

At first Mr. Paderewski accepted this and authorized me to convey the proposition with his approval to President Wilson. Later in the interview he said that he would have to consult his colleagues, which he would do late this afternoon, and that he would call upon me to-morrow morning and inform me of his decision.

Sincerely yours,   Tasker H. Bliss.

P.S. I enclose a letter to the President[2] which I ask you to be good enough to bring to his immediate attention because it relates to the appointment of the above-referred-to Inter-Allied Armistice Commission of which the American members have been appointed but the Allied members of which have not yet been appointed. I hope that the President will secure the appointment of the other members by the Council of Four at the earliest possible moment.

TLS (T. H. Bliss Papers, DLC).
[1] For the text of the message, see T. H. Bliss to GFC, April 18, 1919.
[2] It is missing, but see the minutes of the Council of Four printed at April 18, 1918, 11 a.m.

From Oscar Solomon Straus

Dear Mr. President: Paris 17 April 1919.

Yesterday I received from THE LEAGUE TO ENFORCE PEACE the following cable:

"Please congratulate the President and Colonel House on text of amendment exempting Monroe Doctrine."

Permit me to add my own felicitations upon the admirable result.

I cabled Mr. Taft the text of the Monroe Doctrine amendment and asked for his opinion. This morning I received the following reply:

"For Oscar Straus from Taft." "Monroe clause eminently satisfactory. Polk Acting."

It gives me great pleasure to transmit these messages to you.

I have the honor to be, my dear Mr. President

Sincerely and faithfully yours,   Oscar S. Straus

TLS (WP, DLC).

Two Telegrams to Joseph Patrick Tumulty

Paris, 17 April, 1919.

Please convey following message to Governors Coolidge of Massachusetts, Bartlett of New Hampshire and Beeckman of Rhode Island.[1] QUOTE.

I deeply regret that it seems impossible from this distance for me to play any wise or prudent part in connection with the telephone strike.[2] UNQUOTE.   Woodrow Wilson.

[1] Calvin Coolidge, John Henry Bartlett, and Robert Livingston Beeckman, all Republicans.
[2] Wilson was replying to C. Coolidge *et al.* to WW, April 16, 1919, T telegram (WP, DLC), the text of which reads as follows: "New-England urges your immediate action to relieve from Great Loss by telephone strike."

Paris, April 17, 1919

I hope you will call Mr. Hines' attention to Mr. Glass's objection to any announcement about the railroads until the loan is over,[1] and assure Glass that I will consult him before acting.
                                              Woodrow Wilson.

T telegrams (WP, DLC).
[1] See JPT to WW, April 15, 1919.

To Peter Goelet Gerry

My dear Senator: Paris, 17 April, 1919.

May I not acknowledge to you, and through you, to Senators David Walsh, Key Pittman, John B. Kendrick and T. J. Walsh the receipt of the important letter of March 28th[1] which you united in sending me concerning the Irish business?

I know you will pardon the brief reply and will not think that its brevity indicates any lack of appreciation of the capital importance of the matter your letter dwells upon. I have it very much in mind and am earnestly seeking some way to be useful in the matter, though I must admit it is very difficult to find the way.

Please present my regards to your colleagues and believe me, with warm appreciation,
                        Sincerely yours,   [Woodrow Wilson]

CCL (WP, DLC).
[1] See P. G. Gerry *et al.* to WW, March 28, 1919, Vol. 56.

Gilbert Fairchild Close to Albert Sidney Burleson

My dear Postmaster General: Paris, 17 April, 1919.

The President asks me to thank you for your letter of March 28th and for the full memorandum about the trouble with the wire operators which you were kind enough to send him.[1]
                        Sincerely yours,   [Gilbert F. Close]

CCL (WP, DLC).
¹ See ASB to WW, March 28, 1919, and n. 1 thereto, Vol. 56.

To William Bauchop Wilson

Paris, April 17, 1919

For the Secretary of Labor: Replying to your telegram of the 16th,¹ I am very glad to authorize the following public statement:

"The church organizations of the country having generously united in an effort to assist the employment service of the United States in finding work for returning soldiers and sailors and war workers and having designated Sunday, May 24th as Employment Sunday, I am happy to add my voice to others in an appeal to our fellow countrymen to give their earnest and united support to this and every similar movement. I hope that the people of the country will universally observe Employment Sunday as a day of fresh dedication to the mutual helpfulness which will serve to work out in the months to come the difficult problems of employment and industrial reorganization. In these days of victory we can make no better offering than that of service to the men and women who have won the victory."

Woodrow Wilson.

T telegram (WP, DLC).
¹ WBW to WW, April 16, 1919, T telegram (WP, DLC).

From Carter Glass

*By first aeroplane*¹

Dear Mr. President: Washington April 17, 1919

I am taking advantage of this history-making event—the first flight of an aeroplane across the Atlantic Ocean—to place in your hands sooner than any agency hitherto used could do, the inclosed official copy of the terms of the Victory Liberty Loan.²

An American invention—the aeroplane—first made aerial flight possible to man. I deem it to be a most happy event that Americans, in an American aeroplane, are to be the first to prove that flight from America to Europe is possible.

I regard it as a happy augury that this proof should be given by Americans at this time that the Nations of Europe and the United States of America are closer together physically, just when the League of Nations is to bring them closer in spirit.

The Victory Liberty Loan will be the testimonial of the American people that they appreciate the Victory that made possible this closer union of the world for the greater liberty and happiness of all mankind. I assure you, Mr. President, you may rely on them for that testimonial—they will make the Victory Liberty Loan a success.

Cordially yours,   Carter Glass.

TLS (WP, DLC).
¹ WWhw. At this time, preparations were under way for three United States Navy seaplanes to fly across the Atlantic Ocean. NC-1, NC-3, and NC-4 departed from Rockaway Beach, Long Island, on May 8 for Plymouth, England, via Trepassey, Newfoundland, the Azores, and Lisbon. Bad weather and mechanical difficulties delayed their departure from Trepassey until May 16. NC-4 arrived at Horta, the Azores, on the following day. NC-1 and NC-3 both landed at sea: NC-1 capsized and sank after the rescue of her crew by a Greek ship; NC-3 eventually made its way on the ocean surface to Ponta Delgada, the Azores. After further delays, NC-4, under the command of Lt. Comdr. Albert Cushing Read, completed the journey to Plymouth on May 31, thus becoming, by only two weeks, the first aircraft to cross the Atlantic. The British aviators, John William Alcock and Arthur Whitten Brown, flew nonstop from St. John's Newfoundland, to Clifden, Ireland, on June 14-15. *New York Times*, April 1-June 1, 1919; Archibald D. Turnbull and Clifford L. Lord, *History of United States Naval Aviation* (New Haven, Conn., 1949), pp. 164-70; and Richard K. Smith, *First Across: The U. S. Navy's Transatlantic Flight of 1919* (Annapolis, Md., 1973).
² C. Glass, VICTORY LIBERTY LOAN: *Department Circular No. 138*, April 21, 1919, printed circular (WP, DLC).

From Vance Criswell McCormick, with Enclosure

My dear Mr. President: Paris. April 17, 1919.

I have received your letter of April 16th, enclosing a message from Burleson, in regard to cable censorship.

Since writing you on April 1st that I had taken this matter up with the British, I am glad to be able to advise you that we have made considerable progress, and that tomorrow, April 18th, cable censorship will be abolished as between the United States, and Great Britain, France and Italy, and between the United States, and Central and South America, and that on April 12th, the censorship was abolished to the Orient and all points on the Pacific, excepting Vladivostock. This only leaves censorship between the United States, and neutral and enemy countries in Europe, in accordance with a plan of relaxation approved by Admiral Benson, about ten days ago, a copy of which I am enclosing herewith. I am surprised that Mr. Burleson has not been advised.

Very sincerely yours,   Vance C McCormick

TLS (WP, DLC).

ENCLOSURE

CENSORSHIP
MEMORANDUM

FIRST: All cable censorship between the four associated governments shall be discontinued as of April 18th.

SECOND: All cable censorship to Central, South America and Cuba shall be discontinued as of April 18th.

THIRD: All cable censorship via the Pacific to the Orient except Vladivostok shall cease as of April 18th.

FOURTH: All cables to or from any neutral with whom trade is permitted, shall be censored by the associated government in whose jurisdiction the message shall originate or terminate. These messages shall be free of any other censorship; that is to say they shall be permitted to pass without diversion to censorship except only by the government under whose jurisdiction the message originates or terminates.

FIFTH: All conditions set forth in paragraph four as regards cable censorship shall apply to all countries with which trade is permitted. April 10, 1919.

T MS (WP, DLC).

From the Diary of Dr. Grayson

Friday, April 18, 1919.

The President had breakfast at eight o'clock.

Lloyd-George was back for the resumption of the Big Four sessions of today. As a result quite a bit of progress was made and the Polish boundary question was completely settled and sent over to the experts to be put into the language that will be used in the treaty. The question of the dismantling of Heligoland also was discussed.

I met Lloyd-George and I said: "Mr. Prime Minister, I wish to congratulate you on the speech which you made before Parliament. If you were a Surgeon I would call you a bold operator. If you think there is pus or a cancerous growth, you do not take your scalpel and puncture the edges, but you have the courage to make a bold and free incision." This reference to the manner in which the British Premier had handled Northcliffe in his denunciations of him and his methods in the speech was very pleasing to the Prime Minister, and he told the President later that he had enjoyed very, very much the characterization which I had made in discussing the Northcliffe episode with him. Lloyd-George told the President: "I like the way the Admiral talked about it. He shows that he is not a timid fellow himself."

The President had lunch with Mrs. Wilson, Miss Benham and myself. After lunch the President went for a short motor ride with Mrs. Wilson, returning to resume his conference with the Big Four. When the afternoon conference had adjourned I asked the President what the news was and he said: "Italy is the only one insisting upon claims inconsistent with the principles explicitly laid down as the basis of the peace, and is pressing for settlements more consistent with the processes of the Congress of Vienna than with the present temper of the world. Apparently it has come to the parting of the way."

The President had dinner with Mrs. Wilson and myself, and after dinner he played Canfield, while Mrs. Wilson and I sat and chatted with him until ten o'clock, when he retired.

Mantoux's Notes of a Meeting of the Council of Four

April 18, 1919, 11 a.m.

M. André Tardieu and Lt.-Col. Sir Maurice Hankey are introduced.

Clemenceau. M. Tardieu must propose to us measures to accelerate the work of drafting the preliminaries. If we do not take them, we risk not being prepared for April 25.

Tardieu. The Drafting Committee is doing its best; but it can only study and prepare a certain number of articles per day; this number is far below what would be necessary to finish the work on the twenty-third, which is indispensable if the document must be printed for the twenty-fifth. It would be necessary to increase the number of members of that committee, some being able to devote themselves to the study of territorial clauses, others to the study of economic or financial clauses.

Wilson. I will observe that, in conformity with the instruction that we gave some time ago, nearly all the reports of the commissions now include conclusions drafted in the form that they are to take in the peace treaty. Such are, for example, the conclusions that we have received from the commission on means of communication. In such cases, the work of drafting consists only of inserting completely finished clauses into the treaty.

Lloyd George. The legal specialists whom we have named as members of the Drafting Committee—do they not already have the right to obtain assistance from experts? I believe that it would be enough to remind them of that opportunity which has been given to them.

Hankey. The British representative on the Drafting Committee, Mr. Hurst, asks above all that the heads of government inform them in precise terms of the decisions that they have taken. In some cases, the Drafting Committee finds itself in the presence of two different proposals. For example, concerning the recognition by Germany of the decisions of our prize courts, the Council of Five did not arrive at one conclusion, but at two conclusions, between which a choice must still be made.

Mr. Hurst asks in particular that the Drafting Committee be informed of the text adopted on the question of Danzig, as well as of that relating to the left bank of the Rhine.

Wilson. I have the text relative to Danzig on my table.[1]

Lloyd George. In that case, would you like us to arrive at our decision on that question this morning? About the left bank of the Rhine, you will recall that we have a text which formed part of the military clauses, but which was removed from them because it was thought that it should be placed among the political clauses of the treaty.

Reading of this text according to the draft of the military clauses.

Lloyd George. I have an observation to make on this point. It is provided that the population domiciled on the left bank of the Rhine will be exempt not only from all military obligations in Germany, but from all contributions to the German military budget. Is it to our advantage to reduce the taxes that that population will have to pay? I do not think this arrangement is necessary.

Clemenceau. We will see if it must be maintained.

M. Tardieu and Sir Maurice Hankey withdraw.

Wilson. You will recall our conversation the other day on the subject of the dispute between the Poles and the Ukrainians. It was agreed that General Bliss would make representations in our name to M. Paderewski about the less than conciliatory attitude of the Poles. The General informs me that the Polish and Ukrainian representatives in Paris are prepared to discuss the conditions of an armistice according to our suggestion. It is up to us to designate representatives who would come into the discussion in the name of the Great Powers. Are each of you ready to appoint a delegate to attend the negotiations?

This proposal is adopted.

President Wilson reads the new text on the western frontiers of Poland (question of Danzig and question of Marienwerder):

[1] See S. E. Mezes to WW, April 21, 1919.

Danzig and its territory will be constituted as a free Hanseatic city, under the guarantee of the League of Nations, which will be represented there by a high commissioner. The territory of Danzig will be included in the Polish customs system, Poland having direction of foreign relations and the possession of the railroads, with free use of the port.

The populations of the circles of Stuhm, Riesenburg, and Marienwerder will be consulted by means of a plebiscite, after the complete evacuation by German troops, about their attachment to Poland or to East Prussia.

Polish sovereignty will extend over the entire course of the Vistula. Special rights of transit will be guaranteed to the Germans on the railroad which connects West Prussia to East Prussia, and to the Poles on the line from Danzig to Mlawa.

Lloyd George. One article of your text speaks of Polish sovereignty over the Vistula; it must be clearly understood that this does not confer on Poland the right to forbid use of the river to the inhabitants of Danzig.

Another observation: is it necessary to lay out in the peace treaty all the details of the functioning of the plebiscite? Many cannot be arranged in a satisfactory manner except on the spot, after examination of the local conditions. Would it not be sufficient to say in the treaty that there will be a plebiscite, that this plebiscite will take place by universal suffrage, the right to vote being reserved to persons actually domiciled in the region for a certain period of time? These essential points being well defined, it would be better to leave the rest to the discretion of the international commission which will organize and oversee the plebiscite.

Aside from this I am satisfied with this text, and I do not see what else we could do.

Clemenceau. I must confess to you that I would like to be able to do otherwise in order to give satisfaction to our friends in Poland; but in all sincerity I do not think that is possible.

Lloyd George. Another article that I do not like is the one which demands the dissolution of the workers' and soldiers' councils. The execution of it is not easy.

Clemenceau. That is what we have done in territories which we are occupying.

Lloyd George. Undoubtedly; but we precisely want to avoid having to occupy that remote region.

Wilson. For the expenses of the plebiscite, the text provides that if they exceed what can be reasonably asked of the region itself, the extra costs will be paid by East Prussia.

Lloyd George. Would it not be better to write: "by the country in whose favor the plebiscite will be pronounced"?

Mantoux. M. Tardieu asked me to remind you that the peace treaty with Germany must mention the frontier between Germany and Lithuania. The map prepared by the Commission on Polish Affairs indicates a drawing of that frontier which takes from Germany the strip of territory along the coast of the Baltic Sea north of the Niemen, with the port of Memel.[2]

Lloyd George. It is a question about which we will have to refresh our memory. Is the population Lithuanian?

Mr. Lloyd George goes to consult his secretaries and returns.

Lloyd George. According to the commission's report, I see that the frontier it drew corresponds to the ethnographic line between Germans and Lithuanians and that, on the other hand, Memel is the only outlet to the sea which is available to Lithuania. In these conditions, I believe that we can only adopt the conclusions of the Commission on Polish Affairs.

The conclusions of the Commission on Polish Affairs concerning the German-Lithuanian frontier are adopted.

Wilson. This morning I examined the two treaties between China and Japan on the subject of Kiaochow.[3] The first[4] provided, after the cession of Kiaochow to Japan by the peace treaty, the retrocession to China under certain conditions: opening of the gulf of Kiaochow to Japanese commerce, a Japanese concession to be established at a place chosen by the Japanese government.

Since then, China and Japan concluded another treaty[5] concerning the railroad from Tsinan to Kiaochow, China recovering the civil administration of the territory crossed by this railroad, but sharing the functions of police and administration of the railroad with Japan, as heretofore with Germany.

Lloyd George. For the moment, we only have to see what is

---

[2] Now known as Neman and Klaipeda, respectively.

[3] Wilson had just read THE CLAIM of China . . . , which Koo had sent to him on April 17.

[4] Here Wilson referred to the Sino-Japanese treaties of May 25, 1915, which were the products of Japanese, Chinese, and American negotiations over Japan's so-called Twenty-One Demands on China. The treaty of 1915 relating to Shantung Province, is printed in THE CLAIM of China . . . , in FR 1915, pp. 171-72, and elsewhere. For accounts of the crisis and negotiations, see Arthur S. Link, Wilson: The Struggle for Neutrality, 1914-1915 (Princeton, N. J. 1960), pp. 267-308; Madeleine Chi, China Diplomacy, 1914-1918 (Cambridge, Mass., 1970); James Reed, The Missionary Mind and American East Asia Policy, 1911-1915 (Cambridge, Mass., 1982); and Robert Joseph Gowen, "Great Britain and the Twenty-One Demands of 1915," Journal of Modern History, XLIII (March 1971), 76-106.

[5] Here Wilson referred to a Sino-Japanese exchange dated September 24, 1918, which Wilson read verbatim to the Council of Four on April 22, 1919, 4:30 p.m. This exchange, along with other Sino-Japanese exchanges of the same date, are printed in THE CLAIM of China and is summarized in FR 1918, p. 205.

appropriate to put in our treaty with Germany. I do not know why Kiaochow should not be treated in the same way as all other German territories overseas, which, we have decided, are to be handed over by the Germans to the Great Powers to dispose of as they see fit.

Wilson. That is also Mr. Lansing's opinion, and I think that it is the best solution. It would be useful to have a serious conversation on this subject with the Japanese; it is not in their interest to make an enemy of China; the future of the two countries is closely linked. We must advise the Japanese to be generous toward China and promise them, if they follow our advice, to promote their peaceful relations with the Chinese Republic.

What would permit us to use this language with authority would be to announce that we ourselves are renouncing our spheres of influence in China. I do not believe that the maintenance of these zones has any great advantage, and, on the other hand, we are interested in the maintenance of peace in the Far East. I fear great danger for the world from that corner if we do not take care there.

Lloyd George. We can study the question, on the sole condition that the principle of the open door continues in China.

Wilson. Certainly.

Lloyd George. For my part, I am ready to examine that question.

Wilson. In my opinion, when the Bolshevik fever dies down, Europe will be protected from a great war for a long time, but I fear that it is not the same in the Far East. I would willingly compare the seeds of conflict that are developing there in the dark to sparks hidden under a thick bed of leaves, which smolder gradually for months and grow little by little, invisible, until the moment when, suddenly, those great forest fires explode, as we sometimes see in America. That is what we must try to avoid.

Lloyd George. Then we will tell the Japanese that the formula adopted for Kiaochow will be the same as for all German possessions abroad.

Wilson. If the Japanese are with us, they must submit to the same method as we.

Lloyd George. Concerning the spheres of influence, if China is open to the commerce of all nations, I think the English public will accept our renunciation of a purely nominal privilege.

Mr. Lloyd George's proposal concerning Kiaochow is adopted.

Lloyd George. Must we not also examine the question of reparations which are or are not due to Poland, Rumania, Serbia, Bohemia? I will observe that two thirds of the Poles fought against us during this war and are claiming their part of the reparation for damages which they themselves contributed to causing. On the other hand, should we not consider that they are amply repaid by the possession of regions as rich as the coal basin of Silesia? To receive that province freed from its part of the German debt and then to claim still more indemnities is a bit much. What does M. Orlando think of that?

Orlando. That question touches directly on Italian interests; I have said nothing about it until now because the question is reserved; but obviously the problem is one of those which must be asked. From the political point of view, the territories which were part of the enemy states must be called upon to pay their part of what is owed by those states. First it would be necessary to ask our financial experts what is the capacity to pay of the territories which constituted the Austro-Hungarian Empire, and then to divide the damages among these territories, either proportionally according to their wealth or, if that evaluation should appear too difficult, according to the number of their inhabitants. Each state whose territory is increasing at the expense of the former Austro-Hungarian Monarchy, such as Serbia and Rumania, will have to bear liability for a contribution corresponding to the capacity to pay of the annexed territories.

Serbia, for example, would have an asset for the reparations due her and a liability for a part of what the Austro-Hungarian Empire would have had to pay if it still existed. The same method would be applied to Rumania or to Poland. We must begin by consulting our experts.

Lloyd George. Do you want to tell your financial representative to invite his colleagues in our name to meet to examine that question?

Orlando. He has already spoken to them about it, and they declared themselves ready to proceed with him to that examination, if they are so instructed by their governments.

Lloyd George. If we agree, it is the mandate of the governments that I ask you to communicate to them through your financial expert.

That proposal is adopted.

Wilson. We have also to return to the question of cables. My great concern is to avoid having the essential communications across the Atlantic Ocean as well as across the Pacific Ocean fall under a monopoly. I have already mentioned the case of cables seized by the Japanese, which they wish to keep. These cables cross at the island of Yap, and if that island remained in the hands of the Japanese, mastery of the telegraphic communications of a great part of the Pacific, in particular between the United States and the

Philippines, would belong to them. We must see to it that the means of communication across a great ocean be not placed under the control of a single nation.

It was decided the other day that the Germans would have the right to raise and use those of their cables which were cut during the war, but which were not rerouted in other directions. It is interesting to know where they could place these cables. If, for example, all rights of this kind in the Azores were reserved to English companies, the consequence would be that America's communications with Europe and with western Africa could only take place by English cables, which could lead in the future to tension and difficulties.

Lloyd George. I must tell you that I do not know about this question. Mr. Lansing has studied it closely and Mr. Balfour is informed; I propose that they speak together and submit their conclusions to us.

That proposal is adopted.

Mantoux, I, 270-76.

To Isaiah Bowman

My dear Dr. Bowman: [Paris] 18 April, 1919.

I have received and read with the deepest feeling the letter which you, Mr. Johnson, Mr. Lunt, Mr. Seymour, Mr. Day, and Mr. Young addressed to me under date of yesterday about the Italian claims on the Adriatic. I need not tell you that my own instinct responds to it, and I am deeply obliged to you all six for your reinforcement of judgment in a matter which, like yourselves, I regard as of the most critical importance.

Cordially and sincerely yours,   [Woodrow Wilson]

CCL (WP, DLC).

To Fridtjof Nansen

My dear Dr. Nanzen: [Paris] 18 April, 1919.

Thank you warmly for your letter of yesterday. I am heartily glad to have been of any service and am very much pleased to know that the important matter of getting food to Russia is in such good hands.   Cordially and sincerely yours,   [Woodrow Wilson]

CCL (WP, DLC).

To Henry White

My dear Mr. White: [Paris] 18 April, 1919.

Personally I was ready, and hoped that my colleagues would be, to accept the recommendation of the Waterways Commission with regard to the Kiel Canal,[1] but when I brought it up there was the usual injection of the point of view of the military men, because that recommendation said nothing about the fortification of the canal.

Personally I think that inasmuch as the canal lies entirely within German territory, we ought to confine our demands to what the recommendation referred to contained, but in view of what was said at the conference at the Quai d'Orsay on Wednesday,[2] I did not feel that I could object to referring the matter to the joint consideration of the military advisors and the Commission on Waterways.

Cordially and faithfully yours,   Woodrow Wilson

TLS (J. B. Scott Papers, DGU).
  [1] See n. 1 to the minutes of the Council of Four printed at April 16, 1919.
  [2] See the minutes of the Council of Four and the Council of Foreign Ministers printed at April 16, 1919.

Tasker Howard Bliss to Gilbert Fairchild Close

Dear Mr. Close: Paris April 18th, 1919

Referring to the matter of the Luxembourg plebiscite, the message which I sent to our officer in Luxembourg[1] and which was given to the President by Mr. Balfour, was as follows:

"The Conference is of opinion that it would be desirable for the present to defer the Plebiscite until the general situation can be further considered."

As you know, a telegram was received from our officer near Luxembourg—General SMITH[2]—yesterday saying that the message had been delivered and the Plebiscite was postponed. I am just in receipt from General Smith of the enclosed letter addressed to President Wilson by Mr. REUTER,[3] Minister of State of the Grand Duchy of Luxembourg. You will note from the President's letter that there are two proposed plebiscites—one to determine the economic relations of Luxembourg, and the other to determine whether Luxembourg shall remain a Grand Duchy or become a republic.

As you will see from Mr. REUTER's letter, the Luxembourg Government assumes that the wish of the Conference relates only to the plebiscite in regard to the economic relations of Luxembourg and that it does not relate to the plebiscite to determine the political status of the Luxembourg people. He desires, *as a matter of urgency*, to have President Wilson confirm this interpretation as to the wishes of the Conference, in order that they may proceed with their plebiscite to determine their political status on the date which has already been fixed for it,—to-wit, the 4th of May. If you can secure the President's decison on this and let me know at the earliest possible moment I will get a message through at once to General Smith in order that he may notify the Luxembourg Government. In view of their ready concurrence in the wishes of the Council I think that they are entitled to a speedy reply. Unless you desire to retain it, if you will kindly return to me Mr. REUTER's letter I will file it with the other papers in the case.

Cordially yours,   Tasker H. Bliss.

TLS (WP, DLC).
    ¹ Unidentified.
    ² Brig. Gen. Harry Alexander Smith, officer in charge of civil affairs for the American army of occupation in Germany.
    ³ That is, Émile Reuter.

To Tasker Howard Bliss

My dear General Bliss: [Paris] 18 April, 1919.

I return herewith the letter of Mr. Reuter, the Minister of State of the Grand Duchy of Luxembourg. I have consulted my colleagues about the reply, and it seems to us that to have the plebiscite on either the economic relations of Luxembourg or on its political status as a Grand Duchy would preclude the subsequent consideration of questions which the conference is anxious to have Luxembourg consider on their merits, and I would be very much obliged if you would have this conclusion conveyed to Mr. Reuter with the assurance that it is meant only as an intimation of our sincere desire to assist Luxembourg in the way most acceptable to her in determining her future relationships, and that we would esteem it a distinct service to the conference if the plebiscite in both its forms could be for the present postponed.

Cordially and faithfully yours,   Woodrow Wilson

TLS (T. H. Bliss Papers, DLC).

To Raymond Blaine Fosdick

My dear Mr. Fosdick: Paris, 18 April 1919.

All that I have seen and heard over here in France has but added to my sense of profound appreciation of the vital importance of maintaining in full volume and strength the service of the seven organizations which last fall joined in a united campaign for support,—the Young Men's Christian Association, the Young Women's Christian Association, the National Catholic War Council (Knights of Columbus), the Jewish Welfare Board, the War Camp Community Service, the American Library Association and the Salvation Army, on behalf of our soldiers and sailors. In addition to the needs which existed at the beginning of the War, there are now added and very imperative reasons why this work should be continued during the period of demobilization. The American people showed in a remarkable manner their whole-hearted support of the cause for which their men were fighting when they responded so generously to the appeal of the United War Work Campaign last November, and I earnestly hope that the whole amount then subscribed may be forthcoming, in order that this final helpful and still absolutely necessary ministry on behalf of the men who have given themselves with such rare devotion to the nation's cause may be in every way worthy of their wonderful spirit.

Cordially and sincerely yours,   Woodrow Wilson

TLS (WP, DLC).

From William Christian Bullitt

My dear Mr. President: [Paris] 18 April 1919.

In the House of Commons on April 16th, Mr. Lloyd-George made the following statements:[1]

The PRIME MINISTER.—No; we have had no approaches at all.[2] Of course, there are constantly men coming and going from Russia of all nationalities who are always coming back with their own tales from Russia. But we have had nothing authentic. We have had no approaches of any sort or kind. I have only heard of reports that others have got proposals which they assume have come from authentic quarters, but these have never been put before the Peace Conference by any member of that Conference at all. Therefore, we have not considered them. I think I know what the right hon. gentleman refers to. There was some suggestion that there was [were] some young Americans who had come back. All I can say about that is that it is not for me to judge the value of these communications.[3] But if the President of the United States had attached any value to them he would have brought them before the Conference, and he certainly did not.

I should greatly appreciate it, if you would inform me whether the last sentence of this statement of Mr. Lloyd-George is true or untrue.   Very respectfully yours,   William C. Bullitt.

TLS (WP, DLC).
¹ The following paragraph is a clipping from an unidentified newspaper pasted on the letter.
² Lloyd George's comments were inspired by a number of virulent attacks upon him and/or his government for his or its alleged contacts with the Bolshevik regime in Russia. Henry Wickham Steed, provoked by hints about William C. Bullitt's mission to Russia and a proposed recognition of the Soviet government, wrote editorials published in the Paris edition of the *Daily Mail* on March 27 and 28 which strongly opposed any such policy. These in turn sparked equally strong denunciations of the rumored démarche in the French press. Steed published another scathing editorial on the subject in the London *Times* of April 3. This inspired a British press and parliamentary campaign against any accommodation with the Bolsheviks. In addition, Winston S. Churchill, at this time a member of Lloyd George's cabinet, on April 11 made a strongly anti-Bolshevik speech in London. See Thompson, *Russia, Bolshevism, and the Versailles Peace*, pp. 237-45; Noble, *Policies and Opinions at Paris, 1919*, pp. 287-89; Henry Wickham Steed, *Through Thirty Years, 1892-1922: A Personal Narrative* (2 vols., Garden City, N. Y., 1924), II, 301-307; and Richard H. Ullman, *Britain and the Russian Civil War: November 1918-February 1920* (Princeton, N. J., 1968), pp. 140-44, 152-53.
³ Lloyd George's remarks to this point were disingenuous, to say the least. In fact, Lloyd George had had a breakfast conference with Bullitt on March 27, at which Bullitt's mission to Russia and the Soviet peace proposal he had brought back were discussed at length. Bullitt later testified that he had brought to this breakfast meeting the "official text" of the Soviet proposal and that Lloyd George had stated that he had previously read it in Bullitt's telegram from Helsinki. See W. C. Bullitt to WW, March 16, 1919, Vol. 55. Bullitt also recalled that the Prime Minister had had a copy of the *Daily Mail* containing one of Steed's editorials (mentioned in n. 2 above) and had said: "As long as the British press is doing this kind of thing how can you expect me to be sensible about Russia?" Lloyd George, Bullitt remembered, had then mentioned several conservative British political figures who might be sent to Russia to gather new information which might be more acceptable to British public opinion. Finally, Bullitt recalled, Lloyd George had urged him to publish his report. See Thompson, *op. cit.*, p. 242 and William C. Bullitt, *The Bullitt Mission to Russia: Testimony before the Committee on Foreign Relations United States Senate of William C. Bullitt* (New York, 1919), pp. 66-67.

Two Letters from Tasker Howard Bliss

My dear Mr. President: Paris, April 18th, 1919.

Some three weeks ago General Sir Henry Wilson, the Chief of Staff of the British Imperial Army, came to my apartment at the Hotel de Crillon and informed me that he had that day telegraphed to Mr. Winston Churchill, the British Secretary of State for War, saying that Mr. Lloyd George had directed him to send an order to the British General Ironside¹ at Archangel ordering him to withdraw the expedition in North Russia when the navigation conditions at Archangel would permit. Under date of April 15, 1919, Mr. Poole, the American Charge d'Affaires at Archangel, telegraphed to the American Mission as follows:

"Ironside insists that he is without definite instructions from London concerning policy but there seems to have been approval of the plan discussed in my No. 72² *to help troops of the Northern*

government to perfect the union with Siberia. Ironside says that
the *logical development of this policy will be to advance on Kotlas
as promptly* as possible."[3]

I invite your special attention to the words which I have underlined with the red pencil.

The plan referred to by Mr. Poole in his No. 72 is one by which
the expedition, instead of withdrawing on the opening of navigation,
would advance to Kotlas and thence to Viatka in order to connect
with a friendly Siberian force said to be approaching in that direction.

This matter of playing fast and loose with the plans for the North
Russia expedition is becoming very serious. I think that you should
request from Mr. Lloyd George to see the exact orders which have
been issued to the British Commander at Archangel. Our troops
are under the command of a British Commander. He may make
plans which may so tie up the American forces that they cannot
be withdrawn when navigation opens, notwithstanding the practical pledge which has been given to the American people. I think
that you should have a distinct agreement in writing with Mr. Lloyd
George that the American contingent will be placed safely aboard
transports for home at the earliest possible moment. The American
regiment now with that expedition understands that it will be withdrawn as promised. Any failure to do this will almost certainly bring
on a general mutiny in that regiment. If there is the slightest intention to allow American troops to remain with this expedition
after the opening of navigation fresh troops should have been sent
there before this in order that the regiment now there may be
relieved.

This matter is becoming so serious that there should be a definite
agreement, in writing, between the British and American governments at once.   Very sincerely yours,   Tasker H. Bliss.

[1] That is, Brig. Gen. William Edmund Ironside.
[2] D. C. Poole Jr., to FLP, April 2, 1919, T telegram (SDR, RG 59, 861.00/4207, DNA).
As Poole indicated in the quotation above, this telegram discussed the project to join the
anti-Bolshevik forces in northern Russia with Kolchak's army then advancing eastward
from Siberia.
[3] D. C. Poole Jr., to FLP, April 15, 1919, T telegram (SDR, RG 59, 861.00/4299, DNA).

My dear Mr. President: Paris April 18th, 1919

I informed you yesterday, by my letter addressed to Mr. Close,
that I had had an interview in the morning with Mr. Paderewski,
as directed by you, on the subject of the acceptance by the Poles
of a truce on the same terms and conditions as already accepted
by the Ukrainians. Beyond general expressions of a desire to comply

with your wishes and those of the Council, I could get nothing satisfactory from Mr. Paderewski. He told me that he would consult his colleagues and let me know his decision in a personal interview this morning. Not having heard from him, late in the afternoon I asked Dr. Lord to see him in person and remind him of his promise to give me the necessary information this morning and to ask him when I could receive it as I intended to submit a memorandum on the subject to you to-day. Thereupon, he telephoned to me that he would call upon me at five o'clock. He did so and we had a conference lasting for one hour.

He began with a statement which I asked his permission to have taken down by my stenographer, in order that I might not by any possibility misinterpret his words in communicating them to you. He gave his cordial consent, and I then dictated the following statement which he said were his exact words, in terms and in spirit:

"His Excellency Mr. Paderewski, at an interview this afternoon between 5.00 and 6.00 o'clock, desires me to say to President Wilson that he and his government accept in principle the suggested armistice and express their cordial desire to meet in every way possible the wishes of the President and of the Council. In execution of this idea he has sent a radio this morning to his government in Warsaw requesting them to send a general officer of the Polish Army to Paris as soon as possible in order that with his knowledge of the exact situation as between the Polish and the Ukrainian forces he may arrange the technical details in a way that will be satisfactory to the Polish people."

I asked Mr. Paderewski whether he could not send a radio to his government asking them to direct its commander in the field to enter into a temporary truce with the Ukrainians pending the arrival in Paris of the officer that he had asked to have sent here and pending his subsequent negotiations here. He replied that he could not do this; that if a truce were now entered into the Polish and Ukrainian forces were so near to each other that the latter would flood the Polish camps with Bolshevik propaganda and that the whole Polish army would then go Bolshevik; that the two forces must be separated in some way and this could only be indicated after the arrival of the officer for whom he had sent.

After the long interview that I had with Mr. Paderewski I feel little hope that the great object will be attained,—to wit, a cessation of the military operations in Eastern Galicia pending the determination of the final boundaries in a treaty of peace between Poland and the Powers. If this cannot be assured, there is great danger of a blaze all through South-eastern Europe. General Haller's Polish divisions are now enroute to Poland. It is quite certain that on arrival they will be immediately sent to Lemberg and will overcome the existing balance between the Polish and Ukrainian forces there. In the event of the decisive repulse of the Ukrainian forces there is no telling where the Poles will stop. It is well known that they are quite entirely under the domination of French influence. It is generally believed that following their repulse the Ukrainians will go Bolshevik and we will have lost another of the governments in that critical situation which claims to desire to be an orderly one.

Even assuming that the Polish Government will now act in good faith, it is quite certain that a considerable time must elapse before the Polish officer sent for by Mr. Paderewski can arrive here; and that much more time will elapse before any conclusion can be reached here. Meanwhile, with the reinforcements now going to Poland, that government will probably get entirely beyond control. I suggest that the following may be perfectly appropriate and, possibly, sufficient action by the Council of Four.

Mr. Paderewski should be informed by the Council itself, in the most sympathetic but most positive terms, that having accepted in principle a truce and an armistice which has already been unreservedly accepted by the Ukrainians, the Council has a perfect right and it is its duty to demand of the Polish Government that it immediately order a suspension of arms pending final action by the Council of the Powers. My personal opinion is that Mr. Paderewski should also, and simultaneously, be informed by the Council that the latter will at once take up the question of the definition of the disputed boundaries.

Mr. Paderewski should also be informed that the Council demands that Haller's divisions now proceeding to Poland shall not be sent to Lemberg nor shall they be used to relieve other Polish troops in order that the latter may go to Lemberg.

It seems to me that the situation as it has existed and continues to exist is a manifest affront to the Council. We cannot afford to allow it to be said that the question of boundaries is not being settled by the Council but by the interested nations themselves who hope thus to petrify in advance the decision of the Council. The Ukrainians, as said before, have acccepted unreservedly the proposed truce and armistice. They have a right to the same consideration that would doubtless be given to the Poles were the latter now demanding an armistice. As Haller's divisions, accompanied and preceded by many French officers, are now enroute to Poland where they will arrive within a few days and as their arrival will so strengthen the Poles that they may feel entirely independent of control, I hope that the action of the Council will be taken very promptly. If the Polish Government should not promptly and fully comply with the wishes of the Council, I think that it could be made to comply by a declaraton that all of the supplies now going and to go to it will be stopped.   Sincerely yours,   Tasker H. Bliss.

TLS (WP, DLC).

From William Emmanuel Rappard

Dear Mr. President,   Paris, April 18, 1919

The Swiss Federal Council and the Council of State of the Republic and Canton of Geneva request me to transmit to you and to the other members of the Commission on the League of Nations the expression of their most grateful appreciation of the high honor that has been done to their Country and their City. They wish you to be assured that the people of Switzerland and Geneva fully realize both the honor and the responsibilities which your decision brings to them.

If you could grant me five minutes of your invaluable time, I should deem it a great privilege to be allowed to express their feelings to you in person and to call your attention to a peculiar situation which has arisen in Switzerland with regard to the proposed League of Nations. I believe that you would not have cause to regret a moment's conversation on this topic.

I would not have ventured to ask again for this favor, which I solicited a few days ago through the good offices of Colonel House, had not a mention in this morning's papers led me to believe that only a misunderstanding had deprived me of it yesterday. The papers say that you yesterday at noon received Mr. Calonder, Swiss Minister of Foreign Affairs. As Mr. Calonder has not left Berne for the last three weeks and as I asked to be heard on his behalf, I suppose that some unfortunate error has occur[r]ed.

In the bold hope that you will find a moment to give me to-day, or to-morrow, I am, dear Mr. President, with the assurances of my highest esteem,   Sincerely yours,   William E. Rappard

TLS (WP, DLC).

Sir William Wiseman to Edward Mandell House

Confidential.

Dear Mr. House,   [Paris] 18th April 1919.

In view of the serious situation in Egypt, it is of great importance that the Government of the United States should recognize the British Protectorate.

If the President can see his way to do this at once it will do much to steady native opinion and avoid the terrible consequences which would follow a Holy War.

Mr. Balfour has asked me to take this up with you. It is a matter of great urgency and I hope you will be good enough to bring it to the attention of the President at the earliest moment.

Briefly the facts are as follows:

When Turkey entered the war by her attack on Odessa, and by crossing the Sinai frontier, the British Government declared a Protectorate over Egypt, a necessity imposed by the Turkish challenge, and in order that they might be in a position to take the necessary measures to defend Egyptian territory.

In December 1914 the French Government gave a general recognition of this Protectorate.

In view of the present situation in Egypt it is of great importance that the United States Government should also recognise the Protectorate.

The ceremony of the accession of the New Sultan Fuad[1] last autumn was attended by the heads of the Allied and Neutral missions in Cairo. While this could not be considered as a formal recognition of the British Protectorate, it was an indication of the views held by the Neutral as well as the Allied Governments. The American Charge d'Affaires, Mr. Knabenshue,[2] attended with the rest of his colleagues, and it is understood that the State Department approved of his action.

Mr. Knabenshue's attitude during his tenure of the American agency has been consistently friendly, sympathetic and helpful, and it is understood that he considers local conditions render the recognition of the British Protectorate highly desirable in order to ease the situation and prevent further collisions in Egypt.

General Allenby reports that the situation in Egypt is daily becoming more serious. In order to satisfy public opinion in Egypt, and to bring about a permanent improvement in the situation, it is necessary that a new Egyptian Ministry should be formed on Liberal lines. The Sultan, however, considers that it is not possible to form a new Ministry until certain political concessions can be promised to the Nationalists and until the position of the Egyptian Government can be strengthened by the recognition of the British Protectorate by the United States of America.

The extreme Nationalists are chiefly paid agents of the revolutionary party in Turkey and the Bolshevists. These extremists are making use of the legitimate demands of the Egyptian nationalists for a further measure of self-government, and are also able to take advantage of the unsatisfactory state of the British Protectorate.

They claim that the United States desires that the authority of the Sultan of Turkey shall once more be recognised in Egypt. All sorts of wild statements gain credence: among others that President Wilson is supporting the nationalist agitators in their attempt to stir up a Holy War against the Infidels.

The recognition of the British Protectorate by the United States would help to remove from Egyptian politics the dangerous religious and Bolshevist appeal which is now gaining force. It would also enable the British Government to meet the views of the more moderate nationalist leaders and enable the Sultan to form a Liberal Ministry whose programme would be peace and progress without disorder.   Yours very sincerely,   [William Wiseman]

CCL (W. Wiseman Papers, CtY).
    [1] Fuad I, Sultan of Egypt, formerly Ahmed Fuad Pasha.
    [2] Paul Knabenshue, Consul at Cairo.

From the Diary of Colonel House

April 18, 1919.

Since this is Good Friday I anticipated more or less freedom because I thought people would be too occupied to disturb me. In this I was mistaken for I have seldome [seldom] had a busier day. Lloyd George asked me to lunch with him. The only other guest was Sir Archibald Williams, M.P. from one of the large North of England manufacturing districts. I think George had forgotten that Williams was coming for he put him out just as soon as he had finished his lunch.

George desired to talk about Syria. He is still disturbed about it. He believes the French and Arabs will surely clash. He had been talking to the President about it this morning and the President advised him to take it up with me, and George in turn, advised me to take it up with the French.

What he wants is for us to accept the Mandatory for Syria and let the French have Constantinople. In discussing this with the President afterward, he was afraid the French would intrigue in Constantinople and that it would not be a wise move. He preferred them in Syria where the League could watch them. . . .

The President and I discussed the question of Fiume and I urged him to settle it one way or the other. I have about come to the conclusion that since we cannot please the Italians by compromise, we might as well do what seems best in the judgment of our Experts, and that is to give it directly to the Jugo-Slavs, safe-guarding the right of all those contributary to the port. This solution appealed to the President. I urged him to take it up with Lloyd George and Clemenceau and commit them in order to present a united front. I have not much confidence in his being able to do this, because both Lloyd George and Clemenceau will wish to lay the burden on the President, shielding themselves behind the Pact of London.

We took up the question of the recoginition [recognition] of British Sovereignty in Egypt. Wiseman's letter to me upon this subject will explain the matter. The President agreed to do it with certain limitations. I shall write to Balfour tomorrow, giving him the President's position.

The President handed me a memorandum which our Experts had prepared regarding Dantzig, and asked me to have a few minor changes made.[1] We also discussed Dalmatia and I gave him a memorandum which Mezes prepared on that subject.[2]

While I was with the President, Wiseman telephoned asking if the President objected to having a secretary in at the meetings of the Council of Four. It seems that Lloyd George has told his people that the reason they could not sit in was because of the President's objections. The President readily consented to having one.

[1] For the revised version, see S. E. Mezes to WW, April 21, 1919.

[2] On April 15, 1919, Wilson had asked House to request Mezes to prepare for his consideration "a series of articles providing for the government of Dalmatia within the Treaty of London line in accordance with plans similar to that prepared for the Saar Basin, and providing also for the holding of the plebiscite at the end of 5-10 or 15 years as might seem most appropriate to determine whether the area in question should continue under the administration and control of an agency of the League of Nations or should be incorporated in the Yugo-Slav State."

Mezes and Frank Lord Warrin, Jr., secretary for territorial questions in the A.C.N.P., had prepared the draft articles to which House here refers. The plan of government of the Dalmatian territory in question was indeed modeled after the one for the Saar Basin. Moreover, it followed Wilson's instruction by providing that a plebiscite should be held in 1929, and that the inhabitants of the specified territory should vote upon only two questions—whether they wished to continue to be governed by a League of Nations commission or whether they desired union with Yugoslavia. In the latter event, the five Allied and Associated Powers agreed to cede to Yugoslavia, in accordance with the decision of the League of Nations, "all that territory governed thereby." See the documents printed in Miller, *My Diary at the Conference of Paris*, VIII, 331-34, 379-91.

From the Diary of Ray Stannard Baker

Friday the 18th [April 1919]

I had quite a long talk with the President this evening in his study. . . .

The President was in a rather discouraged mood, I thought. He expects a break with the Italians on the question of Fiume. He met with Lloyd-George & Clemenceau at Clemenceau's office this afternoon & they agreed on a policy which is to be maintained with Orlando & Sonnino when the Italian question comes up to-morrow.

They settled the Polish boundaries to-day.

The President asked me if I thought there was any element of "bluff" still left in Orlando's demands—which amount to an ultimatum—and I told him I thought not. Orlando's political necessity dictates his position. He says that L.G. has served his domestic political situation, Clemenceau his & Wilson his (the Monroe Doctrine) & he wants his necessities also considered.

From the Peace Conference Diary of William Linn Westermann

Friday, April 18 [1919]

Mr. Crane dined with the President on Wednesday. The President had received the document, in abbreviated form,[1] which de Caix[2] left in the office. Crane told of an intercepted wireless which the President had received which showed that the allied governments were stacking the cards against the Interallied Committee which was to go to Syria. As it has turned out it was our abbreviated version of the de Caix document with comment and conclusion against the sending of the Committee.

[1] See the memorandum by W. L. Westermann printed at April 17, 1919.
[2] Robert de Caix de Saint-Aymour, director of *Asie française* and *Afrique française*, and a technical expert on political and diplomatic questions in the French delegation to the peace conference.

From the Diary of Edith Benham

April 18, 1919

Conversation at the table is not so interesting as it was because one of the servants is undoubtedly a spy for the foreign office, and one feels sure things are carried back. The servants are selected by them and are excellent. There is an old head butler and his wife who run the house and are responsible for the linen, etc. I believe the contract for food is let to a restaurant—La Rue. Beside our table Close, Swem and Wagner, the stenographers and Hoover[1] have their meals together in a little dining room off my office, formerly the nursery dining room.

Downstairs an endless lot of people are fed; the servants, the Captain of the French Guard and his Lieutenant. You see all this little square is guarded by the French soldiers. Inside are the American guard, and a certain number of them, and Mr. Close's office force and mine are fed—and splendidly fed all these boys say.

They are devoted to the old maitre d'hotel and his wife whom they say do everything in the world for them, and the old man says they are polite and never drunk. He is a good old soul and does not come in the spy category.

¹ That is, Charles C. Wagner and Irwin Hood Hoover.

To Oscar Solomon Straus

My dear Mr. Straus: [Paris] 18 April, 1919.

I have been very much cheered by your kind letter of yesterday, with the messages which it quotes from the League to Enforce Peace and from Mr. Taft personally, and I want to thank you very warmly for your own kind personal assurances of satisfaction with the results of our work on the Covenant.

Cordially and sincerely yours,   Woodrow Wilson

TLS (O.S. Straus Papers, DLC).

From Robert Lansing

My dear Mr. President: Paris. 18th April, 1919.

I enclose herewith a copy of a telegram stating that a memorial service for the late Ambassador Page is being arranged for April 25th and suggesting that you might wish to send some message in regard to Mr. Page's work which could be read at the meeting. I will be pleased to transmit any message which you may wish to send.¹   Faithfully yours,   Robert Lansing

TLS (WP, DLC).
¹ See GFC to RL, April 19, 1919.

To Gilbert Monell Hitchcock

Paris, April 18, 1919.

Please convey the following to Senator Hitchcock, quote. I am warmly obliged to you for your message.¹ It cheers and encourages me and I am delighted to know that what we have done has so brightened the prospects of the League. unquote.

Woodrow Wilson.

T telegram (WP, DLC).
¹ G. M. Hitchcock to WW, April 16, 1919.

To William Cox Redfield

Paris, 18 April 1919.

For Redfield. I am sincerely sorry that the efforts of the Industrial Board have met with serious check,[1] but I am afraid that it is partly because the public and some members of the Board itself have been under the impression that they were fixing prices and had been invited to do so, whereas, as I am sure you yourself hold, the office of the Board was merely a court of mediation between buyer and seller. In view of this misapprehension, I think it would be wise not to extend the effort into new fields. It is hard to think clearly about such matters at this distance, but I instinctively feel this to be a counsel of prudence.   Woodrow Wilson.

T telegram (WP, DLC).
　[1] Wilson was replying to WCR to WW, April 11, 1919.

To Walker Downer Hines

Paris, 18 April 1919.

For Hines. I have been thinking a great deal about the matter in controversy between the Industrial Board and the Railway Administration and take the liberty of urging that in consultation with Mr. Redfield and his associates you will try to fix a price that you are willing to pay for steel rails, which will not be the lowest price you could demand but the lowest price that you can pay without, in effect, obliging the purchasers of steel in other forms to reimburse the manufacturers by the prices they pay for what the manufacturers will deem they lost in the transactions with the Railway Administration. This is the point of danger and I am sure I can confidently urge upon you the desirability of avoiding such consequences.   Woodrow Wilson.

T telegram (WP, DLC).

From Norman Hezekiah Davis

Dear Mr. President: Paris, 18th April, 1919.

The Secretary of the Treasury has cabled me that all credits established in favor of Italy have been advanced except balances of credits for neutral purchases, and that the amount of credits approved but not yet established is $163,500,000. He states that he hopes to make, at an early date, a final commitment to Italy regarding the future establishment of credits in her favor for war purposes, but that in the meantime it may be advisable formally to commit the Treasury to the possible establishment of credits for Italy of an amount between twenty-four and fifty million dollars, in excess of the amounts already approved by you, so that Italy may meet the following demands:

(a) Outstanding commitments for approved purchases.
(b) Running expenses to June 1st—a trifling amount.
(c) Interest due in May on Italian obligations held by the United States.
(d) Certain claims of our departments.
(e) Further contracts or expenditures during April and May.

The Secretary has accordingly asked me to obtain your approval for the establishment of a credit for Italy up to fifty million dollars, in addition to amounts previously approved by you, and I am therefore enclosing a letter of approval to Secretary Glass for your signature in case it meets with your approval.[1]

Bearing in mind your suggestion regarding the establishment of a credit in favor of the British Government, which would apply equally in this case, I shall suggest to Secretary Glass that he withhold as long as possible the establishment of this credit pending developments here.

I am, my dear Mr. President,
Cordially and sincerely yours,   Norman H. Davis

TLS (WP, DLC).
[1] See WW to N. H. Davis, April 19, 1919.

From Joseph Patrick Tumulty

[The White House] April 18 1919.

#64 War Loan Organization requests following statement from you which has Secretary Glass' approval QUOTE

For two weary years the American people have striven to fulfill the task of saving our civilization. By the exertion of unmeasured power they have quickly brought home the victory without which they would have remained in the field until the last resource had been exhausted.

Bringing to the contest a strength of spirit made doubly strong by the righteousness of their cause, they devoted themselves unswervingly to the prosecution of their undertaking in the full knowledge that no conquest lay in their path excepting the conquest of a kingdom of Right.

Today, the world stands freed of the dismal threat of those archaic systems of militarism which perennially affrighted industrious peoples and vaingloriously cast away the fruitful arrangements of nations.

The heavy stone of war has been rolled away and at this sacred Easter season the promise of a new and radiant peace seems near and intimate. Pleasant avenues to a fresher and larger life open to our people and to our neighbors and the kindly will is among the nations to learn war no more.

But we yet stand only at the gateway of these auspicious times. To enter, we must fulfill to the utmost the engagements we have made. Chief and key among these is the Victory Liberty Loan. Two years ago we pledged our lives and fortunes to the cause for which we have fought. Sixty thousand of our strongest sons have redeemed for us that pledge of blood. To redeem in full faith the pledge of our treasure, the opportunity is offered quickly and gladly to subscribe to the Victory Liberty Loan. UNQUOTE.

Tumulty.

T telegram (WP, DLC).

From Herbert Clark Hoover

Dear Mr. President: [Paris] 18 April 1919.

I have received from you Mr. Redfield's letter with regard to the price of wheat.[1]

This problem divides itself into two distinct stages. The first is with regard to the balance of the 1918 harvest year, that is until the new harvest is available in quantity, say September 1st, 1919; the second is the 1919 harvest year.

Mr. Redfield's proposition is, I understand, that wheat should be allowed to take its normal course in the market, that is at its "world price."

With regard to the first stage, that is, up to the 1st of July, the "world price" is probably $3.00 or $4.00 per bushel as we are now plunged into an effective world shortage by inability to send enough tonnage to the Argentine and Australia to secure supplies from that quarter, and if the control of prices were removed in the United States and if all buyers were allowed to enter that market, the price will go to extremely high levels. We have, in fact, a shortage of thirty million bushels of wheat to supply the demands on us to July 1st. And this, after refusing to make further supplies to Neutrals (in order to force them to the Southern Hemisphere).

You will perhaps recollect that six weeks ago, when Mr. Redfield and his associates demanded that we remove the price control on wheat, pork and cottonseed products, I and my entire staff protested that this was fraught with extreme danger in view of the world situation and the speculative activities that would follow, and that prices would rise. The control of pork products was removed and the price of hogs has ascended from $17.50 to $21.00, and although I have not purchased any pork products for Relief purposes or for Germany since the control was removed, and [sic] I am sure an even worse situation would arise if we removed the fixed price on wheat.

As to the harvest of 1919, as Mr. Redfield points out, there can be only one seller of wheat in the United States, and there will probably be a continuation of consolidated buying abroad. There can, therefore, be no natural flow of supply and demand on which to base any "world price" of wheat. One might approach the problem in two or three ways—none very effective. A guess might be made at the world supplies and the probable world demand. To present appearances the world supply of wheat next harvest will be again insufficient to take care of the world demand assuming always that Europe does not fall into complete anarchy and is able by its products to pay for its bread. Even on this assumption of a shortage, it is impossible to tell what the price should be. In the hands of speculators a shortage of 5% might mean $3.50 wheat as in 1917. In the hands of governments it might mean $1. or $4. depending upon the predilections of the controllers. Another factor that enters into the price of wheat and which has been much overlooked is the factor of currency inflation. Wheat is practically the only commodity under price control today in the United States, and yet all prices are very high and, in fact, although I have not calculated it accurately, I think that it is probable that the ten or twelve principal staples would prove on investigation to be higher on comparative levels to wheat itself. It would not appear, therefore, that the price of wheat can be influencing the price level of other commodities so much as depreciated currency and world shortage. Another method by which the problem might be approached is to make an economic determination from time to time as to what the price level is of say some ten other principal food staples and adjust the price of wheat downward to such level, should they indicate a level below the guaranteed price. Such a procedure would be based on the assumption that there is a free flow of supply and demand in the other staples and as the world controls of these other staples have been largely liquidated this might be possible. On the other hand, the technical difficulties of adjusting the price of wheat downward to the consumer and yet maintain it at the guaranteed price for the producer will require the utmost ingenuity, with the assumption of a uniform high integrity on the part of some hundreds of thousands of people. The wheat of the United States physically cannot come all into the market in one day and placed in the possession of the Government and be resold on the next day at a lower price, but it must naturally flow into the market every day for the whole 365 days, and as near as I can recollect there are about 44,000 wheat buyers in the United States. Each of these buyers would need become a Government agent paying the guaranteed price and reselling at some lower price with a great bureaucracy of watchmen against fraud. A great number of methods have been suggested for handling this technical problem, but none of which have yet appealed to me.

There is another broad problem involved that even assuming the guaranteed price of wheat is higher next year than the world price or the economic price would indicate that it should be, two factors enter into it from a public point of view. The first is that out of probably 1,100,000,000 bushels we shall want to export 500,000,000 bushels. If we take a dollar off of the entire crop, it will cost the Government a billion one hundred million dollars, and of this money we shall have conferred upon the rest of the world five hundred million and I doubt whether the rest of the world would give thanks.

The price of flour on the guaranteed price of wheat should be about $11.00 a barrel wholesale, Atlantic seaboard. The pre-War average price was approximately $5 to $6.00, but if we are to maintain our present wage level and present increased railway rates a reduction in the price of wheat so as to absorb the entire one hundred million dollars would probably not reduce the price of flour below $8.50 a barrel, and at the consumption of the American public this would be a saving to the United States consumer of approximately $350,000,000 at a cost to the Government of $1,100,000,000.

To sum up this very confused and problematical statement, I would say that the same policy would need be pursued with regard to next years wheat that has been pursued in regard to all food emergencies, and that is a consultation between yourself and those whom you can best depend upon for advice from time to time and an adjustment from time to time based on the economic, political and social outlook without any pledges to a definite course of policy.

Yours faithfully,   Herbert Hoover.

TLS (WP, DLC).
    [1] See WW to HCH, April 16, 1919, n. 1.

From Julius Howland Barnes

Washington. April 18, 3 P.M. 1919.

1628. Following for the President from Mr. Julius H. Barnes.

"My dear Mr. President: I appreciate most gratefully your expression of approval of the work of myself and my associates in the Grain Corporation for the past two years under Mr. Hoover, and I shall convey with great pleasure and pride to those associates the personal appreciation you so generously express.[1] We have no misconception regarding the scope of the large problems to be met in administering justly the national wheat price guaranty this year. Only care and patience and a great desire to use influence and authority justly can find the right solution; and with your kind invitation to carry these problems directly to yourself, I accept the responsibility you tender with a sincere desire on my part to discharge its duties in the interest of our whole people; and I shall endeavor to carry into that service also my present associates, possessing already, as I believe they do, the public confidence."

Polk   Acting.

CC telegram (WP, DLC).
  [1] See WW to J. H. Barnes, April 15, 1919.

From William Graves Sharp

My dear Mr President,   Brest, April 18th, 1919.

Just as my boat is about to sail from the shores of France, I wish my last message to be to you. I wish it to be a message bearing testimony to my appreciation of all your kindness and indulgence to me for nearly five years past.

At the same time I would extend my congratulations as well as express my great admiration for the manner in which your leadership has done so much to guide the nations of the world out of the swamps and shadows of traditional intrigues, selfishness and distrust, the existence of which has invariably laid the foundations for new wars, to the light which illumines the higher plains of reason and regard for each other's rights in a Christian spirit of mutual trust and toleration.

In recently reviewing your messages in my early morning hours at home, I have been struck, above all, with their remarkable consistency of purpose from the first neutral message to the last having to do with the armistice questions from the many powers. While changing conditions made the use of different plans necessary in effecting results, yet the underlying principles remained as fixed and as stable as some great shining star, pointing out the only way to the liberation of the world from the plague of future wars. I feel certain that success is about to crown your efforts and the world will soon proclaim you as its deliverer.

As far as the problems of actual war are concerned, only one cloud—the Russian situation—may remain to darken the horizon. I wish that might be automatically solved with the signing of peace; but I fear that is too much to hope for. While such event will have no little influence in bringing about such result, yet as much courage as wisdom will be needed in dealing with it against the foolish and prejudiced cry to not treat with the Bolshevik regime. Yet I feel certain that if another recourse to arms is not to be resorted to, some plan must be evolved by which conversation may be had with its leaders. Much as we must deplore and abhor their atrocities, the need for their cessation becomes all the greater. To thus treat with them involves no recognition of their form or manner of government. In that conversation they must be told to cease murder, to restore an orderly and just government before they can be recognized by the League of Nations. But they should be talked with.

As your exchange of notes preceding the Armistice against the opposition at home and abroad of those who would march to Berlin, ended the war eight months earlier than it would have otherwise ended and before anarchy could further undo all governmental authority, so will a parley with the present Russian regime serve to greatly expedite the urgent need of an early ending of such crimes against humanity.

This is an observation—an expression of opinion—I can not help making, no longer in an official capacity, but just simply as a private American citizen whose study and frequent conversation with those in a position to understand Russian affairs prompt me to make as a duty.

My very best wishes for a shining and enduring success in these last few more days of your labors in such a great humanitarian cause, dear Mr President, I leave with you. Mrs Sharp[1] joins me in kindest regards to Mrs Wilson.

Sincerely yours   W. G. Sharp.

ALS (WP, DLC).
[1] That is, Hallie Clough Sharp.

Cary Travers Grayson to Joseph Patrick Tumulty

[Paris, April 18, 1919]

Please secure from Thompson's drug store and send by pouch two five hundred C.C. bottles Wyeth's phosphates compound without sugar,[1] charge Naval Dispensary.   Grayson.

T telegram (WP, DLC).
[1] Phosphate salts are used primarily as laxatives and purgatives.

Gilbert Fairchild Close to Richard C. Sweet

My dear Mr. Sweet: Paris, 18 April, 1919.

The President asks me to say in reply to your note of April 16th[1] enclosing the cable message which I am returning herewith, that he feels that it would be wise for Mr. Francis to wait before publishing a book at least until the Peace Conference is over and we are in nearer sight of the end. Until things clear up in Russia the President thinks that the less said by officials the better.

Sincerely yours,   [Gilbert F. Close]

CCL (WP, DLC).
[1] R. C. Sweet to GFC, April 16, 1919, TLS (WP, DLC).

From the Diary of Dr. Grayson

Saturday, April 19, 1919.

The President had breakfast at 8:30. After breakfast he worked in his study. Colonel House dropped in to suggest that Mr. Balfour had proposed that notes should be taken of the Big Four meeting. Colonel House told the President that he thought he should have an American to take these notes, and he suggested that in the person of his son-in-law, Gordon Auchincloss, the President would find a very desirable vehicle and that he would be ready any minute he wanted him. The President said: "I thank you for the suggestion." Later on the Colonel called the President on the telephone and wanted to know what time Auchincloss would be required to come up. The President replied that when he wanted him he would let him know. He then arranged with one of his secretaries to come in to take the notes of the meeting.[1]

The Italian claims dealing with the Dalmatian case were presented by Baron Sonnino, the Italian Foreign Minister. They were exactly as had been expected—an attempt on the part of Italy absolutely to grab the entire Adriatic and to sacrifice the new Jugo-Slav Republic,—before it was actually born.

After the morning session adjourned, I asked the President what luck they had had with the problems, and he said that so far as he (the President) was concerned he was adhering to principle. He said that he hated very much to disappoint a man whom he thought so much of as he did of Premier Orlando, but that it was impossible for him to accept the Italian claims which were entirely at variance with the principles that the President had enunciated and which Italy had accepted at the time of the armistice. Although the Italians were pressing their point very strongly, no complete decision had been reached, and the question was put over for a Sunday morning meeting. The President was doing everything he possibly could to force action by the Peace Commissioners, and he himself asked for the Sunday meeting. Lloyd-George had made arrangements to spend Sunday in the devastated regions, but the President told him that he believed in the present state of world-wide unrest there was no excuse for not going ahead with the work and completing the peace program and utilizing every possible minute to do so.

Luncheon was delayed until two o'clock because the President had insisted that the morning session continue until everything possible was cleared up. And this was done. There were no luncheon guests.

After lunch the President, Mrs. Wilson and I went out for a drive to St. Cloud. We were able to make this drive in an open car—the first one since we came to France.

Following the drive, the President went to the Hotel Crillon, where he had directed the American Commissioners to meet with him in the room of Secretary of State Lansing. Following this conference the President went to the War Office, where he, Lloyd-George and Clemenceau considered various matters.

Enroute from the Crillon to the War Office I asked the President if he had made any progress at his conference with his associated Commissioners, and he said: "No, there was a great deal of talking. I went there to get some ideas but I found no one there who had any to suggest."

The President had dinner with Mrs. Wilson and myself. After dinner he played Canfield, while Mrs. Wilson and I chatted with him. The President retired early as he had mapped out a full Sunday.

---

[1] There is no evidence that any American secretary was present at this or at subsequent meetings of the Council of Four.

Hankey's Notes of a Meeting of the Council of Four[1]

President Wilson's House,
Paris, April 19, 1919, 11 a.m.

I.C.-171-D.

1. M. ORLANDO said that he would consider the whole question of Italian claims from the point of view of the resolutions taken by the Supreme Council on other questions. He recognised that there was one Power represented there to-day, namely, the United States of America, which had not taken any part in the Treaty concluded with Italy by France and Great Britain. Consequently, he proposed at the moment to deal with the subject on the hypothesis that no engagements existed. Italy had formulated three definite and distinct claims. He believed these to be in conformity with the general principles which had been adopted by the Supreme Council in dealing with the Peace Treaty. Consequently, he proposed to make a comparison between the principles underlying Italian claims and the general principles on which the Treaty of Peace was being based.

2. Italy's first claim related to her desire for union with the territories on the Italian side of the natural frontiers of Italy. Italy shared with Spain and Scandinavia the distinction of having boundaries more clearly defined by nature than almost any other country on the continent. More than almost any other country Italy possessed a geographical unity being bounded by the sea and the mighty chain of mountains which encircled her northern limits. Consequently, the natural boundary was the water-shed of the mountains and Italy claimed this line as her natural frontier. It was recognised that peoples not of Italian races were included in this territory. This was not an occasion on which to begin a discussion on the precise numbers and he had not the material with him. He would remind his colleagues, however, that everyone, without exception, who had appeared before them to discuss Austrian statistics had agreed that they were untrustworthy. No one had been more vehement on this subject than the Jugo-Slav delegates. Material could be produced to prove that the Austrians had falsified the figures against Italy. He did not know whether the incorporation of these territories in Italy would bring a hundred thousand, more or less, Slavs under Italian rule. Every time, however, that the Peace Conference had had to determine frontiers, or to fix limits of a new state, it had been recognised that the inclusion of different races was not a reason for overriding strong strategic and economic rea-

---

[1] The full text of these minutes is printed in *PPC*, V, 80-94.

sons. He asked that that same principle might be applied to the Italian claims. Pointing to the map, he explained that if the line showing the natural boundary of Istria were adopted, it would be impossible for Trieste, from a strategic point of view, since it would bring Trieste within the range of gun-fire. Even if Italy secured the whole of its claims it would embrace a total population of foreign origin which would be small in comparison with that of other nations. Under the approved scheme, for example, the population would include from 18 hundred thousand to 2 million Germans as compared with a total population of some 25 million Poles, whereas Italy would only have a foreign population of some 6 hundred thousand as compared with a total population of nearly 40 million. The same applied in the case of Roumania, which would include a large Hungarian population, and in the case of Czecho-Slovakia, which would include more than 2 million Germans compared with a total of 10 million Czechs. Hence, Italy considered it within her right to demand the natural frontiers fixed for her by God and the inclusion of certain population of other races should not be a bar. Supposing there had only been 4 or 5 hundred thousand Germans between France and the Rhine, would this, he asked, have been a reason for denying the historical strategic claims of France to the Rhine as a frontier?

3. The second point, M. Orlando continued, related to Fiume. Italy considered that the question of Fiume depended on general frontiers fixed for her. The historic frontier line of Italy passed along the watershed of the mountains and came down to the sea on the Gulf of Quarnero and would embrace Fiume. For Fiume Italy appealed to the principle of self determination of the people. He referred to a historical fact that was insufficiently remembered, that Fiume itself had, before the conclusion of the Armistice, expressed a desire for incorporation in Italy. On the 18th October, 1918, the deputies of Fiume had in the Hungarian Chamber stated that as the Austro-Hungarian Empire was in a state of dissolution, Fiume being a free city demanded union with Italy. Hence Italy was in the presence of a question that had not been raised in the first instance by Italians, and there was a general demand that the declaration by Fiume should be supported. One objection that might be raised was that the principle of self determination was not applicable to a small community. It might be urged, also, that Fiume was not a part of Italy. Nevertheless, Fiume could not be considered as an isolated unit. The principle of self determination ought to apply just as much to little peoples as to great nations, particularly where there was a historical claim. Fiume had a history relating to liberty over its own destinies dating back many centuries. It con-

stituted a small people which might be compared to the State of San Marino which, if the need arose, ought to have the same right of self determination as the peoples of Russia.

Another objection that had been raised to the inclusion of Fiume in Italy was the economic factor. The precedent he would quote here was that of Dantzig. In the case of Dantzig, the demand for annexation by Poland had not been accepted. It had been decided that the rights of the majority of the population of Germany must be respected. In the case of Dantzig, therefore, economic considerations had not been allowed to prevail over national desires. If it were decided that Fiume was to be constituted as a free state like Dantzig, the Italians would say that a procedure had been adopted which was more favourable to the Germans than to the Italians. In the case of Dantzig it could be argued that it was the sole outlet to Poland. This did not apply in the case of Jugo-Slavia which had several other outlets. It could be shown not only that there were several natural harbours left to Jugo-Slavia, but in addition that that country would have a very long coast line. There were some several ports more accessible to Jugo-Slavia than Fiume. Hence he maintained that the concession made to Poland in the case of Dantzig did not apply to Fiume.

Another difference between the two cases was that Dantzig could only serve Poland, whereas only 7% of the capacity of Fiume was used to serve Jugo-Slavia. In fact Jugo-Slavia was only a secondary consideration commercially to Fiume. He had read in the papers that M. Trumbitch[2] had stated before the Supreme Council that 50% of the port of Fiume was devoted to Jugo-Slavia. He had at once telegraphed to the Chamber of Commerce of Fiume which had telegraphed back detailed figures to show that 7% was the correct figure. Supposing, however, that it was 12% or 15%, the fact would not be altered that Fiume was mainly concerned in serving other territories such as Hungary, Galicia and Bohemia. For the above reasons he supposed that if Fiume were treated on the same lines as Dantzig, public opinion would be justified in saying that Italy was being treated worse than the enemy. There was one point of detail which he would mention, not as a serious argument, but as an interesting illustration of the historical independence of Fiume. It was a point of heraldry which could have no value among the Allied and Associated Powers, but which was of some importance in a country like Austria, which had preserved its aristocratic influences. This point was that the various states forming parts of Austria possessed historic escutcheons and among these Fiume was included with its own coat of arms.

[2] That is, Ante Trumbić.

4. Italy's third claim, M. Orlando continued, related to Dalmatia and the Islands off the coast—and he would mention here that the case of the Islands applied also to Istria with which must be considered the large Islands of Cherco and Lussin which were largely Italian in character.

Italy's claims here were of a strategic order. It was not necessary to be a Naval Expert to understand them although they were a question of great interest to Naval Experts. The eastern shores of the Adriatic with their covering Islands and high coast commanded the Adriatic; even if the Naval forces on the Italian side were reduced to the lowest limits necessary for policing the seas, there would always be the possibility of ships setting out from these recesses reaching and bombarding the Italian coast and then returning with little or no damage behind the screen of Islands. He did not wish to enter into too much detail but if the matter were examined analytically it would be found that ships could come from the North or the South to bombard the coast of Italy in the middle Adriatic and return in safety. The recent war had demonstrated this danger. The bombardments on the Italian coast made the greater impression because while the Entente was absolutely mistress of the Seas, it was not mistress of the Adriatic. The Austrians it is true were not able to navigate the Adriatic, neither was Italy. Reinforced by British and French warships, the Italian Fleet had double the force of the Austrians, but nevertheless they were never able to stop these bombardments. The enemy had escaped every time. Italy would never be secure until she had a defensive basis in the middle of the opposite coast.

The strategic argument, however, was not the only one on which Italy based her claims. There was a national question as well. In the course of those conversations it had been stated that historical claims must not be allowed to possess a decisive influence. He, himself, recognized that. There were, however, cases where history must exercise a deep influence. Since historic days right down to the Treaty of Campo Formio[3] Dalmatia had been connected with Italy—first as part of the Roman Empire, subsequently as part of Venice. One factor of the case resulted from the dispositions of nature. The mountains divided the coast from the interior. For this reason the whole culture of Dalmatia gravitated inevitably towards Italy. As he had stated, Dalmatia had been connected with Italy until the Treaty of Campo Formio but Italian influence had lasted much longer than this. He could not state the exact date as he had not the documents with him but he believed that it was until 1881

---

[3] Of 1797, by which Dalmatia, formerly under the control of Venice, was ceded by France to Austria.

that the majority in the Diet of Dalmatia had been Italian. Hence it could not be said that Italy was dating her historical arguments too far in the past. He had in his possession a document copy of which he had communicated to President Wilson, which had been found at Hara and which was dated 1887, and which purported to determine the official language (Dienst Sprache) of the different communes of Dalmatia.[4] This official document ordered that out of 84 communes, nineteen were entitled to speak exclusively Italian; twenty-five were entitled to speak both Italian and Serbo-Croat. This he would point out was information derived not from Italian but from Austrian sources. Some places still preserved an Italian minority, notably Zara, Trau and perhaps Spalato. There still remained in Dalmatia a flourishing Italianism. Was it possible, he asked, after all the sacrifices of the war for Italy to see this Italianism devoted to destruction. What Italy demanded was only a small part of Dalmatia leaving to Yugo-Slavia Spalato, Ragusa, and Cattaro. He considered that this was a very modest demand, and he only asked that the existing agreement in regard to Dalmatia should be adhered to.

5. PRESIDENT WILSON recalled that it had been agreed that he should confer with M. Orlando and through him with his colleagues and he would now state the substance of what he had said. His Italian friends would bear witness that throughout the conversations he had insisted on the same point of view. It had been his privilege as the spokesman of the Associated Powers to initiate the negotiations for peace. The bases of the Peace with Germany had then been clearly laid down. It was not reasonable—and he thought his Italian friends would admit this—to have one basis of Peace with Germany and another set of principles for the Peace with Austria-Hungary, Bulgaria and Turkey. He must assume that the principles in each case would be the same. The whole question resolved itself into this: we were trying to make peace on an entirely new basis and to establish a new order of international relations. At every point the question had to be asked whether the lines of the settlement would square with the new order. No greater question had ever been asked in any negotiations. No body of statesmen had ever before undertaken to make such a settlement. There was a certain claim of argument which must be brushed aside, namely, the economic and strategic argument. Within certain limits he agreed that natural boundaries such as existed in the cases of Spain or Scandinavia (which M. Orlando had referred to) must be taken into consideration. The whole course of life in these regions was deter-

[4] The Editors have been unable to locate this document. Perhaps Wilson returned it to Orlando.

mined by such natural boundaries. The slope of the mountains not only threw the rivers in a certain direction but tended to throw the life of the people in the same direction. These, however, were not strategic nor economic arguments. On these grounds he felt no difficulty in assenting to that part of the Italian claims included in M. Orlando's first point. Nature had swung a great boundary round the north of Italy. It included Trieste and most of the Istrian Peninsula on which Pola lies. He had no great difficulty there in meeting the Italian views.

Outside of these, however, further to the South all the arguments seemed to him to lead the other way. A different watershed was reached. Different racial units were encountered. There were natural associations between the peoples and this brought him to the question of Fiume.

6. From the first it had seemed to him plain that on the side of the Alps on which Fiume lay there was not only a difficult but an entirely new problem. Hitherto Fiume had been linked up with the policy[5] of the Austro-Hungarian Empire. That Empire had been governed by men who were in spirit very similar to the former rulers of Germany and who had been more or less under their domination. In fact they had become their instruments. If the Austro-Hungarian Empire had not gone to pieces the question could not have been difficult to deal with. Now, however, it had disappeared. Hence part of the wisdom of the present situation seemed to build up new States linked in their interest for the future with the new order. These States must indeed become partners in the new order and not be regarded as States under suspicion but as linked in the new international relationship. M. Orlando would remember that at the time that we were trying to detach the Jugo-Slavs from Austria we spoke of them as friends. We could not now speak of them as enemies. By separating from Austria-Hungary they had become connected with the new and disconnected from the old policy[6] and order. M. Orlando had argued the case of Fiume as though it were purely an Italian and Jugo-Slav interest. Fiume was undoubtedly important to Jugo-Slavia whatever the proportion of the Jugo-Slav trade to the whole might be. But above all its importance was that of an international port serving Roumania, Hungary, and Czecho-Slovakia. In the past Hungary had had the principal interest in Fiume. Hence, it had been the policy of Hungary to encourage the Italian element and to use it to check the Slav population round about Fiume. He conjectured that Hungary had encouraged the idea of the autonomy of Fiume as a check to the surrounding Slovak

---

[5] Wilson undoubtedly said "polity."   [6] *Idem.*

population. This did not lead to the natural conclusion that Fiume should be joined to Italy.

Neither did the analogies mentioned by M. Orlando in their application to Fiume lead to such a conclusion. It had been decided to separate Dantzig from Germany. Yet M. Orlando proposed to extend Italian sovereignty to Fiume where it had never existed. If we followed the precedent of Dantzig, therefore, we could not give what Italy desired. All the economic and strategic arguments had been in favour of uniting Dantzig with Poland, yet, in order to give effect to the general principles on which the peace was being based an unscientific method had been adopted and a rough line had been drawn and the principle of plebiscite had been accepted which would probably result in a line of railway connecting Dantzig with Poland traversing German territory. The strategic and economic reasons had therefore been ignored. M. Orlando would recall M. Jules Cambon's powerful arguments in defending the conclusion of the Polish Commission.[7] He would also recall M. Hyman's demand for the inclusion of a strategic railway in Belgium involving a slight modification of the frontier.[8] Both these claims had been rejected because it would have involved the inclusion of Germans in Polish and German territory respectively. To put Fiume inside Italy would be absolutely inconsistent with the new order of international relations. What should be done was a totally different question. The essential point to be borne in mind was that Fiume served the commerce of Czecho-Slovakia, Hungary, Roumania as well as Jugo-Slavia. Hence, it was necessary to establish its free use as an international port. The Italian population at Fiume was not connected with Italy by intervening Italian population. Hence, to unite it with Italy would be an arbitrary act, so inconsistent with the principles on which we were acting that he for one could not concur in it.

7. In regard to Dalmatia, President Wilson continued, the argument most dwelt upon, the argument which Baron Sonnino had most forcibly expressed to him when he first arrived was mainly strategic, that is to say the necessity, from the point of view of naval defence, of giving Italy control of part of the eastern shores. In this case also the new order must either be accepted or not. Under the new order of international relations we united influence with policy to protect territory and to give independence of life. He could not imagine that a Jugo-Slav navy, under the regime of the League of Nations, could ever be a menace to Italy. The only possible risk

7 See the minutes of the Council of Ten printed at March 19, 1919, Vol. 56.
8 See Mantoux's notes of a meeting of the Council of Four, April 16, 1919, 11 a.m.

was an alliance between Jugo-Slavia and some other state and its only possible motive would be to attack Italy.

In his view, one of the essentials of the new order was that the control of the Great Powers should be withdrawn from the Balkans. In the past this had furnished the seeds of war. Germany had sought to plant out sovereigns in the Balkans to be used, as occasion required, for her own purposes. Most of the intrigues against the peace of the world in the Balkans had arisen from this cause. There had been no real independence in the Balkans for these states had been under constant pressure from the Great Powers, and especially from Berlin. Consequently, he was opposed to the lodgment of any great Power in the Balkans. Our rule must be not to interfere in the internal affairs of these states and one of his primary objects was to withdraw the hand of the Great Powers from the Balkans. He regarded this as of capital importance. Hence the strategic argument must be rejected.[9] Military men with their strategic, military, economic arguments had been responsible for the Treaty of 1815. Similarly, military men had been responsible for Alsace-Lorraine. It was military men who had led Europe to one blunder after another. It would be quite detrimental to the peace of the world if Italy insisted on a lodgment on the east coast of the Adriatic. We were now engaged in setting up an international association and Italy would have a part of the leadership therein. If this did not suffice, then two orders would exist—the old and the new. In the right hand would be the new order and in the left hand the old order. We could not drive two horses at once. The people of the United States of America would repudiate it. They were disgusted with the old order. Not only the American people but the people of the whole world were tired of the old system and they would not put up with Governments that supported it. We sometimes spoke in those conversations as though we were masters of Europe. We were not so in reality. If the new order of ideas was not correctly interpreted a most tragical disservice would be done to the world. Hence, he urged his Italian colleagues to remember that they were in the hands of true friends. He would not be serving their interests

---

[9] Mantoux, I, 284-85, rendered the following portion of Wilson's remarks as follows: "The strategic argument was invoked in 1815. It was invoked in 1871. The military advisers who imposed strategic frontiers bear responsibility for some of the gravest mistakes which have been committed in the history of the world. I believe that it would be a danger to the peace of Europe if Italy insisted upon establishing herself on the eastern coast of the Adriatic. We are creating a great League of Nations, in which one of the principal roles is reserved to Italy. If that does not suffice, if it is also necessary at the same time to have recourse to strategic measures, that is because we are trying to combine two irreconcilable systems. As for myself, I cannot drive these two horses at the same time. The people of the United States would not accept seeing the world fall again into its former state, and the governments which do not understand that would learn from their own people that their time has passed."

if he consented to their claims to Fiume and Dalmatia. He was prepared to leave it to history to judge whether he or they were serving Italian interests best. He had been brought up in America, 3,000 miles away, and had passed most of his life there. There had been a time when he had not cared a snap of the fingers what happened in Europe. Now, however, it was his privilege to assist Europe to create a new order. If he should succeed, he could bring all the resources of his people to assist in the task. The claim for Fiume was a recent one put forward only within the last few months. As far as self-determination was concerned, Fiume was only an island of Italian population. If such a principle were adopted generally, we should get spots all over the map. In the case of Bohemia and the Polish frontiers, there was a preservation of historical frontiers; but this was not so in the case of Fiume. There was no analogy here that attached Fiume to Italy.

He could not conclude his remarks without stating the profound solemnity with which he approached the question. He fully recognised its gravity for the Italians. He tried to approach the subject in the most friendly spirit. His conclusion was that of one who wished to serve Italian interests and not of one who wished to oppose them.

8. BARON SONNINO reverted to President Wilson's remarks on the strategic reasons that he, himself, had given to the President for the incorporation of Dalmatia with Italy. The President had said that he could not admit the claim of strategic advantage in establishing the new order. He must point out that Italy had never asked for any strategic advantage from an offensive point of view. All that they had demanded was the necessary and indispensable conditions of defence. He had never even thought of obtaining any possible advantage for offence in the Balkans. All he wished to avoid was the continuance of the tragic history of Italy as open to attack from across the Adriatic. Without this the east coast of Italy was helpless. The League of Nations could not intervene in time. Any fleet established behind the island could defy the fleets of the League of Nations when they arrived, just as in the late war the Austrians defied the fleets of the Entente, which were two or three times their size. The Allied fleets would have destroyed the Austrian fleet, if they could have reached them, but they were unable to. The present situation provided a temptation to war, or at least, to the menace of war. It was perhaps a temptation even to Italy to profit by any favourable situation that might arise to get rid of the danger. The League of Nations might be compared to any civilised community which possessed a police force, but in every town people had to shut their door at nights. Italy could not do without this.

Referring to President Wilson's remarks on the Balkans, BARON SONNINO said that Italy had no desire to mix herself there. Dalmatia, and especially its Northern part, was entirely outside the Balkans. All its economic and commercial relations were on the Italian side of the Adriatic. This was why, in spite of every effort by the Austrians to prevent it, the Italian interest had survived and was still maintained in Zara, Sebenico and Spalato. Until 1859 or 1860 the Italian element in Austria had been numerous enough for Austria to have an interest not to smash it. After the loss of Lombardy, however, and later on in 1866, after the loss of Venetia, all the parliamentary interests in Austria had been Slavonic.

In spite of all sorts of adverse influences, falsification of statistics, etc., Italianism had maintained itself.

After a successful war, in which Italy had lost 500,000 killed and some 900,000 badly wounded; to revert to a worse situation—for Austria had offered Italy the Adige and the islands[10]—would not be explainable to the Italian people. They would not understand why Italy had entered the war. It would be a crime against the Italian people, and he himself would feel remorse towards his people, for whom he was ready to give up everything.

He fully recognised the importance of the League of Nations and the general sentiment that was maturing towards a better state of things, but the League of Nations was a new institution and had many difficulties to face. He would like to know how tomorrow the League of Nations was going to adjust the Russian situation for example? How could it be relied on until it was fully established? In the present state of affairs it would be a crime for Italy to give this up, and it could not be done. Italy was asked to assume great responsibilities in guaranteeing the position of others, and received nothing herself.

PRESIDENT WILSON pointed out that Italy herself received these guarantees.

M. SONNINO said they were not sufficient. On the other side of

---

[10] By "the Adige," Sonnino apparently meant the boundary line between the predominantly German-speaking area of Alto Adige ("Upper Adige," now known as Bolzano) and the largely Italian-speaking area known as the Trentino, or Trento. In a final proposal for a diplomatic settlement with Italy on May 19, 1915, just prior to the Italian declaration of war on May 23, Austria-Hungary had offered to make this line the boundary between Austria and Italy, thus ceding the Trentino to Italy while retaining the Alto Adige. See the maps on pp. 23 and 91 and the text of the Austro-Hungarian proposal on pp. 342-44 of René Albrecht-Carrié, *Italy at the Paris Peace Conference* (New York, 1938).

It is much less clear what Sonnino meant by his reference to "the islands." Count Aldrovandi, in his diary entry covering this meeting of the Council of Four on April 19, at which he was present, says that Sonnino spoke of "certain islands on the Dalmatian coast." *Ibid.*, p. 465. However, the only reference to islands in the Austro-Hungarian proposal of May 19, 1915, was in Article 10 which reads as follows: "On her part Austria-Hungary renounces all claims based on the fact of the Italian occupation of the Dodecanese islands." *Ibid.*, p. 344.

the Adriatic they were close to the Balkanic races who were excitable peoples, much given to intrigue and falsification of documents, etc.

Moreover, the League of Nations had no forces under its direct control.

PRESIDENT WILSON said Baron Sonnino was speaking of a time when the Balkan states were being used by the Great Powers for their own purposes.

M. SONNINO said he mistrusted the Balkan peoples most. Who would say that economic relations would not again link up the Balkans with Central Europe? He was very sorry, and deeply pained with the attitude he had to take. If Italian claims were not satisfied he, who had always sought completely to do his duty, would feel that he had done something contrary to the interests of his people.

(9) M. Clemenceau said that, in listening to President Wilson's speech, he felt we were embarking on a most hazardous enterprise, but with a very noble purpose. We were seeking to detach Europe and the whole world from the old order which had led in the past to conflicts and finally to the recent War which had been the greatest and most horrible of all. It was not possible to change the whole policy of the world at one stroke. This applied to France just as much as to Italy. He would be ready to make concessions to his Allies. They were a people which has merited well of humanity and of civilisation and he felt it right to recall it in this tragic hour. To the powerful arguments given by President Wilson he would add one other. Great Britain and France were bound in advance. The Treaty with Italy had not been signed by him, but it bore the signature of France. In that Treaty Dalmatia had been given to Italy, and this was a fact he could not forget. In the same Treaty, however, Fiume was allotted to Croatia. Italy had at that time no pretentions to Fiume. They had granted it as a gift to the Croats. M. Bazellai[11] had told him that since that time Austria had disappeared, which altered the situation. This was true, but, nevertheless, Italy had signed a document allotting Fiume to Croatia. He was astonished that Italy, while claiming Dalmatia under the Treaty, also claimed Fiume, which had been given to the Croats. Signatures counted no longer. It was impossible for Italy to claim one clause of the Treaty and to cancel another clause. It would be deplorable if his Italian friends on such a pretext should break away from their Allies. He believed they were making a great mistake. It would serve neither their own cause nor the cause of civilisation. We French,

[11] Salvatore Barzilai, not Barzellai, Trieste-born irredentist leader, member of the Italian Parliament since 1890, minister without portfolio for the liberated territories, 1915-1916, at this time a plenipotentiary delegate to the peace conference.

as he had often said, had had to deplore the treatment given to the Italians in the Adriatic. But these moments were past. Now it will be necessary to traverse another critical period. He hoped his Italian friends were not counting too much on the first enthusiasm which would greet this action. Later on the cold and inevitable results would appear when Italy was alienated from her friends. He could not speak of such a matter without the gravest emotion. He could not think of one of the nations who helped to win this War separating from their Allies. We should suffer much, but Italy would suffer even more from such action. (M. Orlando interjected "without doubt.") If the Italian plenipotentiaries should leave, he hoped that after consulting their people the forces of reason would bring them back. He hoped they would make one last effort to come to an agreement. His heart was always with Italy with its great and noble history and its immense services to civilisation. Nevertheless, he must listen to the voice of duty. We could not abandon the principles we had worked for for the good of civilisation. It was impossible for France to adhere to one clause of the Treaty and to denounce another.

M. Orlando recalled that in the beginning of his statement he had declared that, since he was discussing the demands of Italy in the presence of a Power which was not bound by the Treaty, he would examine them on the hypothesis that the Treaty did not exist. If he were only asking his Allies to carry out their engagements, he would not ask for Fiume. In regard to what M. Clemenceau had said, he must express profound anguish in his heart at the suggestion that he was animated by any consideration of popularity or enthusiasm among the people of Italy at the course he was taking. He fully understood the tragic solemnity of the moment. Italy had to choose between two methods of death according as they limited their demands solely to the Treaty or separated themselves from their friends and became isolated from the world. If he had to choose he would prefer death with honour. He recalled that when Henry III had been assassinated the Duke of Guise looked at the body of his friend and said he had not believed he was so tall. He anticipated that Italy would prove so great a corpse that there would now arise a poison which would threaten the whole world.

(10) Mr. Lloyd George said that as the representative of a Power which had signed the Treaty of London, he must express his views. He had not much to add to what M. Clemenceau had said, but in the present grave situation he must express the British point of view, since Great Britain had also been a signatory of the Treaty. His personal position was much the same as M. Clemenceau's,

since he had not been a signatory to the Treaty. He realised the strength of President Wilson's arguments, but he thought he was entitled to say that if we felt scruples about the Italian claims they should have been expressed before Italy had lost half a million gallant lives. He did not think we were entitled to express these doubts after Italy had taken part in the war. He wished to say that Great Britain stood by the Treaty, but that she stood by the whole of the Treaty. The map which he had in his hand attached to the Treaty showed Fiume in Croatia. This was known to Serbia. We could not break one part of the Treaty while standing by the other. On merits he did not understand how the principle of self-determination could be applied. If it was applied at all, it must be applied to the whole area. There must be a plebiscite from Trieste to Spalato. This, however, was not the proposal, which was merely to take the views of the inhabitants of Fiume. It was only proposed to apply it to the ancient town of Fiume itself. If the suburb across the river— a narrow river as he was informed—were included, his information was that the majority would be Jugo-Slav. (Baron Sonnino interjected that the majority would still be Italian.) If M. Orlando's argument in regard to the strategic position of Trieste and its danger from the guns in the hills were applied to Fiume, the Jugo-Slav majority would be overwhelming. The population of the valley was some 100,000 people, of whom only 25,000 were Italians. He could not see that any principle could be established for giving Fiume to Italy. If Fiume were included in Istria, exactly the same would apply. The Italian claim was only valid if applied to a little ancient town where an Italian population had grown to a majority of some 8,000. To give Fiume to Italy would break faith with the Serbs, would break the Treaty on which Italy entered the war, and would break every principle on which the Treaty of Peace was being based. He admitted that the Italian losses had been very heavy, and even appalling. But the French losses had also been very heavy. M. Clemenceau could no doubt evoke a great demonstration by announcing that the French frontier was to rest on the Rhine. Moreover, this was a strategic frontier, and would fulfil long-standing ambitions of France. There were very powerful elements in France which favoured this solution, and M. Clemenceau had to face these. They would urge that France had lost 1,500,000 dead in support of the justice of the claim. As regards the strategic arguments, British towns had also been bombarded. Like the Italians, the British Fleet had not been able to catch the enemy. The Germans, however, had not been able to transport troops across the North Sea. Neither could the Austrians transport them across the Adriatic. In France, however, with the exception of the Rhine, which was merely a military obstacle, there was land all the way between their boundaries and Germany. If our principles were to be extended we should have to re-cast the whole of the principles on which the Treaty of Peace was based and to begin with France. (President Wilson interjected that France had foregone the principle.) How could we apply a different principle to Italy to what we had applied to France and Poland?

M. Clemenceau had spoken of Italy going out of the Conference. This was a very grave decision which he had not been made aware of. What was the reason for it? It was that a population of 25,000 people in a single town had an Italian majority; it was a case where the majority was doubtful if the suburbs were taken into consideration, and where, if the surrounding country were taken into consideration, the population was overwhelmingly against Italy. He asked his Italian friends to consider the position they would create by such action. What would their population do? What would our position be? We thought Italy was in the wrong and was making an indefensible claim. If war and bloodshed should result, what would the position be? Surely, there must be some sanity among statesmen! To break an Alliance over a matter of this kind was inconceivable. If Italy should do so, however, the responsibility would not be ours. We stood by our Treaty and the responsibility would rest with those who broke the Treaty.

Baron Sonnino pointed out that President Wilson did not accept the Treaty.

Mr. Lloyd George said he was speaking for Great Britain only. He recalled that some time ago he had told M. Orlando that the British Cabinet had decided that they would stand by the Pact.

M. Orlando again recalled that at the outset of the meeting he had stated that he would discuss the question as though the Treaty did not exist. If what Mr. Lloyd George said meant that the Conference would take its decision on the basis of the Treaty of London, leaving Fiume to be settled as the Conferrence might think fit, then a new situation would be created, and he would be prepared to discuss it with his colleagues on the Italian Delegation and return to give his reply.

President Wilson said that this solution would place a burden on him that was quite unfair. He did not know and did not feel at liberty to ask whether France and Great Britain considered the Treaty as consistent with the principles on which the Peace Treaty was being based. He was at liberty to say, however, that he himself did not. To discuss the matter on the basis of the Pact of London would be to adopt as a basis a secret treaty. Yet he would be bound to say to the world that we were establishing a new order in which secret treaties were precluded. He could not see his way to make peace with Germany on one principle and with Austria-Hungary on another. The Pact of London was inconsistent with the general principles of the settlement. He knew perfectly well that the Pact of London had been entered into in quite different circumstances, and he did not wish to criticise what had been done. But to suggest that the decision should be taken on the basis of the Treaty of London would draw the United States of America into an impossible situation.

Baron Sonnino said he only asked the Supreme Council to accept the merits of the Pact of London.

President Wilson said he was willing to state, and might have to state, to the world the grounds of his objections. He could not draw the United States into principles contrary to those which now animated them and which had brought them into the War.

Baron Sonnino drew attention to President Wilson's statement of the 21st May, 1918, in which he had admitted the principle of security for Italy.[12]

President Wilson said he did not admit that Dalmatia was essential to the security of Italy. Great Britain was in exactly the same position as Italy. He could not allow the argument, and he had said so frankly at his first interview with Baron Sonnino. It was inconceivable to him that Italy should draw apart from her friends, and he begged that the Italian plenipotentiaries would not decide the question in a hurry. He asked them to take every element into consideration and not tear the country apart from the sacred associations of the present Conference and of the past. He appealed to them with confidence to reconsider the question, and not to think of action which would be one of the most tragic results of the War.

Mr. Lloyd George asked that the Italians would remember one

[12] This was a message from Wilson to the Italian people, read by Robert Lansing at a meeting to celebrate the third anniversary of Italy's entrance into the war at Liberty Hut, Washington, D. C., May 23, 1918. It was also sent to Thomas Nelson Page for presentation to the Italian Foreign Office. Its text is as follows:

"I am sure that I am speaking for the people of the United States in sending to the Italian people warm fraternal greetings upon this the anniversary of the entrance of Italy into this great war in which there is being fought out once for all the irrepressible conflict between free self-government and the dictation of force.

"The people of the United States have looked with profound interest and sympathy upon the efforts and sacrifices of the Italian people, are deeply and sincerely interested in the present and future security of Italy, and are glad to find themselves associated with a people to whom they are bound by so many personal and intimate ties in a struggle whose object is liberation, freedom, the rights of men and nations to live their own lives and determine their own fortunes, the rights of the weak as well as of the strong, and the maintenance of justice by the irresistible force of free nations leagued together in the defense of mankind.

"With ever increasing resolution and force we shall continue to stand together in this sacred common cause. America salutes the gallant Kingdom of Italy and bids her Godspeed. Woodrow Wilson." *Official Bulletin,* II (May 24, 1918), 6.

factor. If they were not present on Friday when the German delegates arrived, the Allies would have no right to put forward a claim for compensation for Italy. This was a matter that they ought to take into consideration.

M. Orlando said that this was a matter that could be corrected at the last moment if Italy did not separate herself.

President Wilson concluded by a final appeal to Italy to take time to consider.

M. Orlando undertook to do so, but said that he was most anxious to have the question settled before he returned to Italy.

(The Meeting was adjourned until
SUNDAY, APRIL 20, *1919, at 10 a.m.)*

T MS (SDR, RG 256, 180.03401/108, DNA).

A Memorandum by Robert Lansing

THE CLIMAX OF FRENCH MILITARISM.
April 19, 1919.

The President at a meeting of the Commissioners today told us confidentially that Clemenceau informed him that Marshal Foch flatly refused to deliver to the Germans the message summoning them to Versailles on the 25th because the left bank of the Rhine not being ceded to France by the treaty he would have nothing to do with it.

As the President recited this defiance of the French Government by the Marshal, his jaw shot out and he said, "If I were Clemenceau, he would never have a chance to refuse again. I would know what to do with him."

Unfortunately for France the "Tiger" is not have [half] as fierce as his name implies. He will undoubtedly make terms with the military crowd and Weygand with his black portfolio and immobile countenance will continue to create situations which require the use of military forces. That is, he will if he can.

T MS (R. Lansing Papers, DLC).

Two Letters to Robert Lansing

My dear Lansing: Paris, 19 April, 1919.

I think this is a good idea,[1] though I must say I do not have as much hopes for its practical usefulness as seem to be entertained by some others. Certainly we can have no objection.

Cordially and faithfully yours,   Woodrow Wilson

TLS (R. Lansing Papers, DLC).
   ¹ Wilson was replying to RL to WW, April 17, 1919.

My dear Lansing: Paris, 19 April, 1919.

   I am clear that our representative on this Committee of Organization should be Samuel Gompers.¹

   In haste,   Faithfully yours,   [Woodrow Wilson]

CCL (WP, DLC).
   ¹ This letter was inspired by H. M. Robinson to WW, April 14, 1919, TLS (WP, DLC).
Robinson had recommended that Gompers be appointed the United States representative
on the International Organizing Committee for the first meeting of the International
Labor Conference to be held in Washington in October 1919. See also Shotwell, *Origins
of the International Labor Organization*, I, 285-88; II, 448-49, 455.

To Vi Kyuin Wellington Koo

My dear Mr. Minister: Paris, 19 April, 1919.

   It was very kind of you to send me a copy of the Chinese Memorandum on the Shantung Question. I have examined it with the greatest interest.

                    Cordially and sincerely, yours,   [Woodrow Wilson]

CCL (WP, DLC).

To Norman Hezekiah Davis

My dear Davis: [Paris] 19 April, 1919.

   We have come to a rather difficult issue with the Italians, and I am going to beg, therefore, that you will cooperate with me in delaying our reply to the Treasury about the fifty million dollar advance to the Italian Government for a few days until the air clears—if it does.

   In haste,   Cordially yours,   [Woodrow Wilson]

CCL (WP, DLC).

From Robert Lansing, with Enclosure

My dear Mr. President: Paris 19 April 1919.

   On April 16th I received a letter from Mr. Henry F. Hollis, a Commissioner of the United States Liquidation Commission in Paris, stating that the American Expeditionary Forces in France had a large amount of surplus arms, ammunition, and field pieces for which England, France, Belgium and Italy have no use, and inquiring whether there would be any objection on the part of our government, or of any other government to making sales to these stocks to good advantage in Spain, Poland and Czecho-Slovakia. I requested an expression of opinion in this matter from General Bliss, whose reply to my inquiry is enclosed herewith.

I beg most earnestly to call your attention to this letter from General Bliss. The sentiments expressed therein are shared wholeheartedly by both Mr. White and myself, and I should be very glad to learn your views in this matter before making a definitive reply to Mr. Hollis.   Faithfully yours,   R. Lansing

TLC (H. White Papers, DLC).

E N C L O S U R E

Tasker Howard Bliss to Robert Lansing

My dear Mr. Secretary: Paris, April 19, 1919.

I do not know anything that more disgusts me, that makes me more sick of the cant and hypocrisy of our peace talk, than the fact that I can offer no reason which anyone else would accept as valid, against your replying to this letter to the effect that so far as I know our government will have no objection to the sale by the Liquidation Commission of these arms, ammunition and artillery "to the governments named or to any other governments which may fairly be considered in the friendly class." In fact the Liquidation Commission was created for that very purpose.

I do not know what limitations are imposed on this matter by the law; but I fear that under the law, it is the unhappy fact that, while we may not sell to an enemy government, we may sell to those who are for the moment friendly to us, even though we know that they are bitterly hostile to each other and at this moment are preparing to fly at each other's throats.

We may sell to Poland though we know that Poland is eagerly preparing a campaign against the Ukraine, the success of which will overthrow a government that is friendly to us and which will make that country Bolshevik, although the Ukrainian Government has declared unreservedly that it will abide by the decisions of the Peace Conference which thus far Poland has declined to do.

We may sell arms to Poland though the head of that government has declared that it will fight Germany if its demands for Dantzig are not fully realized; and that it will fight Czecho-Slovakia if its demands for Teschen are denied. And we may sell to Czecho-Slovakia in order that it may fight Poland for the same object.

And so I might go around the entire wearisome and bloody circle. The arms which we brought to Europe in order to kill militarism and to bring on an era of lasting peace, we are going to sell over the bargain-counter to the new nations which we boasted we were going to usher into a world of peace. It would be bad enough if we sold for cash; but as a matter of fact, we are selling for credit the value of which will depend on the success of purchasers in killing a sufficient number of the neighbors. Our securities will be valid only in proportion as they are stained with blood.

Personally, I would rather be taxed to my last dollar to pay for this material of war if we threw it into the sea than to have it sold for any such purpose.

And why should we not throw it into the sea? What more splendid object lesson could the United States give to the world than to utterly destroy this material? By selling it we will get a bagatelle of its cost to us,—*plus* a long tale of dead men, of maimed bodies, of ruined habitations and devast[at]ed fields, and starving women and children. With the arms, artillery and ammunition that we have already used we—we Americans—have already, in a good cause, destroyed towns and villages, created widows and orphans and have left starving women and children. The cause was good because we believed that we were forever putting an end to the cruel business. Why should we, because we have a little of this material of destruction left over, and in order to save a little money, sell it to the highest bidder (who will be low at the highest) in order to continue the cruel business indefinitely?

But I fear that the hard-headed taxpayer will not listen to these silly sentiments, whether expressed by me or you. Therefore I shall not weary you with more of them.

I wish that the President could recommend to the American people that all weapons and material of destruction that are not required to be taken back to the United States for our own protection should be utterly destroyed. I can conceive of no more magnificent testimony to the American ideal of lasting peace. Let us sell our surplus food and clothing and animals and wagons and motortrucks and tractors and locomotives and railway cars and shops and machinery—everything that makes for the peaceful development of these countries over here—and destroy everything that is used to destroy anything. But I am afraid that the taxpayers would not listen to the President any more than they would to my sentimental twaddle.

I note that you were asked to inform the Liquidation Commission whether "any other Government" would object to the sales suggested by that Commission. I do not know how that can be ascertained except by addressing a diplomatic note to all Governments concerned.   Very sincerely,   T. H. Bliss

CCL (T. H. Bliss Papers, DLC).

From Henry Mauris Robinson

Dear Mr. President: Hotel Crillon, 19 April 1919
Enemy Ships Seized by the United States During the War

The Supplementary Interim Report of Sub-Commission No. 2, Reparation Commission,[1] contains the amendments and statement offered by the United States Delegation, copies of which accompanied my letter of April 14.[2]

It also contains the British and French Contention, copy enclosed.[3]

To comment on their contention is but to reiterate in a slightly different form the position stated by the United States Delegation, that is:

1. Certainly the Enemy Powers should not be permitted to question the validity of the title ships seized as a war measure by any Allied or Associated Power.
2. If the Enemy Powers have no right to question the title, a fortiori, the Allied and Associated Powers should not be permitted to raise the question.
3. It then becomes a request for contribution, and this could only be on the theory that there is some inequity in relation to ships standing by themselves.
4. The contention that the Neutrals could claim a like right does not of course apply, because seizure by a neutral could not be considered a war measure.

The inequities that grow out of a war, as between individuals and nations, are very marked and vary materially with the different subjects involved. The subject of ships on the basis of a contribution should not be considered separately: the question of principle raised would necessitate a thorough survey of the remote and immediate causes of the war, and the part taken by each of the Allied and Associated Powers.

As the British and French contention is based on figures, I am enclosing a graphic presentation of the figures on the different suggested methods.[4] Personally I think figures should not be considered; but that the other principles should control.

                    Very respectfully yours,   Henry M. Robinson

TLS (WP, DLC).

[1] Printed report, dated April 18, 1919 (WP, DLC), printed in Burnett, *Reparation at the Paris Peace Conference*, II, 754-70.

[2] H. M. Robinson to WW, April 14, 1919, TLS, enclosing proposed amendments and statements, T MS, both in WP, DLC.

[3] "British and French Contention," T MS (WP, DLC), printed in Burnett, *op. cit.*, II, 756-57.

[4] "Comparison of Allied War Losses with Total Enemy Tonnage which is Considered for Reparation and Proposed Distribution of This Tonnage by U. S. and by British-French Methods," T MS (WP, DLC).

Edward Mandell House to Arthur James Balfour

Dear Mr. Balfour: Paris, April 19, 1919.

In answer to your enquiry the President has authorized me to inform you that he recognizes the British Protectorate over Egypt which was announced by His Majesty's Government on December 18, 1914.

The President has no objection to this decision being made public as he understands that it may help to the restoration of order and the cessation of further bloodshed in Egypt.

You will no doubt realize, dear Mr. Balfour, that in according this recognition, the President feels constrained to reserve for further discussion the details of formal recognition together with the question of the modification of any rights of the United States Government which this decision on his part may entail.

I am, my dear Mr. Balfour,

Yours very sincere,   E. M. House[1]

TLS (WP, DLC).

[1] A note attached to this letter, dated April 20, 1919, reads as follows: "Colonel House requests that the accompanying letter be brought to the attention of the President." T MS (WP, DLC).

A Memorandum by Michael Idvorsky Pupin[1]

Paris, April 19th, 1919.

MEMORANDUM

The mental attitude of the Yougoslavs now residing in Paris, and also that of the representatives of other small nations who together with the Yougoslavs are anxiously watching the work of the Peace Conference, indicates that President Wilson's principles as laid down in the historical Fourteen Points are their political "credo." I believe, moreover, that the masses of all other nations, including even the Italians, profess to-day the same political faith. President Wilson, they say, will lead them from the desert of international immorality to the promised land of international morality. The most direct proof of this is the fact that the Yougoslav Delegates at the Peace Conference, that is Messrs. Pashitch, Trumbitch, and Vesnitch, declared themselves ready to leave the whole question of the Adriatic in the hands of President Wilson with the assurance that they would abide by the results of his arbitration.

I have been told over and over again that there is not a person in Yougloslavia, in Czecho-Slovakia, and in Poland who does not know perfectly the principles enunciated in President Wilson's Fourteen Points, and does not see in them the foundation for the future life, liberty and persuit of happiness of the peoples in these countries. A young Montenegrin who has just arrived in Paris told me the other day that an old peasant woman met him on the road a few days before he left for Paris and requested him to take to Paris a pair of socks which she had made with her own hands and to present them to President Wilson. He who understand the customs of Montenegro will certainly consider this the most sincere compliment which President Wilson ever received in Europe; it has a wonderfully deep meaning, and I am sure that millions of peasant women of Europe have the same mental attitude as this sincerely grateful Montenegrin peasant. This veneration of President Wilson and of our great country is in my humble opinion the greatest asset which this war has gained for us. We claim no territory and no indemnity as a result of this victorious war, and we can afford to get along without any immediate material gains, because we have made wonderful spiritual gains, and they are the respect, the admiration, and the love of the small peoples who up to yesterday looked upon the great and the powerful nations of the world with fear, suspicion, and mistrust. In their experience the great and the powerful always appeared to them as masters ready to command, to exploit, and to op[p]ress them. To-day for the first time in their history they see in the people of the United States a great nation ready to serve them and to help them. They all understand now that the American Declaration of Independence was not merely a clever academic composition but that it was and is to-day the sincere expression of a people who have a big and a righteous heart, and who were the first to recognize that social and international security rests upon the willingness of the strong to serve and to aid the weak.

It is evident to every American who is watching the course of events connected with the Peace Conference that there is a decided tendency on the part of some of our Allies to persuade the American Peace Delegates to depart from the principles laid down in President Wilson's Fourteen Points, and thus sacrifice our great national asset to which I have referred. For instance, Italy lays claim to a part of Dalmatia and to Fiume. If I understand correctly the argument advanced by the Italians in support of their claims, then it is obvious that our American Peace Delegates would be forced to throw overboard every principle contained in President Wilson's Fourteen Points if they consented to yield to these Italian claims. A similar statement can be made with regard to the Italian claims in Istria, Goritzia and Corinthia. Italy has no better support for these claims than the London pact of 1915, and the additional argument which one hears from time to time that unless these claims are satisfied, the present Italian Government cannot maintain itself. The Yougoslavs, on the other hand, maintain that the London pact is null and void, because it violates President Wilson's principles. They propose to prove this violation by a plebiscite of the people in the territories claimed by Italy. Besides, even a most elementary study of the Italian claims from a purely economic point of view will readily convince a fair-minded student that the Italian claims in Yougoslavlands would, if granted, strangle to death this young and economically still undeveloped state. The Yougoslavs can never agree to the proposition that President Wilson's principles be sacrificed and that thereby they be economically condemned to death for no better reason than to save the present Italian Government. They also maintain that a very short time ago a manifesto was issued by the Socialist Party of Italy,[2] signed by 41 Socialist members of the Italian Parliament, in which the just aspirations of the Italian nation as the Socialists see them were carefully defined but no reference whatever is made in this manifesto to Dalmatia, Fiume, or to the Slovene territories in Istria, Goritzia and Corinthia claimed by the Italian Government. On the contrary *these Socialist members of the Italian Parliament contend that they will force the Paris Peace Conference to fulfill its promises by leaving it to the peoples to determine freely their own destiny.* One who reads this manifesto will infer that there is a large class of people in Italy who will do their best to overthrow the present Italian Government in case that the above mentioned claims of the present Italian Government are satisfied, and this is just the opposite from the contention made occasionally by the present Italian Government and by some of its friends.

Let us suppose for a moment that President Wilson's principles, as enunciated in the historical Fourteen Points, are thrown overboard by the American Peace Delegates and that the Italian Government's claims in Dalmatia, Istria, Goritza and Corinthia are satisfied, what will be the inevitable result? The Yougoslavs will be driven to desperation because they will feel that they have been deserted by their greatest friend of to-day, by the just and generous people of the United States. Despair breeds rebellion, and rebellion means war between the Yougoslavs and Italy. This upheaval would demonstrate to the whole world that in this one spot, at least, the soil upon which it is proposed to build the great structure of a League of Nations is full of quick sands.

There are only two standard bearers in the disturbed and nervous parts of Europe to-day. On the one side we have President Wilson's standard with the historical Fourteen Points written upon it; on the other side stands the standard of the Bolsheviki. No doubt whatever exists in my mind as to what the masses in the Yougoslav countries will do if Italy with her most unreasonable claims forces the lowering of President Wilson's standard around which the Yougoslavs are now gathered.   M. I. Pupin.[3]

TS MS (WP, DLC).

[1] Born in the Banat; naturalized United States citizen; Professor of Electromechanics at Columbia University. At this time he was an adviser to the Yugoslav delegation at the peace conference.

[2] This manifesto, based on resolutions adopted by the Socialist Party of Italy, March 18-22, 1919, among other things, condemned Italian imperialism and demanded that the peace conference give the proletariat the "real disposition of executive power." It is printed in *Avanti* of Milan, April 5, 1919.

[3] Baker handed this memorandum to Wilson on April 22. See the extract from the Diary of Ray Stannard Baker printed at this date.

From the Diary of Edith Benham

April 19, 1919

This morning, now in fact, Orlando is here hearing that he can't, the Italians can't, have Fiume. The P. is unalterably opposed to giving it to them. Lloyd George said they would stand by him, but they changed over night, and it all remains to be seen what they are accepting. The P. has been told that this is all a bluff, that it is the way Italy has always obtained her territory—by a game of bluff. Then I suppose the Italian troops will refuse to withdraw from Fiume and that will mean trouble and then what you[1] prophesied will happen, that the Germans will wait until the Allies begin fighting among themselves. H.S.K.[2] said when he was here that in his aviation conferences the Italians did not like certain things and threatened, like children, to withdraw and he suggested that they could also put in a minority report for consideration when this aviation committee sends in its report for the conference to consider. . . .

Last night for the first time in a month the P. went to the theatre. It was a part English, part French, and the manager had sent word via Close that there would be only the most refined wit permitted. I suppose it was as far as the French can be, but I feared for the worst when the girls began slipping off their garments, and in some little details of the play the wit was not of the Sunday school variety.

It was a beautifully staged thing, and I know the P. enjoyed the decent parts. The English Ambassador and Lady Derby had the next box. He came in to see the P. and Mrs. Wilson and tried to persuade the P. to emulate him in a trip he had made to Fountainebleau for golf, going the fifty miles in an hour and ten minutes! We all agreed heartily we didn't want to drive with him. With him came Sir William Wiseman and Lord Farquhar,[3] one of the two gentlemen who had backed along the corridors of Buckingham Palace in front of the King and Queen and the P. and Mrs. W. through the waste of corridors to the banquet hall.

The P. grew interested in the spy question and had the Secret Service look it up, and they report that the minute he goes out the servants, the men, have occasion to go into his room. Now one of the Secret Service sits in there, or did until he got a strong box in which to put some of his less important papers which he was apt to keep in his desk.

[1] That is, Rear Adm. James Meredith Helm, to whom she was writing the letters which make up this diary.
[2] That is, Rear Adm. Harry Shepard Knapp.
[3] Horace Brand Farquhar, 1st Viscount Farquhar, the Lord Steward.

From the Diary of Colonel House

April 19, 1919.

Last night just as I was going to the Harjes[1] to dinner, Shepardson came to tell me that Hoover had given out to the Press an intemperate statement regarding Russia.[2] I read the statement and it was even worse than Shepardson said it was. I sent Shepardson to Hoover to tell him to please stop it until I could talk with him this morning. It is the most foolish thing I have known Hoover to do yet, although I am somewhat accustomed to an occasional "brain storm" from him. We have been for several weeks trying to get this Russian matter in the shape that it now is and he has helped as much as anyone. Just as soon, however, as we have it signed by the President and three Prime Ministers, Hoover gives out a statement which would absolutely destroy any chance of its success. Whether his action is because of his inordinate desire for publicity, I do not know.

This morning he said he would yield to my judgment, yet this afternoon he sends me a letter containing practically the same statement, excepting that he takes the responsibility upon his own shoulders. I showed this to the President, and to our other Commissioners, and they were unanimous in the opinion that it was a childish thing to do. The President asked me to say to Hoover that he hoped he would not make any statement at the moment because it would be impossible for him to disassociate himself either from our Government or the Governments of the Allies. See Hoover's letter and mine.

The President came to the Crillon at four o'clock to tell of what had happened at the morning meeting in regard to Italy. The *Proces Verbal* of that meeting will tell its own story. After the President left, I suggested to the Commissioners that we all agree to recommend to the President this course:

(1) Accept the line of the Pact of London, as far as it touches the boundaries of the old Austro-Hungarian Empire. Everything south of that including Fiume and Dalmatia to be taken over by the five Powers as Trustees under the League of Nations. The fate of the territory to be determined later when passions cool.

I suggested, however, that an intimation be given Italy now that this territory would probably not be given her, therefore the Italians [Italian] officials could go home and make the best they could of what to them seems a bad situation.

The only reason I suggest such a compromise, if indeed it may be called one, for it merely postpones the action which we have decided upon now, is because if Italy refused to sign the Treaty with Germany and if Japan also refused, and there is some danger of this too, then conditions would be serious. If in addition to Italy's refusal to sign, there should be revolution and Italy should establish a Bolsheviki government, it might upset the equilibrium in both France and England, to say nothing of the United States.

The President told us that Clemenceau had asked Lloyd George and himself to meet with him this afternoon to discuss his differences with Marechal Foch. Foch has grown insubordinate and has refused to deliver an order which Clemenceau instructed him to give the Germans. He is angry because Clemenceau has not insisted, to the breaking up of the Conference, upon a Rhenish republic and an indefinite French occupation of the Rhine. These are serious problems, and I find it hard to exercise my usual philosophy and not worry as to the outcome. I manage to do it, however, for if I do not, I would be unfitted for the day's work.

---

[1] Lt. Col. Henry Herman Harjes and Frederica Berwind Gilpin Harjes. Harjes, born in Paris, was senior partner in Morgan, Harjes & Co., the Paris branch of J. P. Morgan & Co. More recently, he had served as chief liaison officer with the A.E.F.

[2] It was indeed an intemperate statement. Although Hoover began by emphasizing that the primary objective of the United States in eastern Europe was to save the lives of starving people, he added that a second objective was to prevent the spread of anarchy in that area caused by starvation and misery.

This said by way of introduction, Hoover then launched into a scathing denunciation of "Communist" Russia. He then followed with an invidious comparison between the American free-market economy and the Soviet system—"the mixture of theorists, dreamers and murderers." He gave extensive statistics to show the breakdown of railroad transportation and industrial and farm production under the Bolshevik regime. He denounced the Bolshevik leaders as tyrants and murderers, who had used the "criminal classes" and were now disseminating propaganda which was spreading more rapidly than the "bubonic plague." Hoover said that he had no fear that "Communism" would take hold in the United States, but he cautioned that, even in that happy and prosperous country, "Communism offers opportunity to the criminal classes to perpetrate murder, theft, robbery in all of the fine phrases of humanity." Hoover doubted that it would be necessary for the United States to stamp out militarily the Bolshevik tyranny in Russia. In fact, he thought that the pendulum was beginning to swing toward the center in that country. He was even more hopeful that the new states of central and eastern Europe would, with generous assistance, "pull through without a cataclysm." "The chances of accomplishing all these things," Hoover concluded, "are about fifty fifty." T MS (HPL), mistakenly dated April 25, 1919.

As this entry from the House Diary reveals, House read Hoover's statement during the evening of April 18 and urgently requested Hoover not to give it out until he, House, had had a chance to talk with him. This extract and Hoover's letter to House, printed as the following document, also show that House and Hoover conferred during the morning of April 19, that Hoover agreed not to publish his statement, but that, in the afternoon, he sent House a revised version of it. It is printed as the Enclosure with the following letter. It is this version that Wilson read and vetoed and to which Baker refers in the extract from his diary of April 19. Hoover may have been angered by the killing of his statement, as Baker reports, but he calmed down enough to draft an innocuous statement which Wilson could approve. This statement is printed as an Enclosure with WW to HCH, April 23, 1919.

The question of Hoover's motivation in this démarche at once arises. Having just read Nansen's letter to Lenin (printed at April 17, 1919), Hoover probably had in mind two large political considerations. First, he wanted to reassure the American people that the United States Government had no intention of recognizing the Bolshevik regime and, in fact, detested it. It was during this very period that American fears of Communism were beginning to grow by leaps and bounds into what historians have called the first Red Scare. Second, Hoover was certainly not without political ambitions, which had been inflated by much talk of him as a presidential candidate in 1920. Thus, he may well have been pandering to anti-Communist fears for political advantage.

But we think that much more might have been involved. The fact is that, during the struggle over the reply of the Big Four to Nansen (see WW to F. Nansen, April 7, 1919, n. 1), Bullitt had won his two main points—that the food and other relief supplies shipped to Russia should be "solely under the control of the people of Russia themselves" (which meant that the Soviet authorities would control distribution in their domain) and, second, that there should be "a complete suspension of the transfer of troops and military material of all sorts to and within Russian territory." This latter point of course meant that whatever Allied and American troops remained in Russia would have to be withdrawn, since they could not be supplied with additional means of their own protection. Moreover, in the last paragraph of his letter to Lenin (printed at April 17, 1919), Nansen, on his own, virtually offered *de facto* recognition to the Soviet government.

Ironically, Bullitt, on account of his fury at Wilson's refusal to present the Soviet government's proposal (see W. C. Bullitt to WW, March 16, 1919, Vol. 55) to the Council of Four, does not seem to have realized the dimension of his victory. However, Hoover must certainly have well understood the clear implications of the Big Four's reply to Nansen. Was Hoover at this point now attempting to torpedo the Nansen project? Hoover had, in fact, set the wheels of the Nansen plan in motion and had obviously lost control. As the extracts from the House and Baker Diaries of April 19, 1919, reveal, Wilson, House, and Baker were convinced that publication of Hoover's statement would wreck the Nansen project.

Herbert Clark Hoover to Edward Mandell House, with Enclosure

My dear Colonel House: [Paris] 19 April 1919.

Since seeing you this morning I find the following in the "Echo de Paris":

"Our Russian policies,—the last mistake in which we mentioned yesterday—perplexes everyone, even our American friends. While M. Clemenceau affixed his signature to a document approving the project of revictualling Russia and Messrs. Wilson, Lloyd-George and Orlando also signed it, Mr. Hoover, who had officially supported the aforesaid project, received a letter from our Minister of Foreign Affairs conveying the refusal of the French Government."

This is obviously a lie. I also learn that statements went out to the United States from French sources of the same import in an attempt to create an atmosphere that either I or the Americans were supporting the Bolshevik. Our New York office also telegraphs over, apparently disturbed by the reaction that has been created.

I have no objection to making any personal sacrifice necessary to obtain large political objects. I do not, however, think it is fair to the American officials or to the American people that we should not define precisely where we stand on Bolshevism. While I regard the parlor operators who are coquetting with this fire with contempt I do realize that we stand to further the forces of disorder in the United States if we stand still. I do not, however, ask anyone to join in my personal views. Nor do I consider that any enemy resents frank statement of opposition.

I wrote the document in question after three days and nights of careful consideration as to all of its bearings and I have now again had an opportunity to think it over, also with a view of what has happened since and with a large knowledge of certain forms of publicity. I have made certain alterations in the text which relieves everyone else of responsibility. I would be glad if you could take the valuable time necessary to reconsider the matter. It is possible that the whole mission will be driven into making a defensive statement within the next three days, whereas if I make an offensive statement now we will never have to do so. Even if this is not the case, unless we disarm the parlor operators we will have to answer for a stimulus to this clap trap over the next twelve months.

Faithfully yours, Herbert Hoover

TLS (E. M. House Papers, CtY).

E N C L O S U R E

18 April 1919.

It is proposed to feed Russia, subject to, first, guarantees through a strong neutral commission that there is complete justice in distribution. Second, that the Bolshevik are to keep themselves within a certain circumscribed area without any militant action.

The primary reasons for this action are purely humanitarian. Hundreds of thousands of people are dying monthly from starvation, and beyond even this it is the wish of the world that fighting and the killing of men should cease. Other reasons have been also brought to bear. The newly born democracies of Siberia, Kuban, Finland, Esthonia, Lettland, Livonia, Poland, Ruthenia, Roumania, Armenia, Serbia, Bulgaria and Austria, and other nationalities which surround Bolshevik Russia must have a breathing spell to build up some stability. There is little hope of setting any orderly government in these places and of getting their people back to production under which they can raise food and necessities for next year, unless they can be relieved of the constant threat of Bolshevist invasion and the necessity to keep armies in being out of resources founded on misery.

Again many social observers believe that Bolshevism will die out much more quickly in the world if its real character is illuminated and made visible so that all may read, then [than] if it is cooped up in a dark room.

Again, the brunt of this famine in Russia is being thrown by the Bolshevik upon the skilled workmen who refuse to accept their doctrines, upon the merchants, storekeepers and professional classes, and unless food is put into Russia all these classes will be dead before next harvest and there will be little hope of Russia's ever reconstructing herself.

Again the Bolshevik Army is founded on famine and is recruited by the lure of food. The Russians have already amply demonstrated the inability to hold an army together in activity, more especially if there is food elsewhere. There are other reasons of less importance.

The economic and political situation inside Bolshevik Russia to-day is about as bad as it can be. Through the agents of the Food organization, we have made a great deal of inquiry into this internal situation. Several primary facts stand out with great vividness. The first is that Russia is not only normally an extremely well fed country but formerly exported as much food as did the United States, yet today her people are dying in thousands from starvation for no other reason in the world than the fool idea that the processes of production and distribution can be broken down in a country and the population still live. The second outstanding fact is that this mixture of theorists, dreamers and murderers that comprise the Bolshevik Government have themselves at last to some degree realized the infinite calamity that they have brought on their people and are themselves floundering around endeavoring to restore the normal processes of production and distribution. They have abandoned their plan for communal ownership of the land because they found the land would not be planted for a remuneration consisting of phrases like the "common good." They have abandoned the notion that they could abolish banks and financial institutions and have themselves established a series of savings banks because they found people saw no object in working if they could not save their wages. They are themselves offering enormous wages for skilled men because they found skilled men would not do more than common labor for common laborer's wages. They have changed their cry from a crusade to impose so-called reason on to the world to an appeal to Russians to defend the sacred soil of Russia. This latter is fundamentally the most extraordinary change made in their propaganda because under their doctrines and their original hypothesis there were to be no national boundaries,—all the world was to be one grand commune with little communes of no political divisions, all property owned in common and everybody who dared to put his head above the common level to have it promptly shot off.

Under the plan of a Neutral Commission for feeding Russia there is no intention of recognizing the men whose fingers are even today dripping with the blood of hundreds of innocent people of Odessa.

CC MS (E. M. House Papers, CtY).

From the Diary of Ray Stannard Baker

Saturday April 19 [1919]

Hoover got out a red-hot statement regarding the Bolsheviks (whom we are about to feed). We held it back & he is very angry. But why abuse people with whom you are about to negotiate— whom you are about to feed? I also talked with Nansen about his plans.

The rift between the President & Col. House seems to be widening. The Colonel compromises everything away. He has gone so far with the Italians that they are now heralding him as the great man of the conference & comparing him unfavorably with the President. It makes it difficult now for the President. The Colonel is still declaring that if he had the peace to make it could all be done in a day or so—and it could—by giving away everything we came to fight for. . . .

We are torn in our own Commission on the Russian question. At one extreme is Bullitt, strongly in favor of recognizing the Bolsheviks & very bitter because the President held up his statement made after returning from Russia with Steffins. (He spoke with profound authority after having been less than two weeks in Russia!) And at the other extreme is Hoover, who would feed the Russians but is very bitter against the Bolsheviks. He sent down a statement for us to issue but we held it up & it was disapproved by House & Wilson (see scrap-book of this date)

In the meantime, out of the dust & confusion in the East comes news of the steady progress of bolshevism—Austria–Bavaria &c It rumbles westward. Who next? Italy is wobbly, & so is Roumania.

Gilbert Fairchild Close to Robert Lansing

My dear Mr. Secretary: Paris, 19 April, 1919.

The President asks if you will not be kind enough to forward the following message to Mr. Polk in response to your suggestion of April 18th:

"It is a matter of sincere regret to me that I cannot be present to add my tribute and friendship and admiration for Walter Page. He crowned a life of active usefulness by rendering his country a service of unusual distinction and deserves to be held in the affectionate memory of his fellow-countrymen. In a time of exceeding difficulty he acquitted himself with discretion, unwavering fidelity and admirable intelligence.

Woodrow Wilson."[1]
Sincerely yours,   [Gilbert F. Close]

CCL (WP, DLC).
[1] This was sent as RL to FLP, No. 1715, April 21, 1919, T telegram (WP, DLC).

Gilbert Fairchild Close to Joseph Patrick Tumulty

Paris, 19 April, 1919.

President authorizes the following statement over his signature by War Loan Organization. QUOTE

For two anxious years the American people have striven to fulfill the task of saving our civilization STOP By the exertion of unmeasured power they have quickly won the victory without which they would have remained in the field until the last resource had been exhausted. Bringing to the contest a strength of spirit made doubly strong by the righteousness of their cause they devoted themselves unswervingly to the prosecution of their undertaking in the full knowledge that no conquest lay in their path excepting the conquest of right.

Today the world stands freed from the threat of militarism which has so long weighed upon the spirit and the labour of peaceful nations but as yet we stand only at the threshold of happier times. To enter we must fulfill to the utmost the engagements we have made. The Victory Liberty Loan is the indispensable means. Two years ago we pledged our lives and fortunes to the cause for which we have fought. Sixty thousand of our strongest sons have redeemed for us that pledge of blood. To redeem in full faith the promise of this sacrifice we now must give this new evidence of our purpose. WOODROW WILSON. UNQUOTE.   Close.

T telegram (WP, DLC).

From William Bauchop Wilson

Washington Apl 19 1919

Number 65 following from Secretary Wilson quote referring to the personal conversation of Mr H L Kerwin[1] with you this morning during which the present financial condition of the National War Labor Board was called to your attention I wish to state that the presidents allotment of 250,000 dollars on november 25 1918 has been almost entirely exhausted and that consequently the boards need for additional funds with which to conduct its business is very urgent paragraph

Accordingly I have requeste[d] that the President make a further allotment of sixty thousand dollars to the department of labor for mediation purposes from his appropriation for National security and defense which sum will enable the board to dispose of the cases remaining on its docket and handle such other matters as may be submitted to it in the near future end quote.   Tumulty.

T telegram (WP, DLC).
[1] That is, Hugh Leo Kerwin, at this time Director of Conciliation in the Department of Labor.

From William Cox Redfield

Washington, April 19, 1919.

1638. For the President from Redfield.

"Promptly on receipt of your cablegram April 16th, courteous letter was sent Director General Railways by Industrial Board, cordially proposing further conferences to establish common ground as requested by you. Before this letter was received, however, your cablegram April 18th was received. It is only just to Board to state no member of the foregoing has had impression that they were either invited to fix prices or could do so. In view however your suggestion, it seems best in order to clarify business situation and relieve you from further anxiety in matter to disband board. Am assuming, therefore, your approval accept resignations and close matter finally. Will delay two days to avoid possibilities of my misunderstanding your wish."　　　　　　　　　Polk,　Acting.

T telegram (WP, DLC).

From Joseph Patrick Tumulty

The White House, April 19, 1919

#66 New York Sun carries headline this morning Quote Wilson puts U. S. into alliance with Great Britain and France.[1] Unquote. This is bound to cause great deal of criticism and dissatisfaction. Now is the time to kill these vicious stories. Telephone situation still critical but we are hoping for improvement today.

Tumulty

T telegram (WP, DLC).
[1] For a summary of this article, see H. White to WW, April 16, 1919, n. 1.

Joseph Patrick Tumulty to Cary Travers Grayson

The White House, April 19, 1919.

Publication of President's message to New England Governors re telephone strike[1] embarrassed us here. Have been trying to settle matter diplomatically without involving the President but holding out appeal to him as final resort. Announcement that he would not act cripples us somewhat.　　　　　　　　Tumulty.

T telegram (J. P. Tumulty Papers, DLC).
[1] See WW to JPT, April 17, 1919 (first telegram of that date).

From William David Upshaw[1]

Atlanta Ga Apl 19-20 [1919]

On *even* [eve] of Victory Liberty Loan campaign I am gravely concerned about the response in the cotton states. Having spoken in former campaigns I note tragic difference of sentiment especially due to uncertainty and depression concerning price and disastrous losses.[2] Genuinely patriotic men supporting you in League of Nations declare situation would be greatly helped if you would announce that full embargo will be lifted after treaty is signed or before. For the sake of every vital issue involved please be good enough to wire us some encouragement

Wm D Upshaw M C

T telegram (WP, DLC).
    [1] Democratic congressman from Georgia.
    [2] From a high of 32.2 cents per pound on September 1, 1918, the price of cotton had fallen to 24 cents on March 1, 1919, and had risen only slightly to 24.5 cents by April 1. It was, however, to rise considerably during the remainder of 1919 and reached a high of 36.5 cents on November 1. The catastrophic collapse of cotton prices did not occur until the second half of 1920. See United States Department of Agriculture, *Yearbook, 1919* (Washington, 1920), p. 592, and Arthur S. Link, "The Federal Reserve Policy and the Agricultural Depression of 1920-1921," in *The Higher Realism of Woodrow Wilson and Other Essays* (Nashville, Tenn., 1971), pp. 330-31.

Frank Lyon Polk to the American Mission

Washington April 19, 1919

1653. Alexander Berkenheim, Vice-President of the All-Russian Central Union of Consumers' Societies at Moscow, speaking also for American Committee of American Cooperative Societies which has been established at New York, has informed the Department that the Cooperative Societies of Russia are prepared to put their entire organization, both in Russia and in this country, at the disposal of Mr. Hoover in carrying out plan to send foodstuffs to European Russia as indicated in this week's press.

Department would be glad to know whether in connection with upholding Hoover's work a commission will be appointed with Nansen, the explorer, as chairman to undertake distribution of foodstuffs and other needed supplies in Russia and if so what reply Department is to make to proposal of Mr. Berkenheim.

Polk   Acting

T telegram (WP, DLC).

From the Diary of Dr. Grayson

Sunday, April 20, 1919.

The President rose early. Even though it was Easter Sunday, he felt that it was his duty to hold a meeting today as the people were so anxious for a decision, and he therefore decided to devote Sunday to this cause.

At 10:00 o'clock Lloyd-George, Clemenceau, Orlando and Sonnino arrived at the temporary White House and were shown immediately to the President's study. The Italian question—Fiume—

was the subject of discussion. Orlando made his argument why the Italians should have Fiume, and the President explained why he could not agree to that disposition, as it was in conflict with the principles laid down in his Fourteen Points. At the conclusion of the President's remarks Orlando got up out of his chair, walked over to the window, and sobbed and wept. The President personally is very fond of Orlando and has great respect for his integrity and character, and naturally this incident was very distressing. Sonnino then stated that he was the one who had brought Italy into the war on the side of the Allies—and this is generally conceded to be the fact. He recalled what the Austrians had promised Italy if she (Italy) entered the war on the side of the Central Powers, and under the position of the President Italy was not getting much more than if she had remained neutral, and yet she had lost nearly a half million men. He then referred to the line of agreement fixed by the Pact of London. The meeting adjourned at about 12:00 o'clock.

It was a beautiful, sunshiny day, and I persuaded the President to take a walk. He and I went for a stroll. We walked down to the Trocadero, and looked around at the statues of French Kings and other relics of the days of royalty.

On returning to the house the President had lunch with Mrs. Wilson. I had lunch with Mr. Bernard M. Baruch at his chateau near St. Cloud. The President and Mrs. Wilson went for a motor ride in the afternoon. The President returned in time for a conference with Clemenceau at 6:00 o'clock. The conference lasted an hour, and at its conclusion the President and Mrs. Wilson and Miss Benham and I had dinner. I remained with the President and Mrs. Wilson after dinner until about 10:00 o'clock, when the President retired. The President always reads the Bible before retiring.

As Clemenceau was leaving this afternoon I inquired how his health was holding out. He said: "Very good. You know, I go home at seven o'clock, eat a little milk and bread, and then go to bed. I wake up between one and three, and I then prop myself up in bed and read until seven. Then I get up for my breakfast and go out and walk around in my garden. I also go through morning exercises, deep breathing, etc. In this way I keep from getting old." With a twinkle in his eye, he added: "You know, we doctors[1] can't afford to get old."

[1] Clemenceau's father, grandfather, and great grandfather had all been physicians. He, too, had trained for that profession, first at the Preparatory School of Medicine and Pharmacy at Nantes and then at the Faculty of Medicine at the University of Paris, from which he received his diploma in 1865. He practiced medicine only briefly, however. See Jack D. Ellis, *The Early Life of Georges Clemenceau, 1841-1893* (Lawrence, Kan., 1980), pp. 5-62 *passim*.

Hankey's Notes of a Meeting of the Council of Four[1]

President Wilson's House,
I.C.-174A.   Paris, April 20, 1919, 10 a.m.

(1) M. ORLANDO read the following declaration:

"I must maintain all the declarations which I have made so far as the question of Fiume is concerned. In reducing the matter to its minimum terms I must observe to President Wilson that, from the point of view of his noble intention of maintaining peace in the world, he is too eminent a politician not to realise that an essential condition for arriving at this object is that of avoiding between peoples the sentiment of reaction against injustice, which will form, without doubt, the most fatal germ of future wars. But I affirm here that if Fiume is not granted to Italy there will be among the Italian people a reaction of protest and of hatred so violent that it will give rise to the explosion of violent contrasts within a period that is more or less close. I think, then, that the fact that Fiume may not be given to Italy would be extremely fatal just as much to the interests of Italy as to the peace of the world. Nevertheless, since the British and French Allies have declared yesterday that they do not recognise the right of Italy to break the Alliance in the event of her being accorded only what the Treaty of Alliance guarantees her, I am so convinced of my responsibility towards the peace of the world in the event of a rupture of the Alliance to consider it necessary to safeguard myself against every possible accusation in this respect. I declare in consequence formally that, in the event of the Peace Conference guaranteeing to Italy all the rights which the Treaty of London has assured to her, I shall not be obliged to break the Alliance, and I would abstain from every act or deed which could have this signification." (The original of this statement in French is attached. *Appendix I.*)[2]

After a pause, PRESIDENT WILSON said it was incredible to him that the representatives of Italy should take up this position. At the centre of the War there stood three Powers—France, Great Britain, and Italy—which undoubtedly had borne the brunt of the War, especially the two first engaged. Undoubtedly, however, the whole world perceived that the War had been largely undertaken to save these Powers from the intentions of the Central Powers. These Powers, however, had not brought the war to an end. Other Powers had come in which had nothing to do with the Alliance, and were not bound by the Pact of London. These Powers had rendered indispensable assistance; for example, the material and financial

[1] The complete text of these minutes is printed in *PPC*, V, 95-105.
[2] There is a copy of this French text in SDR, RG 256, 180.03401/109, DNA.

assistance of the United States of America had been essential to the successful conclusion of the War. (M. CLEMENCEAU and MR. LLOYD GEORGE interrupted to express agreement in this.) As soon as the United States of America entered the War they declared their principles. These were acclaimed particularly by those peoples to whom they gave a new assurance of peace, namely, the smaller Powers. They were also greeted with acclamation by the peoples of the Great Powers. When he wrote these principles he knew that he was not writing merely his own conscience, but the point of view of the people of the United States of America. These principles were found to be identical with the sentiments of all the great peoples of the Allied and Associated Powers. Otherwise, these principles would have no effect. The world did not ask for the opinions of individuals. What it did ask was that individuals should formulate principles which called to consciousness what every man was feeling. The opinions expressed first by Mr. Lloyd George, and a few days afterwards by himself,[3] had accomplished this. On these principles the United States of America and some other Powers had entered the War. This world conference must, in formulating the peace, express the conclusions of the whole world and not those of a small group, even though he hastened to add the most influential group who had entered earlier into a Treaty. The object of our principles was not to exclude any legitimate natural aspiration. In this connection PRESIDENT WILSON read the following extracts from his Fourteen Points:

"XI. Roumania, Serbia, and Montenegro should be evacuated; occupied territories restored; Serbia accorded free and secure access to the sea; and the relations of the several Balkan States to one another determined by friendly counsel along historically established lines of allegiance and nationality; and international guarantees of the political and economic independence and territorial integrity of the several Balkan States should be entered into."

"IX. A readjustment of the frontiers of Italy should be effected along clearly recognisable lines of nationality."

This, he said, was what we had been attempting to do. If we did not do what M. Orlando had so eloquently referred to and carry out our principles, but were to base ourselves on the Treaty which Italy invoked, we should be raising antagonisms which would never be stamped out until what we were now doing was rectified. Hence, the result of M. Orlando's proposal, namely, that other Powers than

[3] Wilson here referred to Lloyd George's speech on January 5, 1918, about which see British embassy to WW, Jan. 5, 1918, n. 2, Vol. 45, and also of course to his own Fourteen Points Address printed at Jan. 8, 1918, *ibid.*

those bound by it should adhere to the Treaty of London, and if Italy insisted on the carrying out of this Treaty she would stand in the way of peace. The United States of America were not bound, and besides they regarded it as unsuited to the circumstances of the day. If the Austro-Hungarian Empire had survived, his attitude would have been entirely different. For then Italy would have been entitled to every outpost of security. Those dangerous circumstances, however, did not now exist, and though the signatories of the Pact of London did not consider themselves relieved of their undertaking, other Powers need not regard the Pact as binding. He asked his Italian brethren whether they were determined to take action which would result in reducing the chance of peace with Germany, of increasing the risk of the resumption of the War, and of alienating people who had been enthusiastically friendly to Italy. Would they refuse to enter the new circumstances of the world because they could not renew the old circumstances? Without the Pact of London Italy would receive her natural boundaries; the redemption of the Italian population; a restoration of her old glory, and the completion of her integrity. A dream would be realised which, at the beginning of the War, would have seemed too good to be true. The dream had come true by the gallantry of the Italian armies and the force of the world. It was incredible to him, even though he had actually heard it, that Italy should take up this attitude. It was the supreme completing tragedy of the War that Italy should turn her back on her best friends and take up a position of isolation. He deplored it as one whose heart was torn. But as representative of the people of the United States of America he could not violate the principles they had instructed him to carry out in this settlement.

M. ORLANDO said that he ought to declare to President Wilson that if he spoke of the Pact of London it had only been at the last moment and in spite of himself. He had only done so in order to reply to remarks made by Mr. Lloyd George and M. Clemenceau. They had said that he would take too great a responsibility in breaking an Alliance towards a people who say that they are ready to honour their signature and to fulfil their obligations. He had made all possible efforts to demonstrate that the rights of Italy rest within the bounds of reason and remain in the field of argument. No one more than he would regret to rely on the text of a Treaty instead of applying reason. Italy had not been, and was not, intransigent. No way to conciliation had yet been offered to her. In regard to the Fourteen Points, he asked the President to recognise that those relating to Austria-Hungary were obsolete because Austria-Hungary had ceased to exist. Yesterday President Wilson had recognised this himself. The President had interpreted the Fourteen Points as if Serbia had a right to Fiume. As a matter of fact, however, Serbia's extreme ambitions in regard to a sea port had extended to St. Jean de Medua, Alessio, and they had never even dreamed of Ragusa. Now they were assured of far more. He asked President Wilson to bear two things in mind, first, that although those parts of the Fourteen Points applying to Austria-Hungary ceased to be valid after the fall of Austria-Hungary, those relating to Italy remained; and second, that he had made a definite reservation at the beginning of the Peace Conference with the United States of America, through Colonel House, in regard to their application to the Austro-Hungarian Treaty.[4] Consequently, he was not bound by them in the Austro-Hungarian Treaty. President Wilson had said with emotion that the War had been waged for justice and right. Italy also considered that she had fought for justice. There, Italy was on the same ground as President Wilson. He deeply objected to President Wilson's suggestion to the contrary, for Italy also had made war in good faith, and he himself could say that he could sign no peace contrary to justice and right. He had said this not to criticise President Wilson, but to explain his own point of view. President Wilson had concluded that his heart was torn by the separation of Italy. He expressed his deep thanks for this, and he declared that his heart was still more torn. He felt exactly the same sentiment of friendship, loyal and mutual affection and esteem, not only between the two peoples, but between the two men. But he also experienced sentiments of anguish when he thought of his own country. As he had said on the previous day, if he must face death, it must be for a just cause.

PRESIDENT WILSON said that M. Orlando might rest assured that he himself had no misconception as to the Italian motives. It was merely a fundamental difference of policy between them. He fully realised that Italy was not bound by the Fourteen Points in making peace with Austria. He was not inclined to insist on any particular principle in the Fourteen Points, but his position was that he could not make peace with Germany on one set and with Austria on another set of principles. Throughout their consultations the drawing of frontiers had been based on ethnic lines as a principle.

[4] Mantoux, I, 295, renders this sentence as follows: "In the second place, we made, concerning the application of the Fourteen Points to problems which interest us, unequivocal reservations. Colonel House received our communication on this subject. We are not bound by any engagement, and we do not believe that President Wilson is either."

Actually, during the Pre-Armistice negotiations, Orlando did try, from time to time, to enter reservations to Points 9, 10, 11, and 12, but he was outmaneuvered by Colonel House with the support of Lloyd George and failed to have any reservations accepted. See Albrecht-Carrié, *Italy at the Paris Peace Conference*, pp. 60-66.

MR. LLOYD GEORGE regretted that the Supreme Council found itself confronted with the most difficult situation that had faced it since the beginning of the Conference. The question was a very troublesome one, and he could not see a way out. We were first confronted with the possibility that Italy was feeling she could not continue her association with her Allies in making peace, because of this troublesome Austrian question. Another alternative was that the United States of America could not assent to a Treaty based on principles involving a grave departure from those for which she had entered the War. Either way it was a very serious matter. Personally, he did not feel free to discuss the question of merits, because he must respect his bond. [M. Orlando shows signs of the deepest emotion.]⁵ It had been honoured by Italy in blood, treasure, and sacrifice. He would tarnish his country's honour if he receded from it, though no one more than he recognised the President's powerful plea. He realised that it was a very serious matter for Italy to antagonise two of the most powerful races in Europe, the Germans in the Tyrol, and the Slavs in Austria. He, however, was not entitled to discuss that. He wished to put to President Wilson the reason why Italy found it difficult to recede from the Treaty. He had been profoundly impressed by M. Orlando's reasoning, but he had also been greatly moved by what Baron Sonnino had said. Baron Sonnino had been in the War from the very outset, and had taken upon himself a very heavy responsibility in rejecting Austria's terms. What could he say to the people of Italy? If he returned to Italy without the Treaty, he would almost have to leave the country. After incurring heavy losses and large debts he had only got little more than what he could have had without risking a single life. His suggestion was that the representatives of the Powers signatories to the Treaty of London should meet separately to consider President Wilson's grave decision. If, however, Italy could not modify her attitude, he was bound to take his stand by his bond. Anything he could say would be by way of suggestion and appeal only. He asked if President Wilson agreed to this course?

PRESIDENT WILSON assented. He said he felt it to be his duty to mention any counsel of accommodation that had been made to him. He, therefore, asked the question as to whether, supposing Fiume were conceded to the Serbo-Croats, as provided in the Pact of London, and if the lines of the Pact and all within it were, for the time being, handed over to the five Great Powers as trustees to determine its disposition, would the Italian representatives then say they could not consent—always on the assumption of no guarantee

⁵ Mantoux, I, 296.

of ultimate cession to Italy of what lay within the line. There was one point on which he had said that he would make an exception to Italy, that was in the case of the island of Lissa. He recognised, however, that this was only a very small part of the Pact of London. He would not be frank if he held out to the Italian representatives any hope of the assent of the United States of America to the ultimate cession of the islands and other territory involved in the Pact of London to Italy. The proposal he had made, however, would relieve the present difficulty and give the Great Powers further time to consider the matter. As the suggestion had been made to him he would like to know if it had any weight at all with the Italian representatives.

MR. LLOYD GEORGE said he would like time to think the matter over, and he suggested that the signatories of the Treaty should meet on the following day.

BARON SONNINO agreed. He thanks Mr. Lloyd George for his exposition of the Italian point of view. His own responsibility towards his conscience made it necessary—the responsibility of those present towards their own consciences made it necessary that everything possible should be done to try to see a way out. Perhaps he himself was too agitated and pre-occupied to see the whole of the picture. He and M. Orlando consented to meet and examine every point of view and to try to find a way out. It was his duty to do all he could to find a settlement. It had been said that it involved death, moral death to him. He did not care a pin about that. He only thought of his country. It would be said that he had ruined his country, and nothing could trouble a man more than that.

MR. LLOYD GEORGE said that it was really an essential element in the case. Italy had rejected one (the Austrian) offer and accepted another and was now threatened with not having that made good.

PRESIDENT WILSON said that he fully realised that Italy had no imperialistic motives and gave her entire credit for that. He also fully appreciated the tragic personal position in which Baron Sonnino was placed. He honoured him for his steadfastness, which merely verified the steadfastness he had shown throughout the War. If Italy could see a way out consistent with permanent peace, he would like to assist if it were only for personal reasons. He hoped that Baron Sonnino would never think he had ruined his country. He would really have given it a more glorious record and no one could say that he had ruined it.

BARON SONNINO thanked President Wilson for what he had said. The word "imperialistic" had been used. Italy, however, had never had any intention to damage others. She only sought security at home. She asked for no positions from which she could menace her neighbours. In other matters referred to in the London Convention in regard to Greece, Italy had made it clear that she would not take an overbearing position. She merely wished to keep out of dangers. She wanted to keep out of Balkanism, for example. She wanted full freedom to her own commerce, culture, and influence, but not to be drawn into the confluence of Balkan States. She wanted a safe basis for keeping out of these questions. If Italy were to do what President Wilson wanted, she would inevitably be drawn in. Her reasoning might be wrong about this island or that island, but the whole political basis of the Pact of London was Italy's desire to keep out of the danger of being attacked or of the temptation to attack herself in order to forestall a danger. For centuries of her history Italy had been overrun by barbarians—Germans, Austrians, Spaniards, &c. (MR. LLOYD GEORGE interjected that Italy had herself overrun Britain.) The reason was that Italy had fair lands. Now she desired to keep in her own corner of Europe outside it all and President Wilson wanted to stop her.

PRESIDENT WILSON said that if he thought this would be the result he would help.

BARON SONNINO continued that even Fiume, which was outside the Pact of London was not asked for as a means of aggression. Other considerations prevailed here. There had been a movement by Fiume itself that had brought it up. The war undoubtedly had had the effect of over-exciting the feeling of nationality. This was not Italy's fault. Perhaps America had fostered it by putting the principles so clearly. In the discussions about the Pact of London M. Sazonoff[6] had insisted on the names of places being put in, and Italy had conceded without discussion a number of big islands and the port of Segna, in order to give Jugo-Slavia means of defence. He could not see that anything that Italy had done contravened the principles. It was very easy to make principles, but enormous differences arose in their application. It was their application that created differences between people who were agreed on the principles themselves. Even in the settlement of the German Treaty concessions of principle had repeatedly to be made.

(2) M. CLEMENCEAU read a telegram he had received from the German Foreign Office in reply to the invitation to the Germans to come to Versailles on April 25. The gist of this reply was that Germany would send, on the 25th April, Minister Von Haniel, Councillor Von Keller, and Councillor Ernst Smitt.[7] These delegates would

---

[6] That is, Sergei Dmitrievich Sazonov.

[7] Edgar Karl Alfons Haniel von Haimhausen, Friedrich von Keller, and Ernst Schmitt, all members of the German diplomatic service. The telegram mentioned above is printed as the Enclosure with T. H. Bliss to WW, April 20, 1919.

be provided with the necessary powers to receive the text of the proposed Preliminaries of Peace which they would bring back to the German Government. A list was then given of the functionaries and servants who would accompany them.

MR. LLOYD GEORGE said we could not deal with messengers. He was altogether opposed to it. He then invited his colleagues to read a dispatch he had just received from Berlin which threw some light on this question. (*Appendix II.*)

After Prof. Mantoux had read the document in French, MR. LLOYD GEORGE said that it had a most important bearing on the German reply. The suggestion to send more messengers to Versailles was a foolish one, because if not intended as insolent, it was purely futile. If circumstances were such as the British agent suggested in the Paper that had just been read, it might be desirable to force the Germans to choose a Government that could represent them.

PRESIDENT WILSON agreed in Mr. Lloyd George's suggestion that we could not receive mere messengers and must insist on plenipotentiaries.

At M. Clemenceau's request he drafted a reply to be sent to the German Government somewhat on the following lines:

The Allied and Associated Powers cannot receive envoys merely authorised to receive the terms of peace. They must require that the German Government shall send plenipotentiaries fully authorised to deal with the whole question of peace as are the plenipotentiaries of the Allied and Associated Powers. (*The discussion was then adjourned.*)

B./627. APPENDIX II TO I.C. 174.A.[8]

Berlin, 17.4.19.

1. It is becoming increasingly clear that the EBERT-SCHEIDEMANN Government cannot long continue *in its present form.*

Reasons:

a) Great numbers of the rank and file of the Government supporters are going over to the left and joining either the "Independents"[9] or (though to a less extent) the "communists." Both Government and National Versammlung[10] have lost the confidence of the country. The working classes believe that the failure to carry out a socialistic programme is due, not to the inherent difficulties of the problem, but to the presence in the government of bourgeois elements whose sole object is obstruction.

---

[8] The following report was written by Capt. Thomas Gibson, a British military intelligence officer in Berlin.

[9] That is, the Independent Social Democratic party.

[10] The German National Assembly at Weimar.

b) The strikes and disturbances throughout the country are no longer merely food riots or "unemployed" riots but have taken on a definitely political, i.e. anti-SCHEIDEMANN, character (Scheidemann is of course merely regarded as the personification of bourgeois-socialist Government in league with capitalism).

c) The idea of the "Räte"[11] or Soviet system has spread to such an extent and taken such a hold on the popular imagination that it has become impossible to leave it out of consideration. SCHEIDEMANN's attitude on this question is one of the chief causes of his unpopularity.

d) The food that is being sent and such raw materials as there might be a possibility of sending, are not sufficient in quantity, so to change the outward circumstances of the working man's life as to make him forget his dissatisfaction at the incompetence of the Government, whom he makes responsible for all his troubles.

2. Unless the governments modified or remodelled in some way either

a) it will be overthrown before peace is signed—by a general strike or Spartacist coup du main. In this case the Entente is faced with a Germany without any constituted government that can sign the Peace Treaty; or

b) on learning the terms on which the Allies consent to make peace, Scheidemann and Brockdorff-Rantzau will do their best to make a virtue of necessity and leave the stage with the "grand geste" of outraged dignity. It is becoming daily more evident *that this government does not intend to sign* the peace they will be offered. And the National Versammlung is already practising the gestures of sympathy with which it will accompany the exit of its cabinet.

3. If then the Government is overthrown before peace or retires in a body on refusing to sign, there only exist two alternatives for the succession

(i) *a military dictatorship backed by the Right wing*—such a regime could not sign peace on behalf of the country even if it wanted to. It is questionable whether the troops would support it in any large numbers. The result will be civil war and complete anarchy, with sooner or later the necessity of military intervention by the Entente.

(ii) A soviet government probably leading to a Spartacist (or Bolshevik) dictatorship. The result in this case would equally be anarchy and the probable necessity of Entente intervention and occupation.

[11] That is, revolutionary councils.

4. There is one possibility of avoiding either of these extreme results.

Negotiations are being carried on with great energy between the right wing of the "Independents," the majority socialists and the military men who stand behind Noske[12] and constitute his force. The objects are as follows:

1. to remodel the cabinet (retaining EBERT as Reichspräsident) on a purely Socialistic basis including "majority" and "independents."

2. to secure for such a government the support of the troops even supposing Noske himself were removed. It is stated that Captain von PABST,[13] the moving spirit of the present military organisation, is in favour of the plan and would support the government if reconstituted on these lines.

3. to pursuade the "Independents" to abandon that part of their programme which involves the disbanding of the troops. The majority of their leaders have, it is said, now realised the necessity for this.

4. to form a second chamber of the Räte or councils which should have the right of initiative and of veto in legislation. It is argued that the Räte system has developed into a genuine political ideal among the proletariat and unless a far-reaching concession of this kind is made to them there will be no possibility of avoiding the worst evil of a Soviet dictatorship.

5. The two strong arguments in favour of such a reconstitution of the government are as follows:

(1) It would start with the confidence of the country. The proletariats will feel that "*their men*" are at the helm and the bourgeois and capitalists have nothing to say. If "their men" cannot do all the workmen expect, they will realise it cannot be done.

(2) They will be inclined to sign the peace treaty and the second (or Räte) chamber will be likely to bring pressure to bear on the National Versammlung to do so too. If a deadlock ensues, there must be a referendum to the country.

The present government (at any rate Scheidemann and Rantzau) quite evidently *do not intend* to sign the peace treaty. A purely socialist government on these lines would be much more likely to do so.

6. If the Entente does not desire to see the whole country thrown into anarchy there remain only these two possibilities:

1. A military occupation of all Germany by Entente troops. If this were done *at once* it would not be necessary to send more

[12] That is, Gustav Noske.
[13] Capt. Waldemar Pabst, leader of a Free Corps cavalry unit.

than 10 or 12 divisions—provided the action were accompanied by skilful propaganda. If it is done only when anarchy
has spread further, it will need several armies. A purely socialist Government, regarded as a remodelling of the present
government and supported by the Entente in respect of still
further supplies of food, concessions as to the independent
purchase of food, concessions as to the independent purchase
of food by Germany from Neutrals and the importation of the
most necessary raw materials such as cotton, wool, iron-ores
etc.

With regard to raw materials, the Entente is in a position to
control the supply so that only such amounts are imported as
are necessary for Germany's internal needs, so as to avoid any
conceivable danger of dumping.

7.   Should the Entente Governments decide that such a modification of the present Government is desirable, it is suggested that
a hint might be given to Ebert in the form of a confidential note
through, say, the Swiss Minister to the effect that "The Associated
Governments are inclined to form the opinion, on the basis of information received, that the government in its present form does
not enjoy the confidence or represent the feelings of the people,
that under the circumstances they feel that its signature to the
peace treaty does not afford a sufficient guarantee for its execution,
and that though the Associated Governments are far from having
any desire to interfere in Germany's political affairs, they feel they
are entitled to the assurance that the position of the government
with which they are to negotiate is perfectly clear."

8.   A reconstitution of the Government on the above lines would
certainly clear the political atmosphere, and would make it possible
that peace be signed. It could not however stand more than a month,
unless its position were strengthened by an immediate announcement from the Entente that the necessities of the industrial situation were realised and raw materials in considerable quantities
were introduced.

T MS (SDR, RG 256, 180.03401/109, DNA).

A Memorandum by Georges Clemenceau[1]

20 avril [1919]

Texte anglais de la proposition francaise[2]
STIPULATIONS TO BE EMBODIED IN THE TREATY.

Between the Governments of the United States of America, France and Great Britain, it is agreed:

1°) The maintenance or building of fortifications west of a line drawn fifty kilometers east of the Rhine is forbidden to Germany.

2°) The maintenance or assembling of armed forces, either permanently or temporarily, is forbidden within the area defined by Article 1, as well as all military manoeuvres of any kind and the maintenance of physical facilities for mobilization.

3°) Any violation of these conditions to be regarded as an hostile act against the signatories to the treaty and as calculated to disturb the peace of the world.

4°) A pledge by the United States of America and the British Empire to come immediately ⟨with their whole strength⟩* to the assistance of France as soon as any unprovoked movement of agression against her is made by Germany.

5°) This pledge to be subject to the approval of the executive council of the League of Nations and to continue until it is agreed by the contracting powers that the League itself affords sufficient protection.

6°) As long as the present treaty remains in force, a pledge by Germany to ⟨submit herself to any investigation⟩ *respond to any inquiry*[3] that the Council of the League of Nations will deem necessary.

* texte de M. Lloyd George

T MS (WP, DLC).
[1] Deletions by Clemenceau in angle brackets; words in italics added by him.
[2] Clemenceau's hw; all words *sic.*
[3] This might have been Wilson's change.

From Prince Faisal

Dear President Wilson   Paris 20 Avril 1919

Before my departure for Syria, which will be tomorrow evening, I wish, Mr. President, to have the honour of thanking you for your beneficent endeavour in behalf of SYRIA. The ardent hopes of the Syrian people, as well as myself, are that the Great American Republic will always be interested in the welfare of our country.

I am confident that when the Commission visits Syria, it will find a country united in its love and gratitude to America and in the hope that you, Sir, and your great co[u]ntry will not withhold from Syria any possible assistance to give that country a place among the free nations of the world.

I am, Sir,   Very truly yours,   Faissal

TLS (WP, DLC).

From Tasker Howard Bliss, with Enclosure

My dear Mr. President: Paris April 20th, 1919

I am just in receipt of the attached telegram transmitted by General Pershing from General Barnum[1] who is the American representative on the Armistice Commission at Spa.

Sincerely yours,   Tasker H. Bliss.

TLS (WP, DLC).
[1] Brig. Gen. Malvern-Hill Barnum.

E N C L O S U R E

TRANSLATION OF CODE TELEGRAM RECEIVED

From HAEF 17:10 hrs.   At Versailles 20 April, 1919.

Bliss American Section Supreme War Council Versailles

Following telegram received from General Barnum at Spa. "Commander in Chief, General Headquarters, American Expeditionary Forces, France. Number 1045.

Following note was handed over by the German Government under date of 19th April.

'In behalf of the Government Minister, Count Brockdorff Rantzau, I request that the following communication be transmitted to the Allied and Associated Powers:

'The German Government has received the communication of the French President of the Ministry and of the Minister of War of the 18th April. The German Government will send to Versailles for the evening of 25th April, Minister Von Haniel, Privy *Legation* Counselor Von Keller and the acting legation Counselor Schmidtt. The delegates are provided with the necessary plenary powers to receive the text of the draft of the peace preliminaries, which they will carry back at once to the German Government. They will be accompanied with 2 officials, Court Counselors, Walter Reinke and Representative Alfred Luders, as well as by 2 officials, Mr. Julius Schmidt and Mr. Niedek.'[1]   Signed   BARNUM."

Please acknowledge.

Pershing   3:10 p.m.

T MS (WP, DLC).
[1] All four were functionaries in the German Foreign Ministry.

From the Diary of Colonel House

April 20, 1919.

The President tells me that the two Prime Ministers and himself had a trying time yesterday morning with Orlando and Sonnino. Orlando finally broke down and wept copiously and Sonnino was at the point of breaking. Neither would yield an inch and neither would the President, so the situation is just where it was except that the feeling is more intense. They are putting up the strongest sort of demand, and speculation is rife as to whether they will finally yield or whether they will go home without signing the Treaty, as they threaten. Every argument is being used to bring them to reason, but nothing so far has moved them.

From the Diary of Ray Stannard Baker

Sunday the 20th [April 1919]

Big Four this morning on the problem of Fiume. I saw the President afterwards & the situation is indeed acute. Orlando came out looking like a thundercloud. The President said he saw no solution. He will not give an inch. He stands. Tomorrow the Italians meet Lloyd-George & Clemenceau, Wilson remains out.

This is a serious situation. They—Italians, including little fiery Tozzi[1]—came in as usual & their temperature was high. They reflect the Eduard VII![2]

It does not seem possible that the treaty will be ready for the Germans on Friday.

There seems no escape for the world from a kind of general equilibrium of ruin. . . .

Col. House & his easy predictions. Said to the correspondents the other day that he had *long thought* that America ought to take a mandatory for Constantinople! We could make a record there— could clean things up: demonstrate to the entire east. He was quite eloquent about it! *The very next day*, someone having talked to him who really knew about Constantinople, he told the correspondents that he had *changed his view*, that it would be very difficult & expensive to build a free city without a hinterland to support it! He fires off just such immature ideas, not thought out, poorly considered. I firmly believe that his compromising spirit,[3] & his assurances to Orlando, communicated to Italy, has served to fan the flame of Italian nationalism & make it harder for Wilson, now that the real issue is joined.

[1] Capt. Pietro Tozzi, an aide to Orlando, who had recently been on a special mission to the United States to explain Italian territorial claims.

[2] Hotel Edouard VII, the headquarters of the Italian delegation.

[3] About House's latest démarche, see the extract from the House Diary printed at April 19, 1919.

From Edward Mandell House

Dear Governor: Paris 20 April 1919.

When the question of the insertion of labor clauses in the Treaty of Peace comes up for discussion in the Council of Four it might be helpful for you to have the following enclosures at hand:

Number One is a copy of the draft made public at the Plenary Conference.[1] It had been hastily thrown together at the last moment, and all the members of the Labor Commission who saw it in print realized that it would have to be revised.

Number Two is a revision by Prof. Shotwell[2] who has frequently served as a substitute for Hurley on the Commission. It is orderly, logical, and faithful to the spirit of the accepted original.

Number Three is Mr. Balfour's redraft.[3] It is carefully worded and astute; but it would probably be regarded by Labor opinion as reactionary and quite unsatisfactory. Nevertheless, it was accepted yesterday by the British Delegation and Lloyd George will probably propose its adoption.

Number Four is Shotwell's redraft of Balfour's text.[4] It seems to me to be a better and briefer statement. Even this will probably disappoint the hopes of Labor people who naturally expect that any redraft will not affect the substance of the text made public in the Plenary Conference.   Affectionately yours,   E. M. House

TLS (WP, DLC).

[1] PEACE CONFERENCE. REPORT OF THE COMMISSION ON INTERNATIONAL LABOUR LEGISLATION, title page and pp. 24-25 of the printed report (WP, DLC). This was the report presented to the fourth Plenary Session on April 11, 1919, about which see n. 5 to the extract from the Diary of Colonel House printed at April 11, 1919. Pages 24-25 comprise the "Clauses Proposed for Insertion in the Treaty of Peace." A copy of these clauses is printed as an Enclosure with H. M. Robinson to WW, March 24, 1919. Vol. 56.

[2] "*Labour*," n.d., T MS (WP, DLC). A similar, though not identical, draft is printed as part of a memorandum from James T. Shotwell to Colonel House, April 19, 1919, in Shotwell, *Origins of the International Labor Organization*, II, 410-11. The major alteration was in paragraph No. 8. In the T MS, it reads as follows: "All insurance and other monetary benefits or advantages secured to workers and their families by law should be equally available to all those engaged in similar employments." In Shotwell's memorandum of April 19, it is replaced by the following sentence: "The standards set by the laws of any country with respect to the conditions of labor should be applied to foreign workers lawfully resident therein."

[3] "BRITISH EMPIRE DELEGATION. INTERNATIONAL LABOUR LEGISLATION, CLAUSES PROPOSED FOR INSERTION IN THE TREATY OF PEACE. Re-Draft by Mr. Balfour," April 17, 1919, T MS (WP, DLC). This document is identical with that printed in Shotwell, *op.*

cit., I, 213-14, except that the former omits the last clause of the sentence comprising the penultimate paragraph: "whether those categories consist respectively of men and women or of foreigners and native-born." Also, the T MS included a clause proposed to be inserted following the words "League of Nations" in the final paragraph: "and they pledge themselves to do their best to carry them into effect."

[4] "Suggested Redraft of Labour Clauses in the A.J.B. Version," April 17, 1919, T MS (WP, DLC). This document reads as follows:

"Preamble as at present.

"Among these methods and principles the following seem to the High Contracting Parties to be of special importance:

"The right of association for all lawful purposes by the employed as well as by the employers.

"The payment to the employed of a wage adequate to maintain a reasonable standard of life, as this is understood in their time and country.

"The enactment of legislation limiting the conditions of work, based upon the following standards:

"The prohibition of the employment of children under fourteen years of age in industry and commerce.

"The imposition of such limitations on the labour of young persons between the ages of fourteen and eighteen as shall permit the continuation of their education, and secure their physical development.

"The adoption of the forty-eight hour week, with one day holiday.

"The recognition of the right of foreign workers lawfully resident in a country to a share in the protection accorded by law to its own nationals with reference to the regulation of hours, safety, health and payment of wages.

"The adoption in each country of such regulations as will prevent the evils consequent upon different rates of remuneration being habitually given to men and to women for work of equal value.

"While recognizing that these methods and principles are neither complete or final, the High Contracting Parties are of the opinion that they may well serve to guide the policy of the League of Nations; and they pledge themselves to do their best to carry them into effect, making provision to that end for a system of inspection, in which women should take part, in order to secure their adequate enforcement."

Edward Mandell House to Herbert Clark Hoover

My dear Mr. Hoover: Paris, 20 April 1919.

Your letter arrived yesterday afternoon just as the President was coming into the Crillon for a conference. I showed it to him, and he thought that it would be unwise to give such a statement to the Press at this time.

He also felt that, though it might appear as the expression of your own personal views, it would nevertheless be generally interpreted as representing the opinion of the four heads of government who replied to Mr. Nansen's letter, and that they would have to consider more carefully what kind of statement, if any, should be made.   Very sincerely yours,   [E. M. House]

CCL (E. M. House Papers, CtY).

From Albert Sidney Burleson

Washington Apr 20 19

Careful estimates just now furnished me by statistical experts disclose that if wage schedule demanded by Boston operatives was applied throughout United States that it would increase operating expenses of Bell Co alone by nearly forty million dollars and the independents by nearly twelve million dollars This does not include increases for linemen electricians and other male employees Many owners assert that this would seriously impair value of the properties and some that it would practically destroy their value The operatives still refuse to take up their demands through the ordinary channels heretofore used and still provided for carrying such negotiations to final and heretofore satisfactory conclusion I have suffered some embarrassment because of my inability to place before the public the issue just as it is and as I see it for fear that it might in some way hinder you in your purposes The great work you are doing the most important on the worlds stage is too near my heart to permit any action of mine to add a straws weight to the burden you are already carrying Am continuing to receive telegrams from business men throughout the country urging that I do not yield the principle involved that is that the government itself must not be coerced in its actions by the arbitrary dictation of strikers Some while critical of concessions made during the period of actual war earnestly insist that the time has now arrived for firmness No one can forecast where this will lead but I was never more sure of the soundness of my position.   Burleson

T telegram (WP, DLC).

From Joseph Patrick Tumulty

The White House, April 20, 1919.

No. 68 9 P.M. A satisfactory settlement has been reached in the telephone situation.[1] Nothing to worry about. Regards to Mrs. Wilson and yourself.   Tumulty.

T telegram (WP, DLC).

[1] Burleson, on April 16, had asked John Cornelius Koons, the First Assistant Postmaster General and chairman of the Wire Control Board, to go to Boston to assist in the settlement of the telephone strike. Burleson himself on April 17 had placed the operators' wage demand before William Raymond Driver, Jr., the General Manager of the New England Telephone and Telegraph Co., and promised that any solution recommended by Driver would be promptly considered by the Wire Control Board. Following an eight-hour bargaining session on Sunday, April 20, Driver and representatives of the New England Joint Council of Telephone Workers announced that an agreement had been reached and that the operators would return to work on April 21. The operators were to receive $19 per week after seven years of employment. They had previously received $16 per week and had demanded $22. See the *New York Times*, April 17-21, 1919, and John M. Blum, *Joe Tumulty and the Wilson Era* (Boston, 1951), pp. 195-96.

From the Diary of Dr. Grayson

Monday, April 21, 1919.

The President rose early and had breakfast, after which he went to his study. Last night the President had made it plain that inasmuch as Sonnino had raised the question of the Pact of London and announced that Italy stood squarely upon it, he (the President) could not enter into any discussions that involved that agreement. It was an agreement entirely between France and Great Britain for Italy's benefit and had never been submitted to the United States, and the United States had neither approved it nor accepted it as an integral part of the issues of the war. Because of that fact the President suggested it would be well if the Italian delegation met with Clemenceau and Lloyd-George and endeavor to reach an agreement upon the subject. It was rather curious that the Pact of London made no mention as to Fiume. In fact, Fiume, it was originally intended, should remain as Austro-Hungarian territory, because when it was agreed upon there had been no evidence that the Dual Empire would break up as it has. In consequence, the trio met and conferred while the President discussed with the Japanese envoys a number of questions in which Japan was essentially interested, especially the question of China's demand that the Peace Conference relieve her of obligations that had been fixed upon her by Japan during the present war.[1] The Big Three were unable to agree at the morning session. In fact, if anything, they made the situation worse. Orlando and Sonnino declared emphatically that they intended standing on the Pact of London and threatened that if the promises were not carried out they would withdraw and permit other people to come here to handle the Italian side of the question.

The President went to the Crillon Hotel shortly after 11:00 o'clock and held an extended conference with the members of the American Mission in the offices of Secretary of State Lansing. The question of procedure was gone over with the Americans and also the latest reports from Austria showing the spread of Bolshevism there were considered.

Leaving the Peace Commission the President went to see Mr. Bernard M. Baruch, with whom he was closeted from some little time.

Returning to the house the President had as luncheon guests Ambassador to France and Mrs. Hugh Wallace. The conversation at luncheon was entirely informal. After lunch the President had a confidential conference with Ambassador Wallace and told him the conditions which he had met with in connection with the intriguing efforts of French officialdom. He told Mr. Wallace it would

be very wise for him to keep close watch on everything that transpired and keep the American Government closely informed.

While the President was in conference with Ambassador Wallace,
Colonel House put in an appearance. He had been over to visit
Lloyd-George and told the President there was nothing to report
concerning the conference of the Italian question. It is developing
day by day that Colonel House is no longer pulling squarely with
the President. The chief evidence of this is the propaganda campaign which is being carried on by H. Wickman Steed, who is editor
of the London Times. Steed is very friendly with Gordon Auchincloss, Colonel House's son-in-law, and also has the entree to Colonel
House at any hour of the day or night. In fact, one of the chief
causes of complaint of American newspapermen, who are covering
the Conference, is that while they are compelled to cool their heels
sometimes for an hour at a time awaiting the pleasure of Colonel
House, the moment Steed appears he is ushered into the ante-
chamber and Colonel House invariably excuses himself, no matter
with whom he is in conference, to talk with Mr. Steed and outline
to him policies that are being discussed by the American Peace
Delegation. In one of his latest articles sent broadcast and published
in the American newspapers, which accept the service of the Philadelphia Public Ledger's foreign bureau, Mr. Steed has seen fit to
declare that Colonel House "speeds peace" and "is one of the very
few delegates who has made good during the conference." Mr.
Steed declared that House would have had peace by this time if he
had not been taken ill.[2] The facts, however, are interesting. When
the President left France to go home for the adjournment of Congress he left behind him a very definite program, which carried
with it the inclusion of the League of Nations in the Peace Treaty
and a general peace program which if carried through would have
enabled the restoration of normal conditions shortly after he came
back to France. During his absence Colonel House agreed to compromise with Premier Clemenceau on the big questions at issue.
He agreed to the establishment of a Rhinish Republic, which would
act as a buffer state between Germany and France, and the creation
of which would have been in absolute contradiction to President
Wilson's Fourteen Points. He agreed also to the elimination for the
time being at least of the League of Nations constitution, which
President Wilson in season and out of season had insisted was the
only remedy which would prevent a recurrence of world wars. The
result of this was that when the President returned to France he
found a program prepared for him which it was necessary for him
entirely to repudiate. But he also found that certain promises had
been made which were embarrassing but which had to be at least

in part carried out.[3] Therefore, the Steed criticism not only was unjust but was an absolute lie.

After Mr. Wallace left, the Big Four was to have resumed its conference but Premier Orlando failed to put in an appearance. Orlando let it be known that he had no desire to interrupt a further consideration of the Italian situation, and that he was chiefly anxious to have a decision reached. The Italian attitude has become more and more defiant in the last few days due to the belief on the part of certain of the Italian leaders that Italy's massed armies could be used as a potent influence to force the Allies to accept the Italian program in full.

Following the Big Four session, the President, Mrs. Wilson, Miss Benham and myself had dinner, after which we went to the opening of the Palace Theatre. The performance there was a typical French-English play, full of froth, with good-looking girls and beautiful costumes and scenery.[4] The show was not over until midnight, so that the President was very late in returning home.

[1] For the gist of this conversation, see the following document and Wilson's remarks in the minutes of the Council of Four, April 21, 1919, 4 p.m., printed below.

[2] This news report, entitled "THE MILLS OF PEACE, (From Our Political Correspondents)," was datelined Paris, April 6 and appeared in the London *Times* on April 7, 1919. It was reprinted in an abridged form, with the dateline Paris, April 7, in the New York *Sun* and other American newspapers on the following day under the byline of H. Wickham Steed, Editor of the London *Times*. Steed was of course the chief editorial spokesman of Lord Northcliffe.

The report consisted of a long review, sprinkled with harsh denunciations of the Anglo-American leaders at Paris and particularly of Lloyd George, of the lack of progress in the Council of Four during the preceding week. Concerning Colonel House, Steed wrote: "In so far as there is a real improvement in the prospects of the Conference, it is believed to be attributable chiefly to the practical statesmanship of Colonel House, who, in view of President Wilson's indisposition, has once again placed his *savoir faire* and conciliatory temperament at the disposal of the chief peacemakers.

"Colonel House is one of the very few Delegates who have 'made good' during the Conference. It is, indeed, probable that peace would have been made successfully weeks ago but for the unfortunate illness [gall stones] which overtook him at the very outset of the Conference. When he recovered the Council of Ten had already got into bad habits, had set itself up as a primary school at the Quai d'Orsay, and begun to waste the time of the world by receiving elementary instruction in geography and ethnography from representatives of various small nations and nationalities that had special claims to advance. Little could be done to mend matters until Mr. Lloyd George returned to England and the President to America. During their absence Colonel House, who has never found a difficulty in working with his colleagues, because he is a selfless man with no personal axe to grind, brought matters rapidly forward. The delay that has occurred since the return of President Wilson and Mr. Lloyd George has been due chiefly to the upsetting of the good work done during their absence, and to the abandonment of sound methods in favour of 'genial improvisations'—or what Mr. Lloyd George once called 'happy thoughts'—that take no account of the truth that *le mieux est l'ennemi du bien.*

"If there is now a chance that the Conference may be hauled back from the brink of failure on to relatively safe ground, it is mainly due to the efforts of Colonel House and to the salutary effect of the feeling that the Allied peoples are becoming seriously alarmed at the secret manipulations of their chief representatives."

It is difficult to determine the impact of Steed's report upon the Wilson-House relationship. Mrs. Wilson read the version in the Philadelphia *Public Ledger* and asked House directly for an explanation. House replied that he would let Mrs. Wilson know about it the next day but in fact never did talk further about the report with her. She in turn showed the article to Wilson and told him about her interview with the Colonel. Cary T. Grayson, "The Colonel's Folly and the President's Distress," *American Heritage*, xv (Oct. 1964), 99.

According to her own memoir, Mrs. Wilson displayed some anger in her conversation with House. When she related her interview to Wilson, the latter replied: "Oh, I am sorry you hurt House. I would as soon doubt your loyalty as his. All this is another attempt to misrepresent things at home." Mrs. Wilson continues: "All my husband had against the Colonel at this time was what he regarded as a grave error in judgment in failing to stand up against men with whom we wished to be on intimate terms. I remember having said: 'Oh, if Colonel House had only stood firm while you were away none of this would have to be done over. I think he is a perfect jellyfish.' To which Mr. Wilson had replied: 'Well, God made jellyfish, so, as Shakespeare said about a man, therefore let him pass, and don't be too hard on House. It takes a pretty stiff spinal column to stand against the elements centred here.' " Edith Bolling Wilson, *My Memoir* (Indianapolis and New York, 1938, 1939), pp. 251-52.

³ See n. 2 to the extract from the Grayson Diary printed at March 13, 1919, Vol. 55.
⁴ They attended the opening of the Palace Théâtre, an Anglo-French playhouse. The attraction was "Hullo Paris," by Lucien Boyer and Bataille-Henri, with music by Hermann Finck, M. Irving, and André Colomb. Lloyd George, Balfour, and Lord Derby were also honored guests.

From the Diary of Colonel House

April 21, 1919.

I lunched with Lloyd George to discuss the Irish situation, but we took up most of the time in going over the Italian difficulties. I will not go into this as it would be largely repetition. George suggested that a way out might be found by giving Italy the line of the Pact of London to the north of Fiume, as I suggested before, and give them the islands of the Adriatic, but nothing of the mainland of Dalmatia. He proposed this to Orlando yesterday but Orlando refused it pointblank. I thought if George, Clemenceau and the President would put it to them as an ultimatum, it might succeed. George wondered if the President would consent. I undertook to find out and went across the street to discuss it with him.

The President did not like it but said if Clemenceau and George would put it up to him as a recommendation of theirs, and would agree to stick to it as an ultimatum to the Italians, he would consider it. I returned to George's apartment and gave him the President's decision. I left George telephoning to Clemenceau asking him to come a little in advance of the four o'clock meeting.

George pretends to me that he is very firm with the Italians regarding Fiume, but Wiseman tells me that he is not so firm when talking with them. This is a great mistake and gives them hope where there is none. George and I agreed that he should see the Irish American Delegates¹ now in Paris sometime next week when he had more leisure, and to discuss with them the question of bringing to Paris the delegates from the so-called "Irish Republic."

The President came to the Crillon this morning for a conference with the Commission. He read us a statement of the Italiam [Italian] situation which it is his purpose to give out. He was not certain whether to do it immediately or wait until a break actually occurred. I suggested discussing the matter with George and Clemenceau and being governmed [governed] by their advice. I asked him how long he would remain in Paris provided the Germans did not sign the peace and the matter was strung along indefinitely. He said "please do not ask me such a distressing question for I cannot answer it now." He evidently intends to call Congress together around May 15th and to remain at least for awhile afterward.

Prince Feisal came to bid me goodbye. He said he again desired to express the wish that I was stronger physically than I seemed, for he knew what a tremendous influences [influence] for evil I had to resist. He insisted that the Syrian Commission should go as soon as possible. If it did not, he would not be responsible for the peace in that part of the world.

After Feisal left, I wrote the President a letter which is a part of the record, asking him if I should stop Dr. King[2] of Oberlin College whom we selected to go as one of that Commission,[3] and who was about to return to America. The President asked me to stop him which I did. I asked King to get in touch with Charles R. Crane and arrange with the French and British Commissioners for their trip.

[1] That is, Walsh, Dunne, and Ryan.
[2] That is, Henry Churchill King.
[3] About which, see n. 2 to the memorandum printed at March 25, 1919, Vol. 56.

From Edward Mandell House

Dear Governor: Paris, 21 April 1919.

Prince Feisal came in to say goodbye this morning, and left Paris this afternoon.

He told me that Clemenceau and Lloyd George had both told him that the Syrian Commission would leave sometime within the next two weeks. He himself, as you know, is very anxious that the Commission should go; and I am very strongly of the opinion that unless it does go, there will shortly be widespread trouble of a religious and racial character in his part of the world.

In view of these facts, will you not like to have me keep Dr. King here. Otherwise, he plans to leave for America on Thursday.

Affectionately yours, E. M. House

TLS (WP, DLC).

Mantoux's Notes of a British-French-Italian Meeting

April 21, 1919, 10 a.m.

Conversation among the representatives of the Powers signatory to
the Treaty of London of April 26, 1915.

Clemenceau. I am trying to find how we can escape the difficulty;
I see nothing. As for us, the treaty binds us; if our Italian friends
declare that they will adhere to the letter of the treaty, we must
keep our word.

Lloyd George. Undoubtedly, but it would be a serious thing if
the United States did not sign the treaty with Austria-Hungary.
The German populations of the Alto-Adige and the Yugoslav populations of the coast of the Adriatic will remain equally discontented; both will believe that if they become excited, the United
States will be behind them. If the President of the United States
cannot sign the treaty, I see a peril from these two sides. On the
other hand, I do not see how Europe can put itself back in working
order if the United States does not put oil in the machine. We have
made plans to assure ourselves of the support of American credit,
and all our financial advisers agree on the danger of a complete
stagnation of business in Europe if this credit is not available to
us. It is a situation comparable to that of South Africa after the
Boer War. England lent that country 30 million pounds sterling—
which, incidentally, were never repaid—to permit the recovery of
economic activity. Without that, South Africa would have remained
for years in the situation of a devastated and ruined country.

The present problem in Europe is the same; it is essential that
America remain with us all the way. It was difficult to bring them
to us. All things considered, President Wilson has in the course of
these negotiations gone much further in our direction than we had
at first thought possible. He has come over to our views on the
question of indemnities, on the question of the Saar Basin, on many
others besides. In this Italian problem, if it is possible to make a
concession which facilitates his adhesion, I see a favorable outcome.
In the contrary case, it will only be left to us to repeat to you that
we will carry out the treaty if you ask us to. Please believe that we
are only speaking as friends who wish to come to the aid of friends.

Clemenceau. I accept all that Mr. Lloyd George has just said,
and I could take it as my own words. I believed that an arrangement
would be possible in the matter of Fiume; but I have lost that
illusion. When the Italians foreshadowed a renunciation of the treaty
in order to consider the question in its totality, that led to no amel-
ioration. When for his part President Wilson suggested a provisional

solution allowing the problem to be suspended, no favorable result followed.

I had a new conversation yesterday evening with the President of the United States; his position is completely firm. The only advice which I can give you is this: if you want Fiume, see what other concession would be possible for you. I think I find an argument for President Wilson in the negotiations which Italy had with Austria before the rupture of the Triple Alliance. But what Austria offered to Italy in 1915 or nothing is nearly the same thing.[1] No one has the right to say that Italy would receive nothing more today if she should have come out of this war with all of the Trentino, the valley of Isonzo, Trieste, and Istria.

Sonnino. When I spoke of the negotiation with Austria, I neglected to say that one month after the rupture, Austria continued her advances through the intermediary of the Vatican.

Clemenceau. Were you ever offered Trieste? On this side I sought an argument for President Wilson; I did not find any. Even if today you only obtained several points in Dalmatia, you would be in what seems to me to be an excellent position with regard to Italian public opinion.

For my part, I renounced asking for France the frontier of 1814; I renounced asking the permanent occupation of the left bank of the Rhine, and that against the opinion of important people, and at my own risk. So I can offer myself as an example. If Italy takes part in the rest of the negotiations, she will gain numerous advantages, believe me, more considerable than she would have been assured of obtaining at the beginning of the war.

I abide by your wisdom in this matter. Mr. Lloyd George, M. Pichon, and myself, we speak as friends of Italy when we say to you: It is only in this way that there is a solution; accept it, otherwise we are hastening toward the most deplorable consequences: isolation, the work of the war left unfinished, and a powerful ferment of disorder sown in Europe.

Sonnino. President Wilson was categorical about Fiume: he says no. About the rest, he tells us: "Place these territories in the hands of the five powers, and I do not promise you that they will then give them back to Italy."

The conditions which we are asking are those on the basis of which we entered the war. We lost a half million dead; our country is ruined, and all the advantages we expected are being taken away from us. When, in the Armistice agreement, the same frontier as defined by the Treaty of London was indicated as the limit of the

[1] See n. 10 to the minutes of the Council of Four printed at April 19, 1919.

occupation, all of Italy believed that the cause was definitively won and there was no American protest at that time.

Lloyd George. Did President Wilson know about the treaty at that time?

Balfour. Yes.

Sonnino. Put yourself in the point of view of the Italian public. The United States only took part in the war, as far as we are concerned, by lending us money. There was only one American regiment in Italy, which lost only a single man dead. I do not give you that as an argument, but to make you understand the Italian public's impression. We negotiated with you; a third party arrives, which declares that it does not recognize our agreements.

He invokes the League of Nations; so let it go, if it can, and put Russia in order! Let it settle Balkan affairs! He can't change human nature that way.

As for myself, I've always taken pains to calm public opinion. When I went to Rome, after the signing of the Armistice and when they came to my windows to cheer me, I hid, because I sensed strongly that a time of troubles was beginning.

America said nothing to us for five months. Now, after having made concessions right and left to legitimate interests, she wants to recover her virginity at our expense by invoking the purity of principles. How could we accept? We would have disorder and anarchy in our country; I do not see how we could avoid it. All that President Wilson just told us is this: "Place all this in our hands, and I will not give it back to you." That would change the memory that I treasure of these five years into a long remorse. I do not believe I can be reproached for not having been faithful to the Allies.

Lloyd George. You will not be offended if I make a suggestion to you? I read your memorandum,[2] which contains very strong arguments. The principal one is that of Italy's security. The danger which you fear comes from the islands, behind which an enemy fleet can always hide. On the other hand, the difficulties which I fear would only come from the occupation by Italy of the mainland. You would never have peace in that part of the world.

Sonnino. The peoples of the Balkans will have enough to do among themselves.

Lloyd George. You would be forced to maintain a considerable garrison in Dalmatia and to be always on your guard. My proposal is that Italy occupy the islands which lie along the coast, while offering to the Slavic population, if it wishes, to be transported and

[2] That is, Orlando's statement printed in the minutes of the Council of Four, April 19, 1919.

installed on the mainland, which the war has so depopulated. If you have only the islands, that will not impose a heavy military burden on you. Such is the friendly suggestion that I allow myself to make to you.

Sonnino. This question of the islands will raise the same objections, and as for the difficulties which you fear, I believe that they would disappear within the span of two years.

Lloyd George. Do you believe that? There are in Dalmatia 600,000 Croatians against 40,000 Italians.

Sonnino. We are not asking for all Dalmatia.

Orlando. I want to explain to you the reasons for our firmness which, within certain limits, must be absolute.

The first is a reason of practical utility, in the general interest. If I should return to Italy bringing a peace which would provoke an uprising of the population, I would render a serious disservice to the entire world. If President Wilson's opinion prevails, there will be a revolution in Italy, don't doubt it. Recently brawls took place in Rome and in Milan between Bolsheviks and patriots. It is the Bolsheviks who were defeated; in Milan two of them were killed. For this nationalistic element, which is so worked up now, would make revolution if the peace seemed bad to it, and this time the Bolsheviks would be on the same side, because they will always be for revolution in whatever way and under whatever pretext it begins. A satisfied Italy would remain absolutely firm and calm; an Italy deceived and discontented—it will be revolution and a danger for the entire world.

If I return to Rome alone against the entire world, while saying to our people as after Caporetto: "Arise! Have courage! The country can still be saved," I will perhaps be able to hold together the national elements. For that I am counting on the great patriotism of the Italian population. Then you will have Italy in a terrible state, but standing; the evil of it will be less, not only for her, but also for you yourselves.

I could not accept President Wilson's proposal, even as the basis for discussion. The line drawn by President Wilson is the one which was published in 1917 by the *New Europe*,[3] which is a sort of official publication of the Yugoslavs. Now, in the eyes of the Italian, the

[3] Sir Arthur John Evans, "Diagrammatic Map of a Future South Slav State," *The New Europe: A Weekly Review of Foreign Politics*, IV (Oct. 11, 1917), 415-16. The foldout map faces p. 416. It showed Fiume, all of Dalmatia, and all of the islands off the coast of present-day Yugoslavia as part of the "future South Slav State." Evans was a distinguished archeologist with a strong interest in the future of the Yugoslavs. Robert William Seton-Watson and Thomas Garrigue Masaryk had founded *The New Europe* in October 1916 mainly to promote the cause of the independence of Czechoslovakia. It was published in London through October 1920.

Croatian is exactly what the Boche is in the eyes of the French. Imagine how the French would consider a proposal identical to the one which the Germans themselves could make them.

Last January, President Wilson showed me his frontier line and asked me what I thought of it. I answered him: "It is impossible." I begged him to consider that, faced with such a proposal, I could only withdraw from the conference. President Wilson stopped the interpreter and said to him: "Does Mr. Orlando really mean that, in this case, he would withdraw from the conference?" I answered: "Yes, that is precisely what I mean."

For three months, I found myself in a false position. I collaborated with you on the solution of the problems of the peace while President Wilson and myself shared the memory of that conversation. Mr. Lloyd George proposes to us to seek conciliation, and I recognize the fertility of his mind. If our allies can, with President Wilson, arrive at an arrangement which I could decently present to my country, I am completely prepared to follow them. But I think that painful conversations are no longer useful. If Mr. Lloyd George and M. Clemenceau wish, with President Wilson, to make a compromise proposal not putting in question the annexation of Fiume, we wish with all our hearts for the success of their endeavor. If it does not succeed, it will be best for the world that we bring to a close an equivocal and agonizing situation. We will ask for the carrying out of the Pact of London, and it will be up to our allies to give us satisfaction. Until then we will be isolated.

Pichon. Do you have no other proposal to make?

Orlando. It is a matter of finding what to pay for Fiume.

Lloyd George. In this case, I see no hope. For on Fiume, I agree with President Wilson. I absolutely maintain the Pact of London. But the Pact of London provided that Fiume would be given to the Serbs and they know it, and they were our allies. We cannot violate our word to them any more than to you.

Clemenceau. We gave Fiume to the Serbs with you; Italy's signature is at the bottom of the treaty, and I cannot take that city from them.

Lloyd George. That clause is as much a part of the treaty as the others.

Sonnino. If you managed to establish a plan of conciliation, we could see what we would have to abandon. I will recall, on the subject of Serbia, that, when offers were made to Bulgaria to attract her to the side of the Allies, one part of Macedonia was held out to her. To Serbia, the Allies offered Croatia in compensation. But Serbia refused to agree to that arrangement, and the Allies responded that in this case, they were withdrawing their offer. So we can say that Fiume was promised to the Croatians, but not to the Serbs.

Clemenceau. That makes no difference today, and I have promised.

Lloyd George. I am receiving information from our General Staff that, in the event that Fiume is taken from the Croatians and the Serbs, they will not hesitate to fight.

I do not know if it is useful to insist on the suggestion that I just made, which was to ask President Wilson to consent to the cession of the islands to Italy, the remaining mainland to the Yugoslavs?

Sonnino. Without Fiume?

Lloyd George. Without Fiume.

Orlando. It is impossible.

Sonnino. Then we would be renouncing Dalmatia without compensation. We cannot accept. The question of security is undoubtedly the first; but there is also a national question in Dalmatia. The cities on the coast, the civilization, are Italian.

Lloyd George. Is not a large majority of the population Slavic?

Sonnino. Not in the cities. We cannot forget the national and historical reasons which bind us to them. Is it not President Wilson himself who said that the national consideration must take precedence over the economic consideration? Then, why not take account of the 24,000 Italians who live in Fiume, when we are concerned with the fate of 4,000 or 5,000 Germans on the frontier of Belgium?

Lloyd George. I will allow myself to call to your attention that the comparison is not valid. The Germans on the Belgian frontier form one body with the rest of the German population, and it is not the same with the Italians of Fiume.

Balfour. We must take into account the difficulty in which President Wilson finds himself. He will have to justify himself before American public opinion for having consented to the annexation of the entire southern Tyrol to Italy, including the German valleys.

Lloyd George. There is no point in arguing among ourselves, but only in seeking a way to obtain the adhesion of the United States to the treaty. If we do not obtain it, it will be grave.

Balfour. I do not believe that we realize how grave it will be. M. Orlando fears revolution in Italy. But suppose that Italy falls out with the United States, I do not see how the the economic life of the country will be able to continue, and, in that case, how will you avoid social revolution? The danger seems to me at least as great as if you return to Rome with a treaty which, in my opinion, would be perfectly satisfactory. The life of Italy would become an insoluble problem, and it is then that the situation would become dreadful.

Orlando. I recognize the truth of what Mr. Balfour says; but I do not believe that one of the two dangers is more serious than the other, and I still have a hope of avoiding revolution, if I remain with my country. We are a sober people, and we know the art of dying of hunger. The danger being equal, I prefer to stay on the side of justice and of honor.

Mantoux, I, 300-306.

A Draft of a Statement[1]

Statement *in re* Adriatic.   [April 21, 1919]

⟨It should be clearly understood what was proposed to the representatives of Italy and what has formed the basis of their decision.⟩

When Italy entered the war she entered upon the basis of a definite, but private, understanding with Great Britain and France, now known as the Pact of London. Since that time the whole face of circumstance has been altered. Many other powers, great and small, have entered the struggle, with no knowledge of that private understanding. The Austro-Hungarian Empire, then the enemy of Europe, and at whose expense the Pact of London was to be kept in the event of victory, has gone to pieces and no longer exists. Not only that. The several parts of that Empire, it is now agreed by Italy and all her associates, are to be erected into independent states and associated in a League of nations, not with those who were recently our enemies, but with Italy herself and the powers that stood with Italy in the great war for liberty. We are to establish their liberty as well as our own. They are to be among the smaller states whose interests are henceforth to be as scrupulously safeguarded as the interests of the most powerful states.

The war was ended, moreover, by proposing to Germany an armistice and peace which should be founded on certain clearly defined principles which should set up a new order of right and justice. Upon those principles the peace with Germany has been conceived, not only, but formulated. Upon those principles it will be executed. We cannot ask the great body of powers to propose and effect peace with Austria and establish a new basis of independence and right in the states which originally constituted the Austro-Hungarian Empire and in the states of the Balkan group on principles of another kind. ⟨They⟩ We must apply the same principles to the settlement of Europe in those quarters that ⟨they⟩ *we* have applied in the peace with Germany. It was upon the explicit avowal of those principles that the initiative for peace was taken. It is upon ⟨those⟩ *them* that the whole structure of peace must rest.

If those principles are to [be] adhered to, Fiume must serve as the outlet and inlet of the commerce, not of Italy, but of the lands to the north and northeast of ⟨her⟩ *that* port: Hungary, Bohemia, Roumania, and the states of the new Jugo-Slavic group. To assign Fiume to Italy would be to create the feeling that we had deliberately put the port upon which all these countries chiefly depend for their access to the Mediterranean in the hands of a power of which it did not form an integral part and whose sovereignty, if set up there, must inevitably seem foreign, not domestic or identified with the commercial and indutstrial [industrial] life of the regions which the port must serve. It is for that reason, now [no] doubt, that Fiume was not included in the Pact of London but there definitively assigned to the Croatians.

And the reason why the line of the Pact of London swept about many of the islands of the eastern coast of the Adriatic and around the portion of the Dalmatian coast which lies most open to that sea was not only that here and there on those islands and here and there on that coast there are bodies of people of Italian blood and connection but also, and no doubt chiefly, because it was felt that it was necessary for Italy to have a foothold amidst the channels of the eastern Adriatic in order that she might make her own coasts safe against the naval aggression of Austria-Hungary. But Austria-Hungary no longer exists. It is proposed that the fortifications which the Austrian government constructed there shall be razed and permanently destroyed. It is part, also, of the new plan of European order which centres in the League of Nations that the new states erected there shall accept a limitation of armaments which puts aggression out of the question. There can be no fear of the unfair treatment of groups of Italian people there because adequate guarantees will be given, under international sanction, of the equal and equitable treatment of all racial or national minorities.

In brief, every question associated with this settlement wears a new aspect,—a new aspect given it by the very victory for right ⟨in which Italy has played so gallant a part and⟩ for which Italy has made the supreme sacrifice of blood and treasure. Italy, along with the four other great powers, has become one of the chief trustees of the new order which she has played so honourable a part in establishing.

And on the north and northeast her natural frontiers are completely restored, along the whole sweep of the alps from northwest to southeast to the very end of the Istrian peninsula, including all the great watershed within which Trieste and Pola lie and all the

fair regions whose face nature has turned towards the great peninsula upon which the historic life of the Latin people has been
worked out through centuries of famous story ever since Rome was
first set upon her seven hills. Her ancient unity is restored. Her
lines are extended to the great walls which are her natural defence.
It is within her choice to be surrounded by friends; to exhibit to
the newly liberated peoples across the Adriatic that noblest quality
of greatness, magnanimity, friendly generosity, the preference of
justice over interest.

The nations associated with her, the nations that know nothing
of the Pact of London or of any other special understanding that
lies at the beginning of this great struggle, and who have made
their supreme sacrifice also in the interest, not of national advantage
of defence, but of the settled peace of the world, now unite with
her older associates in urging her to assume a leadership which
cannot be mistaken in the new order of Europe. America is Italy's
friend. Her people are drawn, millions strong, from Italy's own fair
countrysides. She is linked in blood as well as in affection with the
Italian people. Such ties can never be broken. And America was
privileged, by the generous commission of her associates in the
war, to initiate the peace we are about to consummate,—to initiate
it upon terms she had herself formulated, and in which I was her
spokesman. The compulsion is upon her to square every decision
she takes a part in with those principles. She can do nothing else.
She trusts Italy, and in her trust believes that Italy will ask nothing
of her that cannot be made unmistakably consistent with these
sacred obligations. Interest is not now in question, but the rights
of peoples, of states new and old, of liberated peoples and and [*sic*]
peoples whose rulers have never accounted them worthy of right:
above all, the right of the world to peace and to such settlements
of interest as shall make peace secure.

These, and these only, are the principles for which America has
fought. These, and these only, are the principles upon which she
can consent to make peace. Only upon these principles, she hopes
and believes, will the people of Italy ask her to make peace.

WWT MS (WP, DLC).
¹ Text in angle brackets deleted by Wilson; text in italics added by him. There are
WWhw and WWsh notes and an outline of this document in WP, DLC.

Hankey's and Mantoux's Notes of a Meeting of the Council of Four[1]

President Wilson's House,
I.C.-175A.   Paris, April 21, 1919, 4 p.m.

[Orlando and Sonnino not present.]

1. MR. LLOYD GEORGE told President Wilson the suggestion he had made at the end of the meeting in the morning, namely, that, in order to give Italy the strategical requirements for her defence, which was the principal case on which the claim for Dalmatia was based, she should be allowed to have the islands off the coast, but not the mainland. Mr. Philip Kerr, he said, had met a Jugo-Slav, who had told him that if the Italians held Fiume the Jugo-Slavs would fight them. If they held Dalmatia there would be sniping. But that he had not expressed any strong views about the islands.

PRESIDENT WILSON said that he himself had talked about the island of Cherso with M. Trumbitch, who had pointed out that, owing to its position across the Gulf of Fiume, the Italians, if they held it, would make trouble up and down the Gulf.

MR. LLOYD GEORGE suggested that, if the Italians held Cherso, there ought to be a stipulation that the channel between that island and Istria should not be regarded as territorial waters. There should be some clause providing for free access through the channel except in time of war.

PRESIDENT WILSON said even then there should be free access if the Jugo-Slavs were neutral.

MR. LLOYD GEORGE said M. Clemenceau, to whom he had spoken, was convinced that the Italians would not accept his proposal. He suggested, therefore, that perhaps Baron Sonnino could be induced to agree by some offer in Asia Minor.

At Mr. Lloyd George's request, M. CLEMENCEAU produced a map giving a new scheme for the distribution of mandates in Turkey, whereby Italy would secure a mandate over a considerable part of Anatolia touching territory mandated to Greece in the region of Smyrna, and the territory mandated with Constantinople, and Armenia.[2]

[1] The complete text of Hankey's minutes is printed in PPC, V, 106-111.
[2] Compare Mantoux, I, 307-308:
"Wilson. Do you think that would suffice to bring him back?
"Lloyd George. I think so. I am well aware of his situation. He took the decision to go to war having a poor country behind him. Italy does not have many natural resources; she has no mines. Nothing as in Alsace and Lorraine; think about all that France will have in iron ore, potassium, etc.
"Wilson. I do not know if Italy would find great resources in Anatolia; but the true difficulty is that the Greeks and the other populations fear the Italians as neighbors. A very picturesque and venerable person, the Patriach of Constantinople, who came to

PRESIDENT WILSON said the real trouble was that the Greeks and everyone else appeared to dread the Italians as neighbours. The Patriarch of Constantinople had called on him the other day and had expressed strong objections to having the Italians as neighbours. He felt great care would have to be exercised in this matter for inasmuch as we were endeavouring to secure the peace of the world we could not enter into any arrangement that would not make for peace.

MR. LLOYD GEORGE suggested there should be an Italian sphere of influence such as the British had in various parts of the world.

PRESIDENT WILSON said that the British Empire, through a long experience, had learned all sorts of lessons and gained all sorts of ideas in administration of this kind, and did not interfere unduly. The Italians, however, had no such experience. The Italians also had no ethnological claim to this territory, such as the Greeks had. In the case of the Greeks, we only desired to make them comfortable masters in their own home. The Italians had not inherited any traditions of colonial administration.

MR. LLOYD GEORGE suggested that the Italians should merely have a sphere of influence and it should be made clear that their authority was limited to commercial and railway development, and that they were not to interfere with the people more than necessary.

PRESIDENT WILSON pointed out the trouble was that the Turks could not govern anyone.

MR. LLOYD GEORGE said that the Turks did not interfere much in railways; they were a quiet docile people except towards Armenians and those whom they did not like.

M. CLEMENCEAU agreed with this.

PRESIDENT WILSON pointed out that he did not like, as it were, paying the Italians for something they had no right to.

MR. LLOYD GEORGE pointed out that there was some strength in the Italian case that they had come into the war on the basis of a certain agreement and that Baron Sonnino's position would be extremely difficult if it were not fulfilled.

M. CLEMENCEAU pointed out the inaccuracy of statements that had been made to the effect that the Italians could have obtained almost as much from Austria without fighting as they were going

---

see me the other day, expressed to me, with the reserve of an ecclesiastic, a very strong feeling against the possibility of seeing the Italians become his neighbors.

"Lloyd George. You remember that M. Vénisélos proposed to give Italy a mandate over all of Anatolia.

"Wilson. Italy lacks experience in the administration of colonies. She would ask for territories only to satisfy her ambition.

"Lloyd George. The Romans were very good governors of colonies.

"Wilson. Unfortunately, the modern Italians are not the Romans."

to obtain in the Treaty as at present contemplated. He had consulted the Green Book[3] on the subject and found that in fact they had been offered very little.

PRESIDENT WILSON suggested that perhaps the Italians might take the line their position being what it was they must go home and report to their Parliament and ask for instructions.

MR. LLOYD GEORGE suggested that it was better politically for them to present Parliament with an accomplished fact. Supposing he were to go and ask the British Parliament for instructions about indemnities, the position would not be very satisfactory. It was better to give Parliament a lead in matters like this.

PRESIDENT WILSON suggested that the Italians would not be in the position of having to say to their Parliament: We have surrendered. On the contrary, they could say: We refused to surrender, but we now want your advice.

There was some further discussion at this point on the subject of the Italian Parliamentary position and generally as to the attitude to be taken towards the Italians in the existing position. It was eventually agreed that Sir Maurice Hankey should be sent to deliver a verbal message to M. Orlando and Baron Sonnino, reminding them of Mr. Lloyd George's proposal made at the end of the morning meeting, which they had now had some time to consider, and asking if they would consider it worth while to meet their colleagues and discuss the question on this basis.

§Mantoux's notes:

Wilson. What will Italy do if M. Orlando and M. Sonnino come to tell her: "We have left the conference"?

Lloyd George. There will be an explosion, delirium, and nothing will do more to encourage the Germans to believe that we are quarreling among ourselves. What has already been said is partly the fault of our press.

Wilson. I think that the only avenue of conduct we can follow is this. Colonel Hankey would write a text on the basis of our proposal, would take it to M. Orlando and ask him if his colleagues and he want to take it into consideration.

Lloyd George. We will tell them that if they want to study this plan, there is a chance of working things out, but that it is the limit beyond which you cannot go.

Wilson. I hardly like to make a compromise with people who are not reasonable. They will always believe that by insisting they will be able to obtain more advantage.

[3] That is, Italy, Ministry of Foreign Affairs, *Diplomatic Documents Submitted to the Italian Parliament by the Minister for Foreign Affairs (Sonnino), Austria-Hungary, Session of the 20th May, 1915* (London, 1915).

Lloyd George. It seems to me that M. Sonnino, despite his obstinacy, would be more tractable. This morning he said: "If we could have the cities of the coast. * * *"

Wilson. We come back to the difficulty.

Lloyd George. These cities are Italian.

Wilson. They contain an Italian element predominant in culture, but not in numbers, whatever be the justifiable suspicion concerning the Austro-Hungarian statistics.

Lloyd George. Can I tell Baron Sonnino that if Asia Minor is divided into spheres of influence regarding economic development, Italy will have her large part?

Wilson. Yes, under a mandate of the League of Nations. But on the other hand, it will be necessary for the Turks to have some sort of government, and, from this point of view, one cannot divide their territory.

Lloyd George. To govern all of Anatolia will be a considerable task.

Wilson. The division of the country would present great difficulties.

Clemenceau. Did the Italians not say this morning that there was no agreement possible if they were not given Fiume?

Lloyd George. M. Sonnino did not say that.

Wilson. Colonel House just learned from Italy that it is about Fiume that the public passion is concentrated, more than about Dalmatia.[4]

Lloyd George. We would be helping M. Sonnino to turn the position of Fiume by saying: "I was obliged to hold myself to the line of the Treaty of London."

Wilson. But he will not have what the Treaty of London promised him. What resulted from your discussion of this morning?

Lloyd George. What I proposed to you: it is the only solution in sight.

Wilson. They must be told that if that suggestion seems to them to be of a kind to be discussed, we are prepared to meet with them and to study it with them. It is a matter of giving them the outposts of the islands, so as to respond to their concern for the security of the Italian coast. That means, moreover, that they would have control of all Yugoslavia from the naval point of view.

Lt. Col. Sir Maurice Hankey is sent to the Hôtel Edouard VII to communicate verbally Mr. Lloyd George's proposal to the Italian plenipotentiaries.

Wilson. Since it is I who create the obstacle to the solution, and

[4] See TNP to EMH, April 17, 1919.

since I am forced to this by my proposal, a time will come when I shall have to explain my attitude and that of America. Toward this end, I have prepared a document which I am going to read to you. . . .[5]

Lloyd George. That is a fine document, which will be useful if the Italian ministers end by going home and taking back to their compatriots only part of what the Treaty of London promised them.

Wilson. I think this statement will also respond to the necessities of the circumstances if the Italians reject our proposals.

Lloyd George. In fact, the document could produce a useful impression in Italy, but only after a certain period of time. For the moment, we need expect only madness.

Wilson. The Italians cannot accuse the United States of being an interested party.

Lloyd George. No, but of taking the side of the Yugoslavs against them.

Wilson. Our tenet is that the Slavs have the same right to independence and to national unity as the Italians themselves.

Lloyd George. Yes, but if a word must be said for the Italians, the Slavs must admit that Italy's sacrifices contributed much to their own liberation, and that did not prevent the Croatians from fighting against us to the end. Except for the Czechoslovaks, the Slavs of Austria played a rather questionable role.

Wilson. It is difficult for the rest of us, free peoples, to understand the state of mind of races which have been oppressed and held under terror for a long time.

Lloyd George. Despite so many persecutions and capital sentences, the Czechs had another attitude.

Wilson. Bohemia had a more independent position in the Empire. It is necessary to understand the situation of populations humbled little by little by oppression.

Lloyd George. How did the Poles of Austria fight?

Clemenceau. I really do not know.

Wilson. About the Poles, I must tell you that I received a report from General Bliss, which indicates that they intend to send General Haller's army to Lemberg.[6] This is contrary to our plans. Should we not inform M. Paderewski that, having accepted in principle the conclusion of a cease fire and an armistice, he must stop hostilities and not permit General Haller's troops to be sent to Lemberg, nor used to relieve other troops, who would receive that same order? If our agents are not listened to, we could, if necessary, threaten to stop the victualing.

[5] Here Wilson reads the statement on the Adriatic question just printed.
[6] See THB to WW, April 18, 1919 (second letter of that date).

Lloyd George. We must avoid throwing the Poles into the arms of the Bolsheviks.

Wilson. Do you see an objection to my proposal?

Lloyd George. We cannot allow General Haller's army to be sent to Lemberg.

Clemenceau. I am of the same mind as you, and I propose to approve President Wilson's suggestion.

Wilson. What is your news from Germany?

Clemenceau. Bad. News received in Lyon by radio denies that the German financial delegates have taken a conciliatory attitude which envisages the signing of most of the clauses of the treaty. That is the gist of it. Tomorrow we shall have the Germans' response to my telegram, and we shall see if they are trying to continue their game.

Lloyd George. In reality, the German government is weak; it is most probable that it will fall. Is it too early to anticipate what we shall do if it refuses?

Wilson. That is difficult, because we do not know how it will refuse; instead of refusing pure and simple, it can adopt a dilatory tactic.

Lloyd George. I think our summons will bring it down to earth. If it does not feel strong enough to send us plenipotentiaries, it will have to be reconstituted, and that is what we should desire.

Wilson. We have the right to say to those who present themselves to us: whom do you represent?

Lloyd George. We must act vigorously. After all, hostilities are only suspended; the war can be resumed after a previous notice of forty-eight hours. It is better to make these people face hard reality, if they are trying to play tricks on us. Then they will fall and they will be replaced by others with whom we can talk. After having fought those great German armies commanded by Hindenburg and Ludendorff, we cannot allow ourselves to be trifled with by politicians of the fourth rank.

Wilson. Maybe, but the true problem is this: how shall we have peace? No one wants the war to be prolonged indefinitely.

Clemenceau. No, none of us; but we can force them to peace by occupying their territory.

Lloyd George. I am not so sure of that. The Germans have a thick skin and will tolerate an occupation better than the French would.

Wilson. Without taking into account that there are people in Germany who fear for their property and would prefer a foreign occupation to a revolution and Bolshevism.

Clemenceau. If you tell them, in case of necessity: "You will have war in forty-eight hours," you will see the effect. §

SIR MAURICE HANKEY reported that he had seen M. Orlando, Baron Sonnino and Count Aldrovandi.[7] He had delivered his message in the very words that President Wilson had used. After recalling Mr. Lloyd George's proposal made at the morning meeting, which they had had some hours to consider, he had asked whether they would consider it worth while to discuss the question of the Italian claims on the basis of the cession of a series of strategic islands off the coast. M. Orlando had asked him if he could give the proposal in writing, but he had replied that he had only authority to deliver a verbal message. The proposal had not commended itself to M. Orlando and Baron Sonnino, who had absolutely rejected it as a basis for discussion. They had said that, of course, they were always prepared to discuss anything with their colleagues if asked to do so, but they would be in the wrong if they encouraged any hopes that his could be a basis for a solution. M. Orlando had elaborated his objections to the proposal a little. He had explained that even from the point of view of defence in its narrower strategic aspects the proposal did not commend itself. He had, however, always regarded defence in the wider aspect of the defence of the Italian populations in the towns on the east of the Adriatic. He mentioned in this connection especially Fiume, but also referred to Zara and Sebenico. Questioned as to the precise terms of Mr. Lloyd George's suggestion, SIR MAURICE HANKEY said he had been given to understand that it did not include islands such as Pago, which were almost part of the mainland, but would doubtless include the other islands allotted to Italy in the Treaty of London. SIR MAURICE HANKEY mentioned that M. Orlando had said that the question had rather retrograded within the last two days, owing to the proposal for the establishment of a free port and city at Fiume similar to that to be established at Dantzig having been dropped.

On the conclusion of SIR MAURICE HANKEY's statement there was some discussion as to the desirability of President Wilson publishing a statement on the subject which he had prepared.

M. CLEMENCEAU and MR. LLOYD GEORGE urged that he should not do so. Their grounds for this were that the statement rather assumed that Italy had closed the door to an agreement and would be regarded as a final act. It would make it difficult for Italy to recede from her position.

PRESIDENT WILSON pointed out that this statement as drafted did not close the door to negotiations, but in deference to his colleagues he had agreed not to publish immediately.

§Mantoux's notes:

[7] For another account of this meeting, see Aldrovandi, *Guerra Diplomatia*, pp. 255-56.

Lt. Col. Sir Maurice Hankey returns from his mission.

Hankey. The Italian ministers did not want to study what I took to them; they were absolutely inflexible. I explained the proposal to them, asking them if they would agree to discuss on that basis. I saw M. Orlando and M. Sonnino: both responded negatively. They asked me if I could give them the plan in writing. I answered no. They say that, even looking at it solely from the point of view of defense, they cannot accept. To tell the truth, what they mean by defense is not only military defense, but the defense of Italian nationality on the coast opposite them.

Wilson. That is not what M. Sonnino said, and that proves that there is no limit to what they are asking.

Hankey. M. Sonnino went so far as to say that that proposal marked a retreat, since the idea of Fiume being constituted into a free port seemed abandoned. Perhaps this was only an enticement for a new discussion.

Lloyd George. If the Yugoslavs keep Dalmatia, Fiume can be constituted as a free city. Besides, I would see a great disadvantage in making it into a Croatian city with Croatian customs.

Wilson. I have thought about this last point: I am still inclined to support the plan to constitute Fiume as a free city, because this plan is advantageous for the interests of the hinterland. I have never closed the door to that proposal.

Lloyd George. What is your impression, Colonel Hankey?

Hankey. I have the impression that the Italians are bluffing a little and that they think you are weakening.

Wilson. What I would rather do is to publish my manifesto in the newspapers of tomorrow morning.

Clemenceau. If you publish it, after that, there will be nothing doing any longer. When the matter is dead and buried, say why, but not before.

Wilson. But then I shall be too late. I can say, in order to clarify the situation, that it seems to me important to indicate what are the views of the United States.

Lloyd George. It will unleash the tempest in Italy. Everything will be topsy-turvey.

Wilson. Meanwhile, the situation remains obscure, and the United States appears to take an unreasonable attitude.

Lloyd George. Two months ago, the French press spoke of me as badly as the Italian press can speak of you.

I thought it was better to keep quiet, and I had only to congratulate myself.

Wilson. But there was a reasonable government here with which we could talk. That is not the case in the matter with which we are dealing.

Clemenceau. I thought the Italians would return.

Lloyd George. My advice is not to budge, to act a little as they, giving them rope, and to limit ourselves to informing them that we are going on to another subject.

Clemenceau. I think that that will soon bring us a visit from M. Sonnino.

Wilson. If the Italians publicly announce their views tomorrow, I do not want to allow them the first shot of the cannon, so to speak.

Lloyd George. I would leave them at peace.

Clemenceau. You will read articles tomorrow in our newspapers, but they will not represent French opinion, I can guarantee you that.

Lloyd George. In England no one is much concerned about that question.

Clemenceau (to Wilson). Wait forty-eight hours and, if there is good reason, say: "Here are my attitude and my reasons."

Wilson. After the debate is over?

Lloyd George. If you do it before, you will cause an explosion; you will raise up all Italian opinion against you.

Wilson. I have not yet presented my point of view to the Italian people, and I limit myself to saying that afterwards they will not ask us for what we cannot permit.

Lloyd George. Yes, but your declaration makes no allusion to our efforts at conciliation, to the last suggestions we have made. It would make all compromise impossible for us. It is better to say these things only when all the doors have been closed. I would coolly invite the Italians to come to discuss tomorrow with the Japanese the question of Kiaochow.

Clemenceau. They will not come. I recall that, when we spoke of sending to the Germans the invitation to come to Versailles, M. Orlando said: "I enter my reservations about my participation as long as the Italian matters have not been settled."

Wilson. Indeed, M. Orlando said that he could not participate in the negotiation with Germany before the Adriatic question is settled.

Lloyd George. I warned the Italians of the consequences which would follow from the financial point of view if they are not represented here when we discuss with Germany the question of reparations. My advice is to invite them to take part in our discussions as if nothing had happened.§

2. PRESIDENT WILSON reported a conversation he had had that morning with Baron Makino and Count Chinda. He had made the

suggestion that Mr. Lansing had already made at the Council of Foreign Ministers, namely, that all claims in the Pacific should be ceded to the Allied and Associated Powers as trustees leaving them to make fair and just dispositions. He had, at the same time, reminded the Japanese Delegates that it had been understood that Japan was to have a mandate for the islands in the north Pacific although he had made a reserve in the case of the island of Yap, which he himself considered should be international. He had suggested that, similarly, in the case of Kiau-Chau, where there was a definite Treaty relating to Kiau-Chau and Shantung, Japan should place the question in the hands of the 5 Powers. He had asked whether there could not be some modification of the Treaty with the consent of both parties. The Powers had no right to force Japan but they had the right to try and persuade her to make some agreement with China on the subject. The Japanese had been very stiff about it. They had said that they would return Kiau-Chau to China, the only reservation being the retention of a residential section and a free port for China. In regard to the railway, they surrendered all control except the joint interest with China in the railway and certain concessions. He had pointed out that China had no capital and had asked whether in that event China could take advantage of this position. They had replied that she could and quoted another instance where they had for 10 years shared some concern of the kind with China, which was run on the same lines. They were absolutely set on obliging China to carry out the bond. They insisted that Germany should resign the whole of her interests in Kiau-Chau to the Japanese and that the Powers should trust Japan to carry out her bargain with China.

MR. LLOYD GEORGE asked why Japan should have a different treatment in regard to Kiau-Chau to what other Powers had in respect to German colonies.

PRESIDENT WILSON said the reason was because in the Treaty it had been made clear that the transfer was to precede the retrocession of the territory to China.

MR. LLOYD GEORGE suggested that it ought to be ceded by the League of Nations.

PRESIDENT WILSON said that the Japanese were too proud to accept this solution. He had then repeated to the Japanese the proposal he had already made to his colleagues that the spheres of influence in China should be abrogated. They had replied that they were ready to do this. They had defined spheres of influence to include the right of putting in troops and extraterritoriality. He thought it would be a great thing if we could get rid of the right of Japan to maintain troops in Kiau-Chau.

MR LLOYD GEORGE said that he thought it was very important that in the Treaty with Germany all the Powers should be put on the same footing. Japan should not have a special position.

PRESIDENT WILSON then read the notes which had been exchanged between China and Japan. The first note[8] from Japan to China had been sent before the entry of China into the war and had been to the effect that when, after the war, the leased territory had been left to the free disposal of Japan the latter would restore it to China under conditions which included a free port in Kiau-Chau Bay: a concession for Japan; the disposal of property was to be effected by mutual arrangement between the two countries. China's answer had merely been to take note and President Wilson did not think the Government had accepted. Another declaration had been made by Japan on September 24th, 1918.[9] Japan then proposed to adjust the questions in Shantung on the following lines:

1. All Japanese troops, except those at Chinan Fu, the terminus of the line, to be withdrawn to Tsingtau.
2. The Chinese Government to be allowed to organise a police force for the railway.
3. The railway to pay for this police.
4. The Japanese to be represented at the headquarters of the police, at the various stations, and at the training establishments for the police.
5. Part of the staff of the railway to be Japanese.
6. The railway to become a Chino-Japanese enterprise.
7. The Japanese civil administration to be abolished.

The Chinese reply had been that she was "pleased to agree in the above mentioned articles." Thus it was not a Treaty but an exchange of notes.

MR. LLOYD GEORGE said that he could see no ground for differentiating in the case of Japan. This territory should be placed on exactly the same footing as all other German territory.

PRESIDENT WILSON said that to be perfectly fair to the Japanese he thought they would interpret this as a challenge of their good faith. He had put it to the Japanese representatives that the peace of the Far East depended more on Chino-Japanese relations than on anything else. China was full of riches. It was clearly to the advantage of Japan to take the most generous position towards China and to show herself as a friend. The interest of the world in China was the "open door." The Japanese had assented and expressed benevolent intentions.

MR. LLOYD GEORGE pointed out that it was the triumph of the

[8] That is, the Sino-Japanese agreements of May 25, 1915.
[9] Again, printed in THE CLAIM of China.

Great Powers in the west that enabled Japan to make this arrangement. He felt strongly that Japan should be in the same position as other States. Otherwise other nations could insist on the same right.

(It was arranged that the next meeting should take place on the following morning at 11 a.m. M. Clemenceau said that he hoped by that time he would have a reply from the Germans. It was agreed that this was a question which would properly be discussed with the Japanese. As, however, M. Clemenceau had certain questions relating to the Western Front to raise, Sir Maurice Hankey was instructed to invite the Japanese for 11:30 a.m. He was also authorised to telephone to Count Aldrovandi to let him know of the Meeting that had been arranged.)

§Mantoux's notes:

Lloyd George. They always accept the principles. When you come to the application, it is different. They do not want to receive anything from the hands of the League of Nations. Nevertheless, we can call to their attention that it is the defeat of Germany in the West which allowed them to keep their gains. If we are not firm on this point, what can I answer Mr. Hughes if he in turn asks to escape from the system of mandates?

Clemenceau. Be careful that Japan does not break with you. If you are prepared for that, all right; but she will break.

Wilson. The Japanese told me with all Oriental courtesy that, if we do not take their side on this article of the treaty, they could not sign the rest.

Lloyd George. Ain't that too bad!

Clemenceau. If that does not sway you, I myself can go no further than you go.

Wilson. We must hear the Japanese tomorrow morning.

Lloyd George. Unless the German response takes all our time. I propose that M. Clemenceau, if he has not received the answer from the Germans, invite the Japanese for tomorrow. If the German reply arrives in the meantime, I would prefer not to involve the Japanese in the discussion.

Clemenceau. Will you invite the Italians?

Wilson. It is difficult in view of the attitude they have taken.

Clemenceau. It is better to show them that our work is continuing.

Lloyd George. I propose to advise them simply that we are placing the Japanese question on the agenda, unless the German response arrives and requires discussion.§

T MS (SDR, RG 256, 180.03401/110, DNA); Mantoux, I, 309-13, 313-15, 317.

To Robert Lansing

My dear Lansing: Paris, 21 April, 1919.

You know, of course, that the British Government is very anxious, in order that it may exercise a quieting effect upon affairs in Egypt, that we should recognize the British Protectorate over Egypt announced by His Majesty's Government on November 18th, 1914, and I am going to take the liberty of suggesting that you make a reply to Mr. Balfour in substance like the following:

"In answer to your inquiry, the President has authorized me to inform you that he recognizes the British Protectorate over Egypt which was announced by His Majesty's Government on November 18, 1914.

"The President has no objection to this decision being made public, as he understands that it may help in the restoration of order and in the prevention of further bloodshed in Egypt.

"You will no doubt realize, my dear Mr. Minister, that in according this recognition, the President must necessarily reserve for further discussion the details of formal recognition, together with the question of a modification of any rights of the United States which this decision on his part may entail."

I hope that this will seem to you to embody the right action and the right tone.

Cordially and sincerely yours,   [Woodrow Wilson]

CCL (WP, DLC).

Robert Lansing to Frank Lyon Polk

[Paris] 21 April 1919.

1722. For Department's information:

I have today in view of necessity of immediate action sent the following telegram to our Agency at Cairo:

"I have delivered today to Mr. Balfour the following letter:

'In answer to your inquiry, the President has authorized me to inform you that he recognizes the British Protectorate over Egypt which was announced by His Majesty's Government on November 18, 1914.

The President has no objection to this decision being made public, as he understands that it may help in the restoration of order and in the prevention of further bloodshed in Egypt.

You will no doubt realize, my dear Mr. Minister, that in according this recognition, the President must necessarily reserve for further discussion the details of formal recognition, together with the question of a modification of any rights of the United States which this decision on his part may entail.'

You may confer with General Allenby as to the best method of giving publicity to the contents of this letter. In that connection I think it is proper that you might indicate that the President and the American people have every sympathy with the legitimate desires of the Egyptian people for a further measure of self-government but that they deplore the effort to obtain such rights by anarchy and violence."   Lansing Ammission.

T telegram (WP, DLC).

To Milenko R. Vesnić

My dear Mr. Minister: Paris, 21 April, 1919.

My attention has been called to the fact that well known Montenegrins are still lying in prisons where they have been placed by Serbian troops.[1] Such circumstances are of course very distressing. I have no means, and perhaps no right, to judge of the causes or the provocations in this case, but perhaps you will allow me as a sincere friend of Serbia to call your attention to the circumstances and to suggest that cordial and satisfactory relations with Montenegro can hardly be established by such means. My heart is so entirely for a course of generosity and friendship that perhaps it is sometimes apt to mislead my head, but my own practical judgment is that a liberal course is always the wise one, particularly with relationships such as we are trying to set up.

It is for these reasons that I venture to call your attention to this matter, and I am sure that I can depend upon your generosity to understand.

Cordially and sincerely yours,   [Woodrow Wilson]

CCL (WP, DLC).
    [1] In Jovan S. Plamenatz (Plamenac) to WW, April 7, 1919, TLS (WP, DLC). Plamenatz was Prime Minister (in exile) of the royal government of Montenegro.

To Henry Mauris Robinson

My dear Mr. Robinson: Paris, 21 April, 1919.

I have your letter of the 19th about the enemies' ships seized by the United States during the war, and thank you for it. I am clear that we must adhere to our position without deviation.

Cordially and sincerely yours,   Woodrow Wilson

TLS (photographic copy, WP, DLC).

To Prince Faisal

My dear Prince Faissal: Paris, 21 April, 1919.

Thank you very cordially for your letter of the 20th which I warmly appreciate. My best wishes will go with you and I hope in every way that is possible to be serviceable to Syria, in whose fortunes I am deeply interested.

Cordially and sincerely yours,   [Woodrow Wilson]

CCL (WP, DLC).

To William Graves Sharp

My dear Friend: Paris, 21 April, 1919.

Just a line to tell you how deeply touched and pleased I was by your parting letter from Brest.[1] It fills me with the deepest gratification to have formed such a friendship. I find my mind going along with yours in your comments upon the Russian situation, and you may be sure that I shall always follow you with the warmest friendship and interest.

In haste,

Cordially and faithfully yours,   [Woodrow Wilson]

CCL (WP, DLC).
   [1] See W. G. Sharp to WW, April 18, 1919.

Two Letters from Tasker Howard Bliss

My dear Mr. President: Paris April 21st, 1919

Referring to the document[1] which you read to the Commission this morning and which was cordially approved by everyone, will you permit me to suggest the following for your consideration?

If a break should come and if your statement should be published after the break, it might possibly be regarded as a *defense* of the American attitude whereas, if it were published in advance of the break it would appeal to the world as the statement of basic principle which would leave the break without any justification in the eyes of the honest part of the world.

From that point of view it would seem that the statement might well be published before the break rather than afterwards,* although other considerations better known to you than to me may make the other course preferable.

Pardon me for intruding this suggestion on you, but after you left Mr. Lansing's rooms this morning I suggested this to him and to Mr. White and they both seemed to think well of it.

Sincerely yours,   Tasker H. Bliss.

* The more so, as some of the clauses in your statement seem to imply that it was made in advance of the break and in the hope of preventing it. T.H.B.

¹ That is, the statement on the Adriatic question just printed.

My dear Mr. President: Paris, April 21. 1919.

A telegram from Mr. Poole, Chargé d'Affaires at Archangel, received on the 18th inst. but not brought to me until to-night, says that the British are sending out reinforcements to Archangel of not less than 12,000 men. He states that their "final objective will be the occupation of Kotlas," several hundred miles farther into the interior, but he also says:

"Ironside informs me that he is arrangeing to evacuate the 339th infantry first of all the troops now here. The ships bringing the new forces will be used and embarkation will occur before June 1st. This will probably obviate further trouble. It will be necessary to retain the American engineer battalion to the end of evacuation."

The 339th infantry is the American regiment now at advanced station south and southeast of Archangel. I do not know whether the statement "it will be necessary to retain the American engineer battalion to the end of evacuation" means that it will be retained only until the end of evacuation of the 339th American regiment of infantry, or whether it means that the American engineer battalion will be retained until the end of the evacuation of all of the forces now in North Russia. It looks to me as though the British do not intend to withdraw their forces, even though the American troops are relieved. Otherwise, I do not understand why the British are sending an additional force of "not less than 12,000 men." I shall endeavor to get further information in regard to this from the British.   Sincerely yours,   Tasker H. Bliss.

TLS (WP, DLC).

From Robert Lansing

My dear Mr. President: Paris, April 21, 1919.

I am sending you enclosed a letter from Minister Lou, the head of the Chinese Delegation, transmitting a memorandum containing certain clauses which China would like to have inserted in the Treaties with Germany and Austria-Hungary.¹

I feel strongly that China's just contention regarding German rights in Shantung should be granted, that is to say that the leasehold of Kiauchow and other German rights in Shantung should revert to China direct.

The Chinese draft expresses this rather verbosely in the 1st and 4th Articles.[2]

The only alternative, as it seems to me, would be that expressed in the general renunciation clause adopted by the Conference of last Thursday afternoon.[3] That clause is in accord with the draft of Major Scott[4] concerning Shantung, sent to you last week, providing for a renunciation by Germany in favor of the Five Allied and Associated Powers.[5]

The paragraphs relating to the general clause mentioned have been marked with blue pencil on pages 4, 5, 6 and 7 of the attached copy of the proces-verbal of the conference, which took place Thursday afternoon, April 17th.

The question of Shantung and Kiauchow came up in connection with the consideration of an article to be inserted in the Peace Treaty whereby Germany agrees to renounce all rights, titles and privileges in territory outside her frontiers as fixed by the present treaty. This article is so drawn as to provide an opportunity for insertion of special clauses relating to particular questions such as Morocco, Egypt, Siam, Liberia, Shantung, etc.

Baron Makino accepted the Article but reserved the right to propose special clauses relating to Shantung and Kiauchow, which he thought should be considered by the Council of Ten and not by the so-called Council of Five. When it was pointed out that no date had been fixed for a meeting of the Council of Ten, Baron Makino stated that he was already engaged in certain pourparlers which he thought might lead to an early settlement of the question.

I understand, however, that the question has since been submitted by the Japanese for your consideration in conference with Mr. Lloyd-George, M. Clemenceau and Signor Orlando.

I am, my dear Mr. President,

Very sincerely yours,   Robert Lansing

TLS (WP, DLC).
  [1] Lou Tseng-tsiang (Lu Cheng-hsiang) to G. Clemenceau, April 16, 1919, TCL, enclosing Chinese Delegation, Preliminary Peace Conference, MEMORANDUM. PROVISIONS FOR INSERTION IN THE PRELIMINARIES OF PEACE WITH GERMANY AND AUSTRIA-HUNGARY, March 1919, printed copy, both in WP, DLC.
  [2] The relevant parts of these articles read as follows:
  Article I: "The state of war between China and Germany having terminated all treaties, conventions, protocols, agreements, contracts and other arrangements between them, consequently all rights, privileges, concessions, immunities and tolerances granted therein, or based thereupon, or accruing therefrom, including notably the leasehold rights of Kiaochow Bay, the Railway and Mining concessions and other rights and options in relation to the Province of Shantung, have reverted to China and or ceased to exist."
  Article IV: "Germany cedes to China all the buildings, wharves, barracks, forts, arms

and munitions of war, vessels of all kinds, marine cables, wireless installations and other public property belonging to the German Government which are found in the German concessions in Tientsin and Hankow and in other parts of Chinese territory including that portion of Kiaochow formerly leased to Germany."

³ That is, the meeting of the Council of Foreign Ministers on April 17. The "general renunciation clause" read as follows:

"In territory outside her frontiers as fixed by the present treaty, Germany renounces all rights, titles and privileges in territory which belonged to her or to her allies, and all rights, titles and privileges whatever their origin which she held as against the Five Allied and Associated Powers or the other belligerent Powers who sign this treaty.

"Germany undertakes immediately to recognize and to conform to the measures which may be taken now or in the future by the five Allied and Associated Powers in agreement where necessary with the Powers in order to carry the above stipulation into effect." *PPC*, IV, 569.

⁴ That is, James Brown Scott.

⁵ Scott's "Proposed Clauses of Renunciation of German Interests in China" read as follows:

"Germany agrees to renounce and hereby renounces to the five Allied and Associate Powers, in favor of China, all claim, title to and interest in any and all concessions and leases of territory and of territorial rights hitherto made by China to Germany, particularly the leasehold rights of Kiaochow Bay, the railways and mining concessions, and all other rights and options in relation to the Province of Shantung, and including in the said renunciation to the five Allied and Associated Powers, in favor of China, all the buildings, wharves, barracks, forts, arms and munitions of war, vessels of all kinds, marine cables, wireless installations, and all other public property belonging to Germany, which are found in the German concessions in Tientsin and Hankow, and in all other parts of Chinese territory, reserving therefrom, however, buildings and establishments used as diplomatic or consular offices or residences.

"When China shall have opened Tsingtao in the leased territory of Kiaochow and certain other suitable places in Shantung Province to foreign trade and residence under conditions which shall be satisfactory to and approved by the five Allied and Associated Powers, the said Powers hereby agree to transfer to China all claims, titles, and interests renounced by Germany in the present article to the said five Powers in favor of China." Undated T MS (SDR, RG 256, 185.1158/66, DNA).

From Vittorio Emanuele Orlando, with Enclosure

My dear President: Paris, April 21st, 1919.

I had learnt from indirect sources that the American Delegation had been badly impressed by reports received from American officials sent to Dalmatia who had given an unfavorable account of the line of conduct followed by our military authorities. As a result of this information I addressed a letter to Colonel House, of which I enclose copy (exhibit 1).

Colonel House, with the fine sense of justice which distinguished [distinguishes] him, allowed one of my secretaries to make enquiries into the grounds of the accusations made against our administration, while in no way violating the secrecy which rightly protects the report of an official.

Among the points noted by my Secretary, the statement which most struck me was that the military administration in Dalmatia had, up to now, deported seven hundred persons, a figure which could not but impress me. I at once telegraphed to Admiral Millo,¹ Governor of Dalmatia, making of him formal enquiry as to the number of persons in regard to whom the Italian authorities had taken police measures: Admiral Millo in reply has sent me the telegram of which I have the honor to hand you a copy enclosed (exhibit 2).[2]

As it is out of question to doubt the statement made by an Italian officer, this reply shows the grave error contained in the information supplied to you, as the real number of persons interned or expelled is very far from considerable when we take into consideration the fact that the territories occupied have a population of some 300,000 inhabitants, and that the occupation has lasted now nearly six months.

It would be easy to show that the measures taken by the Italian authorities in respect of Italian citizens in territories under martial law have been no less numerous than those taken in Dalmatia. In both cases such action is the inevitable result of the exceptional conditions prevailing under military occupation.

Far be it from me, Mr. President, to cast any doubt on the good faith of the officials from whom you have received these reports. It is easy to make a mistake in entire good faith, and this is what has happened in the case before us. Nevertheless, the point is important for it shows how difficult it is even for the most fair-minded and honest people to judge equitably of men and affairs in environments agitated by such deep passions.

I cannot and will not here take up in detail the other matters referred to in the reports under consideration; yet I cannot refrain from commenting on one other point which seems to me very characteristic. It is stated that in the Commercial treaty with Austria-Hungary, Italy favoured the importation of her citrus fruits and wines into Austria-Hungary to the detriment of the interests of the Dalmatian farmers. This is true, but what of it? Dalmatia was part of another State, and of course Italy could not subordinate the protection of her commercial interests to those of a section of a foreign country, however dear to the hearts of Italians. The same situation existed in the case of the Trentino, which is a great wine producing centre, but nobody has used this as an argument against the annexation of the Trentino to Italy. If the intention was to point out that the agricultural products of Dalmatia will be in competition with similar products from Italy, this indeed is true; but it has no bearing on the case in point, as such forms of internal competition occur in all countries. The wine-growers of Sicily compete with those of Tuscany and of Piedmont; the cereals of the South are in keen competition with those of the Po district, and so on and so forth. No one however has ever argued that on this account the union of Sicily with Italy was undesirable.

I feel sure, Mr. President, that your deep sense of fairness will lead you to admit that these arguments and others of a like kind can have no serious influence on the extremely grave questiond [questions] now under discussion.

Please accept, Mr. President, the assurance of my high esteem and consideration.   Sincerely yours   Orlando

TLS (WP, DLC).
  ¹ Adm. Enrico Millo di Casalgiate.
  ² E. Millo di Casalgiate to [V. E. Orlando], n.d., T telegram (WP, DLC). Millo reported that ninety persons had been "interned," four had been "expelled," and one was "in custody" at Lagosta (now Lastovo), an island off the Dalmatian coast. According to Millo, the reasons for these measures were: "Agitation against our occupation and incitement to opposition. Preparation for an propaganda in favor of violence and acts of bolschevism aiming at concentration of bands and 'comitagi.' " "Comitagi" is the Italian derivation of the Turkish word "komitadji," that is, an armed band or guerrilla band.

E N C L O S U R E

Vittorio Emanuele Orlando to Edward Mandell House

Confidential   *Exhibit* ı

My dear Friend: Paris, April ıoth, 1919.

I am informed confidentially by a very trustworthy person that the American delegation has recently received some reports on the attitude of the military authorities in the occupied territories towards the non-Italian populations. These reports, I am told, ascribe to the authorities acts of injustice and persecution towards these populations. My friend added that this had made an unfavorable impression on the Delegation, as indeed, it rightly should.

If my informant is correct, I would most earnestly request you to supply me with full particulars of the events which have given rise to this report, so that I may be able to give all requisite explanations. I feel sure that you will agree with me that this request is justified not only by our friendly relations, but also by that fundamental principle of justice which forbids passing judgement on events until the facts have been made known to the defendant.

For my part, I can assure you positively that the Italian Government has never given instructions which diverge in the slightest degree from the most scrupulous respect of the rights of other nationalities. I have carried this respect, indeed, to a length which some have deemed excessive. Thus, for instance, in some communes where strong Italian minorities exist, the Austrian Government had arranged for the opening of Italian schools. Well, I have gone so far as not to carry out this decision taken by the Austrian Government in behalf of the Italians in order to avoid even the appearance of a departure from the most scrupulous impartiality.

We must therefore face this dilemma: either the facts referred to are justified by circumstances of which your informant may not be aware, in which case it is desirable to make them known; or there is no such justification, in which case it would mean that some official or military commander is at fault in not carrying out my instructions. In this case it is essential that I be informed so that I may take proper steps to bring home to such official his responsibility for disregarding the orders of the Government.

I feel sure that you will appreciate the deep sense of justice which leads me to make this request. Meanwhile, with high esteem and cordial regards, I beg to remain.   [V. E. Orlando]

TCL (WP, DLC).

From Herbert Clark Hoover

My dear Mr. President: Paris, France. April 21, 1919

I enclose you, herewith, memorandum[1] containing the points which I desire to present to the American people, eliminating the whole of my very strong opinions on the whole Bolshevist movement. I do not wish to involve anyone in these latter views, and I think I could satisfy my own conscience by taking an entirely separate early occasion when there is no national or allied question involved to give expression to what I think of the purely social currents that are developing in Europe and their relations to the United States.   Yours faithfully,   Herbert Hoover

TLS (WP, DLC).
[1] It is printed as an Enclosure with WW to HCH, April 23, 1919.

From Herbert Clark Hoover, with Enclosure

Dear Mr. President: [Paris] 21 April 1919.

I enclose you, herewith, memorandum on the note which you handed me today with regard to the situation in Germany.[1] I have put it in the form of a memorandum in case you wish to hand it to one of your colleagues for their edification.

          Faithfully yours,   Herbert Hoover

TLS (WP, DLC).
[1] See Appendix II to the minutes of the Council of Four printed at April 20, 1919, 10 a.m.

ENCLOSURE

MEMORANDUM

21 April 1919.

With regard to the attached memorandum we consider it an extremely able analysis of present state of affairs in Germany. We are not entirely clear as to the method of procedure to avoid a complete Bolshevist government.

We agree that unless something constructive is done at once we shall be ultimately faced with either Bolshevism or Military occupation, or both. Of the intermediate courses proposed in this document, we would certainly agree that any combination of Soviet and Assembly Government that would maintain order and enable the construction of peace would be infinitely preferable.

We do think, however, that the proposed formula to Ebert would be dangerous. It strikes us that the party with whom to open such a suggestion are the Independent Socialists, as these are not Bolshevists in the ordinary sense of the word, and probably come nearer representing the yearnings of the German people at the present time. Ebert, of course, is a Majority Socialist and has two complexions; in the first place, he is a Majority Socialist himself and has a Majority Socialist cabinet under him, and second, as President he could probably summon an Independent Socialist cabinet. If negotiations with Ebert would result in the establishment of such a cabinet there is a possibility of Germany being saved from chaos. It does appear to us, however, that it would be impossible to settle an agreement with the Independent Socialists in advance that they would accept any given treaty of peace. What is desirable is that in the event of the Schiedeman Government (which seems almost certain) refusing to sign the treaty, that Ebert should be guided to create an Independent Socialist cabinet. Whether these gentlemen will be any more inclined to sign the treaty than the former, of course, we do not know, but certainly they stand a better chance of preserving order in Germany today than the Schiedeman cabinet.

We cannot fail to again mention what we consider is one of the absolute fundamentals to constructively handle this situation. You and all of us have proposed, fought and plead for the last three months that the blockade on Germany should be taken off, that these people should be allowed to return to production not only to save themselves from starvation and misery but that there should be awakened in them some resolution for continued National life. The situation in Germany today is to a large degree one of complete abandonment of hope. The people have simply lain down under the threat of Bolshevism in front and the demands of the Allies behind. The people are simply in a state of moral collapse and there is no resurrection from this except through the restoration of the normal processes of economic life and hope. We have for the last month held that it is now too late to save the situation. We do think, however, that it is worth one more great effort to bring the Allied countries to realize that all the bars on exports and imports should be taken down without attempts to special national benefits; that the Germans should be given an assurance that a certain amount of ships and working capital will be left in their hands with which to re-start the National machine.

We feel also from an American point of view that the refusal of the Allies to accept these primary considerations during the last three months leaves them with the total responsibility for what is now impending.

We do not believe that the acceptance of any possible treaty is very probable under present conditions, and we feel certain that the hope of reparation is gradually being extinguished by the continued use of the noose. We do not believe the blockade was ever an effective instrument to force peace; it is effective, however, to force Bolshevism.

T MS (WP, DLC).

From Henry White

Dear Mr. President: Paris 21 April 1919

You may remember my calling your attention this morning, briefly, to the manner in which the Kiel Canal question came before meetings of the Commission on Ports, Waterways and Railways on the 18th and 19th instant.

The original Report of the Commission, of which you approved in your letter to me of the 18th instant, but which had been returned for revision to the Commission by the Council of Four, has been elaborated by a new Report, whereof I enclose a copy for your information and which explains itself.[1] Our effort, throughout, was to avoid any impairment of German sovereignty and is embodied in the British and American proposed Article VII. In this we were stoutly opposed by the French Delegation, chiefly at the instigation of the French Admiralty, whose views in the matter are embodied in the alternative French proposal for that Article. The British, Japanese and Italian Delegations supported our point of view, as it is embodied in Article VII in the Report.

You will note, also, that we reserved the requirement that charges should be limited to the cost of upkeep. It was our opinion that something more than the cost of upkeep might be charged by Germany and that a sufficient limitation was contained in the requirement that charges be equal for the ships of all nations, including those of Germany.

I may add that Admiral Benson opposed any further provision concerning the fortifications of the Canal on the ground that Articles XXXVI and XXXVII, of the Naval Clauses already approved by the Supreme War Council, have sufficiently met the needs of that situation. In this view we were supported by the British and Japanese Delegations and opposed by the Italian and the French. The French proposal will be found under Article VIII in the enclosed Report, and we are opposed to its insertion in the Treaty, for the reasons stated.

Yours very sincerely,   Henry White

P.S. I enclose for your information a copy of the original paragraph which was sent back to the Commission.[2]

TLS (WP, DLC).
[1] "REPORT OF THE SUB-COMMISSION ON THE KIEL CANAL TO THE SUPREME COUNCIL OF THE ALLIES," April, 1919, T MS (WP, DLC).
[2] "The Kiel Canal shall remain under the sovereignty of Germany, subject to the application to this Canal, and to its approaches, of the rules to be formulated later regarding the International Regime of Waterways; especially such rules as concern the freedom of navigation for subjects, property, and flags of all nations at peace with Germany, to the end that no distinction be made between subjects, property, or flags of Germany, and those of all other states at peace with her. This provision shall apply, not only to merchant vessels, but also to warships." T MS (WP, DLC)

From Lord Robert Cecil

My dear Mr. President,   Paris. April 21, 1919.

I venture to lay before you in this note my strongly-held view with reference to the holding of a Plenary Conference on the amended Covenant.

You will remember that at the close of the Conference of February 14 M. Clemenceau stated, quite definitely as I recollect, that an opportunity would be given to members of the Conference who were not members of the Commission to discuss the constitution of the League. I think this leaves us no choice in the matter, even if such discussion were not, as I think it is, desirable in itself.

If you agree, I think no time should be lost in getting the secretariat of the Conference to work to arrange the Plenary Conference for Thursday next, the 24th. Friday is, I understand, already taken up: and if the German delegates are to arrive on the 25th., to hold it on Saturday would lay our Commission open to the charge of delaying the signature of peace.

If you wish to see me on the subject I shall be glad to come either this evening or to-morrow morning.

Yours very sincerely,   Robert Cecil

TLS (WP, DLC).

From Fridtjof Nansen

My dear Mr. President,   Paris April 21st 1919.

May I express my deep gratitude for your very kind letter of April 18th and for the great confidence shown me in encouraging and supporting me in the great task of trying to save the starving and suffering population of northern Russia.[1]

I may say that I fully appreciate the great importance of this matter, and the responsibility which I assume. Feeling keenly my deficiency I can only say that it will be my one desire to do all in my power to show myself worthy of your great confidence.

Believe me, my dear Mr. President,

yours very respectfully   Fridtjof Nansen

ALS (WP, DLC).

[1] That is, the area controlled by the Soviet government. It might be pointed out that Nansen had sent his letter of April 17, 1919, only to Lenin, and not to any other Russian leader.

From George Davis Herron

Dear Mr. President: Geneva, Switzerland April 21st 1919.

The University of Bâle has asked me to give a public oration on the subject of "Wilson." When this invitation first came, I declined, on account of all the circumstances attending the Peace Conference. But the invitation has come a second time, and in some sense the Municipality joins with the University. It is now publicly known that the invitation has been issued, and the circumstances are such that I fear I could not have declined a second time without giving rise to new rumors about the Peace Conference.

It is because of the whole present situation, therefore, that I am asking if you can kindly take a moment and a half a dozen lines to give me some hint of your final feeling about the Conference. It goes without saying that any hint you give me will be held sacredly confidential, and I should not in any way quote you. It is for your sake, and the immeasurable work's sake, that I would ask for some word for my guidance. I should deplore, above all things, that any word of mine should unwittingly add to the burden of the world's confusion which you bear at the present time. I cannot avoid the subject, and whatever I say in this connection will inevitably be a subject of press dispatches throughout Middle Europe.

My feeling about the Conference is one of frank and profound discouragement; all the more so that I know what is taking place in the minds of the peoples in Middle Europe. I feel that the great ends for which you have labored, and which I in my poor way have so ardently supported, have been either so baffled or compromised that nothing now can save European civilisation from utter disintegration in the course of a very few months; and I think that America, unless the peoples are made to understand the burden divinely laid upon them better than they now do, will inevitably be drawn into the pit into which Europe will soon be descending.

Let me say again that I would not think of troubling you if this were a matter merely personal to myself. It is only because it will concern you, without any regard to what I might wish in the matter, and will concern the cause for which you have so exhaustingly worked, that I ask for some hint from you for this occasion.

Thanking you most heartily in advance, I remain,

Most faithfully yours,   George D. Herron

TLS (WP, DLC).

Frank Lyon Polk to Roland Sletor Morris

[Washington] April 21, 1919, noon.

STRICTLY CONFIDENTIAL FOR THE AMBASSADOR.

The following is the text of a secret message for you from Colonel House, who is one of the American representatives on the Commission charged with drawing the Covenant of the League of Nations. This message has been read by Secretary Lansing who authorized you to use the substance thereof discreetly with the Japanese Foreign Office:

QUOTE: I have just learned that Mr. Hughes, Prime Minister of Australia, has issued a statement to the Japanese press to the effect that he, as Prime Minister of Australia, was not responsible for the rejection of the amendment proposed by the Japanese to the covenant of the League of Nations.[1] It seems to me that this statement is calculated to place the blame particularly upon the United States for the rejection of the amendment. His statement is in part as follows: INNERQUOTE: For it is most emphatically untrue to say that Australia alone is responsible for the rejection of the Japanese amendment. Just what happened at the meeting of the commission which rejected the Japanese amendment I do not know but I have been told on good authority that six or seven representatives either recorded their votes against it or abstained from voting at all. Australia had no representatives there. In the face of these facts, it is not only contemptible but absurd to say that Australia is alone responsible for the rejection of the amendment. The Japanese people are not fools but on the other hand very keen and wise people and they will know how to interpret correctly the motives of these so called friends of Japan who have circulated these insidious rumors. End—INNERQUOTE.

Viscount Chinda has just called upon me and has given me a copy of Hughes' statement, a part of which I quoted above. Neither Chinda or Makino are in any doubt as to the attitude of the United States respecting this amendment or as to the attitude of Australia. The true facts of the situation are as follows: Chinda and Makino have frequently conferred with me respecting the form of the amendment and I told them with the approval of the President that the United States would accept the amendment as finally proposed to the Preamble of the Covenant provided the British Government would give assurances that no public attack in the plenary session of the conference or in the press would be made against the amendment. We have done everything we possibly could do to induce the representative of the British Government to give such assurances but our endeavors have never met with any success. The stumbling block has always been the attitude of Hughes of Australia. He has warned the British delegate that if such an amendment was included in the Covenant he would personally denounce it before the plenary session of the conference. The Japanese representatives acting, I believe, under specific instructions from their Government proposed the amendment. At the last meeting of the Commission of the League of Nations the vote on the amendment was eleven votes in favor of the amendment, eighteen members of the Commission being present, the vote in the negative was not demanded but during the discussion Lord Robert Cecil acting in behalf of the British Empire stated that he was acting upon specific instructions and that the amendment was entirely unacceptable to the British Government.[2] President Wilson made a speech of conciliation neither favoring the amendment nor opposing it, but suggesting that the wisest course might be not to press the matter at this time. The flat objection of the British Government made the necessary unanimous vote impossible, the United States therefore was not called upon to vote.   Polk   Acting.

T telegram (R Lansing Papers, DLC).
  [1] It is included in the minutes of the meeting of the League of Nations Commission printed at April 11, 1919.
    [2] Ibid.

From Sidney Edward Mezes, with Enclosure

April 21, 1919.

To: The President
From: Dr. Mezes
Re: Draft of Treaty Articles for Danzig.

I

I am returning this draft[1] with changes according to your instruction of Friday, conveyed by Colonel House, (a) omitting two provisions dealing respectively with Soldiers' and Wor[k]men's Councils and with expenses of plebiscite, (b) making the plebiscite provisions more general and correspondingly increasing the discretion of the Commission, and (c) assuring East Prussians equitable access to, and use of the Vistula.[2]

These changes were made in conference and agreement with Mr. Headlam-Morley of the British Delegation, and *the document as changed by us has been sent by him to the drafting committee of the Conference*, according to his instructions.

I indicate clearly in this text three minor changes we made, the provision dealing with police and protection being the only one of importance, and being, we think, an indispensable corollary that it is necessary to state.

II

I also enclose a copy of recommendations Mr. Headlam-Morley and Colonel Kisch are sending their Prime Minister.

I concur in their conclusions (a) *that a plebiscite in the region East of the Vistula is unnecessary and inadvisable, and that the region should be assigned either to East Prussia or to Poland, and* (b) *that assignment to Poland is preferable.* The Danzig decision is major, this minor; and here the need of Poland is greater.

T MS (WP, DLC).
    [1] It is missing in WP, DLC; however, it is printed as Appendix VII to the minutes of the Council of Four, April 22, 1919, 11 a.m.
    [2] About these issues, see the minutes of the meeting of the Council of Four printed at April 18, 1919, 11 a.m.

E N C L O S U R E

NOTE RELATIVE TO THE SETTLEMENT OF THE DANZIG QUESTION AND THE POLISH FRONTIERS IN EAST AND WEST PRUSSIA.

1. The establishment of a free State of Danzig has been approved by the Council of Four. The terms of the final draft for giving effect to this decision are such that when fully understood they should

go far to satisfy Polish public opinion, (though this is not the case as regards Polish official opinion, which is of little account).

2. It is submitted that the proposal to hold a plebiscite in the MARIENBURG-MARIENWERDER region needs further consideration in the light of the following facts:

(a) In view of the fact that the area in which it is proposed to hold a plebiscite contains over 80% of Germans, the result of such a plebiscite is a foregone conclusion. It appears, therefore, to follow:

    (i) that if the wishes of the inhabitants of this area are the predominant consideration, the area should be definitely assigned to East Prussia;

or (ii) that if considerations other than ethnographic make it of great importance to allot this small area to Poland, it should definitely be so assigned.

(b) With reference to (a) above, the decision to constitute a Free State of Danzig entirely alters the considerations which led the Supreme Council to object to the inclusion of the MA-RIENBURG-MARIENWERDER region in Poland.

(c) The DANZIG-MLAWA-WARSAW railway is the main and by far the shortest line of communication between Danzig and the centre and capital of Poland.

If this railway is allowed to run through territory either Polish or belonging to the State of Danzig, the communications of Poland with the sea can be regarded as adequately secured. If a block of German (East Prussian) territory is interposed astride the railway between Poland and the State of Danzig, such communications could not be regarded as either free or secure.

The matter is therefore one of vital importance to the life and trade of Poland as a whole. On the other hand the assignment of the region in question to East Prussia would not materially assist in maintaining connection between East Prussia and Germany, for which it is impossible to arrange direct territorial access and which is being provided for by other means.

(d) In view of what has been said above, the undersigned recommend that, subject to the modifications involved by the approved draft for constituting a Free State of Danzig, the frontiers of East Prussia (including the boundary of the plebiscite area) as recommended in Report No. 1 of the Polish Commission be adhered to. In submitting this recommendation, it is assumed that the Treaty Clauses will provide for

the fullest possible guarantees for the protection of cultural
minorities.   (sd.) F. H. Kisch.
                          (sd.) J. W. Headlam Morley

T MS (WP, DLC).

From the Peace Conference Diary of Bernard Mannes Baruch

April 21, 1919

I had a conference with Dr. Taussig,[1] who agreed to get the proofs of the entire subject matter of the Economic Commission ready and corrected for me by Wednesday morning, with the O.K. or comments of the various men doing the work.

Colonel House and the President came in, and the President discussed with me the appointment of the two American representatives on the private committee which is to investigate the economic conditions of Europe. I informed him that America had an obligation to fulfill, and that we could not very well depart from Europe and leave the people here in their present condition. I referred more particularly to the smaller and newer countries, which might become so involved with the larger powers that they would be unable to disentangle themselves. I urged that we should help these people, but only to the extent that they would help themselves; that we should not lend money with a free and open hand, but with a stinted hand, in order that the individual might continue to help himself, and in order that the government should not get control of the individuals and industries to the extent of throttling them, but should force them to help themselves.

I told him exactly how the formation of the committee had come about; that Lord Robert Cecil had been at me for some time; that I had insisted to Lord Robert that anything that could be done by the various governments to loosen the blockades and restrictions should first be done; that while I was discussing these matters with Lord Robert, he took up this question with Colonel House, and that he agreed—as the correspondence shows—to appoint a committee of two men each, quite private, to investigate the matters in Europe. Lord Robert was very much annoyed with me, because he thought that I might try to block the matter.

[1] With Wilson's approval, Taussig had come to Paris in March as an economic adviser to the A.C.N.P. See WW to F.W. Taussig, Feb. 27, 1919, TLS (Letterpress Books, WP, DLC), and F. W. Taussig to WW, March 3, 1919, TLS (WP, DLC).

From the Diary of Vance Criswell McCormick

April 21 (Monday) [1919]

Worked in office until 7.30. Russian Problem most interesting as we have agreed to relieve Bolshevist Russia and insist that the Bolshevists stop fighting, when the State Dept. comes along with another proposal to recognize the Omsk government, they getting stronger every day.[1] If we recognize Omsk, will it be breaking faith in regard to proposal of relief through Nansen. Lenine will not agree to stop fighting for food unless we get anti-Bolshevists to agree to stop also. This is hard on Kolchalk as he is winning now. I am going to put this new situation to the President. Unfortunately, almost impossible to have satisfactory talk with the President on this matter on account of other pressing peace terms now concluding.

[1] It is missing in the State Department files. However, it was apparently a telegram from Polk, which was forwarded to McCormick in E. T. Williams to V. C. McCormick, April 18, 1919, TLI (SDR, RG 256, 861.01/11, DNA). Williams commented on the enclosure as follows: "This yellow should have been sent to you. . . . I am convinced that Mr. Polk is right in insisting upon the consideration of the recognition of the Omsk Government. He [Kolchak] is supported by Denikin and by the Archangel Government and by all Siberia. Ivanoff and Semenoff as well as Horvath are not fully satisfied, but they are the imperialistic crowd and we play into their hands by refusing to strengthen Koltchak."

From the Diary of Ray Stannard Baker

Monday April 21 [1919]

I had quite a long talk with Mr. Wilson after the meeting this afternoon. He told me fully about the Adriatic negotiations which are now at complete deadlock. I conveyed to him the message of Orlando sent through Tozzi accounting for the attacks in the Italy press, which Orlando deprecates. Orlando wished to assure the President of his great personal respect & admiration. The President said that he had always liked Orlando & had found him a gentleman & a man of his word. He thought, however, that the Italians had worked themselves up to the point of insanity. He said Orlando told him that a break meant the ruin of Italy, but it was with Italians a "point of honor." The President has prepared a strong statement of the case which he will put out in case a break comes. I was allowed to tell almost nothing to the correspondents this evening. The meeting of the Italian parliament has been postponed until May 6 which will somewhat relieve the situation. The whole matter is very critical. The President also explained to me why they had refused to accept the first delegates named by the Germans.

From the Diary of Edith Benham

April 21, 1919

These are very trying days for the P. with the continual wrangling over the Italian question. L. George and Clemenceau had agreed day before yesterday to stand by him and refuse Fiume to the Italians. This morning—no, yesterday morning—they came and said they had been considering it over night and had decided they must stand by the pact of London. Today the P. said that Orlando, for whom he says he has not only a liking but a real affection— and I haven't often heard him say that—made a very moving speech at the Big 4 conference. He read this speech which was really Italy's ultimatum of what she must have or withdraw, and then when the end came he gave a little gulp, went to the window and sobbed piteously. He said that Sonnino, too, was very moving for he had brought his country into the war and had been responsible for the death of nearly a million (I think the figures are correct) men, and yet it was really a futile sacrifice in view of the fact that the conference would have given Italy a more extended coast line, yet not all she championed. He said, "I shall go home to my people with all these deaths on my conscience."

The P. said if Orlando would only go home to his parliament and tell them the truth he was sure they would be far more respected. He, the P., has written some sort of a statement of O. to make[1] and yet with all that he is afraid to go home. This was after dinner he said this. We always sit in Mrs. W.'s little sitting room downstairs, around the open fire if it is cold, as it was tonight. After he had finished talking, he took us into his room to see the contour maps, and to show what Italy claims and what she will get. He said he thought he would calm himself down by playing solitaire. He always does that when he is tired or annoyed, though he plays at other times, too, but not so absorbedly. Curiously enough he never knew how to play until this Mrs. W. taught him. . . .

Tonight the P. gave us the statement which appears in the papers tomorrow about our attitude to Italy and the question of Fiume. This contains about the same matter which was in his letter for Orlando to read to the Italian parliament and which he said he would not read. The French press he says will be violent about it, for Clemenceau said several papers had been bought up and he knew the price paid for them. He was very bitter about Italy's part in the war and that she had sold herself to the highest bidder. Now, of course, they are refusing to sign the peace negotiations with Germany, if they can't have Fiume. The P. says he fears all this will give heart to the Germans who are naturally anxious to have the Allies fight.

In speaking of the construction of his speeches he said his father had been so careful to drill him in construction and when he wrote anything he arranged his subjects under headings and it was often necessary to rearrange the headings so as to make the whole read well.

¹ That is, Wilson's memorandum on the Adriatic question printed at April 14, 1919.

To Albert Sidney Burleson

Paris, 21 April 1919.

Please convey following to Burleson QUOTE Have greatly sympathized with you in your difficulties. Warmly appreciate the attitude of your cable of yesterday and rejoice to learn through Tumulty that the telephone strike has been settled. END QUOTE.

Woodrow Wilson.

T telegram (WP, DLC).

To Carter Glass

Paris, 21 April, 1919.

For Secretary Glass. Thank you for your cable of the 15th about the issue between the Industrial Board and the Director General of Railways. I had come to exactly the same conclusion.

Woodrow Wilson.

T telegram (WP, DLC).

A Telegram and a Letter to William Cox Redfield

Paris, 21 April 1919.

Tumulty, White House, Washington, D. C.

Please convey following to Redfield QUOTE It is with sincere regret that I learn of the dissolution of the Industrial Board,¹ because I believe that it attempted a very useful piece of work, and I hope that you will convey to the members of the Board an expression of my appreciation of their efforts. But it became evident that what the Board had attempted was in fact so difficult as to be next to impossible and I have learned that the Attorney General entertains conclusive doubts as to the legality of the effort we were so hopefully making. I can therefore only acquiesce in the dissolution of the Board with sincere regret that what we attempted proved impossible. END QUOTE. For Tumulty Greatly appreciate your telegrams. We all join in most affectionate messages.

Woodrow Wilson.

T telegram (WP, DLC).
  [1] See WCR to WW, April 19, 1919.

My dear Mr. Secretary: Paris, 21 April, 1919.

I beg that you will read the enclosed copy of a letter from Mr. Hoover,[1] which seems to me to cover the matter of wheat prices to which you call my attention much more thoroughly than any of the rest of us could cover it, because it is written in view of the whole world situation. Will you not please accept it as my reply to your important letter of April 4th?[2]

With best wishes,

Cordially and sincerely yours,   [Woodrow Wilson]

CCL (WP, DLC).
  [1] HCH to WW, April 18, 1919.
  [2] WCR to WW, April 4, 1919, Vol. 56.

To William Bauchop Wilson

Paris, 21 April 1919.

For Secretary Wilson QUOTE Am very glad to allot sixty thousand dollars to the Department of Labor for mediation purposes from the appropriation for National Security and Defense.[1] END QUOTE.

Woodrow Wilson.

T telegram (WP, DLC).
  [1] Wilson was responding to WBW to WW, April 19, 1919.

Two Telegrams to Joseph Patrick Tumulty

Paris, 21 April 1919.

Please be kind enough to say to William D. Upshaw, Member of Congress from Georgia, that of course there will be no embargo after peace is proclaimed and that in the meantime every restriction which the United States could remove has been removed.

Woodrow Wilson.

Paris, 21 April 1919.

Please say to Julius H. Barnes that his message of the 18th is received and deeply appreciated.   Woodrow Wilson.

T telegrams (WP, DLC).

Cary Travers Grayson to Joseph Patrick Tumulty

Paris (Received April 21, 1919 11:08 a.m.)

The President is not going to do anything inconsistent with League of Nations. Situation still very tense. GEORGE WASHINGTON returns home with troops but arrangements have been made to have at least one transport available each week. In addition battleship ARIZONA, which does not carry soldiers, is held here for emergency.

Love to Mrs. Grayson and birthday greetings to young fellow.[1] Wish him many hundred happy returns. All well.

Grayson.

T telegram (J. P. Tumulty Papers, DLC).
[1] That is, James Gordon Grayson, who was celebrating his first birthday.

From William Shepherd Benson

My dear Mr. President,   Paris, 21 April 1919.

A cable received from the Navy Department announces that you have been pleased to present me with the Distinguished Service Medal for exceptionally meritorious and distinguished service as Chief of Naval Operations throughout the war with the Central Powers.

It gives me unbounded gratification and pleasure to accept this expression of appreciation of my services.

It affords me special personal gratification to know that I have performed this service under a Commander-in-Chief who has done more than any other man in promoting man's humanity to man.

Very sincerely yours,   W. S. Benson

TLS (WP, DLC).

From the Diary of Dr. Grayson

Tuesday, April 22, 1919.

The President arose early and immediately after breakfast went to his study. When the time came for the Big Four to meet, Signor

Orlando, the Italian Premier, failed to put in an appearance. The question of the disposal of the Shantung Peninsula became the order of the day, and the Japanese representatives put in an appearance to argue that inasmuch as the Chinese agreements with the Germans covering the disposal of Kaio Chow ante-dated the war, they automatically reverted to Japan when Japan expelled Germany from the Peninsula. The morning session was devoted to the hearing of the Japanese position, and in the afternoon the Chinese representatives presented briefs demanding that the situation revert back to what it was before Germany forced her entry into Chinese affairs. The Chinese were especially insistent in their arguments declaring that if Japan were allowed to continue under existing circumstances, it would only be a few years before China became entirely a "vassal" state. No decision was reached on the subject, and consideration of it was finally adjourned until tomorrow.

The President, Mrs. Wilson and I had lunch together, and immediately after lunch I said to the President: "You are going to ride in the open car this afternoon, are you not, Mr. President? It is a beautiful, sun-shiny day, and I would suggest that you use the open car." He turned around to me and said: "Who said there is going to be any car?" I smilingly told him that I had said so. At 2:15 he and Mrs. Wilson went out in an open car. In this connection it did me quite a lot of good to realize that after all the President appreciated my care for him. Only this morning my attention had been called to an article that had appeared in an American publication, which said:

"The President went to bed 'by my direction,' announced Admiral Grayson." (Then, sarcastically, the paper added): "May be so, but he (the President) was never known to go anywhere else by anybody else's direction."

This was an entirely erroneous conception of President Wilson's attitude. It is only fair to say from my standpoint, professionally, he is willing at all times to take advice and to accept suggestions. Whenever I speak to him about his health he frequently says: "I really haven't time to follow your suggestion, but if you think that I should do this, all right." Sometimes he jokingly says: "I take orders from you as a health master, but, remember, that I am your Commander-in-Chief, and I always reserve the right to issue orders to you on other matters."

It is rather interesting to recall that the actual quotation which the New York publication commented upon was not only prepared but insisted on by the President himself at the time of his recent illness. At that time I had prepared a simple statement but the

President directed that I should include in it the fact that he "had gone to bed" *by my direction.*

The President and Mrs. Wilson and I had dinner, and during the dinner we discussed the show we attended last night. The President referred to the more amusing characters and repeated some of the dialogues. Before leaving the President at 9:30 he showed me the lines drawn by the secret Pact of London, calling my attention to the subject of Fiume. He has a topographical map in his study of Italy, Jugo-Slavia, and the Dalmatian Coast. He discussed the whole subject with me showing just what Italy was claiming.

After leaving the President I went to the Crillon Hotel to attend a reception given by the Secretary of State and Mrs. Lansing in honor of the new Ambassador to France, Mr. Hugh C. Wallace, and Mrs. Wallace.

A Translation of a Telegram from Keishiro Matsui to Viscount Yasuya Uchida

Paris, April 22, 1919

No. 694 Concerning the resolution of the Shantung problem: Despite the repeated requests of our delegates for discussion of this matter since President Wilson's return to France, Council of Four meetings have been solely taken up with resolving other issues of contention among the powers. Therefore as the date for fixing the preliminary treaty provisions is now fast drawing near, on our part we motivated Balfour to speak up on the urgency of resolving the Shantung problem. As a result, the subject will finally be discussed this week. On April 21, Japanese delegates Makino and Chinda were sent to pay a visit to President Wilson to seek his opinion. The subsequent private meeting lasted an hour or more, during which diverse topics were discussed, as summarized below.

Our delegates first explained generally the peculiar features of Japan's current cabinet organization and her foreign policy, especially that toward China, and ended by advocating the demands of the Imperial government concerning Shantung and requesting the President's support. The President, after listening very carefully, replied as follows. He maintained the premise that, for the sake of the peace treaty, i.e., in creating the terms of a peace treaty designed to preserve a lasting world peace, the powers, in upholding the fundamental principles involved, might inevitably have to rise above their immediate interests. Turning to the pending problem over Fiume, he explained that, out of his concern that the demands of

Italy would result in oppression of Slavic peoples, which would again cause unrest in the future, he had to continue to maintain his opposition. Then, changing the subject, he spoke of the great importance of peace in the Far East to the general prospect for peace in the world and of the record of aggressive actions in China by foreign powers, including Germany, taking advantage of that country's weakness. About relations between China and Japan, it seemed that the Chinese both feared Japan's power and, at the same time, were in great apprehension of Japan's intentions. Certainly these conditions causing the unease of the Chinese people did not contribute to international stability. Therefore, he believed it possible that the territory which Germany was now to give up should first, on the basis of the Lansing proposal, be given over to the Allied countries as a whole, and afterwards, the disposition of these possessions should be decided by treaty provisions based on thorough discussion. He was speaking solely on the basis of his political philosophy and ideals.

Our delegates maintained that the settlement of the Shantung problem was different from the question of other German possessions insofar as China and Japan had the treaty of 1915 which had already stipulated the means of this settlement. In addition, some of the official documents exchanged between the two countries after China's entrance into the war in 1918 also constituted an agreement on the means of putting into effect this arrangement. As some of the terms of these provisions were already in effect, there should be no cause for misunderstanding between the two countries now. In other words, the Shantung problem was only a matter of executing these treaty arrangements, which they explained in detail. Next, they pointed out that this treaty had already been made public in Japan, and the Japanese people believed that at the peace negotiations the Shantung problem would be settled by its provisions. If the peace conference was to use an entirely different method to resolve the problem, naturally this would give an unexpected shock to Japan and arouse the resentment of her people. They explained Japan's position that, if the already existing and clearly stated treaty were disregarded and the problem was decided by a completely different mechanism for settlement, it was difficult to judge whether in the end the plenipotentiaries might not have to forego signing the preliminary treaty. A short while ago, when the Chinese Foreign Minister[1] had stopped in Japan on the way to the peace conference, he had met the Japanese Foreign Minister[2] privately, and some steps toward peaceful cooperation

[1] That is, Lu Cheng-hsiang.
[2] That is, Viscount Uchida.

between the two countries at the peace conference were gained, especially in light of the promise of delivery of aid from Japan to China. He was seemingly very pleased to hear from the Japanese Foreign Minister the pledge to return the leased territory and promises of cooperative aid, and the relationship between China and Japan seemed cooperative and harmonious. But this same plenipotentiary and his delegation have completely reversed this position after arriving in Paris, and the fact is that they are trying to disseminate hostile propaganda attacking Japan. As a result of these distortions, the Shantung problem itself is no longer just a matter of leased territory, but has been transformed into a grave issue in the general political situation in the Far East.

The President seemed to gain some appreciation of our standpoint. Then, again changing the subject, he spoke of the railway problem and his fear that, if the Japanese were to succeed completely to German rights in this area, this would for the Chinese be simply a repetition of the type of oppression Germany had previously exerted. Our representatives replied that the Shantung railway, by agreement with China reached in 1918, was to be undertaken as a Sino-Japanese joint venture, with the extension of railway lines financed by loans from Japan. As for the detailed provisions, the Chinese government was now negotiating them with Japanese financial leaders and, beyond that, a part of these talks had already resulted in the raising of advance money amounting to twenty million yen. The President responded that, while the Shantung railway had from its beginning taken the form of a Sino-German joint venture, this had been in name only, and that it had actually been a purely German railway. What the Chinese feared was that the Japanese would simply substitute themselves in the German role and, just as before, the joint venture would be nominal. On our side we replied that between China and Japan there already existed, in Manchuria and elsewhere, joint ventures like lumbering companies which operated very successfully both in form and substance. China's doubts about this were unfounded. Of course, because the nature of the Shantung railway had originally been viewed as an extension of the leased territory, German political authority, firmly established in its leased possessions, naturally extended into the operation of the railway, and this was the cause of Chinese distress. Now, however, Japan's position would be the opposite. In returning the leased territory to China, the political and military aspects of the railway concession will be extinguished and only the economic aspects will remain. Therefore, the outstanding record of other Sino-Japanese joint ventures should ease all doubts.

However, this issue aside, for Japan to do something like return the leased territories in the name of the Five Powers or other steps which were meaningless or damaging to her credibility would be a grave problem for the Japanese people's reputation and honor, one which they definitely could not accept. The President reiterated that there would be no such damage to or doubts about Japan and stated that the concept of the Allied countries was one that included Japan as one of the Five Powers, so concessions to the Five Powers also embraced the meaning of concessions being made to Japan. By this same reasoning, Japan's mandate rule had already been recognized in the case of the South Pacific islands and other colonial possessions. Our representatives stated that, whereas mandate rule in places like colonies where the native peoples still lacked modern civilization was intended to foster development, in cases like China, a country with a developed culture, disposition of territory had to follow different principles. They strongly argued that the two cases could not be discussed as one.

At this point President Wilson explained his own idealistic inter-pretation of the China problem. In the past, the foreign policy of the Great Powers toward China had been aggressive. (text missing) The Japanese side explained that, during the last period of Japan's China policy, the hard-line approach had gradually weakened, to be replaced by the increasing prevalence of the so-called moderate line's notably sincere Sino-Japanese friendly and cooperative ap-proach. The present Japanese cabinet belongs to this moderate group. The current policy trend represents a significant transitional period for China policy, when the hard line advocated by one group was being rejected. While it was not yet possible to speak among Japan's current political leaders (just as among many leaders of the great powers) of definite legislation concerning such problems as the abolition of spheres of influence, some were advocating this. Japan would also find satisfaction if there were true application of such ideals as the open-door policy and equal opportunity. Indeed, in some instances, Japan's government had indicated a willingness to put into effect the revocation of extraterritoriality on condition that the other powers agreed to do so, and to give aid to China. Now that Japan is prepared to accept such legislation and is not ungenerous in her offers of aid to help China raise her status in the world, it is indeed regrettable and unexpected that the Chinese delegation at the peace conference has singled out Japan for hostile treatment.

The President seemed especially interested in this explanation of Japan's China policy and stated that, regarding this problem, there should be repeated opportunities for our exchanges of opinion. In any case, today's meeting has been very fruitful, and he has learned the details of several important facts. He departed after saying that he must directly meet with Lansing to discuss these subjects.

The evaluation of our members attending this meeting was that the President could not be said to agree completely with Japanese demands or to have a favorable outlook toward Japan. He seemed now to understand the facts of the treaty and the sudden shift in position of the Chinese plenipotentiaries. Lansing, a lawyer by profession who sometimes alludes to the interpretation that the treaty of 1915 was invalidated by China's entry into the war, especially has many connections with American and British reporters and other supporters of the propaganda from the Chinese side. While it cannot be anticipated that the President has come to accept our demands enough to change this interpretation of Lansing, who is so partial to the China sympathizers, we think that we have given him the information and facts with which to understand our position. Before parting, our delegates stressed the reasons for the urgency of completely resolving this problem before the provisional treaty is settled, and the President responded that he fully understood this concern.

Printed in *Nihon gaiko bunsho* [Japanese diplomatic documents] (150 vols. to date, Tokyo, 1926-), 1919, Vol. 3a, pp. 244-47.

From the Diary of Ray Stannard Baker

Tuesday the 22nd [April 1919]

I had a long talk with the President in Mrs. Wilson's sitting room this afternoon. He went fully into the Japanese question as presented during the day. He is also standing like a rock on the Italian question. He says he will not sign the treaty if the Italians are allowed to seize Fiume & the Dalmatian coast. Lloyd-George & Clemenceau, who are more or less bound by the London treaty must either side with him or with the Italians. The President now expects the Italians to break away—& says he would not care so much if it were not for the effect it may have in Germany. He has a kind of still determination—sat by the sunny window, where Mrs. Wilson was at work with bits of crochet-pattern—a huge bunch of white lilacs perfuming the room—& talked to me about decisions which may make or unmake the world. He has given way here & there to get a settlement but has now reached the last trenches. I brought along an interesting article by Dr. Pupin, giving an account of the Italian point of view & describing the devotion of the Serbs to the President—one Serbian woman having knit him a pair of socks. I showed it to Mrs. Wilson, who was much amused by it.

Hankey's and Mantoux's Notes of a Meeting of the
Council of Four[1]

President Wilson's House,
I.C.-175B.   Paris, April 22, 1919, 11 a.m.

[Wilson, Lloyd George, Clemenceau, Hankey, and Mantoux were
present. It was agreed that a committee (Haskins, Headlam-Morley,
and Tardieu) would examine the draft articles prepared by the
French government in regard to Alsace-Lorraine.]

2. PRESIDENT WILSON informed his colleagues that M. Orlando
had sent word that he was unable to be present.

3. M. CLEMENCEAU handed Mr. Lloyd George a copy of a letter
he had written to the Emir Feisal. (*Appendix I.*) The Emir Feisal
had replied that he was satisfied and that he expected soon to be
back in Paris. M. CLEMENCEAU undertook to give Mr. Lloyd George
a copy of the Emir Feisal's letter. He asked what was to be done
about the Commission.

MR. LLOYD GEORGE said that he thought the Commission should
soon start. It was settled so far as he was concerned.

4. M. CLEMENCEAU handed round copies of the German official
reply to the last communication in regard to their coming to Versailles. (*Appendix II.*) He said that he could not undertake to guarantee to the Germans entire free intercourse.

MR. LLOYD GEORGE suggested that they must have communication with their Government at Weimar.

M. CLEMENCEAU agreed.

PRESIDENT WILSON said that was all they asked for.

M. CLEMENCEAU said he would have to take precautions that they
should not have free movement at Versailles as there would be a
serious danger of their being mobbed. He was responsible for their
safety. At M. CLEMENCEAU's request President Wilson drafted the
following note on which the reply should be based: "The Allied and
Associated Powers will, of course, grant to the German Delegates
full freedom of movement for the execution of their mission and
unrestricted telegraphic communication with their Government."
(This was agreed to.)

5. M. CLEMENCEAU handed round the attached draft representing
the agreement reached as regards the demilitarization of the west
bank of the Rhine. (*Appendix III.*)

PRESIDENT WILSON said he had already communicated it to Sir
Maurice Hankey.

[1] The complete text of Hankey's minutes is printed in *PPC*, V, 112-22.

MR. LLOYD GEORGE agreed that it was comprehensive enough.

Appendix III was approved and Sir Maurice Hankey was instructed to send it to the Secretary-General for the Drafting Committee.

6. M. CLEMENCEAU handed round the attached document headed "Articles concerning Guarantees of Execution of the Treaty," which had already been agreed to by President Wilson on April 20th. (*Appendix IV.*)

MR. LLOYD GEORGE commented on the length of the period contemplated for occupation, namely, 15 years, which seemed considerable. He supposed that the British Government was not asked to keep troops there so long.

M. CLEMENCEAU said all he asked was a battalion with the flag.

MR. LLOYD GEORGE said he must insist on the difficulty which the British Government would have in maintaining any larger number of troops. The people of England insisted on the disappearance of compulsory service immediately the war was over. He had had considerable difficulties at home since the election owing to the extension of compulsory service for 12 months.

M. CLEMENCEAU drew attention to the words "by International forces" in Article I, which apparently had not been included in the copy he had left with President Wilson. He said he could not go to his people and say that there were no forces of the Allied and Associated Powers. He only asked for a flag to be shown.

MR. LLOYD GEORGE asked if 15 years was the maximum. He hoped it was not conditioned by the extension of the Treaty. Indemnities, for example, could not be paid within 15 years. He hoped he understood correctly that there would not be any question of retaining forces after that.

M. CLEMENCEAU said that was not the intention.

Appendix IV was agreed to and Sir Maurice Hankey was instructed to forward it to the Secretary-General for the Drafting Committee.[2]

§Mantoux's notes:

Lloyd George. You must not expect that we will leave British troops in Germany for fifteen years.

Clemenceau. I must prepare to write in this text that the occupation will be done by international troops. All that I am asking you for, if absolutely necessary, is to leave me one battalion and a flag.

Lloyd George. You know with what impatience England is waiting for the abolition of compulsory military service. The problem is

---

[2] These articles were approved verbatim by the Drafting Committee and were included as Appendix V to the minutes of the Council of Four printed at April 30, 1919, 11 a.m.

different for France because it is an institution to which your population is accustomed.

Clemenceau. I do not know if the word "international" is found in President Wilson's copy.

Wilson. Why not say that these territories will be occupied for a fixed period of time, without any other indication?

Clemenceau. The Germans will ask by whom. I will also be asked that here. If I do not have your flag beside mine on the left bank of the Rhine, I will not be able to go before our Parliament.

Lloyd George. These fifteen years: are they indicated here as an absolute limit? Can it not vary with the payments made by Germany?

Clemenceau. No, unless Germany refuses to pay. If the League of Nations states that Germany is not fulfilling her commitments, we can prolong or even renew the occupation.

Lloyd George. It's all right; I accept.

Wilson. You also have my assent. §

7. M. CLEMENCEAU handed round a document entitled "Treaty between France and the United States," which had been approved by him and President Wilson on April 20th. (*Appendix V.*)

PRESIDENT WILSON explained to Mr. Lloyd George that he had made a point that it was not wise in this matter to have a tripartite agreement but a Treaty between the United States of America and France and another Treaty between Great Britain and France.

MR. LLOYD GEORGE said he thought that would do for Great Britain and instructed Sir Maurice Hankey to show it to Mr. Balfour.

Subject to Mr. Balfour's agreement, this was accepted.

(Note by the Secretary.)

(*Mr. Balfour agreed to it after the Meeting*)

8. M. CLEMENCEAU handed round an Article concerning the independence of German-Austria. (*Appendix VI.*)

This was accepted and Sir Maurice Hankey was instructed to forward it to the Secretary-General for the Drafting Committee.

9. M. CLEMENCEAU reminded President Wilson that he had undertaken to complete the Articles in regard to Dantzig in accordance with certain alterations that had been agreed.

PRESIDENT WILSON then produced the document in *Appendix VII* and proposed that it should be sent direct to the Drafting Committee.

MR. LLOYD GEORGE agreed and Sir Maurice Hankey was instructed to forward *Appendix VII* to the Secretary-General for the Drafting Committee.

10. PRESIDENT WILSON asked Mr. Lloyd George if the British

Government were sending additional troops to Archangel. He had had a communication from General Bliss[3] which seemed to indicate that the local British Command instead of contemplating withdrawal intended to take steps to link up the Russian forces in the north with those in Siberia, which would involve an advance to Kotlas and Viatka. General Bliss's communication had also suggested that 12,000 British reinforcements were being sent.

MR. LLOYD GEORGE said he thought there must be some misunderstanding. Great importance was attached to secrecy in regard to the withdrawal from north Russia and possibly this was some local bluff to convey the impression that no withdrawal was intended. He did not think that the reinforcements contemplated were nearly so large. He undertook to enquire into the matter.

APPENDIX I TO I.C.175.B.

[Translation[4]]

Copy of Letter From M. Clemenceau to the Emir Feisal

YOUR HIGHNESS: I am happy, on the occasion of your return to the East, to confirm what I said to you in our conversation of Sunday, April 13.

The French Government, desirous of assuring to Syria, as well as to Armenia, Mesopotamia and the other countries of the Orient which have been liberated by the victory of the Entente, a regime of liberty and progress in conformity with the principles by which it has always been inspired and which are the basis of the deliberations of the Peace Conference, declares that it recognizes the right of Syria to independence in the form of a federation of autonomous local communities corresponding to the traditions and wishes of their populations.

France is prepared to give material and moral assistance to this emancipation of Syria.

In referring to the needs of the country and the interests of its people as well as to the historic role which France has played Your Highness recognized that France is the Power qualified to give Syria the assistance of the various advisers necessary to establish order and bring about the progress which the peoples of Syria desire.

When the time comes to work out more detailed plans to assure the collaboration of France with Syria, they should be in conformity with the spirit of our arrangements. I take pleasure, on the occasion of parting from Your Highness, to confirm to you in writing and to

---

[3] T. H. Bliss to WW, April 18, 1919 (first letter of that date).
[4] This translation from *PPC*, V, 115.

testify to the harmony which will not fail to inspire the representatives of France in Syria.

Accept (etc.)   G. CLEMENCEAU
Paris, April 17, 1919.

SPA, April 21, 1919.
18 h.30.

From General NUDANT, President of the C.I.P.A. to Field Marshal FOCH, and PRIME MINISTER, PARIS.

No. 802.

1. German Government supposing that, after the remittance of the project of the preliminaries, it is intended to negotiate on their contents, has appointed as delegates with all the necessary powers: Count BROCKDORFF-RANTZAU, Secretary for Foreign Affairs, Doctor LANDSBERG, Minister of Justice, Mr. GIESBERTS, General-Post-Master, Mr. LEINERT, President of the Prussian National Chamber, Doctor MELCHIOR, Professor SHÜCKING.[5]

Names of the persons who will accompany the delegates will be given later.

2. The German Government is ready to send to VERSAILLES the above mentioned persons if they will be granted their liberty of movement and free use of Telegraph and Telephone for communications with the German Government. The German Government keeps the right of appointing later on experts for certain questions of Peace.

3. Delegates will probably not be able to leave before April 27 or 28.

Continuation of wire 892 of April 21st, 893.

1. The total number of German delegates and suite will be of about 75.

2. Besides, the delegates will be accompanied by a telegraphic personnel of about 40 men, who will organise and use a "central" whose installation has been promised by the French Telegraphical Mission in BERLIN as reciprocity for the installation of a Special Allied "Central" in BERLIN.

3. German Government asks for immediate dispatch to VERSAILLES for the preparation of the installation of the German Delegation, and advanced party composed of Mr. Von WACHENDORF, Conseiller d'Ambassade, Mr. Walter, Inspector of Postal Services

---

[5] The full names of those persons not heretofore identified in this series were Otto Landsberg, Johann Giesberts, Robert Leinert, and Walther Max Adrian Schücking.

and Mr. DUNKER, Food Official.[6] This personnel is actually at SPA and ready to leave at first notice.

APPENDIX III.
INSTRUCTIONS TO DRAFTING COMMITTEE
FOR THE MILITARIZATION OF GERMAN TERRITORY WEST
OF THE RHINE.[7]

The maintenance or building of fortifications west of a line drawn fifty kilometers east of the Rhine forbidden to Germany. The maintenance of armed forces, either permanently or temporarily, forbidden within the area defined above, as well as all military manoeuvers of every kind and the maintenance of physical facilities for mobilization.

Any violation of these conditions to be regarded as an hostile act against the signatories to the treaty and as calculated to disturb the peace of the world.

As long as the present treaty remains in force a pledge by Germany to respond to any enquiry that the Council of the League of Nations may deem necessary.

APPENDIX IV.
ARTICLES CONCERNING THE GUARANTEES OF EXECUTION
OF THE TREATY.

(As approved by President Wilson and M. Clemenceau
on April, 20th)

1. As a guarantee of the execution by Germany of the present treaty, German territories west of the Rhine, including the Bridgeheads, are to be occupied by international forces during fifteen years from signature of the present treaty on.

2. If the conditions of the treaty are executed by Germany, occupation to be successively reduced according to following schedule:

a) to be evacuated after 5 years: the bridgehead of Köln and the territories north of a line running along the Ruhr then along the railroad: Jülich, Düren, Euskirchen, Rheinbach, then the road Rheinbach to Sinzig, and reaching the Rhine at the confluence with the Ahr river (the roads, railroads and localities above mentioned included in the occupied territory).

b) to be evacuated after ten years: the bridgehead of Coblentz and the territories north of line to be drawn from the intersection between the frontiers of Belgium, Germany and Holland, running

---

[6] These three persons cannot be further identified.

[7] That is, concerning the Allied occupation of the left bank of the Rhine.

about 4 Kilometres South of Aix-la-Chapelle, then to and following the crest of Forst Gemünd, then east of the railroad of the Urft Valley, then along Blankenheim, Valdorf, Dreis, Ulmen to and following the Mosel from Bremm to Mohren, then passing along Kappel, Simmern, then following the ridge of the heights between Simmern and the Rhine and reaches the river at Bacharach (all localities, valleys, roads and railroads above mentioned included in the occupied territory.

c) to be evacuated after fifteen years the bridgehead of Mainz, the bridgehead of Kehl and the remainder of German territories still occupied).

3. In case, either during, or after this fifteen years delay, the Interallied Commission of Reparations recognise that Germany refuse to execute the whole or part of the conditions agreed upon by her according to the present treaty, the international re-occupation of part or the whole of the areas defined by Article 2, will take place immediately.

4. If, before fifteen years, Germany meets all the engagements taken by her according to the terms of the present treaty, the withdrawal of the international troops would immediately follow.

APPENDIX V
TREATY
BETWEEN FRANCE AND UNITED STATES
(as approved by President Wilson and M. Clemenceau
on April 20th.)

Between the Governments of the United States of America and the Republic of France it is agreed:

1) Any violation by Germany of the engagements taken by her according to articles N^r [blank] N^r [blank] and N^r [blank] of the present treaty to be regarded as an hostile act against the signatories to the treaty and as calculated to disturb the peace of the world.

2) A pledge to be taken by the United States of America to come immediately to the assistance of France as soon as any unprovoked movement of aggression against her is made by Germany.

3) This pledge to be subject to the approval of the Executive Council of the League of Nations and to continue until it is agreed by the Contracting Powers that the League itself affords sufficient protection.

APPENDIX VI TO I.C.175.B.
ARTICLE CONCERNING THE INDEPENDENCE OF GERMAN AUSTRIA
(as approved by President Wilson and M. Clemenceau on
April 20th.)

Germany recognizes the independence of German Austria within the frontiers as defined by the present treaty.

Draft of Articles to be included in the treaty with Germany agreeing

1) To establish the "Free City of Danzig."

2) To include the Free City of Danzig within the Polish Customs frontiers and make it in fact the port of Poland.

3) To hold a plebiscite in a certain district East of the Vistula.

4) To effect agreements granting to Germany and Poland certain rights to, on and over railways needed by them respectively.

(1. Map attached.)

N.B. If this draft is approved, the treaty articles submitted by the Committee on Polish Affairs, and concurred in by the Central Committee, will have to be revised accordingly.

Article 1. The German Government renounces all rights and title over the following territory in favor of the Five Allied and Associated Great Powers:

Take a line from—

(a) position latitude 54° 22' 25" N; longitude 19° 22' 05" E:

(b) in a direction 159° for a distance of one sea mile:

(c) thence to the Light Beacon at the bend of the Elbinger Channel approximately in latitude 54° 19½' N. Longitude 19° 26' E.

(d) from this Light Beacon to the easternmost mouth of the Nogat River bearing approximately 209°.

Keep on the *thalweg* [downstream] of this river up to its junction with the main stream of the Vistula north of Pieckel, and thence follow the thalweg of the main stream northward to a point 5 miles below the railway bridge at Dirschau. Thence continue in a general westerly direction leaving the village of Muhlbanz on the south, and Rambeltsch on the north, and touching at Klein Golmkau the tip of the salient formed by the boundary of *Kreis* [district] Dirschau. Thence westwards along that boundary to the salient formed west of Boschpohl.

From the tip of the salient west of Boschpohl continue westward, leaving the villages of Neu Fiets and Schatarpi on the south. At a point north of Schatarpi turn north-west to the mid-point of the lake west of Lanken leaving the village of Lanken to the north. Thence continue north and northwest to the northern end of the lake. From there continue almost due north to the southern end of the lake. From there continue almost due north to the southern end of the lake immediately north-east of Pollenschin. Thence pass north-east along the median line of the lake to the northern end of it. From this point continue north to the Stangenwalder forest leaving the village of Kamehlea on the west and Neuendorf on the east. Where the line reaches a point due north-west of the village of

Neuendorf turn north-eastward to the Lappinet lake north of Gross Czapielken leaving Krissau on the northwest and Marschau on the southeast. Thence continue to the north-eastern end of the lake and from there north-eastwards as far as the westernmost point of Lake Ottomin leaving the village of Fidlin on the north-west. Thence continue in a north-north-easterly direction between the villages of Klein Kelpin and Mattern. Thence continue northward through the Olivaer forest leaving the villages of Pelonken, Pulver Muhl and Renneberg on the east to a point one kilometre north of the road between Renneberg and Wittstock. From this point continue north-north-east to the Baltic coast crossing the railway north of Stein-fliess.

In delimiting this line on the spot existing Gemeinde [commune] boundaries should be followed as far as is practicable.

Article 2. The Five Allied and Associated Great Powers undertake to establish the town of Danzig, together with the rest of the territory described in Article 1 as an (independent) Free-City (under the title of Freihansestadt Danzig.)

Article 3. A Constitution for the Free City of Danzig shall be drawn up by the duly appointed representatives of the Free City in agreement with a High Commissioner to be appointed by the League of Nations, and shall be placed under the guarantee of the said League. The High Commissioner will also be charged with the duty of dealing, in the first instance, with all differences arising between Poland and the Free City of Danzig of this Treaty, or any arrangements or agreements made thereunder. The High Commissioner shall reside at Danzig.

Article 4: The Five Allied and Associated Great Powers undertake to negotiate an agreement between the Polish Government and the Free City of Danzig which shall come into force at the same time as the establishment of said Free City.

This agreement will include provisions with the following objects:

(a) To effect the inclusion of the Free City of Danzig within the Polish customs frontiers with the right in Poland of police and protection on land and water against smuggling, always provided that there may be clauses in the agreement establishing a free port area therein.

(b) To ensure to Poland the full and unhampered use and service of all waterways, docks, basins, wharves, and other instrumentalities within the territory of the Free City necessary for Polish import and export.

(c) To ensure to Poland the control and administration of the Vistula and of the whole railway system within said Free City except such street and other railways as serve primarily the needs of the

Free City; and of postal, telegraphic and telephonic communication between the port of Danzig and Poland.

The rights conferred in Article 4(c) shall extend also to the development and improvement of the existing railways and other means of communication therein mentioned, and to the lease or purchase through appropriate processes of such land and other property as may be necessary for these purposes.

(d) To provide against any discrimination within the Free City of Danzig to the detriment of citizens of Poland and other persons of Polish origin or speech.

(e) Such foreign relations as may be necessary for the Free City of Danzig will be conducted by the Polish Government; and citizens of the Free City of Danzig when abroad will be entitled to the diplomatic protection of Poland.

Article 5: On the coming into force of the present Treaty German nationals ordinarily resident in the territory described in Article 1 will ipso facto lose their German nationality and become citizens of the Free City of Danzig.

Article 6: Within a period of two years from the coming into force of the present Treaty German nationals, more than eighteen years old, ordinarily resident in the territory described in Article 1, will have the right to opt for German nationality. They must during the ensuing two years transfer their place of residence into Germany.

Option by a husband will cover his wife and option by parents will cover their children less than eighteen years old.

All persons who exercise the right of option referred to above will be entitled to preserve the immovable property which they possess in the territory described in Article 1.

They may carry with them their movable property of every description.

No export or import duties may be imposed upon them in connection with the removal of such property.

Article 7: All property situated within the territory described in Article 1 belonging to the German Government or to the Government of any German State will pass to the Five Allied and Associated Great Powers for transfer to the Free City of Danzig or to the Polish State, as may be equitably determined by the said Five Allied and Associated Great Powers.

Article 8: In a zone including Kreise Stuhm and Rosenberg, and those parts of Kreise Marienburg and Marienwerder which lie to the East of the Vistula, the inhabitants will be called upon to indicate by a vote by commune (Gemeinde) whether they wish the several communes (Gemeinden) within the territory to belong to Poland or East Prussia.

From the time when the present Treaty takes effect, and within a period which shall not exceed a fortnight, the zone delimited above shall be placed under the authority of an International Commission composed of five members, appointed by the Five Allied and Associated Great Powers, and shall be evacuated by German troops.

This Commission, accompanied by the necessary forces should occasion arise, shall have general powers of administration and shall take whatever measures it may deem proper for holding the plebiscite and assuring the liberty, fairness and secrecy of the vote, following the provisions of this treaty regulating the plebiscite to be held in Allenstein as nearly as may be. All decisions of the Commission shall be taken by a majority vote.

All of the expense incurred by the Commission, whether in the exercise of its own functions or in the administration of the zone subjected to the plebiscite, shall be levied upon the local revenues.

At the conclusion of the vote, the Commission shall communicate to the Five Allied and Associated Great Powers a detailed report of the manner in which the vote was conducted, and a proposal for the line which should be adopted as the frontier of East Prussia in this region, taking account of the desires of the inhabitants as expressed by the vote as well as of the geographic and economic situation of the locality. The Five Allied and Associated Great Powers shall then determine the frontier between East Prussia and Poland in this region, leaving to Poland as a minimum for any section of this river the full and complete control of the Vistula, its east bank included, as far east of the river as may be necessary for its regulation and improvement. The said Great Powers shall at the same time formulate regulations securing to the population of East Prussia equitable access to and use of the Vistula for themselves and their goods and for craft controlled by them or owned by them as may best serve their interests. These determinations of frontier, as well as the regulations just mentioned, are accepted in advance as binding by all parties hereto.

As soon as the administration of the portion of the zone assigned to it shall have been assumed by the authorities of East Prussia and of Poland respectively, the powers of the International Commission shall be terminated.

Article 9. A Commission composed of three members, including the High Commissioner, who shall be Chairman, one member named by Germany, and one member named by Poland, shall be constituted within six months after the time when the present Treaty takes effect, to delimit in the field the lines provided for in the foregoing articles.

The decisions taken by a majority vote of the said commission shall be binding on both parties concerned.

Article 10. The Five Allied and Associated Great Powers agree to negotiate agreements between Poland and Germany by which, whether under the form of a general railroad convention to which both States are partners, or in the form of a special agreement between the two States, there shall be secured, on the one hand to Germany, full and adequate railroad facilities for communication between the rest of Germany and East Prussia over the intervening Polish territory, on the other hand there shall be secured to Poland, in the same way, full and adequate railroad facilities for communication between Poland and the City of Danzig over any German territory that may, on the right bank of the Vistula, intervene between Poland and the City of Danzig.

T MS (SDR, RG 256, 180.03401/111, DNA); Mantoux, I, 319.

From Robert Lansing, with Enclosure

My dear Mr. President: Paris, April 22nd, 1919.

I send enclosed a copy of a communication which I have just received from Viscount Chinda, relating to the restoration to China of the leased territory of Kiaochow, in which he explains the desire of his Government to have the question settled in accordance with the provisions of the notes exchanged May 25, 1915, between China and Japan.[1] The notes to which Viscount Chinda refers are those the signature to which was forced from China by the despatch of troops and the issue of an ultimatum demanding assent within forty-eight hours.

The conditions which to the Viscount seem so simple would leave the kernel to Japan and restore the shell to China.

Faithfully yours,   Robert Lansing

TCL (WP, DLC).
[1] Lansing enclosed, also from Chinda, those portions of the Sino-Japanese treaty of May 25, 1915, relating to Shantung Province.

E N C L O S U R E

Viscount Sutemi Chinda to Robert Lansing

Strictly confidential.

My dear Mr. Secretary,   Paris le 31 [21] Avril, 1919

Adverting to our conversation of today, I wish to state that the conditions upon which Japan and China agreed for restoring the leased territory of Kiaochow to China are very simple, as will be seen from the excerpt from the notes exchanged at Peking on May

25, 1915, between the representatives of the two countries, herein enclosed for your reference. These notes, together with the main treaty, were published at the time and will be found among the documents, we had pleasure of producing at the Conference.

I trust, you would not differ with me, if I say that these conditions are only reasonable. To open the port as a commercial port to foreign trade, to establish a Japanese settlement and an international settlement, to settle questions as to the disposal of German public properties, etc., can only be regarded as quite natural and matters of course and necessity.

As to how soon Kiaochow will be handed back to China, I may say that it ought not to take very much time for Japan and China to make actual arrangements for carrying out the conditions already agreed upon, and I need hardly assure you that my Government will be disposed to reach an agreement as to such actual arrangements with utmost speed upon conclusion of the Peace Treaty with Germany.

You seemed to entertain some apprehension as to the future status of the Province of Shantung, but what Japan and China had actually agreed upon concerns only the running of the Shantung Railway upon the basis of a Sino-Japanese Cooperation, and the loans for two railway lines to be built by China in connection with the Shantung Railway, a portion of which has already been handed over to China by Japanese capitalists. These cannot certainly be looked upon as affecting in any way the status of Shantung. These arrangements were made by an exchange of notes on September 24, 1918, copies of which are also enclosed herein for your perusal.[1]

Trusting the above points have been made clear to you, I beg to remain,   Very sincerely yours,   (Sd) V. CHINDA

TCL (WP, DLC).
[1] S. Gotō to Chang Tsung-hsiang, two letters, and Chang Tsung-hsiang to S. Gotō, two letters, all dated Sept. 24, 1918, TCL (WP, DLC).

Hankey's and Mantoux's Notes of a Meeting of the Council of Four[1]

President Wilson's House,

I.C.-175C.   Paris, April 22, 1919, 11:30 a.m.

PRESIDENT WILSON explained that M. Orlando had written to say that he was unable to be present.
§Mantoux's notes:
Clemenceau (to Wilson). This morning I reread our treaty with Japan: it binds us toward her, as well as Great Britain. I want to warn you about it.§

(1) BARON MAKINO read the following statement:

In January last I had the privilege to present and explain before the Supreme Council Japan's claims[2] which we deemed as just and fair in the light of the circumstances which led Japan to take part in the war and of the actual situations created or found in the regions to which the claims related. I wish to take advantage of the opportunity now offered me to explain more fully that part of our claims which relates to the leased territory of Kiaochow and Germany's rights in respect of Shantung province. As will be remembered the Japanese Government sent an ultimatum to Germany on the 15th of August 1914, inviting her to unconditionally hand over the territory to Japan which she intended to restore to China. Germany failed to give answer within the specified time limit and this obliged Japan to have recourse to military and naval forces. In all those steps we acted in consultation and co-operation with England.

The German stronghold at Kiaochow was captured on the 7th of November, 1914, and has, together with the Shantung Railway, remained to this day under Japanese occupation.

Looking to the eventual termination of the war, Japan approached China in January, 1915, with a view to reaching beforehand an agreement as to the basis of the restitution to China of the leased territory of Kiaochow and of disposing other German rights in relation to Shantung, so that Germany might find no pretext to refuse acquiescence in Japan's demands at the final peace conference and that she might not find it possible to recover her influence in China, thereby becoming again a grave menace to the peace of the Far East.

As a result of the negotiations that ensued, a treaty respecting the Province of Shantung, accompanied by an exchange of notes, was signed on the 25th of May, 1915. In that treaty China engaged to recognise all matters that might be agreed upon between the

[1] The complete text of Hankey's minutes is printed in *PPC*, V, 123-34.
[2] See the minutes of the Council of Ten printed at Jan. 27, 1919, 3 p.m., Vol. 54.

Japanese Government and the German Government respecting the disposition of all the rights, interests and concessions, which Germany possessed vis-à-vis China in relation to the Province of Shantung.

By the exchange of notes, Japan declared to China her willingness, in case she acquired the rights of free disposal of the leased territory of Kiaochow, to restore it to China on the following conditions:

1. Opening of the whole of Kiaochow as commercial port;

2. Establishment of a Japanese settlement in the locality to be designated by the Japanese Government;

3. Establishment, if desired by the Powers, of an international settlement;

4. Arrangement to be made, before the return of the said territory is effected, between the Japanese and Chinese Governments, with respect to the disposal of German public establishments and properties and with regard to the other conditions and procedures.

These terms explain themselves, but a few words on some of the points may be found useful. The Japanese settlement, or concession, whose establishment is provided for under condition 2, refers to only a part of urban District to be set apart for the settling of Japanese as well as other nationalities, including Chinese, under a special system and jurisdiction that are found in many of the principal open ports or marts of China.

In reference to the words "the other conditions and procedures," found in condition 4, I may state that they refer to those minor working conditions and procedures to be determined and observed in effecting the restitution of the Leased Territory to China.

Early in the year 1917, Japan began, in conjunction with her Allied Powers, to direct her efforts in inducing China to sever relations with, and if possible to declare war against Germany. China severed her diplomatic relations with Germany on the 14th of March, 1917, and finally on the 14th of August of the same year, she declared war against the latter; that was more than two years after the signing of the aforementioned treaty between Japan and China had taken place.

Later, on the 24th of September, 1918, more than one year after the declaration of war by China and more than three years after the conclusion of the agreement of the 25th of May, 1915, the Chinese Minister at Tokyo[3] exchanged with the Minister for Foreign Affairs of Japan[4] a series of notes, the translations of which

[3] That is, Chang Tsung-hsiang.
[4] That is, Baron Shimpei Gotō.

have already been presented to the Supreme Council.[5] The notes provide, among other things, for the withdrawal of the Japanese Civil Administration, the management of the Tsingtao-Chinan Railway as a joint Sino-Japanese undertaking upon determination of its ownership, and the guarding and policing of the Railway. The Chinese Minister also solicited the aid of the Japanese Government in the matter of arranging for loans for building two railway lines connecting with the Tsingtao-Chinan Railway and practically coinciding with the lines projected by Germany. To this, the Japanese government consented. The preliminary contract covering these loans was made between the Chinese Government and the Japanese bankers, and the Chinese government actually received from the bankers an advance of twenty million yen according to the terms of this contract.

From the afore-mentioned facts which I have attempted to lay out as clearly as possible, it will be seen:

First, That Japan has undertaken to restitute Kiaochow to China on conditions, none of which can be regarded in any sense as unjust or unfair, considering the part Japan took in disloading [expelling] Germany from Shantung.

Secondly, That the declaration of war by China against Germany could have no relation whatever to the validity of the treaty and the appended agreement which was concluded between Japan and China more than two years prior to the declaration of war, nor could it alter or affect in any wise the situation in connection with which the aforesaid treaty and agreement were made.

Thirdly, That the arrangements of September 1918, which were made more than one year after China's declaration of war, could not have been entered into without presupposing the existence and validity of the treaty of May 1915. Some of the provisions of the former dealt with the subject-matters or furthered the aims, set forth in the latter. In fact, the arrangements of 1918 were intended to be, and are, a supplement and sequel to the treaty of 1915. It is to be noted that China has actually received the advance of twenty million yen according to the terms of the above arrangements.

To those summaries and deductions, I may add that as between Japan and China there is a well-defined course laid out, for effecting the restitution. Any other course would be against the definite arrangement which has been agreed to between the two governments concerned. What Japan now seeks is to obtain from Germany the rights of free disposal of the leased territory and Germany's rights,

[5] About these treaties and exchanges, see THE CLAIM of China . . . , cited in V. K. W. Koo to WW, April 17, 1919, n. 1.

privileges and concessions in relation to Shantung for carrying out the provisions of the treaty of 1915 as well as of the arrangements of 1918.

It is claimed that the declaration of war abrogates *ipso facto* treaties of lease of territory. Such a claim can not be regarded as warranted by the established rules of International Law. From the very nature of the Lease Convention, which provides for the exercise by Germany of rights of Sovereignty within the territory the lease of Kiaochow may be regarded as a cession pure and simple with the exception of the time limit of 99 years. And it is commonly accepted principle that a declaration of war does not abrogate a treaty of cession or other territorial arrangements.

I feel firmly convinced that full justice will be done to the claims of Japan based upon her sacrifices and achievement and upon the fact of actual occupation, involving the sense of national honour.

I now beg to submit to you a draft containing the clauses to be embodied in the Preliminary Peace Treaty with Germany. (Appendix I.)

BARON MAKINO then handed round a draft of the clauses which the Japanese Delegation wished to have included in the Peace Treaty with Germany. He said it has been based on similar clauses inserted in other treaties.

PRESIDENT WILSON asked whether the following cables, mentioned in Article I were referred to in the original concession by China of Kiauchau to Germany, viz:

Tsingtao-Shanghai and Tsingtao-Chefoo.

BARON MAKINO replied they were German concessions, though not in the original concessions. He said they were Government cables.

PRESIDENT WILSON asked if they were submarine all the way to Shantung.

BARON MAKINO said they were the same line—a continuation of the same line.

PRESIDENT WILSON said that he had already taken the liberty of describing as well as he could to M. Clemenceau and Mr. Lloyd George what happened in his conversation with Baron Makino and Viscount Chinda. Their minds, therefore, were in the midst of the subject. He had laid what was in his own mind before all present. He did not know what was the impression formed by Mr. Lloyd George and M. Clemenceau.

MR. LLOYD GEORGE said that so far as Great Britain was concerned they were in the same position towards Japan as towards Italy. They had a definite engagement with Japan, as recorded in the Note of the British Ambassador at Tokio, dated 16th February, 1917.

(Appendix II.) Hence, so far as Great Britain was concerned, there was a definite engagement. The only doubt he felt was as to whether the ultimate destination of Kiauchau was a matter for inclusion in the Treaty with Germany.

In the case of the other German possessions in the Far East the Japanese Government had undertaken to support the British claims South of the Equator, and the British Government had undertaken to support the Japanese claims in the islands North of the Equator. So far as Great Britain was concerned, it was not proposed to press for the immediate allocation of the mandates for these islands, but only for their surrender by Germany to the Allied and Associated Powers. The allocation was left for settlement afterwards.

When the time came, we should have to press the claims of Australia and New Zealand to the islands South of the Equator.

BARON MAKINO said that Japan had expressed her willingness to support the British claims.

MR. LLOYD GEORGE pointed out that if the Japanese claims for the surrender of Kiauchau by Germany were put in the Treaty, Australia might demand the same treatment as regards the islands South of the Equator, and South Africa might make the same claim as regards German South-West Africa. There was hardly time to settle all these details before the treaty with Germany.

VISCOUNT CHINDA said that he did not know if Mr. Lloyd George had in mind that the leased territory of Kiauchau should be put on the same basis of the mandatory system as the South Pacific Islands. In that case the Japanese Delegation thought that Kiauchau ought to be on a definite basis. The mandatory system rested on the basis that those islands were in a state of civilisation which necessitated their being taken care of by other people. This did not apply to the case of Kiauchau.

MR. LLOYD GEORGE said that was true.

VISCOUNT CHINDA, continuing, asked if it was merely proposed to postpone this question: to put it in abeyance? The Japanese Delegation were under an express order for the case that the question was not settled. The Japanese Government had a duty to perform to China in this matter, and they could not carry out their obligation to China unless Kiauchau was handed over to them. The Japanese Delegates were under an express instruction from their Government that unless they were placed in a position to carry out Japan's obligation to China, they were not allowed to sign the Treaty. Consequently, they had no power to agree to a postponement of this question.

BARON MAKINO said that if the Treaty were ignored, it would be a very serious matter for Japan.

VISCOUNT CHINDA said it seemed to them to be a very simple question in its nature. No long deliberations were involved. They could not persuade themselves that the question was one that ought to be postponed.

PRESIDENT WILSON asked if it would be possible for the Japanese Government more particularly to define the arrangements she would expect to maintain with China in the Shantung Province. In the paper he had been given,[6] the statements were sufficiently explicit as regards the town of Kiauchau and the bay of Kiauchau, but not so explicit in regard to the railway and the administration.

VISCOUNT CHINDA said that the notes explained that the administration of the railway would be a joint undertaking.

PRESIDENT WILSON said it was not very explicit. Some further definition was required of the term "joint administration." The document was explicit about the establishment of a police force by China towards the cost of which the railway would make a contribution. He understood that at each station, by which he supposed was meant railway station, as well as at the training school, there would be Japanese. The document did not explain the position to be taken by these Japanese.

VISCOUNT CHINDA said he thought they were only intended to be instructors. He pointed out that there were many foreign instructors in the Chinese administration.

MR. LLOYD GEORGE said there were, in the Customs, for example.

PRESIDENT WILSON said this was part of a series of things which had been imposed on China.

MR. LLOYD GEORGE said they had asked for the Customs officials.

PRESIDENT WILSON said they had done so after a certain experience. He was fairly clear about the railway concession. He asked if there were not included in the lease to Germany certain concessions about exploitations.

VISCOUNT CHINDA suggested mines.

BARON MAKINO said the mines were amalgamated into the railway.

VISCOUNT CHINDA said there were three mines.

BARON MAKINO said that the mines had not paid, and had therefore been amalgamated in the railway, mainly for the use of the railway. The coal was not of very good quality. Germany had given up their concessions. One of the mines was not of much value.

PRESIDENT WILSON asked if there were any great iron deposits.

MR. LLOYD GEORGE suggested they had not been made much use of.

[6] That is, the Enclosure just printed.

PRESIDENT WILSON agreed, not up to the present.

MR. LLOYD GEORGE said he feared that if this arrangement was included in the Treaty, the question of mandatories would have to be settled. This might create difficulties and delays. Other interested parties might complain if this were not done when the Treaty handed over Kiauchau to Japan.

PRESIDENT WILSON said that Viscount Chinda's answer to this had been that the islands were in such state of development as to require someone to look after them, whereas Kiauchau was the case of a concession in a self-governing country. He asked Viscount Chinda if the railway was a joint enterprise with China.

VISCOUNT CHINDA replied in the affirmative.

BARON MAKINO said that Japan had already worked joint undertakings very well with China. In the case of the Sino-Japanese Timber Company, for example, where Japan and China had the same number on the Directorate and where the dividends were paid in equal proportions. There were several similar concerns, the directorates always consisting of equal numbers of both nationals.

PRESIDENT WILSON asked if there were any restrictions on these railways? His interest was to keep open the door with China.

BARON MAKINO said there was nothing in the agreement with China against the open door.

PRESIDENT WILSON pointed out that, as had happened in many instances, he was the only one present whose judgment was entirely independent. His colleagues were both bound by Treaties, although perhaps he might be entitled to question whether Great Britain and Japan had been justified in handing round the islands in the Pacific. This, however, was a private opinion.

MR. LLOYD GEORGE pointed out that they were only the German islands.

PRESIDENT WILSON pointed out that in the circumstances he was the only independent party present. He would like to repeat the point of view which he had urged on the Japanese Delegation a few days before. He was so firmly convinced that the Peace of the Far East centred upon China and Japan that he was more interested from this point of view than any other. He did not wish to see complex engagements that fettered free determination. He was anxious that Japan should show to the world as well as to China that she wanted to give the same independence to China as other nations possessed; that she did not want China to be held in manacles. What would prejudice the peace in the Far East was any relationship that was not trustful. It was already evident that there was not that relationship of mutual trust that was necessary if peace was to be ensured in the Far East. What he feared was that Japan,

by standing merely on her treaty rights, would create the impression
that she was thinking more of her rights than of her duties to China.
The world would never have peace based on treaty rights only
unless there were also recognized to be reciprocal duties between
States. Perhaps he was going a little too fast in existing circumstances but he wished to emphasise the importance in future that
States should think primarily of their duties towards each other.
The central idea of the League of Nations was that States must
support each other even when their interests were not involved.
When the League of Nations was formed then there would be
established a body of partners convenanted to stand up for each
other's rights. The position in which he would like to see Japan,
already the most advanced nation in the Far East with the leadership in enterprise and policy, was that of the leader in the Far
East standing out for these new ideas. There could be no finer nor
more politic role for her. That was what he had to say as the friend
of Japan. When he had seen the Japanese Delegates two days ago
he had said that he was not proposing that Kiauchau should be
detached from the treaty engagements but that it should be ceded
to the Powers as trustees with the understanding that all they were
going to do was to ask how the treaties were to be carried out and
to offer advice as to how this could best be done by mutual agreement. The validity of treaties could not be called in question if they
were modified by agreements between both sides. What he was
after was to attain a more detailed definition as to how Japan was
going to help China as well as to afford an opportunity for invest-
ment in railways etc. He had hoped that by pooling their interest
the several nations that had gained foothold in China (a foothold
that was to the detriment of China's position in the world) might
forego the special position they had acquired and that China might
be put on the same footing as other nations, as sooner or later she
must certainly be. He believed this to be to the interest of everyone
concerned. There was a lot of combustible material in China and
if flames were put to it the fire could not be quenched for China
had a population of four hundred million people. It was symptoms
of that which filled him with anxiety. Baron Makino and Viscount
Chinda knew how deep-seated was the feeling of reverence of China
towards Shantung which was the most sacred Chinese Province
and he dreaded starting a flame there because this reverence was
based upon the very best motives and owing to the traditions of
Confucius and the foundations of intellectual development. He did
not wish to interfere with treaties. As Mr. Lloyd George had remarked earlier, the war had been partly undertaken in order to
establish the sanctity of treaties. Although he yielded to no-one in

this sentiment there were cases he felt where treaties ought not to have been entered into.

BARON MAKINO, referring to President Wilson's remarks in regard to the larger ideas of international relationship, said that the best opinion of Japan was at that point of view. For China, the best opinion in Japan wanted equal opportunities or the "open door." He had convinced himself of this and was very glad of it, for he felt it would be to the advantage of both countries. He recalled, however, that international affairs in China had not always been conducted on very just lines. (Mr. Lloyd George interjected that this was undoubtedly the case.) He did not want to go into past history or to enquire where the responsibility lay, but this had been the source of the present situation. Once the unjust methods had been begun other nations followed. The best opinion, however, in Japan based itself on fairness and justice. Before he left Japan he had had a conversation with one of their older statesmen,[7] who had remarked to him that Japan would have to enter into a good many joint undertakings with China and must content herself to share equally, half and half, in them. This had been one of the most influential men in Japan and he himself shared his views.

PRESIDENT WILSON said that he was satisfied on that point and he hoped Baron Makino would not interpret him to have expressed any doubts. He wanted that principle, however, to be shown in a concrete way to China.

BARON MAKINO then referred to the President's remarks on Shantung. There, Japan had only entered into an agreement, whereas Germany had assumed almost complete sovereignty. All Germany's concessions over and above the agreement between Japan and China would now fall through. There remained only the concession mentioned in the Treaty which had already been discussed. Reverting to the larger views expressed by President Wilson he said that the Minister of Foreign Affairs of Japan,[8] in a speech made at the opening of the session (in January he thought), had sketched the line of policy which was proposed towards China. He had said that the Japanese Government was ready to help and contribute towards anything just that was proposed in China. As regards more concrete matters by which he meant such matters as extraterritoriality, maintenance of foreign troops, spheres of influence and the Boxer Indemnity—the four principal points which China had most at heart—on these matters he gathered from the speech of the Minister of Foreign Affairs that the Japanese Government was ready to discuss them with the Great Powers. These were concrete

[7] Prince Aritomo Yamagata, the leading figure of the Genrō, or Elder Statesmen.
[8] That is, Viscount Yasuya Uchida.

matters which could be worked out with the Great Powers. If this could be done it would do much to allay the feelings of injustice and bad tradition that still were lurking in China. Japan would be glad to discuss these questions. Extraterritoriality was a matter which would take some time. Japan had accomplished it and China could follow her footsteps. In the matter of prisons, for example, considerable progress had already been made in China. As soon as the Powers felt that they could trust Chinese Courts there need be no delay in rectifying matters.

PRESIDENT WILSON asked what was the idea of Japan as to extraterritoriality in the settlement contemplated at Kiaochow.

BARON MAKINO said that as matters stood extraterritoriality was considered as an established principle all through China. If, however, the principle changed, Kiaochow would form no exception.

PRESIDENT WILSON said that he felt that he realised the situation in a fuller light than ever before. He asked whether the Japanese representatives would prefer to draw the Chinese representatives into conference in which they would take part or would they prefer that their colleagues should see them separately. As China was a full member of the Peace Conference final judgment could not be passed without seeing them.

BARON MAKINO said that he did not in the least object to China being heard but he did not want to enter into discussion with them. It was difficult to discuss with people who had preconceived [ideas] to dispel them in one or two conversations. He greatly regretted that they should exist.

VISCOUNT CHINDA represented that Japan had the right to be present when the Chinese Delegates attended although her Delegates did not wish to be drawn into discussion.

After some further discussion it was agreed that:

Japan would not exercise her right to be present and that the best plan would be for the discussion with the Chinese representatives to take place in their absence.

MR. LLOYD GEORGE suggested that the opportunity of the presence of the Japanese delegates should be taken to refer to some of the general questions relating to the Treaty with Germany in which Japan was interested. Up to now the Supreme Council had concerned itself almost entirely with questions of European interest, such as the boundaries of Germany and related questions, the Saar Valley and Dantzig. Other more general questions, such as the League of Nations and Labour had been discussed outside in Commissions. Japan had been consulted about the question of breaches of the laws of war. The great outstanding question was compensation and indemnity.

M. MAKINO said that Japan was interested in this question. She had lost ships and would have a considerable claim. She had representatives on the Reparation Commission.

MR. LLOYD GEORGE said that the Reparation Commission have found great difficulty in reaching agreement; these questions were now being discussed by a special Committee.

PRESIDENT WILSON suggested that the Japanese Delegation should place themselves in communication with Mr. Norman Davis, who was the American representative on a Committee which also included M. Loucheur, Lord Sumner and M. Crespi.

M. MAKINO undertook to do this.

A few further explanations were given of the progress made in the Treaty of Peace.

M. MAKINO said that before the end of the Meeting, he wished to say one word about the form of restitution of Kiau Chow to Japan. The Japanese Government attached supreme importance to the form which had been submitted that morning. To-day, fresh instructions from Government have been received and he could not lay too much stress on the matter.

(The Japanese representatives then withdrew.)

APPENDIX I TO I.C.175.C.
Special Conditions
relative to Shantung Province.
Article I.

Germany renounces, in favour of Japan, all the rights, titles, or privileges—particularly those concerning the territory of Kiaochow, railways, mines and submarine cables—which she acquired, in virtue of the treaty concluded by her with China on the 6 March, 1898 and of all other arrangements relative to Shantung Province.

The Tsingtao-Tsinan Railway, including its branch lines together with its accessories of all kinds, stations, shops fixed materials and rolling stocks, mines, establishments and materials for exploitation of the mines, [are], and shall remain, acquired by Japan, together with the rights and privileges appertaining thereto.

The submarine cables of the State of Germany, from Tsingtao to Shanghai and from Tsingtao to Chefoo, with all the rights, privileges and properties appertaining thereto, shall equally remain acquired by Japan.

Article 2.

The rights of movable and immovable properties possessed by the State of Germany in the territory of Kiaochow, as well as all the rights which she is entitled to claim in consequence of the works or equipments set up, of the expenses disbursed, or of the contracts concluded by her, either directly or indirectly, and concerning the territory, are, and shall remain, acquired by Japan.

APPENDIX II TO I.C.175.C.

British Embassy, Tokyo.

Monsieur le Ministre,   16th February, 1917.

With reference to the subject of our conversation of the 27th ultimo, when your Excellency informed me of the desire of the Imperial Government to receive an assurance that, on the occasion of a Peace Conference, His Britannic Majesty's Government will support the claims of Japan in regard to the disposal of Germany's rights in Shantung and possessions in the Islands North of the Equator, I have the honour, under instructions received from His Britannic Majesty's Principal Secretary of State for Foreign Affairs, to communicate to your Excellency the following message from His Britannic Majesty's Government:

His Majesty's Government accede with pleasure to request of Japanese Government for an assurance that they will support Japan's claims in regard to disposal of Germany's rights in Shantung and possessions in Islands North of Equator on occasion of Peace Conference, it being understood that Japanese Government will, in eventual peace settlement, treat in same spirit Great Britain's claims to German Islands South of Equator. I avail myself of this opportunity, Monsieur le Ministre, to renew to your Excellency the assurance of my highest consideration.

(signed)   CONYNGHAM GREENE. H.B.M. AMBASSADOR

His Excellency
  Viscount Ichiro Motono,
    H.I.J.M. Minister for Foreign Affairs, etc. etc. etc.

T MS (SDR, RG 256, PPC 180.03401/112, DNA); Mantoux, I, 320.

Hankey's and Mantoux's Notes of a Meeting of the Council of Four[1]

President Wilson's House,

I.C.-175D   Paris, April 22, 1919, 4 p.m.

(1) MR. LLOYD GEORGE reported that, on his return from the morning meeting he had found M. Orlando's Chef du Cabinet[2] awaiting him. He had arranged to see M. Orlando in the afternoon and had just come from the interview. M. Orlando had had the intention of writing a letter saying that Italy could not be repre-

---

[1] The complete text of Hankey's minutes is printed in PPC, V, 135-37.
[2] Augusto Battioni.

sented at Versailles when the Germans came unless the Italian claims were conceded. MR. LLOYD GEORGE had said that in that event Italy's claim for reparation could not be put forward. M. Orlando had said that this was a settled matter. MR. LLOYD GEORGE had pointed out that this was not the case, and that a number of questions were outstanding. He asked to whom M. Orlando proposed to entrust Italy's claim against Germany—France, or England, or the United States? He had told him he thought that he was in a very serious situation. He himself and M. Clemenceau stood by their Treaty, but he had told him that if the Treaty was signed without the United States of America it meant disaster. He had pointed out to him that President Wilson was immovable. Moreover, he wanted to present his case to the public immediately. M. Orlando must realize that once President Wilson had done that he could not go back on it, and there would be no chance of conciliation. He had also told him that it was only with the greatest reluctance that President Wilson would consider the idea of handing over the islands to Italy. After that he had asked M. Orlando what he thought about the establishment of a free city in Fiume instead of handing it over to Croatia. M. Orlando had then harked back to Zara, Sebenico, and Spalato.

PRESIDENT WILSON said that Italy would never get these.

MR. LLOYD GEORGE said he had one last suggestion to make, that Fiume should be a free city and that Zara and Sebenico should also be free cities with provision for a plebiscite at the end of three years to ascertain whether they would wish to join the mainland.

PRESIDENT WILSON doubted whether this would help the peace of that coast.

M. CLEMENCEAU feared collisions between the Italians and the Jugo-Slavs.

PRESIDENT WILSON feared that the Slavs would crowd into the free cities and there would be a constant agitation in Italy that this was being done to prejudice the plebiscite.

M. CLEMENCEAU said he would not stand in the way of the proposal if President Wilson would accept.

PRESIDENT WILSON thought that a better plan would be for him to publish the statement which he had prepared, to which he proposed to put a preamble in some such words as the following:

"All aspects of this question should be known before the decision is arrived at."

Those who knew Italian public opinion well thought that this would for the moment inflame Italian public opinion, but that this would be followed by a reaction in which the people would see that it was to their own interest to accept the cooperation of the United

States of America rather than to stand out for the Treaty. Italy, he pointed out, had sent very large numbers of emigrants to the United States of America and every year thousands of these returned to visit their native land. There was a stream of many millions of dollars every year from America to Italy. When the people realized the dangers of the position, as they might in the course of a week or two, opinion would probably change.

MR. LLOYD GEORGE pointed out the danger of bringing back a Giolitti Government[3] in Italy.

At this point the discussion was adjourned to enable the Chinese plenipotentiaries to develop their case on the question of Shantung, which was recorded separately. After the interval, however, there was a further discussion as to the action to be taken in regard to the Italian claims. As a result of this discussion, it was agreed that:

> Mr. Lloyd George should be authorized to see M. Orlando at once and to ascertain from him whether Italy would discuss the following conditions:

(1) Fiume, together with the surrounding territory, to be a free city;
(2) The islands of strategical importance to Italy to be ceded to her, excluding islands such as Pago, which are almost an extension of the mainland;
(3) Zara and Sebenico to be free cities without any definite provision for a plebiscite, but with the power that all countries have under the League of Nations to appeal to the League for an alteration of their boundaries.

§Mantoux's notes:

Clemenceau. Are we returning to the question of Zara and Spalato?

Lloyd George. I would like another discussion with the Italians, to see if they would accept my plan, with free cities on the Dalmatian coast and a plebiscite at the end of fifteen years.

Clemenceau. You would not place these cities under their administration?

Lloyd George. No, but under that of the League of Nations. President Wilson tells us that the Yugoslavs have a majority in these cities.

Wilson. What I said is that the Italian majority was doubtful, although, certainly, the dominant element at least by culture is the Italian element.

Does your plan include the cession of the islands?

Lloyd George. Yes; Italy would have the outer line of islands; Fiume would be a free city.

Clemenceau. What would its customs arrangement be?

---

[3] That is, a government headed by Giovanni Giolitti.

Lloyd George. We would constitute it as a free port for all commerce in transit. From the point of view of strategic protection, Italy would receive satisfaction by the possession of the islands. Zara and Sebenico would be free cities like Fiume.

Wilson. The island of Cherso commands Fiume's roadstead.

Lloyd George. That is why it constitutes a protection for the Italians.

Wilson. With all due respect to the Italians, that is a bad joke.

Clemenceau. We do not owe them Fiume.

Lloyd George. Fiume would be a free port for the use of Hungary and the other countries of the hinterland.

Wilson. I fear a compromise like this one; I fear the consequences. I dread dangerous encounters; I sense the probability of intrigues and conflicts, with the question of Montenegro and with the presence of two religions and three different ethnic groups in these territories.

Lloyd George. Serbs, Croatians, and Slovenes have the same language and same literature.

Clemenceau. It is true that the island of Cherso bars the route of Fiume.

Lloyd George. Yes, but if the Italians adhere to the Treaty of London, we have promised them those islands. Thus, as far as we are concerned, we have nothing more to say.

Wilson. Sir Maurice Hankey transmitted a proposal to them yesterday. Here is another one. If this is also transmitted to the Italians, they will think it enough to hold fast and that we will end up saying that they are right. As for myself, I am not ready to make new proposals to them.

Hankey. I should comment that the Italians never make a proposal, so to speak. They wait for them to be made to them.

Lloyd George. What we really have to decide is whether we want to have M. Orlando or M. Giolitti here within a week.

Wilson. Giolitti would not last.

Lloyd George. Who knows? In any case, at the most crucial moment, Giolitti would intrigue with the Germans.

Clemenceau. We must not forget that at base the Italian Chamber is Giolittian.

Lloyd George. Do you want to let me make a new attempt?

Wilson. Let me publish my document; that could only clear the air.

Lloyd George. Yes, but as a storm would. Our poor Europe is like a land sown with grenades; if you step on it, everything blows up. I think my plan is not impractical, because the Yugoslavs are much less interested in the islands than in the mainland.

Clemenceau. We will let you act.

Lloyd George. It would be a catastrophe if the European Powers and the United States should separate over this unfortunate affair. To tell the truth, I fear much more the question which the presence of a German element in the Italian Tyrol could raise.

Wilson. There is a fatal antagonism between the Italians and the Slavs. If the Slavs have the feeling of an injustice, that will make the chasm unbridgeable and will open the road to Russian influence and to the formation of a Slavic bloc hostile to western Europe.

Lloyd George. I do not think that this sentiment would be provoked by the cession of certain islands.

Wilson. Why not make the cities we have just spoken about into free cities without a plebiscite? I would fear a systematic immigration. We can, it is true, stipulate that the right to vote will be limited to the present inhabitants of those cities.

Lloyd George. We can leave the decision to the League of Nations.

Clemenceau. Who will make the proposal to the Italians?

Lloyd George. I would very much like to try it. Undoubtedly they will say that we have forced their hand.

Clemenceau. This is of no concern to me.

Lloyd George. Nor to me also, if we maintain the peace among ourselves.

Wilson. You will surely admit that it is I who caused America to enter the war, who instructed and formed American opinion little by little. I did it while standing by principles which you know. Baron Sonnino led the Italian people into war to conquer territories. I did it while involving a principle of justice; I believe my claim takes precedence over his.

Lloyd George. In reality, the Italian claim is based primarily on a question of security; she does not pursue the conquest of territories or of great cities, for there are scarcely nothing more than rocks there.

Wilson. What M. Sonnino says to the Italian people is this: "We cannot abandon our brothers." He does not speak to them of strategy; it is an argument for our use. M. Orlando sent me two beautiful volumes showing that Dalmatia, according to its artistic traditions, ought to be Italian. It is by these means that they create popular sentiment.

Lloyd George. I fear much more the difficulties in the Tyrol than those concerning these little islands.§

T MS (SDR, RG 256, 180.03401/113, DNA); Mantoux, I, 337-39.

Hankey's and Mantoux's Notes of a Meeting of the Council of Four[1]

President Wilson's House,
Paris, April 22, 1919, 4:30 p.m.

I.C.-175E. (REVISE)

1. President Wilson said that the Chinese Plenipotentiaries knew the interest he felt in the Kiauchau-Shantung settlement. On the previous day he had a Conference with the Japanese representatives, and this morning they had come to confer. M. Orlando, unfortunately, could not be present. Since he had last seen Mr. Koo, he had carefully read the documents, from which he gathered the following was the chain of events.

Before China entered into the war, there had been an exchange of Notes. He thought in 1915 (Mr. Koo said it was the 25th May). In that exchange of Notes, the Japanese Government had said that when the German rights in Kiauchau were transferred after the war to Japan, Japan would return them to China. The Chinese Government had taken note of this. Subsequently, there had been a further exchange of notes, and he believed, also a treaty although he had only seen Notes, in which the Japanese Government laid down certain conditions. The Chinese Government had accepted these conditions. Great Britain and France (Mr. Lloyd George said that this had occurred between the two exchanges of Notes between China and Japan) had entered into a similar but not identical agreement with Japan to the effect that they would support the claims of the Japanese Government on the Continent and on the islands North of the Equator. In the case of the British Government it had been on the understanding that Japan supported her claim to German islands South of the Equator. Hence, Great Britain and France were in much the same position in the matter.

MR. LLOYD GEORGE explained that at that time the submarine campaign had become very formidable. Most of the British torpedo-boat-destroyers were in the North Sea, and there was a shortage of those craft in the Mediterranean. Japanese help was urgently required, and Japan had asked for this arrangement to be made. We had been very hard pressed, and had agreed.

PRESIDENT WILSON then read extracts from the exchange of Notes printed on page 62 of the Official Claim of China for direct restitution to herself of the leased territory of Kiauchau, etc., circulated by the Chinese Delegation:

"When, after the termination of the present war, the leased territory of Kiauchau Bay is completely left to the free disposal of

[1] The complete text of Hankey's minutes is printed in PPC, V, 138-48.

Japan, the Japanese Government will restore the said leased territory to China under the following conditions."

He then read the following reply of the Chinese Foreign Minister, in which, after rehearsing the whole of the Japanese Note, he had said "In reply, I beg to state that I have taken note of this declaration." He then read an extract from page 82, namely, exchange of Notes dated September 24, 1918:

"The Japanese Government, mindful of the amiable relations between our two countries and out of a spirit of friendly co-operation, propose to adjust all the questions relating to Shantung in accordance with the following articles.

1. Japanese troops along the Kiauchow-Chinan railway, except a contingent of them to be stationed at Chinanfu, shall be withdrawn to Tsingtau.

2. The Chinese Government may organise a Police Force to undertake the policing of the Kiauchow-Chinan railway.

3. The Kiauchow-Chinan Railway is to provide a reasonable amount to defray the expense for the maintenance of the above mentioned Police Force.

4. Japanese are to be employed at the Headquarters of the above-mentioned Police Force, at the principal railway stations, and at the Police Training School.

5. Chinese citizens shall be employed by the Kiauchow-Chinan Railway Administration as part of its Staff.

6. The Kiauchau-Chinan Railway, after its ownership is definitely determined, is to be made a Chino-Japanese joint enterprise.

7. The Civil Administration established by Japan and existing now is to be abolished.

The Japanese Government desires to be advised of the attitude of your Government regarding the above-mentioned proposal."

To this the Chinese Minister had replied:

"In reply I have the honour to state that the Chinese Government are pleased to agree to the above articles proposed by the Japanese Government."

The Chinese Delegation would see, President Wilson continued, the embarrassing position which had been reached. Mr. Lloyd George and M. Clemenceau were bound to support the claims of Japan. Alongside of them the Chinese had their exchange of notes with Japan. He reminded Mr. Koo that when urging his case before the Council of Ten at the Quai d'Orsay, he had maintained that the war cancelled the agreement with the German Government.[2] It did not, however, cancel the agreement between China and the Jap-

[2] See the minutes of the Council of Ten printed at Jan. 28, 1919, 11 a.m., Vol. 54.

anese Government, which had been made before the war. What he had himself urged upon the Japanese was that, as in the case of the Pacific Islands, the leased territory of Kiauchau should be settled by putting it into the hands of the Five Powers as Trustees. He did not suggest that Treaties should be broken, but that it might be possible, in Conference, to bring about an agreement by modifying the Treaty. He also proposed to them that all Governments should renounce the special rights they had acquired in China, so as to put China in a position free from the special limitations which had been imposed upon her. The Japanese were not willing to have Kiauchau handed over to the Five Powers, and the British and French Governments were embarrassed by their Treaties. When he pressed the Japanese for explanations of the meaning of their agreement, they had replied that the exploitation of two coal-mines and one iron-mine had not proved a successful venture, and were now bound up with the railway. They stated, however, that they would withdraw the civil administration; that they would maintain troops only on the termini of the railway; and that if a general agreement was reached, they would withdraw their extraterritoriality. They urged that they wanted a community of interest with the Chinese in the railway, and the only reserve they made was for a residential district in Kiauchau.

Mr. Koo said that the Treaties of 1915 and the subsequent exchange of Notes were the outcome of the 21 demands which Japan had made on China and were all part and parcel of one transaction. He hoped he had made this clear before the Council of Ten. He felt that the Treaties and Notes which had been exchanged after Japan had delivered an ultimatum stood outside of the regular procedure and course of Treaties. They dealt with matters arising out of the war.

MR. LLOYD GEORGE asked what ultimatum he referred to.

PRESIDENT WILSON asked if Mr. Lloyd George had never heard of the twenty-one points.

MR. LLOYD GEORGE said he had not.

MR. KOO said that in January 1915 after the capture of Kiau Chau that port had been opened up to trade; China then asked Japan to withdraw her troops from the interior of the province. The Japanese took occasion to treat this note as though it were an unfriendly act and shortly after sprung on China twenty-one demands divided into five groups—for example, that China should accept Japanese advisers; that they should give up railway concessions in which Western Powers were concerned, and he would draw Mr. Lloyd George's attention to the fact that Great Britain was concerned. China was put in an extremely embarrassing position. She resisted and resisted and only gave up when she was absolutely compelled to. On the 7th May the Japanese sent China an ultimatum in regard to the majority of demands giving China only 48 hours within which to accept; otherwise Japan would consider herself free to take such steps as she thought fit to enforce them. This caused absolute consternation to the Chinese Government which eventually had to submit to force majeure.

MR. LLOYD GEORGE asked if they had not appealed to the United States of America.

PRESIDENT WILSON said they had and the United States had intervened in regard to the infringement of sovereignty and political independence. The whole transaction, however, had been kept extremely secret and the United States only learnt of it in a roundabout way.

MR. KOO said that secrecy had been imposed upon China by Japan under severe penalties. It had been said that Japan had informed the Allied Governments and the United States Government that there had been only 11 Demands; but actually 21 Demands had been made on China. The Chinese Government felt that the Treaties and Notes exchanged as a result of these demands followed by an ultimatum were on a different footing from the ordinary. China had always endeavoured to carry out to the letter all engagements made in good faith. These, however, had been made against China's free will, and the same applied to the notes exchanged in the previous year. For the last four years since they had captured Kiauchau, Japanese troops had penetrated far into the province of Shantung, where there was a population of 36,000,000 people. This had been very uncomfortable for the general population, and the results had been disturbance and trouble. The Chinese Government had protested, and asked Japan to withdraw her troops who were stationed 250 miles up the railway, but they had refused and had established civil administration bureaux in the interior of Shantung and extended their control even over the Chinese people by levying taxes on Chinese people and asserting judicial power over them. The feelings of the Chinese people against the extension of Japanese control were so strong that the Chinese Government felt constrained to take some immediate step to induce Japan to withdraw her troops and remove the civil administration bureaux, the object being to relieve the tense situation until the question could be finally settled at the Peace Conference.

MR. LLOYD GEORGE said that it looked that by the Treaty with China, the Japanse Government would get more than the Germans had had. He asked Mr. Koo which he would prefer—the Treaty with Japan, or the transference to Japan of the German rights?

MR. KOO said that the situation was so difficult that he felt he must speak very frankly. The Japanese position was so close to China, especially in Manchuria, where they occupied a railway which was connected with Pekin, that merely to transfer German rights would create a very serious situation. With the Japanese on the Manchurian railway, and the Shantung railway, Pekin would be—as it were—in a pincers.

PRESIDENT WILSON pointed out that the Japanese claimed that the administration of the Shantung railway would be a joint one, and they proposed to withdraw the Japanese administration.

MR. LLOYD GEORGE said that Mr. Koo had not quite answered his point. Supposing the Great Powers had to decide (and this really was his position since he was bound by a Treaty) between Japan inheriting Germany's rights in Shantung or exercising the rights under the treaty with Japan, which would China prefer? He pointed out that Great Britain was only bound by the rights which Japan inherited from Germany.

PRESIDENT WILSON said that if Japan inherited the German rights, it would involve her retaining the leased territory. He thought Mr. Lloyd George's point was that possibly Japan was claiming greater rights than Germany had exercised. As the British and French Governments had to support the Japanese claim to what Germany had had, they wanted to know whether China would be better off according as Japan could exercise the rights that Germany had or those that she obtained by her Treaty.

MR. LLOYD GEORGE agreed that this was the point, and said the real question was whether the Treaty with Japan was better for China than Germany's rights.

(At this point there was an interval to permit the Chinese plenipotentiaries to confer.)

Mr. KOO said that he had now consulted his colleague. He could make no choice, because both alternatives were unacceptable; he would merely compare them. The Treaty and Notes with Japan provided for restoration of the Leased Territory to China on certain conditions, but such restoration would be only nominal. Between the two, he thought that the German rights were more limited than the rights claimed by Japan under her Treaty and Notes with China. Even mere succession to the German right, however, would create a grave situation for China's future. In claiming direct restitution of German rights, he was not asking for any compensation or remuneration for China as a result of her entry into the war, but only for what was necessary for peace in the Far East. The experience of the last three years made it so clear what the Chinese position would be if Japan was allowed either to succeed to the German rights in Shantung or to retain the rights she claimed under her treaty with China. It was an uncomfortable position both to the Chinese people and the Government. He was not in the least exaggerating, but only saying what was necessary to explain the situation.

PRESIDENT WILSON said that M. Clemenceau and Mr. Lloyd George would bear witness that he had put the Chinese case as well as he could to the Japanese Delegation in the morning. He had emphasised the great need of trust and friendship between Japan and China, which he regarded as essential to peace in the Far East. He had urged that China should be free and unfettered to carry out her development. What he asked now was only a means of getting out of a position that was extremely difficult. In this Conference the United States of America was the only power that was entirely unbound. Great Britain, France, China and Japan were all bound by Treaties. They were bound to keep these Treaties because the war had largely been fought for the purpose of showing that Treaties could not be violated.

MR. LLOYD GEORGE suggested that in the exchange of notes of September 1918, China might have stood out.

MR. KOO said that the exchange of notes in 1918 was the result of the Shantung Treaty, made in consequence of the 21 demands. It was part of the same transaction.

PRESIDENT WILSON said that the exchange of notes had grown out of the previous agreement. He looked for the Shantung Treaty.

MR. KOO said that it was on page 59 of *China's Claim for Direct Restitution of Kiaochow*, etc.

PRESIDENT WILSON read the following extracts from the treaty and said that China had then had to accept and had had no other choice:

"Art. 1—The Chinese Government agrees to give full assent to all matters upon which the Japanese Government may hereafter agree with the German Government relating to the disposition of all rights, interests and concessions which Germany, by virtue of treaties or otherwise, possesses in relation to the Province of Shantung.

"Art. 2—The Chinese Government agrees that as regards the railway to be built by China herself from Chefoo or Lungkow to connect with the Kiaochow-Chinanfu railway, if Germany abandons the privilege of financing the Chefoo-Wehsien line China will approach Japanese capitalists to negotiate for a loan."

MR. LLOYD GEORGE said he would like to have the two positions examined by British, French and American experts, and to learn their views as to which course would be best for China.

M. CLEMENCEAU said he had no objection.

MR. LLOYD GEORGE said that it was also only fair that China should be given more time to consider this question. This seemed to be the only alternative there was to acquiescing in the Treaties between China and Japan. Great Britain and France, however, were not bound by this latter Treaty, but only by their own arrangements with Japan.

§Mantoux's notes:

Lloyd George. Our treaty with the Japanese only provides for the transfer of rights from the Germans to Japan. I would like these two arrangements to be examined and compared by experts, who would tell us which of the two is the more favorable to China. We would also allow the Chinese delegates the time to make this examination. For us this is the only alternative, since we are bound toward Japan by our signature.

If the transfer pure and simple of Germany's rights and privileges to Japan is the solution the least unfavorable to China, that is all that we are bound to grant to Japan. We are not obligated to assure her the benefit of a treaty signed behind our backs and under threat of an ultimatum.

Wilson. I recall what the nature of that ultimatum was. By the twenty-one demands, Japan demanded to furnish the Chinese government her political advisers, to have her portion in the police force of all the large cities; she asked for a monopoly—for half—of the sale of arms and munitions, a preponderant role in the exploitation of the mines of all central China. The Chinese had to accept a part of these conditions.

Lloyd George. Are they still in force?

Koo. Yes; that is why we are asking the conference to support us.§

PRESIDENT WILSON then read the following extracts from the 21 Demands on page 52 and 53 of the Chinese Document.

Group IV.

The Chinese Government engages not to cede or lease to a third Power any harbour or bay or island along the coast of China.

Group V.

"Art. 1.—The Chinese Central Government shall employ influential Japanese as advisers in political, financial, and military affairs.

"Art. 3.—Inasmuch as the Japanese Government and the Chinese Government have had many cases of dispute between Japanese and Chinese police which caused no little misunderstanding, it is for this reason necessary that the police departments of important places (in China) shall be jointly administered by Japanese and Chinese or that the police department of these places shall employ numerous Japanese, so that they may at the same time help to plan for the improvement of the Chinese Police Service.

"Art. 4.—China shall purchase from Japan a fixed amount of munitions of war (say 50% or more of what is needed by the Chinese Government) or that there shall be established in China a Sino-Japanese jointly worked arsenal. Japanese technical experts are to be employed and Japanese material to be purchased."

PRESIDENT WILSON recalled that there were other demands designed to exclude other Powers from the commercial and industrial development; (Mr. Koo said, on page 52.).

PRESIDENT WILSON read Article 1 of the Group III as follows: "The Two Contracting Parties mutually agree that when the opportune moment arrives the Hanyehping Company shall be made a joint concern of the two nations and they further agree that without the previous consent of Japan, China shall not by her act dispose of the rights and property of whatever nature of the said Company nor cause the said Company to dispose freely of the same."

MR. KOO pointed out that the Hanyehping Company was the largest coal and iron mining Company of China, situated in the Yangtze Valley. He requested the reading of Article 2 which, he said, was even more serious.

PRESIDENT WILSON read the following: "Art. 2—The Chinese Government agrees that all mines in the neighborhood of these owned by the Hanyehping Company shall not be permitted, without the consent of the said Company, to be worked by other persons outside the said Company; and further agrees that if it is desired to carry out any undertaking which, it is apprehended, may directly or indirectly affect the interests of the said Company, the consent of the said Company shall first be obtained."

MR. LLOYD GEORGE asked whether China had agreed to this Article.

MR. KOO said that the Chinese Government had had to accept most of the 21 Demands with slight modifications. That was why China was seeking some redress.

PRESIDENT WILSON asked if the following point of view would make any appeal to the Chinese Plenipotentiaries? Hereafter whatever arrangements were made both Japan and China would be members of the League of Nations, which would guarantee their territorial integrity and political independence. That is to say, that these matters would become the concern of the League and China would receive a kind of protection that she had never had before and other nations would have a right which they had never had before to intervene. Before it had been, comparatively speaking, none of our business to interfere in these matters. The Covenant, however, laid down that whatever affected the peace of the world was a matter of concern to the League of Nations and to call attention to such was not an hostile but a friendly act. He, himself, was prepared to advocate at the Council of the League and at the Body of Delegates that the special positions occupied by the various nations in China should be abandoned. Japan declared that she was ready to support this. There would be a forum for advocating these matters. The interests of China could not then be overlooked. He was stating this as an element of security for China in the future if the powers were unable to give her what she wanted now, and he asked the Chinese Delegates to think the matter over. While there was doubt as to the Treaty and Notes between China and Japan, there was no doubt whatsoever as to the agreements entered into by France and Great Britain. Hence, even if the agreements between them and Japan were abandoned, these two Governments were bound to support Japan in getting whatever rights in Shantung Germany had had. Hence, the question which the Chinese Plenipotentiaries had to consider was, would they prefer to retain the rights which Japan had secured in their treaty with her or would they prefer that Japan should inherit the German rights in Shantung.

MR. KOO said that he could not lay too much emphasis on the fact that the Chinese people were now at the parting of the ways. The policy of the Chinese Government was co-operation with Europe and the United States as well as with Japan. If, however, they did not get justice, China might be driven into the arms of Japan. There was a small section in China which believed in Asia for the Asiatics and wanted the closest co-operation with Japan. The position of the Government, however, was that they believed in the justice of the West and that their future lay there. If they failed to get justice there, the consequential re-action might be very great. Further, he wished to suggest that the validity of the arrangements was questionable owing to the following facts: (1) They arose out of the war: (2) China had subsequently come into the war herself: (3) New principles had now been adopted by all the nations as the basis of the peace and the agreements with Japan appeared to be in conflict with them. Consequently, in thanking the Supreme Council for hearing the views of the Chinese Delegation, he wished to state the great importance of attaining a peace which could be relied on to endure for 50 years instead of a peace so unjust that it would only sow the seeds of early discord.

PRESIDENT WILSON said that these were serious considerations, but he would not like Mr. Koo even personally to entertain the idea that there was injustice in an arrangement that was based on treaties which Japan had entered into. The sacredness of treaties had been one of the motives of the war. It had been necessary to show that treaties were not mere scraps of paper. If treaties were inconsistent with the principles on which the peace was being formed, nevertheless we could not undo past obligations. If that principle were acccepted, we should have to go back and France would have the treaty of 1814 and there would be no end to it. He would not like to feel that because we were embarrassed by a treaty we were disregardful of justice. Moreover, the unjust treatment of China in the past had not by any means been confined to Japan. He hoped that the quandary in which the Powers were would be stated to the Chinese people. He hoped that it would be shown to them that the undoing of the trouble depended on China uniting in reality with other nations, including the Western Nations. He felt absolute confidence that the opinion of the world had the greatest sympathy for the realm of China. The heart of the world went out to her 400 millions of people. Much depended on the state of mind of these 400 million people. Any statesmen who ignore their fortunes were playing a dangerous game. But it would not do to identify justice with unfortunate engagements that had been entered into.

MR. KOO said he believed prevention to be better than cure. He thought that it would be better to undo unfortunate engagements now, if they endangered the permanence of the future peace.

MR. LLOYD GEORGE said the object of the war was not that. The war had been fought as much for the East as for the West. China also had been protected by the victory that had been won. If Germany had won the war and had desired Shantung or Pekin, she could have had them. The very doctrine of the mailed fist had been propounded in relation to China. The engagements that had been entered into with Japan had been contracted at a time when the support of that country was urgently needed. He would not say that the war could not have been won without this support. But he could say that Kiauchau could not have been captured without Japanese support. It was a solemn treaty and Great Britain could not turn round to Japan now and say "All right, thank you very much. When we wanted your help, you gave it, but now we think that the treaty was a bad one and should not be carried out." Within the treaties he would go to the utmost limits to protect the position of China. On the League of Nations he would always be prepared to stand up for China against oppression, if there was oppression. China was a nation with a very great past and, he believed, with a still greater future. It would, however, be of no service to her to regard treaties as Bethmann von Hollweg had regarded them, as mere scraps of paper to be turned down when they were not wanted.

M. CLEMENCEAU said that Mr. Koo could take every word that Mr. Lloyd George had said as his also.

PRESIDENT WILSON asked whether assuming for the sake of argument that the engagements were unfortunate nevertheless they had been entered into for the salvation of China, because they had been entered into for the salvation of the world, of which China was a part. In fact, it would be said that the very engagements were instruments for the salvation of China.

MR. KOO said they had been designed apparently to meet a situation in Europe and not in the Far East.

MR. LLOYD GEORGE pointed out that if Germany had won the war in Europe, she would have won it in the Far East also. The world would have been at her feet.

M. CLEMENCEAU agreed.

PRESIDENT WILSON pointed out that the German project was not only domination from Hamburg to Bagdad but also the control of the East. Germany knew China to be rich. Her objects were mostly material. The Kaiser had been the great exponent of what was called the "Yellow Peril." He had wanted to get France and Great Britain out of the way and afterwards to get everything else he could. One result of the war undoubtedly had been to save the Far East in particular, since that was an unexploited part of the world.

MR. LLOYD GEORGE said that he wished to consider the question further before arriving at a decision.

PRESIDENT WILSON asked the Chinese Delegates also to give further consideration to the question and hoped that it could be taken up soon again.

(The Chinese Representatives then withdrew.)
§Mantoux's notes:

Wilson. I realize the apparent contradiction that exists between my stand on this question and my stand on the Italian question. But the difference is that Austria-Hungary has disappeared. If she still existed, I would not oppose execution of the Treaty of London. And the Yugoslavs and Italy are admitted as we are into the League of Nations.

Concerning Japan, it is necessary to do everything to assure that she joins the League of Nations. If she stands aside, she would do all that she could want to do in the Far East. You heard them this morning saying clearly that they will not sign the treaty if the obligations contracted vis-à-vis them are not respected.

Lloyd George. The way in which they have terrorized the Chinese to force them to sign their treaty is one of the most unscrupulous proceedings in all history, especially against a gentle and defenseless people.

Wilson. Yes, but I am above all concerned not to create a chasm between the East and the West.

Lloyd George. That is the strongest argument, and the Chinese do not see that, without us, they would be at the mercy of the Germans today.§

T MS (SDR, RG 256, 180.03401/114, DNA); Mantoux, I, 333, 334.

From the Diary of Edward Thomas Williams

Tuesday [April 22, 1919]

Revised letter to President.[1] Wrote to Gout[2] telling him [about] consortium matter handled by the Embassy.[3] About 6:30 p.m. was sent for by President Wilson, who told me that the Shantung question had been discussed, that Gt Brit & France were bound by their agreements with Japan—that this was a war to enforce treaties & while some were unconscionable, it was a question whether they ought not to be enforced. I asked him if he meant that a treaty extorted by show of force & threats ought to be held binding. He said Japan probably would not admit that it had been obtained that way. I referred to published documents. He said of course if it was as published Japan would not deny it.

We reviewed the situation in Shantung. I pointed out the fact that Japan had already bought up all desirable sites in Kiaochow, that the return was a sham. He had not heard of these purchases.

He asked me to consider and report upon the question: Which would be least injurious to China, enforcement of the 1915 Conventions or enjoyment by Japan of the rights formerly belonging to Germany?

I asked permission to suggest another solution; viz. abrogation of German treaties with China, renunciation by Germany of all rights etc. automatic reversion to China without compensation of all German State property, but a statement that such properties in Shantung, having been taken by Gt Brit & Japan in war & being now held by Japan, the latter would transfer them to China within a year. He said the matter had not been discussed from that angle & asked me to write it out.

Attended reception at night given by Sec'y & Mrs Lansing in honor of Mr & Mrs Wallace—Wallace is new American Ambassador.

Saw Koo who confirmed the situation before the Council of Four also put the same question to him. Told Mr Lansing who agreed with me that these are not the alternatives in the case. It is merely an attempt of Lloyd George to get us to help him out.

Bound diary book (E. T. Williams Papers, CU-B).
  [1] See E. T. Williams to WW, April 24, 1919.
  [2] Jean Étienne Paul Gout, chief of the Asiatic Section of the French Ministry of Foreign Affairs.
  [3] Discussions about a new, or second, consortium of international bankers to assist China, which was to include participation by the United States, had begun in January 1917. Wilson himself had become involved in June 1918. See RL to WW, June 20, 1918 (first letter of that date); WW to RL, June 21, 1918 (second letter of that date); and WW to RL, July 4, 1918, with its Enclosures, all in Vol. 48; and WW to FLP, July 26, 1918, with Enclosure, and WW to RL, Aug. 22, 1918, with Enclosure, all in Vol. 49. For the course of the negotiations, which continued until October 1920, see Roy Watson Curry, *Woodrow Wilson and Far Eastern Policy, 1913-1921* (New York, 1957), pp. 187-204.

To Vittorio Emanuele Orlando

My dear Mr. Prime Minister: Paris, 22 April, 1919.

Thank you for your letter of April 21st about the statements concerning deportations from Dalmatia. You may be sure that my judgment about the general questions we have been discussing has not been guided by the information to which your refer, and I am very glad indeed to have this direct report from your own naval authorities.

With warm regard,

Sincerely yours,   [Woodrow Wilson]

CCL (WP, DLC).

To Herbert Clark Hoover

My dear Hoover: [Paris] 22 April, 1919.

Thank you warmly for your letter of yesterday enclosing your memorandum on the situation in Germany apropos of the British memorandum which I handed you. It will be very serviceable to me indeed.

Cordially and faithfully yours,   Woodrow Wilson

TLS (Hoover Archives, CSt-H).

Two Letters to Tasker Howard Bliss

My dear General Bliss: Paris, 22 April, 1919.

When I took up with Mr. Lloyd George and Mr. Clemenceau the matter of General Ironsides' plans and the Allied plans in general in Archangel and the Archangel district,[1] I found them quite of our mind and purpose. They were disturbed, apparently, by what I told them in outline was your information from Poole, and they both begged that you would put them in possession of all information that you have. I mean Mr. Lloyd George and Mr. Clemenceau. I am sure you will be glad to do so, because they are anxious to cooperate with us in getting the troops out. I would be very much obliged if you would make an outline for them of the information which has disturbed you and me.

Cordially and faithfully yours,   Woodrow Wilson

[1] See THB to WW, April 18, 1919 (first letter of that date).

My dear General Bliss: Paris, 22 April, 1919.

I do not know whether General Kernan has returned or whether he is about to return to Poland, but whether he is there or merely ready to go back, I would be very much obliged if he might be our messenger in conveying to the Polish government just exactly the intimations suggested by you in your letter of April 18th concerning your conference with Mr. Paderewski. I am authorized by Mr. Lloyd George and Mr. Clemenceau to request this of you and General Kernan, and if you will give General Kernan written instructions along the lines of your suggestions in that letter, he is at liberty to convey them as an authoritative message from the representatives of Great Britain, France, and the United States.

Cordially and faithfully yours,   Woodrow Wilson

TLS (T. H. Bliss Papers, DLC).

To William Shepherd Benson

My dear Admiral: Paris, 22 April, 1919.

Replying to your letter of yesterday, you may be sure that it afforded me the greatest pleasure to authorize the presentation to you of the Distinguished Service Medal. I was glad to have such an opportunity to show my estimate of the services you have rendered.   Cordially and faithfully yours,   [Woodrow Wilson]

(WP. DLC).

From Norman Hezekiah Davis

My dear Mr. President: Paris, 22nd April, 1919.

With reference to your letter of April 15th and my reply of the 16th relative to the establishment of further credits in favor of the British Government up to $150,000,000 beyond amounts previously authorized by you, I have just received a cable from the Secretary of the Treasury stating that he has recently effected an arrangement with the British Government whereby it is unnecessary to establish this additional credit, at least for the present, and that he withdraws his request for your approval.

I therefore return herewith the two letters signed by you in approval of these credits and the terms of their extension.

I am, my dear Mr. President,
         Cordially and respectfully yours,   Norman H. Davis

TLS (WP, DLC).

Two Telegrams from Joseph Patrick Tumulty

[The White House, 22 April 1919]

No. 71. Have not delivered your cable to Redfield consenting to dissolution of Industrial Board because of your cable of April eighteenth to Hines asking him again to cooperate with Industrial Board. Hines away from here and am holding up your cable to Redfield until I hear from him whether price adjustment is definitely off. Have you heard from Hines that he could not cooperate along lines suggested in your cable of April eighteenth? The suggestion of price adjustment had such a tonic effect on general business that we ought to exhaust every effort before final dissolution of Board.
                                    Tumulty.

T telegram (WP, DLC).

The White House, 22 April 1919.

General criticism in press of report of alleged secret treaty or agreement between Great Britain and France, to which United States is said to be a party.[1]   Tumulty.

T telegram (J. P. Tumulty Papers, DLC).
   [1] See H. White to WW, April 16, 1919, n. 1. Tumulty's comment to the contrary notwithstanding, editorial comment on the "agreement" had been mixed up to this point. Indeed, some major organs of opinion, such as the *New York Times* and the New York *World*, had printed no editorial on the subject. The *New York Tribune*, April 21, 1919, saw the "alliance" simply as good evidence of the "practical insufficiency" of the League of Nations. The New York *Evening Post*, April 17, 1919, took an almost exactly

opposite position. "An alliance," it said, "is out of the question, since it is neither in Mr. Wilson's power nor in his policy to form such a connection. But if the League of Nations, as now seems certain, is to be the executor of many of the provisions of the peace treaty, America by its adhesion to the League is pledged to common action with the Allies."

Tumulty probably had specifically in mind the editorial, "No Alliance Needed or Advisable," printed in the *Washington Post*, April 21, 1919. "The spirit and structure of the government of the United States," it began, "do not harmonize with leagues and alliances." "The United States," it continued, "is more friendly to France than to any other nation. The life of France will not be taken, if the United States can prevent it. Yet the people of the United States will not enter into an alliance with France or any other nation. That fact ought to be well understood by this time; but if it is not, it will be duly impressed upon any man or any party that attempts to embroil this nation in a compact binding it to perform certain things in the unknown future, under unknown conditions, contingent upon the action of foreigners. The reason why the United States will not enter into an alliance with any nation is simple and clear. It is because this nation can be of more service to its friends and more damaging to its enemies when outside of an alliance than within one. An alliance would mean nothing unless it committed the United States to a certain action under certain contingencies. But the United States cannot advantageously be committed in advance to pursue any fixed course in such an important business as war. This nation must be free to do what is best at the time it is called upon to act."

For other editorial opinions on this subject, see the *Literary Digest*, LXI (May 3, 1919), 20.

Gilbert Fairchild Close to Newton Diehl Baker

My dear Mr. Secretary: Paris, 22 April, 1919.

The President asks me to send you the enclosed letter which he has received from Mr. Garfield[1] concerning a plan for an "industrial cabinet" and to ask you, if you approve of the plan, if you will not be kind enough when you get back to Washington to take the matter up and superintend its inauguration and perfection.

                          Sincerely yours,   [Gilbert F. Close]

CCL (WP, DLC).
    [1] [H. A. Garfield] to WW, April 6, 1919, CCL (H. A. Garfield Papers, DLC). For a brief discussion of the plan for an industrial cabinet, see H. A. Garfield to WW, March 27, 1919, n. 2, Vol. 56.

Gilbert Fairchild Close to Joseph Patrick Tumulty

                                        Paris, 22 April, 1919.

President has today signed one pardon warrant and fifty one warrants of commutation espionage cases as well as all other documents sent from White House on April 9th and April 10th including acceptance of Judge Barney's[1] resignation.

                                        Close.

T telegram (WP, DLC).
    [1] Samuel Stebbins Barney, Associate Justice of the United States Court of Claims.

ADDENDA

[April 9, 1919]

OUTLINE SUGGESTED WITH REGARD TO RESPONSIBILITY
AND PUNISHMENT.

1. All persons guilty of crimes under the laws of war to be tried by military tribunals in the usual way and sentenced, if convicted, to the usual punishments. In case the crime was committed against the nationals of only one of the belligerents, the trial to be by the military tribunals of that belligerent. In case the crime was against the nationals of several of the belligerents, the trial to be by a military tribunal made up out of the personnel of the military tribunals of the belligerents affected. The accused in every case to be entitled to name his own counsel.

2. Request to be made of Holland to deliver the ex-Kaiser into the hands of the Allied and Associated Powers for trial before a special tribunal, that tribunal to consist of five judges, one of such judges to be appointed by each of the five Powers here named; namely, the United States of America, Great Britain, France, Italy and Japan; the offence for which it is proposed to try him not to be described as a violation of criminal law but as a supreme offence against international morality and the sanctity of treaties. The punishment to be determined upon is left to the tribunal selected, which is expected to be guided by the highest motives of international policy with a view to vindicating the solemn obligations of international undertakings and the validity of international morality.

(signed):   G. CLEMENCEAU.

D. LLOYD GEORGE.

V. E. ORLANDO.

WOODROW WILSON.

SAIONJI.[1]

◊

T MS (D. Lloyd George Papers, F/147/8/9, House of Lords Record Office).

[1] Marquis Kimmochi Saionji, Japanese plentipotentiary delegate, who signed this document later.

Two Memoranda by Vi Kyuin Wellington Koo

MEMORANDUM OF A CONVERSATION AT AN AUDIENCE
WITH THE PRESIDENT OF THE UNITED STATES,
WOODROW WILSON, AT THE WHITE HOUSE.

WORLD PEACE AND THE FAR EAST

Nov. 26, 1918.
(2:15 to 2:30 p.m.)

He first greeted me and shook hands with me and asked me to sit down with him on the sofa chair, he on right and I on left. I inquired of his health and he reciprocated, expressing sympathy to me for the loss of Mrs. Koo.[1]

I congratulated him and through him the government and people of the United States on the victory of the American armies in Europe. I added that the government and people of China had been animated with a sincere admiration for the magnificent way in which the United States under his leadership had prosecuted the war and carried it to a victorious conclusion.

He said in reply that he had felt that China had been with the United States in the war and that only her political stress had prevented her from taking a more active part. I said that the Chinese people themselves regretted the political disturbance in China, but I expressed my hope that through it all China would emerge nearer to the goal of true democracy with which the hearts of the Chinese people are attached.

The people of China, I added, entertained the belief that the United States under the President's able leadership would play a very important role in the making of peace as it did in the prosecution of the war.

He said he hoped too, adding that it was comparatively easy to formulate principles for a peace, but their practical application was quite a task, as in the matter of defining territories for the many new-born states in Europe. He referred to Bohemia for example, and dwelt upon the difficulty of finding a boundary for her. But he said the difficulty must be faced, because the principles were important.

I said that China had great hopes for the peace Conference. She had always relied on the friendship and good will of the United States in the crises which she had to undergo in the past. Now during the present period of world reconstruction, particularly at the peace conference where stupendous problems would be dealt

---

[1] Pao-yu T'ang, oldest daughter of T'ang Shao-yi, first Prime Minister of the Republic of China (February-June 1912). She had died of pneumonia following the Spanish influenza in Washington on October 10, 1918.

with, China would rely on the sympathetic support of the United States all the more, in the conviction that the ideas of the Chinese people were in full harmony with those of the United States. China would hope to present certain proposals at the peace conference concerning her territorial integrity, the preservation of her sovereign rights, and her fiscal and economic independence—proposals which, I remarked, were designed, not to secure any material gain or any selfish advantage for herself, but merely to restore to her some of the things which, in the view of the Chinese people, had been wrongfully taken from her. So the people of China were all looking to the President and the great country which he represented for help in the realisation for their just claims and aspirations.

The President said in reply that he had always felt sympathy for China and was interested in the problems of the Far East, for in his opinion peace was more likely to be endangered there than in other parts of the world, in future. He agreed with me that the ideals of China and the United States were along the same lines and said that he would gladly do his best to support China at the peace conference. He said there was one difficulty in the case of China, i.e. there were many secret agreements between the subjects of China and other powers. He thought these agreements were injurious to China and the world, and if they had to be published, they would never have been made at all. He said he would therefore propose at the peace conference that not only secret diplomacy but secret commercial, industrial and financial agreements between subjects of different powers should be prohibited.

I said in reply that this would be particularly conducive to the welfare of China, though as a principle it was bound to be beneficial to the entire world. He said he was working on a plan for the league of nations. His idea was to provide international guarantees for the territorial integrity and political independence of all States. Any change of sovereign rights concerning territory should be effected only with the consent of the League, provided the people themselves were willing to see the change. This would prevent any particular nation from seeking selfish advantage. He also referred to the country "North of You" in Eastern Siberia, which was yet, he said, in a formative stage. He said it should be cared for, too, by international guarantees rather than left to any particular nation to take advantage of it. The principle he had in mind, he said, was that right should be the basis of international relations and not force; force to be used only against the outlaws.

I expressed my endorsement of his principles and said that for one, China which I had the honor to represent in this country would most heartedly support his plans and his principles—as much out of regard for her own welfare as for the interests of the world. I said I assured him of this because I knew the government and the people of China were heartily in favor of a league of nations. Such an institution would more than any other preclude the possibility of international aggressions.

He expressed gratification at the assurance which I had given him and asked me whether I would attend the peace conference. I said that my government had decided to appoint our Foreign Minister Lou[2] as Chairman of the Chinese Delegation and my colleagues at London and Paris as other members. The government had also asked me to be one of the delegates. He said that knowing I was to be present at the conference, he was particularly glad to find this agreement of views between us, and hoped to cooperate with the Chinese delegation at the conference.

When I was to take leave, he urged me to remain and said that he had another matter to speak to me. While the date for the conference was not yet fixed, he said, he was going to have a preliminary conference with the premiers of Great Britain, France and Italy on the essentials of a peace. He assured me that there would be nothing for China to fear from the discussions at this Conference, because he could tell me confidentially that his purpose was merely to urge the governments to accept the 14 principles as the basis of a peace.

I remarked that an informal conference of this nature would facilitate an agreement; and he agreed with me in saying that he could not hope to accomplish this in public where every one would try to stand on pride. I said that the Chinese people's hearts were attached to the principles of peace which the President had enunciated and which, in so enunciating them, he had given expression to the ideals of the world and kindled the hearts of all; and I expressed my hope that he would see to it that the 14 principles would be made applicable to the Far East as well as to other parts of the world. He said that it was probably more difficult to apply to the Far East, but that mere difficulty was no good reason for not applying them there. I asked him to command me if he should, while in France, need any information concerning the Chinese question for his use at the preliminary conference of the four Powers. He said he would avail of my kindness.

In taking leave, I asked him to allow me to wish him a most pleasant voyage across the Atlantic and to hope to have the privilege of calling to pay him respects while in France. He assured me he would be glad to see me there.

---

[2] That is, Lu Cheng-hsiang.

MEMORANDUM OF AN AUDIENCE WITH PRESIDENT WILSON.
MR. LIANG CHI CHAO,[1] MR. KOO AND MR. CARSON CHANG[2] PRESENT,
AT 11 PLACE DES ETATS UNIS.
(March 24, 1919, 2 p.m.)
1. On the League of Nations.
2. On the question of Kiaochow.

1. After exchanging a few personal greetings, Mr. Liang said that the Chinese people were looking to President Wilson for laying a new basis for international intercourse.

The President asked if he was referring to the League of Nations and Mr. Koo replied affirmatively.

The President observed that China was too taking a part in its formation, whereupon Mr. Koo remarked that compared with the task of the President China was playing a relatively small part, though her desire to see the formation of the League was no less keen.

The President thought that for its establishment he was devoting a great deal of his attention to the framing of the Covenant, and was trying to reconcile some of the effects of the present settlement, one of which was to perpetuate the status quo of the situation left by the peace treaty. He admitted that in a way he was responsible for the delay in the drafting of the treaty, as he insisted upon the incorporation of the covenant therein. But he was of opinion that when the League was formed, it would at once have a quieting effect on international aggressions. He asked Mr. Koo if he thought likewise.

Mr. Koo replied that China certainly looked, as she was looking, upon the League of Nations as having a checking influence upon aggressive intentions of one nation upon another.

2. Mr. Koo asked if there was any prospect of an early solution of the question of Kiaochow, particularly before the conclusion of the preliminary treaty of peace.

The President remarked that there would be only one treaty of peace: that he himself had been misled by the term "preliminary treaty of peace." Of course, after the peace treaty was signed, there would be left many questions issuing from the settlements provided in the treaty which would have to be taken up and worked out by commissions before there would be an exchange of ratifications of the treaty. The Allied and Associated Powers themselves were making the preliminaries at present.

[1] Liang Ch'i-ch'ao, an "unofficial" member of the Chinese delegation, who had arrived in Paris in February.
[2] Chang Chia-sen, a close associate of Liang Ch'i-ch'ao. His western name is rendered as Carsun (not Carson) Chang.

Mr. Koo said it was thought at one time that Germany would be asked merely to renounce all the territories and rights which would be asked of her, leaving the distribution of the same to be worked out later by and among the Allied and Associated Powers themselves.

The President said that that was not the idea in his mind. The arrangement mentioned referred to the appointment of mandatories for African German colonies and South Pacific islands. It did not include the Continental territories of Asia. The leased territory of Kiaochow could not be considered as a colony; it was merely a concession granted by China to Germany and remained nominally still under China's sovereignty. Certain questions would have to be settled with Germany and incorporated in the treaty of peace and the Kiaochow question was one which belonged to this class.

He said further that the Japanese delegates had asked him for an interview to discuss the Kiaochow question privately with him before taking it up again at the Council of Ten. Having been so pressed for time, he had not been able to receive them. He knew that Japan had promised to return the territory of Kiaochow to China, but that they wanted to have it returned first to Japan for independent action with China. He asked Mr. Koo if Japan wanted, in proposing this procedure, to keep the railway and return the place of Kiaochow to China.

Mr. Koo said in reply that that must be one of Japan's reasons in asking for the surrender to herself. She probably also wanted to attach conditions to the restoration of the leased territory of Kiaochow to China. One of these conditions as provided in the Shantung treaty made in consequence of the 21 demands would be that Japan should be allowed to set up an exclusive Japanese settlement in the best part of the leased territory. It was generally understood that Japan had already designated the area which she was to occupy, one which would control the terminus of Shantung railway.

The President asked whether any exclusive Japanese settlement would be like the British settlement at Hong Kong.

Mr. Koo said in reply that it would practically amount to that; that this settlement would be under Japanese police and Japanese municipal control, constituting an imperia in imperio. If Japan was to have the railway and exclusive settlement in the best part of the leased territory, it would mean the returning of the shadow to China, while leaving the substance to Japan. China would be getting nothing back.

The President said he could understand it well; that, in other words, China would be getting back nearly [merely] the useless part of the leased area.

Mr. Koo added that as between the railway and the leased territory, China would lay more emphasis on the restoration of the railway, because this line of communication traversed the whole province of Shantung, and by its connections and branches controlled the gateway to Peking. It was like a grip on the throat, threatening the future independence of China. Public opinion in China on this question was singularly united. The Chinese Delegates had received cablegrams from all parts of the country, from the legislatures of the south as well as from those of the north, urging the delegates to stand firm for complete restitution. A satisfactory solution of this question would really mean a great deal to the peace of the Far East.

The President said that he was quite clear in his mind on principles involved in the question: that its solution was important, because when solved one way, it would mean one thing, and when solved the other way, it would mean another thing.

Mr. Koo asked if the Council would call for another hearing from both sides, and the President said that he did not think it necessary, adding that he had understood very clearly from Mr. Koo the reasons and principles upon which China's claim was based.

Mr. Koo asked [the] President to let him know, if he should feel desirous of having some further information about the views of the Chinese delegation. The President said that he had the principles involved very clearly in mind and that if he should try to go into details of the question, then he might feel lost, because he was engaged in the study of so many questions.

Mr. Chang observed that Japan had gone so far as to have removed the floating dock of Tsingtao to Kobe. The President remarked that this could hardly be considered as an illegitimate act. Mr. Koo intimated to Mr. Chang (in Chinese) that his point was not worth while taking up whereupon Mr. Chang refrained.

The President asked Mr. Liang to excuse him for having taken this opportunity to talk with Dr. Koo privately the question of Kiaochow, and expressed his pleasure of having made acquaintance with him, whereupon all rose up to take leave.

T MSS (V. K. W. Koo Papers, NNC).

INDEX

NOTE ON THE INDEX

THE alphabetically arranged analytical table of contents at the front of the volume eliminates duplication, in both contents and index, of references to certain documents, such as letters. Letters are listed in the contents alphabetically by name, and chronologically within each name by page. The subject matter of all letters is, of course, indexed. The Editorial Notes and Wilson's writings are listed in the contents chronologically by page. In addition, the subject matter of both categories is indexed. The index covers all references to books and articles mentioned in text or notes. Footnotes are indexed. Page references to footnotes which place a comma between the page number and "n" cite both text and footnote, thus: "418,n1." On the other hand, absence of the comma indicates reference to the footnote only, thus: "59n1"—the page number denoting where the footnote appears.

The index supplies the fullest known form of names and, for the Wilson and Axson families, relationships as far down as cousins. Persons referred to by nicknames or shortened forms of names can be identified by reference to entries for these forms of the names.

All entries consisting of page numbers only and which refer to concepts, issues and opinions (such as democracy, the tariff, and money trust, leadership, and labor problems), are references to Wilson's speeches and writings. Page references that follow the symbol Δ in such entries refer to the opinions and comments of others who are identified.

Three cumulative contents-index volumes are now in print: Volume 13, which covers Volumes 1-12, Volume 26, which covers Volumes 14-25, and Volume 39, which covers Volumes 27-38.

INDEX

WOODROW WILSON

APPEARANCE AND IMPRESSIONS

APPOINTMENT SUGGESTIONS, APPOINTMENTS, AND RESIGNATIONS

CABINET